S0-AQL-310

Midwifery and Medicine in Boston

Midwifery

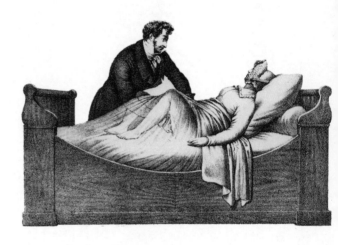

and Medicine in Boston

Walter Channing, M.D. 1786–1876

Amalie M. Kass

Northeastern University Press
Boston

NORTHEASTERN UNIVERSITY PRESS

Copyright 2002 by Amalie M. Kass

All rights reserved. Except for the quotation of short passages for the purposes of criticism and review, no part of this book may be reproduced in any form or by any means, electronic or mechanical, including photocopying, recording, or any information storage and retrieval system now known or to be invented, without written permission of the publisher.

Library of Congress Cataloging-in-Publication Data

Kass, Amalie M., 1928–
  Midwifery and medicine in Boston : Walter Channing, M.D., 1786–1876 / Amalie M. Kass.
     p. ; cm.
  Includes bibliographical references and index.
  ISBN 1–55553–501–1 (cloth : alk. paper)
    1. Channing, Walter, 1786–1876. 2. Physicians—Massachusetts—Biography. 3. Midwifery—Massachusetts—History. 4. Obstetrics—Massachusetts—History. I.
    Title. [DNLM: 1. Channing, Walter, 1786–1876. 2. Physicians—Massachusetts—Biography. 3. Midwifery—history—Massachusetts. 4. Obstetrics—history—Massachusetts. WZ 100
  C4568K 2002]
  R154.C319 K37 2002
  610′.92—dc21
  [B]   2001031726

The image on the title page is courtesy of the Francis A. Countway Library of Medicine.

Designed by Gary Gore

Composed in Berkeley by Coghill Composition Company in Richmond, Virginia. Printed and bound by Thomson-Shore, Inc., in Dexter, Michigan. The paper is Writers Offset, an acid-free sheet.

Manufactured in the United States of America
06   05   04   03   02   5   4   3   2   1

In loving memory of my mother,
Helene Lobe Moses,
And of my grandmothers,
Amelia Bachrach Mann and Rose Levy Moses

Contents

Contents

Illustrations

Acknowledgments

Many people have encouraged, advised, and assisted me during the years it has taken to complete this book. My greatest gratitude goes to three who did not live to see it published. First, to my late husband, Edward H. Kass, for so many things including his enthusiasm for medical history. We had hoped to collaborate on this project and to enjoy again the pleasure of working together. Ed was William Ellery Channing Professor of Medicine at Harvard Medical School, but that chair (and the Channing Laboratory he directed) bears no relationship to the medical career of Walter Channing. Next, to Stephen T. Riley, who was director of the Massachusetts Historical Society when I first began to think about the history of midwifery. He kindly invited me to have a look at the Channing Papers, thereby initiating the research that eventually produced this book. Third, to J. Worth Estes, late professor of pharmacology, medicine, and the history of medicine at Boston University School of Medicine, whose knowledge of the history of medicine was prodigious. Worth set high standards for himself, expecting other people to do the same. He was a mentor and a good friend.

The Francis A. Countway Library of Medicine at Harvard Medical School has almost been a second home and I am grateful to many people there. Thomas Horrocks, Jack Eckert, Lucretia McClure, and the other librarians in Rare Books and Special Collections have been unfailingly helpful. Judith Messerle, library director, has been supportive and a friend. During their many years at the Countway, Richard and Elin Wolfe gave me much assistance. After their move to Philadelphia, Dick read the entire manuscript, pen in hand, even correcting the notes, while Elin has continued to provide encouragement and inimitable insights. Mollie Craig and Madeline Mullen were very helpful in the early years of the project.

Similarly, at the Massachusetts Historical Society there are many people to thank. William Fowler's interest and encouragement are greatly appreciated. Conrad Edick Wright read part of the manuscript and made very helpful suggestions. Peter Drummey is a never-failing source of information, good humor, and great ideas. Over the years, Brenda Lawson, Nicholas Graham, Jennifer Tolpa, and Virginia Smith retrieved, photocopied, and gave cheer.

Philip Cash is exceptionally knowledgeable about medicine in nineteenth-century Boston. He carefully read a large part of the manuscript and made many helpful suggestions. Allan Brandt read the manuscript early in the process; his encouragement and approval spurred me on. My daughter, Anne Hecht, and my friend Cynthia Vartan read the entire manuscript, saving me from numerous incomprehensible sentences. Cynthia's many years' experience as an editor helped reshape the book and I am much indebted to her. Several children-in-law who are physicians, Susan Korrick, Loreta Matheo, and Sean Tunis, advised on points of medical practice. Kristina Jones has been my consultant on topics botanical. Dr. Theodore Barton read the chapters on obstetrics. Dr. Mortimer Greenberg instructed me on puerperal anemia. Dr. Tim Brewer helped me understand the medical problems of Barbara Perkins Channing. Barbara Rosenkrantz and Lilian Handlin gave encouragement in the very early stages of the project. John Harley Warner also gave advice and counsel. Sandra Rosenblum found information on music in the Unitarian church service.

Willard P. Fuller, Jr., kindly provided access to family papers then in his possession, along with his knowledge of family lore. His Channing and Fuller heritage is an extraordinary legacy and he takes good care of it. Joan Fuller Kimball is a neighbor who directed me to Mr. Fuller, while Judith Marriner, another Channing descendant, graciously showed me some of the memorabilia from her side of the family. Francis Dedmond, who has devoted much of his scholarly life to William Ellery Channing II, read the early chapters and urged me to continue. The Reverend Frank Carpenter, who was minister of the Channing Memorial Church in Newport when I began this project, generously shared his knowledge of the Channing and Gibbs families and of Newport history.

I am indebted also to people at many other libraries. At the Schlesinger Library, Kathy Kraft and Jane Knowles have been hospitable and helpful. Anita Israel and others at the Longfellow National Historic Site gave assistance. At the Newport Historical Society, Joan Youngken and Bertram Littlefield answered many questions. Bob Sullivan provided information from the archives of the Brookline Public Library. The Brookline Preservation Commission was also helpful, as were the American Antiquarian Society, American Philosophical Society, Bostonian Society, Boston Public Library, New York Public Library, College of Physicians of Philadelphia, Pierpont Morgan Library, Houghton Library, Widener Library, Andover-Harvard Theological Library, Smith College

Library, Wellesley College Library, Antioch University Library, Boston Museum of Science, Massachusetts State Archives, and the Concord, Massachusetts, Free Public Library. Mark Frazier Lloyd at the University Archives and Record Center, University of Pennsylvania, and Jean Archibald at Edinburgh University Library found records and answered queries. Archivists at the Massachusetts General Hospital and Brigham and Women's Hospital gave access to their collections. Early in the research stage, I benefited from a grant from the American College of Obstetricians and Gynecologists and the help of Susan Rishworth. Megan Marshall graciously shared her knowledge of the Peabody sisters.

Without the steady smile and computer wizardry of Ondine Le Blanc, the manuscript would never have passed muster with the editors at Northeastern University Press. I thank her very much.

Finally, gratitude and devotion to my children, step-children, children-in-law, and grandchildren. They have been hearing about Walter Channing for a long time. I hope they will enjoy meeting him at last.

Chronology

1786   Born in Newport, Rhode Island
1793   Death of William Channing
1803   Channing family moves to Boston
1807   Dismissed from Harvard College; studies medicine with James Jackson
1808   Studies medicine at the University of Pennsylvania
1809   Receives M.D. from University of Pennsylvania
1810   Studies medicine in Edinburgh and London
1811   Begins to practice medicine in Boston
1812   Serves as editor of the *New England Journal of Medicine and Surgery*
1814   Named Fellow of the Massachusetts Medical Society
1815   Appointed Lecturer in Midwifery, Harvard Medical College; marries Barbara Higginson Perkins
1818   Appointed Professor of Midwifery and Medical Jurisprudence
1819   Named dean of the Medical Faculty
1820   *Remarks on the Employment of Females as Practitioners in Midwifery* published by an anonymous physician
1821   Becomes Assistant Physician at Massachusetts General Hospital
1822   Death of Barbara Perkins Channing
1828   Serves as editor of the *Boston Medical and Surgical Journal*
1829   Becomes treasurer of the Massachusetts Medical Society
1830   Joins Boston Society of Natural History
1831   Marries Eliza Wainwright
1832   Establishment of the Boston Lying-in Hospital
1833   Avery trial; gives annual address to the Massachusetts Medical Society
1834   Death of Eliza Wainwright Channing; death of Lucy Ellery Channing
1835   Gives annual address to the Boston Society of Natural History; becomes secretary of the Massachusetts Temperance Society
1836   Gives annual address to the Massachusetts Temperance Society

1839   Relinquishes appointment as physician at Massachusetts General
        Hospital
1841   Marriage of Ellery Channing and Ellen Fuller
1842   Foundation of the Church of the Disciples; death of William Ellery
        Channing; publishes "Notes on Anhæmia"
1843   Publishes *Address on the Prevention of Pauperism*
1844   Publishes *A Plea for Pure Water*
1847   Death of Lucy Bradstreet Channing
1848   Publishes *Treatise on Etherization in Childbirth*
1849   AMA third annual meeting in Boston
1850   Parkman murder trial; Harriot Hunt refused admission to the medical
        school; three black medical students asked to leave the medical school
1851   *New and Old* published
1852   Journey to Europe
1853   Ellery and Ellen Channing separate
1854   Resigns from Harvard medical faculty
1856   Death of Ellen Fuller Channing; becomes president of the Suffolk
        District Medical Society
1857   Report of Committee on Criminal Abortions
1861   Serves as first president of the Obstetrical Society of Boston
1866   Moves to Dorchester
1876   Dies in Brookline, Massachusetts

The CHANNING

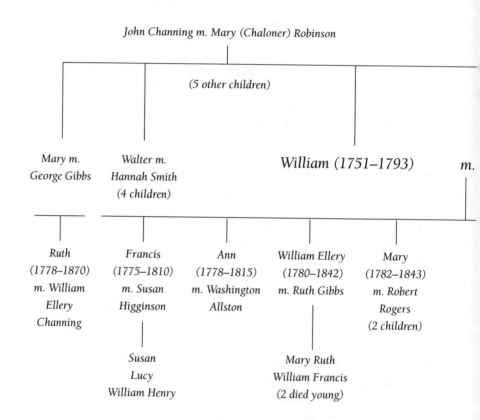

John Channing m. Mary (Chaloner) Robinson

(5 other children)

Mary m.
George Gibbs

Walter m.
Hannah Smith
(4 children)

William (1751–1793)   m.

Ruth
(1778–1870)
m. William
Ellery
Channing

Francis
(1775–1810)
m. Susan
Higginson

Susan
Lucy
William Henry

Ann
(1778–1815)
m. Washington
Allston

William Ellery
(1780–1842)
m. Ruth Gibbs

Mary Ruth
William Francis
(2 died young)

Mary
(1782–1843)
m. Robert
Rogers
(2 children)

F A M I L Y *Tree*

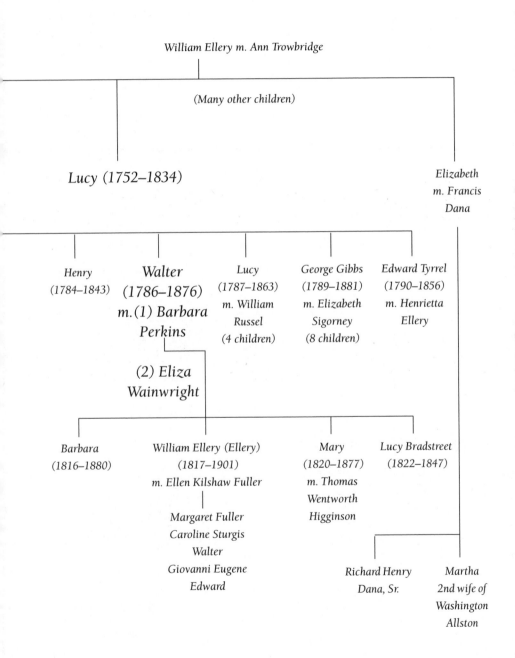

William Ellery m. Ann Trowbridge

(Many other children)

Lucy (1752–1834)

Elizabeth
m. Francis
Dana

Henry
(1784–1843)

Walter
(1786–1876)
m.(1) Barbara
Perkins

Lucy
(1787–1863)
m. William
Russel
(4 children)

George Gibbs
(1789–1881)
m. Elizabeth
Sigorney
(8 children)

Edward Tyrrel
(1790–1856)
m. Henrietta
Ellery

(2) Eliza
Wainwright

Barbara
(1816–1880)

William Ellery (Ellery)
(1817–1901)
m. Ellen Kilshaw Fuller

Mary
(1820–1877)
m. Thomas
Wentworth
Higginson

Lucy Bradstreet
(1822–1847)

Margaret Fuller
Caroline Sturgis
Walter
Giovanni Eugene
Edward

Richard Henry
Dana, Sr.

Martha
2nd wife of
Washington
Allston

Midwifery and Medicine in Boston

Walter Channing, oil by William F. Draper after Joseph
Ames (Harvard Medical Library, Francis A. Countway Library of
Medicine)

Prologue

Little that a man does is remembered after he is dead.

—Walter Channing, Reminiscences

According to a story once told in Boston, a stranger approached a house on Tremont Street asking to see Dr. Channing. He was greeted at the door by a genial man of medium height, with clear gray-blue eyes, florid complexion, and dark hair who replied, "Which Dr. Channing? My brother preaches. I practice."

The Dr. Channing who preached was William Ellery Channing, the most prominent Unitarian of his day, the minister at Boston's Federal Street Church from 1803 until his death in 1842. A liberal theologian, social reformer, and notable essayist, he was greatly admired in his own country and abroad. As the older brother of the other Dr. Channing, he was an important influence on many aspects of his life.

The other Dr. Channing, the brother who responded to the query, was Walter Channing, Boston's leading obstetrician, a professor of midwifery and the dean of the faculty at the Harvard Medical College, well known locally for his commitment to his patients as well as his participation in many movements for the amelioration of social wrongs. Despite his contemporary reputation, he has long been overshadowed by his preaching brother.

For more than fifty years, Walter Channing was the unnamed presence in the lives of countless Boston women. It was an era when women were loath to discuss the realities of their pregnancies and deliveries or their other physical problems. Yet they counted on him to provide as easy and safe a labor as was possible. He was with them too if there were postpartum disorders and provided advice and treatment for their gynecological problems. Channing's expertise and experience, as well as his compassion and concern, led to a

3

reputation among his colleagues and his patients that has since faded from memory.

Channing's story reveals more than the practice of obstetrics or the reproductive lives of nineteenth-century women. He instructed hundreds of young men in "the art of midwifery" as well as in medical jurisprudence and was instrumental in the creation of a lying-in hospital for poor women. His non-obstetrical practice, including nearly two decades as a physician at Boston's only general hospital, was an important part of his career, and his position among the small group of physicians who dominated medicine in antebellum Boston placed him among the most important leaders of the profession. Additionally, his long life coincided with social, economic, and political changes in Boston that were reflected in his personal experiences. Though there were fewer significant changes in the practice of medicine and obstetrics, in at least one—the use of anesthesia in childbirth—he was the major force in its acceptance.

Channing's personal life was complicated. As a member of Boston's intellectual and cultural elite he was acquainted with many of the prominent men and women of his era. His family connections were among the best of Boston society. Friends and colleagues found him witty and cheerful, an excellent conversationalist always ready for fun. Yet beneath this gaiety was a hidden undercurrent of loneliness that often rendered him almost unbearably sad.

At the beginning of the twenty-first century, when childbirth is relatively safe and painless and gynecology provides care that would have been unimaginable in the nineteenth century, the hitherto neglected career of Walter Channing points the way to our own time while revealing a remarkable, multifaceted, nineteenth-century man.

Chapter 1

Youth

> When I was a boy everything was different from what is
> common now. We had just come out of the Revolution
> and all things were new. The times were hard enough.
> Everybody had to work.
>
> —Walter Channing to his grandson, June 17, 1863

N EWPORT was still recovering from the devastation of war when
Walter Channing was born there on April 15, 1786, less than three
years after Great Britain granted independence to the American colonies. The Rhode Island town had suffered severely from occupation by ma-
rauding British troops during the early years of the war, as well as from the
French and American batteries that attempted to dislodge them. Homes and
shops had been destroyed, churches damaged. The exodus of Tory sympathiz-
ers and the flight of families seeking safer environs had reduced the population
to half the prewar number.[1] In the harbor, once a bustling scene of maritime
enterprise, only a few ships were loading or unloading their goods.

For most of the eighteenth century, Newport was a flourishing commercial
and cultural center. Three generations of Channings had helped to make it so.
Walter's great-grandparents, John Channing and Mary Antram, had arrived in
Boston from England in 1712, after a nine-month voyage prolonged by hostilities between the British and the French and a floundering ship that required
repairs en route.[2] They married and soon after moved to Newport, where they
prospered. At his death in 1731, John Channing was known not only for his
success as a merchant, but also for his corpulence, greater than that of any
other man in Newport.[3]

The next generation, Walter's paternal grandparents, were also named
John and Mary Channing. This Mary was born Mary Chaloner and had been

the widow of Dr. James Robinson, the only physician member of the family, tangential though he was, prior to Walter. John Channing, like his father before him, was highly respected in Newport society. He owned a warehouse located directly at the wharf and a dry goods store closer to the center of town. His wife, assisted by several clerks, directed the retail operation, a practice that was not uncommon in pre-Revolutionary New England. The threat posed to Newport's prosperity by British trade policy during the decade before the outbreak of the Revolution incited many merchants to band together in opposition to imperial rule. John Channing was one of the early leaders of the Sons of Liberty in Newport.[4]

Walter's father, William, born in 1751, was the first Channing to opt for higher education and a profession. He studied at Nassau Hall (later Princeton), then returned to Rhode Island to read law and begin a legal practice. In May 1773 he married Lucy Ellery. As tension mounted during the years before the outbreak of hostilities with Great Britain, William Channing was a vociferous champion of colonial rights, and when war broke out he became an officer in one of the volunteer companies formed for the defense of Newport.[5]

On his mother's side, Walter inherited a pedigree equally well suited for his post-Revolutionary generation.[6] Through his grandmother, Ann Remington Ellery, Walter could trace his ancestry to Thomas Dudley, who came to Boston in 1630 on board the *Arbella* with John Winthrop and the original

Channing's birthplace, School Street, Newport, Rhode Island, paper print (The Newport Historical Society)

settlers of Massachusetts Bay Colony. As deputy governor, Dudley took part in the banishments of Roger Williams and Anne Hutchinson, both of whom threatened religious control by the Puritan oligarchy in Massachusetts Bay. Williams then migrated southward to establish the colony of Rhode Island on principles of religious toleration and to attract Englishmen such as the Channings who welcomed religious liberty as well as economic opportunity. The descendants of Thomas Dudley bore illustrious New England names such as Bradstreet, Remington, and Trowbridge and were distinguished governors, judges, and ministers. Anne Bradstreet, Thomas Dudley's oldest daughter, achieved lasting renown as colonial New England's first poet.

Of all his forebears, William Ellery, Walter's maternal grandfather, most clearly embodied the spirit of the Revolution. The Ellerys too had migrated from Massachusetts to Rhode Island during the early years of the eighteenth century and a previous William had been a deputy governor of the colony.[7] Like the Channings, they too acquired wealth as merchants. William Ellery graduated from Harvard College in 1747 and was a successful businessman in his own right until the disruption of trade that accompanied the escalating dispute over British revenue acts and colonial nonimportation agreements forced him to turn to the practice of law so that he could better support his family. Ellery was one of Rhode Island's most active patriots in the years prior to the outbreak of war and in 1776 he was chosen a delegate to the Second Continental Congress. A monthlong horseback journey took him to Philadelphia, where he participated in the deliberations that led to the Declaration of Independence and signed the document on behalf of Rhode Island. In retaliation for that courageous deed, the British burned his house in Newport.[8]

Known thenceforth as "the Signer," Ellery continued as a member of the Continental Congress until 1785 and thus became well acquainted with the important political figures of the new nation.[9] President George Washington appointed him Collector of the Customs for the District of Newport, an office he held until his death in 1820.[10] As the most long-lived of Walter's grandparents, William Ellery was an important influence on Walter and his siblings. From the Signer they learned to venerate Washington, Adams, Hamilton, and the other leaders of the early Republic and became staunch Federalists when political parties developed at the end of the eighteenth century.

Newport's location in Narragansett Bay, at the southern end of Aquidneck Island, with a protected harbor on one side and the Atlantic Ocean on the other, was a great advantage in the development of coastal and overseas trade. Much of its prosperity depended on its pivotal position in the so-called Triangular Trade. Newport shipped vast quantities of rum to the west coast of Africa, where it was exchanged for slaves, who were then transported to sugar plantations in the West Indies. The sugar and molasses produced there by slave labor was shipped north to Newport distilleries, where it was used to manufacture the rum and complete the triangle. Newport's role in the slave trade extended to the sale of black men and women in the southern colonies and to a far lesser degree in Rhode Island itself.[11]

The wealth produced by the slave trade, as well as by conventional seafaring activities and commercial enterprises, enabled Newport's merchants, the Channings included, to live in fine homes and to enjoy the arts, literature, and other intellectual pursuits.[12] The Redwood Library, built at mid-century to resemble a Roman temple and open for public enjoyment, was emblematic of the town's cultural aspirations. The natural beauty of the island, with the open sea stretching eastward, beaches extending for miles around, and rocky ledges above, added to its appeal.

By the year of Walter's birth, slavery had been abolished in Rhode Island and the Channings had freed their own black servants. Some remained with the family, including "the Duchess," so named because of her regal bearing. She was a particular favorite who became a mainstay of the rapidly expanding Channing household.[13]

Walter's father, William, was one of Rhode Island's most admired and popular lawyers. After independence, he served simultaneously as the elected attorney general for Rhode Island and as the appointed United States district attorney. His many civic duties brought esteem but not much remuneration. Lucy Ellery Channing, educated "in the stern school of Puritanism,"[14] was by nature and circumstances forced to be extremely careful with money, a habit she passed on to her children. She was a woman of great firmness and inflexible integrity who detested the slightest deviation from truthfulness. The family was the center of her life, which was made "happy or wrecked" by the success or failure of her children.[15] She claimed their reverence "as an act beneficial to them."[16] They, in turn, cherished her company and welcomed her advice. Lucy was also a woman who observed the social proprieties, entertaining formally at dinner and tea her husband's professional and political friends. Her ready wit, forthright conversation, and genuine interest in those about her were fondly remembered by her children and grandchildren long after her death.[17]

The Channing home on School Street did not reflect Newport's economic troubles. It was large and gracious, befitting the attorney general and his growing family.[18] Francis Dana was born in 1775, Ann in 1778, William Ellery in 1780, Mary in 1782, and Henry in 1784. Following Walter's birth in 1786 came Lucy in 1787, George Gibbs in 1789, and Edward Tyrrel in 1790. Circumstances and individual traits caused each of the boys to follow a different path, Francis to the law, William to the ministry, Henry to trade, Walter to medicine, George to a varied and often problematic career in business, publishing, and the ministry, and Edward to academia. The three girls were expected to marry, and they all did.[19]

Walter remembered his father as "upright in a high sense of the word. He was of a most amiable temper, and though the times exacted an implicit obedience in children . . . yet he was kind and indulgent. I remember he would stop at my school door sometimes before school broke up, and take me home on horseback with him. I feared my father, but there was a lesson of love in the severest of his instructions."[20]

The lessons of love were abruptly ended by his father's death in 1793, when Walter was only seven years old. William Channing's unidentified but fatal illness was sudden and severe. His mind was so deranged that Walter and the other children were kept from his bedside. After his death one of the servants, probably the Duchess, insisted on taking the boy to gaze on what he would "never see again on earth" and

Lucy Ellery Channing, oil by Washington Allston (The Fine Arts Museums of San Francisco, Gift of Mr. and Mrs. John D. Rockefeller, 3d, 1979)

cautioned him "to make this last sad sight an everlasting lesson in virtue and piety." Instead, the child saw only "a face transfigured by death . . . pale, shrunken, dead." Long into adulthood Walter fervently prayed for a vision of his father "such as he was in the happiest days of mine when the light of his countenance was my light, and my joy."[21] Older brothers, a loving grandfather, and myriad uncles could not replace the father so early removed from Walter's life. It was the first of many losses, each depriving him of love, each rendering him more lonely.

Lucy Ellery Channing was left to raise the family alone, but her inner strength and the support of many Channings and Ellerys sustained her and her children. Nonetheless, her financial situation was difficult. William Channing had accumulated a remarkable law library and some real estate, but there was little money.[22] The United States Treasury was unwilling or unable to pay the widow for her husband's service as attorney general and the rents from farmland he had owned were small.[23] Though birth and breeding placed her and her children among the best of Newport society, genteel poverty was the reality of her condition. Francis was in his third year at Harvard when his father died, and William had already left the family circle for New London to

prepare for college under the tutelage of an uncle, the Reverend Henry Channing. Though the two eldest brothers were acutely aware of their obligations
to their mother and the other children, each was expected to continue his
studies, assisted by loans and other subsidies from family connections.[24]

Walter had been named for one of his father's brothers, a Newport merchant who was co-owner of Gibbs and Channing. Uncle Walter's partner and
brother-in-law, George Gibbs (Gibbs had married Mary Channing), was
among the most successful merchants in New England.[25] It was a fortuitous
naming, for Uncle Walter was a wealthy man despite the ups and downs of
commerce during the unsettled postwar period. Thus it was to him that many
members of the family turned for counsel and loans.

Grandfather William Ellery lived less than a mile from the Channings and
he continued to play an important role in the lives of his daughter's children.
"There is nothing that concerns my grandchildren in which I do not feel myself interested," he later wrote. "I rejoice with those of them who do rejoice,
and mourn with those who mourn."[26] The Signer could be a lively and amusing
personality, regaling them with stories of his own youthful escapades and his
adventures en route to sessions of the Continental Congress. He read Latin
and Greek classics as well as English philosophers, historians, poets, and scientists, and he encouraged young Walter's intellectual curiosity while super-
vising some of his studies. "How well is that time," he later recalled, "and those
studies and recitation remembered. Never before nor since, has such or any
intellectual work been to me so wholly attractive, or more cheerfully done."[27]
Walter began to study Greek with his grandfather, and was soon reading "with
some ease."[28] His training in classical languages provided a lifelong ability to
use medical words correctly, even to the point of telling his colleagues when
they strayed from the original Greek.[29]

In contrast to the Channing family, William Ellery opposed slavery, a situation that might have caused conflict with his son-in-law, had he lived longer.
As watchdog of the port, Ellery brought suit against merchants who continued
in the by then illegal slave trade, whereas William Channing, who had treated
his own blacks well and saw nothing wrong with slavery, had been their de-
fender. The antipathy to slavery that Walter and his brother William showed
later in their lives owed much to the influence of their grandfather.

Grandfather Ellery was deeply devout, another trait he passed on to his
progeny. He read the Bible daily throughout his long life and freely demonstrated his familiarity with its verses and his understanding of its lessons. The
family worshiped at the Second Congregational Meeting House, which was
badly desecrated by British soldiers during the occupation of Newport but had
since been restored. The Reverend William Patten, successor to Ezra Stiles,

preached dry, expository sermons on points of Calvinist theology that held little interest for the younger members of the congregation. "We sat shivering in the winter through a long service, in a large barn-like building, without stoves, furnaces, or carpets, listening to discourses which older heads might not always fully comprehend."[30] The service was intolerably tedious and seemed to Walter like "the eternal punishment and eternal misery of which the minister spoke most, especially of the first."[31]

Samuel Hopkins also had a small congregation in Newport and though his extreme Calvinist beliefs had no appeal to the Channings, his doctrine of "disinterested benevolence and self-sacrificing charity . . . [and his] exhaustless love, kindness, and charity" made a lasting impression on young Walter.[32] Despite its Congregational majority, Newport's tradition of religious tolerance meant that from childhood Walter was acquainted with the practices of Jews, Quakers, Baptists, and Episcopalians as well as several other denominations.

William Ellery, by Samuel B. Waugh after Trumbull (courtesy of the National Park Service, Independence National Historical Park)

Though the Sabbath was strictly observed, with no activity permitted but prayer and meditation, Walter and his brothers had plenty of opportunities to play. The beach beckoned in summer and the frozen ponds in winter. Lucy issued firm orders about swimming, and though William obeyed her commands, Walter and his next younger brother, George, were often caught with wet hair and sent supperless to bed. A more dangerous escapade nearly ended in disaster when the two youngsters were skating without permission. Trying to outskate one of the other boys, Walter ventured out on thin ice, fell through, and might have drowned had George not lain down on a safer spot and pushed a long pole out to his older brother. Once again they were punished; Lucy took seriously her solitary responsibility for their conduct and safety.[33]

In his early years, Walter attended a school near home where a Scot named John Frazer was the master. As was customary, Frazer was a strict disciplinarian and the boys, Walter among them, were whipped for infractions of the rules. He was neither an outstanding nor a poor student.[34] However, he was beginning to demonstrate the strong sense of independence and self-direction that characterized his entire life. One day when he was about twelve years old, he entered his mother's wainscoted front parlor smoking a cigar. Queried about his conduct, he showed no embarrassment, asserting only that indeed he was smoking. Lucy must not have been offended, for she indicated that he could do as he pleased.[35] The incident was emblematic of his entire life. His mother's unwillingness to interfere reinforced an emerging insistence on self-reliance. A few years later, he decided to leave school. Again there was no opposition. He claimed that he wanted to assist his mother in the management of the family property, but more likely he was bored by school.

With his days relatively unstructured, Walter showed a romantic flair then still unusual among descendants of New England Puritans. He began by painting, indulging for a brief time the notion that he might become a great artist.[36] When that dream was squashed by unappreciative relatives and friends, he turned to literature, writing poetry, plays, and fiction. Again he received little encouragement, though he continued to pursue his literary interests throughout his life. He spent long and solitary days in the Redwood Library, but the classics and weighty books of philosophy, read without guidance or purpose, made little impression.

He keenly felt the absence of his brother William who, after graduation at the head of his class at Harvard College, spent a year and a half as a tutor in Virginia before returning to Cambridge in 1802 to study divinity. Walter wrote to his serious and scholarly brother about the books he was reading, seeking William's approbation and advice. "Do write me often . . . let your letters be moral essays. I am young, susceptible to every feeling & want the aid of your cool philosophic mind." On occasion he added a plea for small amounts of money so that he might buy a toothbrush or wood to heat his room. "I am a poor fellow," he added, "but heaven may bless my studies & here after any good which it may be in my power to do to man may make it possible for me to repay the kindness of my friends." He was afraid to seek help from Francis, the eldest brother, lest he be accused "of an excellent faculty for begging."[37]

Despite an outward gregariousness, Walter often preferred to withdraw from society. After hours reading at the Redwood Library, he would take off for the beach "and there among the rocks, the sands and the waves indulge in such speculation, as the scene, or my strange studies, or my own fancy might suggest. I have been there in the storm and the calm with wide and boundless ocean before me, nor used I to leave it till in the darkness of evening, nothing remained for me but its ceaseless roar. There was something in this kind of life that strongly attracted me. It inclined me to avoid men."[38]

Gradually, he realized that medicine genuinely interested him. He began to read anatomy, physiology, and medical theory, though without adequate guidance, and soon discovered that "he never studied harder [and] never learned less."[39] With no physicians (except Dr. Robinson) in either the Channing or the Ellery families and none of his brothers sharing a similar interest, Walter had begun on his own, unique path, and should he pursue it he would have to find his way in a world very different from the one he had known. That may well have been part of its attraction for a young man eager to demonstrate his independence.

Nonetheless, he felt compelled to justify his commitment to medicine rather than the more traditional careers in law or the ministry. Writing to William in 1803, he explained that he would study "a profession that has been stigmatized with the character of an irreligious one but by my manner of education I hope to be an exception. A physician can perform too [sic] important duties . . . by an acquaintance with physic he can ease the pains incident to the body & by an acquaintance with the comforts of religion he may make the pains of dying much easier."[40] Not only might he bring relief and solace to the sick and dying, but as a physician he would be fulfilling his duty to society, another of the precepts thoroughly inculcated in young New Englanders like him.

Newport had known distinguished physicians in the past and for several of them Walter Channing had a particular affinity. Dr. William Hunter, a Scot educated at Edinburgh, settled in Newport in 1752 and practiced medicine, including obstetrics, for twenty-four years. Though most of Newport's babies were delivered by midwives in the years before the Revolution, Hunter was reputed to have about fifty childbearing women under his care annually.[41] He also gave a series of anatomy lectures in 1754–1756 deemed to have been the first systematic medical course in the colonies. He included midwifery in his lectures, although the topic was considered inappropriate by many in the community. Channing was born too late ever to have known William Hunter, but he knew enough about him to appreciate his pioneering work, though he would not have approved his strong Tory principles.[42]

Benjamin Waterhouse, one of Newport's most illustrious medical sons, had already abandoned its limited environment by the time Channing was born, but eventually they became well acquainted as instructor and pupil in medicine. During his childhood years, the most important physician was Dr. Isaac Senter, who was called whenever Lucy's home remedies were not sufficient to cure a sick child. Lucy trusted him implicitly and the children loved him despite the harsh medicines he prescribed. To Walter, his "excellent and cultivated mind, his contributions to the *London Medical Journal* . . . his gentleness, his widely reputed professional skill and the large confidence he enjoyed" made him a model to be imitated if at all possible.[43]

As Walter's interest in medicine became known, several local physicians allowed him to accompany them on their visits to patients. Initially he thought surgery would be his calling, but the idea was quickly abandoned when he witnessed two horrific operations. In the first case, he fainted while a young boy's protruding blind eye was incised in an effort to remove nonexistent fluid. The boy suffered horribly from the procedure and others that followed and eventually died of infection and exhaustion.[44] The second case was a compound fracture of the leg, the result of a carriage accident near the Channing home. The victim was brought into the house, where the bone was set. Afterward he was carried to his own house but the leg had to be reset. Tetanus developed and in time this patient too expired, leaving an indelible memory of the agony produced by rampant infection. Thereupon young Walter Channing decided to avoid surgical cases and focused his interest on physic (that is, internal medicine).

In 1803 William Ellery Channing was ordained minister of Boston's Federal Street Church, and shortly thereafter he invited his mother and the children still living in Newport to join him. This meant leaving the familiarity of the home and garden that had given comfort and pleasure, despite their adverse circumstances, and the friends and relatives who had known and sustained them for many years. But Lucy was eager to have her children together again and accepted William's offer.

> [I]t will be very advantageous to your younger Brothers to reside in Boston. Henry when he shall return would there find a home. Walter would be with us while he is studying physic and George, if he cannot be received into a store without my boarding him, can be boarded by me and when Edward shall enter College he will be under our eyes, and we can wash and mend his cloathes. Francis . . . will live in Boston and board with me—and it may be more for your interest and comfort to be with me than to board out. . . . Your GrandPapa says that [it] is more likely that the girls will get good husbands in Boston than at Newport. . . . I shall not object to my sons or daughters marrying when the former can get *good* wives & the latter *good* husbands but matrimony is at present out of the question.[45]

So Lucy became mistress of the house on Berry Street, purchased by the parish to accommodate their new minister's family. William, who continued to feel responsible for the well-being of his entire family, made his salary available for the needs of his younger sisters and brothers and paid board to his mother for lodging him.[46] Newport remained forever an important place in all their lives, reclaimed by frequent visits, especially in summer, to renew family ties and friendships. But it was now a backwater community and could not match the opportunities that Boston offered. Lucy made the right decision. Thenceforth Boston would be the locale for Channing accomplishments. The descendants of merchants and politicians would make their mark in more intellectual pursuits—the ministry, academia, and medicine.[47]

SERIOUS study was necessary if Walter was to pursue a medical career. Medicine was just emerging from its colonial status: the absence of educational requirements and professional standards meant that anyone could call himself a physician and seek patients. Most practitioners, however, had spent several years apprenticed to an experienced physician and had received a certificate of accomplishment from their preceptors, which indicated acceptable morals as well as familiarity with the basic literature of medicine. It was not uncommon for an apprentice to begin training in his mid-teens, with little preliminary education beyond grammar school. The apprenticeship system worked reasonably well for its time, but more formal studies, as in law and the ministry, were necessary if medicine was to achieve recognition as a profession.

The Revolutionary War and establishment of a new nation led to important changes, especially in Boston. The wartime experiences of many physicians had underscored the deficiencies in medical training and several of them sought reform. Dr. John Warren took the lead. Warren, a graduate of Harvard College, had apprenticed in medicine to his brother Joseph, the patriot-physician killed at the Battle of Bunker Hill, and had served as surgeon and head of the army hospital in Boston. In 1781 Warren delivered a series of public lectures on anatomy, similar to lectures he had previously given to his staff. The number of attendees, which included the president of Harvard, and their enthusiasm for the subject affirmed the need for a proper medical school in Massachusetts. (Pennsylvania and New York each had a medical school dating from 1765 and 1767, respectively.)

In 1782, the year following Warren's lectures, the Harvard Corporation voted to create three professorships: anatomy and surgery, physic and theory of medicine, and chemistry and materia medica. They also authorized the granting of medical degrees. Admission to the lectures was restricted to upperclassmen, college graduates, and noncollegians twenty-one years old or more. Those who intended to practice medicine were already apprenticed to physicians and the lectures supplemented the instruction they received from their preceptors. Massachusetts now had the beginnings of formal education leading to a degree in medicine, and Harvard became the third medical school in the nation, the first since independence from England. It was hardly an auspicious beginning, for the school lacked anatomical exhibits and chemical apparatus as well as a medical library, and it had no funds to purchase them, relying instead on the professors' personal accouterments. An earlier legacy from a physician named Ezekiel Hersey eventually provided salaries for two of the professors, but student fees were the primary source of income for the faculty.[48]

The establishment of the Massachusetts Medical Society in 1781 was another attempt to improve professional standards. It was empowered by the legislature to examine candidates for membership but had no power to prevent nonmembers from practicing medicine. For those who sought admission to the society and the cachet membership bestowed, knowledge of Latin and Greek, mathematics and natural science, plus a three-year apprenticeship with a "respectable" physician were considered sufficient preparation.[49] A three-year licentiate period preceded full fellowship. In time, men who held medical degrees from Harvard were entitled to membership without examination.

The beginnings of a medical school at Harvard notwithstanding, the easiest and most economical route to becoming a physician was to pay apprenticeship fees to an acceptable physician, study his medical books, observe some of his cases, and, at the end of three years, be examined by the Censors of the Massachusetts Medical Society. Undoubtedly this was what Lucy had expected when she wrote that "Walter can be with us while he is studying physic." Although college education was not a necessary precursor to a medical career, Walter Channing thought otherwise. An academic degree, he insisted, "would aid my professional progress."[50]

Friends and family tried to dissuade him from his academic ambitions, although Francis and William had attended Harvard and it was assumed that Edward would do the same. Perhaps Walter's previous lack of regular scholarship suggested that he would not take advantage of a college education. Perhaps they did not deem medicine as worthy a profession as the law or ministry.[51] Perhaps there did not seem to be enough money available to support Walter and Edward simultaneously. Nonetheless, he persisted in seeking the same educational opportunities that his brothers had enjoyed and expected the advantage they bestowed to place him at a higher level among Boston's physicians once he completed his training. Fortunately, just when his prospects seemed most bleak, Uncle Walter offered to meet his expenses.

His heretofore haphazard schooling made remedial study necessary before he could be admitted to the college, and so he spent seven months living with a clergyman in Bridgewater, Massachusetts, known to successfully prepare young scholars for college entrance. The Reverend Sanger charged a dollar and a half per week for instruction, board, and incidentals. Initially, Walter was lonely and homesick, his misery intensified by the distance between Bridgewater and the seacoast, with its familiar smell of salt air, but he gradually settled into a routine.[52] By February 1805 his studies with Sanger were sufficient to win him a place among the freshmen who had already spent one term at Harvard. His classmates included his brother Edward and his cousin Richard Henry Dana.[53]

It was a fractious period in the history of Harvard, precipitated by two deaths, those of the Reverend David Tappan, the incumbent Hollis Professor of Divinity, in August 1803 and of Joseph Willard, who had been president of the university for twenty-three years, in September 1804.[54] In recent years New England had experienced increasing tension between orthodox Congregationalists who adhered to Calvinist doctrines, including belief in the wickedness of mankind and a wrathful God, manifest in the Trinity, who punished sinners for their transgressions, and the growing number of more liberal ministers whose theology embraced free will and a merciful God whose Son exemplified the perfection of human existence. Harvard, having been founded in large measure for the education of ministers, was a great battleground for the growing schism that eventually resulted in two denominations, orthodox Trinitarian and Unitarian. The Channings, led by William, would become Unitarians.

Appointments of the Hollis Professor and the president were delayed by a bitter debate, for it was evident that whoever should be selected would determine the character and direction of the university far into the future.[55] The six-member Corporation, responsible for nominating the replacements, was evenly divided between Calvinists and liberals, which led to weeks of intense discussion, repeated balloting, and abortive compromise. In the end the liberal view prevailed and, early in 1805, the Reverend Henry Ware was chosen to be the Hollis Professor of Divinity. Subsequently, the Board of Overseers, also divided between the orthodox and liberals, officially approved the selection. The following year Samuel Webber, Professor of Mathematics, a man "without friends or enemies" but with liberal religious views, was named president.[56]

At the same time, Harvard's governance remained firmly in the hands of Boston's Federalists, who bitterly resented the embargo acts imposed by Jefferson's administration to preserve American neutrality in the growing conflict between France and Great Britain and deeply mistrusted Jeffersonian/Republican admiration for the French. Fearful of the excesses of the French Revolution, sympathetic to British representation of order and stability, and thoroughly angered by the restrictions on trade and commerce on which so many Boston fortunes depended, the men who controlled Harvard, liberal in theology but conservative in politics, represented the same elite class that would dominate Boston business and society for many decades.[57]

How much these controversies affected the students is hard to gauge, for young men are unlikely to pay much attention to affairs that seem to be concerns of their elders. The daily grind of memorization, recitation, and examination was much more compelling than the theological and political issues that surrounded them. Channing and his fellow students were required to study Latin, Greek, grammar, natural science, and mathematics. The faculty was small and the graduating classes never numbered more than forty-five. Law and the ministry were the most acceptable pursuits; the study of medicine was not much encouraged, except for the lectures available in the senior year at the fledgling medical college.[58]

Channing quickly tired of academic life. He was fined three times for absence from public worship and admonished for indecent noise and disorderly conduct at evening commons. He was older than most of the students in his class and this may have contributed to his disenchantment. Despite the months of instruction with Rev. Sanger, he still felt unprepared, and after working hard to avoid embarrassment in the classroom, he began to doubt his reasons for being there. Additionally, he was absent for more than thirteen weeks when illness, diagnosed as typhus fever, forced him to return from Cambridge to the parsonage on Berry Street.[59] The delirium, weakness, headache, lack of appetite, and dependence on others he experienced while ill stuck in his memory for the rest of his life, for he generally prided himself on good health. The true nature of his illness is impossible to ascertain, since fevers and rashes could not then be clearly differentiated. The family physician, Samuel Danforth, thought that the disease was caused by a disturbance of the stomach and prescribed an emetic-cathartic, to which he attributed Channing's eventual recovery.[60]

In Channing's eyes, President Webber was unsuited for his new responsibilities. "He had passed his whole life in the retirement of C. [Cambridge] and in the pursuit of abstract, and exact Science. His favorite pursuits had kept him away from men, and he knew less how to direct the physique and morale of . . . young men than any body in the community."[61] Certainly he was inadequate to deal with the "Rotten Cabbage" rebellion that erupted in March 1807, springtime being then as now the season most propitious for student unrest. The initial problem was "unwholesome . . . nauseous" food, in particular some especially bad cabbage soup that provoked the students to quit the dining hall and form a committee to protest to the college authorities. They cited the filthy appearance of the cook and steward, and the bad meat as well as the offensive soup.

Channing later admitted a secondary cause. "We were predisposed . . . to resist government, and the college fare offered the best reason for rebellion." According to Channing's grandson, writing about the episode more than a hundred years later, "A committee waited upon the immediate head of the college . . . with a sample of the soup in the bowl. One of the committee held the bowl, the chairman made a speech, and my grandfather held a spoonful of the mixture under President Webber's nose." It may well be that the grandson enjoyed imagining his grandfather as an impudent rebel, but it is certain that Walter Channing was heavily involved.[62]

The rebellion quickly assumed political overtones. At first the Corporation demanded that the students withdraw their petition. The students refused. Instead, they issued a public statement that began: "As we, the Students of Harvard University are about to dissolve the ties which have hitherto bound us to that institution, we think that a decent regard to the opinion of the public and especially for those who are more deeply and dearly interested, requires that we should give a fair and impartial statement of the causes which have brought us to this our present, important and unusual resolution."[63] One hundred and forty-seven students signed this "appeal for a cool and impartial decision." Among the juniors were Walter and Edward Channing and Richard Henry Dana.

Everyone in Cambridge and Boston knew well the declaration that the students had imitated. But rebellion against Great Britain was one thing, rebellion against Harvard was another. There was fear that indulging the students would lead to more protests and demands for an even greater variety of food. "Plainness of diet . . . made acceptable by evening sobriety and early rising . . . is the universal rule of this place," opined the adminstration.[64] To the Federalist-controlled Corporation the episode seemed to threaten general disorder, and they were determined to restore authority. Tension increased when they voted to dismiss the students who had taken part in the rebellion, with a provision that those who would acknowledge their effrontery and promise never again to oppose college rules would be readmitted. Fathers and guardians of the rebellious students were summoned to a meeting designed to "reduce [them] to obedience." Many students, among them Edward T. Channing, agreed to seek pardon.[65] Walter did not.

The Rotten Cabbage rebellion had special significance for Channing: "during all this time of trial nobody appeared for me, and I was left pretty much to my own guidance."[66] He ignored advice from some of the family, fearing that it would contradict his stubborn refusal to give in. Their attempted interference reminded him of previous episodes in which he had experienced "much harshness, much severity" when he had expressed his views or opinions on issues with which others disagreed. He did not want to repeat those unpleasant occasions. Instead, he once more made his own decision and stood by it. On April 15, 1807, President Webber signed a formal letter of dismissal sent to William

Ellery Channing. "It appears that your brother Walter Channing was a party in the offence, and that he has not chosen to comply with the terms, required by the Corporation. The painful office therefore devolves on me of announcing to you, that his connexion with the College, pursuant to a vote of the Corporation, is dissolved."[67] By coincidence the letter was written on Walter's twenty-first birthday.

Many years later Walter Channing would advocate a strong liberal arts education as essential preparation for professional life, but in 1807, when he had already begun to tire of college studies and with another year in Cambridge ahead of him, he may well have found the rebellion a good excuse to quit. However, he had his family to face and returned to the parsonage with some trepidation. There his younger sister, Lucy, greeted him with welcome news. "Walter, we have voted not to hear a single word about the late affairs at Cambridge."[68] Whether the family had already forgiven him or had concluded that his conduct had shown the wisdom of their initial opposition to his attendance at college, their apparent lack of interest was consistent with their previous attitude toward his conduct and further strengthened his independent spirit.

But a course had to be charted. He was of legal age, with no money of his own and no inheritance at his disposal. He had not altered his goal, but he had to change the means of achieving it. His interest in medicine remained strong and he well knew he could proceed without the Harvard College degree. He had learned to manage for himself and he quickly formed a plan. On April 20, 1807, he became a pupil of Dr. James Jackson, already one of Boston's leading medical men, who would soon become the quintessential physician in antebellum Boston. It was one of the best decisions he ever made.

Chapter 2 ✐✿

Medical Studies

The medical student is influenced by his age. He cannot
escape the power of the current opinion, and he will
commonly fall into the current practice.

—Walter Channing, "General Introductory Lecture,"
November 4, 1840

CHANNING hitched himself to "a rising star" when he became a pupil
of James Jackson. It was the beginning of a professional and personal
friendship that lasted sixty years. "My master in medicine was—and
is—Dr. James Jackson. . . . And where a wiser or better master?" wrote Channing a few years before Jackson's death in 1867.[1] His admiration never diminished for the mentor whose devotion to his patients, commitment to the
medical profession, and willingness to adapt to new ideas represented the epitome of a nineteenth-century physician.[2] Equally important, Jackson's lucrative
practice was proof that medicine could provide a good living. Channing was
acutely aware of the necessity before him to make money.

Jackson was only nine years older than Channing, but the additional years,
coupled with ambition, superior training, and outstanding ability, had already
launched him on a stellar career. He graduated from Harvard College in 1796,
having attended the medical lectures in his senior year. After a brief hiatus
teaching school, he became a pupil of Dr. Edward Holyoke of Salem, Massachusetts, one of New England's outstanding early physicians and the first president of the Massachusetts Medical Society.

Jackson next spent nine months in London at the United Hospitals of St.
Thomas's and Guy's, an opportunity not enjoyed by many of his contemporaries. In addition to attending the medical lectures and serving as a "dresser"
(surgical assistant), he studied anatomy with Henry Cline and Astley Cooper,

21

considered the foremost surgeons in England. Edward Jenner's remarkable treatise, *An Inquiry into the Causes and Effects of the Variolæ Vaccinæ*, had been recently published and Jackson was quick to recognize that smallpox, a leading cause of sickness and death, could be prevented by vaccination. Assuming the procedure was still unknown in his own country and that he would have a decided advantage by introducing it, he also studied vaccination at St. Pancras Smallpox Hospital.

While in London, Jackson strengthened his friendship with John Collins Warren, another recent Harvard graduate. Warren, son of John Warren, the founder of the medical school at Harvard and its first Professor of Anatomy and Surgery, was also destined for permanent glory in the Boston medical pantheon. For nearly forty years thereafter, Warren and Jackson jointly created the major institutions of antebellum medicine in Boston.[3] By the time Channing became his pupil, Jackson was busily engaged in a growing medical practice greatly facilitated by his British training and by his familiarity with vaccination, though he had been frustrated in his attempt to be the first to bring the procedure to Boston.[4]

Under Jackson's tutelage, Channing applied himself "with unabated industry."[5] The Rotten Cabbage episode had had a sobering effect, focusing his mind as no previous experience had, and he was occupied with subjects that fully engaged his energies. Jackson's collection of medical books, assembled during his months in England, was the core of the instruction.[6] Channing studied twelve or fourteen hours daily, absorbed by anatomy, physiology, chemistry, and materia medica. There were frequent oral examinations. Occasionally he or one of the other pupils compounded prescriptions according to their preceptor's orders.[7] Frivolity was ruled out; there was no time for parties and entertainments, no possibility of leading a fashionable life. Yet Channing found the regimen entirely to his liking, for he could expect that Jackson's guidance would lead to professional success.

Diligent study of anatomy was especially important as a foundation for obstetrics, though there is no indication that Channing was then thinking about a career in that branch of medicine. He did witness a single case of childbirth, at the Almshouse; a friend who was the pupil of the acting physician had been entrusted to deliver the child of a black woman. Channing's role was limited to remaining with the patient when his friend went home for the night and to administering a dose of *secale cornutum* (ergot) to hasten the labor. Asked what he had done while waiting, he laughed and said that he had been "making rye faces."[8]

Jackson also introduced his pupil to morbid anatomy, permitting him to witness a few postmortem dissections and allowing him to attend others in the practice of John Collins Warren.[9] French physicians had recently made morbid anatomy a productive area of medical investigation and Americans were beginning to pay attention. Postmortem dissections enabled them to correlate observations of diseased organs with symptoms shown by the patient during his or her final illness. The students were usually charged with restoring the corpse to its prior state, sewing, washing, and wiping as best they could.[10]

There was no hospital in Boston at the time of Channing's pupilage, so clinical instruction was limited. Neither the Almshouse nor the Dispensary, which might have substituted as clinical settings, permitted regular attendance by Harvard students or by physicians' pupils.[11] Occasionally, he witnessed an accident case or surgery in a patient's home, taking careful notes on the cases he had seen as well as those explicated by his mentor during tutorial sessions. Primarily, though, he had to rely on learning from books. At the time, Jackson was a thorough believer in "heroic medicine," a metaphor for the battle against a disease that was threatening the life of an individual patient. Strong measures were required to defeat disease and heroic medicine relied on plentiful doses of emetics and purgatives. Many years later, when heroic therapeutics had become outmoded, Channing defended his teacher's practice. "There was nothing excessive in the operation of such doses. They surely worked themselves out and off, and the taker only remembered how much good they did him. Patients then were grateful . . . satisfied and gratified with treatment and results."[12]

Even more than the medical knowledge he received from Jackson, Channing was indebted to him for "unbroken kindness." Jackson may well have been the supportive older brother Channing had not known. He was treated "almost like a member of his family" and permitted familiarity with the lifestyle of a successful medical practitioner.[13] He quickly understood that long hours and hard work were necessary, but that a good physician would receive esteem and honor from his patients, his colleagues, and the public.

Jackson was preceptor to several other pupils during the months Channing spent with him, including John Revere, the son of Paul Revere, the revolutionary hero and subsequent mayor of Boston. Like Channing, Revere later studied in Edinburgh and the two were fast friends. Paul Revere paid $233 "for the pupillage of his son for eighteen months."[14] Channing's fees, $150 for fifteen months, were paid by Uncle Walter.[15]

While studying with Jackson, Channing attended the six-week course of medical lectures delivered in Harvard's Holden Chapel. Used as the college lumber room during the British occupation of Boston, this was the space now allotted to the medical professors.[16] John Warren made a strong impression. As Channing later recalled, "By daily and very prolonged lectures he was able

Holden Chapel, Harvard College (courtesy of the Francis A. Countway Library of Medicine)

to communicate excellent knowledge in his branches [anatomy and surgery]. . . . I know of few teachers in America or Europe who is better remembered . . . he knew thoroughly what he wanted to say and said it."[17] Midwifery was discussed during the final lecture only, hardly sufficient preparation for young physicians who would soon have to attend deliveries. In later life, Channing could not recall receiving any instruction in midwifery from John Warren, but that may have been due to the insignificance of the material or to a lapse of his own memory.[18]

What he did remember was "how cheerfully and how laboriously, and dangerously, in the depths of winter, did we labour to supply him with the material for his brilliant anatomical dissections." Until 1831 only the cadavers of executed murderers and men who had engaged in a fatal duel were legally available for dissection in Massachusetts.[19] Hence, "a very severe service devolved upon the medical students. . . . They were to supply the material for anatomical demonstration. . . . One night as I was returning at midnight from some miles distance from the college with the product of a search, a fellow student being also with me in the carriage, it broke down a long distance from our destination. It was agreed that I should wait in the carriage while the other student went for another carriage. It was cold, dark, silent." For three very long hours he waited with the body, and it was well past sunrise before Channing, friend, and corpse were safely back in the anatomical room.[20] Grave robbery was a serious offense, yet medical students such as Channing were willing to risk it for the sake of adequate instruction.

The other two Harvard medical professors made a less favorable impression. Channing found that Aaron Dexter, Professor of Chemistry, did not understand much of his subject. His experiments often failed, though he was seldom embarrassed by repeated fiascoes. Benjamin Waterhouse, Professor of Theory and Practice of Medicine as well as of Materia Medica and Botany, held his classes in the parlor of his home facing the Cambridge Common. No lecture room had been made available to him at the college. The class was not large, so there was ample space, but it was difficult to see the small drawings Waterhouse used to illustrate his lectures.

Channing thought of Waterhouse as "a character" and gave him little respect. Though he had been educated abroad and was more familiar with European medical literature than his colleagues, in Channing's eyes Waterhouse lacked confidence in himself. He was known to change his prescriptions frequently, "going to a patient's house . . . sometimes before the medium was got and before they had been sent to the apothecary, or if sent, follow them there and make a change." Waterhouse never got along with the other medical professors and when a serious clash eventually erupted, Channing did not support his cause.[21] However, he did provide one of the quips Channing never tired of repeating. "Once I asked if he practiced midwifery. Oh no said he. Why not? Because I could not wait for the moving of the waters."[22]

Despite the long hours Channing committed to his medical studies, he took time to develop an interest in mineralogy. He attended a series of lectures delivered by a visiting Frenchman named Godon, and joined frequent expeditions to local sites of geological interest.[23] Like many other intellectually curious men and women of the era, Channing was fascinated by natural science.[24] He continued to acquire mineral specimens throughout his life, regretting that he lacked the money and leisure that would have enabled him to accumulate a significant collection.

After fifteen months with Jackson, Channing decided he was ready for a larger medical arena and resolved to pursue further studies in Philadelphia. It would have been easier for him to remain in the comfortable intimacy of Boston, as did most of his contemporaries. Had he done so, he could have attended a second series of medical lectures, for he had been accepted by the Harvard professors despite his ignominious departure a year or so before. Like other aspiring physicians who wanted formal training and an academic degree, he would soon have qualified for a diploma.[25] Or, if he had not wanted the academic degree, he could have continued with Jackson and received a certificate of competency, been examined and approved by the Massachusetts Medical Society, and begun to seek patients. However, the University of Pennsylvania offered the best medical training in the United States, and Channing assumed that would make a difference in an increasingly competitive profession. Again demonstrating the ambition he had shown when he insisted on attending Harvard College and the independence he had shown when he refused to recant his position vis-à-vis the Harvard Corporation, he borrowed money against the legacy he would eventually receive from his father's small estate, gathered letters of introduction that would be helpful in a new city, and in June 1808 set out for Philadelphia.[26]

PHILADELPHIA, the largest city in the new nation, with a population more than twice that of Boston, presented a sharp contrast to the more provincial town.[27] Indeed, one historian has suggested that Boston was fifteen to twenty-five years behind in just about every aspect of life.[28] Philadelphia had been the cultural center of colonial America and the administrative and financial capital during the Revolution and early years of the Republic and it was now a bustling, cosmopolitan city. For Channing, its importance lay in the hospital and medical school that were well esteemed at home and abroad.

The Pennsylvania Hospital, the only general hospital opened during the colonial period, had been founded in 1751. It offered a clinical setting where diseases of every kind could be seen. From its inception, apprentices were permitted to observe while their preceptors examined patients; when the medical school was established in 1765, its students were required to attend clinical lectures at the hospital, a powerful attraction for Channing.

The Pennsylvania Medical School, the oldest medical school in the nation, was equally appealing to the young man from Boston. It was patterned after the medical school in Edinburgh, which, by the eighteenth century, had replaced Leiden as the foremost medical center of Europe.[29] The Edinburgh faculty was part of a famous university empowered to grant academic degrees to its medical graduates.[30] Under the leadership of William Cullen (1712–1790), instruction was based on a theory of disease that deviated from traditional humoral theory. Humoralism, which had its origins in ancient Greece and Rome, postulated that disease is caused by an imbalance of the bodily fluids (the so-called humors: blood, phlegm, yellow bile, and black bile), and that health can be restored when the humors are balanced and purified by appropriate drugs and diet.

The Edinburgh professors espoused the solidist theory, according to which disease is caused by excitement or irritation of the body's organs and solid tissues. More specifically, Cullen and his disciples believed that irritation of the nervous system causes disease and that cures depend on stimulation or relaxation of nervous tone, again by application of appropriate drugs. John Brown (1735–1788), another of the Edinburgh professoriate, held a theory contrary to Cullen's. Brown taught that disease was the result of excessive action of the blood vessels, and he advocated reducing blood flow to cure disease.[31]

The founder of the Pennsylvania Medical School, John Morgan, had studied medicine in Edinburgh as well as in London and on the Continent. He was particularly impressed by the Scottish system and determined to replicate it when he returned to his native city. In 1765, with the assistance of influential physicians and merchants, he persuaded the trustees of the College of Philadelphia to appoint him Professor of the Theory and Practice of Physic, thus making medicine part of the academic curriculum.[32] Additional appointments soon followed Morgan's, most notably William Shippen, Jr., who had studied anatomy with John and William Hunter and midwifery with Colin Mackenzie in London, and continued his studies in Edinburgh with Alexander Monro (Primus) and William Cullen. Shippen, like Morgan, had received an M.D. from the University of Edinburgh.

When Channing began his studies in Philadelphia, there was a faculty of six professors, all of whom had studied in Edinburgh. A few had also been to London, Paris, and other European medical centers. Of the three contemporary Harvard professors, only Waterhouse had had the benefit of European training. Warren and Dexter, like most of their Boston colleagues, were products of the apprenticeship system. That does not mean that they were necessarily less effective as physicians or teachers, only that they had no academic medical training and tended to impart practical lessons from their personal and sometimes limited experience. European-trained men, who had been exposed to the grand systems and theories that reflected physicians' attempts to discover a unifying explanation for disease, relied heavily on observation and reason rather than experience. Neither group was closer to the truth about the cause and cure of disease. Scientific medical experiments were still relatively uncommon.

Requirements for graduation were fairly rigorous considering the absence of educational standards in colonial America. To receive the M.D. degree, the students had to attend two four-month sessions of lectures in various areas of medical learning, including clinical lectures. (The lectures were not sequential but repeated every year.) Upon completion of the second set of lectures students were examined orally by the professors; they then defended a written thesis.[33] The traditional preceptor system continued in tandem with this formal education, thereby familiarizing the student with the daily practice of medicine.

In addition to greater opportunities to observe disease, diagnoses, and therapeutics at the hospital and to learn from sophisticated medical teachers, Channing now had access to a good medical library, well-equipped anatomical collections, and more cadavers with which to observe and perform dissections.[34] He could also form friendships from among a more varied group of men. Students flocked to Philadelphia from many parts of the country, especially the south. A few were attracted from the West Indies and farther overseas. About 250 men matriculated annually in the medical department of the University of Pennsylvania, a huge difference from the still small student body at Harvard.[35]

In addition to Channing, five other New England men, including two from Massachusetts, enrolled in 1808.[36] It was a significant change. Until very recently, New Englanders had not sought a Philadelphia education, perhaps an indication of parochialism, perhaps a reflection of mutual suspicions. Philadelphians were reputed to be impious, ostentatious, proud, and vain; Yankees were rumored to be sharp dealers, their credentials and scholarship questionable.[37] Few Yankees had ventured so far until 1806, when George Cheyne Shattuck, who had already received a medical degree at Dartmouth, chose to augment his knowledge by spending a year in Philadelphia.[38] Shattuck became a pupil of Benjamin S. Barton, then Professor of Materia Medica and one of the physicians at the hospital.

On Shattuck's recommendation, Channing called on Barton soon after his arrival in the city and was accepted as his pupil. The arrangements were similar to those he had had with James Jackson. He would be expected to assist Barton in whatever way he desired, in exchange for supervision of his studies and the guidance that an older man could provide. Channing was extremely pleased. "He [Barton] converses with the zeal of a man desirous of the reputation of his profession & of exerting the same zeal in others," he wrote to Shattuck. He also accepted Shattuck's advice regarding lodgings and made arrangements to board "with a small but respectable family" on South Street, not far from the hospital.[39]

The industrious habits Channing had acquired with James Jackson were not neglected in Philadelphia. He was soon visiting patients for whom Barton did not have time, a mark of his preceptor's confidence in him. Since the lectures did not begin until November, most of the students had not yet arrived and the hospital was not overcrowded with observers. It was a great opportunity for Channing, who was eager for firsthand encounters with disease. Throughout the summer and autumn months he accompanied the resident house physician on early morning visits and made careful notes on the interesting cases.[40]

On the other hand, his social life differed markedly from that during the previous year in Boston. "Few young men of my age," he later confessed, "experienced a greater change in his habits in some respects, than I did by the removal to Philadelphia. I had lived a life of much seclusion while a pupil with Dr. J. and something of my Newport mode of life had returned. But in the great city, I was called out . . . I visited a good deal, and took much pleasure in the intercourse of life."[41] There was no reason to refuse society, especially when he realized that Philadelphia had "the prettiest, most charming—red cheek'd plump young women" he had ever seen.[42]

In November, Channing began to attend the lectures that would qualify him for the degree. He relished the wide offering of instruction and, in letters to Boston, extolled the "eminent men" who were his teachers.[43] Most notable was Benjamin Rush, Professor of the Practice of Physic and of the Institutes of Medicine and Clinical Medicine, who made as vivid an impression on Channing as he did on everyone, everywhere. William Ellery, the Signer, had made his acquaintance in 1776, when Rush was a member of the Pennsylvania delegation to the Second Continental Congress and also a signer of the Declaration of Independence.[44] Now he was the leading physician and teacher in Philadelphia, "the central light and glory of the school who perhaps never had his equal for the talent of exciting a spirit of investigation in medical students."[45] Channing attended Rush's course each of the two years he was in Philadelphia and often referred to Rush's optimistic, though often misguided, faith in his ability to cure the sick.[46]

Following in the footsteps of his mentors in Edinburgh, especially John Brown, Rush taught that disease was caused by excessive action in the blood vessels, producing fever in most instances, but leading to other symptoms of disease as well. His insistence on the therapeutic necessity of bleeding, which would reduce the action of the hematologic system, and on strong drugs to further deplete the system and reduce internal friction, made him the most extreme and most renowned exponent of heroic medicine.[47] Many students carried Rush's theories to other parts of the country.

The New Englanders were more skeptical. According to Channing, "Well is the medical practice of Philadelphia remembered. It was in the strictest sense depleting. . . . As far as the influence of Dr. Rush extended, v.s. [venesection] and active internal remedies were in daily use. How far this system was adopted by students generally I do not think it had much patronage among those who went from New England."[48] His comment suggests the extravagance of Rush's therapeutic practice, since at the same time Channing admired the more moderate form of heroic medicine practiced by James Jackson and the other Boston physicians.

There was little formal instruction in obstetrics in Philadelphia, a deviation from its Scottish heritage. In Edinburgh, Thomas Young had been appointed Professor of Midwifery in 1756 and was the first British instructor to give a complete obstetrical course to medical students.[49] (Until well into the nineteenth century, the word "midwifery" continued to refer to the study and practice of the medical subject now called "obstetrics." See Chapter 4.) However, the American colonies were far behind in recognizing the need for systematic instruction for male accoucheurs.[50] The neglect was not unreasonable. Until the latter part of the eighteenth century, most American women continued the age-old tradition of calling a female midwife to assist them in the birthing room, and few physicians were engaged for childbirth cases.

William Shippen, Jr., had given particular attention to midwifery studies during his years abroad. Shortly after his return to Philadelphia in 1765, he offered private instruction to midwives, male or female, but there were few subscribers. When appointed to the medical faculty of the university, it was as Professor of Surgery, Anatomy, and Midwifery. As was the case at Harvard, midwifery received scant attention, since surgery and anatomy were more generally useful. Over the years the three subjects were separated from one another and eventually, in June 1810, Thomas Chalkley James was named Professor of Midwifery.[51] By then, Channing had left Philadelphia.

Prior to James's appointment, students who desired more obstetrical training than was available at the medical school could attend one of two private schools that offered instruction and some clinical experience. Channing selected the school run by Thomas Chalkley James and Nathaniel Chapman.[52] Both men were excellent teachers who "did what they could to supply means of practical knowledge of midwifery."[53] Channing had not yet decided to make obstetrics his paramount medical interest, but the fact that he sought the additional instruction suggests at least an incipient interest. James and Chapman allowed their advanced students to attend some deliveries and thus Channing had his first real case in midwifery. He was accompanied by John Shelby, a fellow student from Tennessee.[54]

The case made an indelible memory, as might be expected.[55] It was a long and difficult labor culminating in the birth of a boy, followed quickly by the placenta. The newborn looked dead but a pulse could be felt in the umbilical cord. Channing immediately immersed the baby, with cord and placenta attached, in a bowl of warm water, inflated the lungs artificially, and attempted to stimulate breathing. It seemed an eternity until the baby began to breathe, feebly at first, but in a short time completely naturally. The cord was cut and the child continued well. Channing and his companion were elated. "Our object was not to learn how long the placentary circulation would continue after that organ had been separated from the womb, but to give the little boy the best chance of breathing and of living."[56]

Chapman was pleased by his students' ingenuity but uncertain about the reason for their success. Channing thought that by keeping the baby in water the same temperature as his mother's body and waiting long enough, the placental blood had stimulated the respiratory system. "The changes produced in the blood by the placentary circulation seemed to be as well performed as while that organ was connected with the womb. Perhaps no changes are made [and] the fœtal blood returning to the placenta . . . ultimately nourish[ed] the fœtal system."[57] Regardless of the plausibility of their explanation, it was a remarkable outcome. Channing must have recognized that he had a talent for obstetrics and that the result, a living child and joyful mother, would be rewarding emotionally as well as professionally.

In the spring of 1809, Channing was examined orally by the full body of professors, a step toward receipt of a medical degree. Though he had attended only one set of lectures, he must have persuaded the professors that his attendance at similar lectures in Cambridge constituted a second year. He experienced some anxiety when they inquired about the Rotten Cabbage episode and was greatly relieved when his straightforward answer did not cause trouble. The questions asked by each professor in turn posed no difficulty. On March 23, 1809, he informed William, "I have taken a degree of M.D. at the University and . . . had the expression of satisfaction of the board of faculty for my examination."[58]

Actually, he had not yet received the degree. The following month was spent writing a thesis, which had to be defended in public to complete the requirements for graduation. His subject was "Animal Life," and by his own admission "a poor affair it was." He was attempting to refute Rush's doctrines and the eminent professor did not take kindly to Channing's comments. "Dr. R. remarked in the Hall that the school required no subscriptions to particular articles of medical faith and supported no dogmas[,] but that he did not feel disposed to yield his opinions, in consequence of my objections . . . thus this great matter ended and I was pronounced Doctor in due form."[59]

Having now obtained the degree, Channing decided he could benefit from another year in Philadelphia. His funds, however, were precariously low. He owed fees for graduation and for memberships in the natural history society and a medical society to which he had been elected. Even more ominously, the shoemaker would not return his mended boots until he had paid for them. He wrote home asking his older brothers for help. The appeal emphasized the advantage he would have from additional education at the medical school, "being the first in the country," as well as from further clinical training at the hospital.[60] The brothers sent the money.

He spent much of the summer months attending at the hospital. There was yellow fever on some ships in the harbor and he had an opportunity to see a disease that appeared less frequently in Boston.[61] But the pressure under which he had labored the previous year was considerably reduced. He took time off from medicine to socialize with new friends, to attend lectures on botany and mineralogy, and to make excursions with amateur naturalists in the area around Philadelphia. When the medical lectures resumed in late autumn, he sat through them for a second time. The repetition was tedious and Channing later regretted the time wasted in "a sort of dissipation, a literary luxury." He might have done better to go to New York, where a different medical scene would have been more instructive.

It soon became unmistakably clear that the time for study had ended and that he must begin to earn a living. Nonetheless, Channing hesitated to return home. He feared there were already too many physicians in Boston, that the Massachusetts Medical Society would not accept his credentials, and that, as a Pennsylvania graduate, he would be excluded by provincial Bostonians with their Harvard connections. In short, he worried that he would not attain "fame and that portion of wealth which it is not a sin to wish."[62] A friend advised

Pennsylvania Hospital (courtesy of the Francis A. Countway Library of Medicine)

him to become a surgeon on one of the ships in the China trade. A position of that sort promised a decent salary as well as a share in profits of the voyage.

But the ties of family and images of familiar places prevailed, pulling him back to Boston despite his misgivings. Shortly after his return, he applied to the Massachusetts Medical Society for licensure. His friends, including James Jackson and George Cheyne Shattuck, feared, as he himself did, that "a Harvard rebel" might not be admitted on the basis of his Pennsylvania credentials, and that he would be required to submit to the indignity of an examination.[63] But the contretemps did not occur and, with a recommendation from Benjamin Barton to support his claims of successful study, he was licensed in May 1810.[64] He took a room on Federal Street, not far from William's church and the parsonage, where he could reside with the family. Disappointment soon overwhelmed him. Few patients sought his care.

He blamed his troubles on the insularity of the Boston medical profession. Writing to Barton to thank him for "the kindness and patronage of a father," he cynically contrasted the state of medical science in the two cities. "With you it is a philosophical pursuit. It becomes more interesting, because it is daily improved. With us, sir, it is the medium of subsistence only and second-handed are all our acquisitions." Channing iterated his earlier concerns: "More unfortunate for our science, the influence of family will make moderate talent the means of almost splendid wealth, while more deserving men not so fortunate by *accident* starve or become sycophants."[65]

His accusations were misplaced. His family had influence and he had plenty of talent. William was daily gaining respect and fame as a minister; Francis, enjoying a successful law career, had married Susan Higginson, daughter of one of Boston's most prominent merchant princes; and Uncle Walter had left Newport to live in Boston, where his financial status and social reputation were high. Channing's friends, recognizing his ability and determination, optimistically predicted success.[66] His lack of self-confidence and view of himself as an outsider without benefit of family connections probably stemmed from a fear that the Boston medical establishment would remember the disgrace of the Rotten Cabbage affair or would resent the fact that he had left home for his medical degree—or perhaps both.

However, something had to be done to right the situation. He was not about to abandon a career in medicine, for which he had already invested more than three years and accumulated serious debts. An issue of one of the fashionable periodicals of the time, the *Salmagundi,* probably read during the lonely hours waiting for patients, had convinced him that "crossing the Atlantic [was] a marvelous sharpener of the wits."[67] He applied this notion to his own predicament. "I saw intuitively in this hint a chance of success which nothing I had already done had brought with it, or was likely to bring."[68] He must go abroad to further his medical education. Again the family objected. "[S]imple ridicule . . . was the weapon employed now, and it was meant to have been fatal to the project as it had been when I thought of being a Painter."[69] Once more he persuaded them of the merit of his scheme. Funding was another potential barrier but Aunt Gibbs (Mary Channing Gibbs) was a wealthy woman and Uncle Walter, her brother and the business partner of her late husband, was her financial manager. A loan was arranged and in June 1810, less than three months after his return from Philadelphia, Channing embarked for England, intending to continue afterward to France and other European cities that might be advantageous for further study.[70] He must have been oblivious to the dangers from ongoing war between Britain and France or the possibility of the United States becoming involved in the hostilities, despite nearly a decade in which the United States had struggled to avoid being caught in the titanic clash between the two European powers. In addition to deciding to sail eastward across the Atlantic and to be the first Channing or Ellery to do so, he made another, more fundamental resolution. He would devote his time abroad to the study of obstetrics. Over the preceding fifty or sixty years, increasing numbers of women in Boston had employed physicians instead of female midwives to deliver their babies, and it was said that "this part of the profession is now principally conducted by physicians."[71] The few months in Boston had shown him that a young physician well trained by the masters of British midwifery might have a special niche in the local medical profession.

James Lloyd was the first Boston physician to gain a reputation as an obstetrician. He had studied in London with William Smellie (1697–1763) and William Hunter (1718–1783), England's most prominent teachers of midwifery and anatomy, and, after his return to Boston in 1752, had developed a practice increasingly devoted to obstetrics. During the Revolutionary War, Lloyd's Loyalist sympathies might have had dire consequences, but the admiration of his female patients outweighed popular suspicion of his politics. In his own words, "I never in my life refused to attend a call, even to the poorest class of society . . . cases which often require immediate assistance. If there was only a bed of straw, I saw that it was beaten up and rendered as easy and comfortable as it was possible, and with my own arms invariably laid the delivered woman upon it; . . . and I assure you I have been amply paid by the esteem and affection of my patients."[72]

Lloyd died on March 14, 1810, within days of Channing's return to Boston.[73] He had been preceptor to several other physicians who made obstetrics an important part of their general practice but, except for John Jeffries, none had the added advantage of British training. However, Jeffries was an outright Loyalist who left Boston with the British army in 1775 and took part in campaigns in the southern colonies. He lived in England during the remainder of the war and for several years afterward. Daring to return to Boston, he resumed his practice but was never as highly regarded as Lloyd. Moreover, by Channing's time Jeffries was nearly seventy years old. A replacement would soon be needed.[74] It did not require much imagination to recognize an opportunity, if one wanted to make midwifery one's particular area of medical expertise and if one could secure the special aura of overseas training. But it did require persistence and a willingness to incur more debt.

Physicians in France and England had pioneered male-midwifery during the seventeenth and eighteenth centuries, often with considerable opposition from female midwives, who feared competition in what had been almost exclusively their domain. The Parisian maternity hospitals for poor women received large numbers of cases that allowed physicians to observe the birth process and begin to develop scientific descriptions of normal and abnormal presentations. Dissections and anatomical study also provided a clearer understanding of the organs of parturition than had been possible for most midwives, whose knowledge was based on individual experience at the birthing stool. Obstetrical texts were written for the use of other physicians and for those midwives who could read and wished to improve their skills. In France and other continental nations women continued to deliver most babies, however, primarily because the governments established training programs and licensing requirements for female midwives, thereby sanctioning their continued practice.[75]

The outcome was different in England. Part of the explanation lies in the development of forceps. For centuries, midwives throughout Europe had called on barber-surgeons for assistance in cases of an impacted fetus. With their surgical instruments, these men usually destroyed the baby in an attempt, often unsuccessful, to save the mother.[76] Forceps were a new instrument designed to pull the baby from the birth canal. Peter Chamberlen, a French Huguenot whose family had come to England to avoid religious persecution, is credited with the invention of forceps early in the seventeenth century. He and his descendants kept their instrument a secret for several decades, supposedly by operating under cover of a sheet, but in time other medical men were using forceps, sometimes of their own design. This ability to save children and mothers from life-threatening situations gave physicians an advantage over female midwives, but it is not sufficient to explain why British physicians became so prominent as midwives. Most deliveries do not require forceps or other devices.

In England, as in France, physicians were giving increased attention to the study of anatomy and physiology, and some of them concentrated on female anatomy and the physiology of pregnancy and parturition. In turn these men, most notably William Smellie and William Hunter, taught aspiring physicians what they had learned about obstetrics. The dissemination of midwifery textbooks and establishment of lying-in hospitals for poor women also meant that obstetrics increasingly became part of medical practice. But medicine was exclusively a male profession and, in contrast to the French experience, British midwives, excluded from further education and lacking the support of professional organization or government, were the losers.

Physicians had long been called to attend royal births, even when a midwife performed the actual delivery, and their presence was insurance in case of an emergency. As the middle class expanded and more people were able to purchase physicians' services, the general demand for medical care increased. Women, especially upper- and middle-class women who could afford physicians' fees, preferred medical men who had studied female anatomy, were trained to deliver babies in as safe and pain-free a manner as was then possible, and had the medical knowledge to deal with complications during and following delivery. More than any other factor, women's expectations that a physician-assisted birth would be easier for the mother and would be more likely to produce a successful outcome for mother and child explains the shift from traditional childbirth practices and the replacement of female midwives by medical men.[77]

Channing knew that the tradition of male-midwifery in Europe, coupled with the intellectual and scientific reputation of the Old World, assured instruction superior to any in the United States. London, with its medical schools, hospitals, and private obstetric courses taught by renowned physicians, and Edinburgh, with a Chair of Obstetrics at the university and a lying-in hospital for clinical observation, promised the key to advancement in Boston. Paris, too, might bestow useful lessons, but there could also be difficulties because of language and customs so much more at odds with those of the sons of American colonials. Federalists like Channing would be more naturally at home in Great Britain, despite memories of the war for independence.

CROSSING the Atlantic might "sharpen the wits" but getting there was a terrible ordeal. The "good ship *Nancy,* two hundred tons," took forty-seven days to sail from Boston to England and Channing was dreadfully seasick the entire time. Nearly half a century later, he vividly remembered "the unmitigated and unmitigable horrors of a sailing ship life," and the motion of the ship, ceaselessly plunging downward, then rising on the waves "as if about to change sea for air."[78] When eventually he reached Falmouth, the lush green

English countryside restored his weary spirits. Though some scenes looked familiar, almost everything was new and unexpected. He was "bewitched by the luxury in an English landscape." The English people with their fresh complexions and pleasant manners were "a contradiction to the general remark that John Bull is very reserved, austere and inaccessible to strangers."[79] He was awestruck by the monuments of Shakespeare and other literary giants in Westminster Abbey and by the splendor of the Houses of Parliament.[80]

He had intended to begin his studies in London, but medical lectures were suspended during the summer months and there was little to keep him in the capital. Instead, he continued northward to Edinburgh, where friends from Boston, including John Revere, his companion from Jackson's preceptorship, Isaac Hurd, and Benjamin Lincoln, were already engaged in medical study.[81] Francis Parkman, Sr., father of the noted historian, was present at the university, and Francis Cabot Lowell and his family had taken up residence in the city.[82]

Lowell, who had married Hannah Jackson, a sister of James Jackson, was investigating the operation of textile mills throughout Great Britain. His clandestine observations would enable him to replicate and improve upon the British system when he returned to Massachusetts. In 1812, together with his brother-in-law, Patrick Tracy Jackson, Lowell started the Boston Manufacturing Company in Waltham and thereby laid the foundation for the hugely prosperous New England textile industry. The Lowells provided homelike hospitality to the young men who had come to study at the prestigious university.

The academic year had not begun in Edinburgh either, so there was ample time for sightseeing. Boston and Philadelphia were small towns compared to Edinburgh. Channing was struck by the stark contrasts he could not help observing—beautiful stone buildings in the New Town juxtaposed against the filth of the Old Town, "elegance coupled with disgusting sights." He was dismayed by "houses some of which are what we call 15 stairs high. One family occupies a story and tho' living under the same roof you are as ignorant of your neighbours as if inhabitants of different houses." He had taken lodgings "on the third flat (as it is called)" in one of these buildings in the Old Town.[83]

The lack of order and cleanliness, the crowded living spaces, and extreme poverty were offensive to his New England sensibilities still unaccustomed to urban squalor. He criticized the poor for their indolence, lack of ambition, and reliance on whiskey to relieve their dreary lives, but the sight of starving children and blind beggars wandering through the streets and impoverished women desperately seeking employment was unsettling. For these conditions, he blamed the British political system, particularly the landed aristocracy and an extravagant monarchy. He was also upset by signs of religious intolerance, especially the ruined churches that he attributed to the "reforming zeal" of John Knox and his Presbyterian followers.[84]

Despite such criticisms, it was a wondrous experience for a young New Englander exposed for the first time to the sights and traditions of the Old World. He and Revere made a trek in the Scottish highlands that opened his eyes and stimulated his mind in ways he could not have anticipated. Unfamiliar landscapes, ancient castles, centuries-old legends, local songs and dances, and the simple but impoverished lives of the highlanders produced a romantic vision that he tried to capture in his journal and letters. In keeping with his literary aspirations, he attempted to express his sense of the natural beauty that surrounded him, and if the words seemed to flood onto the pages, they were but an indication of his heightened emotions.

> At times the mist which is always hovering over these bleak elevations, would light upon them and the lake would become a boundless sea. In a moment, the sun would make a break through this obstacle to his glory, and present some little island near enough to threaten, with the assistance of the imagination, instant destruction, at another time the sublime head of Ben Lomond would become alone visible, while the base was still immersed in the ocean of mist, and now we had only to invoke the power just now mentioned and we saw it tumbling on our devoted heads. Then on a sudden you might see the full splendor of light poured on a thousand cliffs, and slowly retiring mountains bringing your vision to the next remote point of prospect.[85]

In late autumn, the academic calendar resumed.[86] Edinburgh University was at the height of its influence, with a notable faculty and students from many parts of the world. Whereas Oxford and Cambridge continued to teach medicine by didactic lectures, without clinical corollaries, and to exclude students who did not adhere to the tenets of the Church of England, Edinburgh and the other Scottish universities, not burdened by these traditions, had long offered wider intellectual and scientific inquiry. "Study has become a fashionable pursuit," Channing wrote to Shattuck, adding that "the professors are quarrelsome dogs among themselves" and that professional jealousy was all too apparent. James Gregory, Professor of the Practice of Physic, had some years previously flogged James Hamilton, Professor of Midwifery, who then sued and recovered damages. The episode continued to fascinate newcomers to Scotland.[87]

Hamilton had succeeded his father, Alexander Hamilton, in the Chair in

Midwifery. He was a powerful lecturer whose vast personal experience in midwifery provided examples for all the points he wished to make. Acknowledged as the leading Scottish obstetrician, he was determined to have midwifery made a required subject in the medical curriculum rather than the elective course it had been. Unfortunately, his controversial style and the enmity it roused among important members of the Faculty Senatus prevented him from reaching that goal until long after Channing had returned home.[88] Nonetheless, Channing was greatly impressed by a professor so totally devoted to his field. "He boldly advanced his principles and defended them with a warmth, adhesiveness and almost vindictive violence rarely witnessed."[89] Despite his attendance at James's and Chapman's lectures in Philadelphia, Channing found that Hamilton required close and respectful attention.

Hamilton also offered his students practical experience at the Edinburgh General Lying-in Hospital, established by his father in 1793. The hospital had twenty beds, primarily for poor women, where Channing could observe and participate in the broad range of obstetrical cases, from normal deliveries that required no intervention to complicated deliveries in which instruments or other assistance was necessary. He witnessed numerous unexpected obstetrical events such as hemorrhage, convulsions, and ruptured uterus. He also learned firsthand the diagnosis and treatment of postpartum difficulties, especially puerperal infection.

Channing concentrated on midwifery to the exclusion of the other medical lectures, and even repeated Hamilton's course in the spring session. However, he did not neglect the nonmedical attractions of Edinburgh that were also certain to "sharpen the wits." There was a continuous stream of intellectual and social activity and Channing, newly arrived from a less sophisticated milieu, did not hesitate to indulge himself. The literary offerings were especially appealing and he attended many of the public readings then much in fashion. He also followed publication of new volumes of the *Edinburgh Encyclopedia*, which he deemed to be "the greatest effort of Scottish genius and industry."[90]

Francis Lowell introduced him to high society. The earl of Buchan, whom he met at Lowell's house, astonished him by asking to see his medical diploma and haranguing him on political subjects. He must have comported himself well enough, for soon after he received an invitation from the earl to a celebration of George Washington's birthday. He became acquainted with Mrs. Anne Grant, an author and essayist who had many friends and admirers in the United States. He met Francis Jeffrey, editor of the *Edinburgh Review*, at a dinner party to which he was invited by Mrs. Grant.[91] He was also introduced to John Leslie, Professor of Mathematics, and they discussed such diverse topics as America, mineralogy, and the effects of rice on blindness.

In short, his Scottish hosts were not only hospitable, they were exceedingly curious about the nation that had separated from Great Britain. This alone might have guaranteed Channing's social success, but he was as eager to make friends as they were. Nor did he neglect the ladies. After he left Edinburgh, a friend informed him that he had been "in company a short time since, with some of the ladies you *particularly* knew, and they spoke of you in such pretty words and expressed such unaffected regret at your departure, that I thought I would instantly take my leave of Scotland with pleasure, if I could flatter myself with being remembered with such tenderness."[92]

In early spring, he bade adieu to Scotland, praising it as "the seat of science and literature . . . above all neighboring states." In the final analysis, he decided, the poverty and loose manners of the lower classes were attributable to the fact that Scotland was a garrisoned country, where soldiers stationed to prevent a possible French invasion were a bad influence on the poor. As colonists, Americans had a long-standing opposition to billeting of British soldiers, and Channing had not forgotten the exploits of his father and grandfather.

When he returned to London, the United Hospitals of St. Thomas's and Guy's with their medical school captured his interest. Astley Cooper, the surgeon with whom James Jackson had studied, provided the anatomy and surgical lectures. Channing found him "far above common men . . . he lectures upon surgery with the persuasion of a rhetorician and makes you *feel* that his art has matter enough to satisfy the mental capacity of most men, for it satisfies his own."[93] He was less enthusiastic about John Haighton, who gave the lectures in midwifery. Haighton's tedious delivery was a marked contrast to the "lively, clever, interesting lectures" he had heard from Hamilton, but he resolved to get as much from them as he could.[94] Later in life, when he had accumulated much obstetrical experience of his own, Channing realized that he had benefited substantially from Haighton's lectures.[95]

Like Hamilton, Haighton had a private midwifery hospital where his students could attend women in childbirth and learn to perform complicated procedures under the eye of their instructor. The students, especially those like Channing who had journeyed from far-off lands, were keenly conscious of their relative lack of knowledge. When a young man from one of Britain's West Indian colonies exerted too much strength during a forceps delivery and actually pulled the woman from the bed onto the floor, Haighton berated him for not knowing better. "If I did," replied the student, "I should not have thought of coming so far to learn."[96] The comment might easily have been made by Channing.

As he prepared to return to Boston, Channing gave considerable thought to the differences he had discerned between medicine as taught and practiced in Scotland and in England, as well as to the future of the profession in the United States. In Edinburgh, he had found that medicine was taught upon a "most liberal plan." The Scots viewed medicine as "the premier branch" and surgery, like apothecary, "as a necessary appendage." The reverse was true in England, where surgery was the preferred branch and medicine was disdained. Astley Cooper himself had expressed doubts as to the usefulness of medicine. Fortunately, in the United States these distinctions, which derived from the medieval guilds that had separated physicians from surgeons and both from apothecaries, did not apply. Though John Morgan had initially proposed that physicians, surgeons, and apothecaries should have separate training at the University of Pennsylvania and should form separate professional bodies, the freewheeling American spirit, which did not welcome limitations on an individual's accomplishments, acted to prevent such distinctions. Channing hoped Americans would continue to avoid British views and practices. He saw no need to separate the branches or "to degrade one to increase the reputation of the other."[97] It must have occurred to him that midwifery, which incorporated medical and surgical skills, would benefit if there were no such distinctions.

As an aspiring physician with his mark to make, he continued to deplore professional jealousy and in-fighting that might inhibit his own success: "If his patient's welfare be the object of his [the physician's] anxiety and unwearied study, how naturally would an union of opinion or cool discussion take the place of that rancor, ill will and jealousy which now disturb the ministrations of the high priest of Apollo even at the very altar. The theater on which a physician has sometimes to appear is the deathbed of a patient . . . to make this the scene of a quarrel is a violence offered to humanity that a man should be ashamed to commit."[98] He hoped professional ethics would prevent such unbecoming conduct.

During the months he had spent in Britain, Channing stayed in touch with home. His letters were circulated among family and friends who were eager for news of his adventure. Edward and William wrote with some frequency. Edward's letters were full of easy banter, cautioning him not to become an Englishman and warning him not to marry an Englishwoman, unless she be rich. The younger brother also assured him that he was deeply missed. "Our late hours in the evening grow silent and cheerless for you are not with us," he wrote.[99]

But there was also unhappy news. In June 1809, while Walter was yet in Philadelphia, his sister Ann had married Washington Allston, still a struggling artist whose talents seemed woefully underappreciated. Allston, born in South Carolina, had gone to school in Newport and was a close friend of the entire Channing family.[100] He had long admired Ann, who reciprocated his attentions, and after seven years of study abroad, he returned to woo the eldest Channing daughter. They were married by William in the parsonage on Berry Street. "A few hours ago," William wrote to Grandfather Ellery, "Washington and Ann, after their long and patient courtship, were united in marriage. We consider this a happy event, but Ann is too important a member of our family to be resigned without something like sorrow."[101] Nearly two years later, it fell to Edward to inform Walter that "Ann's baby had been born and died."[102]

This same letter contained other sorrowful tidings. Francis, the oldest of the Channing siblings, had died November 8, 1810, en route to Rio de Janeiro, but the news had just arrived in Boston. Shortly after Walter's departure for England, Francis had suffered an alarming hemorrhage from the lungs. Though he temporarily recovered, he had been advised to seek a more permanent cure. Leaving their three children with relatives, Francis and his wife, Susan, embarked for South America hoping the sea air and warmer climate would restore his health. He died nineteen days after leaving Boston.[103] "We indeed had reason to fear this event," wrote William to his grandfather, "but hope mingled so much with our fears, that it fell on us almost with the force of an unexpected. . . . It has pleased God even to deny us the melancholy pleasure of having his ashes deposited near us."[104]

There is no record of Walter's reaction to this news, but his grief may have been mitigated by the strain in his relationship with his oldest brother, who had seemed to lack confidence in him and his prospects in medicine. Francis had charge of the funds lent to Walter by Aunt Mary Gibbs and had informed him, during his stay in Edinburgh, that the money had run out and that he must find his way home as best he could. Threatened by penury while three thousand miles from home, Walter turned to Francis Lowell, who immediately assured him of his assistance. "Go to Paris to finish your education and complete your studies abroad; and call on me for the means." The next mail brought the Gibbs money, but the disagreeable matter continued to rankle.[105]

The family assembled in the Berry Street parsonage was overwhelmed with grief. "It is impossible for one who did not see them to conceive the extent and vehemence of their sufferings." Francis's seniority had made him head of the family and they had all looked up to him with "sentiments nearly allied to filial reverence."[106] As the oldest son, Francis was especially cherished by his mother, but William too was deeply pained by the "breach in a family so united as ours" and felt as if "a part of ourselves were torn from us." Edward mourned "the dearest friend I ever had."[107] In time, faith and an acceptance of suffering enabled them to endure the loss.

Walter wound up his London adventure more like a tourist than a medical student. He attended art lectures and exhibitions of recent paintings and described them fully for the benefit of "Brother Allston." He visited Benjamin West, an American expatriate then president of the Royal Academy, who made a lasting impression because of "his youthful vivacity and the zeal with which he regarded his art."[108] He went to scientific lectures by Humphry Davy, perhaps at the Royal Institution. At the House of Commons, he heard William Wilberforce speak against slavery and Henry Grattan speak for Catholic Ireland, two events long remembered by an incipient social reformer.[109] He accumulated medical books and obstetrical instruments for his personal use and for instruction of the students he hoped to have one day. Though Francis Lowell had offered to provide the money for additional study in Paris, it would not have been a prudent move, especially since he was already encumbered by so many debts. Relations between England and France had not improved and travel from one country to the other was difficult. Surely he must have felt a desire to comfort his mother in her bereavement. He had been away a full year, seen many wonderful places, and become acquainted with interesting, talented Scots and Englishmen. Most significantly, he had learned as much as he could from the leading obstetrical teachers in Great Britain. He was twenty-five years old. It was time to return home and begin to practice medicine.

Chapter 3

Launching a Career, 1811–1822

His [Channing's] own talents & industry, aided by *powerful* friends, must ensure him success.

—George C. Shattuck to Jacob Bigelow, 1810

ACCORDING to family legend, Aunt Polly was the only person who sought Channing's recently acquired medical skills when he returned to Boston in the summer of 1811, but when he added "Just Returned from Europe" to the sign outside his door patients began to flock to his waiting room.[1] Thereafter he had more than enough business to keep him fully engaged. Eventually, he paid off the debts that plagued his conscience and strongly affected his outlook on the necessity for hard work. By old age he had become moderately prosperous and took satisfaction from the fact that he was the only Channing to have done so independently of a rich wife.[2]

Legend and family pride aside, it was not so easy to enter the medical profession in Boston. The 1810 *Boston Directory* listed forty-five physicians and surgeons, thirty-nine of whom had been licensed by the Massachusetts Medical Society, serving a population slightly in excess of 33,000.[3] Several of Channing's contemporaries, including equally promising men such as George C. Shattuck and Jacob Bigelow, hesitated to begin their careers in the crowded Boston medical community, where competition was strenuous, internecine strife prevalent, and the cost of living higher than in the smaller towns nearby.[4] Additionally, the local economy was burdened by restrictions on overseas trade.

Channing had three distinctions that propelled his career forward. First, he possessed up-to-date knowledge of British medical teaching and Bostonians were strongly Anglophile in their intellectual and scientific preferences. Second, he had given most of his time abroad to the acquisition of obstetrical knowledge and skill, whereas the other Bostonians who could boast of European training had not concentrated in that part of medicine. There was need for a man with his expertise, though he could never rely exclusively on obstetrics to make a living and would always have an active general practice.

Finally, despite his previous disappointment and fear of rejection, he was already well connected. He had been a Bostonian for eight years, spent two of those years at Harvard among the sons of Boston's finest families, and was well known in society. The increasing favor that his brother William's ministry was receiving, the esteem in which various other Channings, Ellerys, and Danas were held, and his personal familiarity with prominent men like Francis Cabot Lowell gave him a preferred place among the other young men seeking advancement in medicine. He had already been licensed by the medical society and accepted as a member of the Boston Medical Association.[5]

There were several direct ways of attracting patients. Easiest was to rely on family networks far beyond Aunt Polly, whoever she may have been. For some relatives he merely dispensed free advice that they could take or not as they pleased, for despite their medical knowledge it was not uncommon for physicians to be greeted with skepticism. Many people continued to diagnose for themselves and to prefer home remedies. Women were especially prone to rely on experience and to prescribe for their children's ailments. Francis Channing's widow, Susan Higginson Channing, "was often more afraid of the Dr. than the disease as they are very apt to give calomel when something without any of its bad effects might do quite as well." Susan so relied on a recipe for tincture of cinnamon once given her by Dr. Danforth that the apothecary refilled it at her request regardless of need or appropriateness.[6] However, when one of Susan's daughters was very ill, she instinctively turned to Walter. "I attribute her restoration in a great measure to the skill, and still more to the good nursing of Walter. . . . he was here 5 days when she was most ill and sat up with me 4 nights successively. During one of those nights it seemed to me impossible she could have survived many hours, but for the unwearied attentions and applications he made."[7]

Channing attended Uncle Walter and his family daily whenever the children or their parents were unwell, charging a dollar and a half per visit, plus an additional fifty cents if he dispensed medicine.[8] For Tom Searle, a distant kinsman via the Higginson connection, Channing prescribed "as little exercise as possible" and an "application to the feet which raises little blisters." Poor Tom was probably suffering from rheumatic fever, commonly called rheumatism. His sisters attributed his ailment to his having neglected to wear flannel underwear before the cold weather set in.[9] Many other members of Channing's family called on him for advice or active doctoring, including the childbearing sisters, sisters-in-law, and female cousins for whom he cared in miscarriages, stillbirths, and the delivery of healthy babies. Successful treatment of these close relations helped spread word of his ability as well as his character, which was described by one admirer as "so industrious, patient & polite that unless Apollo himself is against him . . . he will get along."[10]

Another way to advertise his skills was to attend at the Almshouse, where the steady numbers of paupers always included a few pregnant women. Channing was not a regularly appointed Almshouse physician but, since childbirth cases could be tedious and even uninteresting, the Almshouse physician and the Harvard professors who had access to Almshouse patients for clinical teaching were often ready to yield their places at the bedside to another man.[11] He had had one such experience during his year with James Jackson. Now, as a more frequent attendant, Channing had the opportunity to make himself better known among physicians who might one day ask him to consult in a complicated private case. He began to keep a list of his midwifery cases in August 1811, just a month after his return. Nearly all the initial cases were at the Almshouse. It was a rude introduction: six of the first seventeen babies died at birth or shortly afterward; one woman died of convulsions following a self-inflicted abortion.[12]

Channing was entering the Boston medical scene at a particularly turbulent time. The original Harvard medical triumvirate, John Warren, Benjamin Waterhouse, and Aaron Dexter, had always had their differences, with Waterhouse consistently the odd man out.[13] His abrasive personality and quarrelsome nature, stimulated by the suspicion (and in some cases the hostility) he encountered when he first arrived in Boston, were as much a cause of his difficulties as were the objective aspects of his life. Waterhouse, a Rhode Island Quaker, had spent the Revolutionary War years abroad studying medicine. This made him less than compatible with Warren, whose religious heritage was Puritan and Congregational,[14] whose brother had died at the Battle of Bunker Hill, and who had himself ably served the patriot cause. Waterhouse's superior medical education, acquired during those years in London, Edinburgh, and Leiden, also set him apart. He was prone to flaunt his cosmopolitan connections in front of the other two, who had trained locally and were doubtless resentful and jealous. Whereas both Dexter and Warren became staunch Federalists during the postwar era, Waterhouse was an increasingly ardent Jeffersonian, eventually espousing democratic ideas that seemed quite radical to his more conservative colleagues.[15] It was a nasty situation.

By 1810 the faculty had increased to six with the appointment of three young men whose European training, enterprise, and connections would make them leaders of the next generation of Boston physicians. Each was inherently unsympathetic to Waterhouse. John Collins Warren, who joined the faculty in 1809 as Adjunct Professor in Anatomy and Surgery, naturally shared his father's animosity toward Waterhouse. John Gorham, Adjunct Professor of Chemistry and Materia Medica, had studied medicine with John Warren prior to study in Europe and had married his daughter. When James Jackson was named to the newly created Professorship of Clinical Medicine in 1810, another anti-Waterhouse voice was added to the faculty.

Jackson had hurried home from London expecting to introduce vaccination to Boston, only to find that Waterhouse had already received cowpox lymph from England and was busily administering it.[16] Two years later Waterhouse succeeded in persuading the Board of Health to conduct one of the earliest clinical trials in medical records. Nineteen boys were vaccinated with cowpox lymph. After an interval of several months, they were inoculated with smallpox material and exposed to contagion at a smallpox hospital on Noddles Island along with two boys who were unvaccinated. None of the vaccinated children developed the disease but the two without immunity became ill.[17] Two of the vaccinated boys were sons of members of the Board of Health. Waterhouse's success added to Jackson's exasperation. His own proposal for a similar experiment had been refused permission.[18]

With the exception of Waterhouse, the medical faculty lived in Boston. The journey across the Charles River to deliver their lectures in Cambridge was time-consuming and tedious, when not made additionally uncomfortable and difficult by wet or wintery weather. At first, Warren and Dexter had to cross the river on the Charlestown ferry and make their way several miles upriver by carriage or on horseback. Later, a series of newly constructed bridges shortened the distance, but since the term lasted from November to March, they continued to be exposed to the elements.[19]

Cambridge was still a village with little to interest medical students, whereas Boston, with its numerous physicians, larger patient population, and intellectual and cultural attractions, offered a more active milieu. If the medical institution associated with Harvard was to grow and prosper, Cambridge was not the best place for it to be. Accordingly, in 1810 the Corporation acceded to a request from the faculty, Waterhouse dissenting, and voted to move the medical school to the Boston side of the river. For the next six years, lectures were held in rooms above an apothecary shop at 49 Marlborough Street (present-day Washington Street), where the younger Warren and John Gorham were already giving private instruction.[20] Now it was Waterhouse who had to come to Boston to deliver his lectures.[21]

The Massachusetts Medical Society, which was quartered in the same location, reflected the same rivalries. Initially the medical society and Harvard had feuded over their respective roles in medical licensure but were eventually reconciled when a Harvard degree and examination by the society were made equally valid. John Warren, with one foot firmly planted in the medical school, was elected president of the medical society in 1804, and he held that position until his death in 1815. His son served as recording secretary from 1805 to 1814, and James Jackson was treasurer from 1807 to 1811.[22] The two younger men poured their personal ambition and their professional goals into the medical society. Together they prepared and published a much needed *Pharmacopœia* that revised and standardized the nomenclature and preparation of medicinal drugs and brought much credit to themselves and the society. Also under their direction, several volumes of the *Medical Communications* of the society were published after a hiatus of sixteen years.[23]

The growing importance of the medical school and the rejuvenation of the medical society aroused the antipathy of many well-respected physicians who resented the clique whose increasing control seemed exclusionary. In February 1811, while Channing was still abroad, they attempted to create a rival medical society to be known as the Massachusetts College of Physicians. It would have the same "powers, privileges and immunities as other medical associations of the like nature and views enjoy."[24] By implication the new society could start a rival medical school. Among those whose names were signatory to the plan was Benjamin Waterhouse, "always happiest when in the opposition."[25]

Legislative hearings for grant of a charter were held in February 1812. Harvard sent President John Thornton Kirkland and John Lowell, one of the Fellows, to protest. The medical society, represented by John Warren and Aaron Dexter, presented its arguments against the proposal. James Jackson spoke on behalf of the medical school. Political differences played an important part in the controversy. The Federalists, party of the status quo, opposed the new society, whereas the Jefferson Republicans, representing the less well established elements of society, favored it. For a while it looked as if the dissidents would receive legislative endorsement, but in the end, after bitter conflict in the State House as well as in the press, on the streets, and in the parlors of Boston and its neighboring towns, the charter was denied.[26] Many years would pass before anyone dared attempt to set up a second medical school in Boston.

Benjamin Waterhouse was soon dismissed as Professor of the Theory and Practice of Physic. The Corporation, long aware of the "lack of harmony" between him and the other professors, was greatly displeased by his support for the College of Physicians and the threat it posed to their institution. The faculty voiced their grievances against him, including his "false, scandalous and malicious libels against the Professor and Adjunct Professor of Anatomy and Surgery."[27]

Waterhouse had anonymously published a sarcastic broadside aimed at "Captain Squirt," who opposed popular desire for a new fire engine. "Captain Squirt" claimed that a new engine would reduce the efficiency of the present engine and that even if he was too old to run to fires, his son, "young Squirt," would do so. On the morning the piece was printed, Waterhouse appeared on the steps of Warren's house, waving it before his nemesis. For this he was roundly cursed by "Captain Squirt." The flagrant hostility between the Warrens and Waterhouse intensified public interest in the affair and added to the uproar.[28] After several lengthy hearings before the Corporation and much perturbation among Waterhouse admirers and opponents, he was officially removed from his chair on May 20, 1812. In September, James Jackson was elected Hersey Professor of the Theory and Practice of Medicine.[29]

CHANNING'S return to Boston could not have been better timed. With so many charges swirling about, and so many changes occurring, he was quickly accepted into the inner circle. His political views, his ties to Boston society, and his personal goals coincided with those of the ruling clique. The problem of a Harvard degree was remedied in the summer of 1812, when Harvard granted him an M.D. degree *ad eundem*, thereby acknowledging that his degree from the University of Pennsylvania entitled him to a similar honor at home.[30] The irony of paying a five-dollar fee for a Harvard degree was not lost on him.

Jackson and John Collins Warren had committed themselves to "inform each other of any causes of discontent" and to work together for "improvement in medicine and other intellectual pursuits."[31] Among those improvements was a medical journal. Theretofore, New England physicians wishing to publish their medical observations or to read case reports of their colleagues had to rely on journals from Philadelphia and New York.[32] Warren and Jackson recognized that a regional periodical would abet the development of the medical profession and, at the same time, promote the interests of the medical school. Channing was invited to be one of the founding editors, along with Gorham and Bigelow. Each brought a special area of expertise as well as his general medical knowledge to the task. Each journal issue was assigned to one of them for general supervision. The editors met monthly to read and critique papers, after "a light supper to aid them in their deliberations."[33]

The *New England Journal of Medicine and Surgery and the Collateral Branches of Science* first appeared in January 1812 and quarterly thereafter. The title page attributed editorship to "a number of physicians" but there was no doubt about their identity. A motto from Francis Bacon proclaimed their scientific intentions: "*Homo naturæ minister et interpres tantum facit et intelligit, quantum de naturæ ordine, re vel mente, observaverit; nec amplius scit aut potest.*"[34] The first issue, intended to attract subscribers by the distinction of its authors and the importance of its contents, contained contributions by John Warren, "Remarks on Angina Pectoris"; James Jackson, "Remarks on the Morbid Effects of Dentition"; John C. Warren, "Cases of Apoplexy with Dissections"; Jacob Bigelow, "Treatment of Injuries Occasioned by Fire"; and Walter Channing, "Remarks on Diseases Resembling Syphilis, with Observations on the Action of those Causes which Produce them." There was also a note reprinted from the *New York Repository* about the first use of spurred rye or ergot in midwifery.[35]

Channing's paper appeared in four parts.[36] His thesis was that many cases assumed to be syphilis and treated aggressively with mercury compounds were "pseudo syphilitic" ulcers that did not require such harsh remedies. "Prudent delay" would enable the physician to determine the true nature of the symptoms and prescribe accordingly. Channing was urging physicians to question their assumptions when diagnosing venereal disease and to "search for new causes" that might lead to better treatment. He justified this cautious approach by citing several British medical authorities whose writings on the subject might not be familiar to his readers.

In subsequent volumes, Channing wrote more frequently on topics that derived from his obstetrical practice.[37] He also reviewed several midwifery texts that had been published in England and France and commented on articles on midwifery submitted by other physicians, several of whom had written directly to him. There were also additional non-obstetrical contributions. "Cases of Delirium Tremens," describing seven cases from his practice, appeared in 1819. It was the earliest significant discussion of the subject in America. Channing's paper acknowledged the work of Thomas Sutton, whose *Tracts on Delirium Tremens*, published in London in 1813, had first described alcoholic delirium tremens.[38]

Channing's next steps toward advancement were made at the medical school. For several years following his return from Britain, he offered lectures at 49 Marlborough Street on the theory and practice of midwifery to private students.[39] Students already enrolled in the medical school, medical apprentices not attending the medical school, and practicing physicians who wanted to avail themselves of the latest obstetrical knowledge took advantage of Channing's training and experience, while he added to his income and his reputation.[40] He was filling an important vacuum, since many Boston physicians had childbirth cases in their general practice.

Midwifery continued to receive scant attention in the regular academic curriculum at Harvard, where, as in Philadelphia, it was incorporated into the anatomy and surgery lectures. However, in 1815, in a reorganization similar to that which occurred in Philadelphia, Harvard created a lectureship in midwifery. The change was driven by John Collins Warren, who wanted to divest himself of responsibility for the midwifery lectures when he assumed his father's chair in anatomy and surgery.

The incumbent professors recommended their friend Walter Channing and the Corporation acceded to their wishes. On May 15, 1815, at the age of twenty-nine, he was appointed Lecturer on Midwifery, with "a claim to such compensation only as he might derive from the fees paid by persons attending his lectures."[41] At the same time, Aaron Dexter was relieved of some of his responsibilities by the creation of a lectureship on materia medica and botany that went to Jacob Bigelow. Both appointments were publicly announced on November 1, 1815, during the ceremonies installing Warren as Hersey Professor of Anatomy and Surgery. Channing and Bigelow declined inaugural ceremonies for their appointments, not wishing to deliver the formal lectures that were expected at such events.[42]

Three years later, they were promoted. Channing was named Professor of Midwifery and Medical Jurisprudence and Bigelow became Professor of Materia Medica. The inclusion of medical jurisprudence reflected the growing sense that a well-educated physician should understand the interaction of the law with medicine, for forensic purposes and for development of public health measures. In Philadelphia, Channing had attended lectures by Benjamin Rush, one of the earliest Americans to advocate the teaching of medical jurisprudence, and this may have influenced the decision to give him those additional responsibilities. An equally plausible explanation is the traditional association of midwifery with legal issues such as bastardy, infanticide, paternity, and rape. In Europe female midwives had long been called as witnesses in such cases.[43]

Channing exalted in his good fortune. Writing to thank his friend Edward Everett, who had used his personal influence on Channing's behalf, he pledged "to make my public life respectable & useful." Perhaps seeing his academic career on an upward trajectory, he also referred to the possibility of a national university where he might someday "make one of its faculty of medicine."[44] The idea of a national university, a favorite idea of John Quincy Adams and other visionaries, would never materialize.

The professorship was more than a personal triumph. It was also proof that a good medical education had to include adequate instruction in midwifery. Channing made sure his course was fully recognized. In 1816 he protested to the Harvard Corporation that the newly revised statutes governing requirements for graduation from the medical school did not include a public examination in midwifery, though materia medica and the traditional subjects were specifically mentioned. The Corporation replied that it had not intended to slight midwifery and agreed that an examination should be required. The exact mode of instruction for that examination was left to the faculty, but Channing was reminded that, since increased numbers of students would benefit the professors, "all necessary instruction" should be provided.[45] The midwifery books, plates, and instruments, as well as an "apparatus for demonstrating labor" that John Warren had used in his lectures, were now added to Channing's own collection of teaching materials.[46]

The medical faculty set its own fee schedule. Students enrolled in Channing's and Bigelow's courses paid ten dollars to each professor. For Gorham and for Jackson the fee was fifteen dollars; for Warren, twenty dollars. The additional time required for the preparations and dissection in anatomy justified Warren's higher fees.[47] When Aaron Dexter resigned in 1816, John Gorham was named Erving Professor of Chemistry and Mineralogy.

Within a few years of the move from Cambridge to Boston, the school outgrew the accommodations on Marlborough Street. Again Warren and Jackson took the lead in a campaign to persuade the Harvard Corporation and the state legislature that public support was necessary and appropriate for the construction of a new building. They made sure to point out that several other states, recognizing the public good that derived from the education of physicians, had seen fit to fund construction of medical school buildings. It helped that Bowdoin and Williams Colleges were also seeking financial assistance from the Commonwealth of Massachusetts.[48]

In 1814 the legislature agreed to appropriate to the three institutions for ten years the revenues from a tax on banks. Harvard's share was $10,000 per year, for a total of $100,000. Of this amount, $20,000 was allotted by the Corporation for purchase of land and for construction and maintenance of a new medical school building on Mason Street, close to the Boston Common and to the residences of the professors. In recognition of the assistance granted by the Commonwealth of Massachusetts, for many years thereafter the school was referred to as the Massachusetts Medical College.[49]

For the next decade the five professors, Warren, Jackson, Gorham, Bigelow, and Channing, *were* the medical school, setting standards, schedules, and course content, with little or no interference from the administrators in Cambridge. Monthly meetings of the medical faculty were held at the professors' homes, sometimes with a convivial dinner afterward.[50] Channing assumed the duties of dean at the beginning of the 1819 term.[51] He filled that post, except for a few scattered occasions, for the next twenty-eight years.

John Collins Warren (courtesy of the Francis A. Countway Library of Medicine)

James Jackson (Portrait Collection, Boston Medical Library, Francis A. Countway Library of Medicine)

As dean of the medical faculty, his obligations in no way compared with those of a modern dean who must devote a major amount of his time to fund-raising and to relations with government officials and agencies. Channing was expected to keep the minutes of faculty meetings and correspond with the Corporation and Overseers on general subjects, including examination times and recommendations for degrees. About the only thing he shared with latter-day deans was that his portrait would one day be conspicuously hung in the administration building of Harvard Medical School. As Warren's biographer declared, "Probably there can nowhere be found in medical biography an instance of greater unity and good feeling, than prevailed among these gentlemen for the whole period of their connection with the College; until, in fact, increasing years, and the claims of extensive practice, caused them, one by one, to retire from the labors of the chair."[52] The acrimony that had characterized the previous generation disappeared as like-minded men were recruited into the oligarchy that dominated all aspects of the profession.

ACCEPTANCE by the Massachusetts Medical Society was another indication of Channing's assimilation in Boston's medical circles. He had become a licentiate in 1810, just before his departure for Britain. Licentiates customarily

John Gorham (courtesy of the Francis A.
Countway Library of Medicine)

Jacob Bigelow ▶ (Portrait Collection, Boston
Medical Library, Francis A. Countway Library of
Medicine)

advanced to fellows after three years of medical practice, but since Channing
was abroad and did not practice the year following his initial election, he had
to wait until 1814 to be named a Fellow of the society. His participation in
society governance was limited. Channing was less politically ambitious than
Warren, less likely to receive general acclaim than Jackson, and, as an obstetrician, less likely to be as widely esteemed as some of his other colleagues. He
never attained leadership of the medical society as they did, but he did serve
over the years as one of the Censors, its librarian, and its treasurer.[53] The last
office was time-consuming and tedious, for he was required to notify members
when their dues were in arrears and to keep society finances in order. In 1820,
along with John Collins Warren and James Thacher, he was elected an Honorary Member of the Rhode Island Medical Society.[54]

The intellectual ferment epitomized by the new generation of physicians
spilled over in many directions. Channing shared with them an enthusiasm
for natural science that flowed from his medical interests as well as from his
inherent curiosity. Both botany and mineralogy had their practical uses as the

basis for materia medica. Every physician prescribed drugs for his patients and had to be familiar with the origins of herbal and mineral medicinals. But there was also the pleasure of investigation, identification, and collection of speci-mens found in their natural environment. Channing's interest in mineralogy had been stimulated by his earlier studies in Cambridge and Philadelphia. His delight in plants received a boost from his preceptor, Benjamin Smith Barton, who was an outstanding botanist, and from the natural history society he joined in Philadelphia. Back in Massachusetts, his favorite pastimes included mineralogical and botanizing excursions to surrounding hills or ponds, which yielded specimens he could add to his own carefully chosen collection.[55]

When Jacob Bigelow organized a local Linnaean Society in 1814, Chan-ning was among the original coterie who shared these enjoyments.[56] Bigelow had already evidenced an unusual talent for botany, giving public lectures on the subject and publishing his *Florula Bostoniensis*.[57] The members of the Linnaean Society, who included many nonphysician amateurs of natural sci-ence, collected and exhibited animal, vegetable, and mineral specimens from all parts of the world, especially items peculiar to the American continent.

One of their more bizarre activities was an investigation of reports of a sea serpent spotted offshore north of Boston. The news had captured the imagina-tion of the public and interest was intense. Descriptions of the strange creature varied widely, some reporting three white rings around its neck, some re-porting that it moved horizontally, others reporting it moved vertically, but everyone attesting to its immense size and rapid motion. The investigating committee took depositions from observers but could reach no conclusions until a three-foot-long serpent killed inland was brought to Boston for further inquiry. Perhaps it was a progeny of the great serpent. The Linnaean commit-tee examined it meticulously but finally, concluding that it was fairly nonde-script, they named it *scoliophis Atlanticus*.[58]

The Linnaean Society soon found that it lacked adequate financial support to maintain and exhibit its collections. A committee composed of Channing, Bigelow, and F. C. Gray offered to give the collection first to the Boston Athenæum, then to Harvard. In both cases they were rejected and the speci-mens were dispersed. The Linnaean Society expired in 1822, but it would be later resurrected under the leadership of John Collins Warren as the Boston Society for Natural History.[59]

Channing was also elected to membership in the American Academy of Arts and Sciences, another indication of recognition by the elite.[60] The acad-emy, which had included physicians from its foundation in 1780, was closely allied with Harvard and with the clergy and merchants who dominated Boston society. Dedicated to "promote most branches of knowledge advantageous to a community," it provided another venue for presentation of papers on scientific topics. These papers reflected little experimental science and did not contribute much to basic science but, by its connections with European learned societies, the academy did help disseminate new knowledge in the still-young nation and encouraged close observation and description of natural phenomena.[61] The academy was a stimulating venue for Channing's interests.

Just as medicine and science received impetus from the younger generation of educated men, the literary scene in Boston was also enlivened by emerging scholars and authors. Some in this group, Edward Everett, George Ticknor, George Bancroft, and Jared Sparks, for example, had studied abroad and returned home full of enthusiasm for the new ideas they had encountered. They were determined to rescue Boston and Cambridge from the intellectual doldrums that they found.[62] The Friday Club was representative of this group. It met at the homes of its members for wide-ranging discussions of essays composed and presented by writers, clergymen, and junior faculty at Harvard. Channing attended regularly, occasionally reading a recent paper.[63] The topics remain unknown, but it is entirely possible that some found their way to publication in the *North American Review*.

This journal, intended to elevate literary and artistic criticism in America, was patterned after the *Westminster Review* and the *Edinburgh Review*, although the editors and contributors intended to promote a vibrant American culture.[64] Edward Tyrrel Channing was involved from the beginning and served as editor for a few years before his appointment in 1819 as Harvard's Boylston Professor of Rhetoric and Oratory.[65] Many members of the Friday Club were part of the enterprise. Walter was a frequent contributor. His essays echoed the call for literary and artistic independence and vitality that was a hallmark of the journal. Since he had spent a year abroad, he felt qualified to compare the American scene with Great Britain's and to exhort his countrymen to break free from cultural dependence on the former mother country.

He also wrote on topics more directly related to medicine. In a eulogy of Caspar Wistar, one of his professors in Philadelphia, he described the characteristics of a physician that, by implication, he considered most worthy: "simplicity of character . . . purity of intention . . . unabated zeal in the cause of science and humanity." The piece gave Channing a chance to praise the University of Pennsylvania, "the most celebrated medical school in our country." The freedom with which he paid tribute to the University of Pennsylvania was further indication that he no longer thought of himself as an outsider.[66]

In a review of a history of ancient medicine originally written by the German historian Kurt Sprengel and since published in a French edition, Channing demonstrated a surprisingly modern understanding of the importance of medical history. The medical historian, he wrote, "should give us the art [of medicine] as it has been, not as it should be." Medical practice, he pointed out, is but a reflection of the particular beliefs of a people at a particular time. Though the medical beliefs described by Sprengle included much superstition and religion, Channing detected the beginnings of "a profession devoted to the study of nature and founding its science on a patient observance and study of intellectual and physical health and disease."[67]

Combining his knowledge of literary personalities with his ideas about health, he also penned an article titled "On the Health of Literary Men." There he criticized the "intellectual forcing" that emphasized excessive study and the acquisition of vast amounts of knowledge by young people at the expense of their physical development. Deploring "premature intellectualism," he argued for more outdoor exercise, recreational activities, and appropriate diet.[68] Channing was taking a position about education and child development that he would repeat on later occasions.

DESPITE creation of a medical journal, reinvigoration of the medical society, an enlarged faculty and better facilities at the medical school, one more institution was needed if the profession was to flourish in Boston—a general hospital. Philadelphia and New York had long had hospitals for inhabitants whose circumstances were such that they could not be cared for at home, though that was eminently preferable. In Boston, the Almshouse had provided minimal medical care for more than a hundred years, but by 1810 large numbers of lunatics and paupers were crowding out the "worthy poor," and it was no longer adequate to meet the needs of the sick, if ever it had been. Biblical commandments to succor the poor and homeless, as well as ordinary sentiments of compassion and civic pride, should have been effective reasons for Bostonians to assist people too ill and too destitute to care for themselves.

By the beginning of the nineteenth century it was equally apparent that hospitals were essential to the progress of medical education and medical science. Physicians and students needed large patient populations for the observation of disease in its many manifestations. The future of the transplanted medical school depended on adequate clinical instruction, one reason for the move from Cambridge. There was ongoing concern that Boston's most promising medical students might prefer to go elsewhere for their training, as Shattuck, Channing, and Bigelow had done. The arrangement whereby members of the medical faculty were permitted to bring students to the Almshouse was not an adequate solution. Nor was the Boston Dispensary, which served the poor on an outpatient basis or sent physicians, not medical students, to their homes.

Lack of support for a hospital was due less to hard-heartedness or civic neglect than to a faltering economy and slow growth in the years after the Revolutionary War. In the early years of the nineteenth century, however, Boston's prosperity and population increased with newly established manufacturing enterprises, improved trade and commerce, and the expansion of banks and insurance companies. Prospects for further economic growth bred a greater awareness of civic responsibility and, for some newly rich men, a desire for respectability and the social standing that contributions to a hospital or membership among its trustees and incorporators could provide.[69]

A circular letter dated August 20, 1810, signed by those inveterate activists John Collins Warren and James Jackson, asked influential Bostonians to support plans for a hospital.[70] They reminded the wealthy of their Christian duty and described the hardships endured by the industrious poor when faced with protracted illness. They made special mention of insanity, an illness that affected all classes and required separation of the afflicted from society. They also emphasized the increased prestige that Boston would receive if it had a first-rate medical school with a suitable hospital for clinical instruction. Their words were well received by men who could make things happen in Boston.

The Massachusetts General Hospital was incorporated the following year by act of the legislature.[71] The governor, lieutenant governor, Speaker of the House, president of the Senate, and chaplains of both legislative houses were named a Board of Visitors with power to appoint four of twelve members of the Board of Trustees. Federalist control of the State House assured a tightly knit board composed of merchants, bankers, and lawyers who shared a strong sense of noblesse oblige.[72]

The Commonwealth committed to sell the Province House, once the residence of the colonial governor, and to contribute the proceeds to the hospital if an additional $100,000 were subscribed privately. Economic and political vicissitudes, including the embargo and the War of 1812, caused some delay, but by July 4, 1818, a site had been selected and enough money received to begin construction.[73] Charles Bulfinch, who had designed the State House, University Hall in Cambridge, and the homes of many wealthy Bostonians, was sent on a tour of hospitals in New York, Philadelphia, and Baltimore.[74] The impressive Greek Revival building he designed was intended to recall the grandeur of ancient republics and remind Bostonians of their civic responsibilities. Its location, on the back side of Beacon Hill and close to the banks of the Charles River, made the hospital easily accessible by boat and by foot. The cleansing breezes from the river promised salutary air.

There was general approval of the hospital despite some concern that it would lead to increased dependency of the poor on the charity of the rich. On the other hand, there was an equal concern that the poor might be unwilling to avail themselves of its facilities. Horror stories about experimentation on the helplessly ill and the use of cadavers by medical students might frighten the very people for whom the new institution was intended. Nonetheless, common sense prevailed. More than a thousand people subscribed to the fund. Boston's leading men, notably William Phillips, David Sears, James Perkins, and Thomas Handasyd Perkins, made generous donations. The physicians gave lesser amounts, as fitted their means. Warren contributed $400, Jackson $420, Channing and Dexter $100 each.[75]

The trustees appointed eight consulting physicians from among the leading nonacademic members of the medical community. James Jackson was designated to be the acting physician, and John Collins Warren the acting surgeon. They would be permitted to bring their students to the hospital. In turn, Jackson nominated Channing to be the assistant physician, not because he expected to be overburdened by the patient load but in case he was ill or otherwise prevented from attendance. To enhance the importance of the position, Jackson intended to give Channing complete responsibility during the summer months, when he would be out of town.[76] Channing was deeply gratified. For the rest of his life, he treasured the recollection of "the morning he called on me and offered me the place of assistant physician to that noble charity in the foundation of which he had exerted so important an agency."[77]

It was another example of the close relationship between him and Jackson as well as the symbiosis of the hospital and the medical school. Neither the physicians nor their assistants received a salary from the hospital and the time they devoted to hospital duties could not be given to paying patients. However, they would be bringing their students to the wards, and that promised a greater number of students enrolled at the medical school and increased fees for the professors.[78] This arrangement could not directly benefit Channing's teaching, for the hospital was not meant to serve pregnant women and there could be no teaching opportunities in midwifery. However, the prosperity of the medical school was very much in his interest, since his fees depended on enrollment. Moreover, his appointment as assistant physician gave him increased exposure in general medicine, while his close relationship with Jackson, reinforced by his new appointment, assured Bostonians that he was a physician to be trusted.

Thus, in every aspect of the medical profession—patient care, faculty status, Fellow and officer of the medical society, editor of the journal, and assistant physician at the new hospital—Channing had fulfilled Shattuck's prediction for his success. He was part of the small but powerful group that had transformed Boston medicine and would provide leadership for the next four decades. The torch had been passed from physicians whose careers had embraced colonial government, revolutionary war, and the establishment of a new nation to men who shared confidence in the future of their nation and their profession. They were better trained than their predecessors had been and were willing to embrace future change. They were energetic and ambitious, involved in a multitude of intellectual and scientific activities, and already well known by colleagues abroad and in other American cities.

Channing never achieved the prominence attained by Warren, Jackson, and Bigelow. This was attributable partly to his personality, which shunned self-aggrandizement, partly to his preference for solitude and quiet pursuits, and partly to the personal tragedies that persisted throughout his life. It was attributable also to his status as professor of midwifery and as a practicing obstetrician. Though there was a compelling need for good obstetrical teaching and practice, the field remained slightly less estimable, perhaps because the patients were women, perhaps because there was a suggestion of uncleanliness or even of prurience about it. Midwifery had long been women's work and in some quarters it still was deemed less "manly" than surgery and medicine. There would always be people who thought it improper for a man to give medical care to women in such intimate circumstances. Channing was admired as the outstanding obstetrician in the Boston community, but that was not enough to push him to the top of the ladder.

Warren, hardworking and determined, endowed with the right name and great ability, was considered "the most eminent surgeon in New England if not in America."[79] James Jackson, a much beloved practitioner, equally involved in every aspect of the advancement of the medical profession, shared first place with him. As for Bigelow, shortly after his return from Philadelphia in 1810 Jackson had invited him to join in his practice, thereby practically guaranteeing his success, though his scientific and intellectual abilities would have marked him for renown without Jackson's patronage.

An indication of the differences among these four can be seen in an estimate of their annual incomes, made by one of their colleagues around 1817. "James Jackson, great and profitable practice [$]10–15,000 . . . J.C. Warren, same as Jackson beside Surgery [$]10–15,000 . . . Jacob Bigelow [$]800 . . . Walter Channing [$]1000–1500." John Gorham, the fifth member of the medical faculty, was reputed to be earning $2,000, "a respectable business."[80]

CHANNING'S marriage to Barbara Higginson Perkins was the capstone of his early success. Even before returning to Boston, he had confided to George C. Shattuck, "We must be married for the women are everything in our calling."[81] Were they clerks or fishmongers, men their age would have been thinking of marriage, but there is no doubt that marriage to the right woman could further a physician's career by assuring the public of his probity. For a physician whose primary clientele were women, a respectable marriage was especially important. A wife with the right family connections brought additional benefits, while a wife whose family was wealthy was even more of a prize for a man who might not become very rich himself.[82]

Channing did not need to wander far or search long to find himself a wife. Barbara Higginson Perkins, more than nine years his junior, was one of the limited set of eligible women with whom he would naturally be acquainted. "Walter Channing with whom we have made acquaintance & who is a charming young man has lent Mamma a Volume of the lectures of Dr. Rush," she confided to her dearest friend less than six months after his return from England.[83] We do not know if his future mother-in-law enjoyed reading Rush's lectures, or if she read them at all. It may well have been a ploy to impress her daughter, for within three more months Barbara had begun to transcribe Walter's European journal into her own leather-bound journal. Soon they were being thought of as a couple, and by the winter of 1814 they were officially engaged.[84]

A virtual spider's web of relatives and friends connected the two. Barbara's aunt, Susan Higginson Channing, widow of Francis, would also be her sister-in-law. Her maternal grandfather, Stephen Higginson, and his family were members of the Federal Street Church and William Ellery Channing had briefly lived in their Brookline summer home. James Jackson was a good friend of her father.[85] Even without so many direct connections it was inevitable that the two should know one another, given the relatively small circle of socially acceptable families in Boston, where everyone knew everyone else and most found marriage partners within that group.

Barbara was the eldest of six children. Her parents, Samuel G. Perkins and Barbara Higginson Perkins, were each of impeccable lineage. Samuel Perkins was the younger brother of Thomas Handasyd Perkins and James Perkins, who made great fortunes trading opium, slaves, rum, otter skins, and just about anything else that could be bought and sold. The China trade, on which much of Boston's prosperity depended, had been especially profitable for them, providing the wealth for their philanthropy and civic leadership. Samuel Perkins was less fortunate in his business enterprises, but he was by no means unsuccessful and, when not engaged in trade, insurance, or other forms of money-making, he devoted his time to horticulture. It became a serious hobby. In 1803 he purchased a small estate in Brookline where he created "an earthly paradise of trees in blossom, bubbling brooks, green verdure and caroling birds."[86]

Barbara Higginson Perkins, the older sister of Susan Higginson Channing and mother of Walter's future wife, was known as one of Boston's great beauties. An admirer recorded that "she looked the queen more than any woman I ever saw. Her throat, neck & bust were beautiful even when past forty years of age . . . she made one feel as if her approbation was of more consequence than that of any one else in society."[87] Talleyrand was reported to have expressed his desire to meet her when he was in Boston.[88] She presided over one of Boston's most fashionable salons, where her brilliant conversation was the equal of her guests' who included many Boston intellectuals and literati.[89] Her father, Stephen Higginson, another of the powerful Federalist merchants, was reputed to be worth more than half a million dollars before he suffered reverses in the latter part of his life.[90]

There are no known portraits of the younger Barbara Higginson Perkins. Friends described her as "pretty." Others thought she was "very lady-like & accomplished in music," and that she "combined cultivation & great excellence of character [and was] among the very few people you would like to have for [a] constant companion." One of her cousins was less flattering, recalling that Barbara and her sister "never had any life in them."[91] The books she chose, sermons of worthy divines, Condillac's *Logic*, and Lord Kamer's *Elements of Criticism*, suggest a serious nature.[92]

Her friends also knew her as frail and sickly. In 1812, when she was "quite unwell and much depressed," her mother took her to Worcester to consult a physician in whom she had confidence. The following summer, when again Barbara was unwell, the family went north to Vermont for the supposed benefit of its clear air. These minimally described episodes suggest the respiratory weakness that became more serious following her marriage.[93]

Walter Channing and Barbara Perkins were married March 21, 1815, by the Reverend Samuel Thacher, minister of New South Church, at the home of the bride's parents.[94] A month before, Boston had received news of peace between the United States and Great Britain, which occasioned great rejoicing and celebration amid hope for a revived economy.[95] With warships no longer inhibiting transatlantic crossings, Samuel and Barbara Perkins soon departed on an extensive European tour, leaving Walter and Barbara to live in their home and supervise the younger Perkins children. Walter rejoiced in his newly acquired marital state, "such a merry breakfast table, such good appetites and spirits at dinner, and playfulness at tea."[96]

Walter was enormously proud of his wife and that same summer, during a rare "moment of professional leisure," he took her to Newport to meet Grandfather Ellery. She was already pregnant.[97] In November she was extremely ill, with symptoms diagnosed by her husband as influenza. A severe cough, lasting more than two weeks, kept her from sleeping. Walter insisted that she remain secluded to prevent her from trying to talk and he treated her with laudanum and a blister.[98] Barbara's illness did not dampen her husband's ardor. Commenting on events of the year in a letter to his sister Lucy, he exalted, "I have relinquished the charms of single blessedness & taken to myself a wife and I almost wish you knew less of my wife, for then I might tell you all I think of her, and something I feel for her. . . . I hope I have not been entirely unworthy of the high and new responsibilities with which it [the past year] has invested me."[99] It is not clear whether the high and new responsibilities refer to his marriage or his appointment at Harvard, for it had indeed been a year with multiple new responsibilities.

The birth of their first child, Barbara Higginson Channing, was duly entered in Channing's List of Midwifery Cases for 1816—"March 13th, Mrs. B. H. Channing, girl, case #84." A professional note was appended, "In Mrs. C.'s case rigidity of the membranes existed."[100] Despite a troublesome pregnancy complicated by general debility, motherhood suited her well. "She makes a sweet little mother and if ever a woman can look and feel happy it is in her present situation," her sister-in-law and aunt Susan commented. Walter was not nearly so serene. All his professional calm was lost where his wife and child were concerned. Only Barbara's ability to make him laugh relieved his excessive anxiety.[101]

That summer found Walter unwell with an intestinal disorder followed by emotional depression. A similar low had occurred shortly after his return from England, when Edward described his brother "overcast with shadow . . . his sorrows of a very peculiar nature," and Susan received a letter "written in a very gloomy state of mind."[102] The earlier melancholy may have been caused by his uncertain future. Now it could well have been triggered by the responsibilities he had assumed and his continued lack of self-confidence. In any case, it was a mood that would return in later years.

Despite pleas from the family, he refused to take a vacation until his in-laws returned, insisting that he must personally relinquish responsibility for their children. But as soon as the Perkinses were back and had gone to Brookline, where his wife and child could join them, Walter was off to New York. There he found relief in the companionship of his sister Lucy, now married to William Russel; it was Lucy to whom he could always confide his innermost concerns.[103]

The journey restored his health, and once he was back in Boston with "his little household," he was ready for "as happy and smooth a voyage through this great ocean of life as man could wish, or at least look for." His fears for the future had been allayed. "In due time," he told Lucy, "I hope to be as well off as my best friends could wish."[104] Boston still presented a bucolic scene, with orchards and flower gardens surrounding many homes, grassy fields throughout the town, and a pond nearby the house Channing and his family occupied.[105]

"Case #104, Mrs. B. H. Channing," was a boy born November 29, 1817, and named William Ellery Channing to honor his paternal grandfather and great-grandfather. He would be known as Ellery. It had been another difficult pregnancy for Barbara. For much of the summer she was too ill to go to Brookline, a refuge she usually enjoyed. Her postpartum recovery was slow; after seven weeks she was too fatigued to socialize and her hand trembled so much she feared no one could read her writing. But the baby was plump and healthy and his older sister chubby, red-cheeked, and good-humored. Little Barbara was also rather self-willed and rough-mannered, which sometimes caused her to "be mistaken for a boy," much to the displeasure of her mother.[106]

Barbara's infirmities became more severe. She began to experience serious problems with her eyes. Her face was peaked and bloodless. There was talk of an ocean voyage, but Walter could not afford the time to accompany her, and with two small children it was out of the question. James Jackson recommended a briefer journey. Fortuitously, William had been invited to deliver the sermon at the upcoming ordination of Jared Sparks as minister to the Unitarian congregation in Baltimore. It was decided that Barbara and her baby should accompany William, along with her sister-in-law Susan. En route they would visit Lucy Russel in New York. Walter was especially anxious for Barbara to consult Dr. Philip Syng Physick, one of his Philadelphia professors, in whose diagnostic and therapeutic skills he had great confidence.

Traveling together for many days by horse-drawn carriage gave Barbara and William the chance to become better acquainted. William was in fine form—conversing, laughing, doing everything he could for the entertainment and comfort of his companions. Barbara's "gentle, sweet and affectionate spirit," her contentment and cheerfulness also delighted the party.[107] They paused in New York, where William encouraged the Russels and their Unitarian friends to establish a liberal church. There is no record of a stopover in Philadelphia or a consultation with Dr. Physick. In Baltimore William delivered a memorable sermon enunciating for posterity the fundamentals of Unitarian doctrine. Thereafter Barbara and some of the others went on to the nation's capital, thus completing a rather remarkable excursion for a young wife and mother so far from home.[108]

Barbara thought the journey did her good, though her eyes remained troublesome. Walter, who was "pretty well tired of living alone & had really grown pale on solitude," welcomed her back.[109] His own health problems resurfaced and he spent a few weeks at Ballston, a popular spa in New York State not far from Saratoga. When he returned he found his wife "quite sick," the result he thought of a chilly excursion in the country. Again she had to keep to her bed. Many Bostonians were concerned for their health that summer. A yellow fever epidemic originating on board one of the ships recently arrived from Africa spread among the houses in the waterfront area, causing alarm throughout the city. Channing's mother and sister fled, though Walter did not sympathize with what seemed to him to be unreasonable apprehension.[110]

It is hazardous to attempt a diagnosis of Barbara's condition based on letters written by her relatives and friends. Some of her symptoms, especially the weak eyes and trembling hands, suggest several diseases attributable to nutritional deficiency, a common condition in an era when the benefits of fresh fruit and vegetables were not understood and such foods were not easily available much of the year.[111] The frequent colds, respiratory ailments, and general fatigue give hints of a predisposition for tuberculosis and knowing the outcome, we can predict that the accumulation of illnesses would lead inexorably to consumption, the disease with which everyone, laity and physicians, was all too familiar. Consumption (phthisis) was the scourge of the nineteenth century, prevalent in all social classes, especially in urban settings. The only prescription was rest and fresh air, which might strengthen resistance. Walter had good reason to be fearful. However, denial is a powerful weapon, especially in the face of a potentially tragic outcome.

Barbara herself was aware of her tenuous future. On the pages of the journal where she had once copied sections of Walter's European journal, she added a long poem, which began

> Not to the rosy maid whom former hours
> Beheld me fondly covet, tune I now
> The melancholy lyre: no more I seek
> Thy aid Hygaia! sought so long in vain.
> But 'tis to thee O sickness! 'tis to thee
> I wake the silent strings, accept the lay.

The "Ode to Sickness" gave full expression to deep feelings of sorrow and pain, but it ended affirmatively.

> For all I bless thee! Thou hast taught my soul
> To rest upon itself; to look beyond
> The narrow bounds of time and fix its hopes
> On the sure basis of eternity.[112]

When she became pregnant for the third time, there was further cause for anxiety. Mary Elizabeth Channing was born July 4, 1820, and was baptized, as her older siblings had been, by William at the Federal Street Church. Barbara had an easier recovery but the eye problems worsened and she feared permanent blindness. For weeks she was not allowed to gaze on her new child and became very depressed. Again Susan Channing described the situation. "She says that all that she has ever endured before is nothing to this. . . . she suffers so much positive pain & is so apprehensive of making them worse by the slightest exertion either of body or mind that she lives in a constant agony. She is perfectly helpless and they are afraid to leave her alone for a minute."[113] When the episode passed, she resumed her maternal duties.

With three children under the age of five, Barbara was fully engaged in their care. Little Bab and Ellery loved stories, especially when read or created by their father, whose fertile imagination produced many enchanting tales. Barbara decided to educate her older daughter at home, following a demanding schedule that began at 9:00 A.M. and ended at 5:00 P.M. There were recitations from the Bible, spelling lessons, and instruction in nature, art, geography, and sewing. One hour a day was set aside for play. Barbara needed patience and gentleness as well as perseverance when dealing with her daughter. Ellery, on the other hand, was "a fine tempered child," though "passionate on contradiction."[114]

By the summer of 1822 Barbara was in the final stages of consumption, spitting blood, breathing with difficulty, often beset with a violent cough. She was also pregnant again. She knew that the outlook was grim and Walter became more fearful. He even hoped for a miscarriage, which might have relieved the added demands on her weakened body. Susan Channing was less pessimistic, explaining, "as pregnancy produces every kind of evil and women live through everything, I can not despair of her."[115] Her mother too refused to think negatively.

As Barbara's disease continued to worsen, Walter, whose fervent affection for his wife and children was evident to all who knew him, watched her gradual decline with ever-increasing apprehension.[116] The baby was born in early October, three or four weeks prematurely. She was named Lucy Bradstreet Channing, but there is no official record of her birth or her baptism, suggesting that Walter and the rest of the family were too distraught to give attention to these formalities.

The final four days of Barbara's life were almost continuous suffering, mitigated by "her angelick patience & gentleness." Even the nurse commented on her fortitude in the face of agony and death. Her frequent spasms were also agonizing for Walter, as well as her mother, sisters, and sister-in-law, who remained by the bedside thinking each breath was the last.[117] When finally she died on October 10 the torture ceased for everyone. Barbara was buried in the Peck and Perkins family mausoleum in the Granary Burying Ground, adjacent to the Boston Common.[118]

Despite the years of warning and final weeks of waiting, Channing could not believe "such a blessing" had been taken from him. He was completely distraught, unable to care for his children and unwilling to remain in the house where he and Barbara had been living.[119] If there had been an unmarried sister, she might have assumed charge of his children and home, but this was not the case. He first considered boarding out, then decided to live with his mother in the house on Berry Street acquired for her by William following his marriage in 1814 to his cousin Ruth Gibbs and their move to Beacon Hill.[120] The children were distributed among relatives: little Barbara to Susan Channing, Mary and the baby (with a nurse) to the Perkins grandparents.[121] The baby was alternately sick and well, causing some to think she would not survive and others to declare her the most beautiful babe ever born. Ellery had already been sent to live with his Forbes cousins in Milton. Aunt Margaret Forbes, a sister of Samuel Perkins, had seven children, the youngest four years Ellery's senior. Nonetheless, it was not a good situation. The Forbes household was more Puritanical than Ellery had known at home, the cousins were not compatible, and his aunt was not affectionate.[122] Ellery was isolated from his father and sisters at a time when he desperately needed love and consolation. The strangeness that became part of his personality may well have had its origins in this unfortunate arrangement.

Channing continued his professional commitments, visiting patients, lecturing at the medical school, attending at the hospital. Otherwise, he spent his time grieving and alone. Friends found his spirits variable. "[H]e seems at times so wretched that it is distressing to be with him."[123] The tragedy was exacerbated by the nearly simultaneous death of William Ellery Channing's small son, left in Boston with a maiden aunt while William and his wife were in Europe. They had made the journey for the sake of William's health, yet the news that awaited them in Rome, the deaths of their child and of a dearly loved sister-in-law, was certain to negate any improvement.

William wrote an extraordinary letter to his brother, whose loss he felt more deeply than his own. "Sweet lovely & full of promise as our little boy was, I cannot but feel that you are the most bereaved & I would rather comfort *you* than speak of myself." He too grieved for Barbara, "so faultless, so spotless that I know not in what I would have changed her. . . . Her heart was a deep calm fountain of love." He had long believed that Walter was "one of the most privileged of men in having such a sharer & guardian of your happiness."

William offered faith in the wisdom of God and hope for reunion in the next world. "We, in the blindness of human love, would have detained her. But suffering had done its purifying work & she was prepared for a higher sphere . . . a spirit such as hers was at this moment needed in the community of the 'just made perfect.' " He feared that his brother's "constitutional sensitiveness" would make grief unbearable and urged him to make "the true use of your suffering." He had much to live for and to enjoy.[124]

William approved Walter's decision to live with their mother, for he could help "support and brighten her last years." Other observers were less certain that the two would be good for each other, since Lucy too could be withdrawn and taciturn.[125] Yet he found a measure of peace and comfort living quietly under her roof, visiting frequently with his children, but avoiding society. He began to accept the situation. "I must be at rest where I am," he wrote to Lucy Russel.

> I look forward to no change in situation or circumstance. My steady pursuit of my professional duties I think will always give me the means of comfortable subsistence for myself & children. . . . there is too little about me or mine to make me an object of interest beyond my mere usefulness and with this & with the sad lessons of my experience constantly before me, I can hardly look or ask for more. To be tolerably cheerful is to me now great gain. There is a sadness which to me is now more nearly allied to happiness than gaiety. It has in it more of the past, & the ultimate future, than of the present, or the tomorrow. . . . I feel lonely Lucy at times beyond yr imagination to comprehend, for I find the dead even among the living.[126]

Chapter 4

Obstetrical Practice

In its practice, midwifery is strictly an art.

—Walter Channing, "Miscellaneous Lecture Notes"

T HE colorless images Channing used in his letter to Lucy Russel, the "steady pursuit of professional duties" and the "mere usefulness" of work, suited the dreary months of solitude but contradicted his usual attitude toward his profession. He sincerely believed that saving women's lives and "adding . . . to the individuals of the human race" contributed to the "happiness of society," and he was proud of his accomplishments.[1] He also recognized that, despite the inflated claims of some physicians about the importance of medical science, success in obstetrics included many nonscientific components.

In the eighteenth and nineteenth centuries, midwife and midwifery, obstetrician and obstetrics, accoucheur and accoucheuse were all common terms that could be and were used interchangeably, though over time obstetrician and obstetrics became dominant.[2] Regardless of nomenclature, obstetrics presented difficulties and provided rewards that distinguished it from general medical practice. The nature of childbirth meant that the physician could be summoned without warning at any time, day or night, and might have to remain with his patient for many hours, even for several days, preventing him from seeing other patients or attending to his personal life. He would be with the woman at a particularly difficult and intimate time, when her fears of pain and death were often stronger than her hopes for a healthy baby. There might be unexpected complications that produced increased anxiety for her family and friends, thus placing additional demands on the physician.

Should a case require the use of instruments, he needed physical strength and stamina in procedures that were often extremely painful for the mother and stressful for everyone present. Turning a fetus or manually removing the placenta put strong pressure on the physician's hands and might cause him pain, though not as severely as for the patient. A stillborn child or a dead mother was grievous for everyone. Channing often reflected on "the death, the sorrow, the wide, wide misery" that were part of obstetrical practice. "To whom else in the common walks of life does death come double in a single act but to the practitioners of midwifery?" he lamented.[3]

Why then would Channing want to make obstetrics the major part of his medical practice? Fundamentally, it contributed to a decent income, though he also needed a substantial general practice, especially in the early years, when he averaged fewer than eighteen midwifery cases per year.[4] But success in obstetrics could help to increase his general practice. Mothers who had placed confidence in him during childbirth and were pleased by the outcome might ask him to be their family physician.[5] The approval of her friends and relatives present at the time of delivery enhanced his reputation. Medical colleagues and female midwives, aware of his ability and experience, called on him for advice and consultation when they encountered problems in their own obstetrical cases, thereby also adding to his business.

There was also the satisfaction he derived from the gratitude of his patients and their families. We will never know how many babies were named Walter while Channing was in practice, but at least one, Walter Channing Cabot, is recorded in the genealogy of the Cabot family and his birth is described in Channing's records.[6] In 1858 Channing received an unexpected and substantial legacy from a woman whom he had successfully delivered by forceps more than thirty years previously.[7] Fathers too were grateful. One described a potential postpartum disaster averted by Channing. The mother was bleeding profusely. "[He] did all that skill and care could do" until exhaustion forced him to send for another physician to help. For seven hours the two alternated applying pressure to arrest the hemorrhage. "I shall never forget their kindness. God reward them for it. . . . Dr. Channing staid all night."[8]

Finally, there was the personal pleasure he experienced when he saved a mother's life or that of her child. Many times he rushed to a woman who was bleeding so badly or was so exhausted from prolonged labor her heart might soon stop beating. In just one example, he was summoned to the bedside of a twenty-six-year-old woman in labor with her second child. She was hemorrhaging, and the physician who had initially been called was so intimidated by the threat of her dying that he was afraid to examine her. Instead, he relied on Channing to determine the cause and to terminate the labor.

Channing "found her almost pulseless; skin white, without blood, —cold; voice feeble; whole appearance, that of extreme exhaustion. I learned she had been flowing six days; that she had lost much blood, —by her report, a gallon. . . . The case was apparently so hopeless, that I took the physician and a friend aside, to communicate my views of it, and to prepare them for the worst result that might follow the only means which promised any good." Upon examining the woman, Channing discovered the placenta firmly attached to a portion of the cervix. "It was at once separated entirely from the uterus, and not the least hemorrhage accompanied the separation." Everyone was relieved. Channing extracted the fetus, already dead for several days, and the mother made a good recovery.[9]

Channing was Boston's leading obstetrician for more than sixty years. There were changes during that long period—changes in the lives of women, in the social and economic character of the city, in medical procedures, and in therapeutics. Yet the fundamental principles that guided Channing as he assisted women in childbirth and provided postpartum care to mothers and their babies, as well as when he attended to gynecological disorders, remained substantially the same.[10]

"PHYSICIAN when called should always ride fast," was Channing's first dictum.[11] Not only did the patient and her family expect immediate attention, but from his point of view, "some of the accidents of labour may manifest themselves very early in the process."[12] Unlike physicians who practiced in rural areas, where the population was widespread, it was not difficult for Channing to reach his patients quickly, often on foot. In later years, as Boston grew in size as well as number of inhabitants, it might take an hour or so and require a horse and carriage to respond to a summons. On the few occasions when he had two patients simultaneously in labor, he kept the carriage "in constant attendance" to shuttle him from one to the other.[13] He usually slept in a small room close by the front door of his house so that the urgent knocking of the husband or friend of an expectant mother would not disturb his family during the night.[14] Boston's streets were so poorly illuminated that he once facetiously appealed for creation of a public "Lamps Department," asking to be appointed chief engineer, "to serve during good behaviour."[15]

Except for paupers at the Almshouse and poor women he saw at the Boston Lying-in Hospital after it opened in 1832, every delivery took place in the home of the laboring woman. Channing brought his basic equipment with him, a female catheter, sharp scissors and strong thread, lard or oil, drugs such as belladonna, ergot, and laudanum, plus a lancet and the instruments he might need in an emergency. In time he brought his stethoscope, and still later he frequently had anesthesia with him. He also used the lancet less often as venesection (bleeding) declined as a medical therapy.

In most homes a room, usually but not always the largest bedroom, had been set aside for the event. Physicians like Channing thought that good ventilation was an important requisite for health and preferred an airy room that was not overheated. A bed would have been prepared, one mattress atop another, covered with a piece of oiled silk, untanned skin, or layers of blankets. If possible, the lower end was raised so that the woman's pelvis would be higher than the rest of her body.[16] He would find his patient fully clothed in loose-fitting garments, a cap upon her head. She might have had a heavy meal shortly before his arrival. He noted one who "had eaten a hearty breakfast of meat and potatoes, while labor was present," and another who had eaten baked beans and huckleberry pie.[17] When it came time for her to be on the bed, a doubled sheet was placed between her abdomen and her clothing so that her "private parts" would be covered.

These of course were ideal arrangements, but not every home could so nicely accommodate childbirth. There were some situations, especially with Dispensary patients whose attending physicians called on Channing for a consultation, when he entered the worst kind of a hovel, putrid smells emanating from the unclean floor and the sometimes equally grimy patient. "The room in which Mrs. —— was confined was very small, without ventilation. Its door opened into another small room, in which was a cooking stove, and in which the family of four children, etc., lived."[18] He adapted to whatever circumstances he found and could if necessary deliver a woman on a pallet or on the floor. He remained in street attire. It would be comforting to think that at least he washed his hands, and perhaps he did, but there is no reference to it in the notes of his lectures or in contemporary obstetrical textbooks.

The relationship between Channing and his patients was based on mutual respect—Channing's respect for women experiencing heightened emotion, pain, and occasional trauma; his patients' respect for Channing's skill, judgment, and empathetic nature. He knew well that dissatisfied women could, and would, dismiss one physician and call in another.

Throughout the years of Channing's practice, women continued to be greatly afraid of pregnancy and labor.[19] Some hesitated to marry, even though they knew that marriage and motherhood were expected of them. They also knew that they would probably be pregnant very soon. "I have always thought that I should not be at all happy during the first year of marriage, imaginary evils are those I most dread," wrote one. Another turned away when it was time for her to leave her parents' home, then almost fainted as she descended the stairs toward the man whom she had married a few hours before.[20] Everyone knew that the nine months of pregnancy would be uncomfortable at best, and full of possible dangers. Labor was almost always painful and could result in temporary or permanent damage to a woman's health. Everyone had a friend, mother, or sister who had died in childbirth; everyone knew a close relative whose baby was born dead or died shortly thereafter. One woman's diary expressed the relief that many felt when they had safely delivered. "At 6 o'clock on 7th January, 1824 I was a mother & experienced the delightful transition from suffering, danger and anxiety to happiness." At last she had been repaid for long months of bad health.[21] Another told her sister she was entitled to have "all the agreeable companions & all the charming things that can be gathered together as compensation for yr. trials and distresses."[22]

Men too were deeply troubled by the dangers and suffering that women endured in childbirth. "I rejoice that Charlotte passed through the perils that environed her without difficulties," wrote William Ellery to his grandson Richard Henry Dana in 1814. Nearly thirty years later his great-grandson Richard Henry Dana, Jr., confided to his journal, "It [childbirth] is an hour of harrowing anxiety. . . . There is surely no pain like it in the world. . . . It is the rending asunder of all but soul & body. . . . What a load from the heart of a husband [when] the precious life of a wife is spared."[23]

The inability of nineteenth-century women to control their fertility meant repeated and frequent pregnancies.[24] For upper-class and middle-class women, there was usually support at the time of childbirth—family members who lived nearby or who came from afar to help during her labor and subsequent confinement, as well as nurses hired especially for the event and weeks of convalescence. For lower-class women who continued to work at home or at menial jobs throughout their pregnancies, there was no assistance except the neighbor women who came in for the labor and delivery and might help with household chores in the days afterward. The presence of additional women had its roots in childbirth customs associated with female midwifery, but physicians too needed their assistance, while the mother received encouragement and comfort from their presence, as she always had.[25] They provided emotional support, massaged her back, wiped her brow, held her hand, and could if needed provide the strength against which she pushed. Channing preferred to have sensible women present and would have liked to exclude some he deemed "excitable," but he was a guest in his patient's home and could not easily influence the choice of attendants. Some husbands remained with their wives throughout labor and delivery.[26]

After hastening to the home of the expectant woman, Channing sometimes found himself waiting until she was ready to see him. For example, he was called at 7:00 A.M. to a woman in her fifth labor, "but was requested merely to be in readiness when labour should be more advanced. I called again about 11 A.M.—as before. At 7 P.M. I saw her for the first time. She was sitting up, complaining of slight pain & would scarcely submit to an examination."[27] In other cases, he was not summoned until the labor was well advanced and his assistance would soon be needed. Or he might make an initial examination, then depart and wait to be summoned again when birth was more imminent. Occasionally everyone misjudged the progress of a labor and the baby had been born by the time Channing reached the bedside. Nonetheless, he tied the cord, made certain the child was well, removed the placenta, and attended to the general comfort of the new mother. If serious complications arose during the delivery or postpartum he remained, in one case for four days and nights.

It might be that Channing was meeting the woman for the first time, for unless there were medical problems during the pregnancy, nineteenth-century women did not seek prenatal care, relying instead on advice from female relatives and friends. On the other hand, many of his patients were women he had delivered before, often several times, and he would be familiar with their previous obstetrical history. "September 29th [1857].—This was Mrs. ——'s fourth labor. I had attended her in all of them, with her family physician. Her first labor was natural. The second was instrumental. The third natural; and the fourth, or last, was instrumental."[28]

Among Channing's patients were members of his family, women related by marriage, and the wives of friends. Thus, he would know something of their general health and temperament if it was a first obstetrical encounter. Familiarity could also preclude his attendance. Elizabeth Bradish, who was a daughter of Aunt Gibbs and thus a cousin of Walter's, engaged Dr. Rand to deliver her child: "[F]rom motives of delicacy she prefer'd him to Walter." However, when her condition became perilous, Rand sent for Channing. Thereafter, Elizabeth "scarcely suffered him to leave her long enough to eat or drink—the very circumstance that made her averse to having him at first, was his greatest recommendation—his being a friend."[29]

First encounter or not, it was important that Channing appear calm and confident. Like other physicians, he assumed that so-called moral influences, the fears and anxiety of the patient or others in the room, might have a deleterious effect on the course of the labor and could even produce unwanted complications. Because the conduct, attitude, and words of the physician could so easily affect her emotional and psychological state, the first imperative was to allay any fears and gain her trust.[30] He would enter the room "coolly . . . [as] if it was a common friendly visit."[31] If she wanted to reveal her fears, he tried to soothe her. In an especially troubling case for which he was asked to consult, "I sat down and talked to the patient, for I was told that she had literally been one (patient). I soon saw I was gaining upon a wearied confidence, and a short time after I was permitted to make an examination."[32] As Boston's immigrant population grew, he used a few words in the patient's language to "bring a smile" to the face of the foreign-born and win her trust.[33] Obstetrics required tact and sensitivity as well as medical knowledge and skill.

He also had to observe strict decorum. "Our conduct," he told his students, "should be marked with delicacy & propriety to those in every class of life."[34] It is an irony of nineteenth-century midwifery that male physicians became prominent at the very time that society increasingly valued female modesty and delicacy.[35] For some women, the thought of revealing their bodies to a man was so abhorrent they refused medical care even when threatened by death. Mrs. L., who had been attended by a midwife during a miscarriage, suffered a retained placenta followed by infection. Nonetheless, she would not permit a physician to examine her until persuaded by her husband that it was absolutely necessary. By then it was too late. Mrs. F. endured postpartum difficulties for four years following her delivery by a midwife, but "[a] strong repugnance to an examination per vaginam . . . prevented her physicians from ascertaining the nature of her case" until her priest advised her to consult several more experienced physicians, Channing among them.[36]

Decorum required that Channing should not remain longer than necessary in the birthing chamber during the early stages of labor. When he first arrived, he limited conversation to "the usual compliments of the day," and to questions about his patient's general health, unless she chose to describe her pregnancy or the progress of the labor. If not, he consulted the female attendants. He could unobtrusively observe superficial signs such as the condition of the woman's skin, tongue, eyes, and pulse, and her general demeanor. Any orders related to bodily functions, such as emptying the bladder and rectum, he transmitted indirectly through the female attendants.[37] When it was time to make a vaginal examination, he asked one of the attendant women to inform the patient. Again, decorum required that he avert his eyes from the woman's body for as long as he could, taking advantage of the sheet that draped her abdomen. He used lard or oil to lubricate his finger. After the examination (called "touching"), sensitivity to the delicate feelings of his patient required he wipe his finger on a towel kept well hidden from view.[38]

ALTHOUGH some physicians did not make vaginal examinations, from embarrassment either on their part or that of their patient, or from prudence or laziness, Channing was certain to examine early, so that he might know the

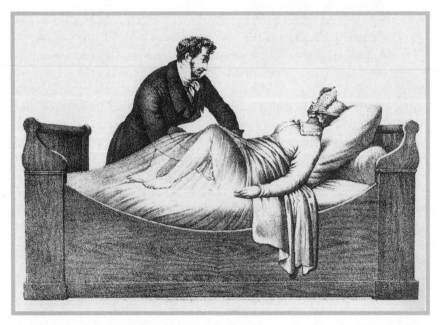

Demonstration of "touching" (from J. P. Maygrier, *Midwifery Illustrated* [New York, 1841], courtesy of the Francis A. Countway Library of Medicine)

condition of the cervix, the presentation of the fetus, and if possible the pressure of the amniotic sac. These would enable him to measure the progress of the labor and to anticipate complications, should they threaten. In retrospect, we now know that vaginal examinations brought increased risk of infection. Fortunately, Channing considered "attempts to assist by too frequent examination" improper conduct and poor obstetrical practice.

Though some obstetrical texts opposed "the preposterous custom of obliging her to walk the floor with a view to increase the pains," Channing was not so dictatorial.[39] His patients sat up or walked the floor to suit themselves during the first stage of labor. Similarly, he could accommodate to the position in which the woman chose to deliver, though most accepted his preference, lying on the left side with their buttocks close to the end of the bed, a pillow between the knees.[40] Nonetheless, he realized that "We must govern ourselves by the customs of the patient and of the country from which she comes." In France women customarily delivered on their backs, in Germany seated on a chair, in Ireland kneeling on hands and knees, and those of his patients who were accustomed to those positions continued to use them.[41]

The most exceptional position in which Channing delivered was with a woman who had devised a complicated arrangement of chairs to suit her needs. Her malformed pelvis made delivery slow and exceedingly painful. By the age of forty-one she had had two miscarriages and sixteen labors. In each, labor began with "a sense of suffocation, anguish, choking, gagging and vomiting, . . . great distress across the upper part of the abdomen . . . and spasmodic twitchings," which lasted ten days or longer. When the "true expulsatory pains" of second-stage labor began, she could not tolerate a horizontal position or lie on a bed. "Three common Winsor chairs are tied strongly together, the bottoms looking towards each other, one behind and one on each side. A matrass is placed on them, and a chair is placed in front for her feet. In this half-sitting, half-lying position, she can exert great power. During uterine efforts she seizes the chairs at her sides and braces herself strongly against them and in this way she gets much advantage."[42] Channing admired her ingenuity and attended her repeatedly.

Relations between Channing and his patients were not always strictly according to the rules. Early in his practice he encountered a particularly distressed woman who "had an iron will and knew how to use it." She had been in labor for six days and Channing was the sixth physician called. She insisted that nothing more be done, for she had suffered unbearably and was prepared to die rather than submit to further procedures. Channing explained that he could save her if permitted to turn the baby in utero and remove it feet first, but she refused. Somehow, he persuaded her to take an emetic in small doses over several hours, expecting it would relieve congestion and he might thereafter secure permission to turn the fetus. She impulsively took the entire dose at once. Copious vomiting ensued during which he placed his hand in the womb, reached the feet, and delivered the baby. Channing's actions may be questionable, but the woman insisted he be her physician in subsequent confinements. On the third day following each delivery she invariably announced, "Well doctor, ye see I'm doing well—first rate. Let us settle. If I want ye again, why I will send for ye!"[43]

In another subterfuge, Channing gave his patient ergot in a cup of souchong tea without her knowledge of the contents. She had been experiencing ineffectual contractions for four days. "Pains very soon came on of a forcing character, I prepared another cup of the tea as before, but before the half hour was over at which I meant to repeat it the labour was over." Channing gave no explanation for his conduct.[44]

Occasionally there were surprises for patient and physician. Channing had been called by a distraught man begging him to hasten to his wife. She had dismissed her regular physician after several days of labor. Channing found her alone in the bedroom. "I have been kilt," she moaned, "butchered, murdered and won't suffer more. There shall not be another hand put to me." She adamantly refused to allow Channing to turn the fetus. Eventually he discovered a dead child lying next to her. "In the absence of her physician spontaneous evolution had taken place and in the severity of her sufferings she had remained unconscious of the birth."[45]

"IN practice the duties of the practitioner are ordinarily simple and few," Channing told his students. "We are for the most part called upon . . . to observe healthful, natural phenomena."[46] He was referring to "natural labors," defined by him and other obstetricians as "completed within twenty-four hours from the dilation of the os uteri, at the full time of utero-gestation, accomplished by the unaided efforts of the womb." Most cases followed this description and indeed there was little to do. He waited for the second stage of labor, noted the advancement of the head, supported the perineum to prevent tearing, and received the child as it emerged. Though the woman might suffer intense pain, until anesthesia was discovered in 1846 little could be done in response to her "cries for help."[47] He was aware that the pain of childbirth was unique. Despite the horrific scenes he sometimes witnessed when men and women endured amputations, cancer, peritonitis, and tooth extractions without relief from pain, he admitted that only a woman could fully appreciate the suffering of childbirth.[48]

Having ascertained that the child was breathing well and that there were no obvious deformities, he cut the umbilical cord, first tying strong thread or string about three inches from the baby's abdomen to prevent bleeding. He then dressed the remaining portion of the cord with a square of cotton, and the newborn was passed to one of the women to be cared for.

Whereas some of his colleagues advised action if the placenta was not quickly thrown off, Channing preferred to wait patiently.[49] Once the placenta was expelled and he made sure no portion remained in the womb, he fixed a cloth swath tightly around the patient's abdomen so the uterus would continue to contract. He and the other attendants then removed the woman's wet garments and the soiled bedclothes and carefully placed her back in the bed. "The patient was now made comfortable and put to bed," was one notation, or, "This patient was so well, that she was soon removed but with great care to her bed, everything being made dry and comfortable about her."[50] He remained in the room as a "mark of attention extremely satisfactory to the woman and her friends" until he was sure she was not experiencing unusual sensations. He usually prescribed a cathartic, relying on the nurse or other attendants to make sure bladder and bowel operated easily. He also recommended a light diet of gruel and broth, bed rest, and minimal company for the first few days following delivery. Contemporary medical theory held that the sympathetic action of one organ on another meant that other parts of the body might be adversely affected by the effort of the uterus in expelling the child and should not be overly taxed. Customarily, he returned twice a day for several days afterward to check on the condition of mother and baby.[51]

Though "it was obviously intended that labour should always be . . . easily terminated," not every delivery went smoothly. As Channing explained to his students, "The circumstances in which women have been placed in the prog- ress of civilization have tended so far to interfere with original design as to render delivery at most a painful, frequently a formidable, & sometimes even a dangerous process."[52] Channing was not alone in believing that American women were healthier than their European counterparts and that newly immi- grant women tended to have more complications in labor and delivery. None- theless, he also believed that urban life with its "excessive refinements" rendered contemporary women less fit for childbearing than their foremothers had been. Women subscribed to this notion, too. "This natural process is said to be an easy one in savage life & in some countries, but it is far otherwise in our state of society whether it be our fault or our misfortune," wrote one woman to her daughter-in-law while recommending she hire a nurse for six weeks following delivery. "Half the sufferings & feeble health of women is occasioned by their undertaking what they are unequal to."[53]

Channing was candid about obstetrical complications. "Few cases are more embarrassing [for the physician] than the difficult ones of midwifery. A constant demand is made upon his physical strength and his mind is at the same time occupied with his responsibility, with the recollections of other similar cases either as they are found in his books or have occurred to him."[54] Like most of his colleagues, he grouped these births in three categories— laborious (more than twenty-four hours' duration, terminated by the sponta- neous efforts of the woman or by assistance from the physician), preternatural (presentation other than the head), and complex (involving convulsions, ex- cessive hemorrhage, ruptured uterus, and other unexpected, life-threatening conditions).[55] Obstetrical complications were uncommon in the practice of most physicians, but this was not true for Channing. A woman who had had a difficult labor would want him to attend her for the next, and midwives and other physicians sought his help when they faced difficulties.

In these "difficult cases of midwifery" Channing usually had to intervene, though he delayed as long as possible, recognizing that nature has a way of rectifying some situations without assistance. In his view, "the patience of medical men cannot be questioned. . . . it prevents all fatigue, all anxiety, hurry and how easily for a long time will the patient submit to the judicious, truly high principled delay."[56] He tried to avoid "meddlesome midwifery," a term used in nineteenth-century obstetrical textbooks to caution practitioners against unnecessary interference in childbirth, as well as by critics of male physicians who practiced obstetrics.

"I was extremely anxious that no unusual or unnecessary interference should be made by frequent examination," he noted in one case, and in another, "The head was low, protruding the perineum. It had been in this position between 1 & 2 hours. As the strength was good, pains powerful, pulse and countenance healthy, no headache, thirst or febrile symptoms present, I recommended further delay."[57] As long as some progress was evident, he did his best to encourage the woman, counting on her female friends and relatives, "the intelligent ones about her, to minister to her mind and provide nutritious food . . . to invigorate the system."[58] By his specifying the "intelligent" friends, we can assume that he found some of the women less than helpful, especially if they engaged in negative speculation or repeated stories that might frighten the woman. He also objected to the traditional midwives' custom of giving "cordials or ardent spirits" to stimulate the labor.

On the other hand, there were many interventions he could and did employ when needed. He eased laborious labors with opium or by bleeding, both of which appeared to relax the patient and gave respite from pain, though excessive use might produce a negative effect.[59] He tried to stimulate ineffective contractions with ergot, though again there was potential harm if it was used inappropriately.[60] Cathartics and enemas were administered in the belief that they would stimulate contractions, or at least prevent "costiveness," or constipation, which was a generally feared symptom of nineteenth-century medicine. If the cervix remained closed, he might try gentle dilation with his finger or by applying belladonna. If the amniotic sac remained intact and seemed to impede progress, he punctured it. He usually performed this with a sharp fingernail, though once he mentioned use of "a large knitting needle with a round blunt end," and another time a wire.[61] When the fetus was sufficiently low in the pelvis, with head first, he employed forceps if the patient had greatly weakened.

When the child presented in a position other than headfirst, Channing initially made sure spontaneous evolution would not occur, then decided whether he could successfully turn and remove the child by the feet. If this was done soon enough, he hoped to shorten the labor and save the life of the child.[62] Turning was excruciatingly painful for the mother, and sometimes painful for the physician whose hand could be in the womb during a strong contraction and might be compressed between the fetus and the uterus. One of the attendant dangers in cases when turning was employed was rupture of the uterus. Channing claimed that he had never experienced rupture as a result of turning, though he did see it as a consultant.

He used instruments, including forceps, lever, hook, and crotchet, as a last resort when turning was not possible, the mother's life was threatened, or the baby was impacted in the pelvis. Several things could produce this last crisis, including malformation of the mother's pelvis (rickets attributable to malnutrition was the primary cause of pelvic deformities), a large fetal head (usually hydrocephalic), or a fetal position that prevented contractions from forcing the child out of the womb. Channing's primary concern was the safety of the mother, even at the expense of the child. Often there were other children who would be semi-orphaned if the mother were to perish. Thus, "if the patient had lost strength, the pulse were low, prostration great," he deemed it imperative to take action.[63] He usually tried forceps first, but if the head remained impacted he might have to compress the skull. Should the pelvic opening be too small to permit removal of the rest of the fetus, he dismembered it, pulling out the parts with the blunt hook.

The decision to use instruments was very difficult, in part because of possible damage to the mother, the baby, or both, and in part because of the horror of such procedures. Until the advent of anesthesia, the mother was conscious. Family or friends in attendance had to witness Channing performing an arduous operation. "The demand for artificial aid must be found in existing circumstances of each case," he wrote. "No department of medicine has such responsibility as this, and the wider the experience so much deeper is felt the responsibility."[64] Channing always sought the opinion and assistance of another physician. The notes for one of his early cases explains that he requested a consultation "in order to relieve the anxiety of the friends, & to divide the responsibility. . . . Dr. Warren met me just after day light." The two physicians delayed action until eleven o'clock, when they "determined to interfere, & to use the lever."[65] Seeking the opinion of another physician was especially important if he had been on the case for many hours and fatigue might impair his judgment.

Before instruments were applied, Channing informed the woman directly or through the attendants. In a few cases she or her family refused permission. "The head was fairly in the pelvis in this case. The labor was slowly proceeding. Suddenly contractions ceased. There was slight hæmorrhage. Sinking rapidly followed. I proposed to deliver by the forceps. Dr. —— strongly advised this measure. The patient would not permit it. She said she was perfectly easy and would sooner die than submit to any operation. It was already too late and she died in a few hours."[66]

If permission was given, the patient was placed on her back, her legs and

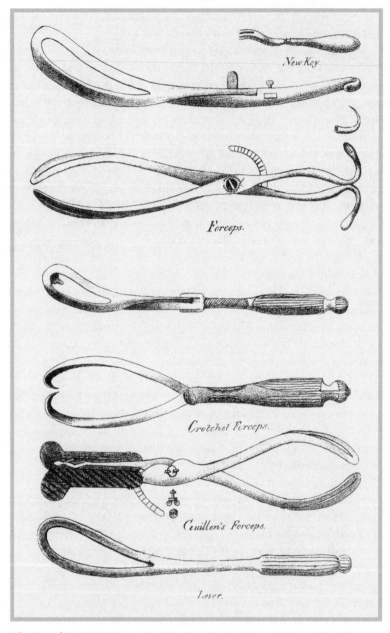

Obstetrical instruments (from J. P. Maygrier, *Midwifery Illustrated* [New York, 1841], courtesy of the Francis A. Countway Library of Medicine)

feet supported by women or consulting physicians seated at the end of the bed.[67] Whatever instrument was to be employed, it was first placed in warm water until it had reached body temperature and was then lubricated with lard or oil. Channing removed his coat, and pushed back his sleeves. He did not wear a special garment for operative midwifery, although his lap might be covered with towels or sheets. His students were instructed to "apply instruments with great care and tenderness" and we can assume he followed his own precept.[68]

Other physicians were more hesitant to use instruments. In the case of his cousin Elizabeth Bradish, Dr. Rand disagreed with Channing's recommendation to use forceps and, since he was the original and senior physician on the case, Channing did not dare disagree with him before the family.[69] Some colleagues made it a principle never to use forceps. One told Channing, "I wait—wait hours and days, nourish, stimulate, encourage, and at length in three or four days, the labor finishes itself. I never give aid; I never will."[70] On the other hand, Channing preferred using instruments rather than risking "injurious if not fatal delay," which might cause a ruptured bladder, rectovaginal fistula, convulsions, puerperal mania, or puerperal fever. "If a properly constructed instrument is employed—if the case be a proper one in which to use it, if it be properly applied, and is properly used . . . in such a case this instrument [forceps] may be as useful and as safe as is any other in the practice of surgery. There must be knowledge and skill in its use."[71]

Some cases required increasingly brutal measures when initial procedures failed. For example, Channing was called when Mrs. B. had been four days in "fruitless" labor and danger seemed imminent. She was "breathing rapidly, skin hot, dry, great thirst, abdomen very tense, full, tender, pulse rapid, small, countenance anxious, irregularly red & white." Channing feared that inflammation would soon set in, if not already present.[72] Ergot had been administered without effect and the head was firmly fixed in the pelvis. Mrs. B. had not felt fetal motion for a day.

> I used the lever & forceps ineffectually. The former was not sufficiently powerful, & the latter could not be so introduced as to lock in such a way as to embrace the head fairly unless by such violence as it was believed would be destructive to the parts within the pelvis. . . . The perforator & crotchet were next used, & such was the difficulty after removing the brain that it was necessary to take away most of the vault of the cranium before the head descended. After the head was born, the pains having entirely subsided, great effort was necessary to bring away the body. The placenta was removed by the hand

after waiting for the womb to act to expel it. Much hemorrhage followed, but this ceased as soon as a bandage was passed round the abdomen.[74]

It is difficult to imagine a case with this degree of horror for everyone involved. Today Mrs. B. would be in a hospital, the dimensions of her pelvis would have been measured, a fetal monitor would observe the baby's vital signs, and she probably would have a living child, delivered by cesarean section within the first twenty-four hours of labor. Cesarean section was known in Channing's time, and a few successful cases could be cited from English and French obstetrical literature, but there is no record that he ever performed one, or contemplated it. Even after anesthesia could have made the operation painless, the danger of infection was so severe it would have been foolhardy to attempt such a dramatic and dangerous procedure.[74] In Mrs. B.'s case, there is no indication of Channing's reaction or of her response to the destruction of her child, who was already dead when instruments were first employed. The sole comment is nondescript: "Mrs. B. suffered somewhat when the milk was about to come, but has since done well, & recovered her usual good health."

The birth of twins was often unexpected, by the mother as well as by Channing. In one situation, "As is the rule, I passed my hand over the abdomen to learn if the womb were contracted and if a second child were in the womb. The abdomen remaining about as large as before the recent delivery, I was satisfied of the presence of another fœtus." The second child was presenting in breech position. "Recollecting that this required more time, and might involve more hazard to the child than a footling presentation, I ruptured the membranes, and easily brought down the feet." Channing reported a happy outcome. "The first was a boy, and the second a brother; and as three girls were living, the first child—a boy—having died in infancy, even a double birth of sons was not painfully, if at all regretted."[75] It was another case that contributed to Channing's satisfaction with obstetrical practice.

Several twin births ended tragically. Mrs. —— hemorrhaged in the aftermath of a fourteen-hour labor and delivery of a dead child. Her regular physician had departed after the delivery despite her bleeding, but was recalled when the emergency became apparent. It was then that he sought assistance from Channing and Dr. David Storer. Upon examination, Channing found another child still in the womb. He and Storer decided forceps should be used immediately and a second dead child was extracted. Each baby weighed more than eight pounds and was more than twenty-two inches long. The original physician claimed he had missed the second fetus because of the size of the first, which was unusually large for a twin. Channing was displeased by these events. "In looking back on this case the question arises what might have been done had it been ascertained immediately after the first birth that another child was in the womb." He answered his own query. "I know of no means as effective as turning," which would have enabled him to remove the second baby before the hemorrhage became so severe. The mother died two hours following Channing's departure from the home.[76]

APART from deliveries requiring internal version or the use of instruments, the obstetrical problems that most severely taxed Channing's ability were excessive hemorrhage, convulsions, and infection. In all these situations, it was imperative that the child be delivered quickly, and he employed the various means of expediting labor described above to avert disaster. Hemorrhage, for example, could occur before labor or during the early stages, either because the placenta was attached at the mouth of the uterus (placenta previa) or because it had already separated from the uterus. If hemorrhage occurred after delivery it was usually because the placenta, or some part of it, had not detached.

In either situation, obstetrical measures were taken to address the cause of the bleeding, but if it persisted or if its cause was unknown, Channing resorted to a variety of medical measures, depending on his judgment of each case. For some he used ice or cold compresses, externally or internally; for some he applied pressure on the abdomen or perineum; for some he administered drugs such as acetate of lead, sulfate of alum, or sulfate of copper. Occasionally, he gave ergot postpartum to induce contraction of the uterus and thereby to expel the placenta or constrict the blood vessels. Though Channing was aware of experiments with blood transfusion made by James Blundell, who had succeeded Haighton in the chair of midwifery at Guy's Hospital Medical School, he did not attempt such a daring procedure.[77]

Convulsions were frightening for everyone. Sometimes they were accompanied by edema, sometimes not, but since no one understood eclampsia it was not easy to predict their onset. Convulsions were attributed to several causes: general irritability of the system, plethora (excessive blood and other bodily fluids), or an overloaded stomach. Channing recommended treatment by "liberal depletion," that is, evacuation of the bladder, strong cathartics, leeches, and venesection, plus shaving the head and applying cold compresses. Toward the end of his career, he and other physicians used chloroform or ether to control convulsions. By then they were also examining urine for the telltale evidence of excess albumin, a sign of pre-eclampsia.

If infection occurred, Channing used the full panoply of nineteenth-century medical treatments: bleeding, emetics, cathartics, purgatives, diuretics, blisters, cupping, fomentations, catheters, injections, and enemas. Mrs. Gurney had developed puerperal fever during or following delivery. Channing kept detailed notes on her disease from February 20, 1829, when he gave orders for mercurial cathartics at bedtime, through March 7, when she "continued to sink and died at 12 M." He visited morning and evening almost every one of those sixteen days. He observed an irregular pulse and a thick, dry tongue. Her sleep was fitful, her head hurt, her abdomen was tense and painful, and she was troubled by dyspnea (shortness of breath) and a cough. There were occasional paroxysms. Channing examined by stethoscope, but found "nothing uncommon."

He prescribed daily cathartics and frequent enemas and emetics, intended to cleanse her system of the unknown impurity that was causing the disease. She received an opiate nightly to produce sleep. She was bled, cupped at the temples, blistered at the abdomen, rubbed with ointments as well as with lard. For a few days she seemed to improve, then became drowsy and languid, which in retrospect is hardly surprising, considering how much her system was depleted by bleeding, enemas, and emetics. She complained of numbness and pain in her hands. Channing asked Dr. W. (probably Warren, possibly Ware) to see her with him, "and we conclude to vesicate [blister] abdomen and give salut. tart. antimon. to nausea." By March 5, "diarrhea and sinking" had set in, and she expired two days later.[78]

Would Mrs. Gurney have survived if she had not received such heroic medical treatment? Perhaps, if her general health had been good and the infection not too virulent. In that case, the extreme measures Channing prescribed so severely weakened her that she was less able to recover. On the other hand, if the infection was severe and she had no resistance to the spread of disease, she would not have survived, and though her final days would have been free from harsh drugs and unpleasant procedures, she would have experienced fever, pain, and extreme discomfort. It is, unfortunately, a moot point.

From Channing's viewpoint, he was doing what he thought was appropriate in her case. "[A]ll our means of treatment," he wrote, "are precisely the same with those which are ordinarily employed in medical management of disease."[79] His prescriptions and treatments were not capricious but were grounded in commonly accepted theory about disease, its causes, and its treatment. Since patients with similar diseases often recovered, it was as easy for them to assume that the physician had cured them as it is for us to assume the opposite.

The rate of maternal mortality in Channing's practice is unknown except among 195 cases described in a list of his midwifery cases from 1811 to 1822. Two of eighteen women who had miscarriages died. One was in her fourth month and had had a previous attack of severe dysentery, which may have caused the miscarriage and led to septic shock or renal failure. The other died of convulsions. Of the 177 full-term deliveries there were eight deaths (just over 4 percent), five due to infection, and one each to convulsions, dysentery, and tuberculosis. In two cases of infection the mother recovered.

The mortality rate among the babies delivered in those early years of Channing's practice is also known. Forty-one full-term babies died (nearly 23 percent of the total), fourteen stillborn and twenty-seven soon after birth. Half the stillbirths and infant deaths occurred in the first three years of his practice, when he was delivering primarily poor women. It is possible that he was less proficient in those early years, but it is more likely that these numbers are evidence of higher death rates among poor children. Neonatal morbidity and mortality in poor populations at the end of the twentieth century would seem to corroborate this interpretation.[80]

On the other hand, he also saved babies born with the cord wrapped round the neck, slipping it upward as the child emerged. He revived stillborn babies by artificial respiration, blowing directly into the mouth of the child to inflate the lungs and stimulate breathing. He also had a system of his own that he described for his students. "Dr. C. says best to have a pipe and having this fixed to bellows which will fill the lungs. But the inflation must be gradual. The quantity of air required is very small."[81] External applications, such as cold water poured over the child, were also used to produce respiration. Additionally, he removed the extra thumb on one child's fist and treated the abscessed breasts of lactating women. In a few cases of spina bifida, he drained fluid accumulating at the base of the spine in unsuccessful attempts to save the children's lives.[82]

IN addition to midwifery, Channing's practice included many gynecological cases, though the word *gynecology* did not become part of his vocabulary until late in life.[83] Instead, *diseases of women* or *diseases of the uterine system* were commonly used to refer to the malfunctions and diseases associated with the female reproductive system. They were not yet the subject of a separate medical or surgical specialty but were treated by general practitioners, especially by men like Channing who were more familiar with women's physiology and anatomy. Nor were these disorders treated by aggressive surgery, as would become more prevalent by the end of the nineteenth century.

These cases, he told his students, "require much patience and time." They included menstrual difficulties; diseases of the bladder; fistulas; prolapsed, inverted, and retroverted uteri; cysts, polyps, and cancerous growths. Many were the result of pregnancy and childbirth, through accidents or medical misman-agement. Some physicians shunned such cases, especially the malignant tu-mors that seemed incurable. Channing took a more positive approach. He believed it was wrong to abandon these patients, "simply because such diseases have got a bad name. I have always treated them as I would other diseases." He ceased his care only "because at length it appeared obvious that no benefit was coming of treatment, or the patient, or more frequently her friends, have thought farther care, or farther expense, unnecessary."[84]

Diagnoses were limited by inadequate examinations and the absence of pathological analysis of diseased tissue. Channing was working without bene-fit of X ray and other modern technology and he usually was treating his patients in their homes. Use of the speculum was not common until the latter part of his career. Lighting was poor. Some women were satisfactorily cured, some could be treated only symptomatically, and other cases were hopeless.

Women with gynecological problems were often reticent to seek help or to submit to examination for embarrassing problems. The prospect of painful treatments with no certainty of success also kept them away. A case of inverted uterus makes the point. "I was called to see a woman in Oliver St. . . . . She had come from a distance, and because it was sleighing time she could travel easily. . . . Her state was explained to her, and also the operation her safety demanded. She said she would think about it, and I might call again in the morning. I did, but she was gone—cleaned out. The talk of an operation had just half fright-ened her to death; she took to her sleigh with a will and evacuated."[85]

On the other hand, their injuries left many women less choice than they wished. Channing examined Mrs. ―― a year after the birth of a child and found her uterus inverted by the careless action of a physician who had im-properly removed the placenta. She had been hemorrhaging frequently ever since and was forced to wean her baby. "She wished to know what was her trouble, and I told her that an operation was the only thing that would save her. Might she not die of the operation? She was told she might. The hazard was distinctly stated." She refused to risk it. Several months later, Channing was called back. Bleeding persisted, she was severely emaciated, and "could not last much longer. She was ready for anything. Arrangements were made . . . and the operation was done successfully." Her original physician refused to attend, maintaining that the "suspected dislocation did not exist."[86]

This "operation" consisted of removing the uterus by ligature. A cord was applied through a double cannula to the base of the womb and tightened daily until the organ had atrophied and was sloughed off. Women who endured this kind of operation had to be courageous as well as desperate, for it was exceedingly painful and could produce gangrene and other unwanted effects. The same procedure was used to remove polyps and other uterine growths. Caustic drugs and astringents were sometimes applied instead, and occasionally forceps were used to remove a small polyp. In that situation there was the additional danger of hemorrhage. Channing did not perform genuine surgery and left repair of fistulae to George Hayward, one of John Collins Warren's protégés who became Professor of Surgery as well as surgeon at the Massachusetts General Hospital.[87]

A patient with bladder problems was particularly pathetic. She worked long hours, seated the entire time, in a shop that did not have a water closet. Excessive retention of urine led in time to incontinence and a diseased bladder. "She had to give up work—to keep at home—and at length to go to bed and keep there. . . . it was serious, too, to have to give up work for by that she lived." Channing prescribed according to a favorite remedy of his old friend Dr. Danforth, and eventually Miss —— was cured. She returned to "steady and well-paid-for employment, and excellent necessary accommodations." Channing implored the editors of the *Boston Medical and Surgical Journal* to do all they could "to remove the occasion of so much danger and distress as Miss —— encountered" by campaigning for public water closets.[88]

DEPENDENT as he was on the income from his obstetrical practice, Channing was naturally concerned about fees. The Boston Medical Association regularly published minimum fees to protect physicians from undercutting one another. When he began his practice, the daytime minimum fee for midwifery was twelve dollars; if the physician was engaged during any part of the night the minimum charge was fifteen dollars.[89] By 1820, fees had increased slightly to fifteen and twenty dollars. Three visits postpartum were included in the initial charge; thereafter visits were charged as they were in ordinary medical cases. By comparison, the association mandated fees no less than a dollar and a half for an ordinary medical visit, eight dollars for a nighttime call, eight dollars for amputations of fingers or toes and for excision of small tumors, ten dollars for a case of gonorrhea, fifteen dollars for a case of syphilis, and forty dollars for capital operations. Physicians were advised to collect their money immediately after their attendance, suggesting perhaps that a husband who received the physician's bill might neglect his obligation once mother and child were out of danger.[90]

Fear of competition from irregular practitioners such as homeopaths or Thompsonians (a medical sect that relied on botanical therapies) who might undercut regular medical men meant that the fees established by the Boston Medical Association were not much altered for many years. In 1855 a proposal was made to charge "for a case of Midwifery, in the day-time, $15.00, instead of from $10.00 to $20.00, as it now stands; if any part of the attendance be in the night, $25.00 instead of from $15.00 to $25.00 as it now stands." As Boston's leading obstetrician, Channing objected to the insignificant changes and proposed that the fee for attendance on a case of midwifery range from fifteen to thirty dollars. He realized that general practitioners were also badly paid and urged that all fees be raised. His proposal was supported by the *Boston Medical and Surgical Journal*, which claimed that physicians were underpaid relative to other professions. The *Journal* also cautioned its readers not to outprice themselves in a market that was challenged by irregular practitioners.[91]

The Boston Medical Association also regulated fees for consultants in midwifery cases. "If, in any case of midwifery, a second physician is called in consultation, both the attending and consulting physician shall charge at least the usual fee for delivery." If he did not remain in attendance on the case, but merely gave his advice and departed, the consultant's fee was to be smaller. Though this arrangement could double the cost to the patient, it was a boon for Channing, who was frequently called in consultation.

There were also implicit rules of etiquette between attending physicians and consultants, and in most instances Channing obeyed them carefully. The language he used shows this politesse. "Dr. Y. desired me to see the patient with him, which I did with pleasure." "He [Dr. ——] advised that I should be called in and the next day I saw the patient." In another consultation, "[I] said to Dr. —— that with his permission I would make an effort to deliver. He begged I would do so."[92] Initially, Channing knew most of the physicians in Boston and there was a collegial relationship with the men who asked his advice. As the city and the medical community grew, however, he was less familiar with other physicians and sometimes more critical of their conduct. This was especially true of physicians who had not attended his classes and of homeopathic physicians.

He also received inquiries from physicians in neighboring states who had been his students or knew him by reputation and wanted his advice. He responded by letter, although occasionally he journeyed to another part of New England to examine a patient, and, if necessary, perform the required procedure. He even went to see a patient in the almshouse of a neighboring town. On one occasion he refused to attend an out-of-town patient, explaining that he would not "leave such a patient until it was either clear she was safe or her case was entirely hopeless," and he could not remain so long away from home.

In turn, when he himself solicited assistance, Channing relied on colleagues he knew well, men such as John Collins Warren, James Jackson, and

John Ware. He became especially dependent on Charles G. Putnam, a son-in-law of James Jackson, who took a strong interest in obstetrics and gynecology.

Not every consultation went well. Channing did not hesitate to criticize physicians whose misdiagnoses, mismanagement, or hasty departure caused problems that he was asked to redress. He was especially short-tempered with a physician who had accused him of negligence in removal of the placenta. Channing had already departed when the patient began to experience severe uterine pains. "Dr. ——, being much nearer than I was, was sent for . . . [and] soon after his arrival a large and very solid coagulum was expelled. He at once pronounced it the placenta which I had left in the womb, having first broken off the cord." Channing enlisted the testimony of the nurse, who had not yet disposed of the placenta. She displayed it, with cord attached, to refute the allegation—though not to quell Channing's indignation.[93]

John Barnard Swett Jackson, who subsequently became Professor of Pathological Anatomy at Harvard, had several encounters with Channing. In one, Channing used the perforator to reduce a fetal skull. Jackson thought more ergot would have solved the problem and that instruments were "entirely unnecessary." Another time, Jackson questioned whether a baby was already dead when the decision was made to perforate the head and break an arm to facilitate passage of the shoulders. Five physicians had been involved in this case, but Channing had performed the final procedures.[94]

Channing did not, however, refuse to admit to his errors. "Mistakes may and have been made. And who is not liable to make them?" he confessed to his students.[95] "I did not examine the abdomen, an oversight I readily acknowledge. I much regret omitting this which is often so important a means of diagnosis," he wrote apropos a consultation in which the uterus ruptured and the patient died.[96] He was frequently surprised by an unexpected outcome. Why had an apparently healthy newborn expired? Why did a mother have convulsions during delivery? Why did another who seemed to be recovering well following labor develop fever and die? He was keenly aware of the imperfection of his knowledge, of the unanswered questions regarding conception, gestation, labor, and disease that remained a great mystery. "These questions or some of them remain unsettled, as if it were a design in the obscurity in which they have been involved, to offer for human investigation inexhaustible subjects of interesting inquiry."[97] Postmortem examinations sometimes explained *what* happened, but not *why*.

In his long career, Channing maintained his curiosity about these questions. Some were solved during his lifetime, though most remained unanswered. He also altered some procedures according to new ideas about disease and therapy. But the fundamentals of obstetrics could not change until bacteriology revolutionized the understanding, treatment, and prevention of infection; endocrinology began to explain the development and workings of the reproductive system; embryology shed light on fetal development; and radiology permitted the physician to view the interior of the body.

A description of Channing's obstetrical practice would be greatly enhanced if it included more words from the women who were his patients. However, though nineteenth-century women wrote to their friends about their fears of pregnancy and childbirth and confided their concerns in their journals, they were remarkably silent about the particulars of the experience. Nonetheless, it is not unreasonable to conclude that his patients liked him, that they trusted him, and that he in turn liked and trusted them. Though his case notes occasionally show class or racial bias, especially if the woman displayed slovenly conduct, there are also kindly remarks about lower-class women and sympathy for the difficulties of their lives. Many of Channing's patients were lower-class women who worked in small shops, light manufacturing, and domestic service. The care they received was as thoughtful as that offered the women on Beacon Hill.

As the years passed and he accumulated the wisdom of experience, he became increasingly understanding of life's complications and tried to help some women who had got themselves in difficulties. He was willing to call a baby "prematurely born" to spare its mother the embarrassment of a child conceived before marriage, and to help a teenage mother bury her dead child without public scrutiny. "He is a happy physician," he wrote, "who is conversant with the causes of things."[98]

Channing worked hard, often sacrificing his obligations to his own family because he expected a patient to go into labor or because he was already engaged in a delivery that required many days' attendance. At the age of seventy he was still staying the night if a case required it, still questioning events, still trying to learn and understand the mystery of childbirth. Obstetrics in any age is limited by medical knowledge and technology, by women's desire for safety as well as their views of their bodies and their role in society. Channing's obstetrical practice was bound by the same parameters, but enhanced by his commitment to his patients and his certainty of the importance of his profession.

Chapter 5

The Hospitals

I can never forget the results to myself of this long hospital service. . . . I learned in it what has done most to render me in any sense useful to those who have given me their confidence.

—Walter Channing to N. I. Bowditch, October 7, 1851

BY September 1, 1821, construction of the Massachusetts General Hospital was complete and it was ready to receive patients. Two days later, a thirty-year-old man diagnosed with syphilis was admitted.[1] He was still there a month later, when the attending physician, James Jackson, named Walter Channing to be the assistant physician. "I entered the service of the Hospital almost literally at its opening," he proudly recalled, "and . . . attended the very first patient who was received within its walls." Channing remained a member of the staff for more than seventeen years, eventually as attending physician.[2] His long hospital service was an important part of his career, augmenting his esteem for the medical profession, his "reverence for its character, its objects, its results."[3]

Despite the fact that Channing was increasingly associated with midwifery, Jackson's choice made sense. He was better acquainted with hospital practice than most physicians in Boston, having spent many of his student days at the hospitals in Philadelphia, Edinburgh, and London. The other promising men among his professional generation, including Bigelow and Ware, had not had the advantage of study abroad. It was a well-deserved compliment from Jackson, who remained satisfied with his assistant and annually requested renewal of the appointment. "I nominate Dr. Channing for re-election from a conviction that I shall thereby best promote the real welfare of the hospital," he wrote to the trustees in 1828.[4]

Massachusetts General Hospital (courtesy of the Francis A. Countway Library of Medicine)

Hospital physicians were an elite group in American medicine, and Channing benefited from the reflected glory of his chief. Frequent contacts with the trustees and with the consulting physicians who were occasionally asked for advice further enhanced his reputation, "until he was one of the best known physicians of the Boston community."[5] Hospital duties also increased his sympathy for the poor and reinforced his social concerns. Admission required a visit by the physician or surgeon to the home of the patient, where, it was assumed, he could better judge real need. Channing was thus forced to witness more squalor than private practice or Dispensary patients provided. The tragic experiences of some patients became part of their medical histories. One young woman who spent six weeks in the hospital was diagnosed with amenorrhea (cessation of menstrual periods for abnormal reasons) and an unspecified "affection of the lungs." Most of her life had been spent sewing straw, "which obliged her to sit a good deal."[6] Another patient, a domestic servant only thirteen years old, was brought to the hospital with a concussion resulting from a bad fall. She had been abandoned by her parents, did not know if she had brothers or sisters, and had no one to take care of her.[7]

Channing often spent an hour or so at the hospital even on days when Jackson was attending. During the late spring and summer months, when Jackson left town for his country retreat, Channing had complete responsibility for the medical wards.[8] He listened to the complaints and medical histories of newly admitted patients, made an initial diagnosis, and prescribed whatever drugs, blisters, diet, baths, or other treatment he deemed appropriate. For the men and women already in the hospital, he visited daily to observe their conditions and adjust their therapies. The house physician, appointed annually by Jackson and John Collins Warren from among the recent medical school graduates, followed Channing's instructions and kept records of the medical history and daily care for each patient.[9]

Ideally, the hospital was viewed as a family, and was often referred to as "the house," with the trustees in the role of beneficent but exacting parents, limiting expenditures, enforcing order, and demanding good conduct from the patients and staff.[10] The hospital was meant to replicate the care more fortunate people would receive at home, albeit with fewer luxuries. As an early hospital report explained, "The poor patients under the care of skilful, intelligent, and eminent surgeons and physicians, are watched over by faithful and attentive nurses, and in truth the minor officers and domestics . . . continue to give the *sick poor* all the comfort and relief with all the chances of restoration, which the kindness of friends or the influence of money can command for those favoured with both."[11]

Two trustees regularly visited the wards each week, preferably when no one from the staff was present, to hear patients' comments and complaints. "The committee cannot but record their satisfaction at the order, neatness and regularity of everything in the house and at the unwearied attention of the Superintendent & all connected with this establishment," was typical of their comments.[12] They also approved admissions, determined the weekly fee assigned to each patient on the basis of his or her ability to pay, and certified that free patients were indeed among the "deserving" poor.[13] Members of the Visiting Committee served two-month staggered terms, which enabled them to become well acquainted with the patients, follow their progress or lack of progress, and approve the physicians' recommendations for discharge. Since patients often remained in the hospital for many weeks or months, the increased intimacy between visiting trustees and the dependent sick promoted the sense of family.[14]

The apothecary, nurses, house physician, and house surgeon were the faithful servants in this house for the sick. Except for the nurses, they were governed by hospital rules that required them, as well as the superintendent, to live within its walls and to seek permission of the superintendent whenever they wished to be away. Although antebellum nurses have been viewed retrospectively as little more than charwomen (and indeed this was often the case), a few who attended the sick at the Massachusetts General had enough understanding of disease to receive praise from some of the physicians. According to Oliver Wendell Holmes, "a clinical dialogue between Dr. Jackson and Miss Rebecca Taylor, sometime nurse in the Massachusetts General Hospital, a mistress in her calling, was as good questioning and answering as one would be like to hear outside of the court-room."[15]

The attending physician and surgeon, together with their assistants, ranked above the rest of the staff. No one was supposed to interfere or dictate to them regarding patient care. Nonetheless, their freedom was limited to the treatment of the patients. In all other matters, the trustees had the ultimate control that any proper Boston father would have in his own house.[16] The physicians could and did offer advice on tangential issues such as arrangement of the wards, ventilation, window shades, assignment of free beds, and patient diet, but the trustees made the final decisions. Indeed, they supervised every aspect of hospital life from purchase of surgical instruments, the cost and quality of food, denial of admission to alcoholics and "colored" people, and rules of conduct. They forbade Sunday visitors who might produce "an unfavorable excitement in the patients" during religious service.[17] They even directed the superintendent "to place a label on the principal doors of the Hospital requiring persons to shut them softly."[18]

Boston was still sufficiently small and society sufficiently circumscribed for Channing to live among, worship with, and share the same outlook as the bankers, merchants, clergymen, and Harvard professors who served as trustees. He was familiar with many, for at various times the board included Perkins and Higginson relatives and some of his personal friends. Most trustees were Federalists in politics and Unitarians in religion, as was he. Though committed in their daily lives to the accumulation and conservation of wealth, they sincerely felt their responsibilities for the less fortunate. Perhaps some helped the poor as a way to maintain a steady labor force and defuse threats to social stability, as has been asserted by a few historians, but many others, like Channing, were genuinely compassionate.[19]

Nonetheless, he too believed that careful adherence to rules and regulations promoted the welfare of the patients as well as "the reputation and usefulness of the establishment." When, for example, he unexpectedly arrived at the hospital to find the house physician, the house surgeon, and the apothecary absent from the premises, he quickly sent a lengthy letter to Warren urging that the regulations be revised so that such a travesty would not occur again. He also recommended a small salary of a hundred or a hundred fifty dollars per annum for the house physician and surgeon, thinking it would provide an incentive for better behavior and compensation for obeying house rules. It was the first attempt to remunerate the otherwise unpaid medical staff. The trustees responded with revised guidelines for conduct and responsibilities of the staff and an annual grant of fifty dollars to house officers upon completion of their appointments.[20]

The number of patients admitted annually was not large. The second patient, a twenty-five-year-old man with chronic diarrhea and fever, did not enter until September 20. He was discharged on October 13. The first female patient, age twenty-eight, described as suffering "tremors of the whole body though not violent, weakness in knees and some strabismus [a vision problem]," came to the hospital November 7 and was discharged December 2, "at her own request . . . greatly relieved she thinks by the bath at 96 degrees."[21] During the four months from the inception of care through December 31, 1821, only eighteen patients were admitted. In the following year there were 122, and in 1823 the hospital had 207 patients.[22] By 1838, Channing's final year of attendance at the hospital, 380 patients were admitted, males outnumbering females 255 to 125.[23] The increase reflected the growing acceptance of a general hospital among the sick poor who began to suppress their fears about medical experimentation and dissection and to recognize the benefits they might enjoy.

The wealthier class showed its support by continuing to make donations and bequests. As the hospital became more respectable there were patients who could pay partial or full board. One, an elderly gentleman who had been an officer during the Revolutionary War and a judge in the Massachusetts courts, not only paid board but was billed by Channing personally for extra services he had rendered. The Visiting Committee had to approve the payment of what was still an uncommon event.[24]

Nonetheless, charity patients continued to predominate. To provide for the charity cases, free beds had been created by contributions from philanthropic individuals and institutions. Among the male patients in 1838, charity and paying, the greatest number were laborers or mechanics, followed by sailors, clerks, and minors. Domestic servants predominated among the female patients. Most patients were in their twenties and thirties, with only a few teenagers and elderly. By then, the trustee reports had begun to indicate increasing numbers of Irish among the free patients. By strict economy, which greatly pleased the trustees, weekly expenses per patient were $5.38, an amount that had increased only slightly since the early years. Most of the money went for food, supplies, and the wages of the nurses and housekeeping personnel. Expenditures for medicines were less than 8 percent—technology had not yet begun to affect hospital costs. And, to prevent charity patients from succumbing to the immorality of dependence, those who had sufficiently recovered were expected to do some housework on the wards.[25]

Frequently listed among the patients were members of the hospital staff who became ill from close contact with infectious patients. Their children too became patients. The four children of the superintendent, ages ten, eleven, thirteen, and fifteen, were hospitalized during January 1825 with cough, sore throat, chills and fever, sweating, vomiting, and soreness in the chest. Ipecac was prescribed and all four recovered rapidly.[26] Their father was less fortunate and died a few months later. Nurses were especially vulnerable, but even the cook had to be treated for dizziness, swelling of the eyelids and face, trembling, and inability to walk up stairs.

With a weekly average of forty-three men and women in the hospital, some of whom were surgical patients and not his responsibility, Channing was not overly taxed by his daily rounds. Nonetheless, the hospital offered the chance to see a great assortment of diseases, often aggravated by poverty and neglect.[27] Within one seven-week period he encountered patients diagnosed with phthisis, typhus, cachexia, pleurisy, pox, uterine tumor, dyspepsia, catarrh, epilepsy, dysentery, prolapsus uteri, fever and ague, lung fever, and palsy.[28] Private practice might include an equal variety of ailments, but the hospital experience encapsulated what would otherwise require a professional lifetime.

Annual hospital death rates were below 10 percent, in part because most patients suffered from adult chronic diseases, while the often fatal infectious diseases of childhood were still, even among the poor, treated at home.[29] As a rule, smallpox patients were sent to the municipal pesthouse (a house of quarantine), although one case did make its way into the hospital, causing immense concern for patients, especially young patients, who had never been vaccinated. Some of the more adult patients and staff feared their previous vaccinations would no longer be protective. Channing immediately vaccinated "every one who felt the least anxiety," and no one else was infected.[30]

Cholera, another potentially epidemic disease, threatened Boston and the rest of the country in 1832. It had already terrorized large parts of Western Europe and Great Britain and was expected to arrive by some unknown transmissible manner aboard the ships and merchandise that made the Atlantic crossing. Like officials in every other port city, those in Boston expected large numbers of cholera patients, and the Massachusetts General Hospital was advised to expect an overflow from a municipal facility especially created for the emergency. However, these same officials also took effective steps to clean up the city. Though there was no commonly accepted explanation for the spread of cholera, experience had demonstrated an association of epidemic disease with the open sewers and accumulated filth that blighted urban areas. Drains were flushed, streets were swept, garbage and other refuse were disposed of. These measures succeeded so well that despite the alarm, Boston was one of the few American cities that escaped the cholera epidemic. There were only seventy-eight cholera deaths in Boston in 1832, a marked contrast to about three thousand deaths in New York.[31]

Erysipelas (an acute infection of the skin and subcutaneous tissues) was always a threat in hospital environments. We now understand that erysipelas is caused by a virulent strain of the streptococcus and can be fatal, especially among the elderly, surgical patients, and puerperal women. In Channing's time erysipelas was known to be contagious, but no one understood the cause. Prevention was the best defense. When an outbreak occurred in 1826 and five deaths ensued, the medical staff advised the trustees to move the patients to other quarters and close the hospital. Once this had been accomplished, the superintendent and housekeeping staff undertook a "thorough purification by fumigation or otherwise," washing first with sulphur, then with chlorine, whitewashing and repainting the wards, washing the furniture and airing the mattresses.[32] Subsequent outbreaks were treated less strenuously but always with attention to ventilation, cleanliness, and isolation of infected patients. One such, a sailor whom Channing had admitted to the hospital after first examining him on board a ship in the harbor, was isolated in separate quarters with a newly acquired French disinfecting machine for company.[33]

For most of the patients at the Massachusetts General Hospital, it was the decent food, warm shelter, cleanliness, rest, and escape from the unhealthy environment associated with poverty that allowed patients to leave the hospital "well," "much relieved," or "relieved," as reported in hospital statistics. Their long stays in the hospital abetted that process. Those who fared less successfully were categorized as "not relieved" or "unfit." The bodies of those who died in the hospital were returned to their families. If there was no family, the city assumed responsibility for burial. Postmortems were not uncommon, as might be expected in a hospital staffed by academic physicians. Channing sometimes performed autopsies and otherwise was a frequent attendant. Here again was an opportunity to learn about disease.

During the years of Channing's service, a quiet revolution was occurring in medical therapeutics. Though Channing associated Jackson with heroic medical treatments at the time of his apprenticeship, he recognized that his mentor was never as strong an advocate of drastic therapeutics as were Benjamin Rush and other medical men of that generation.[34] Over time, careful observation rather than tradition and theory convinced Jackson and his colleagues that the debilitating effects of cathartics and bleeding did not of themselves cure the sick. At the medical school, Jackson taught a theory of "expectant treatment" that held that the course of every disease was fixed and that there was little the physician could do to alter it. Rather than attempt to interfere in the body's natural struggle against disease, the physician's first task was to make the patient comfortable and encourage recovery with fresh air, sensible clothing, exercise, and cleanliness.[35]

Thus, the treatments prescribed by Jackson, and Channing as his deputy, were gentler than might be expected. They continued to use cathartics for digestive ailments, but in milder doses and for shorter periods than before. They relied on bloodletting in the beginning stages of pneumonia but not otherwise. Leeches were sometimes ordered for headache and local pain, but discarded if not effective. Opium and guaiac (derived from the resin of a tree native to the West Indies) were prescribed for persistent diarrheas or bloody stools, fevers were treated with quinine, local inflammations with cantharides (or Spanish fly, a dried beetle used as a counter-irritant). But they recognized that the facilities of the hospital did much to relieve people who would otherwise have had to recover while living in filthy surroundings. Digestive ailments responded well to an improved diet; respiratory ailments to "the pure air and clean apartments."[36]

In the decade of the 1830s Boston began to feel the impact of French medical teaching, especially that of Pierre Louis, whose "numerical method" was based on observation of many cases of the same disease and analysis of the effectiveness of therapies used for them. Recent American medical graduates as well as established physicians, including some from Boston, went to Paris to study with Louis and other eminent French medical professors, much as the previous generation had gone to London and Edinburgh. The Paris hospitals, with their large patient populations, offered the opportunity to corroborate Louis's studies and to observe the benefits of bedside teaching.[37] James Jackson, Jr., J. Mason Warren (a son of John Collins Warren), and Oliver Wendell Holmes were among those whose exposure to Louis and the Paris school of medicine confirmed what Jackson and others had long suspected.

Jacob Bigelow, who visited Paris in 1833, enunciated the new teaching two years later at the annual meeting of the Massachusetts Medical Society. "On the Self-limited Diseases," Bigelow's exposition on the ability of nature to cure many diseases, was a straightforward call for therapeutic moderation. He urged his colleagues to refrain from interfering with nature's curative powers, though he also recognized that with some diseases the physician's measures could make a difference. Bigelow's prominence in Boston's medical circles strengthened the impact of his essay.[38]

The difficulty physicians faced, having begun to doubt the efficacy of bleeding, purging, and dosing with mercurials and other toxic medicines, was that they had nothing with which to replace them. Knowing what does not work does not necessarily mean knowing what will work. Even the greater understanding of the etiology of infectious diseases that followed the path-breaking work of Pasteur, Koch, and Lister at the end of the nineteenth century would not significantly reduce morbidity and mortality until the development of antimicrobial agents in the middle of the twentieth century. Nor do we yet know how to cure some of the infectious diseases that have recently appeared and many noninfectious diseases such as cancer. Channing and the other hospital physicians thus continued to rely on the customary therapeutics, using moderation and caution; but they were forced by the necessity of "doing something" to prescribe treatments we look back upon with horror.

Hospital practice did not add much to Channing's expertise in obstetrics and the diseases of women. Some of the female patients were diagnosed with various menstrual disorders that may well have been symptoms of underlying disease that could not be explained. For example, the headaches, dizziness, abscesses on the side of the neck, chest pain following meals, confused vision, and hearing loss of one patient were attributed to amenorrhea, though she subsequently developed a cough, swollen tonsils, and abdominal pain. Even more mysterious, for no obvious reason she gradually recovered.[39] Other women were treated for postpartum hemorrhage, prolapsed uterus, ovarian tumors, and other all-too-common female disorders. Obstetric cases were rare. When a nineteen-year-old woman entered the hospital on November 15, 1823, the house physician noted that she "looks daily to be confined." She had developed complications during the previous four weeks, including syncope (fainting) and repeated threats of convulsions, for which she was bled. On the 29th she delivered a nine-pound daughter "with relative ease." The house physician attended the birth. The following day another paroxysm occurred, but by December 14 she had recovered and was discharged.[40]

It is unclear how the new mother came to be admitted to the Massachusetts General Hospital. The New York Hospital had had a lying-in department since 1801, and the Pennsylvania Hospital since 1803. They also permitted midwifery instruction on the wards.[41] But Boston's civic leaders and philanthropists were less eager to offer their medical facilities to childbearing women. If it had once been difficult for them to accept their responsibilities toward friendless strangers stranded in their city—widows without families to care for them, or the worthy poor who served as domestic servants and common laborers—it remained difficult for them to assume additional obligations on behalf of poor women seeking a clean, safe place in which to deliver their babies. Nor were they sympathetic to the idea of using the hospital for instruction in midwifery, a serious restraint on Channing's income. Whereas Warren and Jackson could bring their students to the hospital for clinical teaching, and could charge additional fees for that instruction, Channing and his students did not have a similar advantage. In the early years of the hospital, clinical midwifery instruction was briefly considered but just as rapidly abandoned.[42]

NONETHELESS, there were well-intentioned people in Boston who recognized the need for a lying-in facility where homeless or impoverished women would be subjected to less degrading attitudes and receive better medical care than at the House of Industry, the new name for the old Almshouse. The initial impetus came from the Humane Society, which had supported the General Hospital from its inception, contributing five thousand dollars to the original subscription and making subsequent donations for free beds.

The Humane Society, founded in 1786, was originally dedicated to resuscitation of drowning victims and others in danger of asphyxiation or suffocation. It provided equipment to restore breathing and sponsored education aimed at preventing drowning and other accidents. Many physicians were among its early officers, including John Warren and Aaron Dexter. Benjamin Waterhouse had been involved in the initial conversations. Over the years, its assets increased more rapidly than expenditures and the officers began to seek additional purposes for its funds.[43]

In September 1830 a committee led by the Reverend Charles Lowell and including Dr. George Hayward, then the junior surgeon at the hospital, was asked for recommendations "in aid of some other humane and charitable object." The committee soon reported back that "they knew of no object more deserving, or more needed in the present condition of the community, than an establishment for Lying-in women."[44] They proposed that five thousand dollars be appropriated by the society on condition that an additional twelve thousand dollars be raised for the same purpose. When Lowell and his associates asked the hospital trustees to collaborate in the enterprise, they were politely but firmly rejected. Though the trustees agreed that a lying-in ward was highly desirable, they excused themselves from contributing to its construction and support because of "the present state of the funds at their disposal."[45]

In view of the response of the trustees to a request for an obstetrical department made nearly fifteen years later by John Collins Warren and Jacob Bigelow, it is questionable whether the trustees answered Lowell honestly. In 1845 Warren and Bigelow made a strong plea for clinical instruction in midwifery so that graduating students would not start medical practice without having ever witnessed a delivery.[46] The trustees replied by conceding the need for clinical training, but they refused to allow it in their hospital. They did not think it would succeed because respectable married women, even though impoverished, would not want to deliver in a ward where medical students and unmarried women were present. Nor would "young females in the City who, from being unprotected & exposed to temptation, fall into a situation in which a charity of this sort would be a protection and a boon" further degrade themselves or "proclaim their fall" by using it.

The trustees predicted that only the worst sorts of females, "women of notoriously bad habits . . . and females brought up in the lowest abodes of misery . . . whose inheritance has been sin," would dare to use the facility. If these women were admitted to a maternity ward, the poor but virtuous women for whom "female chastity is considered the highest virtue" would stay away from the medical and surgical wards. In short, only "the lowest class of women" (read prostitutes), who had nothing to lose from public shame, would avail themselves of a lying-in facility, and, by doing so, they would drive away sick women whom the hospital was meant to serve. As for instruction, the trustees assumed that pregnant inmates of the House of Industry and Dispensary patients delivering their babies at home would be suitable subjects.[47]

The attitudes expressed by the trustees, representative as they were of contemporary views of chastity, marriage, and female virtue, remained so prevalent that no further attempt was made to introduce obstetrics at the Massachusetts General Hospital for the remainder of the century. The argument they did not use, though hindsight renders it more appropriate, is that the patients in a lying-in ward, even if it was in a separate part of the hospital or in a special building, would have been exposed to infection and the possibility of high rates of morbidity and mortality. The Pennsylvania Hospital had experienced several epidemics of puerperal fever and European hospitals were renowned for the dangers on their maternity wards.

Though the offer from the Humane Society was rejected by the Massachusetts General Hospital, it attracted notice from another charity looking for worthy organizations to support. The Massachusetts Charitable Fire Society was founded a few years after the Humane Society to assist people whose homes were damaged or destroyed by fire, a common enough event in an era when buildings were constructed of easily flammable materials and there were no insurance companies to compensate owners for their losses. By judicious management its funds too had grown, especially since improved building materials and fire-fighting equipment and the advent of private insurance companies reduced the need for their help.[48] Like the Humane Society, the Charitable Fire Society had made annual contributions toward free beds at the hospital. When asked to join them in the creation of a lying-in hospital for indigent women, the Charitable Fire Society responded affirmatively. Its charter was amended by the legislature to permit expenditure of funds for such a purpose.

Subsequently the two organizations, established forty years previously for very different purposes but faithful to a tradition of civic responsibility and obligation to the less fortunate, contributed five thousand dollars each toward the establishment of the Boston Lying-in Hospital. In return, each organization was entitled to name two trustees. Additional subscriptions brought the assets to more than fifteen thousand dollars.[49]

The idea of a private lying-in hospital was relatively new in the United States. New York had had a series of small lying-in establishments, of which only the New York Female Asylum for Lying-In Women was extant when the Boston Lying-in Hospital opened its doors. In Philadelphia, the Lying-In Charity had just begun to provide obstetric care and to train women in obstetrical nursing.[50] Thus, despite the recalcitrance of the trustees of the General Hospital, Boston was a leader in the recognition of the need to provide free obstetrical care for poor women. A small brick building, once a private home, on the west side of Washington Street was purchased. To the rear was a garden where the matron raised vegetables to feed the patients and to sell for the benefit of the hospital. The establishment was meant to be homelike, restful, and secluded, though one wonders if the seclusion was entirely for peace and quiet. The hospital was located at the southernmost limit of Boston, where a narrow strip of land connected it to Roxbury and towns to the south. Perhaps the founders and trustees preferred to shelter their clients in a remote part of the city where they would be less offensive to the neighbors.

And where was Walter Channing while all these plans were hatched? His name does not appear in the official correspondence, act of incorporation, or list of officers. The only reference in his personal correspondence is a casual remark made in a letter to James Jackson, Jr., then a student in Paris, written shortly after the hospital opened. "We have a small Lying in Infirmary established at last and I think this will be useful here."[51] Yet he is generally considered the founder of the hospital, his name is permanently associated with its origins, and his portrait hangs prominently in the lobby of today's Brigham and Women's Hospital, successor to the Boston Lying-in.[52] In October 1940 Frederick Irving, an obstetrician and amateur historian who had a long association with the Boston Lying-in Hospital, established "Walter Channing Day" to commemorate the anniversary of the first patient at the hospital. Channing, he said, should "be venerated because he founded this hospital."[53]

Channing was indeed a friend of many members of the Charitable Fire Society. Samuel Perkins, his father-in-law, was one of the earliest members, served on the committee that secured legislation permitting the charter change, and was one of the initial hospital trustees designated to represent the society.[54] Perhaps, as Irving suggested, Channing persuaded him and his colleagues to add their funds to those already offered by the Humane Society. He may also have been instrumental in the offer from the Humane Society, for he was equally familiar with the men on its board. George Hayward was on the staff of the Massachusetts General Hospital and had been a frequent contributor to the *New England Journal* while Channing was editor. More than anyone else in Boston, Channing understood the need of poor women for "such comforts and attentions as the necessities of the puerperal state require," and he would have been a powerful influence on the charitable men who decided to help them.[55]

In most respects the Lying-in Hospital was patterned after the General Hospital. The house physician, appointed from the recent medical school class by the attending physicians, was required to live on the premises, free beds were made available through the income on hospital investments and the charity of benefactors, and visitors were strictly limited. The only significant differences were general supervision from a matron rather than a superintendent and the appointment of twenty-four directresses who visited weekly, much as the Trustee Visiting Committee did at the General Hospital. The participation of directresses was expected to add "delicacy to the benevolent objects of the institution" and assure the public that the hospital did not condone immoral conduct.[56]

The trustees, all male, also visited regularly to check on the matron and give their approval to the establishment. To make certain the hospital was not seen as a haven for "fallen females," the *Rules and Regulations* specified that "none but married women, or recent widows, known to be of good moral character" were to be admitted.[57] It was important that the hospital not give "the least encouragement to Vice or immorality."[58] In further acceptance of conventional morality, medical students were not permitted at the Boston Lying-in. How much this bothered Channing is not certain. As dean of the medical school faculty in 1845, he informed the trustees of the Massachusetts General that his colleagues "retain their original impressions on the subject," even though they accepted the decision not to create a lying-in department. Thirty years later he continued to deplore the absence of clinical obstetrics in the medical curriculum and urged his colleagues in the Boston Obstetrical Society to remedy the situation.[59] On the other hand, he was enough of a realist in 1832 to know that the new hospital would never have community support if it did not conform to contemporary mores.

The trustees of the Lying-in Hospital named Channing attending physician, along with Enoch Hale, a close friend and colleague.[60] John Collins Warren, Jacob Bigelow, and George Hayward were designated consulting physicians. Edward Hook, a recent graduate of the medical school, was the first resident physician, responsible for admitting patients and keeping case records.

Despite the incorporators' claims of urgency, the hospital was never fully occupied. From the admission of the first patient on October 24, 1832, until the hospital closed in 1854 prior to its removal to a different location, there were only 650 patients, an average of twenty-seven per year.[61] In most months only four or five women were in residence. Like the patients at the Massachusetts General, they tended to stay for long periods, often arriving many weeks before term. It was not uncommon for the resident physician to note "reckoning doubtful" when a woman claimed that she did not know when she had had her last menstrual period or when she first felt "quickening." Perhaps many women did not. Or perhaps they feigned ignorance because they wanted early admission.

One woman entered the hospital seven weeks before her labor began. The resident physician noted that she "has been remarkably well. Enters now from anxiety or ignorance."[62] Middle-class women who delivered at home usually enjoyed the luxury of reduced responsibilities before delivery, and poor women would have had similar or perhaps even greater need of respite. Additionally and despite the Rules and Regulations, the hospital provided a haven for unmarried women in the final weeks of pregnancy when they could not hide their condition. Nonetheless, the trustees resented the evidence of patients seeming to convert the hospital into a free boardinghouse, even though they usually worked in the house or garden until the onset of labor.[63] Some patients remained longer after delivery than deemed necessary by the physicians. Susan Brown gave birth on September 17, 1837, and was discharged October 3, but remained three additional days although she had three children already at home.[64] Middle-class women would have expected a lengthy convalescence, yet the trustees were uncomfortable with Susan's apparent malingering. Most patients were charity cases, but those who could afford some minimal payment were charged accordingly.

The requirement that they be either married or recently widowed was honored more in the breach. The number of women claiming widowhood or desertion by unworthy husbands was unusually high, and the management made little or no attempt to verify their stories. The directresses and trustees also meant to demonstrate Christian compassion by placing patients in "good homes," as either domestic servants or wet nurses, if they had no place to go following discharge. What happened to the babies of those women is unknown.

If some of the women did not fulfill the requirement regarding wedlock, all seem to have been poor. "On account of great poverty, has been subject for a few days to many and great privations," was the notation in one case history.[65] Abigail Carner, nineteen years old, was admitted eight days after the birth of her baby "because of her destitute situation." Sophia Yorke had four other children and was "accustomed to hard work." Margaret Boga, a washerwoman with three children, "has worked very hard lately." Mercy Sparhawk Goodenow "is at present in a delicate state of health caused by laborious exertions for the support of her family, has had 5 children, including twins."[66] One patient, "her mind much excited," had had seven daughters and claimed her husband had died two weeks before she entered the hospital. Another, age forty-seven and among the oldest ever admitted, had had eleven children, of whom only six were still living. She said she had recently been abandoned by her husband, "an intemperate man."[67] For the women who had so many children at home, both the respite from the harsh conditions of their daily lives and the relative cleanliness and peacefulness of the Lying-in must have been particularly welcome.

Hospital records also reveal women who had been beaten by their husbands. One young woman, a recent immigrant, fearful and frequently delirious, had been told by "an old hag" that she would die in childbirth and her baby would be given to strangers to be raised. Neither event occurred.[68] Enough women returned to the hospital for a subsequent confinement to indicate that they had been satisfied by their experiences there. On the other hand, Sarah Currier was "anxious to go out" two weeks after the birth of her baby, complaining that she had not regained her strength, apparently thinking "she wont [sic] get it here."[69] Several others left without permission from the attending physician as required by the bylaws of the institution. Despite general satisfaction, some patients clearly resented the strict regulations.[70]

Women who went to the Lying-in Hospital must have wondered what awaited them, for there was nothing comparable to it in New England. On the whole, despite the rules and regulations and occasional complaints about cleanliness, they found good care and sympathetic attendants who provided shelter and decent food during the weeks of waiting, encouraged them through labor, and gave advice and medical care as needed to mother and child during the postpartum weeks. The physicians usually agreed to their desires for special foods, particularly if they were ill following delivery. Thus, there were orders such as "Desires salt fish, may have it," "wishes meat or broth, may have weak mutton broth," and "may have lemonade to drink."[71] Of course, we do not know how many requests may have been denied.

The first patient was Mary Connor, age twenty-one. Her marital status was not indicated in the hospital records, which did note that she had been in domestic service. The physicians ordered her "to exercise as usual and have for diet plain, nutritious food." Mary lived in the hospital for seven and a half weeks until her baby, a seven-pound girl, was born on December 8. Four days later she was allowed to sit up for an hour, and she gradually increased her activity until discharge on the 19th. She had the hospital to herself until December 1, when Maria Gregg, "domestic, age 19, has had one child," doubled the patient load.

Mary Connor was relatively healthy during the weeks she awaited the birth of her child, but other women required treatment for problems ranging from the usual aches and pains of pregnancy to severe coughs, delirium, and

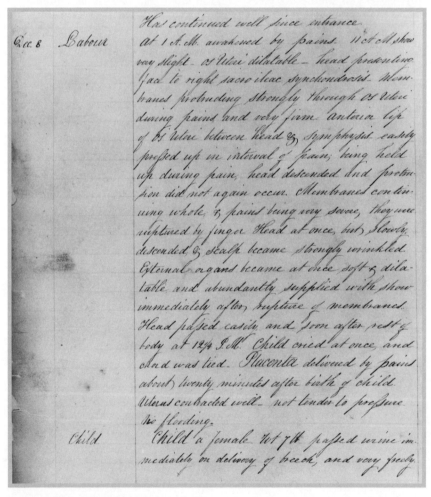

Boston Lying-in Hospital case report, 1832 (courtesy of the Boston Medical Library, Francis A. Countway Library of Medicine)

convulsions. Their hospital records reveal daily attention to their complaints and disorders, with particular regard for proper diet and prevention of constipation.

Although most were already resident in the hospital when labor began, a few arrived when they were experiencing frequent pains. "Sarah Oakes, age 29, domestic, has done housework to last evening. This morning in bed the waters came away after which [she] walked from her residence to the Hospital—a distance of three-fourths of a mile. . . . baby born quarter past eight A.M." Another "has walked today about eight miles and feeling some pain thought best to enter." Two and a half hours later, her daughter was born.[72]

Poor women could be as modest as rich women. Roxanna Frost, age thirty-two, refused an examination until well into labor "when the parts were found somewhat dilated and membranes protruding." She delivered an hour later.[73] To avoid embarrassment to physician or patient, the nurse examined the women following delivery and reported her observations to Channing or Hale for his prescriptions. Thus, on March 8, 1838, "patient has (by report of nurse) a swelling on inside of thigh about the size of a dollar which is very painful"; on March 1, 1838, "nurse reports that there is an excoriation of the perineum, extending around the anus and vulva and downwards between the thighs." The latter wound, caused by pressure of the child's head, which had to be perforated in order to terminate the labor, was dressed with a cloth dipped in a dilute solution of sodium chloride and a bread-and-water poultice.[74] Some domestic medical treatments, reminiscent of female midwifery, remained popular and were prescribed by medical men.

The procedures during labor and delivery at the Lying-in did not vary from those noted in Channing's private practice or from those of other contemporary obstetricians.[75] Patients usually delivered on the left side, but there were exceptions and some delivered on their knees. In most cases, neither Channing nor Hale examined vaginally until labor had been under way long enough for dilation to have occurred. If the amniotic sac was protruding but had not broken, they ruptured it with a fingernail, as was common practice. Ergot was administered for long labors, especially when contractions were not forcing the child through the birth canal. If convulsions threatened or occurred, the usual treatments were attempted: bleeding, blisters, sinapisms (mustard plasters), ice to the head, or antispasmodic drugs such as valerian and asafetida.

Instruments were used much less frequently at the Lying-in than in Channing's private practice, however. In 173 cases from 1832 to the end of 1838, the years when Channing was on the staff, instruments were noted only five times.[76] Poor women might be expected to have increased rates of nutritional deficiencies and pelvic deformities and thus to require more instrumental deliveries. In several cases, labor continued for many days yet instruments were not used. Perhaps there was insufficient dilation to permit the safe application of forceps. Perhaps the physicians imputed greater forbearance to the women at the hospital. But Channing's private practice included poor women in complicated cases requiring obstetrical instruments, so it is difficult to compare the hospital patients with other patients in a meaningful way. In any case, none of the noninstrumented hospital patients died.[77]

Rates of maternal morbidity and mortality at the Lying-in Hospital during Channing's tenure were lower than those he noted during his early years of practice, the only period for which there are consistent records.[78] There were four maternal fatalities among the 173 deliveries at the Lying-in, one attributable to preexisting disease, the others to puerperal fever.[79] In at least ten other cases, symptoms of infection were noted and the women recovered. Some instances of puerperal fever were extremely severe. One woman was clearly identified as Channing's patient and the records of her case did not flatter him. Her fast pulse, abdominal tympany, and extreme diarrhea could have been caused by infection or by physician error, for the placental membrane had not been entirely removed. A creosote solution, which caused much irritation, was injected into her vagina to reduce the offensive odors caused by rotting tissue. She also had a urethral fistula, which led to catheterization and subsequent vaginal infection. As if all this was not enough, the poor woman developed a severe infection of the parotid gland—mumps. Yet she recovered fully and was discharged from the hospital four and a half months after entering, nearly ten weeks following delivery of a stillborn baby.[80]

This relatively successful record regarding puerperal fever is an important aspect of the early history of the hospital, since other maternity hospitals experienced serious epidemics and their reputations for high mortality rates were well known. It may be that the Boston Lying-in took more precautions. One thing that clearly favored it was the small number of patients present at any one time. For example, when Isabelle Johnson was diagnosed with peritonitis on February 19, 1837, there were no other patients in the hospital. She had already begun to recover by the 25th, although she was not discharged until March 18. Meanwhile, Anne Taylor entered the hospital on March 6 and Mary Tully on the 18th. Neither delivered until long after Isabelle Johnson had gone. Neither they nor the next patient developed disease, but Serena Dunnell, who entered on April 5 and delivered on June 9, was diagnosed with peritonitis on June 13. She too recovered. The next two entrants did not get sick. Thus, there were three cases following Isabelle Johnson with no sign of infection, then one moderately infected, and two that were not. Perhaps neither Johnson nor

Dunnell was infected by a virulent strain of the streptococcus, or perhaps each had sufficient stamina to withstand the disease.

A year previously, when the hospital was more crowded and seven women entered in a one-month period, there were four cases of and two deaths from puerperal fever.[81] It was episodes and contradictions like these that added to physicians' inability to understand the infectious nature of puerperal fever or to decide how best to cure it. Channing addressed the Boston Society for Medical Improvement on the quandary, pointing out that "some bore bleeding well and were benefitted by it, one, which did not bear venesection was treated with sedatives and did well; fatal case was bled."[82]

Infant mortality also was significantly lower at the Lying-in than in Channing's beginning practice, when 23 percent died, mostly at the Almshouse.[83] At the Lying-in Hospital fewer than 11 percent either were stillborn or died shortly after birth. These statistics more than justified the founders' intentions, since their clientele was composed primarily of poor and destitute women similar to the Almshouse and Dispensary patients. The prolonged care received at the Lying-in, especially during the month prior to delivery, the relative cleanliness during and after delivery, and decent food and shelter during convalescence contributed to the successful record.

This does not mean that the hospital did not have its share of mistakes and tragedies. Some stillborn babies died because there was no way to foresee that the umbilical cord was too tightly wound around their necks. Others suffered trauma that might have been avoided if instruments had been used or used more promptly. But there were also stillborns successfully revived when cold spirits were "dashed" on them or they received artificial respiration. Three premature babies died, although the staff had covered them with flannel blankets and kept them in warm rooms. Each weighed less than four pounds.

What may have been an egregious error involved three babies born in the autumn of 1838.[84] In each instance, the mother was not able to nurse and the infants were fed milk mixed with sweetened water. Within a few hours each began to show signs of great distress: twitching, fits, and paroxysms of pain. They also had unusually dark green stools. By the third case the house physician began to note the similarities with the two previous babies. The babies were treated with various compounds of ipecac, opium, and magnesium intended to relieve intestinal disturbance, as well as by frictions over the chest, cold cloths at the head, flannel coverings at the feet, and soap and oil enemas. Despite such apparently heroic efforts, two died. The autopsy of one revealed a full bladder distended with bile, stomach lined with thick, dark-colored mucus, the small intestine filled with meconium. Could contaminated milk or impure water have been the cause of death? It seems more than likely.

Many babies were diagnosed with ophthalmia (an eye inflammation), for which they were treated with silver nitrate and mild mercurial ointments. Many also had aphthea (or thrush, a fungal infection of the mouth and tongue), which was thought to be caused by poor digestion. These newborns received small doses of magnesia to purge the bowels. The increased incidence of these neonatal infections may have been due to infection of the birth canal or poor hygiene postpartum.

Hospital staff did everything they could to facilitate breast-feeding. Leeches were applied to painful and abscessed breasts. If a mother's nipples were inverted, several methods were used: a breast glass, a breast pump, or, if neither was effective, an older, stronger infant was placed on the breast to suckle and stimulate the flow of milk. In almost all these cases, the physicians "discharged mother and child well."

IN the summer of 1838, Channing terminated his formal association with the Lying-in Hospital but remained many years longer as a consulting physician. He also decided to give up his appointment at the Massachusetts General Hospital, where he had been serving as one of three attending physicians, a post to which he was elevated in 1836.[85] Late in the autumn, he sent a letter of resignation to the trustees. We do not know whether the letter was a formal statement or whether it contained some regrettable remarks. In January 1839 he wrote a second letter requesting that the prior one be destroyed and that he not be considered for the next annual appointment.[86] It was a strange way of ending his association with the hospital.

We can only speculate about the reason for these almost simultaneous withdrawals from hospital service. Channing was over fifty years old and may well have found himself too widely committed or less willing to exert himself so strenuously. Perhaps he was experiencing another period of depression or was angry about something. In any case, he needed to pay careful attention to his income. There were extra expenses for Lucy, the daughter who was always sickly, and there was continuous concern about Ellery's future. The two older daughters were still unmarried and he was responsible for them too.

Despite the mystery of his resignation from the Massachusetts General, Channing expected to be named one of the consulting physicians, since it was the custom to make those appointments from among the men once on the staff. To his surprise, his expectations were not realized. Instead, John Homans filled the next vacancy, though he had no previous association with "the house." The episode was an embarrassment to some of the trustees who seem not to have realized what had happened. Two stopped Channing on the street to explain that he had simply been forgotten. Channing did not admit his chagrin though he was keenly disappointed. Instead, he praised Homans as "an excellent physician and a personal friend," which indeed he was. Equally inexplicable, the trustees' minutes for February 10, 1839, included an expression of appreciation of Channing for his "long and faithful services," which was never transmitted. Channing remained unaware of the recognition until a history of the hospital published in 1845 referred to the matter.[87] It seems unlikely that, after being at the hospital from the very beginning, a fixture since its opening days, Channing should have been forgotten. A more plausible explanation is that he no longer had a champion in Jackson, who had retired two years previously. Or it may be that his tendency toward self-deprecation prevented his name from being considered, whereas the other physicians were more aggressive. Another possibility is that Channing's increased association with obstetrics made him less desirable as a general physician.

In any case, he took the news philosophically, noting in his memoirs, "little a man does is remembered after he is dead."[88] This included his important service to the Massachusetts General Hospital. On the other hand, he continues to be remembered, long after death, as the founder and guiding personality during the early years of the Boston Lying-in Hospital.

Chapter 6

The Education of Physicians

I am such a true lover of lecturing that I should miss much
pleasure if I did so divide my labours.

—Walter Channing to James Jackson, Jr., November 22, 1832

C HANNING gave his initial introductory lecture on the theory and
practice of midwifery promptly at 9:00 A.M. on the first Wednesday in
November 1815. It was an occasion he would repeat annually for the
next thirty-eight years.[1] When he began to teach, the medical school was still
quartered above White's Apothecary store, but construction of a new building
was already under way. The new medical college, inaugurated in the autumn
of 1816, was on Mason Street, not far from the Boston Common, where cows
still grazed in summer and young Bostonians sped along a snow-packed sled-
ding track in winter.[2]

The new building offered many amenities not found in previous locations
of the school. Channing, Bigelow, and Jackson lectured in a spacious room
furnished with mahogany tables and warm carpets, the aspiring physicians
seated before them on circular raised tiers. In the nearby chemistry laboratory,
Gorham and his successors performed simple experiments, not always successfully. The floor above was Warren's domain: an anatomical theater adorned
with replicas of the Apollo Belvedere and Venus de Medici, two dissecting
rooms, and an anatomical museum. The students may have hoped that the
statues were intended to illustrate the lectures, but a life-sized skeleton hanging from the ceiling gave greater reality to the human form and to the business
before them. Skylights set in the roof dome illuminated the theater and distinguished the college from buildings around it.[3] There was also a library, which

initially held about five hundred volumes, primarily texts donated by the professors to supplement their lectures.[4]

The students were intrigued by the Professor of Midwifery. According to a student in the early years, Channing "popped up through the side door . . . mounted the rostrum . . . gave a pretty good introductory and ended precisely at ten of the clock."[5]

William Wellington, a student in 1835, described a similar scene. "He came fresh from his morning's drive, bright, cheery, and in the best of spirits. The first impression was a favorable one. He was a fluent, at times an eloquent speaker. He graphically described the bones of the female pelvis, and clothed them with flesh and blood; he was full of fun and anecdote; his manner was pleasant and interesting. The lecture reminded one of a refreshing easterly breeze, in a dry, hot, summer's day. The hour passed rapidly away; he briskly put on his coat, and disappeared as suddenly as he came, leaving us almost spellbound."[6]

That Channing was a good speaker should be no surprise, given the talents of his two brothers, one Boston's most popular preacher and the other the Boylston Professor of Rhetoric.[7] That he could be eloquent is equally plausible, for he was a keen student of poetry and the classics, especially Shakespeare, and understood the importance of cadence and literary style. That he enjoyed the limelight of the podium could also be expected. When Fanny Kemble, a famous British actress, came to Boston on one of her many dramatic tours, Channing read Macbeth to her Lady Macbeth in a public performance.[8] Later

Massachusetts Medical College (courtesy of the Francis A. Countway Library of Medicine)

in life, he occasionally conducted the service and delivered the sermon at the Church of the Disciples, which he joined when William Ellery Channing ceased his active ministry at the Federal Street Church.

But Wellington discovered that the initial éclat of Channing's lectures began to fade. "[T]he promise of this first lecture was hardly fulfilled in the sequel. As the course proceeded, the lectures were apt to be discursive. The doctor was rarely tedious; but he was erratic, and not always edifying." In his publications and letters, too, Channing had a tendency to stray from the immediate subject, and used such convoluted sentences the reader was often left to puzzle meaning from verbiage. His students quickly learned that "he could be easily diverted from his main subject, and use up his time in speaking of some recent theory."[9] They also came to admire his "profound acquaintance with the older obstetrical writers."[10]

The Professor of Midwifery was appreciated for his wit as well as his erudition. According to another anecdote, he was fully engaged in a description of puerperal convulsions when an organ-grinder appeared beneath the open window. Presently the strains of a popular air began to mingle with Channing's words. "For a while the battle was evenly contested, the honors going first to the organ-grinder and then to Dr. Channing who, completely drowned out, at last sat down and said, 'Gentlemen, Apollo was the god of music as well as of physic.' "[11]

The students recognized that Channing was totally committed to their instruction. "This afternoon attended an extra lecture by Dr. Channing exhibiting some important operations in his branch of the profession," one student noted in his diary.[12] "Dr. Channing . . . has invited us to call at his room where he will answer any questions or discuss any subject relating to his branch of the profession," another told his preceptor, adding, "His hour never drags— nor fails to interest."[13] However, Channing did not invite them to his home to celebrate the close of the academic session, as was the custom with some of his colleagues. Bigelow served "wine, brandy, nuts & fruits," and Warren provided "an entertainment . . . a pretty splendid treat." A student who arrived late at Warren's Park Street residence regretted that he could enjoy only "a small portion of the conviviality of the evening."[14] Channing's family situation and his persistent concern for his pocketbook were not conducive to such hospitality.

There were a few students with money to spend on the theaters and other entertainments that Boston offered, and their sometimes riotous behavior became the stereotype of medical student life. For most, however, the cost of their education and the seriousness of their pursuits prevented much indulgence. Despite what now seem low fees, the young men who came to the

Massachusetts Medical College from the small towns and farms of New England found that the total expenditure for three (later four) months of instruction, room, board, books, and transportation to and from Boston was quite high. Tickets for the five sets of lectures came to seventy dollars; board was about three dollars per week, with extra charges for firewood and laundry. Additionally, the students were simultaneously under the tutelage of a preceptor whom they also paid for instruction. Some cynically accused "Medicine, Doctors, & everything connected with them" of being interested only in the fees. The seventy-dollar fee in 1825 would equal about one thousand dollars in year 2000 dollars.[15] There were additional charges for the diploma, and if a student left Boston at the end of the term in March, there was the further expense of returning to Cambridge in August for the graduation ceremonies.[16]

Most of the students were purposeful, not only because their education was costly but because they fully expected that their studies would enable them to contribute to society. "Feeling the responsibility which I am soon to take upon myself, it being no less than the lives & health of my fellow creatures & the necessity of being prepared to discharge my duty to my fellow beings with propriety, I have been so deeply & so constantly occupied with my scientific pursuits that I have neglected concerns of eternal importance to myself," William Workman confided to his diary as he assessed his progress on his twenty-seventh birthday.[17] Workman allowed himself time on Sunday to attend morning and afternoon church service, and thus looked after those "concerns of eternal importance," but for the most part he stayed close to his books. Others, equally imbued with the significance of their ambitions, found that the study of medicine could be perplexing. John G. Metcalf complained that the student "will often find himself lost or bewildered among the mazes and labyrinths of the half an hundred of fantastic or visionary hypotheses, or turn with disappointment and disgust from the fruitless endeavor of reconciling two opposite and incontrovertible theories." These difficulties, he added, "can only be surmounted by years of tedious and unremitting application."[18] Channing encouraged the notion that continuous study was required of physicians in practice as well as of students preparing for a career in medicine.

Channing took his teaching duties seriously. Just as there is a stereotypic nineteenth-century medical student, be he boisterous and irreverent or heartless and cynical, who is belied by sober and earnest men like Workman and Metcalf, so there is a stereotypic nineteenth-century medical professor, interested only in the fees he would collect, repeating his lectures year after year and scorning new ideas. There is some truth in this picture because the fees were an important part of Channing's income and little new obstetrical knowledge was produced during these years. However, it is equally true that Channing boasted of the pleasure he derived from lecturing and reworked his notes annually.

Occasionally, he found himself torn between a patient in the final stage of labor and the students awaiting his appearance in the lecture room. Called to a case in which a fetal arm presented, he solved the dilemma by turning the fetus and rapidly delivering it, "thus arriving on time at the medical school."[19] Another day a potentially serious accident failed to prevent his appearance. Inexplicably devoted to fast, unwieldy horses, Channing was unable to control a runaway beast that was pulling his sleigh down the steep incline of Beacon Hill en route to Mason Street. Horse, sleigh, and driver were upturned. In his own words, he was "soon extricated from this helpless situation by several gentlemen, and walked to deliver his lecture at the medical college." Once again, his students did not miss instruction (we do not know what happened to the horse).[20]

Over the years, the sequence and content of the lectures did not change very much, and Channing regularly repeated some of his favorite anecdotes. This was rather boring for students forced by degree requirements to sit through a second year of instruction that did not differ markedly from the first. One complained that Channing and Gorham "go on pretty much after the old sort," and that a story illustrative of the importance of midwifery "was not much improved since last year."[21] It was not until the 1870s that a graded curriculum was introduced, with courses designed to build one upon another. Nonetheless, Channing updated his lectures with references to recent cases in his own and his colleagues' practices and with citations from articles in the latest British and American medical journals. If he disagreed with any of them, he said so. If he had no preference, he might describe the opinions of several writers.

The class met three times per week.[22] Channing usually introduced the course with a simple declaration: "Midwifery is that branch of medicine which treats of conception and its consequences." This was followed by an explanation: though a branch of medicine distinct from surgery and physic, midwifery includes aspects of both (anatomy, physiology, pathology, and therapeutics). He emphasized the need to understand conception, pregnancy, and delivery "in the healthy and the diseased state," in ordinary and in abnormal situations. Finally, he made extensive remarks about the importance of the knowledge he was about to impart and exhorted the students to pay careful attention.

There was no textbook. Instead, Channing recommended significant writers from William Smellie through William P. Dewees, and included the two Frenchwomen, Madame Boivin and Madame LaChapelle, whom he credited with having greater empathy with parturient women than men could have.

Denman, Hamilton, Burns, Merriman, Conquest, and Ramsbotham were also suggested, as well as Baudeloque. Though familiar with French obstetrical teaching, Channing was more comfortable with the British school, in which he had trained. Thus, his students were expected to learn Denman's categories of labor: natural, laborious, preternatural, and complex, but did not have to memorize Baudeloque's six classifications of the position of the fetal head or his rationale for aggressive use of forceps.[23]

Throughout the course Channing attempted to provide historical context to his lectures. He gave the full story of the use of forceps from their earliest development by Peter Chamberlen and his descendants. He summarized theories about conception or menstruation from the ancient Greeks to the present, though it was obvious that much remained obscure. His explanation of the mysteries of conception reveals the state of contemporary medical science: "at a certain time after the congress of the sexes, the precise one however we are ignorant of, an ovum, containing an embryo, a mere speck in existence, is found in the cavity of the uterus."[24]

Over the many years of Channing's professorship, the medical school term was extended from thirteen to seventeen weeks. This allowed him to embellish the course with additional examples, but the general outline remained the same. About half the lectures were devoted to the anatomy of the female pelvis and fetal head, the physiology of conception and menstruation (as then understood), and the pathologies associated with female reproductive organs, including menstrual problems, tumors, and cancers. These lectures were meant to prepare his students to treat "diseases of women" as best they could, given the limitations of knowledge and therapy.

Around the midpoint in the lectures, he began to discuss pregnancy and some of its possible complications, including spontaneous abortion, or miscarriage. Thereafter came a series of lectures on labor, the conduct of the physician during labor, and the many possible interventions that might be needed. He could not offer a complete explanation of labor: neither he nor anyone else understood anything about the hormones that initiate labor and cause the uterus to contract. He could only describe mechanical changes. "Labour begins because and when the cervix is obliterated by the growth of the fœtus or for its accommodation . . . because the os at the moment when the obliteration is perfect begins to open or . . . has become dilatable." As for the second stage of labor, "Force drives the fœtal head downward."[25]

The final sessions were devoted to rupture of the uterus, inversion of the uterus, hemorrhage, convulsions, puerperal fever, and phlegmasia dolens (thrombophlebitis causing swelling of one or both legs, called milk leg when it appeared in a recently delivered woman). He indicated his personal preferences for various styles of forceps and other instruments, even specifying the name of the designer. He recommended prescriptions for specific situations. He also called attention to advice offered in British and American texts. The lectures were highly practical, intended to prepare beginning physicians to expect an uneventful delivery but be able to meet any complication that might occur.[26]

The course was almost entirely didactic, which was expected in an era when professors were meant to provide a comprehensive overview of medical theory and practice and preceptors were expected to introduce the students to patient care.[27] But Channing understood that the students' interest was heightened by visual examples. He illustrated the lectures with wax models of the external and internal parts of generation, the different stages of pregnancy and labor, and the organs associated with the female pelvis. Some of these models he had ordered from Italy, where the art of medical moulage was best developed. Others came from Paris. As pathological anatomy became more widespread, he also showed specimens of diseased reproductive organs, the placenta and cord in various states, and fetuses "from as large as a fly to last month of pregnancy."[28]

John Bernard Swett Jackson, a nephew of James Jackson who later became the first Professor of Pathological Anatomy at Harvard, frequently saved autopsy specimens for him. Channing referred to this collection of wax models and specimens as "his museum of midwifery," and he was eager to have the items properly displayed at the medical school. In 1835 there was talk of creating a midwifery museum in conjunction with increased space for Warren's anatomical collection. When Channing realized that he personally would have to meet the expenses involved, he decided to "forego this most important want in my department." As always, the fear of spending more money than he thought he could afford kept him from realizing a potential benefit.[29]

Clinical instruction in midwifery was out of the question. As Wellington recalled, "Once or twice . . . we were treated to a little practical midwifery. A female pelvis was placed upon the table. The head of a rag baby was thrust into it. It was our duty to ascertain the presentations, and to deliver with the forceps."[30] According to Channing's lecture notes, he used "a machine," presumably a female pelvis with gravid uterus to demonstrate labor and delivery, and he showed the students how to use various instruments needed "for overcoming difficulties." Channing allowed two lecture periods for this exercise, dividing the class so that each man had a chance to "acquire manual skill sufficient for all practical purposes."[31]

Outside the medical school, preceptors occasionally entrusted childbirth cases to their students. There might also be a chance for observation or real experience if a student was well connected with a Dispensary physician, or, as had happened to Channing himself, with a physician at the House of Industry.[32] In his other teaching role, as a preceptor, Channing advertised "clinical opportunities" to students genuinely interested in obstetrical practice, but there is no evidence that such instruction occurred.[33]

Subsequent commentators have been critical of the inexperience of new physicians when they had to face the reality of labor and delivery in their first case of childbirth.[34] However, conservative Bostonians would hardly have condoned a violation of female modesty by allowing students entry into the birthing chamber of a "respectable" patient, and the Boston Lying-in Hospital refused to permit midwifery students to observe its patients. There was a tacit assumption (or fear) that young, unmarried men would take a prurient interest in such scenes and might even be sexually aroused by them. John Collins Warren had to assure Harvard's President Kirkland that "we will cover the female parts" when Dr. Channing's wax preparations arrived from Europe.[35] Instruction was somewhat more liberal at the Obstetrical Institute of Philadelphia, organized in 1837. There, anatomical models were used throughout the course, and after eleven weeks of instruction each student was assigned a woman to follow from the final weeks of her pregnancy through delivery and postpartum visits.[36]

By the middle of the century reform was under way. In 1850 Dr. James Platt White flew in the face of conventional mores by holding the first clinical demonstration in midwifery at Buffalo Medical College in New York. The patient was a recent immigrant, unmarried and pregnant for the second time, who was brought from the poorhouse to the medical school to live with the family of the janitor several days before her estimated confinement. When labor began, twenty students examined the patient, listened to the fetal heart, and witnessed the delivery. News of the event produced an uproar. A local physician wrote angrily to the local newspaper about the "salacious stares" and "meretricious curiosity" of the medical students, condemning a precedent "set for outrage indiscriminate." To protect his reputation, White sued for libel but lost the case when he could not prove the identity of the author. Other physicians were equally disapproving of clinical instruction. A committee of the American Medical Association argued that a physician had to learn to work by touch alone and was otherwise unfit to practice.[37]

White did have his champions, including Austin Flint, editor of the *Buffalo Medical Journal*, who commended the propriety of "better preparing those soon to become practitioners of medicine for the responsible duties of the accoucheur."[38] The editor of the *Boston Medical and Surgical Journal* also supported "demonstrative midwifery," as White's innovation was called, pointing out that most European lying-in hospitals had permitted such instruction for many years; he urged "the use of all legitimate and appropriate means of acquiring that skill upon which our happiness and hopes may in a great measure depend."[39]

Demonstrative midwifery was not incorporated into Channing's course. Though he had benefited from clinical experience in London and Edinburgh, he acquiesced in the refusal of the Massachusetts General to admit midwifery cases and submitted to the policy of the Lying-in Hospital that forbade medical students. Instead of opposing conventional mores, he stressed the importance of book learning, insisting that study of the texts provided the essential foundation of medical knowledge and that a student must be well prepared intellectually before he could benefit from observation. "Where does he acquire that knowledge? From books . . . from books alone. We claim for our profession that it is an intellectual one, that it is the mind and the whole mind that is to be devoted to it, in order that it may be worthy of our highest nature. A man who discourages reading, hard & laborious study in our profession, is not of us."[40] This, of course, is the way Channing had studied medicine with James Jackson.

The controversy over demonstrative midwifery continued in the decades following White's revolutionary act, with many physicians and laymen remaining adamantly opposed, primarily on grounds of morality and the preservation of female modesty. Channing was more open to change after his retirement from the faculty in 1854. Belatedly recognizing the deficiencies of didactic instruction, he urged his obstetrical colleagues to promote clinical training.[41] He gave his wholehearted approval to the obstetric clinic that Dr. Gunning Bedford had created at University Medical College in New York and to Bedford's weekly clinical lectures. By innuendo he even criticized the Boston Lying-in Hospital for not allowing students to observe there. "[T]his, so-called, respect for the feelings of patients did not preserve this institution from dissolution," he wrote in 1862, referring to the closure of the hospital when it had been unable to attract sufficient numbers of patients.[42]

MEDICAL jurisprudence occupied a secondary role in Channing's teaching, as it did in the curriculum of all medical schools.[43] There was neither sufficient time nor sufficient demand to warrant more attention. Examination in medical jurisprudence was not a requirement for graduation, and students could not be expected to devote themselves to a course that had no immediate rewards. Channing did not offer it every year, but when he did he scheduled additional hours for eight lectures on the subject.[44] They did not produce additional fees. Few people seem to have objected until 1851, when David Humphreys Storer, soon to succeed to Channing's chair, lamented the absence of methodical instruction in medical jurisprudence. Storer was reacting in part to the increase of crime in mid-century Boston, "caused in a great measure by the vast hordes of ignorant and abandoned foreign paupers who are daily swarming to our shores."[45] Storer must have assumed that the study of medical jurisprudence would produce physicians better equipped to testify against the immigrant criminals and well-trained medical examiners who could reveal their dastardly acts.

Perhaps Channing remembered listening to Benjamin Rush's lectures on medical jurisprudence when he prepared his own course, but he gave little credit to the Philadelphian. Rush had divided the subject into forensic medicine (criminal injuries, poisons, accidental deaths, and aberrant sexual situations) and public health (epidemic diseases, safe water and healthy foods, and the sources of harmful air). Colleagues at other medical schools included medical ethics in their syllabi. Channing was more concerned with protecting his professional colleagues from embarrassing and awkward legal situations, especially when they testified in court. "The medical witness must study books on medical jurisprudence," he once commented. "He must attend lectures about it, as a branch of his professional education."[46] Channing assumed that physicians would be impartial, that their knowledge and experience uniquely fit them to reveal "the Truth." He worried about the implications of their testimony, because they would be dealing with the life or death of the accused. "What we may say in court is treated with sacredness, and with beauty," he wrote in a fit of idealism.[47] It took several personal experiences as an expert witness himself for Channing to realize that the adversarial justice system often renders "truth" a questionable and relative notion.

He has been described as "an insightful and effective professor who maintained strong interests in and commitments to research in medical jurisprudence through his entire career."[48] His lectures showed that he had studied strictly legal texts, such as Glassford's *Principles of Evidence* and Reid's *Inquiry*, as well as the literature on medical jurisprudence.[49] He relied heavily on a two-volume text, *Elements of Medical Jurisprudence*, published in 1823 by Theodoric Beck, Professor of the Institutes of Medicine and Lecturer in Medical Jurisprudence at the College of Physicians and Surgeons of the Western District of New York. Reprinted twelve times, Beck's tome remained the standard in American medical schools for more than thirty years. Channing also quoted freely from the European masters of medical jurisprudence, especially the French school, which was particularly noted for contributions in toxicology and insanity.

He divided his lectures on medical jurisprudence into four broad areas:

first, legal issues that relate to human reproduction (what he called "continuance of the species"), for example, age of puberty, marriage, divorce, impotence, sterility, legitimacy; second, insanity, described by him as the incapacity of the individual to conduct himself responsibly and manage his affairs properly; third, acts of violence such as homicide, suicide, and infanticide; and fourth, "all those not in the above," which included death from apoplexy or lightning, drowning, and unexplained instances of sickness or death where the physician had to examine the victim and decide on cause.[50] The students must have found these lectures fascinating, with the shocking tales of illegitimate birth, abortion, incest, seduction, and rape that illustrated them. There were graphic stories of poisoning, hanging, murder, feticide, infanticide, and accidental death, even death from spontaneous combustion. Channing had examples for every crime. He recounted trials in which he had appeared as a witness and retold the legends of great murder trials in England and early Boston. Among his favorites, repeated many times over the years, were the trial of John Donellan, Esq., for the willful murder of Sir Theodosius Edward Alloesley Boughton, Bart., in London in 1781, and the trial of T. A. Selfridge, Esq., charged with killing a Harvard student, Charles Austin, on the streets of Boston in 1806.[51]

Channing wanted to prepare his students for the courtroom, where he feared they would be placed at an unexpected disadvantage. He warned that daily practice, when "the physician can expect to be in control," was no preparation for the tensions of a criminal trial, where his authority and competence would surely be questioned and he could be intentionally provoked or submitted to abusive inquiries. Channing urged his listeners to prepare carefully for evidence that could be presented by the opposing lawyers and to take plenty of time when responding to questions. He even suggested dropping names of well-known physicians to impress a jury and other ploys to protect themselves on the witness stand.

Malpractice suits were another topic to which he gave much attention. Jacksonian notions of democracy and equality promoted distrust of all elite institutions, including the medical profession, during the 1830s and 1840s. One result was an increase in medical malpractice cases.[52] Channing was naturally protective of professional colleagues who had to defend themselves in court. His views echoed those of a Pennsylvania jurist who had ruled that the legal responsibility of the physician is limited by the personal responsibility of the patient. As Channing explained, the physician possesses "a reasonable degree of professional skill which he exercises with reasonable care and diligence." He is expected to use his best judgment, but he cannot guarantee the outcome of his ministrations. Too many variables, from the conduct of nurses and other attendants to the actions of patients themselves, produce unwanted results and lead to outcomes for which the physician has no responsibility. "The patient," Channing taught, "must be responsible for all else; if he desires the highest degree of skill and care, he must secure it himself."[53] To further shelter the profession, Channing urged that physicians accused of malpractice be judged by other physicians, much as members of the clergy or the military are tried by their peers.

IN addition to giving practical lessons in midwifery and medical jurisprudence, Channing used the lecture podium to inspire the young men seated before him with his own vision of the profession they had chosen. He liked to quote Cicero: "In nothing does a man so nearly approach to the immortal Gods, as in giving health to mortals."[54] But the public image of physicians was less exalted. Though the number of medical schools proliferated during the nineteenth century, many were proprietary enterprises with minimum standards for admission, poor instruction, and lax graduation requirements. Since they were competing for students, their managers feared losing business if their schools were too demanding.

Admittedly, requirements at Harvard were more stringent than at the smaller schools, but that did not always guarantee high performance. Channing usually gave a brief oral test partway through his course. No one was reported to have failed.[55] Final examinations were perfunctory and superficial. Candidates for degrees appeared one at a time before the assembled professors and were asked a few questions relative to each specialty. Their responses in these brief interviews were taken as an indication of their knowledge and fitness for medical practice. They then wrote a dissertation "on some subject connected with medicine," submitted it to the appropriate professor for approval, and read it in public. Each student was allowed ten minutes for his oral presentation, so the papers cannot have been long. They were based entirely on secondary sources and usually summarized current theory on a particular medical issue. The students did not engage in experimentation or research, as would later be required in academia.[56] There had been little change since Channing's years as a medical student.

Apart from the skepticism caused by poorly educated physicians, the public was increasingly disenchanted with harsh medical therapies that often made the patient miserable and just as often did not cure. Jackson and Bigelow might urge milder therapeutics, but they had nothing specific to offer in place of heroic medicines, and patients expected something. A number of unorthodox medical sects, including homeopathy, hydropathy, and botanic medicine, gained popularity by offering alternative treatments.[57] The Massachusetts Medical Society had never had the power to prevent nonmembers from practicing. Now botanics and homeopaths as well as men with degrees from unknown medical schools were competing with Fellows of the society. Even acknowledged charlatans could call themselves physicians.

The confusion and suspicion led Channing to address the problem in one of his concluding lectures to the midwifery course. "I am not standing here in defense of medicine as a certain science," he asserted. "We have too often occasion to acknowledge to ourselves if not to others how ignorant we are, and death is too often the termination of disease to have it for a moment a question whether medicines will always cure or no." But he feared that doubt and skepticism would "spread over the whole & fair domain" of the profession.[58] Channing was determined to have his students share his own pride in a profession that seemed to him to be unjustly maligned.

Embedded in his lectures were eloquent words about the physician's role in the promotion of individual happiness and "the general good." There was praise for the "observer of nature, trained and prepared to understand human activity . . . his researches after truth are . . . wider and deeper than those of other men."[59] And there were exhortations to pursue medical studies beyond graduation. "To secure to our profession a true place in our own respect & confidence . . . let us give to it our nights & our days. Be true to it & to those who place . . . their lives in our hands."[60]

Every five years or so, Channing had an opportunity to deliver the general introductory lecture that initiated the academic session. It was an honor that rotated among the medical faculty on a more or less regular basis. Practicing physicians and laymen were in the audience along with the students. The speaker was expected to fire the students with enthusiasm for the profession they were entering and to espouse the highest ideals of medicine for the general public. It was not easy to find new and different ways of saying the same thing. Channing relied on frequent allusion to past masters, Latin quotations, and lines from Shakespeare to inspire lofty purposes and convey his personal pleasure in the profession he had chosen.

His comments bore a strong autobiographical character. Medicine, he insisted, has been "the means of doing good, much good to others."[61] He emphasized professional duty. "The physician must be a self-denyer," cheerfully sacrificing his time and energy for his profession and its obligations. With great sincerity, he urged the neophytes to "carry sunshine to the dark chambers of sickness & if it beam not from our countenances, it must be in our hearts, and come out with our words."[62] Would that the medical profession might always exemplify similar values.

There was a spiritual quality and an idealism in some of these lectures not found in those of his colleagues. Thus, when speaking of Matthew Baillie (1761–1823), an eminent London physician, he referred to "exalted dignity . . . celestial brightness . . . the divine in him."[63] In urging students to "love thought" that they might do something "to remove the charge of a mechanical age, deprive the external of some of its power and minister widely to the upwakening and outward showing of the spiritual," he was revealing his own view of man as well as his distaste for mechanistic views.[64] "The physician studies Life—that mysterious essence or principle which in himself and in all other living beings constitutes and is the distinguishing circumstance between them and all other existences."[65] These words from lectures delivered in the later years of his teaching career hint at the influence of the Transcendentalists and coincide with his personal involvement in liberal religious groups.

CHANNING'S teaching commitments extended well beyond the academic term at the medical college. He had offered private instruction in midwifery during the few years between his return from England and his appointment at Harvard; in subsequent years, still recognizing the need and having space available at the medical college, he again gave a summer course for physicians' private pupils and others who might want to augment their knowledge of "the obstetric art." Sometimes his course included "diseases of children."[66]

He was also a preceptor, as was common with all the faculty. Acquisition of the medical degree still required, in addition to two years' attendance at lectures, three years of tutelage with a physician who provided exposure to daily practice, instruction in the preparation of drugs, and supervision for reading medical texts. This, of course, is the same scenario as Channing's pupilage with Jackson and Barton. During the 1820s and 1830s, however, medical education in urban centers like Boston became relatively more sophisticated. As some physicians acquired knowledge and experience in particular aspects of medicine and as the demand for clinical instruction became more acute, it was difficult for a single physician to provide all the training that an ambitious young man might desire. The preceptor system began to change.[67]

Channing and Jackson were quick to realize that their affiliation with the Massachusetts General Hospital gave them access to clinical facilities that most other preceptors lacked. In 1825 they began what Channing later described as "a private school for professional education . . . the first school at the time amongst us." The primary attractions were the opportunity to use Channing and Jackson's joint collection of medical books and plates, which were kept at Channing's house, supervision of students' reading by experienced teachers, and hospital visits during the eight or nine months when the medical school was not in session.[68] Over the first five years, fifty young men enrolled, and there was a steady stream of students thereafter. Many listed Jackson and Channing as joint preceptors when they matriculated at the medical college.[69] Some were not affiliated with the college, for it was still possible to spend three years with a preceptor and submit to examination by the Massachusetts Medical Society. A few young men who did not reside in Boston may well have spent only a few months with Channing and Jackson and had a local preceptor.

The success of Jackson and Channing's "private school" was not lost on other physicians with similar advantages to offer. By 1830, John Collins Warren, George Hayward, and Enoch Hale, Jr., were offering a medical course that emphasized anatomy and surgery, an area in which Jackson and Channing were deficient. Their students too had access to the hospital.[70] Not to be outdone, Channing and Jackson added three colleagues to their roster: John Ware, George W. Otis, Jr., and Winslow Lewis, Jr. Ware had recently been appointed an assistant physician at the hospital along with Channing. Otis, who had briefly served as an assistant surgeon at the hospital, taught surgery; Lewis, who had studied for several years in London and Paris, offered instruction in anatomy.[71] Channing added chemistry to midwifery and diseases of women and children. Thus, the private school mimicked the curriculum offered at the medical college.

Channing, Jackson, and their colleagues charged a hundred dollars for nine months of private instruction, more or less the same amount individual preceptors usually received. To avoid being undercut by the Warren group, who asked twenty-five dollars less, they persuaded their competitors to raise their fees to the same level.[72] Students without family in Boston or surrounding towns were at a disadvantage, because they had additional expenses for board. This helps explain why men such as William Workman and John G. Metcalf, who lived many miles from Boston, returned home to their local preceptors after the session ended in March.

Many of Jackson and Channing's students were destined to became well known in Boston's medical circles. Over the years, there were two representatives of Jackson's family (John B. S. Jackson and James Jackson, Jr.) and three of Channing's relations (Charles Stedman, Francis J. Higginson, and Francis Dana, Jr.). Oliver Wendell Holmes and Henry Ingersol Bowditch, each a prominent figure in the next generation of physicians, studied with them, as did Edward Hook during the months prior to his appointment as first resident physician at the Lying-in Hospital.[73]

In 1835 the editor of the *Boston Medical and Surgical Journal* paid tribute to "two of the best private schools for medical instruction . . . the one conducted by Dr. Channing and his talented associates and the other by Dr. Hale in conjunction with gentlemen of acknowledged acquirements."[74] Their success quickly bred imitation. More private schools sprang up, also offering a complete course of study and clinical instruction at a variety of venues—the Chelsea Marine Hospital, the Eye and Ear Infirmary, the Dispensary, and the House of Industry.[75] The last claimed to offer special instruction in diseases of the heart and lungs.

After passage of the Anatomy Act in 1831, Channing and his associates were able to give increased emphasis to instruction in anatomy. Until that time, only the bodies of executed murderers and men who had engaged in fatal duels could legally be procured for dissection.[76] The public considered "anatomizing" to be a sinful desecration of the body. Warren was often threatened with personal attack and sometimes feared that the medical college might be damaged by an irate mob bent on stopping the practice. The university disclaimed any association with the teaching of dissection, although the fact that it occurred was common knowledge.[77] It had taken years of public education and persistent lobbying by the Massachusetts Medical Society before the legislature was persuaded to enact the new law, the first anatomy act in the nation. It permitted the transfer of unclaimed bodies that would otherwise have to be buried at public expense to medical institutions for teaching purposes. Thereafter, cadavers were more readily available to medical students, and the private medical schools were better able to provide demonstrations and practical instruction in dissection.[78]

After 1834 Jackson was no longer associated with the school, which by then was quartered in Winslow Lewis's house.[79] George Cheyne Shattuck, Channing's longtime friend, a popular practitioner, and president of the Massachusetts Medical Society, joined the group in 1838.[80] By adding his name to the school, Channing and his associates may well have been trying to meet emerging competition. Channing continued the management functions, receiving inquiries and applications.

In September of that year, another private medical school appeared that was destined to outshine all that had come before. The Tremont Street School was founded by Jacob Bigelow, Edward Reynolds, David H. Storer, and Oliver Wendell Holmes. Already fifty years old, Bigelow was Channing's contemporary, but the other three represented the next generation, ready to take a more active role in Boston medical circles and impatient with a system that perpetuated the same leadership decade after decade. Instead of teaching at home, as Warren, Channing, and Lewis did, they rented rooms above an apothecary shop at 33 Tremont Row, available to the students from 6 A.M. to 10 P.M. for reading, recitation, and examination. They also had a private dissecting room in the rear of a nearby savings bank. Through Bigelow and Reynolds, the students had access to the hospital for clinical teaching.

The Tremont Street School flourished. Fifteen students enrolled the first year; by 1855 there were fifty-two, about one-third of the Harvard medical class. The faculty also expanded and the course offerings became more diverse, matching the new medical science being imported from Europe. Students had opportunities for instruction in comparative anatomy, diseases of the skin, pathological anatomy, surgical pathology, and diseases of the eye. Holmes gave lessons on auscultation and percussion (diagnosis by listening to sounds of internal organs), as well as microscopical anatomy. Storer provided lectures in midwifery and offered instruction in the application of obstetrical instruments, using a machine and models similar to Channing's.[81]

The Tremont Street School had a great appeal to the current crop of medical students and rapidly eclipsed the other private schools. Its faculty were energetic and ambitious, familiar with the medical theories and techniques that had made Paris the medical center of the Western world. By 1840 Ware and Shattuck had given up private instruction and Winslow Lewis was teaching anatomy by himself.[82] Channing and Otis continued their collaboration for a few more years but eventually they, too, abandoned private teaching.

The Tremont Street School soon became an adjunct to the Harvard Medical College. From the end of March to the beginning of November (the so-called summer term), the teachers reinforced and elaborated on the lectures regularly delivered at the medical school. When the medical school was in session, they offered intensive tutorials to supplement the lectures and quizzed the students regularly. Over time, several from the Tremont faculty, notably Holmes, J. B. S. Jackson, and Storer, received appointments at the Harvard Medical College.

The success of the Tremont Street School inspired still another group of young physicians. The Boylston Medical School, incorporated in 1847, offered a graded, three-year course of instruction patterned on the European model. This was a true innovation, as it eliminated the repetition of lectures and substituted a well-planned succession of courses that built one on the other. After seven years of successful operation, it applied to the legislature for degree-granting privileges. The Harvard faculty argued against their petition, but this time they did not prevail. However, the Boylston School never conferred a medical degree. Responding to the possibility of competition, Harvard made modest reforms by increasing the term and absorbing the most promising young teachers from the Boylston School into its own faculty. The Boylston Medical School also disappeared from the scene.[83]

WITH an expanded student body, faculty, and curriculum, it was obvious that more space was needed at the medical college. Equally apparent was the importance of clinical instruction and the advantage of proximity to the hospital. Therefore, rather than enlarge the building on Mason Street, the faculty accepted an offer from George Parkman, a graduate of Harvard College and of the medical school who had abandoned medicine for real estate, of land adjacent to the Massachusetts General Hospital.[84] The school moved into a new building on Grove Street in time for the 1846 academic session. It was rumored that the building on Mason Street was to be refitted as an infirmary for children and infants, but instead the Boston Society of Natural History acquired it to house its ever-growing collections.[85] It cannot have been a coincidence that John Collins Warren was a leader of the Society of Natural History.

Channing witnessed these changes philosophically. Within a year he resigned as dean, having served almost three decades as faculty scribe. Oliver Wendell Holmes, recently named Parkman Professor of Anatomy and Physiology, succeeded him. Thus Holmes, and not Channing, was on the spot for the extraordinary scandal that rocked the medical school and the city of Boston in 1849, when the same George Parkman was brutally murdered. Holmes also had to lead the faculty through two disturbing challenges from outsiders seeking admission to the school.[86] During Channing's deanship there had been no dramatic issues to be dealt with. Most serious often seemed to be the choice of color for the admission tickets sold each year to the students.

By 1854 Channing was ready to retire from the faculty as well.[87] Many years previously, when it was rumored that John Collins Warren might accept a professorship in New York, Channing had asked Warren to use his influence if "the chair I fill here" was also vacant in New York. If so, he went on, "I shall certainly ask to be appointed to it."[88] Warren did not accept the offer from New York and Channing's idea of moving became moot. He did not pursue it on his own. It is difficult to take his remark seriously, just as it is difficult to imagine that Warren would have considered the move. Both were deeply rooted in Boston society, attached by family, friends, and colleagues to teaching, medical practice, and good works in the comfortable environment they knew so very well.

When Channing submitted his resignation in September 1854, he and Bigelow were the only remaining members of the intimate group they had joined in 1815.[89] Though the school term had been lengthened to seventeen weeks, he was receiving the same fees as he had for thirteen weeks, thirty years before. His course was now called "Obstetrics and Medical Jurisprudence."[90] The lectures included reference to the use of ether in difficult labors and advocated greater caution against puerperal fever, but little else had changed.

The conclusion of Channing's teaching career brought praise from the *Boston Medical and Surgical Journal*, which remarked on his "fluent and pleasant teaching [that] will be long remembered by many who have received their medical education at this College."[91] The president and Fellows of the university expressed perfunctory appreciation for his "long and faithful services." He did not receive the usual accolades from his colleagues. There was no farewell dinner, no flattering speeches. When Jacob Bigelow resigned the following year, David Humphreys Storer, Channing's replacement, was effusive in his tribute to "the most distinguished member of this school—who possessed our undivided esteem, in whose judgment we all confided, of whose varied attainments we are all proud."[92]

Channing's almost forty years' dedication and loyalty to the medical college, his steadfast commitment to teaching, and his unfailing interest in his students remained unacknowledged. Not having written a textbook, his name would not be permanently affixed to midwifery instruction. Yet the generations of men who listened to his lectures and observed his demonstrations were as well prepared for practice as any in this country, and better than most. One can teach only what there is to learn; Channing did it well.

Chapter 7

The Middle Years, 1822–1840

You and I have been sojourning pilgrims here so long that we need not be too confident, and failure has crossed our path so often & in such form that hope comes if at all, with such wise misgiving that disappointment brings not all with it which it otherwise might.

—Walter Channing to Richard Henry Dana, December 19, 1839

THE year 1822 brought a distinct change to Boston. For almost two centuries the town meeting system of government had provided all male property holders the opportunity to vote on taxes and local ordinances.[1] This participatory process served a small and homogeneous populace well enough, but it was not adequate to meet the demands of nineteenth-century urban life. The population had swelled by nearly a third just in the decade since Channing's return from England. There had also been an expansion of living space, as the mudflats along the Charles River and Massachusetts Bay were reclaimed and developed for building lots. More people and increased acreage led to a demand for urban services such as efficient removal of garbage and filth from the streets, an improved water supply, and better police and fire protection. In 1822, by act of the legislature, Boston received a new charter as a city with an elected mayor, aldermen, and common council whose greater power and authority promised improvements and further growth.

The economy was also in transition. Shipping and trade, the two primary sources of wealth in the eighteenth and early years of the nineteenth centuries, were rapidly being displaced by manufacturing and the financial institutions that support industrial enterprise. Many new residents had come to Boston from the farms and small towns of New England seeking jobs and prosperity. With less pronounced reliance on the maritime activity of the harbor and dockside streets, and increased congestion in older parts of the city, affluent families began to move to cleaner, airier neighborhoods near the Common and in the West End.

An energetic and optimistic spirit pervaded society. Despite increased heterogeneity, the political scene was more harmonious than it had been in the previous decade, when the Federalists, threatened by those who advocated Jefferson's more democratic views, had struggled to maintain their control. The so-called "Era of Good Feelings," ushered onto the national stage by the election of President James Monroe in 1816, had its repercussions in Boston, where partisan animosity was tempered by common purpose. John Phillips and Josiah Quincy, the first and second mayors of Boston, quickly initiated programs that improved sanitation, safety, and public health and gained general approval from the citizenry.

The Congregationalists, descendants of the original Puritan stock who had dominated Boston's religious life until the turn of the century, were becoming more tolerant of the Unitarians. Indeed, many of the original Congregational churches now had Unitarian ministers. Moreover, the majority of the leaders in business, cultural activities, and philanthropy were Unitarians. Other religious groups, notably the Baptists, Episcopalians, and Roman Catholics, were gradually increasing their communicants. And, in this same period, the intellectual and literary elite were well on their way toward making Boston "the Athens of America."

For Walter Channing, 1822 was less promising. His personal happiness seemed irrevocably destroyed. Despondency permeated many of his thoughts. He was one of the few in Boston who did not celebrate the anniversary of the Battle of Bunker Hill. He was offended by the pageantry that disturbed the "sepulchre of those who sleep on that hill" and was displeased by the manner in which the few still-living veterans were brought out for public display. "They too," he told Lucy Russel, "belong to the dead" and like the dead should not be troubled.[2]

Confronted by his persistent sorrow and adamant refusal to speak about Barbara, the children were afraid to ask about their mother.[3] He remained incapable of resuming direct care of them. The girls continued to be shuffled among family in Boston, Brookline, Milton, and Nahant. When they were old enough, first Barbara and then Mary attended Sophia Dana's school in Cambridge, where they developed a close affection with their cousin and schoolmistress, who would later be one of the founders of Brook Farm. Susan Channing assumed the major responsibility for Lucy, who won her genuine affection and caused her persistent worries about the child's health. Walter's involvement was limited to brief visits and affectionate letters sprinkled with fatherly advice about drawing lessons and writing books.[4]

Ellery was sent off to Round Hill, a boarding school in western Massachusetts run by Joseph Green Cogswell and George Bancroft.[5] Grandmother Perkins was a friend of Bancroft, who greatly admired her beauty and charm; this may have been one reason the school was selected for Ellery. Additionally, the Forbes cousins had been scholars there and many other sons of good Boston families were among the pupils. Round Hill was designed to challenge traditional educational theories by abolishing punishments and emphasizing individual achievement, physical exercise, and outdoor activities. Ellery was not quite seven years old when he arrived there. He remained a lonely, solitary child, happy only during the hours spent wandering among the hills that surrounded the school or musing along the banks of the Connecticut River. There, a motherless boy far from home and family, he acquired a sympathy with nature that remained a powerful theme in his life. When it became clear that Round Hill was inappropriate, he was enrolled in a small private academy in Brookline close to the home of his maternal grandparents.[6] He was not much happier there and in time unexplained difficulties led to his departure from that school.[7]

Already young Ellery was demonstrating peculiarities that puzzled his father and alarmed other members of the family. William counseled patience, "a feature of the parental character of God," and warned Walter that "we can not advance ourselves more than in subjecting ourselves to the discipline which a right discharge of parental duty requires."[8] Walter was willing to be patient but he was at a loss when it came to recognizing what his parental duty required.

Lucy Channing's decision to give up housekeeping and live with her daughter Mary (now Mrs. Robert Rogers) in one of the newer houses on Beacon Hill forced Walter to seek independent lodgings. In 1825 he rented a fine brick house at the corner of Common and School Streets. It placed him in an up-and-coming, stylish area; within a few years, Common Street was renamed Tremont Street and the city's best hotel, the Tremont House, and its most popular theater, the Tremont Theater, were built across the street from his house. The new arrangement gave him a consulting room in a fashionable part of the city and space for the private medical teaching he was about to share with James Jackson. He was close to Beacon Hill, where his mother, his sister, and William were living. He was also near the Granary Burial Ground, where Barbara lay.[9]

He was often morose and depressed and spent many long nights talking to himself "in grand monologues." The romantic poets assuaged some of his misery, especially Coleridge, whose works he read aloud in the company of his nephew William Henry Channing. To William Henry, an impressionable divinity student, their hours of intimate conversation revealed a man who was a "latent Poet, mystic philosopher and aspiring Saint."[10] A long letter from Walter to Lucy Russel, replete with self-pity and despair, ended with the hope that life after death would bring peace. "How glorious is that state of living in which this divine principle shall know no interruption in its progress, in the society of angels, in the worship of a *visible* God."[11]

Richard Henry Dana, Channing's cousin, boyhood friend, and companion in the "Rotten Cabbage" episode, may have understood him better than anyone. Their lives had sad congruities. Dana's wife died from consumption about six months before Barbara, leaving four motherless children just as there were four motherless Channings.[12] Unlike Walter's situation, however, Dana's unmarried sisters moved in and assumed responsibility for raising the children. Dana, too, was pampered and cared for by the women. Channing, on the other hand, felt bereft and solitary. With his cousin he shared his "blue moods," as well as a mutual passion for literature.[13]

At Dana's suggestion, Channing wrote an essay reviewing a series of lectures given by an English literary and scientific scholar for publication in a new journal, *United States Review and Literary Gazette*.[14] The Boston editor, Charles Folsom, found it too "Wordsworthian." Only Dana's revision and approval from the co-editor, William Cullen Bryant, prevented rejection of Channing's essay.[15]

To Dana he could also reveal his growing belief in, and dependence on, the beneficence of God. "I must be in the midst of God's universe . . . filled with its immensity, its beauty, and its glory, a partaker in my capacity of an infinite and endless good. . . . Is it not cause of true gratitude that we can find, or believe there exists here, enough of good, of a spiritual influence, to make life desirable and happy."[16] Walter was clearly reflecting the influence of William's creed, which provided the relief he so desperately needed to get on with his life and the consolation he would need even more when future losses and trials nearly overwhelmed him.

AND, of course, life went on. There was plenty of extra space in his house, so he rented rooms to some of his bachelor friends. With them he was more convivial and outgoing. Jared Sparks, who had abandoned his Baltimore pulpit and returned to Boston to edit the *North American Review* and begin a career as a historian, moved in toward the end of 1826. Eventually James Perkins, Channing's young brother-in-law, and Edward Lowell, a son of Francis Cabot Lowell, who had befriended Channing in Edinburgh, also lodged with him.

Channing formed a particularly close friendship with Sparks and the two men spent many quiet evenings together discussing literature, religion, and politics.[17] They were deeply stirred by the Greek struggle for national independence and the glorious tales of Samuel Gridley Howe, who had fought with the Greek army. Channing was part of a local committee raising money for food and other supplies for the relief of beleaguered Greeks. He also wrote two book reviews that Sparks published in the *North American Review.*[18] Their late-night colloquies, abetted by tobacco and whiskey, often ended with a toast to "the health of the morning star."[19]

With his patients he was as kind and considerate as ever.[20] He continued to diagnose and prescribe for relatives, by mail if they were away from Boston. William, always fearful for his own health and that of his wife and children, was especially dependent for advice and comfort. The mere fact that Walter was aware of his ailments reassured other members of the family, who never ceased to worry about the health of their frail brother.[21] Hospital duties, medical lectures, private teaching, and an ever-growing practice kept him so busy that he saw his children even less often. Susan was frequently miffed by his seeming inattention, especially to little Lucy.[22]

One of his most interesting patients was Sophia Peabody, who would later marry Nathaniel Hawthorne. Sophia was nineteen years old when Channing became her "dear Doctor." She had suffered migraine headaches and other assorted ailments for several years and spent most of her time confined to her bedchamber.[23] Channing offered her sympathy and understanding, in addition to recommendations about diet, exercise, and intellectual activity. By urging Sophia to enjoy the seaside and to study Italian, he gently coaxed her out of the lethargy that had become a part of her existence. As she recovered her health and spirits, he encouraged her artistic endeavors and eventually persuaded her to attempt a recuperative journey to Cuba.[24] They became good friends. Boston society was not large and their social worlds intersected through mutual acquaintances.[25]

Channing was also physician to many children, among whom one so greatly engaged his attention and his compassion that he published details of the case and continued to ruminate over it many times thereafter.[26] Despite a sorry outcome, he was gratified by his ability to diagnose an unsuspected disease using careful observation and the stethoscope, still a relatively new clinical tool. The patient was a five-year-old boy who complained of a painful knee in the spring of 1834. Initially, Channing found nothing remarkable in his condition, which the parents attributed to a fall. He was summoned again on the Fourth of July when the child seemed less well, but saw no reason why the family should not depart as planned for their summer home, not far from

Boston. Two days later he hurried there himself. The child was now more severely ill, with cough, fever, and pain in the abdomen. He recommended that the family return to Boston so that he might continue to supervise the case.

Channing paid particular attention to the child's chest. Relying on auscultation and percussion for clues about the state of his heart and lungs, Channing determined that the child had pericarditis. His sore knee, along with the abdominal pain, cough, and the respiratory sounds, indicated that rheumatic fever was the underlying disease causing the coronary inflammation. Channing visited frequently, often playing with the child while observing his ups and downs.

Despite every effort, which included administration of cathartics, enemas, leeches, and camphor liniments, and consultations with Jacob Bigelow, the child died within the month. Autopsy revealed that Channing's diagnosis was correct. Rheumatism or rheumatic fever was a prevalent nineteenth-century disease that caused chronic arthritis as well as damage to the heart, and eventually death. Channing was not unfamiliar with its manifestations, but he was surprised and saddened by the fatal outcome in such a young child. Medical research since Channing's time has identified streptococcal infection as the cause of rheumatic fever.[27]

Other obligations began to intrude, obligations that brought him back into the intellectual life of the community. He joined his brothers William and Edward, along with George Ticknor, William Russell, Elizabeth Peabody, and others in a Society of Education that discussed the educational ideas Ticknor had brought back from Europe.[28] With friends who had once been members of the Linnaean Society, he helped create the Boston Society of Natural History. The first meeting was held at his house and he served as chairman until permanent officers were selected.[29] The society inherited a portion of the collections of the defunct Linnaean Society and proceeded to add further specimens and books. In addition to semimonthly meetings, frequent lectures were scheduled to encourage popular enthusiasm for natural science.[30] This society prospered, an indication of greater scientific sophistication and interest among Boston's intellectuals.

Channing was asked to deliver a series of lectures on public health for the Society for the Diffusion of Useful Knowledge, which had recently formed under the leadership of Daniel Webster and Edward Everett. This august group of Boston highbrows met at the Boston Athenæum, a splendid building on Pearl Street, once the home of Barbara Channing's uncle James Perkins. In his opening lecture, Channing used the relationship of physical health and mental activity to elaborate on some of the educational theories being discussed by the Society of Education. He criticized the existing educational system for

overemphasizing intellectual development at the expense of physical development, using the ancient Greeks as an example of a society that recognized the
importance of both kinds of training. In a subsequent lecture he talked about
the need for a municipal supply of pure water. This time the Romans were
extolled for their system of aqueducts. Both were topics to which he would
return in subsequent years. The lectures were meant for an audience seeking
instruction on topics of general interest. Channing's references to ancient history and cultures attested to his familiarity with the classics, but some in the
audience thought his comments were neither "well adapted" nor particularly
instructive. Fortunately, they found that his discourses were not too long.[31]

MORE direct professional activities also recaptured his interests. Foremost
was the *New England Journal of Medicine and Surgery*, launched at the beginning of Channing's professional career. By the mid-1820s it was floundering.
Warren and Jackson had ceased to contribute, leaving John Ware and Channing as the editors.[32] Channing continued to write articles based on his general
and obstetrical practice, as well as lengthy reviews of obstetrical texts.[33] Ware,
too, was working overtime but subscriptions fell off, especially when competition emerged from a new journal, the *Boston Medical Intelligencer*, which appeared in 1823. The *Intelligencer* was the first weekly medical journal in the
United States, suggesting more medical news than there was. It mimicked the
format of the senior journal, publishing extracts from foreign and national
medical journals, local medical cases and information, and original articles on
various diseases and therapies. For a brief time the editor tried to broaden its
appeal with papers on physical education and the preservation of health.

Essentially, though, the two journals were destroying each other.[34] The
potential market was hardly large enough for one medical journal, much less
two that were so similar. In 1828 Channing, Ware, and John Collins Warren
purchased the *Medical Intelligencer* for six hundred dollars. Warren contributed two-thirds of the purchase price. They then merged the two publications
under a new title, the *Boston Medical and Surgical Journal*.[35] In the first issue,
the editors promised that "the list of subscribers being now large, it will go
forward in some shape or other; and efforts will not be wanting to make it
useful."

Channing did not have a large investment in the new journal but, confronted by the responsibility for a weekly publication, he had to work harder
than before. Volume 1 showed the close relationship between the editors and
the Massachusetts General Hospital. At the top of the first page of each issue
was a sketch of the hospital building, and there were numerous case reports,

Channing preparing those from the medical department. He also contributed articles based on his private practice, as did Warren and Jackson.[36]

It was an arrangement that did not last long. Ware was especially unhappy. He had taken responsibility for the day-to-day management and found he had to devote more time to the enterprise than he had anticipated. He had expected to use his share of the earnings to acquire greater equity. But there were no profits, only unmet expenses, unpaid subscriptions, and a publisher, John Cotton, who was unwilling to collect them. After a year, the three editors began negotiations with Cotton, who eventually bought them out at a loss.[37] With more consistent leadership and, in time, with more physicians practicing in the region, the *Boston Medical and Surgical Journal* survived well into the twentieth century, when it was purchased by the Massachusetts Medical Society and became its official publication. In 1924 the name changed to the *New England Journal of Medicine.*[38]

The Massachusetts Medical Society also captured Channing's renewed energy. He became secretary of the Board of Censors as well as treasurer. In the first capacity he was required to judge the qualifications of applicants to the society. In the second, a more onerous position, he was responsible for receipts, expenditures, and investment of funds. He kept meticulous records and was especially assiduous collecting dues from forgetful members.[39] He proved to be as watchful of the society's funds and as frugal in spending them as he was with his own. It was a sign of his competence, as well as his willingness to serve, that he was reelected treasurer annually from 1828 to 1840.[40]

I T was just as well that Channing was released from his editorial duties. He had resumed an active social life, despite the disclaimers he insisted on making. One of the oddities of Channing's personality is the contradiction between his self-image as lonely and solitary and his friends' descriptions of him as gregarious and convivial. He complained about his "small breakfast and the even smaller dinner," eaten alone while the servant puttered nearby. Yet, according to observers, "Dr. Walter Channing *never* provided a dinner for himself for *nine years* until he married Eliza Wainwright—*he knew* he was always welcome and he dined at one place every Friday, and at another every other Wednesday, etc., for he could not go round his circle of friends in a week." He moaned about life in "lonely halls and parlours," yet he admitted suffering "headache from oysters & porter at a small supper party." He claimed to "pant & long for quiet," but he was a regular at George Ticknor's lively Sunday night gatherings, where he was welcomed as a "kind and genial family physician."[41]

Was he feeling sorry for himself when he complained? Did the company

of good friends relieve his loneliness? Undoubtedly both sentiments were operating, as they had since Channing's boyhood. There can be little doubt that
he became dissatisfied with bachelorhood. "This state of single blessedness is
a dull affair," he confessed to Jared Sparks. He felt unequal to the "petty troubles" associated with housekeeping and made the mistake of encouraging his
daughter Barbara to assume those duties, although at the age of fourteen she
was too young for the task.[42] He needed a wife, as he had needed a wife when
he married Barbara Perkins, but now he was fifteen years older and had four
children who should be living at home with him.

In the spring of 1831 Walter informed the family that he was engaged to
Miss Eliza Wainwright, a woman admired by many Bostonians for her family
connections and her virtuous character. The news was happily received by his
relations, with the possible exception of Barbara, who had been led to expect
to be mistress of her father's house. Mary was quickly won over by visits with
Eliza to the confectioner's shop, and Lucy was "mightily tickled" by the idea
of a new mama. No one could be certain how Ellery would respond to the new
situation. Eliza faced real challenges as wife to a longstanding "bachelor" with
many professional obligations, stepmother to four hitherto wandering children, and new member of a discriminating family of Channings, Ellerys, and
Perkinses. Fortunately, she was a woman with uncommonly good judgment.[43]

Eliza was born in 1794 in Liverpool, England, where her English father,
Peter Wainwright, was an agent for Samuel Cabot, one of Boston's merchant
princes. The family, which included two brothers, returned to Boston when
Eliza was about ten years old. Her mother was the daughter of the Reverend
Jonathan Mayhew, an early critic of Calvinism and precursor of the liberal
Christianity that William Ellery Channing represented. Mayhew also preached
resistance to authority and enunciated the principles of free civil government
that helped inspire Bostonians to consider independence.[44] Elizabeth Mayhew,
his wife and the maternal grandmother of Eliza Wainwright, was born into the
Clarke family that practiced medicine in Massachusetts for many generations
from the earliest days of the colony.[45] Eliza's mother was reputed to have inherited the argumentative talents of her clergyman father and to be too democratic
in her opinions for some of the Federalists who ruled Boston society. Nonetheless, she had many friends in Boston, as did her daughter, and they visited
back and forth with the best families.

Walter probably met Eliza shortly after his marriage to Barbara. Both
young women were special friends of Eliza Quincy, who thought them "among
the very few people you would like to have for constant companions." They
seem to have been unassuming and pleasant young women, in contrast with
their more assertive mothers. Like Barbara, Eliza Wainwright played the piano

well and happily entertained her friends with the music of Haydn and other popular composers.[46] Another of her intimate friends was Eliza Cabot, a daughter of Samuel Cabot, who appreciated her devotion to duty and her self-sacrificing nature.[47]

Despite the Congregational heritage derived from the Reverend Mayhew, his namesake, Eliza's brother Jonathan Mayhew Wainwright, took orders in the Episcopal Church and for a few years was rector of Trinity Church in Boston.[48] Eliza was greatly attached to the family of her second brother, Peter Wainwright, with whom she lived in Roxbury. It was there that she and Walter Channing were married on September 6, 1831.[49]

Eliza assumed her new duties with some diffidence, uncertain as to her ultimate success. Yet she quickly became "mother" to the children, who were reassembled to live at their father's house. She provided the stability that Barbara craved, smoothed Mary's rough edges, and managed to disarm Ellery of some of his eccentricities. Ellery, in turn, responded to her with unexpected affection.[50] She watched over William with the same concern shown him by the rest of the family, endeared herself to her new mother-in-law, and became a good friend to Susan Channing and her daughters.[51]

Walter was reinvigorated by his expanded household, which could now welcome his friends and extensive family for dinners and holiday festivities. Professionally he had never been busier. He lectured three mornings a week at the medical school and was spending more time than before in preparation. "If I do not teach my class something," he wrote to James Jackson, Jr., "I shall not think that it was all my own fault."[52] The private medical school was flourishing with Ware, Otis, and Lewis now supplementing the instruction he and James Jackson, Sr., offered. The pupils continued to study at his house. Jackson was spending more time away from Boston, which put additional responsibilities on Channing at the Massachusetts General Hospital. Negotiations for the Lying-in Hospital were reaching their culmination, which meant meetings with the Board of Directors over organizational matters and patient care, as well as medical obligations once the facility opened on Washington Street.

In May 1833 Channing delivered the address at the annual meeting of the Massachusetts Medical Society. It was an ambiguous honor since Jacob Bigelow had already been invited; he accepted, then changed his mind when he decided to go to Europe.[53] Channing agreed to fill in. The medical society had not featured a general lecture at its two most recent annual meetings and attendance had dropped off. Now, the prospect of a keynote talk brought out a respectable audience, including physicians from the western part of the state. At the conclusion of Channing's address, the society moved on to the Exchange for an elegant dinner, followed by a reception at the home of the current president, John Collins Warren.

Channing titled his talk "On Irritable Uterus."[54] It was the first time an annual discourse had been directed to a gynecological topic, signifying greater interest in the physiology of the female reproductive system and a willingness to discuss in public subjects often considered taboo in American medical circles.[55] He acknowledged several British authors whose work on female disorders had informed his own ideas, as well as his obligation to William P. Dewees, Professor of Obstetrics at the University of Pennsylvania. Channing described the irritable uterus as a diseased organ indicating "an excited sensibility." The pressure it produced could lead to pain or distress and might indicate fatigue, overexertion, or misuse of a pessary. An irritable uterus could cause "certain functional derangements," especially problems related to the menstrual cycle. An interesting aspect of the talk was the relationship of the reproductive system to problems of female physiology, including headache, rapid pulse, chest pain, paleness, and "flabby flesh." Contemporary medical theory taught that health depended on the proper relationship of all the bodily organs, so his association of the uterus with general health was perfectly acceptable. It also made his topic pertinent to the general practice of the physicians in the audience. Later in the nineteenth century, when there was more medical specialization, gynecologists and neurologists would continue to associate the uterus with emotional disorders and physiological distress of women, and some would advocate extraordinary surgical treatments as therapy.[56]

The outbreak of cholera in 1832 added to Channing's responsibilities. Though Boston was spared the worst of the epidemic, there were some serious local cases. Channing had been attending a meeting of the Wednesday Night Club, another of Boston's many short-lived social groups, when his good friend and neighbor, J. Greely Stevenson, was called away to see a cholera patient.[57] Channing decided to go along for his first encounter with the disease that such fear and damage worldwide. There was little that could be done to control the extreme diarrhea, intense vomiting, thirst, cramps, and violent muscular spasms that characterized cholera, but successful venous injections of warm saltwater had been reported in some of the British medical journals. With little to lose, and with approval from Channing, as well as Jackson, Bigelow, and Ware, who were asked to consult, Stevenson decided to use this procedure with his patient.[58] Three pints were injected into a vein of the left arm. Encouraged by the effect, the physicians decided a second injection was in order. Channing and Ware opened a vein in the left ankle and administered more of the solution. Channing remained two nights by the bedside to observe the result of this radical treatment, which provided temporary improvement but did not prevent death.[59]

For the next several months, Channing saw more cholera cases, usually in the poorest parts of the city. In one cellar room, he found a man prostrated on his miserable bed, wet and cold on the outside, burning up within, speaking with difficulty. His only complaint was thirst. Channing instructed his wife to fill a large bucket with ice from a shop nearby, add water, provide the sick man with a dipper, and let him drink as much water as he wished. The woman did as directed. When Channing returned the following morning the patient was convalescent. "How much did you drink? Two bucket-fulls, yer honor—and God bless you." Channing had read about this remedy in a report of cholera in India. Evidently it worked, and though he did not know why, he considered the cure a triumph and repeated the story in several publications.[60]

CHANNING frequently appeared in court as an expert witness, but in no trial more sensational than *Rhode Island v. Ephraim K. Avery*, described by the press as having "excited the public mind to a degree hitherto unexampled in the judicial annals of our country."[61] The case was heard during a special term of the state Supreme Court held in Newport during May and June 1833. Avery, a thirty-seven-year-old Methodist minister, stood accused of the murder of Sarah Maria Cornell, a young factory worker whose bruised and battered body, suspended from a rope affixed to a haystack pole, had been found on a farm in Tiverton, Rhode Island, just south of Fall River, Massachusetts, on December 21, 1832.[62]

Suicide was the original explanation, but when an autopsy revealed that Sarah Cornell was pregnant and when incriminating letters and notes were found hidden among her few possessions, the Reverend Avery became the prime suspect, as father of the unborn child and as murderer of its mother. Some years previously, Sarah had attended Avery's church in Lowell, Massachusetts, where she was working in the Appleton textile mills. By the time she moved to Fall River and found a mill job there, Avery had been reassigned to a church in nearby Bristol, Rhode Island. They had been seen together several times in suspicious circumstances, most notably at a revival meeting at the end of August.

Everything about the case gave it national celebrity—a small, defenseless girl mercilessly strangled to prevent revelation of her pregnancy, and a tall, dark-haired minister with an invalid wife and two small children, accused of sexual transgression and murder. The melodrama was further embellished by an irate mob that threatened to lynch Avery before he had been formally charged with the crime and by his subsequent flight to New Hampshire, where he was discovered and apprehended by a freewheeling deputy sheriff.[63]

An undercurrent of Puritan repugnance toward the excesses of evangelical enthusiasm helped convince a large segment of the public that Avery was a lascivious hypocrite. He often preached at campground revival meetings, where repentant men and women seeking redemption and rebirth in Jesus gathered in the summer months, often in the company of the less virtuous seeking excitement and entertainment or opportunities for petty crime. Traditional churchgoers found these religious meetings offensive and suspected the worst of the participants. But another part of the public was convinced that Sarah was a "bad girl," guilty of a long list of sins and misdemeanors, including lewd conduct, fornication, stealing, lying, and destruction of mill property.

Avery was defended by Jeremiah Mason, reputed to be the most clever and expensive lawyer in New England, with the possible exception of Daniel Webster.[64] Mason and his team of attorneys had been hired by the New England Conference of the Methodist Episcopal Church, which was nearly bankrupted by the expenses it incurred on behalf of Brother Avery. The prosecution was aided by the leading citizens of Fall River, who feared that Sarah's death might raise questions about the "mill girls" for whose virtue the factory owners were supposed to be responsible. Both sides sent agents throughout Massachusetts and Rhode Island seeking witnesses who could destroy the character of the victim or the accused.

The trial, characterized by Channing as "the longest trial on record except that of Warren Hastings," lasted twenty-eight days.[65] A crowd of five hundred spectators and reporters from as far as Philadelphia filled the lower hall of the State House on Newport Parade, where the trial was held. More than a hundred men were called before an impartial jury could be empaneled. There were 111 witnesses testifying for the prosecution and 128 for the defense. Channing described "all sorts of swearing . . . confusion was on all sides and it became impossible with such an unmanageable mass to make such a presentation of it to court or jury, as could subserve the purposes of justice."[66] Chief Justice Samuel Eddy forbade the press from publishing any details until a verdict was reached.

The State presented evidence to show that Avery and Sarah were intimately acquainted and to connect his movements on the day of the murder from his home in Bristol to the farm in Tiverton. Several physicians testified that Sarah had been violated and beaten prior to death. Rope marks on her neck and the clove knot with which the noose was attached clearly pointed to foul play.

The defense revealed that Sarah was neither virtuous nor naive. She had long been infected with gonorrhea. She had spoken of revenge for her dismissal from Avery's church in Lowell. She was reported to have mentioned suicide as a way out of her shame. Several physicians whom she had consulted about her disease and later about her pregnancy thought her deranged. They also raised doubts about the age of the fetus, which they estimated to be more than five months. The implication was that Avery could not have been the father if, as alleged, he had seduced her at a camp meeting four months prior to her death.

Channing was one of the final witnesses for the defense. Despite some initial misgivings, he had been persuaded by Mason that his testimony could help acquit an innocent man. He was not eager to be away from home, even in a place as congenial to him as Newport, but after consulting one of his medical colleagues on some of the points in the case, he was convinced of Avery's innocence and the usefulness of his appearance. Ellery went with him. He later commented on the "villainous aspect of the culprit" whom his father was there to defend.[67]

Channing took the witness stand on Saturday morning, May 25. His professorial title and his expertise in medical jurisprudence and in midwifery were expected to impress judge and jury. The previous medical witnesses were local practitioners who did not have the reputation his education and experience implied. None had the same familiarity with postmortem examinations.[68]

Sarah's body had been exhumed and examined three days after death and again thirty-six days after death. Channing testified that examination of a body so long interred would not yield reliable evidence. He rejected the idea of a failed forced abortion, rape, or strangulation prior to hanging, insisting that unusual spots observed in the pelvic area were marks of postmortem blood normally seen in a cadaver. He also testified that the rope marks on Sarah's neck, the knot by which the rope had been fastened, and the position in which her body was found were not uncommon to suicides.

The remainder of his testimony focused on the length of Sarah's pregnancy. He cited the opinions of many medical writers to support the argument that the size of the fetus indicated it had been conceived several months before she and Avery met at the camp meeting. Channing even brought a few fetal specimens with him should the court ask for further proof. It did not. Final questions from the defense attorneys addressed the possibility that "females of bad character were more irregular in the recurrence of the natural indisposition than those who are virtuous." Channing replied that he believed that hypothesis to be true, and that "a woman of ill fame" whose menses were irregular would have difficulty judging herself pregnant or not. Asked if children of parents who have been affected by venereal disease are "as large or as healthy as those of virtuous parents," Channing responded that they are not, implying that Sarah's fetus might have been even older than suggested by its weight and length.[69]

When cross-examined Channing did not do well. A young physician, "a vehement witness for the government," had been passing notes to the attorney general throughout Channing's testimony.[70] These scribbles were quickly transformed into questions that confused and embarrassed him. The attorney general peppered him with conflicting statements about fetal size drawn from the same authorities Channing had cited in his original testimony and pushed him to admit that evidence provided by the postmortem examination was inconclusive. The chief justice reprimanded him for trying to avoid answering some of the trickier questions. By the time the grueling interrogation was over, Channing had been forced to qualify or amend some of his previous statements. Though the Boston Medical and Surgical Journal complimented him for "one of the best sustained expositions of medical opinion to a jury we have ever seen," a modern commentator describes it as "the kind of medical testimony that the court had come to expect: long, detailed, and inconclusive."[71]

Though he regularly lectured to his students about the difficulties of courtroom appearances, warning them against trick questions and aggressive lawyers, in this situation Channing seemed as inexperienced as a novice physician. He left the witness stand completely exhausted, his voice husky, his appetite gone. He was uncertain how much time had elapsed since he had been sworn in, but the courthouse clock indicated more than three hours. He left Newport with Ellery as quickly as possible.

Walking down State Street several days later, he encountered an acquaintance who announced, "Well, you have saved his life."[72] Whether an accusation or praise, it was the first Channing knew that Avery had been acquitted. Though his testimony may have helped, it was Mason and his team of lawyers who had saved Avery by utterly destroying Sarah's reputation and by placing enough doubt in the minds of the jury to prevent a guilty verdict. If Avery did not commit the murder, no other suspect was suggested at the time. And though the defense wanted the jury to believe that Sarah had spoken of revenge and suicide, it is unlikely that she could have accomplished suicide in the manner by which she died, Channing's testimony notwithstanding. Years after the trial Mason was asked whether he thought Avery was innocent. It was an unexpected interrogatory, to which Mason was reported to have replied, "Upon my word, I never thought of it in that light before."[73]

Channing soon learned that others held him responsible for an unjust acquittal. He woke on Sunday morning to find, swinging from a rope outside his house, an effigy dressed in full black with a paper sticking out of the coat pocket inscribed, "Confession of the Murder." A crowd gathered to gaze at the dummy but after a while it was lowered by a group of boys, who kicked it around the neighborhood until church bells announced that it was time to go to meeting.[74]

The effigy on Tremont Street was not unique. Mobs of young men often roamed Boston's streets on the slightest pretext of injury or injustice, and effigies were a common indicator of their anger. About the same time, a hostile crowd threatened a Methodist worship meeting on the assumption that Avery was present. A justice of the peace had to be called to disperse them.[75] A week later, when Avery did appear on the streets of Boston, he was accosted by another angry mob. Only the assistance of a shopkeeper who dragged him inside his store saved him from harm.[76]

Gradually, however, Boston lost interest in the scandal. The anniversary of the Battle of Bunker Hill was approaching and there was another celebration to anticipate.[77] President Andrew Jackson was expected to visit the city shortly afterward, and though his Democratic Party was not generally favored in Boston, he had been General Jackson, hero of the Battle of New Orleans, and had recently been reelected to a second term as the nation's chief executive. The threat of cholera had not entirely disappeared. The Avery case and Channing's role in it soon passed into oblivion.

CHANNING was in high spirits. Marriage agreed with him and he delighted in the ease with which his four children had reentered his life. Eliza reported that he was "bright, cheerful and making all happy around him."[78] His happiness was augmented when Eliza let it be known that she was expecting a child. She looked toward motherhood, "full of hope and joy," with no visible anxiety though she was nearly forty years old and it was her first pregnancy.[79] It was assumed that Walter would deliver the baby. Eliza had "perfect confidence" in her husband's skill.

Labor began later than anticipated.[80] The pains were moderate but continued for several days and nights without progress. Although Eliza became increasingly fatigued, Walter did not seem to be alarmed. Several women in the family kept her company. Kind words were uttered by everyone, most especially by Eliza herself, who conversed affectionately with the children. Barbara brought fresh flowers, which Eliza gratefully held as long as she could. Her suffering intensified. After three days, Walter decided that the baby could not be born by natural means and that instruments must be used.[81] He expected the child might be dead but did not foresee danger for his wife. Eliza may have had more ominous premonitions, for she spoke with those around her about her confidence in Christianity, assuring them that she had complete faith in

Tremont Street looking south; Channing's house was on the left corner, facing Tremont Street (courtesy of the Bostonian Society/Old State House)

the truth of life after death. She also spoke with justifiable pride of her accomplishments as wife and mother over the past three years.

Channing insisted on performing the operation himself though wiser heads should have counseled against it. Nor did he request assistance from another physician, as was customary. As he feared, the child, a boy, was dead. But his confidence for Eliza's safety was not shaken and it seemed as if the dead child would be the only loss. Within a short while, however, there were signs of grave problems. Eliza was hemorrhaging. Now greatly alarmed, Channing summoned James Jackson. Eliza was very weak, but, still mindful of her husband and the children, she indicated that there was a letter for him in her desk, and that her cousin Elizabeth Howard should be sent for to help with the children. Again, she reassured the mournful family clustered around her that she was prepared to die. Within another half hour, she expired.

Walter fell apart. He had not slept during the days and nights while Eliza was enduring a difficult labor. He had exerted all his strength to extract a dead child, his own. He had watched his wife bleed uncontrollably and die in the throes of convulsive spasms. Unable to face what had happened, he became completely irrational. He began to lament his terrible fate—both his youngest son and his oldest son were dead! Ellery tried to assure him that he was alive, but his father continued to reproach him for dying. The boy was shattered. The dreadful scene went on and on until William intervened. He alone was able to soothe his brother, reminding him that Eliza's steadfast faith showed them all how to bear her loss.[82] Eventually, William persuaded him to rest.

Next morning, Walter had regained some composure. His confidence in a wise Creator remained unshaken. At breakfast he read from the prayer book, as was his daily custom, and Elizabeth Howard read from Scripture. But the burden was almost unbearable. He had not been able to save the lives of his wife and unborn child despite his knowledge of obstetrics and his years of practice. All his expertise was of no avail. That eventually he did resume work and continued to care for women threatened by the unpredictability of life and death is testimony to his extraordinary resilience and a remarkable devotion to his calling.

The tragedy was compounded by the effect on the children. They had lost their second mother, to whom they had become as devoted as if she had been their natural mother. Ellery was profoundly troubled. After a boyhood bereft of emotional attachment, in his early teens he had found genuine affection in his relationship with Eliza. The new loss reinforced his previous penchant for solitude. He drew back from common social intercourse, refusing to express his feelings or to engage in ordinary forms of conduct. He was especially wary of his father, whose outbreak had deeply wounded him.[83]

Eliza had prepared Barbara to assume her place, should ever anything happen to her. The young woman, just eighteen years old, was ready to take on her duties toward her father and the rest of the family. It became the defining feature of her life. Though Barbara's possibilities for marriage and children equaled those of any other woman, she devoted herself instead to the wishes of her father and the well-being of her sisters and brother. She made sure her father's household ran smoothly and catered to his whims for another forty years. When he was unable or unwilling to give affection and time to Lucy, Barbara filled in. Eventually, she would become a surrogate mother to Ellery's children. Eliza's example remained a powerful influence on Barbara's life, a gift "which time will not deprive us of if we keep the chain of memory bright."[84]

There was general concern that Mrs. Lucy Channing would be unable to bear Eliza's death. She had recently suffered a slight stroke, brought on by news that her son George had experienced another business failure. William offered to inform his mother about Eliza, confident that a lifetime of calamities would enable her to bear one more. But Lucy knew before he uttered a word.

"Eliza is dead!" she cried. "Oh my God! Is that valuable life taken—and mine spared!" Her emotional outburst was almost too much for the normally reserved William.[85]

If Boston was distressed by Eliza's death, it was overwhelmed five days later by the equally untimely and unexpected death of James Jackson, Jr. The young man had returned the previous summer from two years of medical study in Europe and received his M.D. degree in February 1834. Everyone predicted a brilliant career for him, especially his father, who was inordinately but justifiably proud of his only son. James had been a great favorite of Pierre Louis at the Ecole de Médecine and was expected to promote French medical theories in Boston. He had already conducted important medical research, including observations on the cholera epidemic in Paris. But on the very day he planned to begin practice, the talented young doctor became ill with typhoid fever and though there was a temporary recuperation, he developed dysentery and died March 27, age twenty-four.[86]

Channing had known James as the son of his most cherished colleague, as a student, and as a friend. He had sent Channing several interesting papers on puerperal fever while he was abroad.[87] Channing was looking forward to welcoming him to the profession. This loss following so closely the death of Eliza added to his affliction.

When William Ellery Channing ascended the pulpit on Easter Sunday, shortly after the dual tragedies, the coincidence with celebration of the Resurrection led him to pose the question many were asking. What happens to "the good, the strong, the useful, the youthful full of hope & promise" when they are taken by death? One of Eliza's closest friends described, in her own words, William's discourse on the ultimate fate of the human soul.[88] The dead would first see Jesus and be welcomed by him to his father's house. "And what must be the infinite love & joy with which he must welcome those who had been saved from the perils & trials of this life through his means, who have been purified & elevated to everlasting felicity by himself." Channing assured his congregants that "heaven must also be a state of intellectual exertion & progress & of endless activity & benevolence. The lovers of their race might be sent on errands of mercy to other spheres." Most heartening, however, was William's assurance that "they should see God."

William's seraphic expression, his unearthly tone, and the intensity of his faith strengthened the meaning of his words and gave comfort to the Channings, the Jacksons, and their friends. He was convinced that the "pure and elevated" souls of the departed retained memories of their earthly home and an interest in those left behind. Channing's sermon, at least as reported by Eliza Follen, described heaven as many of his congregants would have liked it to be and gave solace to the bereaved, for whom disease remained mysterious and the possibility of unexpected death was ever present. Walter too looked up "with a holy & confiding trust towards that Heaven where his treasure is." Eliza's bright smile and loving nature were thus rendered immortal.[89]

Though Lucy Channing survived the initial impact of Eliza's death, she too was soon taken "from languor and suffering to rest and happiness."[90] The family was convinced that the loss of Eliza hastened her death; she was eighty-two years old. As his mother's physician, Walter watched over her final days, grateful that she died "with the greatest tranquility."[91] But Lucy's death added to his own despair and loneliness. She had been a "bosom friend" who saw his defects as well as his good qualities. She had encouraged him in his career and always had his best interests in mind. As long as she was alive there was someone to whom he could confide his secret troubles and his secret joys. He had depended on her constant affection and her good judgment. Now, like Eliza, she was gone and there was no one who understood him as they had, no one to whom he could turn for companionship, guidance, and solace. It was indeed "a widespread woe."[92]

DESPITE the quick succession of severe losses, once the initial shock had subsided Channing recovered more rapidly than might have been expected. Again death had taken people very dear to him, but experience had taught that he must continue to fully participate in life. His children could not be sent off to live with relatives, his patients relied on him, his students expected him to teach with enthusiasm, and his colleagues counted on him to take part in the professional activities that normally engaged them all.

Nonprofessional interests also prevailed. He agreed to deliver the annual address to the Society of Natural History, urging continued support for its activities.[93] A few months later, in a lecture delivered to the American Institute of Instruction, he discussed the importance of natural history as a key to understanding the beauty of the universe and the means of attaining philosophical truth.[94] In his remarks, Channing alluded to the ideas of Wordsworth, Coleridge, and other English poets he admired, writers whose exaltation of nature and transcendentalist ideas had begun to influence New Englanders. The study of natural history, he told his audience, enables one to grasp the meaning of harmony, solitude, beauty, and goodness. On a more practical level, he urged Americans to make natural history collections accessible to all classes of society, rather than the exclusive province of the wealthy. Whereas Channing's initial enthusiasm for natural history had been as a collector of mineral specimens, the intervening twenty years had made him both appreciative of its metaphysical influence and an advocate of its social utility.

Walter Channing (courtesy of the Colonial Society of Massachusetts)

He continued to see patients with the same diligence he had always shown for his work.[95] Indeed, work became a panacea for loneliness and sometimes an excuse to avoid unpleasant obligations. This was especially true with Lucy, who often caused her father great anxiety. The circumstances of her birth, the many years she had lived apart from him, and her congenital frailty made it difficult for him to deal appropriately with her.[96] She first attended the Temple School, close by on Tremont Street, where Bronson Alcott and Elizabeth Peabody sought to fashion young minds according to Alcott's idiosyncratic ideas about the education of children.[97] Like most of Alcott's projects, the Temple

School failed. A few years later, Lucy was sent off to the Berkshires to live with Elizabeth and Charles Sedgwick and attend Elizabeth Sedgwick's school.[98] Her father hoped she would develop physically and mentally among a lively family whose reputation for intellectual accomplishment was widely acclaimed. Despite repeated promises, he never visited her there, pleading that "the bell keeps ringing night and day & I fear I shall not be able to leave the sick folk so long as a journey to Lenox would require."[99]

The autumn following Eliza's death, Ellery enrolled at Harvard. He stayed only three months. The elevated position of his family in the Harvard community may have contributed to his feelings of inadequacy and discomfort but, just as likely, his inability to accept discipline and his distaste for rules made him a poor candidate for college life.[100] There had been little change at Harvard since his father's student days, despite repeated calls for curricular and pedagogic reform. Ellery found recitation of standard texts to be utterly boring. He was affronted by the requirement of regular attendance at religious services and angered by the arbitrary (or so he thought) manner in which grades were given. Rather than face the distinct possibility of failure, he left before the end of the first term.[101]

Ellery's departure might seem to replicate his father's dismissal from Harvard thirty years previously, but there were important differences. The son was an individualist, rebelling against societal norms. Walter had been part of a general student rebellion against authority, but he had had no desire to separate himself from society and after his expulsion he immediately apprenticed to Jackson. He was perplexed by Ellery, who had no alternative plan and spent the next few years living at home, reading without apparent direction, and writing poetry. Occasionally, confused and purposeless, the youth put a knapsack on his back and made "a ramble" in the mountains of New Hampshire or the hills of western Massachusetts. He claimed to be willing to fend for himself, though in truth he knew his father was not likely to let him get into too much trouble.

Walter realized that his son had suffered twice from loss of a mother and that he himself had been unable to supply the warmth and companionship a growing boy requires. He also knew that some of Ellery's characteristics were not unlike his own. He too had been a youthful romantic, he too had embraced the wonder of nature. He had read aimlessly in the Redwood Library and, like his son, he had dreamed of becoming a poet. In fact, he had never stopped writing poetry and pursuing other literary interests. In his case, however, the need to be self-supporting and make a living had forced him to prepare for a worthy profession. But he was willing to grant his son the latitude that he had not enjoyed. He indulged Ellery's inertia and unwillingness to engage in normal societal intercourse, though even he sometimes admitted that he was "such a queer boy."[102]

Channing deeply loved his children. Their company cheered him when they were at home and he missed them when they were away at school or visiting with relatives. Then he wrote frequent, sometimes plaintive letters, confessing in one, "I wish dear Lucy and dear Mary I had been taught better to write. . . . But I love you both so dearly, and rejoice so much in your happiness and well doing, that I can say so, so say that you cannot but understand all I say, all I mean, all I hope and all I trust to."[103]

The children partially filled the void in his emotional life, while professional obligations and a growing involvement in social reform occupied his time. In the middle of his sixth decade, Channing was a busy physician and an active citizen who still had many contributions to make to his patients, his profession, and the betterment of society.

8 🖋

Puerperal Fever

Of all acute diseases, the plague excepted, the puerperal
fever is perhaps the most dangerous.

—Walter Channing, Miscellaneous Lecture Notes

I T is almost impossible, when most American babies are born in clinical
settings where antisepsis is routine and anesthesia is available, to contem-
plate the fear with which nineteenth-century women faced the suffering,
disease, and death they associated with childbirth. The most uneventful delivery had its painful moments, and prolonged labors or instrumented births
were certain to be extremely painful. Stalwart women might bear pain with
little complaint, yet they faced the next pregnancy with vivid memories of
their prior distress. Women with less self-control moaned and groaned as uterine contractions forced the baby through the birth canal and often screamed
aloud as their bodies seemed to be torn apart. One of Channing's patients,
normally confident and well mannered, was so distraught that, in the midst of
bodily agony and mental terror, she sat up in bed crying out, "I am scared!"[1]

Their families shared their apprehension. "This is no light matter when it
comes home to you in yr own family. There is so much anxiety & real danger
that it is quite painful & I wish it were well over," confessed Channing's
nephew William Henry Channing while awaiting the delivery of his sister's
first child.[2] It was not uncommon for a woman to confess "unspeakable emotions of thankfulness to the Being who had preserved [her] through the hour
of danger" or for her relatives to admit similar feelings of relief and gratitude.[3]
Having delivered a healthy baby, mothers still faced potential complications
postpartum. None was more worrisome than the possibility of puerperal fever

156

(also called childbed fever), which was frequently fatal. Though there are no reliable statistics to confirm the extent of nineteenth-century maternal mortality, the fact that so many people feared childbirth attests to the reality of their concerns.[4]

Two events occurred in Boston during the 1840s that presaged the better obstetrical care that eventually meliorated women's lives. Oliver Wendell Holmes's 1843 paper on puerperal fever provided a logical explanation for the transmission of the dread disease and unequivocal rules for its prevention. He did not identify the infecting agent, and there would be no effective cure for another hundred years, but his essay was an important beacon lighting the way toward safer childbirth. Three years later, the demonstration of surgical anesthesia at the Massachusetts General Hospital led in a short time to its use in obstetrics. Anesthetic relief of the pangs of childbirth altered the centuries-old assumption that pain was an inevitable part of parturition and eventually permitted more radical obstetric and gynecological procedures. The decade marked a high point in Boston medical circles and in the professional life of Walter Channing.

Channing had wrestled with puerperal fever from the earliest years of his practice.[5] It was a disease that confounded and distressed him, as it did most physicians. A patient who had been safely delivered and was looking forward to motherhood might suddenly develop alarming symptoms that could be erratic in their development and sometimes subsided, but often led to a painful death. The symptoms might appear before or during delivery, within twenty-four hours after delivery, or a week later. Usually, but not always, the disease began with a severe chill followed by high fever, rapid pulse, headache, and acute pain in the pelvic area. The abdomen would swell and became exquisitely tender to the slightest touch. The pulse became more rapid and less distinguishable, respiration was difficult, and the patient became restless and disassociated from her surroundings. Sometimes a rash appeared. Nausea and vomiting, often of the most repugnant contents, frequently occurred. Death might take place within a few days or several weeks later. At autopsy, evidence of the disease might be confined to her uterus, be seen in her peritoneum, or found in other parts of her body.[6] Death rates varied too, reaching as high as 80 to 90 percent in some European lying-in hospitals.[7]

By Channing's time, British physicians had written convincingly that puerperal fever was a specific disease, rather than one of the generic fevers and agues that described so many disorders. They also recognized that it appeared in the private practice of midwives and physicians as well as in maternity hospitals and that it could be sporadic as well as epidemic.

But there was little agreement on the nature of the disease. Was it autogenic, that is, due to something within the woman's body, such as retained lochia (blood and mucus discharged from the vagina following delivery of a baby) or remnants of the placenta? Was it caused by environmental factors such as weather and climate? Was it the effect of poisons rising from bad air or putrid substances? Was it contagious in the traditional sense of disease transmitted from patient to patient, by either direct or indirect contact?[8]

Toward the end of the eighteenth century, Alexander Gordon, a Scottish physician, witnessed an outbreak of puerperal fever in Aberdeen and in 1795 he published a significant treatise on the subject.[9] Gordon is credited with being the first writer to affirm the contagious nature of the disease as well as the means of its transmission. Previously, puerperal fever had been thought to attack women congregated in cities, whereas the epidemic in Aberdeen spread to women in nearby villages and on remote farms. By listing seventy-seven cases along with the name of the midwife or physician (including himself) who delivered the baby or the nurse present during the lying-in period, Gordon showed that specific attendants were carrying the disease from patient to patient. He claimed that he could "foretell what women would be affected with the disease, upon hearing by what midwife they were to be delivered, or by what nurse they were to be attended during their lying-in." In almost every instance, Gordon's prediction came true.[10]

To prevent further spread of the disease, Gordon advised that "the patient's apparel and bed-clothes ought, either to be burnt, or thoroughly purified; and the nurses and physicians, who have attended patients affected with the Puerperal Fever, ought carefully to wash themselves, and to get their apparel properly fumigated, before it be put on again."[11] He also suggested that there was a connection between cases of erysipelas (an acute infection of the skin and subcutaneous tissues) and puerperal fever, though he did not know what the common poison might be. These parts of his message were largely ignored, perhaps because of the enmity he aroused among the midwives and nurses whose names appeared in his treatise.

Gordon recommended drastic bleeding and purging, especially in early stages of the disease, as the most effective cure. The women and midwives of Aberdeen opposed these active remedies, believing that the epidemic was an ephemeral fever known as "the Weed," for which bleeding and purging were deemed inappropriate treatment.[12] However, the therapeutic portion of his treatise coincided well with contemporary medical theory and was accepted by many physicians. The medical writers who followed Gordon focused on variations of treatment, but they did not come any closer to understanding the nature of puerperal fever.

Channing had read all the authorities. Initially, he subscribed to the notion that unfavorable conditions during pregnancy predisposed some women to the disease. Inadequate diet or lack of exercise might lead to costiveness (constipation) and thus to the retention of poisons. Too much exercise could cause pulmonary disease or hemorrhage and weaken a woman's constitution. Despondency and other psychological factors could also render her susceptible to disease.[13] Channing knew from experience that puerperal fever often followed a prolonged or complicated labor, and he advocated taking measures to hasten delivery if danger threatened. He speculated, too, about phlegmasia dolens, wondering if the inflammation of the veins was somehow related to puerperal fever.[14]

He was not convinced of the contagious nature of the disease, but was willing to accept as reasonable "removing the patient from the society and attendance of those, who have either visited or nursed patients ill of puerperal fever."[15] Like everyone else, he was basing his ideas on cause and effect as observed in his own practice and described by other writers. Also like everyone else, he remained confused.

In his lectures Channing gave careful attention to the symptoms of puerperal fever. Because the initial abdominal pain was often mistaken for the harmless contractions that commonly follow delivery, it was important for young physicians to recognize the distinguishing features of puerperal fever and take immediate steps to combat it. Most experts agreed that there was a better chance of recovery if treatment was started on the first or second day of the disease. But there was disagreement as to the most effective mode of treatment, which ranged from extreme measures (bleeding, purging, emetics, application of moist heat, and enemas) to milder therapies (gentle laxatives and tonics).

Channing favored Alexander Gordon, who "assures us that the disease in his hands was more frequently cured, than in those of any other man's."[16] Gordon's success depended on beginning treatment early with "great doses of jalap with calomel till diarrhaea come in" and copious bleeding from each arm, repeated if necessary.[17] Channing's case notes confirm that he bled, purged, induced vomiting, and blistered in a desperate attempt to reverse the course of the disease. Once the patient had begun to sink and there was no reason to hope for recovery, the drastic measures were replaced by opiates and wine to support whatever strength remained and relieve the pain. But deep down, he had little hope for much success with any treatment.[18]

His later lectures reflect the same uncertainty. He could not believe puerperal fever was contagious in the ordinary sense of the term (passed directly from patient to patient), primarily because it was not transmitted from puerperal women to males or non-pregnant women, whereas infectious diseases such as smallpox knew no such distinctions. At the same time he suspected that it might be contagious in a different sense. Again, Gordon was instructive, as was John Haighton, whose lectures he had attended in London. Haighton taught that nurses (he did not refer to doctors) might communicate the disease from one person to another in their clothing. Since good ventilation and thorough cleansing were often effective in controlling epidemic puerperal fever in hospital settings, Channing could also support arguments that "some epidemic state of the air" might be at least part of the cause.[19]

Puerperal fever was a frequent topic at the meetings of the Boston Society for Medical Improvement. This professional association, like medical societies in numerous localities, combined professional concerns and continuing medical education with collegiality and sociability. Organized in 1828, it met biweekly at the homes of its members to exchange information on recent cases, discuss topics of common interest, and listen to prepared papers on contemporary medical questions.[20] The anniversary dinner, regularly held each February, was an occasion for much good food and drink, accompanied by extravagant merriment. After one annual dinner, Oliver Wendell Holmes, in his capacity as secretary, noted that the company parted at an early hour of the morning "with mutual good wishes, and the proud consciousness that each was able to reach his own domicile unassisted, and unconvoyed."[21] Another year, Channing entertained his colleagues with "a sketch of an auscultator run mad as the pure pathologico-numerico-expectorante observer."[22]

Channing had been one of the earliest invited to join this select group.[23] Curiously, he was assigned to the committee on Medical Chemistry, Pharmacy, and Materia Medica rather than the committee on Midwifery. He was also a member of the standing committee charged with arrangements for the cabinet, or museum, of the society, where "well labeled" anatomical and pathological specimens were to be displayed.[24] Obstetrical cases were frequently discussed at the meetings since all the members faced similar problems and dilemmas in their day-to-day practice.

The assigned topic for March 29, 1830 (a meeting held at Channing's house), was "Varieties and treatment of puerperal fever." The subject was particularly pertinent because several cases had recently occurred in Boston and its environs. One physician had lost five puerperal patients "in pretty quick succession," yet during the same period of time he had attended other women who did not become ill. Perhaps there were different varieties of puerperal fever, some contagious and some not. The members were not able to reach a conclusion. They did agree, however, that the inflammation seemed to be "of an erysipelas nature" and that there probably was a correlation in a case where a husband was "violently seized" with erysipelas and his wife developed puerperal fever.[25]

In the years that followed, Channing and his colleagues brought additional cases of puerperal fever to the attention of the society. In these reports too, the treatment and outcome of each case were carefully described. It was clear that everyone was baffled by the question of contagion. They recognized that the disease occurred in clusters and that there might be a surge in incidence followed by a temporary disappearance, but they remained unable to explain these phenomena.

On June 27, 1842, Channing read his notes on thirteen fatal cases of puerperal fever he had recently seen in Boston and vicinity.[26] In the discussion that followed, mention was made of an outbreak of erysipelas and two cases of puerperal fever in a nearby town. Someone mentioned that the disease was then prevalent in New York. In early October Channing reported a woman with severe puerperal fever whom he had been asked to see that afternoon. Having recently read about a case of puerperal fever occurring in a house where typhus fever was also present, he suggested that this woman's illness might be related to typhus fever, which had been in her house for four weeks.[27]

At the same meeting, Dr. John Fisher detailed an alarming sequence of events: the autopsy of a woman who had died of puerperal fever; severe inflammation in the arm, high fever, nausea, chest pains, and general prostration of the physician who had performed the dissection; the subsequent death of a student who had assisted in the dissection and had attended the infected physician in his illness; and the sickness of a second student who attended the dissection. Interest in the subject quickened.[28] At the end of November, Channing described another case to which he had recently been called. Puerperal fever had appeared thirty-six hours postpartum and the woman was dead two days later.[29]

Oliver Wendell Holmes, one of the younger members of the society, was much affected by the increasing reports of disease and death among newly delivered mothers and intrigued by the unresolved questions regarding transmission of the disease. He began to examine authoritative treatises, medical texts, and journal articles, seeking the common threads that might tie the cases together.[30]

At both January meetings, puerperal fever dominated the discussion. Channing reported additional cases, and John B. S. Jackson announced that a Dr. Barker of Lynn had died "from a dissection wound" incurred during the autopsy of a puerperal fever patient. The progress of his illness was similar to puerperal fever: rigor followed by intense heat, ardent thirst, pain and swelling of the shoulder, and gradual sinking.[31] Jackson had been Dr. Barker's physi-

Oliver Wendell Holmes (Portrait
Collection, Harvard Medical Library, Francis
A. Countway Library of Medicine)

cian. Troubled by the outcome, he asked the opinion of the society "as to the contagion of Puerperal Fever, and the probability of physicians communicating it from one patient to another." So animated was the conversation that the members agreed to continue it at the following meeting.[32] The stage was thus set for Holmes to deliver his paper "The Contagiousness of Puerperal Fever," which became, in time, one of the classics of American medical literature.[33]

Holmes presented a well-reasoned and carefully constructed argument to support the theory that puerperal fever was a contagious disease, transmitted from patient to patient by the attendant, be it physician, midwife, or nurse. His paper was based on published reports of puerperal fever epidemics, but no previous investigator had made such a broad survey of the literature. He quoted extensively from Alexander Gordon, who had presented a similar thesis based on his experience, and excerpted treatises of Charles White and John Armstrong that also showed a correlation between the incidence of disease and particular physicians' practices. Numerous authors and articles from the *London Medical Gazette*, the *Lancet*, and other British medical journals were cited. The evidence was overwhelming: repeated incidence of puerperal fever in a single physician's practice and horrendous epidemics in lying-in hospitals, where row after row of parturient women were examined and delivered by the same attendants. Holmes discounted the negative argument that because puerperal fever did not appear in every case a suspicious physician attended or in every hospital patient, it could not be contagious. "It signifies nothing that wise and experienced practitioners have sometimes doubted the reality of the danger in question; no man has the right to doubt it any longer."

Holmes had also accumulated evidence from American medical journals and from correspondence with physicians in the Boston area who sent him thorough descriptions of puerperal fever cases in their practices. He had asked them for details: had they changed clothing between sick calls, had they attended erysipelas cases at the same time, were there any extenuating circumstances such as geographic or climatological influences that might bear on the incidence of puerperal fever? Their responses corroborated its contagious nature. He also recounted example after example in which postmortem examinations of puerperal fever patients were followed by the appearance of the disease in subsequent parturient women.

Holmes was outraged by the imputed misconduct of his colleagues and had no tolerance for anyone who might disagree with him. He was particularly critical of medical teachers who neglected to inform their students and colleagues about the terrible dangers inherent in puerperal fever or, even worse, completely ignored the subject. In that context, he praised his own professor of midwifery. "It gives me pleasure," he wrote, "to remember that, while the doctrine has been unceremoniously discredited in one of the leading journals, and made very light of by teachers in two of the principal medical schools of this country, Dr. Channing has for many years inculcated, and enforced by examples, the danger to be apprehended and the precautions to be taken in the disease under consideration."[34] Holmes had nicely exonerated him from not giving sufficient attention to puerperal fever in his lectures and practice. Yet Channing was still not convinced on the subject of contagion.[35]

Holmes concluded his paper with a passionate plea for strict adherence to practices that would prevent a "private pestilence," as he called the transmission of puerperal fever by physicians. He demanded that physicians who expected to attend midwifery cases not take an active part in autopsies of puerperal fever or erysipelas victims and that they take thorough precautions even if only present at such autopsies. If a physician encountered puerperal fever in his practice, he must "consider the next female he attends in labor, unless some weeks, at least, have elapsed, as in danger of being infected by him, and it is his duty to take every precaution to diminish her risk of disease and death." This might mean that the physician would have to give up his midwifery practice for a month, even longer, yet Holmes did not equivocate. "The time has come when the existence of a *private pestilence* in the sphere of a single physician should be looked upon not as a misfortune but a crime; and in the knowledge of such occurrences, the duties of the practitioner to his profession, should give way to his paramount obligations to society."

The eloquence of Holmes's prose far outstripped its science. Although he had accumulated abundant data to convincingly demonstrate the correlation of puerperal fever cases and attendant, and the probable connection with erysipelas and wound fever, he could not explain *what* was carried from patient to patient, or from cadaver to dissector to patient. Indeed, a few years later when Ignaz Semmelweis, the physician in charge of the maternity wards at the Vienna General Hospital, proved the contagiousness of puerperal fever empirically by requiring that the medical students wash their hands with chloride of lime before examining parturient patients and thereby reduced maternal fatalities within a month from 18 percent to 2.45 percent, he first

attributed the disease to "cadaveric poisons." Semmelweis subsequently referred to "decomposing animal organic matter," but he was no closer to the
correct explanation.[36]

Not until the advent of bacteriology in the 1860s and 1870s could the
etiology of puerperal fever be clearly understood. It was Pasteur who, in 1879,
identified the streptococcus as the cause of puerperal fever as well as erysipelas
and the deadly septic disease that so frequently followed a dissection wound.
It took many more years until the streptococcus was better understood and
the particular strain most frequently associated with puerperal fever was identified. The work of Joseph Lister and the acceptance of antisepsis and aseptic
procedures confirmed Holmes's and Semmelweis's demands for cleanliness in
the birthing room, including cleanliness on the part of the physician, and
made it easier to prevent puerperal fever. Nonetheless, until the sulfa drugs
were discovered in the 1930s and penicillin became available in the 1940s,
there were no reliable cures should the disease occur.[37]

Thus, although Holmes was thoroughly convinced that physicians were
the agents of transmission, and the subsequent acceptance of germ theory
makes his case self-evident, it remained difficult for many in the profession to
accept his argument. It was, after all, a terrible indictment of their conduct.
The minutes of the Society for Medical Improvement do not record the comments that followed Holmes's presentation. There is only the terse statement,
"it was voted that Dr. Holmes be requested to publish the paper which he had
just read."[38] The litany of puerperal fever deaths grew that very same night,
with Dr. Storer announcing recent cases that had occurred in the practices of
Dr. Thaxter of Dorchester and Dr. Flint of Boston.

Channing was not present when Holmes read his landmark paper. It was
not uncommon for him to miss a meeting. The vagaries of midwifery practice
often constrained his other activities. He also had personal problems to dis-
tract him. His brother Henry and his youngest daughter, Lucy, were both invalids at his house and may well have prevented his attendance at a meeting
so clearly interesting to him.[39] No doubt he soon heard about the paper, for its
conclusions were certain to provoke lively debate in the medical community.
He did attend the next meeting of the society, on February 27, where he reported an outbreak of puerperal fever in Charlestown.[40]

Ten fatal cases had appeared in the practice of a single physician, four
more cases in the practice of another. Channing had been asked to visit a
woman in the neighborhood who became ill shortly after her labor began and
was afraid that she too would die. He happily reported that she did not. During
the discussion, Channing remarked that, though he had been a consultant in
many of the fatal cases, "in his own practice he had had no case of puerperal

fever." Furthermore, he had consulted with Dr. Flint, whose puerperal fever cases had been reported at the previous meeting, and took charge of his midwifery patients after Flint left town, presumably because of the outbreak in his practice. "They all did well," Channing added. Thus, despite the persuasiveness of Holmes's data, the experience of individual physicians made it difficult to accept his conclusions.

At a meeting in March of the following year, Channing read a prepared paper "containing several facts to show that puerperal fever is not always contagious."[41] It is unfortunate that the manuscript for the paper does not exist, for it would help us know exactly what facts Channing referred to. But there is no question that there were many examples in which a physician had a single case of puerperal fever in an otherwise busy midwifery practice. The minutes of the meeting reveal only Channing's comment that "from his own experience he would never hesitate to visit other patients and take charge of women in labor, when attending puerperal fever cases as consulting physician." Consulting physicians did not necessarily examine puerperal fever patients; they observed and offered opinions.

Channing's experience in Charlestown, as well as his experience with Dr. Flint's patients, wherein none of his own patients became ill, substantiated his position. Holmes, however, did not accept this reasoning. Though he had admitted that the contagion of puerperal fever was not always followed by disease, and that there might be some forms of the disease that were not contagious, he would not have a member of the medical profession risk a single woman's life.

The more Channing considered Holmes's theory, the more it seemed correct. He had no doubt of the similarity of puerperal fever and erysipelas. Too many physicians who had been ill with erysipelas themselves, or had attended erysipelas patients, had subsequent obstetric cases in which the woman, and sometimes the infant, died.[42] During a serious outbreak in 1849, he became aware of a physician who had attended a case of phlegmonous erysipelas and afterward lost four puerperal patients, one after the other. At Channing's suggestion, the Society for Medical Improvement asked him, Dr. David Storer, and Dr. Charles Putnam to collect further data about physician responsibility for transmission of puerperal fever and better ways of treating the disease.[43] The committee polled their colleagues, asking whether erysipelas, scarlet fever, and measles had occurred in their practices or their localities simultaneously with puerperal fever; whether puerperal fever had been contagious; and whether physicians called in consultation had communicated the disease. Questions such as these would not have been asked prior to Holmes's paper.

As responses came in, a misperception occurred that threatened to damage

Channing's reputation. All the recent cases were rumored to be his! He wrote immediately to the editor of the *Boston Medical and Surgical Journal*, refuting the attribution. "It so happens that I have not had a single case of this disease in my practice and so have lost none. . . . I have seen in consultation some cases of puerperal fever, and this more than once, but have in no instance communicated the disease."[44] He had become increasingly cautious, as well as defensive, avoiding puerperal fever consultations as much as possible and refraining from entering the sickroom if he could do so.[45] He also made sure that the nurses who assisted in his cases and remained with the woman after delivery changed their clothing frequently.[46] Like many physicians in Boston, he was fearful "of conveying that certain something" which proved disastrous to parturient women.[47]

Holmes's paper, published as it was in a fledgling journal that expired within a year, did not produce the acclaim he might have wished for it. Although some physicians such as Channing were gradually persuaded, there was disbelief and antipathy from others who were angered by the accusation of a young practitioner that they might be transmitting disease to women they thought they were helping. Holmes's lack of expertise in obstetrics made him an easy target.[48] His paper was roundly attacked by Charles D. Meigs and Hugh L. Hodge, both well-respected professors of obstetrics in Philadelphia.

Hodge indignantly assured his students that they could never be "the minister of evil," that they could never "convey, in any possible manner, a horrible virus so destructive in its effects and so mysterious in its operations as that attributed to puerperal fever."[49] Meigs characterized Holmes's essay as "the jejune and fizenless dreamings" of a sophomoric writer and told his medical students that he preferred to attribute puerperal fever "to accident, or Providence, of which I can form a conception, rather than to a contagion of which I cannot form any clear idea."[50] Again, in retrospect it is easy to accuse the noncontagionists of stupidity, but we must remember that these were physicians who could not accept an explanation that discredited their profession yet had no scientific theory to support it.[51]

Holmes responded to these and other attacks by republishing his paper in 1855, with a different title and an introduction that stoutly defended his theory against the Philadelphians' disparagement.[52] "I am too much in earnest," he wrote with zealous fervor, "for either humility or vanity, but I do entreat those who hold the keys of life and death to listen to me also for this once. . . . I beg to be heard in behalf of the women whose lives are at stake, until some stronger voice shall plead for them."

The reappearance of Holmes's essay made a greater impact than the original paper. The attention it now received prompted Channing to send comments to the *Boston Medical and Surgical Journal*.[53] Using examples from his practice and those of several colleagues, plus citations from the British writers whom he particularly admired, Channing affirmed the contagious nature of puerperal fever, its likely transmission by physicians, and its strong correlation with erysipelas.[54] He suggested that the accepted therapeutic modalities, bleeding and strong drugs, be replaced by sulfate of quinine, which had been successfully used by a colleague and was becoming more popular in general medicine.[55] But he could not refrain from asking the fundamental questions that continued to perplex him. "Whence the FIRST CASE?" What is the "specific cause which is nothing else, and can be nothing else than itself?" The second, third, and fourth cases could be explained by transmission from patient to patient via the physician, but what initiated the string of cases? The answer, Channing said, "has in it the whole history of a contagious disease." His questions remained unanswered and unanswerable until bacteriology explained the specific cause of the first case.

He had come to a full realization that "the whole profession, at whatever sacrifice it may be required, [must] be ready to do all in its power to prevent the communication of so fatal a malady." Many years later, when Oliver Wendell Holmes referred to Channing as having "the open and receptive intelligence belonging to his name as a birthright," he may well have been referring to the evolution of Channing's ideas about puerperal fever.[56]

Chapter 9

Obstetrical Anesthesia

> May we not . . . look with confidence to the time when labor
> will be accomplished with an ease, a freedom from suffering,
> quite as great as has hitherto been the pain which has ac-
> companied it, and which has been regarded as its necessary
> condition?
>
> —Walter Channing, "A Case of Inhalation of Ether in Instrumental
> Labor," 1847

ON October 16, 1846, an operation for removal of a tumor from the neck of a young, impecunious printer named Edward Gilbert Abbott marked one of the great achievements of nineteenth-century medicine. John Collins Warren was scheduled to perform the procedure at the Massachusetts General Hospital. He had agreed to allow William T. G. Morton an opportunity to demonstrate the effectiveness of a still unnamed vapor in rendering the patient insensible and thus preventing pain during the operation. Morton, a dentist, had been experimenting for some time with compounds that would make dental operations painless. While Warren and the assembled physicians watched, he placed a glass tube close to the mouth and nose of the patient and instructed him to inhale. In four or five minutes Abbott seemed to be asleep and Warren began to operate. His patient was not entirely motionless or silent throughout the surgery, but he did not feel pain. Afterward, Abbott reported that he was aware of a blunt instrument being drawn across his neck, not the sharp knife with which Warren had incised his flesh.[1] Warren reportedly immortalized the event by proclaiming, "Gentlemen, this is no humbug."[2]

Morton intended to keep the formula a secret, expecting to reap huge profits by selling or licensing the compound to other physicians. He was quickly disabused of that idea, for it was not difficult to figure out what the vapor was. The name he had chosen for it, "Letheon," was abandoned when Oliver Wendell Holmes suggested "anesthesia," a word derived from Greek and used by Dioscorides in the first century A.D. to describe drug-induced insensibility.[3]

Few medical discoveries have contributed more to the betterment of human existence than this one. Though other gases, including nitrous oxide, or "laughing gas," had long been known to induce temporary loss of sensation and bitter controversy would rage for decades about the "real" discoverer of anesthesia, Morton's success with sulphuric ether, its use in subsequent operations at the hospital, and its rapid application in surgery and dentistry in many parts of the world made the first ether operation a historic occasion.[4]

Though Channing had hesitated to accept new ideas about the spread of puerperal fever, he soon took the lead in recognizing the benefits of anesthesia for obstetrical practice. He had not witnessed Morton's demonstration, for he was no longer on the staff of the hospital, nor was he accustomed to attend surgical procedures. Neither was he present when anesthesia was first administered in a case of childbirth. But he was the first American physician to use it in an instrumented delivery and was so convinced of its merit by the success of that case that he rapidly became the nation's leading champion of anesthesia for women in labor and delivery.

News of Morton's accomplishment spread like wildfire in the Boston medical community.[5] Henry J. Bigelow (son of Jacob Bigelow), a prominent surgeon present at the dramatic first operation, announced "the recent discovery & practice of the inhalation of a vapor so as to produce insensibility" to the American Academy of Arts and Sciences on November 3 and to the Boston Society for Medical Improvement on November 9.[6] Channing heard the full story there, though he was undoubtedly already aware of the news. The *Boston Medical and Surgical Journal* published the younger Bigelow's paper ten days later.[7]

Reports of the extraordinary drug quickly reached Europe. Jacob Bigelow described it for a friend in London, who informed his colleagues at University Hospital.[8] There, on December 21, Robert Liston performed the first anesthetized surgical procedure in England and predicted that within six months no operation would be done without it.[9] A Harvard medical graduate wrote to colleagues in Paris and they too began to experiment with it.[10] Soon German and Russian physicians were similarly engaged.

A young Scot, James Y. Simpson, recently appointed Professor of Midwifery in Edinburgh, hastened to London to see for himself the effect of anesthesia in surgical operations.[11] Simpson immediately understood the possibilities for instrumented deliveries, and shortly after his return to Edinburgh he performed the first recorded obstetrical operation in which anesthesia was administered. He had selected his initial case carefully because no one knew whether ether would halt uterine contractions. The woman whom Simpson chose had a severely deformed pelvis and he knew he would have to turn the fetus and extract it feet first. Contractions would not be essential to the success of the operation; in fact, their cessation might make it easier. He discovered, however, that contractions did not stop, while the patient remained completely insensible to the pain of a potentially excruciating maneuver. Simpson concluded that the discovery of anesthesia had enormous potential in the practice of midwifery.[12]

Now news traveled across the Atlantic in the other direction. Reports of Simpson's initial achievement and his subsequent success using anesthesia in normal deliveries as well as in operative midwifery soon reached Boston. But, whereas the use of anesthesia in America was promoted by surgeons and dentists, for whom the screams and writhing of their patients made their work difficult emotionally as well as technically, the first trial of anesthesia in childbirth was due to the courage and determination of a woman.[13]

Fanny Appleton Longfellow, the wife of the poet Henry Wadsworth Longfellow, wanted to have ether administered during her third labor. She knew that anesthesia had been successfully used for childbirth in Britain and in Paris.[14] But local physicians, uncertain of the effect on mother and child, had not yet dared to try it. She had no friends who could describe a similar experience. Indeed, she risked criticism from many women who would not have approved such an unconventional act.[15]

Boston's dentists had become experienced with ether in the few months since Morton showed how easily it obliterated pain. Among them was Nathan Cooley Keep, whom Longfellow engaged for his wife's confinement. Keep had received a medical degree from Harvard in 1827. His particular interest in dental medicine led to an association with Morton and thus to extensive familiarity with anesthesia. A few weeks before he was asked to administer ether to Fanny Longfellow, he addressed a communication to the *Boston Medical and Surgical Journal* describing the apparatus necessary for its administration.[16] When Fanny's labor began on April 7, 1847, Keep was summoned to Craigie House, the Longfellow home in Cambridge, where a midwife was already present to "manage the case" and deliver the baby.[17]

Keep's description of the event was succinct, but it spoke to the questions on everyone's mind.

> Five and a half hours having elapsed from the commencement of labor, her pains . . . becoming severe, the vapor of ether was inhaled by the nose and exhaled by the mouth. The patient had no difficulty in taking the vapor in this manner. . . . In the course of twenty minutes

Fanny Longfellow with her sons, Charles and Ernest, 1849 (courtesy of the
National Park Service, Longfellow National Historic Site)

four pains had occurred without suffering, the vapor of ether being
administered between each pain. Consciousness was unimpaired and
labor not retarded. Inhalation was then suspended that a comparison
might be made between the effective force of the throes with and without the vapor of ether. No material difference was detected, but the
distress of the patient was great. Inhalation was resumed, but the
progress of the labor was so rapid that time could not be found for
sufficient inhalation to bring the system perfectly under its influence;
still the sufferings of the last moments were greatly mitigated. . . . No
unpleasant symptoms occurred, and the result was highly satisfactory.[18]

Longfellow was greatly relieved by the success of a trial that might have had an unhappy outcome. Within hours of the birth he announced to a friend, "The great experiment has been tried, and with grand success. . . . The *Ether* was heroically inhaled."[19] He also described the event for his mother, Zilpah Longfellow. "Fanny was courageous enough to be the first in this part of the world to inhale the vapor of Ether, under similar circumstances. The effect was magical. All pain instantly ceased; though the labor continued; and while under the effect of the vapor, there was a delightful sensation of repose! Only when the phial of ether was removed, did she become conscious of pain. The trial proves, that the new-discovered *Letheon* may be used not only with perfect safety in such cases, but with most beneficial results afterwards. Fanny has never before seemed so quiet and well after a confinement."[20]

Though Longfellow's family and friends scolded him for permitting his wife to take such a risk, especially since the physicians were not using it in their midwifery cases, Henry was so satisfied that the day after the birth he went to Boston to have the stump of a double tooth extracted under anesthesia by Dr. Keep.[21] Fanny was equally pleased, telling her sister-in-law, "Two other ladies, I know, have since followed my example successfully, and I feel proud to be the pioneer to less suffering for poor, weak womankind. This is certainly the greatest blessing of this age, and I am glad to have lived at the time of its coming and in the country which gives it to the world."[22]

Though Fanny Longfellow had been delivered without mishap and reports from Europe were encouraging, there were very real concerns. No one understood how anesthesia worked, although animal experiments indicated that it was transmitted to parts of the brain that control consciousness and sensation. If this was true, might it also induce puerperal convulsions? Might it affect other organs, cause complications, and threaten the health of the mother? Surgery and dentistry had shown that the voluntary muscles ceased to function during its use. Would uterine contractions halt or be less effective? Was anesthesia inhaled by the mother safe for the baby? For how long might it be safely administered? Surgical and dental operations were relatively quick, whereas labor could last for hours. What was the proper dosage? What was the best way to administer it during childbirth? Was chloroform, which Simpson had begun to use instead of sulphuric ether, preferable to ether, which had been accepted by surgeons and dentists in Boston? Finally, was there a physiological necessity for pain in childbirth which made all the other questions moot?

There were also cultural assumptions about pain in childbirth. Most prominent was the precept that labor was the punishment women were ordained to suffer because of Eve's sin in the Garden of Eden: "I will greatly multiply thy pain and thy travail, in pain thou shalt bring forth children."[23] A different but commonly accepted belief was that middle-class women had become "weak" from their soft, less-demanding lives and were just more sensitive to pain than women in primitive societies and lower-class women in the Western world. Finally, there were those who took a psychological approach and asserted that the pain a woman suffered while giving birth was a positive good. It helped her to bond with her child and prepared her for motherhood. Most of these views, it must be said, were expressed by men. Women may have accepted their weak status, as Fanny Longfellow did when she felt "proud to be the pioneer to less suffering for poor, weak womankind," but many were as eager as she to have relief.

CHANNING had long regretted his inability to offer women a magic potion that would reduce their agony and lessen their fears. If a patient seemed especially troubled, he might prescribe opium compounds. He could also resort to bleeding, which sometimes relieved pain, especially if enough blood was drawn to cause partial or complete loss of consciousness, but venesection was less acceptable than it once had been. He relied primarily on rapport with his patients and his calm, confident demeanor to lessen anxiety, reduce tension, and thus relieve their pain.

There is no indication that either Fanny or Henry Longfellow sought Channing's advice. But he was aware of the success with which anesthesia was being used for obstetrics in Edinburgh and Paris. At the meeting of the Society for Medical Improvement on April 26, he heard Dr. John Homans describe an obstetrical case in which he had used ether "with mitigation of the pains." Homans mentioned that the patient's breath retained an ether smell for a week after delivery, but otherwise he was satisfied with the outcome.[24]

Thus on May 7, when Dr. W. E. Townsend asked Channing to consult in a difficult case, he was predisposed to learn for himself how effective ether could be. He saw Townsend's patient, Mrs. H., age twenty-three, around 9:00 A.M. She had had severe pains for more than thirty-three hours, but her cervix had hardly dilated. Townsend had prescribed an opiate and she was resting. Channing predicted that the labor would be protracted and painful, but he advised waiting to make sure that the use of instruments could not be avoided. When he returned at noon, there had been little progress. He recommended belladonna be applied to speed dilation. A few hours later, Townsend appeared at Channing's door seeking further advice. They agreed that it was "a very fair case for the use of ether." Townsend went off to get the ether and a sponge and met Channing at the patient's house.

By now Mrs. H. was in serious trouble. She had been in labor about forty-two hours. Though the cervix was more dilated, her pulse had risen to 120 beats per minute and was feeble. In faltering syllables, unable to speak above a whisper, she pleaded for help. Channing applied forceps without difficulty but when he began to pull, she screamed with pain. At that point, Channing instructed Townsend to apply the sponge, saturated with ether, to her mouth and nose.

This he did, and in about a minute she was under the full influence of the ether. The first inspiration produced a slight cough, as if the larynx had been irritated. . . . The next noticeable effect, and which was quite an early one, was a sudden movement of the body, such as is made sometimes when one is falling asleep, and has consciousness enough to know this, and to rouse the will into sufficient action to prevent it. It was involuntary, still it did not convey the idea of being spasmodic, in any morbid understanding of the term. She was directed to open her eyes, to answer questions, etc., but gave not the least evidence of consciousness of anything said. I now proceeded to extract.[25]

Mrs. H. did not say a word as the operation continued. Nor was there any reduction in the expulsive action of her uterus. For a while it seemed all would go well, but again the child's head became firmly fixed in the pelvis and Channing could not use forceps without risking damage to Mrs. H. The effect of the ether had diminished and she regained consciousness. "Put it to my mouth—I shall faint—you must," she murmured. Channing sent for a resupply. Meanwhile, he perforated the child's head and tried to continue extraction using the hook. Once again Mrs. H. cried out in pain and he had to stop. "The repose had been entire since consciousness had returned. She thought she was delivered. Said that she had *sense*, knew that she was alive, after the sponge was put to her mouth, but that she had no *feeling* after, and knew not what had happened. She had passed the time in most entire freedom from all pain. She said that there had been light before her eyes, and buzzing in her ears, that she had been in another world."[26] When the sponge was reapplied, Mrs. H. lost consciousness again and Channing continued to extract the child. The uterus did not cease to contract, but progress was slow and ether was administered several more times. The child had been dead for some hours. Mrs. H. recovered consciousness soon after it was born and reported her ignorance of everything that had happened.

Throughout the delivery, Channing paid minute attention to his patient's respiration, color, and pulse as well as her emotional response to the anesthesia. For several days afterward he continued to monitor her condition, looking for any indication that the ether had caused problems. He found none. She slept well, her pulse was good, tongue moist, head clear, and she was completely comfortable. In fact, she recovered more rapidly than might be expected after a difficult forty-eight-hour labor. As usual, there was no reference to sorrow over the dead child.

When Channing published this first case report of operative midwifery using anesthesia in the United States, he gave all the details. He knew well how important it was. Homans had been brief in his description to the Society for Medical Improvement and had not produced a written record. As a professor in a respected medical school and as the best-known obstetrician in New England, Channing's comments regarding the safety and efficacy of ether would receive careful attention from colleagues throughout the country and in Britain. He composed a full account, which he read to the society on May 10 and published in the *Boston Medical and Surgical Journal* on May 18, 1847. To his surprise, the paper earned him a reputation for being the first American to administer anesthesia in midwifery, a claim he readily disavowed.[27]

Within a week Channing reported a second forceps case in which he used anesthesia. This time, a nine-pound boy was born alive. Recalling that the birthing room was saturated with ether vapor in Mrs. H.'s case, he had covered the sponge with brown paper. As the patient emerged from unconsciousness, she babbled on about her happy dreams and wanted to know why anesthesia had not been used before. The following day she remembered absolutely nothing, the dreams, Channing's presence, or the application of instruments. As with Mrs. H., Channing had deliberately applied the forceps before inhalation of the ether so that the possibility of injury could be reported by the patient.[28]

From then on, his experience with ether continued to grow, as did his enthusiasm. He arranged to have the first two cases reprinted in a single pamphlet for wider dissemination.[29] In mid-June he reported three more cases in the *Boston Medical and Surgical Journal* and soon after that he published another pamphlet, *Six Cases of Inhalation of Ether in Labor*, for the benefit of colleagues who did not subscribe to the journal.[30] He justified each example by the severity of the pains, duration of the labor, or the need to use instruments.

He was learning from every case. In one, he gave ether intermittently over nine hours, longer than ever before. The patient asked for it when she thought she needed it and threw the sponge aside as soon as she felt it taking effect. Channing was astonished by her control of the situation as well as by her effusive gratitude "for this means of comfort." Her family was less pleased, because she suffered bad headaches and chest pains afterward. Channing had not been informed of these potentially dangerous conditions, so he cautioned his readers "to learn if peculiarities exist in patients, or if morbid predispositions may be supposed to belong to them" before giving anesthesia.

He was also struck by the behavior of his patients. Mrs. R. initially refused to accept the sponge, but, once she was under its influence, it was difficult to persuade her to give it up. After the delivery, she sang, talked, and swung her arms in the air. When she heard the baby cry, she put her hands to her abdomen as if to learn what had happened and was astonished to find the child born. Mrs. W. cried out, "I am dying, I am dying," when ether was first given to her but murmured, "How beautiful, how beautiful," throughout the rest of the labor. None of the women remembered the ordeal they had gone through.

Channing was rapidly becoming a crusader for anesthesia. If he encountered problems during or after a delivery, he assumed they were not different from nonanesthetic obstetrics and could not be attributed to the vapor. He did not mention the nausea, hoarseness, or offensively sweet smell often associated with ether. By the end of June, several local physicians were using it in their obstetrical practices. By the end of November, Channing had attended forty cases of his own, more than any other physician in Boston, probably more than any in the United States.[31] But doubts remained. The editor of the *Boston Medical and Surgical Journal* warned about the danger of "serious mischief" and recommended that ether should be reserved "for the most difficult and trying circumstances."[32] Some physicians reported fainting and hysteria or diminished and arrested contractions. There were notices of deaths from chloroform administered in surgical and dental cases. Well-esteemed obstetricians were expressing their opposition, citing physiological and psychological reasons for not using it. Channing decided he must respond to these negative comments and began to plan what would be his most ambitious and most important published work, *A Treatise on Etherization in Childbirth, illustrated by Five hundred and eighty-one Cases.*[33]

Today a federal government agency evaluates scientific data based on clinical trials and is required by law to approve a new medical procedure. In the mid-nineteenth century there was no formal system to determine the efficacy and safety of medical innovations. Evidence was anecdotal. Physicians offered medical treatment on the basis of their individual training, experience, and preferences. Patients and their families would be influenced by rumors and the opinions of their friends. Channing decided it was incumbent on him to accumulate as much data about obstetrical anesthesia as he could, aggregate the results, and make a rational judgment about its benefits and dangers.

The concept was similar to the "numerical method" introduced to American medicine by the disciples of Pierre Louis. Channing's study did not require sophisticated mathematical analysis, but it was nonetheless one of the earliest examples in the United States of large numbers of similar events used to test a medical hypothesis.[34] His personal experience undoubtedly predisposed him to a favorable conclusion, but by soliciting information from many colleagues, some of whom he did not personally know, he expected more valid results.

The quotation on the title page of the work, "Give me the facts . . . your reasonings are the mere guesswork of the imagination," was the motif of his research.[35]

Forty-five physicians responded in writing to eleven questions Channing posed in a letter asking about their experience with anesthesia, whether ether or chloroform.[36] Some reported only one or two cases, while others, such as John Homans, had used it almost as often as Channing. Channing assembled the data in three tables, to which he added extensive commentary and a fourth table for comparison with nonanesthetized deliveries.

The first table summarized 516 cases of "natural labor," that is, head presentations delivered without instruments or other assistance. Forty-five were from his own practice. Many were long and painful labors. There were no maternal fatalities. Five stillbirths could be explained without reference to anesthesia. None of the physicians reported an "apparent danger" during delivery. There were examples of diminished contractions, even cessation of contractions, when anesthesia was first given, but they had resumed, often more efficiently than before. Channing assured his readers that serious problems were not likely to result from those events. Ether was used two times more frequently than chloroform, though several physicians expressed a strong preference for chloroform. Smaller quantities were required, making it easier to carry to the patient's home. It also had a less offensive odor, took effect more rapidly, permitted a quicker return to consciousness, and could not be detected on the breath of the child.

There were no standard answers to questions about quantity, length of use, or time elapsed before the anesthetic took effect. To Channing's query about "special effects, physical, moral, and intellectual, in individual cases," the answers ranged from "no special effects" to "pleasant effects." One physician described "nervous excitement with laughing" for five patients, "expressions of delight" for another five, and "hysterical screaming in two for a short time." He added that all his patients were eager to continue inhalation. There were many accounts of reduced muscular tension, less exhaustion, quicker labors, reduced after-pains, and an easier, quicker "getting up." Everything pointed to proof that anesthesia did not pose a danger in "natural labor." To the contrary, it had many positive benefits.

Tables 2 and 3 listed cases of instrumental, preternatural, and complicated labor. Channing endeavored to include every case of this kind that had occurred in Boston and vicinity since obstetrical anesthesia had been introduced. He had himself participated in twenty-eight of this group. He analyzed these cases and twenty-four more that had been communicated to him by other physicians. Forty percent were forceps deliveries; the rest included craniotomies, convulsions, breech and arm presentations, hemorrhages, and twins. There were four maternal fatalities, less than 8 percent, all attributed to convulsions. Six additional women with convulsions recovered. Among the babies, there were nineteen stillbirths, just over 37 percent.

Channing compared these maternal fatalities and stillbirths with similar labors without anesthesia. There were fifteen maternal fatalities and seventeen stillbirths in eighteen cases where anesthesia was not used. Channing was particularly gratified by evidence that anesthesia made turning in breech and arm presentations easier and less dangerous. There were no dead mothers or babies in this group and the hands of the physicians were less pained or damaged by the force of uterine contractions. Fortified with these data, Channing declared anesthetized deliveries in operative midwifery were also safe for mother and child.[37]

Many of the physicians included personal remarks with their responses. Dr. Erasmus D. Miller wrote, "I know of no better criterion, in its administration, than to trust to the wishes of the woman."[38] Some women did not want an anesthetized birth, "preferring to trust to their powers of endurance" even when they knew that the physician had brought chloroform or ether with him.[39] A patient in South Boston rejected a second dose of ether because she wanted "to complete labor in the natural way."[40] Others obstinately refused relief until the pains became unbearable. A woman in Salem, Massachusetts, learned about anesthesia from friends in Boston and had expected to use it until she was dissuaded by the women assembled to help with the birth. Eventually, worn out and depressed by the severity of the pains, she reasserted herself and begged for anything that would alleviate her suffering.[41]

"Chloroform-phobia" was attributed by Dr. Folts to the husband and friends of Mrs. L. In the first stage of her labor they refused to allow its use, but her agony during the second stage of labor and the physician's pleas on her behalf forced them to relent. When chloroform was administered, however, Mrs. L. became extremely talkative, frightening her husband so badly that he demanded a halt. Again she begged for relief and again Mr. L. gave in. A healthy child was born and everything went well until the husband became alarmed once more because his wife was sleeping so peacefully.[42]

Physicians' enthusiasm for anesthesia was not uniform. Some willingly used it in just about every case, while others, like Dr. Miller, used it only if the woman insisted. There were physicians who restricted it to operative obstetrics and a few who remained skeptical even though they had not had a negative experience. Dr. W. Strong wrote, "I have been opposed to its use, and have only yielded to importunity, when I gave it; and this not because I had seen any bad effect, but because I prefer to pursue old methods, which have been found safe and sufficient, in preference to enter upon the use of an untried remedy."[43] Jacob Bigelow summarized the opinion of many of his colleagues by commenting that obstetrical anesthesia was "an experiment not yet settled in all its bearings, but promising much for the relief of human suffering."[44]

Channing did not share his restraint. There were many reasons for his enthusiasm. He had taught toxicology as part of his course in medical jurisprudence and chemistry at his private medical school and was familiar with the potential effects of anesthetic gases. The fact that "[t]he remedy of pain was discovered in this city" appealed to his local pride.[45] Finally, but perhaps most important, his zealous promotion of anesthesia satisfied his humanitarian instincts. The volume, he wrote, "treats of a noble subject, *the remedy of pain.* After ages of suffering and of frequently and long intermitted pursuit of such a remedy, one has been discovered."[46] He was convinced by his data that anesthesia in childbirth was safe and effective.

Channing wanted to make sure physicians used anesthesia correctly, and he included instructions in the *Treatise.*[47] He insisted that the anesthetic agent, whether ether or chloroform, must be pure. To illustrate the proper mode of administering it, he provided a sketch of a conical device, manufactured according to his instructions by a local instrument maker. Unlike Simpson, who used large quantities of anesthesia, he advocated moderate dosage. "Entire etherization," he advised, "is unnecessary in midwifery, except in instrumental and other difficult cases."[48]

Anxious that his numerical method might not be sufficiently reassuring for his medical audience, Channing devoted a large part of the treatise to the physiological and neurological effects of anesthesia. He attempted to explain the tingling in the fingers that patients often experienced, as well as dizziness, confusion, and noises in the head. He reported animal experiments that seemed to corroborate his understanding of the mechanism of anesthetic agents, and he praised new investigations regarding consciousness and sensibility. Channing was a compassionate physician, but he was not a scientist, and much of this discussion makes little sense in the light of subsequent developments in our understanding of physiology.

He had been forced by use of the new agent to reconsider his assumptions about the mechanism of childbirth and produced some interesting though mistaken conjectures. For instance, to counter the argument that pain is a necessary component of labor, he developed his own explanation of parturient pains, asserting that contractions of the uterus do not cause pain any more than contractions of the bladder or rectum cause pain. Instead, he suggested that pain is produced by the opposition encountered by the fetus as it descends through the pelvis. With anesthesia, he wrote, there is no pain because the

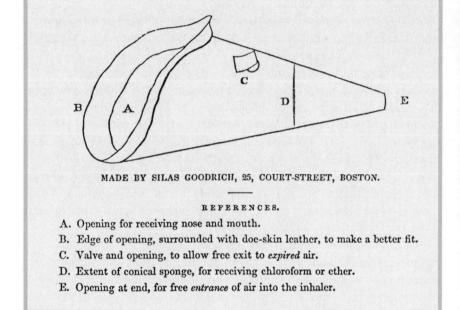

MADE BY SILAS GOODRICH, 25, COURT-STREET, BOSTON.

REFERENCES.

A. Opening for receiving nose and mouth.

B. Edge of opening, surrounded with doe-skin leather, to make a better fit.

C. Valve and opening, to allow free exit to *expired* air.

D. Extent of conical sponge, for receiving chloroform or ether.

E. Opening at end, for free *entrance* of air into the inhaler.

Ether cone (illustration from Walter Channing, *Treatise on Etherization in Childbirth*)

muscles do not resist the expulsive power of the uterus. In another original observation, he maintained that cervical dilation is not caused by pressure of the fetal head or amniotic sac or by any "mechanical action," though his alternative interpretation, that dilation of the os uteri is "functional," that is, a physiological process, did not explain much, either.

To the argument that "labor pains are not so severe as to authorize the use of an agent of unknown power to destroy sensibility," Channing suggested that the gentleman who made this statement had never given birth and probably had never witnessed a birth. To those who feared that etherization might injure the newborn, he again relied on his experience and his data, claiming that ether reduced the number of stillbirths and that the children he had delivered were "fully equal, in health, growth, and mind, to those who have been born in the midst and pressure of the severest pain." He had followed those children since birth, questioning the mothers about the development of their newest born, and observing them for himself.

He also tackled moral objections. Not surprisingly, anesthetic substances were being abused for the emotional high they give. Reports of "ether parties" and of young girls breathing chloroform for private amusement were damaging the drugs' reputation as materia medica. Channing had no patience with such behavior, which in some instances had nearly been fatal, but he was equally impatient with the argument that such foolishness should impede the use of anesthesia in appropriate situations.

As for religious objections to the use of anesthesia in childbirth, Channing was familiar with the dialogue between Simpson and Scottish churchmen who had severely chastised him for transgressing the divine decree regarding the "primeval curse." Simpson was a linguist, philologist, and Biblical scholar as well as a scientist and physician. He had reinterpreted the Hebrew text, reading "sorrow" not as the sensation of pain, but as the "muscular toil and effort" associated with childbirth.[49]

Channing took a different, entirely idiosyncratic position in the theological dispute. He pointed out that Scripture was often used to discredit many kinds of "moral improvement," meaning in this case the social causes he supported. The peace movement, for example, could be contradicted by the wars of the Israelites or temperance reform by the marriage at Cana. Channing found better Scriptural support for peace and temperance, as well as for anesthesia, in his certainty that the Creator had endowed man with the intellectual capacity to improve his existence, including his health. Then, and in a remarkable bit of Biblical exegesis, Channing suggested that "Eve's curse" might refer to "the sorrow caused by the wickedness of children, when grown up." He probably did not intend to reveal the sorrow caused by his own child, Ellery, but the possible coincidence cannot be ignored.

Channing decided he needed support for these arguments from a recognized authority and consulted Professor George Rapall Noyes of the Harvard Divinity School.[50] Noyes, esteemed for his Biblical scholarship, furnished two letters, which Channing included in the *Treatise*. The professor took issue with Simpson's philological explanation of "sorrow" and with Channing's suggestion about wicked children, arguing instead that the birth of children had been a joyful occasion for Eve. But he did offer Scriptural support for the notion that human ingenuity used for the relief of pain is "the use of God-given means by God-given powers."[51]

Channing knew that the most powerful opposition to anesthesia in childbirth came from Professor Charles D. Meigs of Philadelphia, as obstinate on this subject as he was on puerperal fever. Meigs had already clashed with Simpson, and an exchange of their letters had been published in medical journals.[52] He argued that anesthesia was potentially life threatening because it could affect the medulla oblongata, the portion of the brain thought to control what he termed the *"nœud vital,"* or life force.[53] "I fear," he wrote to Simpson, the primary champion of chloroform, "that, in all cases of chloroformal anaesthesia, there remains but one irrevocable step more to the grave." Since no one understood the physiological process by which anesthesia produced insensibility and memory loss and there had been fatalities in non-obstetric cases, his point could not be totally dismissed.

Meigs insisted that pain in labor was essential to the physiology of the birth process, a "most desirable, salutary, and conservative manifestation of the life force," and that a mother risked her life and her health if she chose to avoid it. He counted on her sense of pain to help him follow the progress of the labor and to assist him in operative obstetrics.[54] In a statement typical of the pompous and melodramatic utterances for which he already was well known, Meigs summarized his personal sentiments: "Should I exhibit the remedy for pain to a thousand patients in labour, merely to prevent the physiological pain, and for no other motive—and if I should in consequence destroy only one of them, I should feel disposed to clothe me in sack-cloth, and cast ashes on my head for the remainder of my days. What sufficient motive have I to risk the life or the death of one in a thousand, in a questionable attempt to abrogate one of the general conditions of man?"[55]

Meigs's explanation of his refusal to make use of "the remedy for pain" included a reference to "Dr. Channing, Dr. Homans, and other practitioners, who make use of it very commonly." Channing realized that Meigs had placed himself in an untenable position because, never having used it or seen it used in midwifery, he had no personal experience with anesthesia. How could he be so certain of the negative effects? To make sure, he sent Meigs a copy of the interrogatory letter with which he queried his colleagues in Boston. Meigs obliged with a long reply, which Channing published in the *Treatise*. Though the tone of his letter was deferential, Meigs did not retreat: "I hold myself in readiness to yield to conviction upon sufficient evidence of the necessity and propriety of etherization in midwifery; but I beg leave to say, that this is a case in which I should hardly yield my opinions to the force of statistical returns, because I have no doubt of some physiological and therefore needful and useful connection of the pain and powers of parturition, the inconveniences of which are really less considerable than has by some been supposed."[56]

Channing intended the *Treatise on Etherization in Childbirth*, with its analyses of nearly six hundred cases, as a powerful answer to Meigs and to other physicians who still doubted the wisdom of anesthesia in midwifery. He worked rapidly so the book might reach the public as quickly as possible. More careful editing would have improved it. There are redundancies, contradictions, and a few errors in fact. Nonetheless, though overwritten and faulty in the light of subsequent, more sophisticated statistical and epidemiological methods, Channing's presentation did what he hoped—it reassured the profession and the public that anesthesia was safe for mother and child.

Most reactions to publication of the *Treatise* were friendly. A woman who had suffered agonizing pain during her lying-in wrote to congratulate him. Most doctors, she said, were satisfied to study the process of labor but unwilling to relieve pain. At last, there was a physician "above the imputation of quackery" who offered relief. She urged Channing to continue to do everything he could to "disseminate confidence" in ether.[57] J. F. B. Flagg, a surgeon-dentist, recommended the book "to all who are desirous of obtaining information that must add much to their happiness."[58]

The *Boston Medical and Surgical Journal* changed its critical tone, enthusiastically urging "perusal of each and every case" mentioned in the book and praising "the timely production of this mass of evidence in proof of the true value of etherization in midwifery." There were rumors that a strongly negative review would soon appear, aimed either at "the total annihilation of the author or . . . at the destruction of the heretical doctrine he has put forth." Channing was so certain of the validity of his argument that he had no fear of the impending threat. It seems not to have materialized.[59]

Edward Warren, a younger brother of John Collins Warren and a physician himself, discussed the *Treatise* in the *North American Review*.[60] (It is possible that Warren's close association with the leading figure in the introduction of surgical anesthesia colored his opinion.) He strongly supported anesthesia for "individuals of the softer sex," for whom there is "so great a degree of physical as well as mental sensibility, that they cannot bear a great amount or long continuance of pain." Warren recognized that Channing's effusive advocacy of anesthesia was similar to his zeal for social reform, but he was certain of the objectivity and impartiality of his investigation. Warren was satisfied that the evidence Channing had accumulated proved his case and that people still in doubt could reach their own conclusions after reading the book

There were also more guarded appraisals. Daniel F. Condie, a Philadelphian with a large obstetrical practice, wrote a long review for the *American Journal of the Medical Sciences* that echoed the concerns of Meigs and other conservative physicians about the possibility of death in an etherized patient, the necessity of pain, and the diminution of uterine contractions. Condie wanted a degree of certainty about safety and efficacy that no one, certainly not Channing, could produce. Indeed, Channing's extravagant enthusiasm for anesthesia and his willingness to dismiss the possibility of harm made it difficult for men like Condie to accept his arguments at face value. All he could do was to thank him for "having collected much of this evidence."[61]

The strangest voice raised in opposition to anesthesia was that of Samuel Gregory. Gregory had attended a few medical lectures while a student at Yale, but he knew very little about medical practice. After graduating in 1840, he

embarked on a career as a pamphleteer and itinerant lecturer on many subjects, including mesmerism, phrenology, physiology, personal hygiene, and
the dangers of masturbation. When he began to criticize the practice of obstetrics by male physicians, calling them men-midwives and accusing them of
indecent conduct and harmful procedures, he moved on to a larger stage. His
call for the renewal of female midwifery and adequate education for women
who wished to be midwives resonated with fathers and husbands who feared
that the modesty of their daughters and wives was being compromised by the
presence of medical men in the birthing room.[62]

There was nothing wrong with Gregory's desire to promote female midwifery. There were always women who preferred to be delivered by a midwife
and other women who wanted midwifery training. But his lurid accusations of
licentiousness, cruelty, and butchery on the part of male accoucheurs did not
endear him to the medical profession, whose opposition to female physicians
and midwives was strengthened by Gregory's rhetoric.

The elaborate title of Gregory's best-known pamphlet reveals the tenor of
his argument: *Man-Midwifery Exposed and Corrected; or, The Employment of
Men to Attend Women in Childbirth, and in other delicate Circumstances, shown
to be a modern innovation unnecessary, unnatural and injurious to the physical
Welfare of the Community, and Pernicious in its influence on Professional and
Public Morality, and the Whole Proven by numerous facts, and the testimony of
the most eminent physicians in Boston, New York, and other places; and the Education and Employment of Midwives Recommended; together with remarks on the
use and abuse of ether, and Dr. Channing's "Cases of Inhalation of Ether in
Labor."*[63] It had been published in Boston a few months before Channing's
Treatise went to press.

In addition to delivering a scathing attack on physicians who engaged in
obstetrical practice, Gregory cast serious doubts on the safety or necessity of
obstetrical anesthesia. To demonstrate the pernicious effects of male midwifery, he reinterpreted the six cases described in Channing's early pamphlet.
Gregory was careful to exonerate Channing of deliberate misconduct, since
"the eminent professor" had been called when the women were already exhausted from excessively long labor. The problem, as he saw it, was that other
men had been in attendance during the previous days and nights, subjecting
their patients to frequent vaginal examinations, inserting catheters, applying
ointments, and otherwise proceeding according to the "shameful, detestable,
and dangerous" rules of man-midwifery.[64] In Gregory's view, these women,
naturally modest, delicate, and sensitive, would not have had such long and
painful labors if they had not been embarrassed and frightened by the presence
of a man. Remove men from the birthing room and there would be no need

for ether, catheters, ergot, or instruments. If the mother experienced pain it was salutary and would be forgotten once she was happily delivered.

Gregory did not neglect arguments about the dangers of ether, including the possibility of suffocation, poisoning, and organic disease. He reported a case of a dentist who "violated" his female patient while she was anesthetized. He suggested that "animal magnetism" and intoxication produced the same insensibility and indifference as ether, with the same potential for violating female propriety. Gregory's writings reinforced the views of Bostonians opposed to anesthesia and to the presence of physicians in the birthing room, but they had little effect on the medical profession itself.

THE Committee on Obstetrics of the newly organized American Medical Association focused on etherization in its 1849 annual report. With some colleagues still questioning the safety and usefulness of anesthesia in childbirth, Channing's "most unexpectedly favorable" conclusions played a large part in the deliberations. The committee deemed his analysis, based on "the largest number of cases . . . yet published," the most valuable contribution to the literature on the subject.[65] Accounts from other physicians in the United States and Europe were imprecise and less accurate. The committee report repeated many of Channing's statistics as well as his explanation for the disparity between the number of deaths in anesthetized surgical cases and the complete absence of deaths in obstetrics. Channing had suggested that the more moderate use of anesthesia in obstetrics, where consciousness need not be completely lost, made it less dangerous than in surgery, where it was administered in advance of pain.

These reports of occasional fatalities in surgical procedures where chloroform was used continued to impede acceptance of obstetrical anesthesia even though "no one woman has yet lost her life in consequence of the pains of her labour having been controlled by etherization." The committee felt bound to include negative opinions in its generally favorable report and let physicians decide for themselves. The one application to which it gave unequivocal approval was for control of puerperal convulsions, since the purpose was not relief of pain but cure of disease.

Channing continued to promote the acceptance of anesthesia. He frequently reported additional cases to the Society for Medical Improvement, including one of inverted uterus and another of placenta previa. In both, anesthesia permitted him to perform life-saving operations.[66] By 1851 he was ready to state that he considered it "his duty" to use it in all cases of parturition and that he greatly preferred ether to chloroform.[67] There was still no unanimity among his colleagues. Nearly all the patients of J. Mason Warren asked for and received it, while Jacob Bigelow used it in about half of his cases. Others who had never been enthusiastic were using it less. Newspaper accounts of accidental deaths during ether-sniffing parties continued to frighten many people.

Channing's enthusiasm seemed boundless. In a paper read to the Society for Medical Improvement, he described a series of cases in which chloroform was applied externally on the skin to relieve various aches and ills. His incredulous colleagues queried him on the assertion, particularly Channing's insistence that the relief had been permanent. This produced a lengthy discussion about the sensitivity of skin tissue and further questions about the properties of anesthesia. Channing remained steadfast in his claims, though he did not convince the others.[68]

In his medical lectures Channing boldly proclaimed the virtues of anesthesia while decrying physicians who continued to deny it to their patients. "The woman may inhale ether and both for the child and for herself the better will the labour proceed. Whether however she gets this help and solace will much depend upon the whim, the prejudice, or the jealousy of the medical attendant, male or female. I say jealousy because it really does seem that there is to some minds a fear that labour will not be painful enough to fulfil the prophecies or secure a good getting up."[69]

His views about obstetrical anesthesia helped increase his business. Women whose physicians were unenthusiastic about anesthesia now asked Channing to attend them in childbirth and to bring along the necessary vapors.[70] Neither anesthesiology nor obstetrics was a medical specialty. Channing administered the anesthetic and delivered the baby, unlike the situation in which Nathan Cooley Keep's role was to anesthetize Fanny Longfellow and the midwife delivered the child. Since Channing did not insist on anesthesia with unwilling women, there was little danger of losing business. Though he did not experience maternal fatalities as a result of anesthesia, tragedies did occur in other physicians' practices, more frequently with chloroform than with ether. Skepticism remained. Even the example of Queen Victoria, who used chloroform in the birth of her eighth child in 1853, did not completely eliminate the opposition.

Channing's advocacy of anesthesia is his most important contribution to the practice of obstetrics. His was the vision to recognize the potential benefits of anesthesia as well as the wisdom to make a thorough study of the risks. His obligation, as he saw it, was to the women who need not "submit to a suffering which is unnecessary as it is . . . cruel."[71] Channing's endeavors, like those of Simpson, were the beginning of a long process of scientific and medical investigation that eventually included anesthesiology, neurology, and physiology and was meant to free women from the pain, anxiety, and fear that had previously accompanied childbirth.

10 𝒵

Social Reform

What is Reform, that word so widely said,
But re-creation of both heart and head?
What but the *self*, which feels its sterling sway,
Can the full measure of its tribute pay?

—Walter Channing, "Reform," in *New and Old*

S OCIAL reform was very much in the air during the four decades preceding the Civil War, coincident with the middle years of Channing's
life. Temperance, universal peace, women's rights, public education,
urban poverty, prison conditions, and better care for the blind, deaf, and insane vied for attention from thoughtful people who could not ignore the problems that were afflicting their communities. The abolition of slavery was
especially compelling, eventually overshadowing all other issues.

Reform-minded men and women like Channing, confident of the righteousness of whatever cause they espoused, organized locally and nationally
to work for change. They spoke from pulpit and podium, issued periodicals
and tracts, held small meetings and convened vast assemblies, lobbied legislators and harangued other government officials. Their assumptions about the
ultimate perfectability of American society reflected a faith in the promise of a
still-new nation where improvement was assumed, innovation was welcome,
and the principles of Christian ethics were expected to prevail.

Boston was especially receptive to the enthusiasm for reform. It was no
coincidence that the city was home to many leaders in the movement. Horace
Mann, Samuel Gridley Howe, Dorothea Dix, William Lloyd Garrison, and
Wendell Phillips are still familiar names, but there were numerous others, less
well known today but famed in their own era, who unstintingly gave their
energy, time, and money to the work of reform. For one thing, Boston's Con-

gregational and Unitarian churches had a long tradition of charity and social responsibility that continued to inspire many of their ministers and congregants.[1] Additionally, the sense of noblesse oblige that had led to the creation of institutions such as the Massachusetts General Hospital remained a powerful force among the intellectual and political leaders of the city. They could not ignore the distressing social conditions emerging from the early stages of an industrial economy, the influx of immigrants living in wretched conditions, or the suffering among the physically and mentally ill. Nor could Bostonians escape the influence of the Transcendentalists, whose writings, lectures, and sermons extolled the spiritual nature of man and criticized the materialistic culture emerging around them.

Channing's resonance with reform sprang from the fundamental values that shaped his life. First was his commitment to liberal Christianity. His faith in Jesus as his spiritual guide and ethical master led naturally to love for the poor and downtrodden, to relief for the inebriate, to abhorrence of human bondage, and to an unwavering acceptance of universal peace. These religious strains in his reformist activities were, of course, closely tied to the influence of his brother, who spent much of his life reflecting on the meaning of righteousness and benevolence and was known throughout the city for his social concerns. But the brothers took very different roles. William, chronically unwell and compelled to safeguard his limited strength, advocated the morality of reform through sermons, speeches, and essays. Walter, robust and energetic, participated actively in a variety of reform movements. Indeed, the broad range of his concern is suggested by the newspapers and journals to which he subscribed: the *Prisoner's Friend, Orphans Journal,* the *Washingtonian, Voice of Industry,* the *Harbinger,* the *American Temperance Journal,* the *Christian World,* the *Liberator,* and the *American Anti-Slavery Standard.*[2]

Channing's reformist impulse was also a consequence of his commitment to the promotion of health and his experiences as a physician.[3] Several of the issues that captured his interest, temperance and poverty for example, had a strong public health component that demanded remedy. Hospital attendance, consultations for Dispensary cases, and visits to homes of the rich and the poor gave insights about the relationship of social conditions to disease that he could not ignore. Physicians in other parts of the country were conspicuous as reformers, one going so far as to claim that "medicine is a physical science, but a social profession"; but apart from the temperance movement, in which the medical profession was much involved, Channing was one of the few physicians in Boston who spoke out for change.[4] Nonetheless, he was recognized in the medical press for his "active benevolence in every work and cause which promises to better the moral or physical state of mankind."[5]

Finally, Channing's reformism was imbedded in his personality. He was a genuinely compassionate man, troubled by human suffering. As a young boy he had embraced physic so that he might "ease the pains incident to the body"[6] and thereafter had devoted himself to that purpose. Now in middle age, he embraced reform so that he might act on behalf of less powerful elements in society and ameliorate social conditions causing pain to the soul as well as the body.

Channing was involved with temperance more prominently and for a longer period than with any other reform movement.[7] Since colonial times, Bostonians had been consumers of large quantities of liquor and their habits had not changed in the years following the Revolution. Wine, cordials, beer, cider, whiskey, and rum

William Ellery Channing (courtesy of the Bostonian Society/Old State House)

were part of daily life, whether served from the mahogany sideboards of wealthy merchants or in the rough taverns frequented by working men.[8] The city was reported to have one licensed grog shop for every twenty-one males above the age of twenty.[9] Intemperance was assumed to cause disease, insanity, and family instability throughout society and to be responsible for crime, poverty, and degeneracy among the lower classes. There was ample evidence to support these views, simplistic as they may seem.

Massachusetts was in the vanguard of a national crusade against liquor. The Massachusetts Society for the Suppression of Intemperance was founded in 1813. Most of the leadership came from the clergy, but there were physicians among them, including John Warren, who lent his prestige as guardian of public health to the society's efforts to "discountenance and suppress the too free use of ardent spirits, and kindred vices."[10] The society was minimally effective, relying only on appeals to rational behavior and self-discipline to reduce excessive use of strong liquor. The temperance movement became more vigorous when evangelical ministers such as the Reverend Lyman Beecher began to deliver fiery sermons calling for total abstinence and demanding legislation that would "banish ardent spirits from the list of lawful objects of commerce."[11]

When John Collins Warren assumed the presidency of the Massachusetts

Society for the Suppression of Intemperance in 1827, the argument shifted. More than forty years previously, Benjamin Rush had called for temperance reform on medical grounds. His *Inquiry into the Effect of Ardent Spirits upon the Human Mind and Body* was reprinted eight times between the end of the Revolution and 1815.[12] Now Rush's message was resurrected and elaborated as Warren and his associates sought to educate the public about the effect of intemperance on health.[13]

It was a difficult position to uphold. Most people honestly believed that wine and other spirits aided bodily functions, including digestion and circula-tion of the blood. Many upper-class ladies and gentlemen were known to de-pend on a daily dose of tinctures and elixirs that contained an alcoholic base.[14] It was also assumed that heavy manual labor, be it on the farm, docks, or city streets, was facilitated by regular use of strong drink. Employers encouraged their employees to imbibe during work hours and the army and navy provided a daily liquor ration to their men. To add to the quandary, physicians fre-quently prescribed spirits medicinally. If they were going to be consistent in their opposition to alcohol, they had to demonstrate that drink was harmful to the body and that good health could be maintained without it.

In response to appeals from Warren and other spokesmen for temperance, the Massachusetts Medical Society declared the "use of *ardent spirits* unhealthy [and] inconsistent with a vigorous action of the bodily and mental powers" and recommended entire abstinence to all classes of the community. In a series of resolutions intended to correct the "insidious" opinion that the use of alco-hol contributes to health, the physicians pledged themselves "to discontinue the employment of spiritous preparations of medicine, whenever they can find substitutes; and, when compelled to use them for any great length of time, to warn the patient of the danger of forming an unconquerable and fatal habit."[15]

Like most of his friends, Channing was not always opposed to moderate drinking. "Scuppernong and mountain dew" had enlivened the long bachelor evenings with Jared Sparks, and after Sparks left Channing's house to make room for Eliza, he retained a standing invitation from his newly remarried friend to return for the enjoyment of some "excellent whiskey."[16] However, as the advocates for temperance became more determined and his medical col-leagues became more involved, Channing altered his attitude and personal behavior. He was aware of the medical and social problems caused by excessive use of alcohol. His paper on delirium tremens, published in 1819, had shown his familiarity with the effects of inebriation. Now he began to advise his stu-dents that "the physician is eminently a teacher of temperance for he best knows the moral & physical ruin produced by intemperance."[17]

Channing was especially intrigued by the efforts of the Reverend Joseph

Tuckerman to "cure" intemperance with "medicine."[18] Tuckerman, a Unitarian minister who had assumed a special mission to the urban poor, visited regularly among Boston's most destitute men and women, many of whom were hopeless alcoholics. He viewed intemperance as "a diseased appetite or a diseased state of the stomach, or of the imagination." From that premise, Tuckerman reasoned that medication could temporarily cure the drunkard of his disease and that the subsequent period of sobriety would give time for moral suasion to produce a permanent cure.

Channing accompanied Tuckerman on his rounds so he that might see for himself the effect of the medicine the minister was dispensing. Most likely, the concoctions were whiskey, rum, or beer to which a powder had been added that produced such severe gastrointestinal effects the "patient" willingly gave up alcohol.[19] Channing approached the "patients" clinically, observing their appearance and inquiring about immediate and remote effects of the medication. He too believed that an "appetite for alcohol" could become an obsession and was optimistic about the possibilities for a cure. However, Tuckerman soon turned his attention to other problems and there was little follow-up from clergyman or physician.

Channing quickly realized that intemperance had social effects far beyond the health of individual men and women and decided to join in the work of the Massachusetts Society for the Suppression of Intemperance. He began speaking publicly about the benefits of complete abstinence although his position was ambiguous, for he had not yet become a teetotaler. Like many of the clergymen opposed to alcohol, he too used religious metaphors, referring to intemperance as "the origin of all sin" and to abstinence as "victory over [the] greatest enemy."[20]

Though support for complete abstinence spread throughout the nation, the Massachusetts Society for the Suppression of Intemperance, reorganized in 1831 as the Massachusetts Temperance Society, maintained its more moderate course. Its members were required to adopt the "short pledge," which proscribed distilled alcohol but did not prohibit wine and other fermented drinks as required by the "long pledge."[21] It was a position that suited Channing's views. In 1834 he published an essay advocating the moral nature of temperance reform and opposing political and legal remedies.[22] He also described the deleterious effects of alcohol on various parts of the human body, including "watery and almost useless" blood and enlarged organs surrounded by fat. The mind, he asserted, is particularly damaged by alcohol, with depression, violence, insanity, and suicide its inevitable consequences.

Channing soon emerged as a leader of the Massachusetts Temperance Society, becoming first a member of the council and then, in 1835, the secretary.[23] At the annual meeting the following year he gave the major address.[24] His speech included repeated appeals for "noble action." He called for "the active direction of the spiritual nature to [remove] an evil which, in its very self, tends to the destruction of the moral and the intellectual . . . [and] the deep desolation of the soul." He exhorted his audience to rely on education rather than on legislation that would limit or prohibit the sale of intoxicating drink. "Let moral truth [be] the great remedy, and true respect for others be in their hearts, on their lips, and in all their writings," he urged his fellow temperance workers.

Channing feared the potential schism between those who insisted that wine, beer, and cider be considered intoxicating drinks and those who remained adamantly opposed to teetotalism. He urged both groups to remain united. "The field is a wide one," he insisted, "and offers numberless occasions for useful action." He correctly perceived an increased tendency in social reform, as well as in politics and religion, to "see nothing to respect or to approve in those who differ," and an unwillingness to compromise that might impede efforts to curtail intemperance, "the fruitful mother of so vast evil . . . the consummation of misery." Personally, he was moving in the direction of total abstinence.

Channing's call for compromise and moral suasion went unheeded. The Massachusetts Temperance Society was considerably weakened by its refusal to accept teetotalism or to agree to the necessity for legal prohibition. The Massachusetts Temperance Union, formed in February 1838 by representatives of several separate temperance societies, became the first statewide total abstinence society.[25] With John Collins Warren on an extended vacation in Europe, Channing assumed responsibility for joining in its campaign for legal prohibition.[26] In response to intense public pressure, the Massachusetts legislature passed the so-called Fifteen-Gallon Law, which prohibited the sale of distilled liquor in quantities less than fifteen gallons.

The law was intended to prevent consumption by the glass in taverns and retail sale of small quantities to be drunk at home. However, since the lower class was more likely to be affected by the law than the wealthy, who could afford to purchase large amounts of liquor, the implication was clear: it was the poor who needed to be saved from their own transgressions. Spies and informers were employed by the temperance societies to collect evidence of violations of the law, though Channing disapproved such underhanded methods.[27] Distillers, liquor dealers, and proprietors of saloons, inns, and entertainment halls had always opposed the temperance movement, but now there was widespread condemnation of a law that seemed unfair and might mean closure of one's favorite tavern.[28] Massive opposition erupted, including mob violence,

forcing the political parties to take a stand on an issue they would have preferred to avoid. Less than two years after passage, the Fifteen-Gallon Law was
repealed.[29]

As an officer of the Massachusetts Temperance Society, Channing had
been a member of the committee that helped move the bill through the legislature.[30] It was a departure from his usual apolitical view, but he campaigned
with uncustomary determination. Once the law was enacted, he defended it in
annual reports of the society. He also spoke in its favor at a meeting of the
Temperance Society of Harvard University, where he recalled the "wasted time
and neglected opportunity" of his own student days when intoxication was
part of college life.[31] Now he was in a missionary as well as a medical mood,
praising the temperance movement for saving souls and lives, while at the
same time urging discipline and self-control on the young men in his audience.

The excitement and controversy created by the Fifteen-Gallon Law exposed Channing to public ridicule and criticism. It was just the kind of environment in which William Ellery Channing's faith in moral and religious
principles was most supportive. He offered sympathy and encouragement to
his brother's cries of abuse and assuaged some of his hurt feelings.[32] But Walter
had learned the futility of political action and the wisdom of his preference for
education, example, and appeals to the higher nature of man to combat social
ills.

Repeal of the Fifteen-Gallon Law forced a return to those principles. In
1842 he became the first (and only) president of the Massachusetts Washington Total Abstinence Society, which differed significantly from the more
widely known Washingtonian societies.[33] The latter were composed primarily
of reformed drunkards and sympathetic reformers eager to restore habitual
inebriates to society. These Washingtonians relied on public confessions, pic-
nics, parades, and other popular forms of entertainment to persuade alcoholics
and "down-and-outers" to forswear liquor and sign the pledge.

Channing's group was very different. They intended to collect statistics on
intemperance from every part of the state, including numbers, sex, and ages
of the reformed and the intemperate, effect of intemperance on property and
poverty, conditions in jails and almshouses, the number of distilleries in operation and discontinued, effect of reform on health, disease, and mortality, and
several other social conditions. Why the society named itself similarly to the
better-known Washingtonians is unclear, especially since they carefully distinguished their activities from those of the other group. Some statistics were
collected and published, but the society quickly accumulated more debts than
it could meet from annual contributions that came to less than four hundred

dollars. The real significance of the Washington Total Abstinence Society lay in its use of statistics as a way to understand a social problem.[34] It may have prepared Channing for his statistical approach to the risks and benefits of anesthesia in childbirth.

Channing remained committed to the cause. He was often an orator at temperance meetings, where the excitement of a crowd and his personal enthusiasm produced an emotional high. He described one such experience to his daughter Lucy: "Last Sunday I went to Dorchester Heights just before evg & there in the old Fort, in the open air, the sea and wide land before and around me, the blue sky above & the setting sun in the 'drooping West' a crowd of men & women & children neigh, I spoke of Temperance. I never spoke so well. It seemed to me as if inspiration had come in the pure air from heaven & I spoke as if moved by the Spirit."[35] An observer at another of Channing's public addresses was less rhapsodic, referring to one of the participants as "the reformed gambler" and to Channing as "the reformed Doctor, that has left his bad & good practices too."[36] But Channing could illustrate his message with examples from that medical practice, especially from cases of sick children whose drunken fathers had abandoned their families or had reduced them to desperate poverty.

Membership certificate, Massachusetts Washington Total Abstinence Society (courtesy of the Boston Medical Library, Francis A. Countway Library of Medicine)

In his personal life he now "practiced" abstinence. An English visitor in Boston, John Shaw, eager to express his appreciation to Channing for curing him "of a very violent attack of the cholera of the worst kind," invited him to dine at the Tremont Hotel.[37] The Englishman was unaware that his guest was a teetotaler. Champagne was offered round the table. Channing "refused in the most marked and decided manner, by a most peculiar and horrified expression of countenance . . . and put his hand over his glass as an effectual stopper to any further proceeding of that course which might have effectually damaged the character of a distinguished lecturer . . . of temperance." Neither guest nor host made any comment, though the Englishman was greatly embarrassed by the incident.

Channing's active participation in organized temperance activity ended in 1848, when he ceased being secretary of the Massachusetts Temperance Society. He had not ceased believing that temperance reform was "a noble mission, its object the redemption of the souls and of the bodies of men from a degradation, a sin, which includes within it, or may become the fearful cause of all other delinquencies." He also remained convinced that intemperance was a moral issue that could be solved only by appealing to "man's highest responsibleness." Like his brother and other Unitarian theologians, he believed that man is "the depository of the fruit of God . . . a being of infinite dignity and of awful power." Just as the Almighty had given man the intellectual capacity to improve his health through science and medicine, so he had given him understanding with which to abandon intemperance.[38]

CLOSELY allied to Channing's passion for temperance was his dedication to improving Boston's water. The lack of good water was often cited as a reason for intemperance, as well as for other physical complaints. Boston's households depended on private cisterns and underground wells or on water from Jamaica Pond that flowed through pitch-pine logs to the homes of paying customers. There was no guarantee of its purity or of an adequate supply.

The water problem became more severe as the city grew. More people meant more demand. Increased congestion, more horse-drawn vehicles, and the proliferation of bad housing created filth in the streets and alleys and overtaxed the drains and sewers. Reclamation of land along the harbor and in the coves caused infiltration of brackish saltwater into wells. The coal that heated the city, the increased number of industrial establishments, and the railroad engines that had recently appeared on the scene produced soot and grime that seeped into the water supply.

Beginning in the 1830s the city began consultations on an improved water system, and various medical groups, including the editors of the *Boston Medi-*

cal and Surgical Journal and the Boston Medical Association, urged them
onward.[39] In 1837, when Channing was an officer, the Massachusetts Temperance Society added its support with a resolution emphasizing "the importance
of an abundant and constant supply of pure water, as a means of temperance
and health."[40] But progress was slow, thwarted by the perennial debate over
private versus public responsibility, with the corollary issues of increased debt
and appropriate use of tax dollars and the pervasive belief that private enterprise could better provide the water. Not everyone thought the system as it
existed was seriously bad. After all, Boston had escaped the major epidemics,
including the worst of the cholera scare.

Many Bostonians—engineers, scientists, and inventors as well as physicians—were engaged in discussions of proposals for a better water system.[41]
Channing attended some of the meetings and published two essays on the
subject.[42] The themes he struck came from his own experience: the danger to
health caused by the proximity of wells to sewage and outhouses, the effect of
saltwater incursions, and the consequences of shortages that forced the poor
to spend their small income on water essential for cooking, housecleaning,
and personal hygiene. Whereas many influential men in Boston could speak
theoretically about the problems, his familiarity with the unwashed bodies,
filthy clothing, and disgusting habitations of the poor and with the relationship among lack of water, intemperance, poverty, and crime gave his arguments an extra cachet.

In refuting some of the objections to a municipal water system, Channing
also showed the extent to which he had begun to think about the responsibility of the community for the welfare of all its inhabitants. A city, he wrote,
"should be the patron of its own great, permanent, universal interests. These
should be committed to the charge of no other corporation, company, nor
individual. The water it drinks, the air it breathes, the light which blesses it,
neither of these should be given in charge to any man, or body of men."[43] This
view was a marked departure from his usual distrust of government and distaste for paying taxes.

Debate over the water supply became increasingly acrimonious, but in
1846 the city finally decided to construct an eighteen-mile aqueduct from
Long Pond (subsequently renamed Lake Cochituate) and a delivery system to
distribute the water throughout the city.[44] Two years later, when the water-
works were complete, there was an extravagant celebration. All the church
bells in the city rang, cannon were fired, and there were fireworks, parades,
and speeches galore. A huge crowd assembled on the Common, where, in
response to a signal from the mayor, a magnificent new fountain threw clear
water eighty feet into the air. Among his many arguments for the project,

Channing had referred to "water as a means of ornament." "Construct fountains in public places," he urged. "Give to the public eye these beautiful objects, and you give tone and purity to the public heart."[45] Evidently Bostonians agreed with him.

DURING the 1840s and early 1850s, Channing engaged in a spate of activities aimed at improving the lives of the poor. He had first encountered the hopelessness and misery of poverty while a student in Edinburgh. It was a human situation for which he was not prepared; in the new American republic it was assumed that most people could and would better their lives. When he returned to Boston, endemic poverty was not yet an obvious social problem. The Overseers of the Poor supervised relief for the "unworthy poor" (homeless men and women who were intemperate, vicious, or chronically unemployed) and for the "worthy poor" (the elderly, widows, orphans, and the sick). Both groups were confined to the Almshouse, where work was required of everyone. Channing's obstetrical practice among the women who gave birth at the Almshouse introduced a measure of reality to his social conscience.[46]

The economic changes that occurred in the following decades produced more urgent problems. Men and women from rural New England and Europe, attracted by jobs in the new mills and factories and in construction of railroads, bridges, and dams, swelled the population. New homes were built for the more affluent classes and there was a growing demand for domestic ser-

Water celebration, Boston Common, October 25, 1848 (courtesy of the Bostonian Society/Old State House)

vants. Included among the newcomers to Boston were thousands of unskilled, uneducated immigrants whose habits and customs were sharply at variance with the traditional way of life among the city's hitherto homogeneous population. Bad housing produced rampant squalor, with several families living in a single, poorly ventilated room and others forced to make do in damp cellars. Inadequate sanitation added to the smells and filth of the streets. Ill-clad children, prostitutes, beggars, and thieves contributed to the realization that an underclass was rapidly changing the city and threatening to destroy its sense of well-being. The economic downturn that followed the Panic of 1837 only made conditions worse.[47]

The differences between rich and poor were clearly visible in the contrast between the spacious homes on Tremont Street, where Walter lived, or on Mt. Vernon Street, where William lived, and the jam-packed rooms in the alleys off Broad Street or the shanties thrown together in swamps and marshland. While the mayor and city council struggled for power with the Overseers of the Poor and the governor and legislature debated the wisdom of taking action, clergymen and private philanthropic groups began to address the problem.[48] Joseph Tuckerman's ministry to the poor was emulated by other clergymen and well-meaning citizens who also walked through squalid neighborhoods, stepped into smelly hovels, comforted malnourished babies, and confronted drunken adults.[49]

Channing was familiar with the same scenes but his analysis of the problem was unusual.[50] Most nineteenth-century reformers, not unlike many who came after them, blamed the poor for their plight. If they were not so lazy, if they were less ignorant, and of course if they gave up alcohol, they could provide for themselves and their families. Channing rejected that position. He refused to join cause with effect, or to view the poor as degraded beings. Pauperism, he insisted, was the consequence of a society whose values, habits, and institutions created the conditions for poverty and perpetuated its existence. Channing was not the only one troubled by the growth of an entrepreneurial society, with its emphasis on material values and competition, but few argued that contemporary Boston was to blame for the large numbers of paupers struggling to live in its midst. Whereas Emerson and the Transcendentalists urged improvement of the individual, and Ripley, Alcott, and other utopians tried to fashion ideal communities in remote settings, Channing sought to change the attitudes and institutions of the upper and middle classes.[51] In a long lecture, delivered in 1843 at the annual meeting of the Boston Society for the Prevention of Pauperism, Channing expounded his critique.[52]

"We have left the old and well-beaten track which has for ages carried the inquirer into the causes of poverty . . . that we may look to the social condition which we have so long tolerated, that we may learn if it does not contain in itself, and in its wide and disastrous relations, the whole and true causes of that poverty." First he examined the social institutions and customs that foster exclusivity and "build higher and stronger the partition walls between men." Rich and poor now lived in separate parts of the city. They attended separate churches. Even when the wealthy tried to help, they did not personally visit the poor but distributed their aid through intermediary agents. This remote form of charity meant that the benefactor did not fully understand "the deeper misery of the soul," while at the same time it debased and demoralized the people for whom it was intended.

He also blamed politics for the existence of poverty. This included the bounties and laws that encouraged and protected the production and sale of intoxicating liquor, the national debt and other policies that destabilized the economy and caused unemployment, and the restriction of voting rights that excluded the poor from the political process. By allowing a few to control the political system and by ignoring the needs of the majority of the laboring class, society was encouraging "the production of pauperism." Even the educational system, "in which manual labor, a practical knowledge of farming, or the mechanic arts, forms no part," was at fault.[53]

An unusual, but not unexpected, aspect of Channing's critique was the attention he gave to poor women with families to support.[54] He knew that many worked long hours for small wages that barely met the daily need for food. Should they become seriously ill from their "long and exhausting toil," unemployment, dependency, and pauperism were certain to follow. As evidence he offered "facts from my own personal observation of the effects of over-work, which prove all I say, and I have them from others, professional men, who have witnessed the same results in large masses of laborers."

Channing was an astute critic but he lacked the ability to suggest creative solutions. Improved education and better housing for the poor were standard fare. So was the notion of migration to the western states. Channing described prosperous farms created by "mind and muscle . . . brought into productive action," contrasting them with the crowded conditions and lack of jobs in cities. And whereas he did not blame the poor for their condition, he did urge them to adopt habits of frugality and self-reliance that would prevent pauperism. These were of course a reflection of his personal ethos and that of his own social class.[55] His distrust of cities and nostalgia for the simplicity of rural life were also common themes in American culture during this period of rapid social change.

For the truly destitute part of society, the penniless, orphans, homeless children and feeble elderly, the sick, the maimed, and the insane, he recommended the House of Industry. He had visited this recently constructed version of the Almshouse and felt sufficiently optimistic to praise its "ample acres, its pure air, and bright sunlight about it, sheltering, and comforting poverty, in all its kinds, and characters." Despite his criticism of the walls separating the social classes, he ended up approving the removal of the indolent from the temptations of sin and crime and the forced employment of those who would not work otherwise.[56]

Nonetheless, Channing remained faithful to his own values. The ultimate solution to poverty lay in recognition of the "great truth of the essential identity in all men of moral and intellectual power . . . the same spirit . . . the same capacity for all development and the same capacity for the highest reaches, and growth, in heaven. . . . It is in the true recognition of a spiritual brotherhood, that the poor are to be brought into the great human family."

Channing had prepared a much longer lecture than could be delivered in the forty minutes allotted to him. The audience was small and he was preaching to the converted. Receipts from the collection box passed at the conclusion of the meeting yielded $27.23. Undeterred by the small collection and encouraged by his associates, he decided to publish the entire address.[57] It came to more than eighty-four pages, for he had read widely on the topic and included many references. Its staccato phrases and convoluted prose suggest that his thoughts simply poured from his pen. But no one could doubt his sincerity. As he confessed many years later, "I do not remember a day in my varied life when I was not able to minister to the wants of the poor, and that fact in my life's history . . . has been the source of the best and most enduring happiness of my long life."[58]

And minister to their wants he did. For the next ten years, he was closely involved with several small organizations whose benevolent activities were inspired by the religious and social predispositions of their members. From 1843 to 1848 he was president of the Boston Employment Society, one of several charitable organizations working to alleviate poverty through job placement.[59] In addition to finding "labor for the poor man," the society sought "masters to educate and train indigent, unruly, vagrant, and orphan boys."[60] It also attempted to expose the false advertisements of the Intelligence Offices that lured unsuspecting people from rural areas to Boston with promises of jobs and riches, thereby swelling the numbers of unemployed. In five years, 8,602 men applied to the society for help and 2,963 were placed, an indication of the difficulty many well-intentioned reformers faced.

It was particularly difficult to assist the Irish, who lacked employable skills and, as the society itself acknowledged, were victims of prejudice. They were deemed to be almost uncivilized, "due to want of humanizing stimulants driven by oppression and starvation," and deficient in ordinary intelligence, despite "strong hands, and generally good hearts." Nonetheless, the society wanted to help, especially since the new arrivals might otherwise become nuisances to the community. Their attitude toward immigrant Irish, cruel as it seems, was better than that of most other Bostonians, who had nothing positive to say about them.[61] When the Employment Society became part of the Society for the Prevention of Pauperism, Channing served for many years as a director of that organization.[62]

The Boston Society for Aiding Discharged Convicts also attracted his attention. He was president for seven years, giving generously of his time and money.[63] His associates were some of Boston's prominent Unitarian reformers, including Samuel Gridley Howe and John A. Andrew.[64] The society aimed to prevent recidivism by providing ex-prisoners with housing, employment, and loans. It succeeded reasonably well in a difficult environment where ex-convicts were automatically looked upon with suspicion. Nonetheless, the society managed annually to assist around a hundred men seeking its advice and aid. A plan to create a temporary residence for recently released prisoners was rejected by the Committee of Public Charities as "inexpedient and a hazardous experiment."[65]

A more unusual attempt to combat poverty was the work of a small group that called itself the Committee on the Expediency of Providing Better Tenements for the Poor.[66] Channing's brother-in-law Stephen H. Perkins was a member, along with the Reverend Charles F. Barnard, Dr. Henry I. Bowditch, Channing, and three others. They had been asked to consider the issue by the members of the Warren Street Chapel, where Barnard, a Unitarian minister and disciple of William Ellery Channing, conducted his ministry to the poor.

The committee gathered information from England as well as from other American cities and concluded that Boston had almost as many people per acre, more inhabitants per dwelling unit, and greater childhood mortality than the major industrial cities of Britain. Moreover, rents were higher in Boston than elsewhere. Poor housing was blamed for many social evils, especially higher incidence of illness and mortality. Not surprisingly, the worst effects were found among the Irish immigrants, where 61.66 children per 100 died before the age of five![67]

The report offered an explanation of disease reflecting the medical theories of Channing and Bowditch. It quoted Boston's superintendent of burials: "the influx of unacclimated foreign immigrants, and the great number of families crowded into the houses in . . . densely populated parts of the city, render the air very impure, and expose the infants, who are compelled to breath [sic] it to disease and death. The influences of such circumstances are not confined to the places where they exist, but they are extended to the population in the neighborhood; and epidemics are generated which are no doubt injurious to the general health of the city."[68] The committee also pointed out that, just as excessive crowding was detrimental to the health of the poor, it also affected their moral nature, which "gradually accustoms itself to the sight of evil."

Channing and his associates proposed construction of a large number of rental apartments, to be located in areas where immigrants were working or could find jobs. Financing would come from private investors rather than "charitable subscriptions." They provided estimates of the cost of land and construction and of potential rents that would make such investments attractive. The planners were confident that tenants would pay their rent punctually if they received full value for their money. To make sure the apartments were adequate, the committee also provided detailed suggestions about outhouses, coal bins, number of rooms, height of buildings, heating, and ventilation.

They also recommended the experiment for its social effects. In phrases reminiscent of Channing's *Address on Pauperism*, they pointed out that there would be no risk of "collateral injury such as in many forms of charity goes so far to offset the more obvious benefits." The poor would not be degraded and there might be "a more healthy kind of intercourse between them and the rich; by which each might see more of the good qualities of the other, and the existing process of estrangement be at least checked." There is no indication of a response to their proposal. It nonetheless demonstrated recognition by nineteenth-century reformers of an intransigent social problem that remains unsolved.

Channing was a meliorist, hopeful that the sincere efforts of good men and women would eliminate the worst problems of poverty. His goal was a harmonious society, physically healthy and spiritually strong, embodying the habits and mores he valued in his own life. To that end, he was greatly concerned for the welfare of that segment of the working class referred to as mechanics. These were the artisans, craftsmen, and small manufacturers whose products provided the basis for a commercial economy.[69] It was already apparent that the growing system of large-scale manufacturing would severely affect their future.

Channing's primary access to this group was through the Mechanic Apprentices' Library Association, which encouraged the education and moral improvement of young workingmen.[70] Formed in 1820 under the auspices of the Massachusetts Charitable Mechanic Association, the Apprentices' Library Association sought to equip the young men "for responsible positions in life" by offering lectures, instruction in elocution and debating, and a library that eventually held three thousand books.[71] Many notables spoke at their meetings, including William Ellery Channing, whose 1840 lecture "On the Eleva-tion of the Laboring Classes" enunciated his views on the importance of work and the necessity for education and self-improvement. Ralph Waldo Emerson's lecture the following year, "Man the Reformer," is one of his best-known es-says.

Walter addressed the apprentice mechanics on two occasions, in 1845 and ten years later, in 1855.[72] His first lecture, titled "My Own Times, or 'Tis Fifty Years Since," began with a history lesson, albeit history subjectively interpret-ed. He wanted to impress the young men in his audience with the significance of the Revolutionary War, "a civil war which tore the colony from the mother country, the child from the arms of the parent," and with the importance of Washington and the other heroes whose leadership in war and peace had en-sured the success of the new nation.

Drawing on childhood memories, he vividly described the first president's visit to Newport and his friendship with his father. Channing also talked about his grandfather, who "received from Washington an important and responsible office . . . and held his office under five successive presidents." The nostalgia extended to recollections of his Newport boyhood, when there was strict disci-pline in family, church, and school and authority was respected—an old ploy when instructing the next generation. Nor did he omit praise for the old ap-prenticeship system, which built character and "rendered the young man a more accomplished mechanic."

Channing's history lesson included comments on more recent events. He had nothing but disdain for contemporary politics and the partisan strife that had replaced the initial harmony. However, his discourse concluded with ex-travagant praise for the "age of reform," the age in which the young men listen-ing to his words were living.

> I have hope, and I have profound faith in my age, in your age, in this country's age. It is an age of moral and spiritual life. . . . The hard crust which has slowly gathered over the soul, the heart of man, of society, is swelling and heaving with the living fires below. When I look around me, I am reminded by the signs of the times, of those regions of extinct volcanoes, which lie barren and desolate. . . . But the internal fires are not put out. They are getting nearer and nearer to the surface . . . and in some places they are already gleaming through the surrounding darkness. . . . Who does not rejoice in the promise of a brighter, better day—in the coming of that glorious king-dom in which dwelleth righteousness?

Social reform, particularly the causes to which he was committed—peace, temperance, antislavery, and concern for the poor—were harbingers of that glorious day.

It was a talk intended to enlighten and energize an audience that would not have known the leaders and events of Channing's "own times." He exhorted his youthful listeners to "study the universal tradition of humanity" as well as "the tradition of your epoch and of your nation. . . . You must be not only MAN, but a man of your age, you must also act as well as speak." It was his fervent hope they would recognize their duty to society and respond to its demands with reverence for God and love for humanity.

Over the years Channing continued to meet with the Mechanic Apprentices and to encourage their efforts at self-improvement. He contributed books to their library and took particular delight in his friendship with young men so different from his students and colleagues.[73] His second lecture, titled "The Law of Compensations," was more obtuse. Emerson had published his essay "Compensation" some fifteen years previously, but the only similarity between the two addresses was that one word. Emerson spoke of compensation as a universal principle of balance that transforms evil, pain, and sorrow into goodness, virtue, and truth.[74] Channing applied the notion of compensation to fields as diverse as geography, astronomy, physiology, and politics, and to topics as varied as the peacefulness of death, the sympathetic qualities of women, and the horrors of warfare. It was at best a demonstration of his personal confidence in human reason, and if he confused the young men in his audience, they should at least have departed feeling confident in their capacity to improve their lives.[75]

CHANNING'S reputation for seeking to better "the moral state of mankind" was nowhere more apparent than in his response to the calls for universal peace that were part of the general clamor for reform. "Peace," he believed, "is the ground principle of religion . . . the object of the coming of Christ . . . the common bond uniting into one great whole all true reforms."[76]

One of the earliest and most unusual advocates for peace was his professor Benjamin Rush, who once proposed a cabinet-level Peace Office to counterbalance the influence of the War Department. The Massachusetts Peace Society, created in 1815 largely through the efforts of Noah Worcester and other Unitarian ministers, including William Ellery Channing, relied on lectures, sermons, and tracts to convince the public that warfare was antithetical to the fundamental teachings of Jesus and intolerable among Christian nations. The movement had its national organization in the American Peace Society, created in 1828. There were also close associations with pacifists in Europe.[77]

Despite its appeal to utopians like the Channings, the peace movement was not widely accepted. Compulsory arbitration of international disputes was an esoteric concept for most Americans. Nor was any policy that abandoned the expansion of the nation's borders destined for great popularity. Ironically, those who were attracted to the cause quarreled among themselves about the degree of change they thought necessary to achieve their aims. Conservatives within the movement sought to preserve its public image by concentrating on the prevention of offensive wars among nations. The moderates opposed offensive and defensive wars. The most radical preached nonresistance to all forms of violence and elimination of all political and societal restraints on individual freedom.

Channing did not bother with these fine points. His commitment flowed from the negative effects of war on individuals and on nations and from his desire that Christ's message might find acceptance throughout the world. His role in the movement was as an advocate rather than an activist.[78] In 1844 he delivered the major address at the annual meeting of the American Peace Society. Though he was a substitute for the original speaker, he readily accepted the chance to share his thoughts on a topic about which he had strong opinions. He had been mulling it over for a long time and had no difficulty getting his thoughts on paper. So certain was he of the rectitude of his ideas, he refused to alter the manuscript for publication despite criticism from some of the press.[79]

It was an emotional address with histrionic overtones. Perhaps his poetry readings within the family circle and his love for the theater stimulated the vivid images with which he condemned centuries of warfare and glorified peace. War, he said, has its origins in the unchristian, unmanly spirit of those who prepare for it and allow it to happen. Without this spirit, war "would moulder in the long peace,—the everlasting reign of manly, noble, heroic love. The grass would again wave over the walls of your island-fort, yonder, or the ocean surge would cover its battlements again, with the ancient, lately disturbed sand. The requiem of the soft-rolling wave would there woo the weary sea-bird to rest, or the ocean storm tell of its harmless power. How majestic, how sublime, the movements of nature, in the mightiest displays of the divine power! We hear them in the voice of God, and man is still!"

Channing buttressed his argument with multiple examples from history and contemporary politics and with acerbic descriptions of military recruitment and training that he hoped would dissuade young men from enlisting. Channing's ardor for peace conflicted with his equally passionate opposition to slavery and, as the nation became increasingly belligerent during the antebellum decades, it became difficult for him to face the growing political crisis.

He was not the only one in Boston who faced a dilemma over slavery, at least in the early part of the antislavery crusade. Many thoughtful people, William Ellery Channing among them, knew that human bondage was wrong, but they were alarmed by the threat to an orderly society and the danger to national union implied by the fiery rhetoric of abolitionists such as David Walker and William Lloyd Garrison, who demanded an immediate end to slavery.[80] Other Bostonians, whose interests made them staunch advocates of property rights, were sympathetic to the property rights of slaveholders. Still others were overt or covert racists opposed to freedom for black men and women. But the overwhelming reason for an unwillingness to confront the issue of slavery was the dependence of New England's economy on a steady supply of southern cotton for its textile mills and on southern markets for its manufactures.

None of this affected Walter's position. His concern for the oppressed and belief in the common humanity of all men and women made him a natural opponent of slavery. This antipathy was additionally strengthened by fond memories of the black servants who had cared for him as a child and of grandfather William Ellery's vigorous aversion to the slave trade.[81] Nor did he mind being outside the mainstream. Though his role in abolition was minimal, no one among his family, friends, or colleagues could misunderstand his views.

Passage of a tariff bill favoring southern interests brought this expostulation: "Slavery is triumphant—! and cotton mills shake a little! . . . they might all tumble down in their shake, could they but take slavery with them."[82] Proposals for extension of slavery into the western territories infuriated him, as did the neighbors who did not share his anger. When the Mexican War grabbed headlines, he refused to permit newspaper reports of "that folly and sin" into his house. The hostilities were an insult to his pacifist beliefs as well as to his antislavery views.[83]

Channing publicly voiced his opposition to slavery on several occasions. In 1842, at the Grand Convention of Freemen called to protest the arrest of George Latimer, an escaped slave who had been living in Boston for several years, he made an impromptu speech, inspired by "the holy purpose of the day." His remarks were enthusiastically received by the audience. After successfully mediating a procedural dispute that threatened to disrupt the meeting, he was invited to preside over the next session but, because he expected to be called to the bedside of a patient, he declined.[84]

His reputation as a spokesman against slavery led to an invitation from Concord to take part in a ceremony commemorating the tenth anniversary of emancipation in the British West Indies. Ralph Waldo Emerson was to be the main orator, but several others, including Channing, were asked to make addi-

tional remarks and thus "give to *freedom* its mighty cheer." To his disappointment, it rained and he decided it would not be worthwhile to travel the twenty
miles from Boston to Concord. Unfortunately, he misjudged the zeal of the
women who organized the event and quickly arranged to move the celebration
indoors.[85]

Two years later, in 1846, Channing participated in a meeting at Faneuil
Hall that honored the memory of Charles T. Torrey, a minister who had helped
runaway slaves escape to Canada. Torrey had been repeatedly arrested and was
finally imprisoned in Virginia. His death from mistreatment by his jailors
caused a furor among Boston abolitionists, who arranged for his burial at Mt.
Auburn Cemetery. Channing was asked to read a poem written for the occasion by James Russell Lowell.[86] Again his dramatic talents served well as he
declaimed:

> Woe worth the hour when it is crime
>   To plead the poor dumb bondsman's cause,
> When all that makes the heart sublime,
> The glorious throbs that conquer time,
>   Are traitors to our cruel laws!

There were five more verses to be recited before he concluded,

> God doth not so bring round his ends
> But waits the ripened time, and sends
> His mercy to the oppressor's heart.

Despite the enthusiasm of the participants, none of these events attracted
a large audience, for Boston was still ambivalent in its antislavery sentiments.
Controversy at the medical school about the admission of black students was
an additional sign that Channing was out of step with many associates, including his faculty colleagues. In the fall of 1850, three "colored men" were admitted to the lectures.[87] Two were sponsored by the Massachusetts Colonization
Society, an affiliate of the American Colonization Society that had founded
Liberia as a homeland for ex-slaves. They were expected to serve as physicians
in that African outpost after completing their studies. The third was Martin
Delany, who had studied medicine as an apprentice to physicians in Pittsburgh
but wanted the professional advantages of an academic degree. Early in December, the faculty received a series of written protests signed by a large group
of students who claimed that the presence of blacks was "highly detrimental
to the interests, and welfare, of the Institution of which we are members, cal-

culated alike to lower its reputation in this and other parts of the country, to lessen the value of a diploma from it, and to diminish the number of its students."[88] The students wanted the blacks dismissed.

Initially the faculty was unwilling to acquiesce to their demands. On December 17, they voted not to revoke their arrangement with the Colonization Society, asserting that anyone who had purchased tickets for the lectures was entitled to attend them. Channing suggested the faculty seek advice from the president and Fellows of the Harvard Corporation, but his recommendation was rejected. Student protest continued and the matter was reconsidered. Unwilling to arouse public disfavor, the faculty capitulated. On a resolution that it was "inexpedient, after the present course, to admit colored students to attendance on the medical lectures," Drs. Bigelow, Jackson, Holmes, and Bigelow, Jr., voted in the affirmative. Only John Ware and Channing voted against dismissal.[89] The three black men departed.[90]

Passage of the Fugitive Slave Law in 1850 and the Kansas-Nebraska Act in 1854 heightened Channing's opposition to southern political and economic power. He feared "despotism in America," and declared his "passionate dislike for the stranglehold" exerted by the three-fifths rule.[91] Many people who had been lukewarm on slavery were shaken by the threat to free soil and free labor in the western territories. Channing's daughter Barbara, unalterably opposed to slavery, was one of many who found an answer in the platform of the newly emerging Republican party. Others, already active abolitionists, abandoned their earlier commitment to nonviolence.

When another escaped slave, Anthony Burns, was caught and jailed pending extradition to Virginia, a mob attacked the courthouse in an attempt to free him. One of the instigators of the action was the Reverend Thomas Wentworth Higginson, who had married Channing's daughter Mary. Both Mary and her father had encouraged Higginson's commitment to reform as well as his alignment with the liberal wing of Unitarianism.[92] Initially an advocate of moral suasion and peaceable protest, Higginson was among those who had become increasingly radical.

A courthouse guard was killed in the assault. Higginson was charged with being part of a mob assembled "to disturb the peace . . . riotously beset and attack the Court House . . . break the glass in the windows . . . force in and break open one of the doors of said Court House . . . fire and discharge sundry fire-arms . . . and . . . utter loud outcries and hurrahs."[93] Channing put up bail for his son-in-law, although as a pacifist he was dismayed by Higginson's conduct.[94] After more legal proceedings, Anthony Burns was shipped back to Virginia.[95] Procedural complications prevented Higginson from ever coming to trial. He became even more of an extremist and subsequently made two trips to assist the beleaguered antislavery settlers in Kansas. Two years later, he was one of the "Secret Six" who financed and abetted John Brown's raid at Harper's Ferry and befriended Brown's wife.

Channing, on the other hand, was disgusted by the bloodshed. "I am a non-resistant," he declared.[96] When the war finally came he did his best to pretend it did not exist. Though other pacifists managed to overcome their principles, he bitterly decried "this most wretched Christ & God denying war."[97] He blamed the politicians for the debacle, just as he blamed them for causing poverty and other social evils. He had not voted in a presidential election since 1840. The victor then was William Henry Harrison, who died after thirty days in office. "Would that some of his successors, nay, all of them, had reigned no longer," was Channing's final word on presidential power.[98] The weariness of advancing years, a nation split apart, and the growing toll of dead and wounded made him more cynical and more quirky than ever.[99]

His son-in-law relished the war. Higginson served as an officer in one of the Massachusetts regiments until he was offered command of the first unit of former slaves incorporated into the army. Higginson enjoyed every moment of that experience.[100] Yet Channing admonished him with a reminder of God's refusal to allow King David to build the temple in Jerusalem: "Thou art a man of war, and sheddest man's blood. Thou shalt not build a temple to my name."[101] Higginson had fairly well abandoned his clerical career in favor of literature and politics, but he cannot have been pleased by the disapproval of his father-in-law.

Nor did Channing have confidence in Lincoln, who, in his view, did not live up to the standards of his Federalist heroes. Lincoln, he wrote to his daughter Mary, could not be an effective wartime president because he had never participated in a war! Consistency was not one of Channing's strong points. Nonetheless, when Lincoln was assassinated, Channing composed one of his most poignant verses:

> *Within a month! How soon he died!*
> *The echo was not over*
> *Of the artillery's roar.*
> *The wide welcome of a nation's pride.*

> *Poor, heart-torn land, thy honored son*
> *Upon thy altar laid*
> *Himself, thy cause to aid.*
> *His noblest offering for thy benezon* [sic].

We were not worthy such a head.
   He died a sacrifice
   And in his grave he lies
Safe from the faithless living, with the dead.

Now ever honored chief, farewell!
   I mourn thy sudden fall.
   My tears endew thy pall.
Let history's ample page thy story tell.[102]

Chapter 11

"Action of a Man's Whole Nature," 1840–1854

Time makes itself. The more a man does, the more a man can do.

—Walter Channing, "Retrospectus"

D ESPITE his occasional complaints of ennui, Channing's life bustled with activity. He had multiple professional duties: daily medical practice, lectures at the medical school, publications on medical topics, and professional meetings. And there were many commitments of a more personal nature: social reform, Unitarian affairs, literary compositions, and continuous interchange with friends and family. How did he do it? "Be only alive early every day, winter and summer, the sleepy Sunday mornings—every morning between 4 and 5 o'clock," he advised. "Go to your professional work at nine and you get about five hours to use of which other men know nothing. If you take in a newspaper, which I do not, never read it til after dinner—my toilette is never elaborate beyond reason or need and my hasty breakfast is soon dispatched."[1]

The early hours were often spent writing and reading. As a member of the Boston Athenæum, a well-stocked private library, he had access to a wide array of publications. Channing was an omnivorous if eclectic reader: the Gospel and contemporary religious works, American and foreign medical journals, history and biography, literary classics, and pamphlets concerning social issues. He read carefully, agreed or argued with the authors, noted passages he wanted to remember, and referred to them in speeches, publications, and correspondence.

He also claimed to make time by neglecting the clubs, parties, dinners, balls, and regular exchange of visits considered de rigueur in Boston society. Nor did he waste many days on vacation and travel, though most of his colleagues took long summer holidays. Some, such as John Collins Warren and Jacob Bigelow, made extensive journeys to Europe. Channing was seldom out of town. Except for professional consultations within New England, a few visits to Newport, and a week in the White Mountains of New Hampshire, until he was finally persuaded to visit Europe in 1852 he remained fixed "in this to me very dull city of Boston."[2] With habitual self-pity, he felt he was "living a hermit like life," giving little pleasure to others.[3]

Though he still portrayed himself as lonely and may well have avoided high society, Channing was no more solitary than he had ever been. He was a frequent guest of friends and family, crossing the river to dine in Cambridge with old acquaintances such as Jared Sparks, who had become president of Harvard, or with the Edward Channings.[4] He maintained a warm relationship with the Perkinses in Brookline and the Wainwrights in Roxbury, and was often in their company. Nephews and nieces were welcomed to the house on Tremont Street, where lively conversation partly compensated for a spartan table. Friends unexpectedly stopped by, inviting him to dine, and he in turn made impromptu visits, often at teatime, to his neighbors or relatives. Though he described himself as abstemious, and perhaps at home he was, many meals out and much rich food occasionally led to indigestion.[5] In his later years, he seems even to have abandoned teetotalism. It is no wonder that friends sought his company, for though he referred to his gloomy, sad existence, those who knew him socially and professionally saluted him as a man born for fun. His exuberant vivacity, humor, and irrepressible gaiety were legendary.[6]

These inconsistencies indicate what a complicated man he was. Channing's mind encompassed many ideas as it moved from religion to literature to science and medicine, producing an erratic, sometimes contradictory image. After Eliza's death, the permanent absence of a confidant reinforced his longstanding belief that he had no one to depend on, driving him further within himself. Emotional tension brought on by family problems led to periods of despondency. "I have been brought thus far on in life, under a discipline which has often been stern, & sometimes very sad," he lamented in a letter to a friend.[7] By his sixties, he was beginning to refer to himself as an old man, to yearn for an end to his weary labors, and to anticipate the "rest of the people of God."[8] His forecasts were decidedly premature, for there were many productive years still ahead. But having seen so much death in his family and his profession, he did not expect he would live to be ninety. The sadness would invariably dissipate, and vigor would return as his natural enthusiasm and his romantic sensibility exerted their effect. Beneath the morose words and thoughts was a warm and gentle man who bore heavy burdens throughout a long life.

One of the heaviest of those burdens was Ellery, a persistent worry as well as a permanent enigma. Now in his early twenties, unwilling, or unable, to focus his interests and talents, he continued to wander from place to place, sometimes engaged in social intercourse, more often quite solitary. Intrigued by tales of fertile land in the west, he joined distant relations in Illinois, purchased 160 acres, spent a few months contemplating a farmer's life, and then quickly abandoned the scheme. He turned up next in western Massachusetts, where he stayed long enough to woo Kate Sedgwick, a daughter of Charles and Elizabeth Sedgwick, with whom Lucy Channing had lived as a pupil of Mrs. Sedgwick. Kate found Ellery an amusing companion but decided he had "a queer brain," and she did not reciprocate his overtures.[9] Sometimes his father knew where he was; more often he did not.

Despite his vagabond existence, Ellery continued to write poetry and gained a champion in Ralph Waldo Emerson, who thought "his lines betray a highly poetical temperament and a sunny sweetness of thought and feeling." Emerson also recognized that, by ignoring the rules of spelling and grammar and neglecting to revise and polish his lines, Ellery often came close to abusing poetic license.[10] But he was sufficiently impressed by the promise of "inward music" and "authentic inspiration" to send some of the poems to Margaret Fuller for publication in the *Dial*, the new quarterly that, for a brief time, captured the essence of transcendentalism.[11] Ellery's father should have been pleased by his son's modest success, especially since he had literary aspirations himself, but if he was, Ellery's strange behavior was a more compelling influence on their relationship.

By February 1841 Ellery was in Cincinnati, where his uncle James Perkins was a minister for a small group of Unitarians, as well as a schoolmaster and minister to the poor.[12] Ellery began to study law but speedily recognized that it did not suit him. He tried journalism with more success, and assisted with Perkins's charitable work. In August he met Ellen Kilshaw Fuller, another Bostonian, two years younger than he, who had just arrived in Cincinnati. They were immediately and passionately attracted to one another, announced their engagement quickly thereafter, and were married in less than two months.

Ellen, like Ellery, had left Boston seeking work and independence in the west and had come to Cincinnati after months of wandering, in her case, from Kentucky to New Orleans and back to Ohio. She had several teaching positions along the way and hoped for pupils at James Perkins's school. She too came from an illustrious family. Her father had held various posts in Massachusetts state government and had served in the U.S. Congress; unlike the Channings,

Ellery Channing (courtesy of Judith C. Marriner)   Ellen Kilshaw Fuller Channing (courtesy of
Willard P. Fuller, Jr.)

he suffered serious financial losses, and his death in 1835 left the family impoverished. Ellen's older sister Margaret, intellectual extraordinaire, literary
critic, teacher and journalist, editor of the *Dial*, friend and confidante of Emerson and the transcendentalist circle, personified antebellum feminism by pro-
posing that women should live freely and independently, neither controlled by
nor subordinate to men.[13] Ellen was not as well educated or brilliant as Margaret and she did not share her sister's feminist ideology, but she had other
feminine qualities that her sister lacked—beauty and charm. Ellery thought
she had "the deepest, surest, strongest character" he had ever known and believed he had found the security he longed for. With uncharacteristic candor,
he revealed that Ellen "loves me so much, so deeply, so truly, that I feel, a
homeless wanderer so long, in her arms that I am under the shelter as of a
wide-spreading tree."[14]

News of their intention to marry caused a great stir in Boston. Ellery's
sisters put their best gloss on the situation, hoping that Ellen would be a good
influence on him. Mary told friends that Ellen's love "will help to bring in play
latent power, which he has never had sufficient motive before for bringing in
action." Barbara expected her to provide the "constant & tender companionship" Ellery so badly needed.[15] Walter wrote a letter to the engaged couple that

was "full of kindness" for Ellen.[16] But word quickly got out that the sisters and their father felt dreadful about the engagement. Well they might: among other things, it was a scandalous breach of etiquette to decide to marry without prior approval of both families. In this case such a step was even odder, since neither Ellery nor Ellen had any money and they would be dependent on an allowance from his father.[17] Margaret Fuller made no secret of her reaction to "a connexion . . . so precipitately formed" and wrote Emerson that she felt "overshadowed by it as by a deep tragedy that I foresee but, as if in a dream, cannot lift my hand to prevent."[18] Little did she know how prophetic were her sentiments.

No one could prevent the wedding.[19] Perkins thought Ellen was "suffering the practical results of—what I can only call Emersonianism,—as it presents itself to young minds and hearts.—She has felt a divine inspiration to marry Ellery, and at once; she has tho't it true womanly virtue to act out her feelings and impulses,—not to thwart her nature."[20] If Uncle James was correct in his evaluation of Ellen, it was most certainly a marriage of kindred souls.

There was another close resemblance. Like Barbara Perkins Channing, the mother-in-law she never knew, she was frail and frequently unwell, with symptoms suggestive of rheumatic illness and lung disease. She often complained of neuralgia, painful vision, and recurrent paroxysms, as Barbara had done during her short life. Neither Barbara nor Ellen was unique to her generation. Rheumatic fever and tuberculosis were leading causes of morbidity and mortality throughout the nineteenth century, yet the similar symptoms of Ellery's mother and his wife, coupled with the pain Ellery had borne since the death of his mother, suggests not only that he was repeating his father's pattern, but that he had found in Ellen the mother he needed. Subsequent events would pose similar questions.

Shortly after their marriage Ellery and Ellen returned to Boston, where his father and sisters received them warmly. They settled in Concord, the town west of Boston that was home to Ralph Waldo Emerson, Henry David Thoreau, and other literary figures. For a brief time it seemed an idyllic life for the newlywed couple. Ellery had the companionship of Emerson and Nathaniel Hawthorne; Thoreau became his closest friend. Sam Ward, a loyal admirer from their student days at Round Hill, subsidized publication of a small book of his poetry, while Margaret Fuller and Emerson saw to it that additional poems and some prose pieces appeared in the *Dial*. Ellen was kindly accepted by her neighbors, had a few private pupils, and was content.

Their first child, Margaret Fuller Channing, was born in May 1844.[21] Ellery was unable to face the responsibility or to deal with the commotion a fretful baby brings to a household and took off for the White Mountains. It was a pattern that would be repeated in subsequent pregnancies and was aggravated by persistent poverty, Ellen's feeble health, and Ellery's increasing irascibility.[22] He could not work steadily at anything that paid, shunned helping around the house, and became ever more abusive of Ellen and the children.

Throughout, Ellery's family remained supportive. Ellen lived with them on several occasions and the children spent weeks at a time with their aunts and grandpapa. Barbara was a frequent visitor to Concord, often for long periods when Ellen desperately needed her assistance with babies, cooking, and other household chores. After Mary's marriage in 1847 to her cousin Thomas Wentworth Higginson, he too tried to help, seeking lecture opportunities for his "brilliant & eccentric cousin & brother-in-law" and counseling Ellen during her moments of despair.[23] Ellen in turn was affectionate with her sisters-in-law and devoted to "father," as she quickly came to call Walter Channing. He provided encouragement when she was overwhelmed by feelings of helplessness and was generous to her and the children.[24] The first son was named for him. But the outlook for Ellery, Ellen, and their ever-increasing brood of children was not encouraging. Nor, by extension, was it reassuring for Walter.

THOUGH the situation in Concord caused chronic anxiety, several deaths in the family created more immediate sorrows. William Ellery Channing, beloved brother and revered uncle, esteemed by most Bostonians and genuinely adored by many of them,[25] died October 2, 1842, in Bennington, Vermont. He had spent the summer in western Massachusetts enjoying the natural beauty of the Berkshires and the sociability of good friends, and he was on his way back to Boston when detained by illness.[26] The diagnosis was typhoid fever. Walter was summoned and hastened to the Walloomsac Inn, where William lay weak and feverish.

It was a memorable reunion, more tender and affectionate than any previous encounter between them.[27] As Walter approached the bed and took his brother's hand, William raised his eyes and asked Walter to kiss his forehead. Walter had recently complained that the Channings were "a timid" family, too sensitive to express their real feelings for each other.[28] Now he was face to face with the most ethereal, least forthcoming of the brothers, who was offering the love Walter longed to share. He received the welcome as if William were blessing him.

Over the next several days and nights he remained close by the sickbed. When William was sufficiently strong, they conversed on topics dear to each— the plight of the poor, the absence of self-sacrifice among the rich, and the misplaced emphasis in contemporary society on the accumulation of wealth. Above all they talked about God and faith in his infinite power. Never before had they had such an extended and penetrating exchange. Nor had Walter ever experienced so profoundly the holiness and beauty that William seemed to personify. He saw his brother not as a frail and mortal being, but as a manifestation of the perfection of God and his Son. The holiness of these hours stirred him to try to live as William had done "in the spiritual and the Everlasting," a vow Walter met by more actively helping the poor.

William's condition did not improve, but there did not seem to be an immediate crisis. William's favorite nephew, William Henry Channing, arrived on the scene, enabling Walter to return to Boston, his patients, and his daughters, who anxiously awaited him.[29] William died peacefully six days later. His body was taken back to Boston by railroad for a funeral service at the Federal Street Church and burial at Mt. Auburn Cemetery.

Walter was less deeply affected by the death of his sister Mary the following summer and of his brother Henry a few months later. Mary had married Robert Rogers, a merchant whose recurrent financial difficulties caused much consternation among their relatives. Rogers had died in 1839. There were two children.[30] Walter was fond of his sister and wanted to help but did not know what was appropriate.[31] Little is known about Henry's life. He seems to have had personal problems, emotional, mental, or both. William Ellery Channing had worried about "his singular inconsistencies, a mixture of vanity and want of self respect."[32] His mother supported him while she was alive, and her small legacy was his primary means of support after her death. Henry was a frequent visitor at the house on Tremont Street, where he was welcomed by Walter and his children and often stayed for several months. His permanent residence was in North Bridgewater, a small town south of Boston, where he died of consumption on October 13, 1843.[33] The family was full of remorse once they realized that they could no longer make up for the neglect Henry had received during his lifetime or thank him for many kindnesses to them. They gathered at Walter's house for the funeral and rode out to Cambridge, where Henry was buried near William Ellery Channing and Mary Rogers in the family plot.

The death of Walter's brother-in-law and friend, the artist Washington Allston, brought sorrow to all the Channings.[34] Walter had been studying in Philadelphia when Allston and his oldest sister, Ann, were married. In the summer of 1811, as Walter was returning from Britain, Allston and Ann departed for London, hoping Allston's work would be better appreciated in the cosmopolitan capital than in provincial Boston. Ann's unexpected death in 1815 was a dreadful blow.[35] Allston came back to Boston and eventually married Martha Dana, a sister of Richard Henry Dana, Sr. Walter was a great admirer of Allston's work and owned several canvases and drawings.[36] Many of Allston's contemporaries, as well as later art historians, thought he never achieved his full potential, perhaps because Bostonians did not provide the financial support an artist required, perhaps because he was chronically ill, perhaps because he worked and reworked his canvases incessantly and left major paintings unfinished.

Channing wrote a long obituary of Allston for the *Christian World*.[37] Having known the deceased since his childhood years, he had a treasury of memories to share. His praise for Allston's "genius" was profuse, as was his regret that Boston had not provided an environment more conducive to the success of such a great artist. He tried to convey the honesty and sincerity that were the hallmarks of Allston's character. Though Channing had been overcome with grief while composing the obituary, it was sensitively written with less hyperbole than often appeared in his prose.

The final loss in this series of mournful events was the death of Channing's youngest daughter. Lucy was continually feeble throughout her short life, with frequent attacks of rheumatism, neuralgia, and dyspepsia (indigestion). She was often excitable and could be difficult, eager to get well but depressed by the bleak future before her. Her father and others in the family hovered over her in vain attempts to lessen her pain and cheer her spirits. Aunt Susan recommended the hydropathic cure that had become fashionable in Brattleboro, Vermont. Cousin William Francis Channing, though trained in orthodox medicine, employed mesmerism.[38] Lucy was a willing subject but did not benefit from the experiment. Her father preferred more traditional but equally ineffective treatments, applying blisters and prescribing beef tea, fresh air, and exercise. More important, he tried by a combination of humor and affection to encourage her to enjoy life as best she could.

By the summer of 1847 hope waned. All the signs of terminal consumption were present. Lucy had difficulty eating and suffered continuous pain; after ten weeks in bed she was reduced to a skeleton.[39] Her father hoped she might rally as she had in previous crises, but he was not optimistic. With Barbara and Mary as her nurses, she was moved to rented rooms in Milton, where cooler weather and complete quiet might relieve her discomfort.[40] Instead, her cough became so much worse that Walter feared she would suffocate. He spent Sunday, August 1, with them, then returned to the city, having prescribed laudanum to control the cough. Lucy accepted the inevitable and managed to whisper farewell messages for her father and friends and to comfort her grieving sisters. She lapsed into unconsciousness and, as they had fervently hoped, died peacefully several hours later on Monday morning, August 2.[41]

Walter was simultaneously relieved and heartsick. "The weary one is at rest . . . her blessed soul in Peace," he wrote to Lucy Russel, adding, "He who has not lost a child has not learned what love and death are."[42] Once again, he faced the existential questions about life and death. He had witnessed so much misery—"life in its hunger, its thirst, its nakedness, its prison, its ignorance, its sickness, its suffering, its death"—and now the tragedy of Lucy's brief life, twenty-four years of pain and sorrow. He struggled to make sense of it all and, as before, religion provided the answers. Lucy's life was not without meaning if, as a consequence, he and others learned to transform misery and death into happiness and goodness. "God does not mean to take evil & woe & sin and suffering out of the world, for he has not brought them into it. He means that you and I in an infinite self sacrifice should make the desert blossom as the rose, and our sad and heavy-laden sisters and brothers to smile in the midst of all the inevitable & the miserable."

It was a view of Christianity very different from that of previous generations, who saw evil as a necessary part of the world and the sinfulness of mankind as the cause. Walter firmly believed in "man's agency in the universe of God." He learned from Lucy's death, as he had learned when William died, that he must love others and work for the betterment of society, following as best he could Jesus' teachings and example. It was a perspective that reinforced his already strong commitment to social reform as well as a philosophy that helped him accept the personal misfortunes of his life. It was also consonant with his Unitarian beliefs as they were defined during William's lifetime and as they evolved during the 1840s.

THE anxiety created by the Transcendentalists' rejection of conventional religion and the uneasiness engendered by issues of social reform had major repercussions among Boston's Unitarians. On the right were the economic and political conservatives, fortified by their privileged position in society, opposed to new ideas. On the left were the liberals who found Unitarian churches cold and lifeless, the ministers unimaginative, the worship service uninspiring, and the congregants unreceptive to reform. "Corpse-cold Unitarianism," Emerson called it, and although Unitarianism remained a religion of the heart for some people, many agreed with him.[43] Some, inspired by transcendentalism, gave up religion for philosophy. Some formed utopian communities like Brook Farm, dedicated to principles of simplicity, harmony, and a classless society. A few took dramatic steps in a different direction, abandoning Unitarianism entirely for the rituals and doctrines of Catholicism or Episcopalianism.[44] Still others, like Channing, preferred to remain closer to the mainstream but sought a Unitarian church more hospitable to their progressive ideas.

When James Freeman Clarke returned to Boston in 1840 after seven years spent ministering to a small Unitarian congregation in Louisville, Kentucky, he had little difficulty attracting the attention of people who were dissatisfied with the current scene but not willing to abandon the fundamentals of Unitarian doctrine.[45] Clarke had spent much of his time in the west studying Scripture and refining his religious beliefs. He accepted traditional Unitarian tenets: the existence of a supernatural order with God as its first element; Jesus as the son of God and the son of man, the perfect manifestation of God and the fullest expression of human nature; and miracles as confirmation of the supernatural power of Christ. To these he added ideas inspired by the Transcendentalists: a God found in nature, the value of innate perceptions or intuition, the unity of the world, and the immanence of God in the world. In discussions of his beliefs and his plans for a church, he was encouraged by William Ellery Channing, who had not lost the interest in new ideas and new ways of religious expression that had characterized his own journey in Unitarianism. William enthusiastically recommended the young minister to family and friends who shared his affinity for spiritual growth.[46]

Clarke wanted an inclusive church where any Christian man or woman would be welcome and where the congregants actively participated in the worship service. They would sing the hymns instead of listening to the performance of organist and choir. They would read the psalms and prayers aloud rather than having the minister recite them. Occasionally, lay members might give the sermon. The church he envisaged would not be a formal organization, but a social entity or family with prayer meetings, Bible study, and discussion groups that met during the week. It would be a "free" church of worshipers, sustained by voluntary contributions rather than the fees and rents traditionally charged to pewholders who, by virtue of their ownership of church property, controlled church policy. Its members would make Christianity an active principle in their daily lives, offering love and comfort to one another, providing aid and support to the unfortunate around them. Clarke's biographer characterizes him as holding "a warm vision of man inspired by his noble intuitions, steadily climbing toward spiritual and moral perfection."[47] It was a vision that appealed to Walter Channing.

Late in 1841, Channing attended three sermons in which Clarke explained his ideas for a new and reinvigorated church. He was immediately persuaded and eagerly took part in the planning sessions that followed. Despite the ferment that greeted some of the minister's proposals, Channing seemed happier and more content than ever before.[48] The first social meeting was held at his house on March 16, when the conversation focused on the order of worship.[49] By April there was a coherent group of men and women ready to adopt a simple pledge and give a name to their church: "Our faith is in Jesus Christ, the Son of God, and we do hereby unite ourselves into a Church of his Disciples, that we may co-operate together in the study and practice of Christianity." Clarke's name was first among those who signed, followed by Nathaniel

Peabody and his daughters, Elizabeth, Sophia, and Mary. George G. Channing was next in line, then Mary Channing and Walter Channing. Barbara's name was fifteenth on the list of forty-eight signatures.[50]

Initially, Walter was heavily involved in the Church of the Disciples. He preached at evening meetings and on Sunday if Clarke was ill or away. He was named to a committee appointed to find more suitable space for worship than the public halls in which the congregation had been gathering. The weekly social meetings frequently convened at his house. Discussion topics ranged from accumulation of wealth, luxury, public amusements, and the power of example to sin, the love of God, the resurrection, and the example of Christ.[51] The participants also addressed contemporary issues, asking if the present organization of society was compatible with the requirements of Christianity and whether the existing arrangements of labor and trade were consistent with the commandment to love thy neighbor as thyself. These conversations fed Channing's concern for the plight of the poor and informed his activities on their behalf.[52] Church members were equally sympathetic to his views on temperance, prison reform, and the abolition of slavery.

The new church had its rocky moments, too. There was a brief quarrel about lay preaching. Objections were made to the innovative practice of sermons delivered on the Lord's Day by persons not officially ordained. Channing was bitterly disappointed by the possibility of a return to "poor and dour conventionalisms," for he firmly believed that one of the most important changes had been ending the "ancient, the almost eternal, silence of People." However, fearful for the long-term welfare of the new church, he urged Clarke to abandon this particular reform lest an unbridgeable gulf divide the membership.[53] In time, the issue was resolved and lay preaching continued.

A more serious disruption occurred in 1845. Theodore Parker, minister of the Unitarian church in West Roxbury and a brilliant and eloquent preacher, had greatly offended most Unitarians by his radical views. "Christianity," he claimed, "is a simple thing, very simple. It is pure morality, absolute pure religion, the love of man; the love of God acting without let or hindrance." In his view, everything else, all church forms and rituals, all theological doctrines, including the authority of the Bible and supernatural power of Jesus, are transient and uncertain.[54]

For several years after Parker enunciated his extreme ideas, the other Unitarian ministers in Boston tried to exclude him from church fellowship by refusing to exchange pulpits with him, hoping thereby to silence his ideas. James Freeman Clarke did not agree with Parker, but he believed that Parker should be free to express his views. As the exclusion policy gained strength, Clarke took a bold step, announcing that he intended to exchange pulpits with

Parker. The reaction was swift. A self-appointed committee at the Church of the Disciples urged him to change his mind. When that failed, there were numerous meetings and fierce debates among the entire membership. Clarke maintained that he had the right as pastor to make an exchange and that controversial ideas should be heard. Eventually he prevailed. Parker preached at the Church of the Disciples while Clarke assumed the pulpit at Parker's church. Neither sermon was the least bit inflammatory. However, sixteen members of the Church of the Disciples resigned their memberships as a final act of disapproval. George G. Channing was among them, although he was one of Clarke's close friends, an important leader in Bible study classes, and editor of the *Christian World*, the weekly newspaper founded by Clarke and his followers.[55]

Walter did not leave the Church of the Disciples.[56] He continued to conduct the service if needed and to preside over Bible class.[57] Ellery and Ellen had joined in November 1842 and their two oldest children were baptized by Clarke at Walter's home in 1847. Thomas Wentworth Higginson became a member in 1844, having been introduced by Mary Channing. Their wedding, in September 1847, was celebrated by Clarke, also at Channing's home. Clarke's diaries record numerous pastoral visits to Lucy, Mary, and especially Barbara, who more than any other Channing depended on him for spiritual advice and personal counsel.[58]

Walter had found a spiritual home in the Church of the Disciples.[59] It met his need for friendship and fellowship, reinforced his social concerns, and stimulated his religious nature. "Christianity," he later wrote, "is the most solemn, the sublime fact in the spiritual history of a universe!"[60] He accepted Jesus as the Savior and as the epitome of a perfect life. That was enough for him. He had little interest in the fine points of theology, which in his view served only to separate one Protestant sect from another and ended by destroying the essence of religion. The practical implications of Jesus' example were more important to him. He professed that his duty as a Christian was to eliminate selfish thoughts and deeds from his life, just as his duty as a physician was to eliminate physical maladies from the lives of the sick.

CHANNING found spiritual comfort in the Church of the Disciples and social purpose in reform, but his primary focus was, and always would be, medicine. For one thing, despite the frequency with which he criticized others for their acquisition of wealth, he needed the income his practice provided. His financial obligations could not be neglected. He was responsible for the support of his daughters, for Ellery and his family, to whom he had pledged an annual allowance of four hundred dollars and made additional gifts, and for other members of the family who also turned to him for help. They assumed that as a physician he was wealthier than he in fact was. Also, although he complained about the unpleasant aspects of daily work in "the hot days of summer and cold nights of winter," he was compulsive about serving the patients who continued to rely on him.[61]

Was Channing's renown as a social reformer detrimental to his business? Did he risk offending families whose income depended on the liquor trade or slave products, who belonged to the merchant class or supported military and naval organizations? There is no way to be certain. On the other hand, he did acquire patients among his friends at the Church of the Disciples. For example, he was physician to James Clarke's children and obstetrician for the wife of John Andrew, for whom he also recommended a nurse when the time came for her lying-in.[62] Additionally, he gave time and free medical advice to some of the poor members of the church, occasionally supplementing professional acts with words of spiritual comfort. When a patient asked if there was anything he could offer in addition to a prescription, he recited long passages from the Book of John.[63]

In any case, his practice kept him very busy, so much so that Barbara, who became his housekeeper and sole companion after Mary's marriage, was soon "sick of a Dr.'s life."[64] The growth of the city meant that his patients were more widely dispersed and he was dependent on horse and carriage to reach them. There were also patients who did not live in Boston but whose expectation of a personal visit meant travel to more distant sites such as Providence and Haverhill; the railroad made those journeys possible.[65] His personal interest meant a lot to his patients, since there was often little else he could do. Though physicians were somewhat readier than previously to trust in nature, and he sometimes prescribed less harsh medicine than he had earlier in his career, medical theory had not changed greatly. Most doctors, Channing among them, continued to believe that they must treat the patient, not a specific disease, and that they must understand her entire constitution, her daily habits, and the environment in which she lived in order to make an accurate diagnosis and prescribe the best remedy.[66]

Many hours of his busy life were devoted to writing on medical subjects. Most important were the treatise and papers on anesthesia in childbirth, but there were many other pieces in which he offered his familiarity with uterine disease to instruct less experienced physicians or recommended new texts that he thought were important additions to the field of obstetrics. In three instances he volunteered memorials to deceased colleagues whom he had admired. All of these appeared in the *Boston Medical and Surgical Journal*.[67]

For his friends in the Society for Medical Improvement who had launched the *New England Quarterly Journal of Medicine and Surgery*, the journal in which Oliver Wendell Holmes published his paper on puerperal fever, he prepared an extensive essay on puerperal anemia. Medical bibliographers and historians of obstetrics credit it as the first known description of this disorder.[68] Channing's analysis was based on his observations in seventeen cases and on evidence revealed by autopsy. The first seven cases were not related to pregnancy or childbirth (one patient was male), but the symptoms were similar to those in the puerperal cases. Some of these nonpuerperal patients recovered, leading Channing to ponder the reason for their survival, in contrast to 100 percent fatality among the ten puerperal patients. Was there a connection between anemia and childbirth that made it a different disease?

Channing described "a strange malady which pursued its progress with so little severe suffering, over which medicine had no control, and the end of which was so certain." The common symptoms were white, marblelike skin, colorless lips, blanched tongue and gums. The blood was pink rather than red and the veins were flatter than usual. Some of the patients reported occasional noise in the head, presumed to be caused by cerebral circulation, but had no other distress. Increased heart rate was also common. Postmortem dissections revealed no lesions of the internal organs, but the tissues were bloodless or nearly so. Remedies had included a diet of meat and meat extracts, wine and alcoholic stimulants, and iron sulphate. Except for one case, the disease did not appear until after delivery, in several as much as three weeks later. There had been no excessive blood loss during pregnancy, at delivery, or postpartum.[69]

Anemia, an insufficiency of red blood cells and hemoglobin necessary for the transport of oxygen, can have several causes, including iron deficiency, vitamin deficiency (including folic acid deficiency), blood loss, and underlying disease such as tuberculosis, heart disease, or a peptic ulcer. By Channing's time it had been described in the medical literature but was poorly understood. Channing's contribution was to focus on a set of related cases that appeared subsequent to childbirth and in which all the patients died. In this he was unique. He wondered if the puerperal condition was somehow related to the unexpected onset and fatal outcome of the disease. From the evidence before him he concluded that the problem lay in the process of blood formation. How that related to the physiology of pregnancy and parturition he did not know.[70] In his paper "Notes on Anhæmia," he wrote, "It is the purpose of this paper to show that some connection subsists between the puerperal state and anhæmia, either as to predisposition, cause, or character and tendency of the malady, in order to lead to a more faithful study of the whole subject than it has received."

The paper on anemia shows Channing at his best. From his wide practice and frequent consultancies he had observed a large number of similar cases that suggested questions about anemia and its relation to the puerperal state. His familiarity with the literature provided the substrate for his observations of the disease. His arguments were cogently presented with fewer asides than usual. He distinguished anemia in these cases from anemia that may follow excessive hemorrhaging, from heart disease, and from chlorosis (a form of anemia found in young girls). He did not offer false hopes or propose a treatment other than sustaining the patient as long as possible. He rejected the possibility of blood transfusion, fearing the risk of "filling almost empty vessels with a fluid so unlike that which already circulates in them, and which *their own functions* have produced." Perhaps the risk would be worthwhile if it gained time for resumption of the production of healthful blood, but Channing was unconvinced.

Channing lacked the tools for further investigation. Microscopes had only recently been improved sufficiently to study blood, and there were still no methods available to quantify its components.[71] Nor did he have the training and temperament to do investigative research. During the next century, scientists would develop appropriate techniques and produce the knowledge that led to a better understanding of the relationship of pregnancy to anemia.[72]

Only one other paper written during this period is worthy of attention, not because it was as significant as that on anemia, but because it shows Channing's continuing concern for the health and morals of society. He wrote it for a new journal intended to instruct the general public in "the laws of health" that must be observed for successful living. "Physical Education" explained the damage society suffers when it does not observe the laws of health.[73] In words reminiscent of his article for the *North American Review* on the health of literary men and his lecture in 1829 to the Boston Society for Diffusion of Useful Knowledge, he reiterated his belief in sound physical development as the prerequisite for serious academic study. He also argued for healthy habits and the cultivation of high moral, intellectual, and religious principles on the assumption that they would determine the physical and mental health of the next generation. For instance, Channing urged the avoidance of luxury and indolence to prevent transmission of gout; temperance, prevention of marriages among cousins, and sympathetic attention to the needs of children to interrupt generational predispositions to insanity.

He saved his strongest warning for venereal disease, "which has its growth and continuance in licentiousness, in illicit indulgence. . . . [It] attacks and kills the unborn child. It destroys the life of the young. It appears in later life, in forms, which, having resemblances to other diseases, may escape the popular knowledge, but concerning which, the judicious physician cannot be in doubt." He was surprisingly sympathetic to "the wretched women . . . seduced by money into sin and deemed loathsome and abhorrent to the sense, and to the heart." European nations had enacted legislation to control syphilis by licensing brothels and requiring examinations of prostitutes. Channing was uncomfortable with the moral implications of these laws, though he understood their purpose. He would have preferred to see the community condemn promiscuity, refuse to admit "base and infamous men" to high society, and correct the ignorance that denied the existence of such a terrible scourge. "While such things be," he concluded, "you can do but little to prevent the transmission of the most terrible diseases, and the infliction of measureless misery."

In addition to patient care and medical publications, Channing continued to participate at meetings of the Society for Medical Improvement and to attend the Massachusetts Medical Society. At the medical school, there were monthly meetings of the faculty, during which, as dean, he took the minutes and reported on the occasional administrative duties that went with the position. Lectures continued as they had since he first ascended the podium. When John Collins Warren resigned as Hersey Professor of Anatomy and Surgery at the conclusion of the spring 1847 term, his responsibilities were divided between Oliver Wendell Holmes, who became Parkman Professor of Anatomy and Physiology at the medical school, and Jeffries Wyman, who was named Hersey Professor of Anatomy in Cambridge. Henry J. Bigelow was already Professor of Surgery. The following September Channing resigned as dean and Oliver Wendell Holmes assumed those duties (see Chapter 6).[74] Lucy's death the previous month may have contributed to Channing's decision. When the trial of John W. Webster for the murder of George Parkman heaped scandal and opprobrium on the faculty three years later, Channing was no longer in a position to speak for the medical school or to take much part in the extraordinary events that followed. Yet he could hardly ignore the excitement that swirled around his colleagues and threatened to destroy the reputation of the medical school.[75]

In 1850, following a series of events almost too bizarre to be believed, John White Webster, Erving Professor of Chemistry, a friend and associate who shared Channing's interest in mineralogy, was accused, tried, and executed for the murder of George Parkman, a physician and benefactor whose gift of land enabled construction of the new medical school building and in whose honor the Professorship of Anatomy was named.[76] Parkman was a wealthy and powerful figure in Boston, having abandoned medicine for real estate. His properties included some of the city's worst slums. He had lent money to Webster, an affable, unassuming man who lived in Cambridge with his wife and three daughters and whose expenditures on luxuries for his family and his personal scientific collections were greater than his income. When Webster was unable to repay, Parkman began to hound him, interrupting his lectures, accosting him on the street and in his laboratory, and generally making his life miserable.

Parkman disappeared November 23, 1849. It was known that he had gone to the medical school for an appointment with Webster, but he was not seen thereafter. Days passed and suspicions grew until grisly evidence found in the furnace, stoves, and privy vault beneath White's laboratory revealed parts of a body that had been incinerated or eroded by caustic materials. Only the dental plates and gold fillings provided positive proof that the remains were Parkman's.[77] Webster, the obvious suspect, was arrested.

As the official historian of Harvard Medical School recounted the episode, there followed "a period of grievous mortification and distress for all Harvard Men."[78] Lectures at the medical college were suspended while the premises were searched, and large crowds gathered outside waiting for revelations of the gory discoveries. Henry J. Bigelow accompanied the police as they examined Webster's laboratory and other areas of the building. At the coroner's request, a postmortem examination and identification of the recovered parts were made by several Harvard medical instructors. They also testified at the trial, as did Holmes, Nathan Cooley Keep, and W. T. G. Morton.[79]

Webster continued to profess his innocence, though he did not testify in court. His lawyers relied on character witnesses, including Jared Sparks, president of the university and a Cambridge neighbor of Webster, who described him as an honest, gentle person. Conviction was a foregone conclusion despite the circumstantial nature of the evidence. Webster subsequently confessed that he had asked Parkman to his laboratory on the fatal day to "beg further time and indulgence for the sake of my family." When Parkman vehemently rejected the request, threatening to destroy his career and ruin his reputation, Webster seized a heavy wooden stick and "dealt him an instantaneous blow with all the force that passion could give it." Parkman fell dead upon the floor. Overwhelmed by the horror of the deed and terrified by the possibility of discovery, Webster had used his knowledge of anatomy and chemistry to dispose of the body.

It took a long time for the medical faculty to recover from the Parkman murder. That "a man who has been in the highest walks of society, esteemed as one of the pillars of science, and a professor in Harvard University, the first and oldest institution of learning in America," should commit such a heinous crime was bad enough.[80] That his victim, also a member of the medical profession, should have acted in such an ungentlemanly manner as Parkman had done when seeking repayment added to the shame. The details of mutilation may well have added to popular fears of postmortem examinations and increased suspicions of the medical profession. Five thousand people were reported to have surged into the building when it was opened for the public to view the scene of the crime. Huge crowds fought for seats at the eleven-day trial, which caught the attention of the entire nation. The historian Philip Cash has suggested that the adverse publicity was one reason the faculty was unwilling to fight public opinion later in the year when the admission of black students further threatened the reputation of the school.[81]

Channing received a plaintive letter from Webster asking his old friend to visit him while he was awaiting execution.[82] There is no record of Channing's appearing at the jail but, given his usual kindness and his friendship with the condemned man, perhaps he did. It is even more likely that Channing's opposition to capital punishment made it difficult for him to accept the sentence. Webster was executed by the hangman's noose in the courtyard of the Leverett Street jail, less than half a mile from the medical school, on August 30, 1850.

SINCE boyhood, Channing had spent much of his leisure time writing poetry, and as he slipped into old age he continued to draw pleasure from "lines with rhyming ends." "Apollo our muse is also muse of art, poetry," he explained, referring to the mythological alliance of medicine with the arts to justify his inspiration.[83] In his later years, it was one more way "to fill a lonely hour on time's receding shore," to meditate on the sorrows and joys of life, and to commemorate people and events with special meaning for him. In 1851 he assembled sixty-eight poems in a small book titled *New and Old*.[84] It appeared anonymously, as he did not want to acknowledge his authorship. It was probably just as well, since the poems have little literary value and are noteworthy only because they demonstrate another facet of his personality.[85] Despite his desire for anonymity, he was enormously pleased with his literary efforts.

The poems abound with subjects drawn from nature, "Sunrise," for example, and "A Summer's Day," and images of mountain views and ocean storms. Ballads based on stories of deserted lighthouses, lost children, and unrequited love add a narrative element. More than twenty of the poems were inspired by memories of England and Scotland. Social issues were captured in sonnets on reform, the spirit of war, capital punishment, the almshouse, and the jail.

Many of the themes were personal.

> *What luxury doth lie in Loneliness!*
> *Companionship of silent thought,—the dead!*[86]

Or,

> Would that the God in man in truth would rise,
> Show the Divine in living excellence;[87]

And,

> He who doth others help doth help himself;
> In his used power the revelation find,
> Of treasures far beyond all other pelf[88]

Channing received notes and letters of thanks from friends to whom he had sent the book and was gratified by their kind words.[89] None of the literary critics commented on it, which was probably fortunate.

FOR years, friends and family had been urging Channing to get away from Boston, to put his cares behind him and enjoy new experiences. He regularly procrastinated, pleading that financial responsibilities prevented him from taking a holiday, that his patients could not spare him, or that other professional obligations took precedence. Suddenly, in 1851, his attitude altered. Living in a large house with only Barbara for company was dreary, especially since she was often absent, visiting relatives or helping care for Ellery's family. Moreover, the house needed repairs that would be expensive and inconvenient. He made an unexpected decision: he rented the house and moved to Somerset Street, around the corner from the State House, to board with "attentive and judicious hosts." Boarding out was not unusual. Many highly respectable people found it more convenient than housekeeping and more congenial than being alone. For Channing there was the further inducement of financial gain—he received more income in rent than he paid for lodging.[90]

The time was thus right for travel. Money was less worrisome, Barbara could stay with friends, and he could be away during the long summer months when his classes did not meet. He made elaborate plans for a European tour that took him from Liverpool to Moscow, from Copenhagen to Vienna, from Paris to Madrid, and concluded with a long visit with James Simpson in Edinburgh. James Jackson provided letters of introduction and Jared Sparks penned a recommendation informing foreigners that Channing was traveling for personal pleasure and for opportunities to make scientific observations.[91] He could hardly believe he was going. "My preparations seem to be making for somebody else, not for me," he confessed to Lucy Russel.[92]

He embarked May 12, 1852.[93] In only one respect did this journey replicate his travels in 1810, for again he was distressingly seasick, whether cross-ing the Atlantic Ocean or on the Baltic Sea. This time, however, he gave himself a whiff of chloroform to relieve the worst of his misery. Everything else was new and tremendously exciting. The contrast with his experiences forty years earlier, when he was a young man fresh out of medical school and had limited his travel to parts of England and Scotland, added to his sense of wonder. Europe had changed in forty years and so had he.

The extent of his tour was remarkable and, for the era, unusual. Not many Bostonians ventured as far east as Russia or included Denmark in their itiner-aries.[94] Channing traveled with a courier who made arrangements for transpor-tation and hotels, managed the luggage, and acted as a guide when Channing desired his company. Channing obstinately insisted on second- or third-class travel, to save money, to satisfy his eccentricities, and to have as much expo-sure as possible to the variety of European life. He also avoided guidebooks, preferring to see for himself and make his own judgments. The long summer days at northern latitudes gave extra hours of light and he was out and about, early in the morning and late at night, observing everyone and everything, attentive to the sounds and smells that made the adventure so different from his customary life. He got lost, missed trains, squeezed onto the narrow seats of stagecoaches, and interrogated everyone with whom he came in contact, even when there was no common language. "My every-day life was new," he wrote, "and to an intensity of degree . . . which my somewhat long and varied experience in living had never paralleled."[95]

Among Europe's greatest attractions for Channing were the fine arts. All his life, he had had to restrain his appreciation for art, as there was little opportunity to visit museums or patronize artists in New England. Washing-ton Allston had been a partial substitute, but he could not satisfy what now emerged as a passion. Channing had read about European artists, especially Thorvaldsen, Denmark's most famous sculptor, and Murillo, a renowned painter of the Spanish Baroque. Now he could study their works "at home"; he included Copenhagen and Madrid in the tour to do so. He spent many days at the Louvre and the Hermitage, in castles and palaces, absorbing "the beauty and truth" expressed by centuries of artistic endeavor. Ecclesiastical architec-ture, from the small churches in Austrian villages to the grand cathedrals in Paris and Moscow, was another fascination, despite his heritage of Puritan simplicity.

Channing also noted things he deplored as he made his way across the Continent and back again. One was the emphasis on warfare, seen in monu-ments to fallen heroes, celebrations of military victories, and the continuing traditions of conscription and standing armies. Another was the difficult lives of poor women. He knew from his professional experience how much impoverished American women suffered and could not help observing the same phenomenon in Europe. On farms and in villages women assumed heavy burdens, made more severe because so many men were on military duty. He observed them making hay, binding wheat, and loading carts. He saw them working on the railways and in brickyards. Women even worked as porters, carrying luggage on their shoulders or heads. In an uncharacteristic fashion, he left large tips for Belgian lace makers whom he observed working in silence for small wages, their vision and general health endangered by the intensity of their labor.

As should be expected, Channing devoted a considerable amount of his time to pursuing his medical interests. He had letters of introduction to directors of hospitals and insane asylums, important physicians, and medical professors in every country he visited. Considering how little he had seen of medical institutions in the United States and how limited was his personal familiarity with American medical men, it was an extraordinary opportunity. Hospitals with 1,800 beds offered a remarkable array of diseases. He had long discussions about dry gangrene, scurvy, and pulmonary disease and made extensive inquiries about diagnostic techniques, therapeutics, and rates of cure. He took notes on the minutiae of hospital life, such as the arrangement of beds, patient diet, cleanliness, and nursing. In Russian military hospitals he was sufficiently impressed by the efficiency of daily examinations to recommend the system to his colleagues in Boston. At the maternity hospital in St. Petersburg, he saw "an ingenious apparatus contrived to preserve a uniform temperature for new-born, feeble, or premature babies" unlike anything he knew at home.

In Paris he called on Baron Louis, whose work had so greatly influenced American therapeutics. Channing brought greetings from James Jackson and they reminisced about Jackson's son and the other Americans who had studied medicine in Paris. Louis did not speak English and Channing's poor French "was not so good as [Louis's] whole ignorance," yet their interview proceeded well. Channing attributed the success of his visit to the baron's "native courtesy and kindness" and celebrated his "great privilege to see and to know him."[96]

The large European maternity hospitals were notorious for epidemics of puerperal fever. In Copenhagen he learned that there had been no cases of disease since preventive policies were instituted. Only half the hospital was in use while the other half was being painted, whitewashed, and thoroughly ventilated. Patients were housed in separate rooms that were also cleaned and purified between cases. The Danes had installed a complicated ventilation system to rid the air of any contagion. In Vienna, by contrast, he was told that ventilation had no effect on the spread of fever and that the least clean and less well aired wards also had the least disease. In neither place did he and his hosts discuss Semmelweis's work on puerperal fever, although the Danish physician, identified as Dr. Lever by Channing,[97] and the Viennese, Doctors Arneth and Braun, were familiar with the effectiveness of Semmelweis's prophylactic measures.[98] Nor, as far as we know, did Channing bring Holmes's paper into the conversation.

Channing was impressed by the beneficial results of the Danish procedures, which he attributed to cleanliness of bedding and equipment and to ventilation and purification of the air.[99] He did not realize that the absence of puerperal fever in the less clean, less airy Viennese ward was the result of midwives' delivering patients there, whereas the patients in the other ward were examined and delivered by medical students carrying infectious matter on their hands. Nonetheless, he was prepared to advocate the preventive measures he had seen. "Much labor and some expense are and must be involved in such arrangements for the health of puerperal women. . . . Especially should they be spared the hazard of death after an ordinarily most safe function, by being placed within the easy, almost necessary reach of a most malignant disease."[100]

The highlight of Channing's vacation was his visit with Simpson in Edinburgh. He had expected to stay at a hotel, make a brief visit with Simpson, and go on to Ireland for his final week abroad. Instead, Simpson welcomed him as a friend and colleague, insisting that he be a guest in his home and inviting him to attend his daily clinic, observe operations at the hospital, and accompany him on patient visits. Simpson's energy and enthusiasm were overwhelming. His knowledge and skill were equally impressive. "He gave me daily opportunities for the observation and study of diseases, such as I have never before met with."[101] He also introduced his guest to many of his colleagues, including James Syme, Robert Christison, and William Sharpey.[102]

There was much to learn from Simpson's gynecology practice, for the Scot was more daring and inventive than Channing and his associates.[103] He was better trained in surgery and did not hesitate to use surgical techniques to remove uterine growths in cases where Channing would have relied on the ligature. Channing observed Simpson perform an os-uterotomy, an operation intended to combat dysmenorrhea and sterility by enlarging the opening to the womb. Channing was accustomed to meeting the same problem by inserting a sponge tent into the cervix. He was also introduced to gynecological and obstetrical instruments that Simpson had designed, including new pessaries and knives.

Simpson and Channing engaged in a lengthy conversation about anesthesia, Simpson making a strong case for chloroform, Channing explaining his preference for sulphuric ether. He listened attentively to Simpson's claims and even visited the chemists recommended by Simpson for the purity of their chloroform. He concluded that both anesthetic agents were safe in obstetrical cases but that chloroform was decidedly the better antidote for convulsions. Nonetheless, he continued to believe that sulphuric ether posed less potential for harm.[104]

Edinburgh as he saw it in Simpson's company was further evidence of the changes that had occurred since Channing had studied obstetrics there more than forty years previously. He wondered if it might have been better not to go abroad so early in his career, when he was inexperienced and unable to figure out what he needed to know. Now, after decades spent in practice and teaching, he could ask productive questions, make intelligent comparisons, and engage in fruitful conversation with his professional peers. The intellectual stimulation he enjoyed in Edinburgh was a fitting finale to his months in Europe.

Channing returned home much improved in all respects. He seemed younger and a newly acquired mustache gave his face greater style.[105] His natural enthusiasm for the creative spirit of mankind had been rekindled by the glories of the past and examples of material improvement he had observed. He plunged into preparation of a paper describing the medical aspects of his European experiences and read it at a meeting of the Society for Medical Improvement in October.[106] A more detailed version was published two months later in the *Boston Medical and Surgical Journal*. It took four more years for him to transform his travel journal into a book.

Exhilarated by his journey, he now persuaded Barbara that she too must go abroad. It was not proper for her to travel alone, but a group of Bostonians, including Uncle Stephen Perkins and several other relatives, had plans to spend a year in Italy and urged Barbara to join them.[107] She departed in September 1853. It was fortunate that she got away when she did, for within a few months the situation between Ellery and Ellen had completely deteriorated. Had Barbara been closer she would have been as devastated as was her father. The events that followed were among the most painful in his life, leading to many alterations and adjustments.

Chapter 12 *❦*

The Medical Profession at Mid-Century

We are told that the ancient reverence in which medicine
was held, is decayed, and that the public confidence in it is
lessened.

—Walter Channing, "Of the Medical Profession, and of its
Preparation," 1845

D
ESPITE having devoted the greater part of his life to the multiple
demands of a profession he loved, in the mid-1840s Channing had to
admit that medicine faced serious challenges. Inspirational phrases
uttered from the lecture podium or published in textbooks and journals were
not enough to assure public confidence in the skills of physicians. Competition from unorthodox medical sects and charlatans posed an economic threat
and raised troubling ethical questions. New views on birth control and abortion,
popular interest in health and physiology, and a growing call for admission
of women to the profession necessitated a reexamination of his assumptions
regarding medical ethics and traditions.

Distrust of the medical profession was largely a reaction to the harsh
drugs, bleeding, cathartics, and other therapies of "heroic medicine." One result was the success of unorthodox medical sects, especially hydropathy and
homeopathy, which became increasingly popular during the mid-century decades. There were several hydropathic or water-cure establishments in New
England, including a large resort in Brattleboro, Vermont, that was acclaimed
by Susan Higginson Channing and her daughters, as well as by literary lights
such as Harriet Beecher Stowe and her sister Catherine Beecher.[1] Homeopathy
was even more widely accepted.[2] The Massachusetts Homeopathic Fraternity,
a loose association of homeopathic practitioners, was flourishing despite opposition from the Massachusetts Medical Society.[3] Channing scorned both sects,

234

which claimed that allopathic (regular) medicine was dangerous, rejected academic medical training, and condemned traditional therapeutics. Their views were an affront to his personal integrity as well as to the profession he honored.[4]

"Of all modern hobby-horsical revivals," he disdainfully wrote, "perhaps no one has been harder ridden than the water cure." He lampooned the fashionable establishments, with their lavish hotels, lawns, groves, hills, and lakes, and the rituals that required their patrons to drink large quantities of water, submerge themselves in hot baths, douse themselves with cold showers, and spend many hours encased in wet packs. In his view, hydropathy was not a cure but an entertainment and a solace for women who preferred to be invalids. Modern historians have been kinder to the women who embraced hydropathy. As summarized by Susan Cayleff, it offered them "an all-encompassing, accessible, and empowering medical and social ideology that valued them for their 'innate' characteristics, for their abilities as individuals, and for their central importance in the campaign to reform American health and living habits."[5]

Channing was even more scathing about homeopathy. The notion that infinitesimal doses of like substances can cure disease was completely antithetical to every theory of regular medicine as well as to common sense, and he had absolutely no patience with it. "We are treating of matters in which are involved the grave questions of death and life. . . . The homeopathist . . . investigates nothing. He asks not for the disease during life nor seeks to confirm or amend the record after death."[6] Channing charged the homeopaths with preventing cures and refusing to prescribe opium and other anodynes to relieve the pain of terminal illness.

He was particularly incensed by their crusade against cathartics since, according to his beliefs, costiveness frequently caused or exacerbated disease.[7] He accused them of dishonesty, having known cases in which homeopaths prescribed larger doses than he would have given, and others in which they permitted a regular physician to prescribe a course of medication, hoping that a cure would ensue. He claimed to have witnessed chicanery when a washtub filled with water was placed beneath a sickbed to "cause the waters to flow." The water was changed day and night, but the patient died in agony from severe urinary disease.

The Massachusetts Medical Society frowned on members who had anything to do with unorthodox medical practitioners.[8] Channing generally adhered to their rule, but if called by a homeopath to consult in a difficult obstetrical case he would not refuse. Experience had shown him that homeopaths frequently lacked skill with forceps and other instruments and that death might occur if he did not try to help. He had also known cases in which the "infinitesimal" did not control hemorrhaging or facilitate the expulsion of an undelivered placenta. Again, "death would have occurred before homeopathic remedies would have emptied the womb, or established permanent contraction."[9]

To ridicule the pretenses of homeopathy he once ate all the pills in a homeopathic medicine box that he had found beneath a patient's bed.[10] Then, having taken so much "medicine," he predicted he would enjoy good health far into the future. Neither the homeopath nor the patient was amused. To the homeopathic claim that drinking seawater was the best cure for seasickness, Channing retorted that it would be better to prescribe a homeopathic dose of land, since most people recovered as soon as they were on land.

Channing's impassioned criticisms of unorthodox sects were indicative of the defensive position regular medical men had assumed throughout the nation. The absence of licensing in nearly all the states, the poor education medical students received in proprietary schools more concerned with profits than instruction, the lack of adequate clinical training, and the frequently unethical conduct of many practitioners were a source of embarrassment to physicians who valued high standards. Boston, with its respect for authority and intellectual endeavor, was less affected than other parts of the country. The tight control of the Warrens, Jacksons, and Bigelows had prevented creation of competitive medical schools, and the Massachusetts Medical Society had maintained professional standards. However, there was no guarantee that Boston's medical men would be forever protected from the poor reputation of physicians in other parts of the country. Indeed, the inroads of the homeopaths suggested otherwise.

Interest in a national medical association that would improve the image of the profession had begun to emerge in the 1830s. During the early 1840s several attempts were made, without much effect, to form a permanent organization. A more promising meeting held in New York in May 1846 led to the official launching of the American Medical Association in Philadelphia the following year. More than three hundred delegates, representing their state medical societies and various medical colleges, approved motions supporting higher standards of medical education and ethics. Channing's friend and professor Nathaniel Chapman was elected the first president. Channing was appointed in absentia to the committee on obstetrics, a testimony to his reputation, but there is no evidence that he made any contribution.[11]

In 1849 Boston hosted the third annual meeting of the AMA, which attracted about 450 delegates from all parts of the country.[12] For four days, Bostonians did their best to impress the guests. There were sessions at the Lowell Institute and in the chamber of the Massachusetts House of Representatives. Mayor John Preston Bigelow (no relation to the medical Bigelows) greeted

STANDING: JOHN COLE HAYDEN, DAVID HUMPHREYS STORER, ZABDIEL BOYLSTON ADAMS
JOHN BARNARD SWEET JACKSON, CHARLES GIDEON PUTNAM, JOHN HOMANS
SITTING: SOLOMON DAVIS TOWNSEND, EDWARD REYNOLDS, DAVID OSGOOD, JOHN WARE
JACOB BIGELOW, WALTER CHANNING.

Group of medical men, Boston (courtesy of the Massachusetts Historical Society)

them at the Revere House, Boston's premier reception hall. They were feted in the homes of John Collins Warren, Jacob Bigelow, George Hayward, and John Homans, and by Abbott Lawrence, the textile magnate and a leading citizen. They visited the medical school, the hospital, the Eye and Ear Infirmary, the Society of Natural History, the Massachusetts Historical Society, the museum of the Society for Medical Improvement, and the Boston Museum. They were also welcomed at the college in Cambridge and at the McLean Asylum in Somerville.

Channing, officially a delegate of the Boston Lying-in Hospital, reported on the events for the *Boston Medical and Surgical Journal*.[13] Not surprisingly, he thought the convention "one of the most important, if not the most important, meetings ever held in this city." It was a unique opportunity for him to meet physicians from distant places and compare notes. Like many of the delegates, he was especially interested in a report of the education committee that recommended the addition of two months to the school year. Harvard's faculty did not favor the proposal. The experience of schools that had tried a longer term indicated that many students would continue to leave at the end of four months and that the expense of added time and effort had not been rewarded. An unacknowledged but more significant reason for unwillingness to extend the lecture term was fear that more students would choose to attend proprietary schools, which had minimal requirements for attendance. Boston's Tremont and Boylston medical schools were closely allied with Harvard, but there was always danger of competition from less friendly establishments.

Channing's report included details of one of the speeches delivered at the end of the meeting. The delegate described an omnibus ride in which he and his colleagues were rescued from ignorance by "a lady [who] saw that we were strangers . . . and at once began to tell us all we wanted to know, and after a manner so intelligible, so lady-like, so truly grateful, that we at once saw the whole secret of New England power. It is, Mr. Chairman, it is in the women." As a Bostonian well acquainted with the women in the city, Channing was pleased to repeat these words for his readers.

Channing did not remain an active member of the AMA. He was named a delegate to the next meeting in Cincinnati, but chose not to attend. He was also asked by Meigs to contribute to a report on diseases of the cervix for the 1852 meeting. Meigs tried to get Channing's attention by pointing out that "the brethren are not fully appreciative of the importance of the subject" and urged him to discuss the necessity, propriety, and morality of physical diagnosis for these disorders. He especially wanted Channing to "allude to the embarrassments . . . arising from the delicacy of those relations that exist between the physician and patient." Channing did not take up the challenge and Meigs was forced to prepare the report himself.[14]

These early years of the American Medical Association did not produce much more than increased familiarity and exchange among the better-educated, more progressive physicians. Without strong state medical societies or state regulatory agencies that could enforce standards, there was no way to restrict badly trained men who had the legal right to call themselves doctors or to curb quacks and charlatans who offered questionable remedies to a badly informed public. Held back by the conservativism of some of its faculty and distracted by the Civil War, Harvard Medical School did not seriously reform its curriculum or raise its standards until the 1870s, when Charles W. Eliot, newly installed as president of the university, forced dramatic changes. A nine-month lecture period, graded courses that moved the student through increasingly complex material, and written examinations were the initial result of his leadership.[15]

THE growing number of abortions was one of the more complicated issues facing the medical profession at mid-century. It was a new and deeply disturbing phenomenon that evoked strong reactions from many physicians. Channing believed that abortion was legally and morally wrong, as well as a threat to the health of the mother, but it was easier to make a statement of principle than to act consistently in daily medical practice.[16]

In his lectures on medical jurisprudence Channing had always defined feticide as "willful murder of the fœtus by internal remedies . . . *after the child has manifested life.*"[17] This notion of "quickening" was an important legal principle, established in English common law and adopted by courts in the United States. Before quickening (the point at which a pregnant woman first feels fetal movement), the fetus was thought not yet alive and thus abortion was not murder. After quickening, deliberate destruction of the fetus was destruction of life and a criminal act. A physician might have to testify in court regarding the gestational age of a fetus or postmortem evidence of criminal abortion, and Channing's instruction contained important information. However, prosecution for abortion was rare. The law required proof of an intention to destroy life, resulting in few convictions and even fewer sentences.

Despite the public and legal acceptance of quickening as the determining indicator of fetal life, leading writers on obstetrics, medical ethics, and medical jurisprudence had long realized that it was a fallacious concept.[18] Channing referred to feticide after the fetus had shown life as the "crime augmented."[19] Like other medical experts, he recognized that quickening had no physiological relationship to life but was the mother's perception of previously undetected fetal motion. There was no agreement on the exact onset of life, any more than there is today.

In his midwifery lectures, Channing talked about the various ways women could end a pregnancy regardless of how far it had advanced: the herbs and drugs reputed to bring on an abortion and the cold baths, exposure to inclement weather, tight lacing, strenuous exercise, violent emetics, douches, injections, even external blows to the abdomen, that were thought to result in expulsion of the fetus. He was preparing his students to treat complications when an attempted abortion went awry and to know the dangers to be avoided if a woman wanted to prevent a miscarriage.[20]

During the first several decades of Channing's career, abortion was not an issue. No doubt some of his patients had attempted to terminate pregnancies and he was called to deal with subsequent unexpected hemorrhaging or infection. Several of his early cases involved "imprudent" women who aborted in the third or fourth month of gestation.[21] But society did not pay much attention to such events, which were relatively few and far between. Most people associated abortion with unmarried women who wanted to avoid the shame and guilt of pregnancy and the stigma associated with illegitimacy. Indeed, there was often some sympathy for these unfortunate women.

A marked change occurred toward the middle of the century, when it became apparent that the number of abortions was rising significantly. Even more alarming was evidence that the increase was attributable to married women from the middle and upper classes. Unlike the poor women whose babies would be illegitimate, these were women who had decided that large families could cause undue financial burdens or emotional stress and wanted to find other outlets for their own energies and talents. With contraceptive methods still unreliable, they were using abortion to limit family size, avoid having a child in the first years of marriage, or better space their pregnancies. Other married women chose abortion rather than endure another difficult pregnancy or dangerous delivery.[22] Husbands often agreed, the judicial system paid scant attention, and the Protestant clergy was silent on the subject.

The changing nature of abortion practices had a direct impact on Channing and his colleagues. They were being asked to facilitate abortions by women from whom they did not expect such unseemly requests. Most refused, as they would have refused a similar request from an unmarried woman. Professional ethics forbade physicians to perform abortions.[23] Yet they knew that some irregular physicians and midwives were doing so, and they may have feared a consequent loss of their own practice. Even more disturbing, regular physicians were treating many more cases of incomplete and botched abortions as well as the infections, bleeding, and pain that often followed. The newspapers carried frequent advertisements from men and women untrained in obstetrics offering relief of "blocked menses" or cures for "female diseases."[24]

The surge in abortions was reported in the *Boston Medical and Surgical Journal*, whose editor was appalled by the "abominable vice."[25] It was also discussed in professional circles, including meetings of the Society for Medical Improvement, at which Channing relayed the story of a woman who aborted herself by eating a pound of ergot, and Charles E. Ware exhibited a diseased uterus taken at autopsy from a woman who had dosed herself with oil of tansy or hemlock.[26] Henry I. Bowditch showed his colleagues a box of pills sold by the infamous abortionist Madame Restell, who had a thriving business in Boston as well as in New York and Philadelphia. Henry J. Bigelow complained that abortifacients were readily available for nominal sums.[27]

On May 12, 1851, the Society for Medical Improvement devoted most of the evening to a discussion of the "astonishing frequency" of abortion in Boston.[28] Channing led off by describing three cases he had seen within the preceding fortnight. Severe hemorrhaging and persistent vomiting had caused fear for these patients' recovery. One had been previously treated by a homeopath whose remedies were inadequate to the gravity of the situation, leaving Channing to save the woman's life. Other members of the society described attempted abortions that produced convulsions and fistulas.

Shifting from medicine to morals, Channing expressed astonishment that increased abortions were occurring among "respectable and married women" who did not wish to have more children or wanted to avoid suffering in labor. Another physician present knew of a couple who sought an abortion because they wanted to preserve the figure and personal appearance of the wife, a handsome woman "of refined manners." At the age of sixty-five, having devoted his life to assisting women in childbirth, Channing could not comprehend this new breed of women "who from ignorance . . . allow this crime to be committed upon them, and not only *allow* but *solicit* it to be done." He felt it was incumbent on the medical profession to make a public statement strong enough to curtail the practice. Physicians understood that the fetus at any age was a living being and, more than any other segment of society, they knew that internal abortifacients and instrumented abortions could be dangerous.

Channing's remarks provided several important motifs to the argument against abortion. First, he was reinforcing the notion that abortion before quickening was unacceptable.[29] Second, in much the way he viewed prohibition of alcohol, he had little confidence in legal remedies for abortion. In 1845 the Massachusetts legislature had enacted a new law making abortion a felony if the woman died and a misdemeanor if she did not, but conviction still required proof of intention. Only the woman herself could testify about intention, which was impossible if she died and unlikely if she survived.[30] Third, he placed his hopes on physicians, whom he urged to inform the public about the error of abortion.

Channing's message was mild compared with the onslaught of anti-abortion activity that emerged a few years later. In 1855 David Humphreys Storer, who succeeded Channing as Professor of Midwifery and Medical Jurisprudence, used the occasion of the annual introductory lecture at the medical school to add an impassioned condemnation of abortion and contraception to the usual exhortations about the nobility of the medical profession and the necessity for diligence and devotion to its purposes.[31] He accused women who terminated a pregnancy of "a crime in the sight of the law" and "a sin in the sight of [their] Maker." He spoke of "an existing, and universally acknowledged evil," of "vice and unholy transactions," and of his horror "that the female can so completely unsex herself, that her sensibilities can be so entirely blunted, that any conceivable circumstances can compel her to welcome such degradation."

Storer used medical theory to reinforce his objections. It was his view that according to the "laws" of female physiology, the uterus "requires that a certain specified time shall be occupied in perfecting its most important work" while "the system of the mother [is] gradually being prepared for the approaching event." To interfere with these natural processes and force the uterus to expel its contents before the determined time could lead to physical disease and mental depression. He also criticized contraception, explaining that incomplete intercourse was unnatural and could cause organic disease.[32]

This rendering of female physiology was a marked departure from that held by Channing and other physicians of his generation. In deference to members of the faculty who were disturbed by the impropriety of these topics, Storer was persuaded not to include the paragraphs on abortion and contraception in the published version of his lecture. However, the *Boston Medical and Surgical Journal* included them in its report of the lecture, and there were many people present at the time of its delivery who further publicized his views.[33]

David Humphreys Storer remained committed to moral suasion to restrict abortion, assuming, as did Channing, that "the laws of the land, with all their penalties annexed, can do but little to abolish the crime." Not so Storer's son, Horatio, who transformed the criminalization of abortion into the "physicians' crusade" associated with his name.[34] Horatio had graduated from Harvard Medical School and spent a year abroad studying obstetrics and gynecology in Paris and Edinburgh. Channing had provided the younger Storer with an introduction to James Y. Simpson, whom he had praised in the midwifery lectures Horatio attended.[35] A friendship immediately developed between the Bostonian and the Scot, much like that between Channing and Simpson. In this case, however, the visitor remained in Edinburgh for nearly a year, studying gynecology with Simpson while becoming convinced of the advantages of chloroform over ether.

Storer was ambitious, looking for a cause that would bring him to the forefront of the profession. He was also pugnacious, eager to outwit and outdo any adversary he encountered. He was angry about the suppression of his father's introductory lecture and humiliated by his father's willingness to accept the restrictions placed on its publication. A campaign against abortion suited his combative personality and accorded with his conviction that willful destruction of fetal life at any stage was murder.

Storer began his offensive by soliciting information from physicians in many parts of the nation about the incidence of abortion and enforcement of legal remedies. He then sought approval from the Suffolk District Medical Society for strict anti-abortion laws that he, as chairman of a special committee, had drafted. He expected the local society to forward his report to the state medical society for its approval and recommendation to the legislature.[36]

These initial efforts of Horatio Storer coincided with Channing's term as president of the Suffolk District Medical Society. Strangely, despite his earlier appeal to his colleagues to speak out against abortion, there is no indication that he took part in the discussions, which were very heated. Storer's controversial recommendations were eventually approved by a small margin and presented at the annual meeting of the Massachusetts Medical Society. Here, too, Channing was present. As one of the senior physicians attending, he offered after-dinner remarks that were well received by his colleagues, but there is no record of his participation in the long debate over Storer's proposals, although they were the major business before the society.[37]

Horatio Storer was only moderately successful in persuading physicians in Massachusetts to join his crusade. Though most agreed with his goal, his extreme positions were offensive to many who did not share his zeal. For instance, Storer proposed severe punishment for women who sought abortion. "[T]he wretch who had caused the death of her offspring, perhaps by her own hand, should be made to suffer corresponding exposure and punishment," he asserted, adding, "if married, as is too often the case, her crime should be considered as infinitely increased." But there were physicians who continued to sympathize with unmarried women desperate to avoid shame and who were not prepared to see middle-class and upper-class married women sentenced to the House of Correction for aborting an unwanted fetus, even if it was wrong.

Furthermore, most Massachusetts physicians, including Channing, placed the life of the mother ahead of the life of the baby in cases where one had to be sacrificed. Storer did not agree, insisting that an abortion to save the life of the mother was a crime against the unborn child. As for "premature deliveries" performed more than one time for the same woman, Storer declared that "the lusts of man or woman should not be pandered to in this way. The man should be castrated or the child have a chance. The mother is responsible if she puts her own life in danger and the crime is against the child."[38]

Channing's views on abortion were milder and more complicated.[39] In theory he was intolerant of an act he called "feticide" and "unborn-child-killing." He accused women of self-indulgence for using abortion to avoid the annoyance of pregnancy or the bother of a new baby, asserting "they will kill, or get killed, the most sacred of human instincts." He warned about uterine diseases, disturbed function of other organs, and possible sterility that might follow an abortion.

On the other hand, his first obligation was as a physician, not as a moralist. He avoided the metaphors he had used for intemperance twenty years previously. "He is not always the wisest priest who harps too much upon sin . . . men and women tire of it."[40] He knew enough about the psychology of women to realize that if a woman desired an abortion she would get it. "You may talk yourself dumb, and accomplish nothing," he admitted. He did not approve but he understood their motives: memories of the illness and dangers that sometimes accompanied labor, inability to nurse and the consequent sickening or

death of a child, or lack of enough money to support a family. He was especially cognizant of the deep shame that pregnancy and illegitimate birth caused
an unmarried woman. "No one but a physician can understand what are the
mental states of such persons—how nearly they approach to, if they do not
reach, that of insanity."[41] Too often he had encountered intensely emotional
scenes: tears, eloquent entreaties, even offers of money. When he attempted to
explain the dangers of the procedure, as well as the criminal nature of the act,
he was usually unable to convince the woman, who, he knew, would find
someone else to perform the abortion or might try to do it herself.

Though he refused to perform abortions, his disapprobation did not extend to refusing medical care to women who developed complications afterward. The paramount duty of the physician, he insisted, is to cure disease
"under whatever forms or circumstances produced."[42] He responded quickly
when summoned and remained as long as needed, even though he sometimes
lost the continued patronage of a patient or her family when the case concluded. Few respectable men and women wanted to face the shame that abortion implied. Called to a young married woman who had eaten a quarter-
pound of spurred rye in an effort to self-abort, he treated her severe pains,
hemorrhage, and respiratory distress until the embryo was expelled, and he
continued to treat her until she had fully recovered. He never saw or heard
from her again. This was also the consequence of a more complicated case.
Hastily summoned to a young housemaid who had nearly bled to death following an abortion, Channing learned she had been made pregnant by her em-
ployer, a man who had long been Channing's patient. After Channing saved
the girl's life, the man never spoke to him again.

He did approve abortions and premature deliveries for women whose
health was so seriously endangered that continuation of a pregnancy posed a
genuine threat to her life. He treated excessive vomiting with nitrate of silver,
though he knew it could also produce an abortion. He induced premature
labor for women who had a small or deformed pelvis and for whom delivery
at term would be disastrous. (If born after the seventh month, the child had a
chance of surviving, but if the deformity was too great to permit delivery at
that point, he advised inducing labor earlier.) And in a typical Channing move,
he submitted a poignant article to the *Boston Medical and Surgical Journal*
describing the death of Charlotte Brontë, the English novelist who suffered
extreme nausea in pregnancy and was reported to have expired from dehydra-
tion, starvation, and exhaustion. Channing wrote that a miscarriage should
have been induced to save her life.[43] Channing's conflict on abortion shows
him grappling with a new and unexpected social question. Professional ethics
condemned abortion, as did his personal moral code. He was a Christian and

a pacifist who did not condone killing in any situation. Abortion, he told his students year after year, "violates both divine and human law."[44] Added to this were contemporary assumptions about the evolution of civilization. To countenance abortion would be a step backward. Savages and heathens practiced abortion to placate their gods or to limit population growth, but Western civilization, he argued, had long since abandoned such barbarous practices.[45]

As a physician he had spent a lifetime providing medical care to women and thought he understood them well. He had helped them in easy labors and difficult deliveries, he had witnessed immense joy and great heartache. He knew that there were some motives that almost justified nontherapeutic abortions. But he was also dismayed to find that "from a wholly selfish motive to save herself from the pains of labour or the troubles [and] the inconveniences of maternal offices," there were women who violated "the best, the most beautiful" part of their nature. Moral education, not punitive legislation, was the best solution. "Let women be taught that the being within them is a living being, capable of an infinite development, and of an immortal life—and they would shrink as from murder from its voluntary destruction."[46] His confidence that women could be persuaded to recognize the error of abortion was typical of his expectation that intemperance could be eliminated and universal peace could be established by the same means. His view of the role of women was not different from the prevailing attitudes of most men and women of his generation. Even some leaders of the feminist movement, including physicians such as Elizabeth Blackwell and Marie Zakrzewska, opposed abortion. As for the men responsible for the pregnancy of unmarried women, Channing thought it was their duty to marry even when class differences made such a union socially unacceptable.

In the long run, the extreme anti-abortionists prevailed. Storer was an astute strategist who recognized the potential of the fledgling AMA as a vehicle for promoting his ideas. Since the AMA wanted to curtail the influence of irregular practitioners, and homeopaths, midwives, and other alternative providers were reputed to be notorious abortionists, it was not difficult to conflate professional rivalries with the crusade against abortion. Storer was named chairman of an AMA committee on abortion, and with his leadership the organization endorsed stringent anti-abortion laws that were subsequently enacted by most of the states.[47] Storer's use of statistics demonstrating the relative increase of births among foreign-born families now resident in the country and the decrease in birth rates among white, Protestant, native-born women fed the fears of legislators and journalists that the nation was experiencing a demographic transformation. By the end of the nineteenth century the illegality

of abortion had become public policy in the United States and remained so for
another seventy years.

QUESTIONS about women's "nature" and their role in society were largely
evoked by the nineteenth-century feminist movement, which was aimed at
reforming many aspects of women's lives, including political disenfranchise-
ment, lack of property rights, and unequal educational opportunity. It was a
social cause for which Channing evinced little concern. He claimed to be completely uninterested in politics and disgusted by partisan strife, so he was not
likely to be sympathetic to women wanting to vote and run for office. The
issues around divorce and ownership of property would not have held much
attraction for him either, though his will explicitly designated his daughters,
Barbara and Mary, as heirs in their own right.[48] Since he believed that women
who procured abortions were misguided and that motherhood should be their
paramount duty, he was not apt to favor other roles for women, at least not
for married women. Despite these views, however, by the end of his career he
had developed some sympathy with the women who sought entry to the medical profession, and he actively supported the few in Boston who made the
attempt.

The mid-century movement to admit women to the profession and Channing's reaction to it must be seen in the context of a pamphlet titled *Remarks
on the Employment of Females as Practitioners in Midwifery*, published in Boston
in 1820.[49] It was written anonymously by "A Physician" whose objections to
women practicing midwifery mirrored the sentiments of most physicians in
Boston and were indicative of attitudes that pervaded society for many years
after.[50] Though never proved, authorship has frequently been attributed to
Channing.

The pamphlet appeared shortly after the arrival in Boston of Janet Alexander, a Scottish midwife with excellent credentials and exceptional local patronage. Mrs. Alexander had been instructed in midwifery by James Hamilton, the
Edinburgh professor with whom Channing had studied a decade previously.[51]
She had been invited to Boston by John Collins Warren and James Jackson,
who wanted to discontinue their obstetrical practice, which often required
long, tiring hours and sometimes prevented them from giving adequate attention to other patients.[52] Both men earned more money than any other physician in the city and could easily afford to give up obstetrics. Since it was
generally agreed that there were no longer any midwives in Boston, Warren
had briefly considered a plan to educate women to replace Jackson and himself
but abandoned the idea as impractical.[53]

Mrs. Alexander began to advertise for clients.[54] It was public knowledge that Warren and Jackson favored her success, and it could be expected that many women would prefer to have a well-educated female attend them in childbirth. It was likely that physicians, especially the younger men just beginning their careers, would lose some of their midwifery practice to her. A special meeting of the Boston Medical Association considered measures "to prevent the irregular practice of midwifery." After much discussion the question was submitted to a committee for further investigation.[55] There is no known record of the committee's deliberations, but the pamphlet was published not long after. It was intended for husbands as well as for their wives.

The anonymous author acknowledged that female midwives had many qualities that might lead women to prefer their presence in the birthing room but, from his point of view, practitioners of midwifery must thoroughly understand "the profession of medicine as a whole." Although for the most part "nature is sufficient for her own ends and needs no assistance from art," the author was certain that the potential for difficulties in labor and delivery or postpartum that require assistance or intervention, the need to anticipate possible problems before they occur, and the close relationship between uterine function and other bodily organs required "the same knowledge, the same education, the same mental resources" as any other part of medicine.[56] These assumptions led him to posit a fundamental question that outweighed every other consideration. "[C]an the practice of midwifery," he asked, "be carried on with equal safety by female as by male practitioners?" The answer was direct and unequivocal. "Both the character and the education of women disqualify them for the office." The problem was not that women are intellectually inferior to men or more incompetent, but that because of their "moral qualities" (read: feminine nature) they cannot handle the difficult situations that may occur in childbirth. Women are passive beings, a commendable trait that enables them to endure suffering and to witness it in others, but they lack the "active power of mind," have less ability to restrain their sympathetic nature, and are more disposed to acute sensibility than men are. Women cannot act decisively and quickly. In a crisis, when immediate action is required, they must lean on others more dependable than they.[57]

The feminine qualities that make a woman unsuitable for midwifery practice also preclude her from acquiring the education she needs to assure safety to mother and child. It is difficult enough for male medical students to subdue their emotions when facing disease and death, but the qualities that make women different, their delicacy, refinement, and feminine sensibilities, would be completely destroyed in the dissecting room or in the hospital.[58]

The anonymous physician also provided arguments showing the dire consequences that would ensue if midwives were to regain a significant role in obstetrical care. Women less well trained than Mrs. Alexander would quickly emerge and would attract patients for themselves. Accustomed to midwives in obstetrical cases, women would hesitate to seek physicians for other medical problems. Eventually, women and medical men would lose the personal relations that should normally follow a well-managed childbirth, and everyone would suffer.

Faced with the opposition to Mrs. Alexander, Warren and Jackson "agreed to give her up."[59] Nonetheless, she remained in the city and developed an active practice, especially among women in the upper class. Her daughter became a midwife and was also employed by many Boston women. Though Janet Alexander was reputed never to have lost a patient, the daughter was less fortunate. She was implicated in a tragic case referred to Channing, though excused for being young and inexperienced.[60]

The identity of the author of *Remarks on the Employment of Females as Practitioners in Midwifery* remains a mystery. Other than Channing, John Ware has been cited by librarians and historians.[61] There are good reasons why either he or Channing could have been responsible.[62] For Channing's part, as a young man still making his mark in medicine and expecting midwifery to be an important part of his practice, there would have been strong personal reasons to object to competition from female midwives. A comment in the text about the time devoted to obstetrics by men "who have any inclination for literary pursuits" might help identify him as the author.

However, there is equally—if not more—compelling evidence that Ware wrote the piece. Like Channing, he too needed to make a living from medical practice. More to the point, he was named as the author fifty years later by George H. Lyman in an address that he read at the 1875 annual meeting of the Massachusetts Medical Society.[63] Lyman devoted a large part of his remarks to criticism of the contemporary feminist thrust toward educating women for the medical profession. He reminded his listeners that more than fifty years before, "the propriety of the employment of women as midwives seems to have agitated the profession and community in this vicinity. Among others the matter was reviewed by Dr. John Ware, whose opinion was clearly against it." Lyman quoted extensively from *Remarks on the Employment of Females* to support his own position.

Ware's comments in the introductory lecture he gave to the medical students in 1850 support his authorship of the pamphlet. Responding to proposals to educate women for professional careers in medicine, he reiterated many of the arguments written thirty years previously. "The general practice of medicine," he told the male students, "would be found unsuited to her physical, intellectual, and moral constitution."[64] Of course, there were many men who objected to medical education for women in 1850, just as there were others who criticized female midwives in 1820.

A third possibility is that the author was neither Ware nor Channing. Both were closely allied to James Jackson, which might have made it difficult to take a stand against his wishes regarding Mrs. Alexander. Perhaps the pamphlet was written by another, unsuspected physician or by the committee of the Boston Medical Association that investigated the matter. In any case, the arguments used to disparage women as midwives were not unique to the anonymous physician. They represent beliefs that prevailed throughout the nineteenth century, despite or because of the simultaneous efforts of a small group of feminists to open doors to women.

SAMUEL Gregory, already mentioned as an opponent of obstetrical anesthesia, turned these arguments upside down in his campaign to establish a school for female midwives.[65] For Gregory, women's feminine qualities, their sensibilities, their sympathy with pain, and their ability to wait patiently through the long hours of labor, made them eminently more suitable midwifery attendants than men. Educating women as midwives would restore "those delicate duties which Scripture and history, reason and propriety, all proclaim are hers."[66]

Gregory's appeal for the education of female midwives was also an appeal for restoration of female modesty and social propriety, which he claimed were violated by the presence of men at childbirth. His passionate rhetoric was laced with serious charges against physicians, including incompetence, unnecessary interference with the natural process of birth, lack of decorum, and immoral conduct. His success in winning support for his school was as much a reflection of public concern about the abilities of the profession and suspicion about the character of its members as it was an indication of an interest in promoting educational and occupational opportunities for women. Nonetheless, Gregory gathered sufficient support from fearful husbands and fathers and from advocates of women's rights to inaugurate the Boston Female Medical College, the first medical school for women in the United States.

The initial class of twelve women who entered in November 1848 studied obstetrics, diseases of women and children, physiology, and hygiene. At the completion of the course, they received certificates of proficiency in midwifery. It was difficult to find qualified teachers willing to be part of such an unusual enterprise, especially since Gregory had disparaged the medical profession so severely, but two practicing physicians who shared an interest in issues of women's health were hired.[67] Soon his feminist backers were demanding an enlarged curriculum that would provide a complete medical education to women. When the school was reorganized as the New England Female Medical

College in 1856 it was empowered to confer medical degrees on its graduates, who by then were taking a full medical course.[68]

Inception of the Boston Female Medical College coincided with some of the major milestones in the feminist movement. Elizabeth Blackwell, the first woman to obtain a medical degree in the United States, had begun her studies at Geneva Medical College in New York in the autumn of 1847. A second medical college for women, the Pennsylvania Women's Medical College, was established in 1850, largely through the efforts of Philadelphia's Quaker community. The first Woman's Rights Convention was held in Seneca Falls, New York, in July 1848. That same year the astronomer Maria Mitchell became the first woman elected to the American Academy of Arts and Sciences and to the Association for the Advancement of Science. Margaret Fuller, the sister of Ellen Channing, had already established herself as the most prominent intellectual spokeswoman for feminism. Women, especially middle-class, white Protestant women, were beginning to claim their rightful place in society. Women making choices about contraception and abortion were demonstrating independence in their private lives.[69]

If Channing was the author of the pamphlet condemning female midwifery, or if he agreed with its thesis, by 1847 he had begun to moderate his views. He was starting to show sympathy for a much more daring concept than that of female midwives. One of his final acts as dean of the medical college was to inquire at the July faculty meeting whether a woman could be admitted to the lectures and examined for a degree in medicine. In taking this step, he may have been influenced by some of the younger members of his family. Barbara was always interested in women's issues, Mary's new husband held many liberal views, and his nephews William Henry Channing and William Francis Channing were friends of Elizabeth Blackwell.[70] Perhaps he had decided to begin discussion of a topic that was gaining interest as a result of Gregory's lectures and publications. Channing's query was forwarded to President Everett and the Harvard Corporation, which replied on August 14 that it "did not deem it advisable to alter the existing regulations of the Medical School, which imply that the students are exclusively of the male sex."[71]

In November the new dean, Oliver Wendell Holmes, received a request from Harriot Kezia Hunt for permission to attend the lectures. Hunt had studied "naturalist" medicine, another sect that relied on good nursing, hygiene, diet, exercise, and rest, instead of orthodox therapeutics. She already had a successful practice, primarily among women and children, but wanted the "scientific light" that would advance her professionally. It is ironic that Hunt wanted instruction in allopathic (regular) medicine. Either she recognized the benefit of orthodox medical theory or she thought its authority would further her career.[72]

Holmes forwarded her request to the president and governing Fellows in Cambridge, suggesting that it be approved and adding that the applicant was "of mature age and might be safely trusted so far as appearances go." The reply was brusque. "[I]t is inexpedient to reconsider the vote of the Corporation of the 14th August relative to a similar request."[73]

Three years later, buoyed by the increased activity in the feminist movement and by her own participation at the first national women's rights convention in nearby Worcester, Massachusetts, Hunt reapplied to Harvard. This time she specified that she wanted only to attend the lectures, but did not intend to qualify for a degree. She also made clear that her interest was providing medical care to women. This acceptance of societal norms was meant to silence the opposition. In Hunt's words, "Delicacy, propriety, and necessity require for woman one of her own sex, properly educated, to consult with in many cases."[74] On November 23, 1850, the faculty voted 5–2 to admit her if her acceptance was not "deemed inconsistent with the statutes." Jacob Bigelow and John B. S. Jackson cast the negative votes. Oliver Wendell Holmes, Walter Channing, Henry J. Bigelow, John Ware, and E. H. Horsford voted in the affirmative.[75] If Channing or Ware had written the anonymous pamphlet in 1820, by 1850 both were willing to consider a woman student. Within the week the president and Fellows reversed their previous position, finding "no objection arising from the Statutes of the Medical School to admitting female Students to their Lectures."[76]

It would appear that Channing's query, made three years previously for whatever reason, had reached fruition. Elizabeth Blackwell had completed her course at Geneva Medical College without any scandal erupting. In April 1849 she embarked from Boston for additional training in Europe, and while waiting for departure of the steamer, she had a visit from William F. Channing, a strong proponent of women's rights, accompanied by "his medical uncle, Dr. Channing."[77] The number of women practicing medicine in Boston without formal academic instruction was increasing, and the New England Female Medical College was educating its third set of students. The editor of the *Boston Medical and Surgical Journal*, commenting on Hunt's first application to the anatomical lectures, had asked, "Why should not well-educated females be admitted?"[78] It looked as if the medical faculty and the governing boards of Harvard were catching up with liberal opinion. Alas, the students had not.

Hunt's admission coincided with the admission of the three black students. The bitter reaction to that radical move has already been discussed. The possibility of a woman present at the lectures added fuel to the white men's outrage. They addressed a stinging protest to the faculty, objecting "to having the company of any female forced upon us, who is disposed to unsex herself, and to sacrifice her modesty, by appearing with men in the medical lecture room."[79] Several professors quietly urged Hunt to postpone her attendance and she acquiesced.[80] Shortly thereafter the Harvard Corporation endorsed a resolution forbidding the admission of women to the medical school. Despite numerous subsequent attempts to persuade Harvard to change that policy and despite the admission of women to many other medical schools throughout the country, Harvard did not accept women medical students until 1944, when the shortage of well-qualified male applicants caused by World War II forced the governing boards to recognize the need for change. Eighty-eight women sought admission and in September 1945 twelve of them began their medical studies at Harvard.[81] It is worth noting, however, that at least in the case of Harriot Hunt, it was not the medical faculty that prevented her from attending the lectures but the students and the authorities in Cambridge.

The inability of the medical school to admit female or black students is added proof of the competitive nature of medical education and the weakness of the profession as a whole. Had their demands not been met, the students might have withdrawn from Harvard and matriculated in medical schools more to their liking. Neither the faculty, who derived financial benefit from their positions, nor the administration, beholden as it was to Boston's merchants and clergy, could risk offending the students, whether or not they agreed with their views. Coupled with the Parkman murder and execution of Professor Webster, it was a difficult time for Harvard Medical College and for the medical profession.

Channing had another opportunity to demonstrate support for women physicians when Marie Zakrzewska came to Boston in 1859 to be Professor of Obstetrics and Diseases of Women at the New England Female Medical College. Zakrzewska, or Dr. Zak as she was usually called, had trained in midwifery at the Charité in Berlin, where she was subsequently appointed chief midwife and professor. Opposition from the male faculty forced her to resign those posts and go to the United States, where she hoped to become a physician. After a difficult year in New York, Zakrzewska met Elizabeth Blackwell, who was struggling to operate a small dispensary for poor women and children on the East Side. With encouragement from Blackwell and financial assistance from other feminists, Dr. Zak enrolled in medicine at Western Reserve College in Cleveland, where Emily Blackwell, Elizabeth's younger sister, had received a degree in 1854. After completing her studies in 1856, Dr. Zak returned to New York and worked with the Blackwell sisters at the New York Infirmary for

Women and Children, the first hospital in the United States staffed by women. Two years later she accepted an offer from Boston.[82]

Almost from the beginning Dr. Zak and Samuel Gregory were at loggerheads. Gregory's limited understanding of medical education, his more traditional views of women, and his alliance with homeopathy clashed with Dr. Zak's insistence on rigorous medical education, her belief that women should enter the profession as equals to men, and her commitment to regular medicine. Nor could she tolerate Gregory's constant financial difficulties and his disdain for the profession. Within a few years she resigned from the New England Female Medical College and, supported by Boston's feminists, male and female, established the New England Hospital for Women and Children. It was the first women's hospital in New England and second in the nation, after the Blackwells' New York Infirmary. In its early years the fate of the hospital was problematical, despite the enthusiasm of the feminists. Most members of the medical profession, and the general public too, had little tolerance for a hospital dedicated to the training of female physicians, even though they provided care only for members of their own sex.

The New England Hospital for Women and Children opened July 1, 1862, in rented space in the South End. Superficially, it imitated the pattern of other voluntary hospitals like the Massachusetts General. Most patients were poor, the trustees took an active role in the day-to-day operation of the hospital, and the medical staff were unpaid. The glaring difference, of course, was that the patients, students, and medical staff were all women, as were the directors and administrators.[83]

Dr. Zak's high standards and insistence on the practice of regular medicine, plus her pragmatism and administrative abilities, earned her the respect of several important physicians, Channing among them, who were willing to flout convention. By and large it was the same small group that supported the antislavery movement and other liberal causes.[84] Several, like Channing, belonged to James Freeman Clarke's Church of the Disciples. Channing provided Dr. Zak with "good will and assistance" in developing her private practice and was one of several who urged her to apply for membership in the Massachusetts Medical Society (she was refused). In 1864 he signed an appeal for funds for a new hospital building and made several small donations.[85]

Dr. Zak's feminist ideology did not prevent her from asking men to assist the hospital as consultants. Initially, she had no alternative if she was to meet her own standards of excellence, especially in surgery. Samuel Cabot was the first consulting surgeon and John Ware the first consulting physician.[86] When Ware died in 1864, he was replaced by Channing, "the most eminent obstetrician in the city," according to the hospital publicist.[87] Hospital records do not reveal Channing's taking part in any cases, but a letter from him to Dr. Zak, dated June 2, 1864, reveals his approval of an operation she performed and that he had observed. "I write also to say that if at any time I can do anything to aid you in the performance of your important duties, I shall be always ready and happy to do so."[88] Channing continued to be listed as one of the consulting physicians until 1870, by which time he had moved out of the city and was in his eighties.

The New England Hospital for Women and Children provided one solution to the demand of women for medical education, albeit one that suited the time and place and may have contributed to approval from men like Channing. Zakrzewska and her associates maintained a separatist position, training women apart from men, providing medical care for women and children but not for men. They practiced obstetrics, gynecology, and pediatrics, fields of medicine that were consonant with the domestic role of women in society. It may have been less difficult for Channing and other men to accept women under those limitations, especially when they proved their ability. The hospital successfully trained nurses as well as physicians. Its patients received care equal to if not better than that available at other Boston hospitals. The New England Hospital flourished for a hundred years, by which time the acceptance of women in medical education and the participation of women in all fields of medicine made its existence superfluous.

A final note must be added regarding a very different kind of medical education for women, the mid-century phenomenon of female physiological societies.[89] Emerging as part of the antebellum movement for health reform, physiological societies offered women an opportunity to study the "laws of health" so that they might better fill their duties as wives, mothers, and nurses within their families. In contrast to the New England Female Medical College and the New England Hospital, there was nothing revolutionary about these groups, though critics suspected a subterfuge to educate midwives and physicians. Indeed, the physiological societies suited the prevalent acceptance of women's domestic role as guardians of the health and well-being of their families and had their greatest appeal to middle-class women with leisure time.

The Boston Ladies' Physiological Institute grew out of discussions about women's physiology led by Harriot Hunt from 1843 to 1848 and the offer of a course of lectures to women "for the promotion of useful knowledge among their own sex," by a Professor Charles P. Bronson. Bronson proposed a donation of anatomical models if the women raised $1000 and formed a permanent society. This was accomplished, and over the following years the institute held regular lectures, developed a library of journals and books related to health and medicine, and created a nursing referral service.[90]

Channing was invited several times to lecture to the group. He repeatedly declined, though he did send them his book on etherization. Finally, in February 1857 he agreed to give a lecture, although his topic was not recorded. He had previously been unsympathetic to popular instruction in diagnosis and treatment of disease. Now he was encouraging women who had formed an effective organization and were acquiring knowledge about their bodies, about sickness and care of the sick, and about the rules of health that were supposed to assure happiness for their families. It was another small step in social reform.

Channing's career ended just as the late nineteenth-century discoveries in bacteriology and physiology were getting under way. Though physicians such as he recognized the problems inherent in their profession and understood the need for change, it was the newer scientific medicine that eventually led to improved medical education, more effective therapies, and increased public confidence in America's physicians.

Chapter 13 🌰

Retirement and Repose

An old man will look on the present gratefully and to the
future with hope.

—Walter Channing to Lucy Russel, July 21, 1856

E LLERY and Ellen's fourth child, Giovanni Eugene Channing, was born
in June 1853.[1] The addition of another baby in a household already
strained by Ellery's erratic behavior made the family dynamic more difficult than ever. He despised his home, "the old shed I live in overnight, the
rat trap I shelter in with its mouldy boards & rot & decay."[2] The great outdoors, "bravely swept & cleaned," became his "real parlor & kitchen," and he
spent most of his time in solitary walks and excursions with Thoreau and
Emerson. Ellen recovered slowly from her confinement. Desperately in need
of help with household chores, discouraged by her husband's self-indulgence
and frightened by his moodiness, she began to consider a separation. She
sought advice from Walter but, torn between loyalty to his son and affection
for Ellen and the children, he was incapable of helping her make a decision.
Her brother-in-law Thomas Wentworth Higginson was a more reliable confidant. He provided Ellen with understanding and support while Mary tried to
calm her anxious father.[3]

Ellery became more and more difficult. He berated Ellen for spending too
much money, though it was only through her scrimping that they managed at
all. He objected when she tried to read Scripture to the children, then accused
her of making them hate him. He called her vile names, spoke abusively to his
daughters, and spent the nights pacing endlessly about the house. There were
threats of violence, followed by retreat to the solitude of his small chamber.

Finally, Ellen felt too anxious for her own safety and the welfare of the children to endure the situation any longer. "My poor heart & brain are lacerated & wearied till I feel that if God would only take me to rest it would be the greatest joy," she sorrowfully wrote to Higginson.[4] Before taking an irrevocable step, she wanted assurance that her father-in-law would continue to help her and the children and that he would never be alienated from them. Wentworth explained the situation to Walter, who unhappily agreed that it would be better for everyone to end the anguish. The older children were sent to Fuller relatives. On November 17 Higginson went to Concord, put Ellen and the two younger children into a carriage, and took off for his home in Worcester, where Mary awaited them. Ellery remained secluded upstairs in his small room as they drove away.[5]

Walter suffered acutely throughout the drama. He found it impossible to face Ellen, though he was well aware of the misery Ellery had caused; he promised the financial support she would need. But his greater concern was for his son, his only son, "how beloved by his mother, how sick in his childhood."[6] It was the end of any hope he had ever had for Ellery's happiness. Everyone sympathized with Ellen, and Walter imagined his son deserted by the rest of society.[7] Who would take care of him? He certainly could not take care of himself. Knowing how unstable Ellery was, Walter was afraid he might go mad. Indeed, some people thought he had been insane for a long time. His extreme moodiness, his irrational conduct toward his wife and children, and his total incapacity for sustained relationships with them seemed too bizarre to admit of any other explanation.[8] A century later, Freudian psychologists might suggest that Ellery's hateful conduct toward Ellen was punishment by substitution of the mother who had abandoned him.[9]

Walter lapsed into melancholy as he viewed "the daily return in new dress of the old sorrow."[10] He could not avoid blaming himself for his son's appalling conduct. Should he have been stricter or more lenient with him? Was it a mistake to have sent him to live with the Forbeses or to Round Hill School? Should he have prevented the marriage? He could think of nothing more dreadful than the separation of husband and wife, father and children. He felt sorry for himself too, for his solitary condition, for the absence of a loving son who might comfort him in his old age, and for his inability to undo the tragedy. A quarrel with Ellery over his annual allowance further soured their relationship.[11] Barbara's absence added to his loneliness. He knew he would have to provide a home, at least a temporary home, to some of the children, but he did not know how he could do it without her help.

Ellen stayed in Worcester long enough to feel safe from Ellery, who for a while threatened to forcibly recover the children. Once that danger had subsided, and Ellery remained alone in Concord visited occasionally by his father, she rented a house in Dorchester, then a village south of Boston, where she reassembled the children and began to look forward to a quiet life. Her health was still precarious.

Channing was worn down by the emotional turmoil. To add to his distress, the tragedy coincided with the beginning of the academic year. It was his turn to give the introductory lecture, which meant he must try to inspire another cohort of medical students with lofty sentiments. He succeeded, somehow and the students asked to have his words published. Channing was flattered but declined the request because "no copy of my lecture exists, but in the mind of its author."[12] Then John Ware became ill and Channing had to assume additional teaching duties. After forty years of professional work, he found it depressing to deal day after day with sickness, sorrow, and the complaints of his patients. Living in the boardinghouse was intolerably lonely. Mary, often unwell, had a severe bout of rheumatism. She was so seriously incapacitated that Channing offered to take her to Europe or any other place where she might find help.[13] Barbara's return gave a temporary respite to his cares, but the prospect of continued obligations was too much. At the age of sixty-eight, it was time to give some of them up. In September 1854 he resigned from the medical school, the Massachusetts Medical Society, and the American Academy of Arts and Sciences.[14] He also ceased attending meetings of the Society for Medical Improvement.

Termination of his responsibilities at the medical school and the medical society was a relief and soothed his spirits, but Channing had no intention of abandoning all his professional activities. When rumors spread that he was planning another trip abroad, he hurriedly wrote a letter to the *Boston Medical and Surgical Journal*, letting colleagues and patients know that he hoped to remain employable "here at home."[15] Specifically, he expected to continue practicing medicine for many more years. Though he ceased paying dues to the Massachusetts Medical Society and used his resignation as an excuse for not reading a paper promised for the September meeting of the Suffolk District Medical Society, he continued to attend meetings when it suited him. Indeed, he was a frequent participant and served for two years, 1856–1858, as president of the district society. Similarly, he was named one of the consulting physicians both at the Boston Lying-in Hospital when it reopened in 1855 in an enlarged facility in the South End, and, as already noted, at the New England Hospital for Women and Children in the 1860s.[16]

Increased leisure permitted more time for writing. Initially he kept busy transforming his European journal into a book.[17] Fearful that it might be "excessively dry," he included everything that seemed interesting to him, which meant vivid reminiscences of many remarkable experiences and stimulating friendships.[18] He asked Wentworth Higginson to edit the manuscript, but his son-in-law was unable to persuade him to reduce the verbiage or correct his peculiar, sometimes obscure, style. A reviewer praised "a remarkable book of travels," but he also took its author to task for numerous digressions and disquisitions, "a jerking, broken, and fantastic rhetoric," and serious errors in usage and spelling.[19] One such misspelling, "St. Goatherd" instead of St. Gotthard, was probably an intended pun on Channing's part. The author was relieved to have the book completed and in print.

He then embarked on another book, tentatively titled "Autobiography of a Physician," but he did not get very far with it.[20] Instead, he inundated the *Boston Medical and Surgical Journal* with frequent contributions that ranged from anecdotes of his previous experiences in obstetrics and medicine and notes on contemporary cases to book reviews and tributes to departed colleagues. He seemed to be using the journal as a substitute for the lecture room, sharing years of study and practical experience. Many readers could find wisdom, guidance, and humor in these pieces. They also discovered a man becoming less pretentious, even a bit Rabelaisian. In "A Fragment of Medical Autobiography, or a Case Reported by the Patient," he described a sudden and severe intestinal disorder that left him, the patient, "as weak as a rag-baby." No detail was omitted. First the "conflict between wind and water in the whole bowel region," next the "matter puked up, blacker than thirty crows . . . its taste perfectly horrible; in quantity, monstrous." And on and on. Concluding that the sickness was some kind of cholera, he then launched into a recital of several cases of Asiatic cholera he had treated more than thirty years previously.[21]

In 1860, when there was a significant increase in the incidence of smallpox in Boston and Channing had several smallpox patients in his practice, he wrote to reassure the public about the safety of vaccination. For many years Boston had not had an effective vaccination program and many people did not have immunity from the disease. Nonetheless, there was fear that vaccinations could be the cause of disease, making it difficult to halt its spread. Drawing on his knowledge of James Jackson's role in the introduction of cowpox lymph fifty years previously and on his own experiences as a vaccinator, Channing tried to assure his readers that they could trust vaccination to protect them.[22]

In a satirical paper, he warned against spiritualism, which became a popular fad in the years before the Civil War. Believers relied on séances for advice from physicians already in the other world. Channing's account of cases "for which relief has been sought from dwellers in heaven" included interviews with several of his departed colleagues, leading him to wonder what "superior knowledge" they had acquired since quitting medical practice on earth.[23]

He also repeated his warnings about the dangers of "meddlesome midwifery," pointing to recent consultations in which he had been summoned to rectify mistakes of other physicians. "To examine, in order 'to see what may be done' . . . without preparation for what we may encounter in our uterine explorations, and especially without such knowledge as will enable us to know what actually exists, may only increase the peril, or lead to efforts which may precipitate a fatal result." Too often he had arrived too late to save the patient.[24]

Not content to rest on his laurels, Channing continued to question unexplained symptoms, faulty diagnoses, and unexpected outcomes. The most unusual example was a paper titled "The Bed Case."[25] It describes a strange malady, limited to women, that Channing had named for its most prominent symptom: the patient remained in bed, sometimes for years, though no life-threatening organic disease could be discerned. It was the only time in his long career that Channing dealt directly with women's diseases that were entirely psychological. "The mind had yielded to the body. That absorption into one's self, which comes of such maladies, was complete. Complaint had become a natural language, and spoke out on all occasions. The mind had weakened in regard to its best uses. Its whole power had come to be directed to the disease, and to a perpetual effort to show how grave it was, and how impossible it was for the patient to be other than she was."[26] Some patients appeared to be in excellent health; others exhibited signs of chronic illness or complained of severe pain in various parts of their bodies. Some displayed inert or twisted limbs, still others lay on one side only and refused to budge. Despite varied manifestations, Channing believed the pathology to be the same in all Bed Cases.

Channing attended many such women, often after other physicians, friends, or family members failed to cure them. He also collected case reports from physicians who had encountered similar situations. He decided it was pointless to try to argue the patient out of bed and focused on gaining her confidence. If there were physical problems, pain, lack of appetite, or sleeplessness, for example, he addressed them by changes in diet, fresh air, and drugs. Eventually, but not always, he succeeded when the patient herself recognized change in her circumstances and of her own volition got out of the bed, out of the bedroom, and eventually out of the house.

Channing thought he was addressing a problem that had not hitherto been adequately discussed. This was an exaggeration, since "invalidism" was not uncommon among middle-class and upper-class women and many nineteenth-century physicians had described similar female disorders, usually ascribing them to uterine problems. Even diseases of other organs, such as the heart or the stomach, were assumed to be indications of "reflex action" originating with the womb. Hippocrates wrote that a woman is defined by her womb, and many female disorders were classified as "hysteria," from the Greek for "wandering uterus." Channing had himself urged that in all chronic female disorders, especially obscure diseases, the physician must consider the condition of "that organ which makes her just what she is."[27] In *The Bed Case* (a pamphlet based on his original journal article) he repeated that notion and devoted many paragraphs to diseases of the womb that might explain the patient's obsessive need to remain in bed.

Where *The Bed Case* differed, and what makes it a strange essay, was Channing's attempt to describe a distinct disease, requiring its own etiology and its own cure. He distinguished Bed Case from hysteria, neuralgia, rheumatism, and palsy, as well as from insanity or monomania. Bed Case, he concluded, is "an imaginary affection," a mental phenomenon, a disease of the mind, sometimes but not always preceded by organic disease. He recognized that it could be "a refuge from a thousand annoyances," a sort of "moral and intellectual hibernation." Ultimately, the cure resided in the patient. When she had regained the will to leave the bed and resume the habits of daily life, the disease would have been conquered.

It is a rambling paper but an indication that, in these later years, Channing was more overtly influenced by views of women as defined by the uterus than he had previously demonstrated. For a variety of reasons, some traceable to the growth of gynecology and others to the same societal changes that produced opposition to birth control and abortion, many physicians shared a similar view.[28] Though Bed Case, if there is such a disease, could be attributed to psychosocial causes, Channing's treatment distinguished him from colleagues who attempted to cure "hysterical" or "neurasthenic" women by gynecological surgery, mesmerism, galvinism, electricity, even confinement in insane asylums.[29] His certainty that Bed Case was a disease of the mind is not very different from subsequent psychiatric interpretations.

THE retirement years brought unexpected honors, including a substantial legacy. A chance meeting on the street one day in 1858 prompted a physician friend to ask if he had heard about "the will." Channing had not. Whereupon his friend explained that he had been present at the deathbed of Dr. Hildreth's widow and that her will named Channing as heir to half her property. Channing was incredulous, for though he remembered his colleague Charles Hildreth well enough, he had only a vague memory of the widow, who had been a patient many years before.[30] She, however, remembered that Channing saved her life during a hazardous delivery and that, because her husband was a professional colleague, he had not charged for the visit. The legacy was a belated expression of gratitude.[31] Her other legatee was the Reverend Theodore Snow, who had married one of her friends. Her property was estimated to be worth between fifty and sixty thousand dollars.[32]

Elizabeth Hildreth had not included her relatives in the will, as retribution for their opposition to her marriage. Now they offered not to contest the legacies if Channing and Snow would grant them a portion. Channing was unwilling to compromise, arguing that Mrs. Hildreth "had not meant to leave a dollar of her fortune to her relations" but had bequeathed the whole estate (with the exception of certain small legacies) to him and Snow and their heirs forever.[33]

Everyone soon knew about Channing's good fortune. Even the *Boston Medical and Surgical Journal* reported it, undoubtedly hoping that other grateful patients would be similarly inspired to honor their physicians.[34] Channing was tremendously pleased. Part of the legacy was in real estate, yielding an annual income.[35] Channing was reputed to be a poor businessman, although he had been a meticulous treasurer for the Massachusetts Medical Society. He admitted that he did not keep good records of fees or debts due to him, relying instead on the honesty of his patients and friends. He once lost several hundred dollars through a forgery he refused to prosecute.[36] Despite his apparent nonchalance, over the years he made good investments in bank and railroad stocks; although he relied on Barbara, his nephew Charles Channing, and the lawyers to manage his money, by old age he was very pleased with himself for accumulating a modest estate.[37]

Retirement elevated Channing to the rank of a "venerable" member of the profession, as is often the case when gratuitous praise is bestowed on elders. He was toasted at annual dinners of the Massachusetts Medical Society— though perhaps not entirely as he would have wished. One year, botanical imagery suffused the citation: "Our friend, Dr. Walter Channing—Though somewhat 'fallen into the sere and yellow leaf,' we are glad to find that he has not yet taken his place in the genus *Gualtheria procumbens*."[38] At a subsequent dinner, he was saluted in an obstetrical idiom. "We see before us to-day, one who has been in labor for more than fifty years; protracted, tedious, however may have been his travail, he exhibits no symptoms of *nervous exhaustion*, he presents no appearance of *puerperal mania* but displays the same vivacity and other peculiarities, which characterized him when we listened to his instructions thirty-five years ago. We rejoice to see him here and rejoice to know that he still labors, well."[39]

More unexpected was his election in 1860 as an Honorary Fellow of the Obstetrical Society of London. The society had been recently founded and

Channing was proud to be recognized as one of two Americans worthy of membership.[40] The other was Fordyce Barker, an outstanding obstetrician in New York who later became the first president of the American Gynecological Society. Shortly after the news of Channing's honor became public, a small group of Boston physicians interested in obstetrics and diseases of women began discussions that led to the creation in 1861 of the Boston Obstetrical Society, the first of its kind in the United States.[41] It would be too much to claim a direct relationship between the events, but the Bostonians were aware of the London society and recognized its potential benefits.[42] Channing readily attended the preliminary meetings. He had already decided that "it would be exceedingly pleasant to me to meet with a few of those with whom I could enjoy free conversation upon matters of professional interest," recognizing that "such exercise of thought and uses of observation would be mutually pleasant and useful."[43] The Obstetrical Society could fill a void left in his life by his resignation from the Society for Medical Improvement.

Channing attended the organizational meeting December 7, 1860, but had to leave early when he was called away to a case of labor. He also missed a lively debate at the next meeting. Since the Society for Medical Improvement and the Society for Medical Observation had fared well without elected officers, there were doubts about the necessity for a president and two vice presidents in the new organization. When a vote was taken to accept the plan for officers, it was with the understanding that they "would enable us to honor distinguished men of the profession" and provide the éclat needed to bring the society to national attention.[44]

Not unexpectedly, Channing was elected president, David Humphreys Storer and Charles Putnam the vice presidents. In his acceptance remarks, Channing referred to the encouraging results "already obtained by a kindred Society in the city of London." He urged the members to aim to "bring together facts and data in regard to obstetric medicine so that disease might be the more readily and certainly diagnosed and treated," pointing out that obstetric phenomena were not being approached with the same clarity and knowledge as other parts of medical science. In that spirit, he offered to prepare a paper himself for delivery at the following meeting.[45]

When the society next convened Channing explained that he had been unable to complete the promised paper, which he had intended to be a discussion of puerperal convulsions. Instead, he gave a brief sketch of the points he planned to present and then led a dialogue in which the members gave their ideas about the subject, especially in regard to the connection between edema, albuminous urine, and convulsions. There was little agreement among the responders, who had seen convulsions with and without edema, with and without albuminous urine, in strong, robust women and in weak, delicate women. Some treated with chloroform, others with ether, some hastened the labor and others were decidedly against such a course. If Channing hoped the society would clarify obstetrical knowledge, it was going to take a long time.

At this same meeting, a subsequent debate about delivery of the placenta gave Channing the chance to describe "two cases which he had seen when the children had lived for a length of time independent of respiration of the lungs."[46] First, he recounted the story of the child he and John Shelby had saved when they were students in Philadelphia. It was one of Channing's favorite anecdotes, repeated here and several other times, always with details of the immersion of the newborn in warm water while the placenta was still attached. The second case concerned a woman who delivered without any assistance, the child and placenta still encased in the membrane.

Some of the younger men present did not enjoy Channing's style. One later wrote,

> Our first president was a peculiar man,—a *genius*; learned, and at times eloquent in speech; and not unlike others in his specialty, somewhat unbalanced and rather erratic. He promised freely, with the fullest intention; not unfrequently coming short in fulfilment. We did not get the promised paper! Instead, we had an interesting impromptu discussion among the members, supplemented by an animated harangue by the President, with some of his "remarkable cases," on a subject incidentally brought before the meeting.[47]

Channing was better prepared in July when he read a paper titled "Concealed accidental hemorrhage at the close of Pregnancy."

During its early years, the society could do little to promote obstetrics within the larger medical discipline, but those who attended had a chance to inform colleagues about interesting cases and seek their reassurance or advice. The minutes of the meetings disclose a broad array of topics, everything from peritoneal tears, internal hemorrhage, and milk leg to the appropriateness of abortion in a case of excessive nausea. Puerperal convulsions continued to receive a lot of attention.[48]

Membership was limited to twenty-five, but there were seldom more than ten men present at any meeting. In addition to the small number of physicians willing to devote their time to obstetrical discussions, the overwhelming distraction of the Civil War nearly put an end to the society. It was resuscitated by the decision to shift the meetings from the rooms of the Massachusetts

Medical Society to the homes of members, where refreshments and sociability enlivened the evenings.[49]

Channing was reelected president in January 1864, but at the following meeting he announced his intention to resign the post. Acknowledging the "sense of advantage . . . derived from a name everywhere held in honor," the society then elected him emeritus president. He continued to attend from time to time, recalling cases from the past, offering insights gleaned from current cases, always asking his colleagues for their ideas. He made his final appearance in October 1865, when he described a case of retained placenta he had seen in Edinburgh and another he had recently attended with Dr. David Humphreys Storer.

The Boston Obstetrical Society grew slowly over the next decades.[50] As physicians became more research-oriented, there were occasional papers based on original findings, but most of the discussion came from clinical experiences.[51] New York had its first obstetrical society in 1864, Philadelphia in 1868. The American Gynecological Society was founded in New York in 1876 and the American Association of Obstetricians and Gynecologists in 1888. Thus, at the end of Channing's life obstetrics and gynecology were acquiring sufficient status to merit their own organizations, but medical specialties such as we have today, with hospital residencies in obstetrics and gynecology and certification by a specialty board, did not emerge until 1930.[52] Throughout most of the nineteenth century, specialism was frowned on. With the exception of surgeons, it was assumed that physicians should be generalists, capable of caring for all diseases and medical conditions other than those of the eye, ear, and skin, and venereal disease.[53]

In 1864 Channing was made an honorary member of the Edinburgh Obstetrical Society, a tribute for which he could thank his friend James Y. Simpson, who had created the organization in 1840 and dominated it for many years.[54] He was also named an honorary member of the Boston Gynecological Society, a more dubious honor, since it was the creation of Horatio Storer and thus had acquired some of the opprobrium with which he was viewed in Boston medical circles.[55]

CHANNING practiced medicine and obstetrics for another ten years following his retirement from the faculty. Some things did not change. He continued to adhere to professional standards, staying with the patient as long as needed, exercising caution when the diagnosis was uncertain, relying on past experience and contemporary information to make decisions. He remained an advocate for anesthesia in difficult labors, in operative obstetrics, and for control of convulsions.[56] James Jackson was still his "master in medicine," respectfully deferred to, continually admired. "How pleasant it is to see him in his old age," Channing wrote when Jackson was eighty-four years old, "walking the streets slowly but surely . . . to give aid and relief where they may be given." Despite Jackson's advanced years, Channing occasionally asked him to consult and together they rode the horse-drawn streetcars if a patient lived too far for them to walk.[57]

Though he acknowledged that heroic medicine was less popular than it had been, he had not completely relinquished his faith in its therapeutic value and did not hesitate to prescribe strong drugs in some situations. In 1854 a male patient asked about the side effects of pills Channing had given him. "I have a perfect confidence in yr judgment in these things & wd not mind a still greater amount of unpleasant sensations if I am to be benefitted in the end." The unpleasant sensations included dizziness, headache, stupor, throbbing in the ears, stiffness about the neck and throat, lameness of the jaws, bursting of the eyes from their sockets, lassitude, and loss of appetite.[58]

Although Channing's belief in "active treatment" extended to other situations, he was not oblivious to newer ideas and adapted when he thought it appropriate. He no longer prescribed cathartics immediately after delivery, accepting John Collins Warren's warning against unnecessary disruption of the system.[59] He rarely bled his patients. He recommended ice as an effective treatment for pain. Newly designed forceps and innovative enema tubes were added to his instrument kit.[60]

As he aged, he had few new patients and relied on consultations for most of his practice. There were more gynecological cases than earlier, although this may only be an artifact of the papers Channing published after retirement, since no casebooks exist. He wrote twelve papers on gynecological problems not directly related to pregnancy or delivery (though often a delayed consequence thereof) and used recent cases as illustrations. Diagnosis and treatment of these disorders required vaginal examinations, by sight as well as by touch. Channing used a speculum with a fenestra, or window, in the tube, insisting, "when an examination of the diseased part is made, the discovery of the nature of the malady is at once made. The sight and the touch should be both employed."[61] Although the Committee on Obstetrics of the AMA endorsed the speculum as early as 1849, many physicians continued to criticize its use as unnecessary and an improper affront to female modesty.[62]

Some of the increase in the number of his gynecological cases can be attributed to the availability of anesthesia, which could ease the woman's shame and reduce the pain of the procedure. Women who had learned about their reproductive system from self-help manuals or lectures at the Ladies' Physiological Institute might decide that some female conditions were not necessarily inevitable or irremediable. The pioneering work of Marion Sims, Thomas Addis Emmett, and Edmund R. Peaslee in New York was known to the profession and helped encourage Channing as he tried to assist some of his own patients. Channing had met Peaslee during a trip to New Hampshire, where they discussed methods of reducing uterine inversions.[63] In Boston, Horatio Storer was leading the fight for acceptance of more drastic gynecological surgery. Nonetheless, Channing continued to shy away from the more dramatic surgical procedures being undertaken by the new generation of gynecologists.

Overall, though, his practice was diminishing. Channing nevertheless continued to respond with his customary energy. At the age of seventy-five he struggled to save the life of a woman who had been neglected by the midwife who delivered her and maltreated by the botanic and homeopathic doctors called when complications developed. Channing observed severe vomiting, difficult breathing, and a weak pulse. He diagnosed retained placenta and suspected that additional problems might be the result of previous abdominal disease. He remained until midnight, administering stimulants at first and opiates later, struggling to stop the bleeding, waiting for expulsion of the placenta. He was there early the following morning and again in the afternoon, four times the next day, 6:00 A.M. and 5:00 P.M. the fourth day, and early the morning of the fifth day, when the woman died.[64]

Three years later, at the age of seventy-eight, he was called around 4:00 A.M. to a woman living nearby on Mt. Vernon Street. She was well past her due date and had begun to hemorrhage. Recognizing the limitations of his years and thinking he might need help, Channing quickly sent for one of the younger men, Dr. Francis Minot, who assisted him in turning and delivering the child.[65]

Channing's final major public appearance was an address on Asiatic cholera delivered at the 1866 annual meeting of the Massachusetts Medical Society.[66] Another cholera epidemic was threatening Boston and physicians were once more debating the fundamental questions of contagion and prevention.[67] Most concluded that cholera was not contagious, often for the same reasons that made it hard to accept puerperal fever as contagious. Channing's manuscript shows how closely he followed the debate and how profitably he used his leisure time.

He recounted the history of the disease from its earliest known appearance in India and transmission across Europe to the succession of epidemics in the United States. Channing was familiar with John Snow's demonstration of the relationship of cholera to polluted water, and with Pettenkofer's theory that land saturated and fermented by polluted water produced the cholera toxin, but, like many others, he had doubts about their applicability in all instances.

Though he cautioned that people living in the Back Bay section of town, where damp cellars rested on filled land, might be among the first to get cholera, he continued to believe that poisoned air "filled with morbid processes" was more likely to cause diseases such as cholera.

Channing urged prevention to forestall another epidemic. A nutritious diet and clean, well-ventilated neighborhoods were essential. But he did not neglect the issues of wealth and poverty that continued to concern him. Citing statistics and information he had gathered from British and American journals, he demonstrated that cholera was less likely to strike among the rich, who lived in the higher parts of the city, which had more salubrious air as well as better water and less polluted land. The poor, lacking decent food, water, and housing and confined to marshy areas of the city, were certain to be disproportionately affected.

CHANNING might have spent the final decades of his life as befitted an elderly and respected physician: gradual loss of patients, slow withdrawal from professional activities, and quiet years in a peaceful environment. The reality was different. In 1856, at the age of seventy, he found himself responsible for five grandchildren, an unexpected event that simultaneously brightened and complicated the remaining years of his life.

Ellen's decision to separate from Ellery seemed irrevocable when made in 1853. The pleasant atmosphere surrounding her little house in Dorchester provided "repose and peace from the terrible tempests" that had made the previous years unbearable.[68] Financial assistance from her father-in-law, supplemented from time to time by Wentworth Higginson and her brothers, kept the children clothed and fed, while moral support tenderly provided by her mother and by Mary Higginson and Barbara sustained her determination to remain apart from Ellery. There were frequent visits back and forth between the children and their grandfather and long periods when the oldest child, Marnie (Margaret Fuller Channing), lived with the Higginsons.

Yet the initial attraction Ellen felt for Ellery was not completely quiescent. As the months passed, she began to experience "a little feeling that there was still some life somewhere in my system . . . and the tho't of Ellery forced itself more & more upon me, day or night he would not leave me." In the summer of 1855, when she realized that she loved him "tenderly as when I stood by his side & received the nuptial benediction," she wrote to tell him so. Though the problems that had caused the separation, Ellery's inability to accept responsibility, uncertain income, noisy children, and a sickly wife, had not disappeared, Ellen recognized that she was "his only friend to whom he had ever unfolded himself." She wanted to "take care of him like a mother," and to ask him to "lay your head on my heart."[69] If he could behave himself, it would be preferable for the children to have their father living with them, and she was certain that he would be a happier man. More letters were exchanged, Ellery began to visit, and by October he was living once more with his wife and children.

Neither the Channings nor the Fullers thought it was a good idea, but Ellen was as headstrong as she had been when she decided to marry Ellery. However, she was not so foolish as to ignore the need to protect herself and the children should the marriage revert to its previous perilous state. A legal document was drawn up guaranteeing custody of the children, the household goods, and half her husband's income to her. Ellery signed reluctantly, as did Higginson, who acted as trustee on Ellen's behalf, though he had serious misgivings about the whole business.

To everyone's amazement, Ellery seemed quite reformed. He attended church regularly, was kind to the children, and, mirabile dictu, had a steady job as assistant editor of the New Bedford Mercury. He rented a room in that city less than sixty miles to the south, but regularly visited his family. Another child, the fifth, was born prematurely on June 15, 1856. It was, as Barbara quite aptly put it, "a much to be deplored event."[70] She was herself badly conflicted by a desire to help Ellen and her obligations to her father, whom she could no longer leave for an extended period. "It leaves him so lonely," she reminded Lucy Russel, "and, you know he is older than he was."[71]

Ellen remained weak. Her chronic cough worsened and there were undiagnosed problems ascribed to internal inflammation. She spent the summer quietly with various members of the Fuller family, and on September 19 came to Walter and Barbara, who had moved to a small house at 45 Bowdoin Street, still close to the top of Beacon Hill. Marnie was with her, the other children having been sent to relatives. On Sunday Ellery visited and then returned to New Bedford. Everyone realized the gravity of her condition but, unable to accept the inevitable, they hoped she would live a few months more. The following evening, while Barbara was helping her into bed, she began to struggle for breath. Walter came quickly. They held her close, applied hot towels to her chest, gave her sips of brandy, and did everything they could to relieve her distress. All their efforts were futile. Ellen's strength dwindled and she died "very gently." Walter turned next to comfort Barbara, who was overcome by the suddenness of the death and distraught by thoughts of the immense loss the children would have to endure. He was as tender toward her as he had been with Ellen.[72]

Whatever memories the scene may have reawakened for Walter, the coincidences were uncanny. The deaths of two young women who had suffered for years from consumption, motherless children—the youngest in each case but a few months old—and a father unable to face his responsibilities. Ellery was hastily summoned. Barbara met him in the basement and assisted him to her room where he remained secluded from everyone but the older children. The house was thronged with mournful family and friends. James Freeman Clarke conducted a service that assuaged some of the grief. Then the children, Ellery, Barbara, and Walter rode in the lead carriage to Mt. Auburn Cemetery, where Ellen was buried, surrounded by flowers, in the Fuller family plot.[73] She was thirty-six years old.

It took several months to sort out plans for the children. At first Ellery indicated that he wanted them with him, but the notion quickly dissipated. His father felt totally incapable of making plans. Higginson had been designated as trustee for the children, so he negotiated with the Fullers. He hoped they would share the responsibilities and expenses that lay ahead. They found many excuses for not doing so, insisting they could accept only a supervisory role. They expected Walter to assume the financial burdens. "They are his only grandchildren, he has adequate means; the law imposes upon the father, and, if he fails, upon the grandfather, the support of grandchildren."[74] In the end, Walter Jr. lived in Wayland with his uncle Richard Fuller, Marnie in Worcester with the Higginsons, and Caroline and Eugene on Beacon Hill with Walter and Barbara. The baby, named Edward for his great-uncle Edward Tyrrel Channing who had died a few months before, boarded with a family in Abington until he was old enough to return to his grandfather's house.[75]

Channing often found the five children, all less than thirteen years old at the time of Ellen's death, more than he could deal with. He complained about noise, commotion, and unruly behavior. At times he was so weary from it all that he feared for his health and begged relief from others in the family.[76] Barbara received the brunt of his exasperation. He blamed her for taking time away from the house for good works. She was so busy "with church and with a Home for fallen women and a Home for fallen men, she literally has no time for the unfallen," he grumbled. Barbara's obsession with abolitionism, her support for an end to union with slave states, and her fervid admiration for John Brown added to her father's aggravation.[77]

At other times, he was paying for new skates, helping with Marnie's expenses, and admiring Eugene, who he thought resembled William Ellery Channing "in the delicacy and beauty of his face."[78] He wrote loving notes to "Walty" with dollar bills enclosed, and signed them "Grumpa." He worried that Carrie lived too much alone with no chance for "moral, intellectual, or physical development." By deed and example, he tried to teach them the importance of hard work, lessons he had been unable to impart to his son. When any of the boys showed the slightest sign of repeating Ellery's ways, he inter-vened to prevent it. He knew he had no choice but to support "all these chil-dren," and ended up hoping "they may be made better by what I do."[79] In truth, he loved them deeply. He also had to admit that Barbara was extraordinary in her devotion to the children.

In the midst of these burdens, Channing continued to send an allowance to Ellery, who had resumed his solitary life in Concord. His friendship with Thoreau flourished. During the final months of Thoreau's life, Ellery was so attentive to the dying man his biographer charged him with "solicitude [that] exceeded anything he had ever accorded his own family."[80] There was little contact with the children, who grew up almost without his realizing it. His father continued to yearn for Ellery's companionship and love.[81]

AFTER so much turmoil, Channing's final years were relatively uneventful. He had always been nostalgic for Newport. He visited from time to time but never as enthusiastically as in August 1859, when the city hosted a reunion for its sons and daughters who now lived elsewhere. It was a splendid occa-sion. Several thousand Newport natives returned from all parts of the country for a full day and evening of festivities. There was a grand parade, a booming artillery salute, flags representing the states from which the visitors had come, fireworks, two immense tents, an elegant dinner, multiple toasts, and effusive speeches. As one of the prominent guests, Channing had been invited to reply to the first toast on behalf of the "returned sons and daughters" of Newport. With characteristic passion, he reminisced about his childhood and his abid-ing love for "*home*, the place of our birth, the land of our fathers . . . where in a word we were made, and from which no new birth can *remake* us."[82] His exhilaration did not quickly subside after his return to Boston. There he amused himself with thoughts of "a house near the sea" where he could "pass what of life remains for me in my native place."[83]

Channing might never have given up medical practice but for a decision he made to move from the city to Dorchester. Yet it was time for full retire-ment. Edward Channing, whose admitted tinkering with facts renders his memoir questionable, despite his illustrious career as a historian and professor at Harvard, wrote that his grandfather was ready to abandon practice when he was no longer certain which drugs were poison and which were not.[84] Walter gave other reasons for leaving his patients. "I am quite tired of roaming about Boston, with its bricks & pavements for green pastures—its horizon the width of a street, & its firmament as large as a french pocket handkerchief," he com-plained to Mary Higginson. "Is it to be wondered at that we are here in Boston, our 180,000, in a spot just 3 by 1, & not a foot bigger. I am sick—dead sick at this imprisonment."[85] He also resented Boston's tax rates.

The house on Tremont Street had been rented out for many years, but in 1866 Channing sold it to Harvey D. Parker for $65,000.[86] Parker owned a hotel around the corner on School Street that had gradually expanded until it abutted Channing's house. By combining the properties, he had access to and from a major thoroughfare. Parker added several more floors to his buildings, including what had been Channing's house, and for many years thereafter the Parker House was considered Boston's most elegant hotel.[87]

Dorchester was still the uncrowded, rural town that had earlier attracted Ellen. Channing purchased a house on a hill overlooking Dorchester Bay, which promised the sight and sounds of the ocean.[88] It was surrounded by an orchard and a garden, a special delight for Barbara, who spent much of her time outdoors. The grandchildren could play in the bucolic surroundings, though they were expected to harvest the fruit and help with other chores.[89] Channing was reinvigorated by country life. He was no longer bothered by neighbors whose proximity impinged on his privacy. Instead, he spent his days in his quiet "book room," where the sound of the wind was like a "harp of a thousand strings," interrupted only by the occasional bark of a distant dog. His eightieth birthday celebration was marked by gifts of books, pictures, delicacies, and "beautiful flowers from beautiful ladies."[90]

Occasionally, he attended meetings of the Norfolk District Medical Society. Requested to talk about his experiences, he decided to discuss dysmenorrhea, which, as he put it, "was looked upon as almost the despair of medicine." Channing described several treatments, including a remedy that women frequently used for relief from painful menses: gin and black pepper, sometimes taken in strong enough doses to produce drunkenness. His own preference was a pill he had often prescribed that included quinine sulfate, extract of belladonna, and extract of coniine (conium). He reported that it had been very successful.[91]

Dorchester was close to Milton, where George Channing, his only surviving sibling, lived with his four daughters. Walter and George dined together on a regular basis, renewing a relationship that had lapsed in recent years. Edward Tyrrel Channing had died in 1856, surrounded by his books and other academic accouterments, and Lucy Russel in 1863.[92] Walter had never made the long-promised visit to his sister in New York.

Professional colleagues were also gone. George Cheyne Shattuck, who had preceded him as a student at the University of Pennsylvania, died in 1854, John Collins Warren two years later, and George Hayward, another prominent surgeon, in 1863. When John Ware died the following year, Channing wrote

View of Savin Hill, Dorchester (courtesy of the Massachusetts Historical Society)

"some men can afford to lose such a friend, I could not."[93] Finally, James Jackson, mentor, friend, and consummate physician, died in 1867, just before his ninetieth birthday. Jacob Bigelow was the only notable physician of Channing's generation to outlive him.

Yet he could look with confidence on the next generation of medical men, which included his eldest grandson and namesake. Channing was especially

Walter Channing (courtesy of the Massachusetts Historical Society)

fond of Walter Jr., and encouraged him to follow whatever career he chose. It
was a compliment to his grandfather as well as an indication of the young
man's talents that he settled on medicine. His grandfather was elated, and
began addressing letters to "W.C. Dr. to Be," advising him to recopy his notes
into a blank book after each lecture, a practice that had served him well in
Philadelphia.[94] Remembering the debts with which he had been saddled when
he was a young man, Channing cheerfully paid for Walter's education at Harvard and for an additional year of European training.[95] In the 1870s Germany
and Austria attracted bright, ambitious American physicians, just as Paris had

been the medical mecca of the 1830s and 1840s and as Britain had appealed
to Channing and the men of his generation.[96]

Channing met old age with equanimity. To commemorate his eighty-second birthday, he composed a poem that began,

> And I have made my last, last journey now,
> And the long voyage of Life is nearly oer,
> I come with withered locks upon my brow
> To lay me weary on life's welcome shore.

The next verses celebrated his youthful years, full of promise, with dreams of friendship, love, beauty, and fame. He continued,

> And whither now has fled that happy dream?
> Where, where that spring that never had a cloud!
> O, sad the story of life's troubled stream!
> With shipwreck everywhere, and death and shroud!

In the next stanza he denied having known relief from past suffering but concluded with a thought that "spreads a calm" and "whispers peace":

> It is the promise of Immortal Youth.—
> The Resurrection of Life's earliest spring,
> Which in its work of ever living Truth,
> A solace for all woe doth daily bring.
>
> Then come again to me that youth's bright hour,
> Oh give me to that age and spring again!
> I'll yield myself to their prophetic power,
> And in the present, find their endless reign.[97]

After living contentedly in Dorchester for five years, Channing was dismayed when the town lost its independent status and was annexed by Boston.[98] Rather than resubmit to the tax collector, he sold his house and moved to Brookline, where the Perkinses and Higginsons had owned estates in his younger years. The town was contiguous with the western edge of Boston and boasted a refined atmosphere of gracious homes and open space. Channing's granddaughter Caroline had married Follen Cabot and was already living there. Marnie, now more properly called Margaret, was engaged to Thacher

Loring. Channing provided the money for her to purchase a home on High Street, close by the Cabots.[99] Shortly thereafter, he rented a house just a few doors away. It was his final home.[100]

He should have been content. He had earlier admitted that the grandchildren were his "chief joy."[101] Now there were frequent visits with Caroline, Margaret, and their growing families. His younger grandsons were affectionate and good company. On occasion they even provided nursing care. Other relatives and old friends were in close proximity.[102] Barbara was unfailing in her devotion. But the idiosyncracies and infirmities of old age crept up. Channing bitterly regretted having left Boston, where there were "libraries—books—men & women . . . matters for interest & thought," and criticized Brookline, "nothing but a receptacle for flies and bugs."[103] He fretted about money, especially after the disastrous Boston fire in 1872, which destroyed hundreds of buildings and ruined many businesses. A series of falls, bad headaches, and gastrointestinal attacks added to his woes. He became more erratic and disorganized.

In October 1874 the family obtained a probate court order naming a legal guardian to administer Channing's financial affairs. Perhaps he had become so overwrought about money the family feared he might do something foolish with his assets.[104] Perhaps Barbara needed to be relieved of an additional responsibility when she was already fully occupied caring for an irascible old man. In any case, the lawyer specified as guardian had already been designated by Channing as executor of his will and trustee for his children and grandchildren of the estate they were to inherit after his death.[105]

Occasional visits from George brightened the dreary days. The brothers took turns reciting familiar passages from Scripture that gave comfort to each. On Walter's ninetieth birthday, April 15, 1876, visitors found him alert and relatively cheerful. He marked the occasion by reading aloud one of his favorite chapters from the Epistles.[106]

Channing died of "old age" on July 27, within weeks of the centennial celebration of the signing of the Declaration of Independence.[107] It was a fitting departure for a man who had grown up in the shadow of the Revolution. His friend and pastor, James Freeman Clarke, officiated at a funeral service at his home and at the burial in Mt. Auburn. In a sermon preached shortly afterward, Clarke compared him to Luke, the beloved physician, rewarded by the "affection which gathers around him" for the toil and anxiety of a medical life.[108]

In his old age, Channing often pondered the lessons of his years in medicine. He had not lost his fascination with the profession he had chosen. It satisfied his great need to be useful. He had helped bring new lives into the world, he had given relief to the sick and the dying, and he had endeavored to

prevent disease. It satisfied his hopes for the future as he conscientiously instructed several generations of young physicians. And it was intellectually
challenging. Medicine asked perplexing questions: "What is life? What is
growth? What is this perpetual motion and how [is it] sustained?" Channing
never found the answer to those questions, but he did know what living is. "It
is action, action of a man's whole nature, the moral, the intellectual and the
physical."[109] Thus had he struggled to live.

Notes

Abbreviations in Notes

Repositories:
Countway Library   Countway Library of Medicine, Harvard Medical School, Harvard
University
BPL   Boston Public Library
MHS   Massachusetts Historical Society, Boston, Mass.

All from Channing Family Collection, Massachusetts Historical Society
WC Papers II   Walter Channing Papers II
WC Papers III   Walter Channing Papers III
WEC Papers   William Ellery Channing Papers
CF Papers   Channing Family Papers
CF Papers II   Channing Family Papers II

Other MHS Collections
HCC Papers   Higginson-Cabot-Channing Papers
JCW Papers   John Collins Warren Papers

Periodicals:
BMSJ   Boston Medical and Surgical Journal
NEJMS   New England Journal of Medicine and Surgery

Notes to Chapter 1

1. Newport's population was 11,000 in 1775, 5,299 in 1776, and 5,530 in 1782. Elaine Forman Crane, *A Dependent People: Newport, Rhode Island in the Revolutionary Era* (New York: Fordham University Press, 1985), pp. 157–68; Carl Bridenbaugh, *Cities in Revolt: Urban Life in America, 1743–1776* (New York: Alfred A. Knopf, 1955), pp. 216–17.

2. Deposition of Mary Channing, July 21, 173[2], CF Papers II.

3. Henry Channing to Edward T. Channing, August 3, 1835, CF Papers II.

4. Ibid.

5. Ibid.

6. William Henry Channing, *Life of William Ellery Channing, D.D.* (Boston: American Unitarian Association, 1880), pp. 4–5; Henry Channing to Edward T. Channing, August 3, 1835, August 8, 1835, CF Papers II.

7. Notes on Ellery genealogy, Newport Historical Society, Newport, R.I.

8. Thomas Wentworth Higginson, "A Revolutionary Congressman on Horseback," in *Travellers and Outlaws: Episodes in American History* (Boston: Lee and Shephard, 1889), pp. 57–87.

9. William Ellery to Richard Henry Dana, March 10, 1819, Dana Family Papers, MHS. There was a two-year hiatus, 1781–1783, in Ellery's membership in Congress. *Biographical Directory of the American Congress, 1774–1949* (Washington: U.S. Government Printing Office, 1950), p. 1125.

10. Channing, *Life of William Ellery Channing*, pp. 1–4; Edward T. Channing, "Life of William Ellery," in *The Library of American Biography*, conducted by Jared Sparks (Boston: Hilliard, Gray, 1836), pp. 87–159; William M. Fowler, Jr., *William Ellery: A Rhode Island Politico and Lord of Admiralty* (Metuchen, N.J.: Scarecrow Press, 1973).

11. Crane, *A Dependent People*, pp. 34–37.

12. George Champlin Mason, *Newport Illustrated* (New York: D. Appleton, 1854); Sheila Steinberg and Cathleen McGuigan, *Rhode Island: An Historical Guide* (Providence, R.I.: Bicentennial Foundation, 1976), pp. 180–221; William G. McLoughlin, *Rhode Island* (New York: W. W. Norton, 1978), pp. 50–108; Dirk J. Struik, *The Origins of American Science (New England)* (New York: Cameron Associates, 1957), pp. 16–18. According to McLoughlin, Rhode Island had a higher proportion of slaves than any other New England colony. Slaves were used on sheep and dairy farms in a "plantation system" (p. 65).

13. I thank Frank Carpenter for sending me the manuscript of his paper, "The Truth about the Duchess."

14. George G. Channing, *Early Recollections of Newport, R.I., from the Years 1793 to 1811* (Newport, R.I.: A. J. Ward; Charles E. Hammett, Jr., 1868), p. 26.

15. Lucy Ellery Channing to Mary Channing, August 1, [1794], CF Papers II.

16. George G. Channing, *Early Recollections*, pp. 26–29.

17. Elizabeth Parsons Channing, *Autobiography and Diary* (Boston: American Unitarian Association, 1907), p. 1.

18. The house at 24 School Street was used after 1867 as the Home for Friendless Children and is today headquarters for Child and Family Services of Newport County, a social service agency.

19. Henry's career is difficult to trace, perhaps because he was less ambitious than his brothers, perhaps because he lacked their intellectual abilities. He seems to have held a series of jobs, remained a bachelor, and was always a worry for his mother. See Chapter 11.

20. WC, "Written by Walter Channing, (M.D.)" (memoir), typescript, p. 2, courtesy of Willard P. Fuller, Jr. (cited hereafter as Memoir).

Channing left at least three accounts of his boyhood and school years and the sequence of events varies among them. The Memoir was written in 1823, primarily for Channing's children. A manuscript titled "Medicine," in WC Papers II, bears no date or indication of its intended audience. "An Address to a Society for Obstetric Improvement," also in WC Papers II, bears no date either, but may have been written for a meeting of the Obstetrical Society of Boston. "Recollections of a Hitherto Truthful Man," written by a grandson, Edward Channing, in 1929, contains stories and his own remembrances of WC. I have tried to make a coherent account from these disparate sources and to be as accurate as they allow.

21. WC, Memoir, pp. 2–3. Many years later, in a poem written about the funeral of his brother William Ellery Channing, Channing recalled his sentiments at the funeral of his father.

I backward look, and in my boyish time,
Now sixty years and more, a funeral was,
Which in my memory freshly lingers still,
And may not leave it; in that, a mourner,
But of years too few to feel what I had lost,
And rather filled with wonder than with grief.
The hearse, the coffin, pall, and bearers there,
Made to my sense and thought a spectacle.
([WC], *New and Old* [Boston: n.p., 1851], p. 27).

22. Part of the Channing real estate became Hammersmith Farm, later renowned as the childhood home of Jacqueline Bouvier Kennedy Onassis. This and other pieces of real estate, once properties belonging to Tories, had been purchased by William Channing from the state during or after the Revolution. I thank Frank Carpenter for this information.

23. See Lucy Channing to Alexander Hamilton and Judge Wilson, December 1793; William Ellery to Alexander Hamilton, December 22, 1794; William Ellery to Oliver Wolcott, May 28, 1795; Oliver Wolcott to William Ellery, January 13, 1796, CF Papers II.

24. Jack Mendelsohn, *Channing the Reluctant Radical* (Boston: Little, Brown, 1971), pp. 19–30.

25. George G. Channing, *Early Recollections*, pp. 133–35. Most of Gibbs and Channing's shipping was done from Bristol, R.I., or Salem and Boston, Mass. Newport never regained the economic prominence it had enjoyed before the war. My thanks to staff members of the Newport Historical Society for suggestions on this point.

26. William Ellery to Martha Dana, November 8, 1817, Dana Family Papers, MHS. Martha Dana's mother was another daughter of William Ellery. Her family and the Channings were particularly close.

27. WC, Medicine, WC Papers II.

28. WC to William Ellery Channing, n.d., WC Papers II.

29. For example, writing about hydrosis and hydrotic fever, Channing explained, "I have spelled them according to their Greek derivation." Similarly he insisted on *anhœmia*, explaining that the usual spelling, *anœmia*, is incorrect.

30. WC, "My Own Times, or 'Tis Fifty Years Since," *Monthly Miscellany and Journal of Health* 1 (1846): 14–24, 38–47, 65–72, quotation p. 40; George G. Channing, *Early Recollections*, p. 74.

31. "Address of Dr. Walter Channing, at the Re-Union at Newport, in Behalf of its Returned Sons and Daughters," in *Re-Union of the Sons and Daughters of Newport, R.I., August 23, 1859,* by George C. Mason (Newport, R.I.: Fred. A. Pratt, 1859), pp. 76–77. Cited hereafter as "Newport Reunion Address."

32. WC, "My Own Times," p. 40; WC, "Newport Reunion Address," pp. 79–82. The doctrine of disinterested benevolence had a long history in New England. Nonetheless, Walter Channing consistently praised Hopkins for the emphasis he gave to it, perhaps not fully understanding Hopkins's role in that tradition. Conrad Edick Wright, *The Transformation of Charity in Postrevolutionary New England* (Boston: Northeastern University Press, 1992), pp. 16–47, esp. 42–47. See also Conrad Wright, *The Liberal Christians: Essays on American Unitarian History* (Boston: Beacon Press, 1970), pp. 22–33.

33. Elizabeth Parsons Channing, *Kindling Thoughts, Aspects of the Present, Fore-gleams*

of the Future Life (Boston: G. H. Ellis, 1892), p. 201; George G. Channing, *Early Recollections*, pp. 30–32.

34. WC, Memoir, p. 4. One of Channing's classmates was Oliver Hazard Perry, the hero of the Battle of Lake Erie during the War of 1812. WC, "Newport Reunion Address," p. 91.

35. Edward Channing, "Recollections of a Hitherto Truthful Man," typescript, courtesy of Willard P. Fuller, Jr. Channing continued to smoke cigars for most of his life.

36. There is no evidence of any artistic talent in Channing, including none of the anatomical or other medical drawings often produced by physicians. Channing later attributed his flirtation with art to the influence of Washington Allston, who attended school in Newport, where he became a particular friend of William Ellery Channing. Allston later married the Channings' sister Ann. [WC], "Washington Allston," *Christian World*, July 22, 1843.

37. WC to William E. Channing, April 25, 180[0?]; WC to W. E. Channing, October 13, 1802; WC to William E. Channing, July 1803; WC to William E. Channing, n.d., WC Papers II.

38. WC, Memoir, p. 8.

39. Ibid., p. 5.

40. WC to William Ellery Channing, June 1803, WC Papers II.

41. Ezra Stiles, *The Literary Diary of Ezra Stiles, DD., LL.D.*, ed. Franklin B. Dexter, 3 vols. (New York: Charles Scribner's Sons, 1901), 1:489. I am indebted to Philip Cash for this information.

42. "Early Physicians of Newport, R.I.," *BMSJ* 61 (1859): 125–26. See also Howard S. Browne, "Newport's Revolutionary Physicians," *Newport History* 54 (Winter 1981): 19–24, which is very unfavorable to Hunter. Newport's William Hunter (1729–1777) claimed to be related to the famous medical brothers William and John Hunter of Glasgow and London. William Hunter was the leading British obstetrician of his time and a consultant to the aristocracy. He made major contributions to obstetrical knowledge with publication of *The Anatomy of the Gravid Uterus* in 1774. He is also remembered for his Great Windmill Street anatomic theater and museum, which significantly advanced the study of anatomy. Fielding H. Garrison, *An Introduction to the History of Medicine*, 4th ed. (Philadelphia: W. B. Saunders, 1929), pp. 339–40.

43. WC, Medicine, WC Papers II. See also Browne, *Newport's Revolutionary Physicians*, pp. 15–19; and George G. Channing, *Early Recollections*, p. 127.

44. WC, Medicine. Channing later wrote that the boy probably suffered from a medullary sarcoma, a diagnosis not known at the time of the operation.

45. Lucy Channing to William Ellery Channing, September 2, 1803, William Ellery Channing Papers, CF Papers.

46. William Henry Channing, *Life of William Ellery Channing*, pp. 110–11; Charles T. Brooks, *William Ellery Channing: A Centennial Memory* (Boston: Roberts Brothers, 1880), pp. 96–97.

47. John Adams made this point about the post-Revolutionary generation very elegantly when he wrote, "I must study Politicks and War that my sons may have liberty to Study Mathematicks and Philosophy. My sons ought to study Mathematicks and Philosophy, Geography, natural History, Naval Architecture, navigation, Commerce and Agriculture, in order to give their Children a right to study Painting, Poetry, Musick, Architecture, Statuary, Tapestry and Porcelaine." John Adams to Abigail Adams, after May 12, 1780, in *Adams Family Correspondence*, ed. L. H. Butterfield et al. (Cambridge, Mass.: Harvard University Press, 1963–   ), 3:341–42. My thanks to Celeste Walker for verifying this quotation for me.

48. Henry K. Beecher and Mark D. Altschule, *Medicine at Harvard: The First 300 Years* (Hanover, N.H.: University Press of New England, 1977), pp. 27–31; Samuel Eliot Morison, *Three Centuries of Harvard* (Cambridge, Mass.: Belknap Press of Harvard University Press, 1963), pp. 167–73. The Hersey bequest was later enlarged by additional contributions from his widow and other members of the family. See Sidney Willard, *Memories of Youth and Manhood*, 2 vols. (Cambridge, Mass.: John Bartlett, 1855), 1:165.

49. Walter Burrage, *A History of the Massachusetts Medical Society, 1781–1922* (Norwood, Mass.: privately printed, 1923); Josiah Bartlett, "A Dissertation on the Progress of Medical Science in the Commonwealth of Massachusetts," *Medical Communications and Dissertations* 2 (1813): 243. See also Philip Cash, "The Professionalization of Boston Medicine, 1760–1803," in *Medicine in Colonial Massachusetts, 1620–1820*, ed. Philip Cash, Eric H. Christianson, and J. Worth Estes (Boston: Colonial Society of Massachusetts, 1980), pp. 69–100.

50. WC, Medicine, WC Papers II.

51. "In selecting a profession, college graduates of that day were mostly limited to the three then called 'learned professions,' Divinity, Law and Medicine. Of these the legal profession was considered as affording scope for the highest intellectual qualifications, and was most resorted to by those who aspired to distinguished social position. On the other hand, the duller class of candidates for the future favor of the public, were content to limit their ambition to a quiet, though sometimes precarious tenure in a country parish." Jacob Bigelow, quoted in George B. Ellis, "Memoir of Jacob Bigelow, M.D., LL.D.," *Proceedings of the Massachusetts Historical Society* 17 (1879–80): 391. Harvard did not yet grant a degree in law. Francis Channing received a bachelor's degree from Harvard before reading law with his uncle Francis Dana.

52. WC, Memoir, pp. 14–15. This was probably the Reverend Zedekiah Sanger, D.D., minister in Bridgewater for thirty-two years, from 1788 till his death in 1820. See *The Bridgewater Book* (Boston: George H. Ellis, 1899), p. 21.

53. Harvard University, Harvard College Faculty Records, vol. 7, "Catalogue of freshmen admitted in 1804," pp. 330, 338, Harvard University Archives. Richard Henry Dana (1787–1879) was a son of Francis Dana, a Revolutionary patriot, statesman, and chief justice of Massachusetts, and Elizabeth Ellery, a sister of Lucy Ellery Channing. He was a good friend of Walter and of Edward Tyrrel Channing. Dana achieved fame as an essayist and poet and as the father of Richard Henry Dana, Jr., who wrote *Two Years before the Mast. New England Historical and Genealogical Register* 8 (1854): 318; *American National Biography* (1999), 6:65–66.

54. Though designated a college during the pre-Revolution years, Harvard was recognized as a university by the constitution of the Commonwealth that went into effect in 1780. Inauguration of the medical school in 1782 was the first step in creating a true university. See Morison, *Three Centuries of Harvard*, pp. 160–61, 167.

55. Conrad Wright, "The Election of Henry Ware: Two Contemporary Accounts, edited with commentary," *Harvard Library Bulletin* 17 (1969): 245–78.

56. Morison, *Three Centuries of Harvard*, p. 190.

57. See, for example, Ronald Story, *The Forging of an Aristocracy: Harvard and the Boston Upper Class, 1800–1870* (Middletown, Conn.: Wesleyan University Press, 1980); E. Digby Baltzell, *Puritan Boston and Quaker Philadelphia: Two Protestant Ethics and the Spirit of Class Authority and Leadership* (New York: Free Press, 1979).

58. For a brief period just before and after the Revolution, more Harvard graduates

pursued medicine than the ministry. I thank Philip Cash for this information. By Channing's time this was not the case. Additionally, many graduates intended to follow their fathers' careers as merchants and bankers.

59. Described by Channing in "A Fragment of a Medical Autobiography, or a Case Reported by the Patient," *BMSJ* 71 (1865): 252. Typhus and typhoid were used interchangeably to describe serious fevers that could be diagnosed only by symptoms.

60. WC, Miscellaneous notes, WC Papers II.

61. WC, Memoir, p. 18.

62. Edward Channing, "Recollections of a Hitherto Truthful Man," p. 4.

63. Harvard University, Commons Papers, "A Statement of Facts Relative to the Late Proceedings in Harvard College, Cambridge," published by the students, Boston, April 10, 1807, Harvard University Archives.

64. Harvard University, Corporation Papers, vol. 4, 1795–1810, April 3, 1807; Harvard University, Corporation Papers, Report of a Committee of the Corporation of Harvard College, May 19, 1807, Harvard University Archives.

65. WC, Memoir, pp. 18–23; Edward Channing, "Recollections of a Hitherto Truthful Man," p. 4. In time most of the rebellious students received a Harvard bachelor's degree, Walter's *ad eundem* in 1867. Edward Tyrrel, who recanted, did not receive a B.A., but this did not prevent him from becoming the Boylston Professor of Rhetoric, a post he held from 1819 to 1851. See also Willard, *Memories of Youth and Manhood*, 2:192–99; "Journal of John Gallison," typescript, Harvard University Archives; *A Narrative of the Proceedings of the Corporation of Harvard College Relative to the Late Disorder in That Seminary* (Cambridge, Mass.: W. Hilliard, 1807).

66. WC, Memoir, p. 20.

67. Edward Channing, "Recollections of a Hitherto Truthful Man," p. 4.

68. WC, Memoir, p. 23.

Notes to Chapter 2

1. WC, "Smallpox," *BMSJ* 62 (1860): 89–95.

2. WC, Medicine, WC Papers II.

3. Jackson received a B.M. (Bachelor of Medicine degree) from Harvard in 1802 and an M.D. seven years later, as was the custom at the time. Until 1811, when this practice was altered, seven years' evidence of medical proficiency and a Latin dissertation were required before the M.D. was bestowed. Morison, *Three Centuries of Harvard*, pp. 170–71; James Jackson Putnam, *A Memoir of Dr. James Jackson* (Boston: Houghton, Mifflin, 1905); George R. Minot, "James Jackson as a Professor of Medicine," *New England Journal of Medicine* 208 (1933): 254–58. For Edward Augustus Holyoke, see Stephen W. Williams, *American Medical Biography or Memoirs of Eminent Physicians* (reprint, New York: Milford House, 1967), pp. 251–75.

4. Jackson had hoped to introduce vaccination to Boston but was preempted by Dr. Benjamin Waterhouse, who had received a copy of Jenner's book, *An Inquiry into the Causes and Effects of the Variolæ Vaccinæ* (1798), early in 1799 from Dr. John Lettsom. Waterhouse sent an announcement of the discovery to the *Columbian Centinal*, where it was published on March 12, 1799. By the time of Jackson's return, Waterhouse had received cowpox lymph from England and had already vaccinated his son and other members of his household. Jackson was doubly disappointed when the vaccine he brought home with him was not

effective and he had to acquire another supply. Beecher and Altschule, *Medicine at Harvard*, p. 43; Howard A. Kelly and Walter L. Burrage, *American Medical Biography* (Baltimore: Norman Remington Co., 1920), p. 1201.

5. WC, Medicine; WC, Memoir, pp. 25–27.

6. At this period there were few American medical books or American editions of foreign medical texts.

7. WC, "The Late John Revere," *BMSJ* 36 (1847): 292–95.

8. WC, Notes for an Address to a Society for Obstetrical Improvement. *Secale cornutum,* or ergot, a fungus found on rye plants, had long been known to stimulate contractions and speed labor, as well as to control hemorrhage, but it was also recognized that it could be dangerous to mother and child. John Stearns is usually credited with reintroducing it in 1807, when he reported the successful use of powdered ergot, giving strict caveats regarding presentation of the fetus lest swift action of the drug bring unexpected consequences. Stearns's work was publicized the following year in the *Medical Repository*, and a protracted argument ensued among physicians regarding the safe use of ergot in obstetrics. Channing's reference suggests either that the physician for whom he was acting was already aware of this publication or that he had been using ergot before Stearns's work was known. See Harold Speert, *Obstetrics and Gynecology in America: A History* (Chicago: American College of Obstetricians and Gynecologists, 1980), pp. 181–82.

9. WC, Notes for an Address to a Society for Obstetrical Improvement. Channing wrote of "Dr. Warren," not specifying father or son. The son, John Collins Warren, is the more likely candidate, since Jackson and the younger Warren were close associates.

10. WC, "A Case," *BMSJ* 69 (1863): 329.

11. Boston's Overseers of the Poor had granted limited access to the Almshouse to students of the Harvard medical professors but not to those of private physicians. The Boston Dispensary was a private charity that provided free medical care to the poor, who were treated in their homes by physicians appointed annually by the Board of Managers. Thomas F. Harrington, *The Harvard Medical School: A History, Narrative and Documentary, 1782–1905*, 3 vols. (New York: Lewis Publishers, 1905), 1:300–301; Robert W. Greenleaf, *An Historical Report of the Boston Dispensary for One Hundred and One Years, 1796–1897* (Brookline, Mass.: Riverdale Press, 1898).

12. WC, "A Case from an Old Common-Place Book," *BMSJ* 67 (1862–63): 212–14.

13. WC, Memoir, p. 26.

14. James Jackson, Receipt, December 18, 1807, Revere Family Papers, MHS.

15. WC to George Gibbs Channing, October 5, 1868, WC Papers II. This amount is based on Channing's recollection in 1868 and may not be accurate. There seems to be no reason why Revere should have paid more than Channing, unless Jackson based his fees on ability to pay.

16. Morison, *Three Centuries of Harvard*, p. 170.

17. WC, Miscellaneous notes, WC Papers II.

18. WC, Memoir, p. 27; Notes for an Address to a Society for Obstetrical Improvement.

19. WC, Notes for an Address to a Society for Obstetrical Improvement. For anatomy laws, see Frederick C. Waite, "The Development of Anatomical Laws in the States of New England," *New England Journal of Medicine* 233 (1945): 716–26; Whitfield J. Bell, "Medicine in Boston and Philadelphia: Comparisons and Contrasts, 1750–1820," in Cash et al., *Medicine in Colonial Massachusetts, 1620–1820*, pp. 166–67.

20. WC, Miscellaneous notes, WC Papers II.

21. Channing's recollections of Waterhouse are different from most interpretations of Waterhouse's personality. They were probably colored by Channing's devotion to James Jackson, who had been outplayed in the smallpox controversy and became a strong critic of Waterhouse. See note 4 above and Chapter 3.

22. WC, Miscellaneous notes, WC Papers II.

23. Godon had arrived in Boston from Paris with letters of recommendation and quickly attracted a small class to his geological and mineralogical lectures. Many of those who participated, Channing included, maintained an interest in these topics throughout their lives. See John Collins Warren, *Address to the Boston Society of Natural History* ([Boston]: J. Wilson & Son, 1853), pp. 5–6.

24. WC, Memoir. For the interest in and importance of geology, see Charles Couloston Gillispie, *Genesis and Geology* (New York: Harper and Row, 1951).

25. As pointed out in note 3 above, Harvard did not grant the M.D. degree until 1811. Channing would have qualified for a Bachelor in Medicine. The Doctor of Medicine degree offered by Pennsylvania would have been an additional incentive to study there.

26. WC to George Gibbs Channing, October 5, 1868, WC Papers II.

27. E. Digby Baltzell, *Puritan Boston and Quaker Philadelphia*; Bell, "Medicine in Boston and Philadelphia," pp. 159–83. Boston's population in 1810 was 32,896. Oscar Handlin, *Boston's Immigrants* (Cambridge, Mass.: Belknap Press of Harvard University Press, 1959), p. 239.

28. Bell, "Medicine in Boston and Philadelphia," pp. 161–62.

29. George W. Corner, *Two Centuries of Medicine: A History of the School of Medicine, University of Pennsylvania* (Philadelphia: J. B. Lippincott, 1965), pp. 1–21; Lisa Rosner, "Thistle on the Delaware: Edinburgh Medical Education and Philadelphia Practice, 1800–1825," *Social Medicine* 5 (1992): 9–42.

30. This was not the situation in London, where hospitals and private teachers provided perfectly good instruction, but there were no university connections. Thus, London students did not receive academic degrees. Oxford and Cambridge were the only degree-granting universities at this time.

31. Lester S. King, *Transformations in American Medicine, from Benjamin Rush to William Osler* (Baltimore: Johns Hopkins University Press, 1991), pp. 19–22, 43–50; Corner, *Two Centuries of Medicine*, p. 67.

32. The College of Philadelphia was renamed the University of the State of Pennsylvania during the Revolutionary War, and after some confusion the medical faculty became part of the university. See Corner, *Two Centuries of Medicine*, pp. 35–37; *Catalogue of Medical Graduates of the University of Pennsylvania with an Historical Sketch of the Origin, Progress and Present State of the Medical Department* (Philadelphia: printed by Lydia R. Bailey, 1836).

33. One advantage for students in Philadelphia was that the thesis could be written in Latin or English, whereas in Edinburgh Latin was still a requirement.

34. Joseph Carson, *A History of the Medical Department of the University of Pennsylvania* (Philadelphia: Lindsay and Blakiston, 1869); Leonard K. Eaton, "Medicine in Philadelphia and Boston, 1805–1830," *Pennsylvania Magazine of Historical Biography* 75 (1951): 66–75.

35. Many of the men who studied at the medical school were not candidates for the degree. "Ledger of Medical Matriculation, 1806–1815," University Archives and Records Center, University of Pennsylvania. I am grateful to Mark Frazier Lloyd, director of the Archives and Records Center, for supplying me with this information. See also Rosner, "Thistle on the Delaware," p. 24; Bell, "Medicine in Boston and Philadelphia," p. 176.

36. The Massachusetts men were Reuben Mussey and Thomas Keegan. In addition, there were three from other New England states. "Ledger of Medical Matriculation, 1806–1815," University Archives and Records Center, University of Pennsylvania.

37. Bell, "Medicine in Boston and Philadelphia," p. 179–80; Eaton, "Medicine in Philadelphia and Boston"; George C. Shattuck to Roswell Shurtleff, November 10, 1806, Shattuck Papers, MHS.

38. Nathan Smith, founder of the medical school at Dartmouth, had been Shattuck's teacher. Shattuck's name is 173rd in a list of 260 matriculants in November 1806. He received the degree of Doctor of Medicine on April 10, 1807, along with 30 other young men. "Ledger of Medical Matriculation, 1806–1815," University Archives and Records Center, University of Pennsylvania. See also *Catalogue of Medical Graduates of the University of Pennsylvania*; Edward Jarvis, "Memoir of the Life and Character of George Cheyne Shattuck," read before the American Statistical Association, April 12, 1854; Howard A. Kelly, *Cyclopedia of Medical Biography* (Philadelphia: W. B. Saunders, 1912), 2:361–62.

39. WC to George C. Shattuck, n.d. [August 1808], Shattuck Papers, MHS. Also WC to Mrs. Lucy Channing, n.d., WC Papers II. Not everyone was as enthusiastic about Barton. Jacob Bigelow, also a pupil of Barton, characterized him as "egotistical, a bad reader and speaker." Vincent Bowditch, *Life and Correspondence of Henry Ingersoll Bowditch* (Boston: Houghton, Mifflin, 1902), 2:285.

40. WC, Medicine.

41. WC, Memoir, pp. 29–30.

42. WC to Edmund Flagg, November 30, 1808, B MS, misc., Countway Library.

43. WC to Francis D. Channing, March 8, [1809], WC Papers II. In addition to Barton and Rush, the faculty included Caspar Wistar, Professor of Anatomy and Midwifery; Philip Syng Physick, Professor of Surgery; John Syng Dorsey (Physick's nephew), Adjunct Professor of Surgery; and James Woodhouse, Professor of Chemistry. Woodhouse died in 1809 and was succeeded the following year by James Redman Coxe. Corner, *Two Centuries of Medicine*, pp. 49–54.

44. Rush described Ellery as "A lawyer somewhat cynical in his temper, but a faithful friend to the liberties of his country. He seldom spoke in Congress, but frequently amused himself in writing epigrams on the speakers which were generally witty and pertinent and sometimes poetical." "Travels through Life," in *The Autobiography of Benjamin Rush*, ed. George W. Corner (Princeton, N.J.: Princeton University Press for the American Philosophical Society, 1948), p. 145. Walter Channing too was noted for his wit, a trait he may have inherited from his grandfather.

45. "University of Pennsylvania," *Western Medical Gazette* 2 (1834): 233–37.

46. WC, "Never Too Late to Mend," *BMSJ* 61 (1859): 109–13, 135–43, reference to Rush p. 109.

47. King, *Transformations in American Medicine*, pp. 49–55; Richard H. Shryock, *Medicine in America: Historical Essays* (Baltimore: Johns Hopkins University Press, 1966), pp. 233–51; Corner, *Two Centuries of Medicine*, pp. 32–48; John Duffy, *The Healers: A History of American Medicine* (Urbana: University of Illinois Press, 1979), pp. 89–97. Rush has been criticized for many aspects of his teaching, including his inability to consider alternative theories and his ignorance of newer investigative methods, such as pathologic anatomy.

48. WC, Medicine.

49. Young, like the other professors in Edinburgh, was appointed by the town council, not by the university, which was governed by the Faculty Senatus, to which he was not

admitted. Nonetheless, Young succeeded in dissipating popular prejudice against formal instruction of midwives. If the Senatus did not consider obstetrics sufficiently academic to admit him to their ranks, the town council understood that the health of women would be better protected by well-trained physicians. See Alexander Grant, *The Story of the University of Edinburgh during its First Three Hundred Years*, 2 vols. (London: Longmans, Green & Co., 1884), 2:414–16.

50. Young was preceded as professor by Joseph Gibson and Robert Smith, but their instruction was aimed at midwives and not at male physicians. John D. Comrie, *History of Scottish Medicine*, 2d ed., 2 vols. (London: Wellcome Historical Medical Museum, 1932), 1:299–300; Grant, *Story of the University of Edinburgh*, 2:414–15.

51. At King's College in New York, where the second medical school was created during the colonial period, John Van Brugh Tennant was appointed Professor of Midwifery in 1767. His influence was negligible. Subsequently, midwifery instruction was part of instruction in other medical subjects, as it was in Pennsylvania. Samuel Bard, Professor of Midwifery and of the Theory and Practice of Medicine, was the first American to write an obstetrical textbook, which reached five editions. King's College became Columbia College after the Revolution, but the medical school did not prosper. In 1807 the College of Physicians and Surgeons was chartered and its faculty eventually joined with the group at Columbia. Speert, *Obstetrics and Gynecology in America*, pp. 73–75; Irving S. Cutter and Henry R. Viets, *A Short History of Midwifery* (Philadelphia: W. B. Saunders, 1964), pp. 147–51.

52. Speert, *Obstetrics and Gynecology in America*, pp. 72–73. For Chapman, see Kelly, *Cyclopedia of American Medical Biography*, 1:171–72; Samuel D. Gross, ed., *Lives of Eminent American Physicians and Surgeons of the Nineteenth Century* (Philadelphia: Lindsay & Blakiston, 1861), pp. 663–78; Corner, *Two Centuries of Medicine*, pp. 66–67. For James, see Corner, *Two Centuries of Medicine*, pp. 55–56, 86; Carson, *History of the Medical Department*, pp. 114–15; Lewis C. Scheffey, "The Earlier History and the Transition Period of Obstetrics and Gynecology in Philadelphia," *Annals of Medical History*, 3d ser., 2 (1940): 215–24.

53. WC, Notes for an Address to a Society for Obstetrical Improvement.

54. Shelby was the son of a governor of Tennessee.

55. Channing delighted in recounting the story and did so many times. See, for example, WC, "Cases," *BMSJ* 54 (1856): 389–95, 431–36, esp. 434–35; Obstetrical Society of Boston, Records, March 2, 1861, Countway Library.

56. WC, "Cases," *BMSJ* 54 (1856): 434.

57. Ibid., p. 435.

58. WC Papers II.

59. WC, Memoir, p. 32. No copy of the thesis is known to exist. I am grateful to Mark Frazier Lloyd, director of the Archives and Records Center, University of Pennsylvania, for this information. The university conferred the degree of Doctor of Medicine on April 20, 1809, to sixty-two men, including Channing.

60. WC to William Ellery Channing, March 23, [1809]; WC to Francis D. Channing, March 8, [1809], WC Papers II. Channing signed the letter to William with "M.D." at his signature.

61. WC, "Cases from My Notebook," *BMSJ* 62 (1860): 517–24, esp. 521. For yellow fever, see John Duffy, *The Sanitarians* (Urbana: University of Illinois Press, 1990), pp. 38–47; John B. Blake, *Public Health in the Town of Boston, 1630–1822* (Cambridge, Mass.: Harvard University Press, 1959), Chapters 8 and 10.

62. WC to George C. Shattuck, November 16, 1809, Shattuck Papers, MHS.

63. George Cheyne Shattuck to Jacob Bigelow, n.d. [1810], B MS c25.2, Countway Library.

64. WC to Benjamin Barton, March 20, [1810]; WC to Benjamin Barton, May 1810, American Philosophical Society Library. On May 31, 1810, the Censors of the Massachusetts Medical Society "voted to license Walter Channing, M.D., of Boston." Massachusetts Medical Society, Record of the Meetings of the Censors, Countway Library. Licensure was not the same as fellowship. Channing was admitted as a Fellow in 1814. Massachusetts Medical Society, *A Catalogue of the Honorary and Past and Present Fellows, 1781–1931* (Boston: Massachusetts Medical Society, 1931). The hiatus between licensure and fellowship was not uncommon. In 1810 Channing was also admitted to the Boston Medical Association, which was primarily concerned with regulating fees. Boston Medical Association, List of Members, Countway Library.

65. WC to Barton, March 20, [1810], American Philosophical Society Library. Jacob Bigelow, another Bostonian, who graduated from the University of Pennsylvania the year after Channing, also despaired of success when he returned home. Fortunately, Jackson took him into his practice, thereby assuring Bigelow's success. My thanks to Richard Wolfe for reminding me of the similarity.

66. George Cheyne Shattuck to Jacob Bigelow, n.d. [1810], B MS c25.2, Countway Library.

67. *Salmagundi; or, The Whim-Whams and Opinions of Launcelot Langstaff, Esq. and Others*, a humorous periodical edited by Washington Irving, William Irving, and James Kirk Paulding, published twenty numbers between January 1807 and January 1808. Its bias was Federalist and conservative, but the wit and whimsy were considerable. See William Rose Benet, ed., *The Reader's Encyclopedia*, 3d ed. (London: A. & C. Black, 1988), p. 860; "Washington Irving," in *Dictionary of American Biography*, 9:505–11.

68. WC, Notes for an Address to a Society for Obstetrical Improvement.

69. WC, Memoir, p. 36.

70. For Walter Channing, Esq., and the Gibbs fortune, see Frank Carpenter, "Paradise Held: William Ellery Channing and the Legacy of Oakland," *Newport History* 65 (1994): 90–127.

71. Bartlett, "Dissertation on the Progress of Medical Science in the Commonwealth of Massachusetts," p. 243.

72. "Dr. Ephraim Eliot's Account of the Physicians of Boston," *Proceedings of the Massachusetts Historical Society* 7 (1863): 177–84. Lloyd had a large general practice, in addition to midwifery, and was one of the founders of the Massachusetts Medical Society. See also James Thacher, *American Medical Biography* (Boston: Richardson & Lord and Cotton & Bernard, 1828), pp. 359–76; Kelly and Burrage, *Dictionary of American Medical Biography*, 2:751; "Notice of the Late James Lloyd," *NEJMS* 2 (1813): 2.

73. George Lovering Bowen, *James Lloyd II, M.D. (1728–1810) and His Family on Lloyd's Neck* (n.p.: privately printed, 1988), pp. 180–82. In his memorial sermon, Dr. J. S. J. Gardiner, rector of Trinity Church, offered the following praise of Lloyd: "There is probably no physician now living, to whom so many individuals have been under professional obligations. The publick have lost in him a practitioner of the first-rate skill and respectability . . . a gentleman of consummate good-breeding." In Bowen, *James Lloyd II*, p. 182.

74. For Jeffries as Lloyd's pupil, see Philip Cash, "The Professionalization of Boston Medicine," in Cash et al., *Medicine in Colonial Massachusetts*, p. 77; "Sketch of the Medical Life of the late Dr. John Jeffries," *NEJMS* 9 (1820): 63–72. Jeffries had an unusual career. He

accompanied the British troops when they left Boston for Halifax in 1776, rendered medical service during the campaign against the southern colonies, then went to England, where he remained until 1789. During the years in England his practice was almost entirely in midwifery and diseases of children, but he found time to learn ballooning and made the first aerial voyage across the English Channel to France. When he returned to Boston, he experienced initial animosity because of his wartime politics, but these soon vanished in the face of his superior medical skills. He was reported to have had nearly two thousand cases of midwifery between 1790 and his death in 1819, and to have lost only one patient.

75. Richard W. Wertz and Dorothy C. Wertz, *Lying-In: A History of Childbirth in America* (New York: Free Press, 1977), pp. 30–34; Adrian Wilson, *The Making of Man-midwifery: Childbirth in England, 1660–1770* (Cambridge, Mass.: Harvard University Press, 1995), p. 5; Hilary Marland, ed., *The Art of Midwifery: Early Modern Midwives in Europe* (London and New York: Routledge, 1993). For a full account of the career of one of the most important French midwives, see Nina Rattner Gelbart, *The King's Midwife: A History and Mystery of Madame du Coudray* (Berkeley: University of California Press, 1998).

76. Wilson, *Making of Man-midwifery*, is the most recent and best-researched study of this subject. See also Marland, *Art of Midwifery*; Thomas R. Forbes, "The Regulation of English Midwives in the Sixteenth and Seventeenth Centuries," *Medical History* 8 (1964): 235–44; Thomas R. Forbes, "The Regulation of English Midwives in the Eighteenth and Nineteenth Centuries," *Medical History* 15 (1971): 352–62; Barbara Brandon Schnorrenberg, "Is Childbirth Any Place for a Woman? The Decline of Midwifery in Eighteenth-Century England," in *Studies in Eighteenth-Century Culture* 10 (1981): 393–408; David Harley, "Historians as Demonologists: The Myth of the Midwife-witch," *Social History of Medicine* 3 (1990): 1–26.

77. There is an extensive literature on the change from midwives to male obstetrical care. For a balanced account, see Judith Walzer Leavitt, *Brought to Bed: Childbearing in America, 1750–1950* (New York: Oxford University Press, 1986); Wilson, *Making of Man-midwifery*; Irvine Loudon, "The Making of Man-Midwifery, Essay Review," *Bulletin of the History of Medicine* 70 (1996): 507–15. Other sources more critical of the shift from midwife to male physician are Judith Barrett Litoff, *American Midwives, 1860 to the Present* (Westport, Conn.: Greenwood Press, 1978); Wertz and Wertz, *Lying-In*; Jane B. Donegan, *Women and Men Midwives: Medicine, Morality and Misogyny in Early America* (Westport, Conn.: Greenwood Press, 1978). For the development of the demand for medical care, including obstetric care from medical men, in eighteenth-century Britain, see Irvine Loudon, *Medical Care and the General Practitioner, 1750–1850* (Oxford: Clarendon Press, 1986); W. F. Bynum and Roy Porter, eds., *William Hunter and the Eighteenth-Century Medical World* (Cambridge: Cambridge University Press, 1985); Roy Porter, ed., *Patients and Practitioners: Lay Perceptions of Medicine in Pre-industrial Society* (Cambridge: Cambridge University Press, 1985).

78. WC, *A Physician's Vacation* (Boston: Ticknor and Fields, 1856), pp. 2–4.

79. WC, Journal, transcribed by Barbara Perkins Channing, WC Papers III. *New and Old*, a book of poetry published anonymously by Channing in 1851, included twenty-three poems that recalled persons, places, and incidents from his months in England and Scotland. Since the poems are based on memory, and the facts altered to fit the rhymes, I prefer to rely on the journal written at the time to describe Channing's year abroad.

80. WC to Mrs. Lucy Channing, July 20, 1810, August 2, [1810], WC Papers II.

81. WC to George Cheyne Shattuck, August 16, 1810, Shattuck Papers, MHS; WC, "The Late John Revere," *BMSJ* 36 (1847): 292–95.

82. For Lowell, see C. David Heymann, *American Aristocracy: The Lives and Times of James Russell, Amy and Robert Lowell* (New York: Dodd, Mead, 1980), pp. 19–20.

83. During his months in Edinburgh, Channing lodged on College Street, just opposite the college gate. See WC, *New and Old*, p. 110.

84. WC, Journal, WC Papers III.

85. WC, Sketch of a Short Tour into the Highlands of Scotland in the Autumn of 1810, typescript, courtesy of Willard P. Fuller, Jr.

86. Walter Channing was one of 116 who registered for the winter 1810 course on obstetrics. He also registered for the spring 1811 course, indicating that this was his second sitting for the course. Courtesy Iain Milne, librarian, Royal College of Physicians, Edinburgh. He gave his residence as Newport, R.I. At the University of Pennsylvania he had registered as from Massachusetts. Perhaps his failure to attract patients in Boston had persuaded him that his stronger attachment was with Newport.

87. WC to George Cheyne Shattuck, September 16, 1810, Shattuck Papers, MHS. For Hamilton, see J. H. Young, "James Hamilton (1767–1839), Obstetrician and Controversialist," *Medical History* 7 (1963): 62–73; T. N. MacGregor, "The Rise and Development of the Edinburgh School of Obstetrics and Gynæcology, and its Contribution to British Obstetrics," *Journal of Obstetrics and Gynæcology of the British Empire* 66 (1959): 998–1105; John Sturrock, "Early Maternity Hospitals in Edinburgh (1756–1879)," *Journal of Obstetrics and Gynæcology of the British Empire* 65 (1958): 122–31.

88. Hamilton antagonized the Senatus (faculty senate), which had refused to include the Professor of Midwifery among them, by appealing to the Edinburgh Town Council, which had the right to require that he be made a member of the Senatus. The Town Council so decreed in 1824, but continued opposition from the Senatus prevented Hamilton from taking his place among them for another year. It was not until 1830 that the study of midwifery was made a compulsory requirement for graduation. See Comrie, *History of Scottish Medicine*, 2:485–88; Grant, *Story of the University of Edinburgh*, 2:417–19.

89. WC, Notes for an Address to a Society for Obstetrical Improvement. Despite his pugnacious personality, Hamilton was respected for supporting the Lying-in Hospital at his own expense and for refusing to desert his poorer patients in the city in order to attend wealthy women waiting to be confined in their country estates. "They must come to me" was his reply to their entreaties. Grant, *Story of the University of Edinburgh*, 2:417–19.

90. WC to George Cheyne Shattuck, September 16, 1810, Shattuck Papers, MHS.

91. For Anne MacVicar Grant (1755–1838), see *Dictionary of National Biography* (1967), 8:376–78.

92. Isaac Hurd to WC, March 15, 1811, WC Papers II.

93. WC to George C. Shattuck, April 20, 1811, Shattuck Papers, MHS. For Astley Cooper, see Samuel Wilks and G. T. Bettany, *A Biographical History of Guy's Hospital* (London: Ward, Lock, Bowden & Co., 1892), pp. 317–29; for Haighton, see Wilks and Bettany, *Biographical History of Guy's Hospital*, pp. 363–65; H. C. Cameron, *Mr. Guy's Hospital, 1726–1948* (London: Longmans, Green, 1954), p. 160.

94. WC to George C. Shattuck, April 20, 1811. According to Cameron, *Mr. Guy's Hospital*, Haighton was a good teacher and a magnificent lecturer. His primary medical interest was physiology and he had been the first lecturer in physiology at Guy's before taking on the midwifery lectures.

95. "While arguing from my own experience, I am bound to refer to that of others. I only refer to my master in midwifery Dr. John Haighton of London whose whole experience

showed the safety of induced labour in all periods of pregnancy." WC to George Shore, n.d., Countway Library. I am grateful to Richard Wolfe for bringing this letter to my attention. Similarly, Channing also wrote, "Nearly half a century ago, it was our privilege to attend the midwifery lectures of Dr. John Haighton in London; and a better lecturer than Haighton, is not in our memory." WC, "Death of Charlotte Bronte," *BMSJ* 57 (1857): 96.

96. WC, Notes for an Address to a Society for Obstetrical Improvement.

97. WC to George C. Shattuck, April 20, 1811, Shattuck Papers, MHS.

98. Ibid.

99. Edward T. Channing to WC, July 10, 1810, December 24, 1810, CF Papers II; Edward T. Channing to WC, March 30, 1811, WC Papers II.

100. Allston did portraits of several members of the family, including Lucy Ellery Channing, Ann Channing Allston, Francis Dana Channing, and William Ellery Channing.

101. William Henry Channing, *Life of William Ellery Channing*, p. 314.

102. Edward Tyrrel Channing to WC, March 30, 1811, WC Papers II.

103. William Henry Channing, *Life of William Ellery Channing*, pp. 314–17: Susan Higginson Channing to Louise Higginson, November 30, 1810, January 9, 1811, HCC Papers.

104. William Ellery Channing to William Ellery, March 13, 1811, WEC Papers.

105. WC to George Gibbs Channing, March 26, 1872, WC Papers II. Walter was not the only one to find Francis difficult. George Ticknor described the "severity in his character" and "that frigid and repulsive atmosphere in which he seemed delighted to involve himself and with which . . . I used frequently to be offended." George Ticknor to Edmund Flagg, May 17, 1811, Ms Am 547(1), BPL.

106. George Ticknor to Edmund Flagg, May 17, 1811, Ms Am 547(1), BPL.

107. William Ellery Channing to William Ellery, March 13, 1811, WEC Papers, MHS; [Edward T. Channing], November 10, 1812, HCC Papers.

108. WC, Miscellaneous draft manuscript, WC Papers II.

109. WC, "My Own Times."

Notes to Chapter 3

1. The identity of Aunt Polly, referred to by Edward Channing, "Recollections of a Hitherto Truthful Man," p. 5, remains a mystery.

2. Oliver Wendell Holmes, in a letter to his father written from Paris in 1835 to urge continued financial support for his medical studies, added, "remember that Dr. Channing is said to have been years in debt for his European residence." Eleanor M. Tilton, *Amiable Autocrat: A Biography of Dr. Oliver Wendell Holmes* (New York: Henry Schuman, 1947), p. 131. William Ellery Channing's wealth came from his wife, who was also his first cousin, Ruth Gibbs. Edward Tyrrel Channing also married a cousin, Henrietta Ellery, whose Newport family had some wealth. Neither of Channing's wives was wealthy in her own right.

3. *The Boston Directory* (Boston: Edward Cotton, 1810); Handlin, *Boston's Immigrants*, p. 238. Demand for medical care was far less at the beginning of the nineteenth century than it is at present. National statistics for 1995 indicate 274 physicians per 100,000 resident population in the United States, or 1 to 365. Boston, with forty-five physicians and 33,000 people in 1810, had a ratio of 1 to 733. U.S. Bureau of the Census, Current Population Reports, Series p-25, Nos. 107b, 104, and 1127, Washington, D.C.: U.S. Government Printing Office, March 1992 and 1995 and August 1985.

4. George E. Ellis, "Memoir of Jacob Bigelow, M.D., LL.D.," *Proceedings of the Massachusetts Historical Society* 17 (1879–80): 383–467.

5. Boston Medical Association, List of Members, Countway Library. The Boston Medical Association was founded in 1806 to set minimum fees for various medical and surgical cases and otherwise supervise the ethical behavior of its members. It replaced the Boston Medical Society, which was founded in 1780 but had lapsed. *Rules and Regulations of the Boston Medical Association* (Boston: Printed by J. Belcher, 1811). See also Mark S. Blumberg, "Medical Society Regulation of Fees in Boston 1780–1820," *Journal of the History of Medicine and Allied Sciences* 39 (1984): 303–38.

6. Susan Higginson Channing to Fanny Searle, [September 1810], HCC Papers.

7. Susan Higginson Channing to Fanny Searle, [August 1813], HCC Papers. The correspondence does not explain the nature of the illness or of Walter's cure.

8. Walter Channing to W. Channing, 1813, 1819, CF Papers II.

9. Catherine Searle to Fanny Searle, n.d., b MS Am 1175, Houghton Library, Harvard University.

10. Barbara Perkins Higginson to Lucy Russel, August 31, [1813], WC Papers II.

11. The university had long sought permission from the Overseers of the Poor for the medical professors to give clinical lectures at the Almshouse Hospital, which usually had about fifty patients, medical and surgical. In 1810, permission was granted. James Jackson, newly appointed lecturer in clinical medicine, gave the first clinical lectures there. Draft of a Petition to Overseers of the Poor of the Town of Boston, May 1810; Overseers of the Poor, July 26, 1810; Vote of Professors of Harvard University attendant on the Almshouse, October 20, 1810; Notice of Medical Institution, September 5, 1810, JCW Papers; Harrington, *Harvard Medical School*, 1:300–301, 362.

12. WC, List of Midwifery Cases, WC Papers III. See also Amalie M. Kass, "The Obstetrical Casebook of Walter Channing, 1811–1822," *Bulletin of the History of Medicine* 67 (1993): 494–523. John Ware later wrote about his obstetrical experience at the Almshouse: "Puerperal women in the Almshouse when they are young and healthy subjects do commonly very well, although their infants, which are generally illegitimate, from the neglect and carelessness of their mothers combined with the confined air of the place, are seldom healthy." John Ware, "Account of some Puerperal Cases, which Occurred at the Boston Almshouse during the Winter of 1823–24," *NEJMS* 14 (1825): 13–20.

13. Philip Cash, "Professionalization of Boston Medicine," in Cash et al., *Medicine in Colonial Massachusetts*, pp. 87–88. See also Philip Cash, "Setting the Stage: Dr. Benjamin Waterhouse's Reception in Boston, 1782–1788," *Journal of the History of Medicine and Allied Sciences* 47 (1992): 5–28; Philip Cash and Yoshio Higomoto, "Further Information Concerning Dr. Benjamin Waterhouse's Appointment as Harvard's First Professor of Medicine," *Journal of the History of Medicine and Allied Sciences* 49 (1994): 419–28; Beecher and Altschule, *Medicine at Harvard*, pp. 40–45; Benjamin Waterhouse, Memoirs, H MS b16.6, Countway Library.

14. Warren's wife was a lapsed Quaker born in Newport, but these affinities with Waterhouse did not gain Warren's admiration for his adversary.

15. Philip Cash, whose long-awaited biography of Benjamin Waterhouse will soon be published, points out that until 1810 Waterhouse had been an Adams Federalist. Waterhouse became acquainted with Adams and his sons in Holland when Adams was negotiating recognition and loans for the American cause.

16. Putnam, *Memoir of Dr. James Jackson*, pp. 223–29.

17. Such an experiment would be considered highly unethical in present-day medical circles. Nor would the public permit it.

18. It should be noted that Jackson was young and inexperienced when he proposed a vaccination experiment to the Board of Health. Waterhouse's involvement with vaccination was also problematic. He attempted to establish a monopoly on the vaccine by charging physicians using the material a percentage of their fees. On the other hand, he convinced Thomas Jefferson about the importance of vaccination, which led the president to promote it in Virginia and nationally. Channing regularly gave Jackson credit for promoting vaccination in Massachusetts. See WC, "Smallpox," *BMSJ* 62 (1860): 89–95. For Waterhouse and vaccination, see Bartlett, "Dissertation on the Progress of Medical Science in the Commonwealth of Massachusetts," pp. 258–59; Duffy, *Healers*, pp. 163–64; Beecher and Altschule, *Medicine at Harvard*, pp. 43–44; John B. Blake, *Benjamin Waterhouse and the Introduction of Vaccination: A Reappraisal* (Philadelphia: University of Pennsylvania Press, 1957).

19. Willard, *Memories of Youth and Manhood*, 1:165–74; Walter Muir Whitehill, *Boston: A Topographical History* (Cambridge, Mass.: Belknap Press of Harvard University Press, 1963), pp. 48–52.

20. The university stipulated that lectures in anatomy and chemistry be offered annually to the senior undergraduates and that the fees formerly received by the professors from those students be thenceforth allotted to the university. See Harrington, *Harvard Medical School*, 1:357–58.

21. Philip Cash suggests that Waterhouse took up temporary residence in Boston until his dismissal two years later.

22. Both Warren and Jackson served as president at a later time.

23. Burrage, *History of the Massachusetts Medical Society*, pp. 74–77.

24. Ibid., pp. 77–81; Harrington, *Harvard Medical School*, 1:379–96.

25. Burrage, *History of the Massachusetts Medical Society*, p. 78. See also Samuel A. Green, *History of Medicine in Massachusetts: A Centennial Address delivered before the Massachusetts Medical Society at Cambridge, June 7, 1881* (Boston: A. Williams, 1881), pp. 111–17.

26. Edward Warren, *Life of John Collins Warren with the Autobiography and Journals*, 2 vols. (Boston: Ticknor and Fields, 1860), 1:104–7.

27. Harrington, *Harvard Medical School*, 1:389.

28. Morison, *Three Centuries of Harvard*, pp. 222–23. The findings of the committee appointed to investigate the charges against Waterhouse enumerated other scurrilous attacks on his opponents.

29. Harrington, *Harvard Medical School*, 1:386–91; Burrage, *History of the Massachusetts Medical Society*, pp. 77–81.

30. Harvard University, Records of the Overseers, vol. 5, October 29, 1805–October 8, 1812; Harvard University, Corporation Records, vol. 5, 1810–1819, August 20, 1812, Harvard University Archives. *Ad eundem gradum* is Latin for "to the same degree." In American colleges a degree recipient of one institution was allowed to take the same degree at another, on payment of a fee. By this he was admitted to the same privileges as a graduate of his adopted alma mater.

31. Burrage, *History of the Massachusetts Medical Society*, p. 70.

32. The *Medical Repository*, first published in New York in 1797, was the first real medical periodical to appear in the United States. Other journals that preceded the *New England Journal* are the *Philadelphia Medical and Surgical Journal* (1803), *Philadelphia Medical Museum* (1804), *American Medical and Philosophical Register* (New York, 1810), and *The*

Eclectic Repository (Philadelphia, 1810). Richard Harrison Shryock, *Medicine and Society in America: 1660–1820* (Ithaca: Cornell University Press, 1962), pp. 36–37. Baltimore also boasted two short-lived journals, the *Baltimore Medical and Physical Recorder* (1809) and the *Baltimore Medical and Philosophical Lyceum* (1811). Joseph Garland, "Medical Journalism in New England, 1788–1924," *BMSJ* 190 (1924): 865–79.

33. Warren, *Life of John Collins Warren,* 1:79, 117; Putnam, *Memoir of Dr. James Jackson,* p. 281. See also WC to Benjamin Vaughn, March 19, 1816, Benjamin Vaughn Papers, American Philosophical Society, in which Channing expresses his regret for "errors of sense and type which disfigured the last number [of the Journal]. I do this the more freely, because it was my lot to be its Editor. The perpetual labour of lecturing while it was printing, & while all the articles of the Review were composing, left no time for the correction of the manuscripts, or of the press. This is the cause of its various errors, not an excuse for them."

34. "Man, being the servant and interpreter of nature, can do and understand so much and so much only as he has observed in fact or in thought of the course of nature; beyond this he neither knows anything nor can do anything." *Novum Organum.* Translation from Edwin A. Burtt, ed., *The English Philosophers from Bacon to Mill* (New York: Random House, Modern Library Edition, 1939), p. 28.

35. See note 8, Chapter 2.

36. WC, "Remarks on Diseases Resembling Syphilis, with Observations on the Action of Those Causes Which Produce Them," *NEJMS* 1 (1812): 65–68, 139–50, 245–50, 377–82. This paper was subsequently excerpted in the *London Medical and Physical Journal* 29 (1813): 60.

37. "Puerperal Fever with Diarrhaea," *NEJMS* 2 (1813): 232–44; "Practical Remarks on Some of the Predisposing Causes, and Prevention, of Puerperal Fever, with Cases," *NEJMS* 6 (1817): 157–69; "A Case of Arm Presentation, with Remarks," *NEJMS* 11 (1822): 30–37; "Case of Inversio Uteri with Comments," *NEJMS* 11 (1822): 264–69. Non-obstetrical articles included "Spontaneous Hæmorrhage," *NEJMS* 4 (1815): 306–18; "A Case of Alarming Hæmorrhage, from the Extraction of a Tooth," *NEJMS* 6 (1817): 235–37; "A Topographical Sketch of Nahant, with Comparative Meteorological Tables for July, August, and September, 1820, with Some Observations on Its Advantages as a Watering Place," *NEJMS* 10 (1821): 22–35; "An Account of Some of the Agents, Medicinal or Mechanical, which Have Been Applied Externally, in the Treatment of Diseases; with Notices of Some of the Writings which Have Been Particularly Devoted to This Subject," *NEJMS* 10 (1821): 250–64, 321–37. The article about Nahant, extolling the healthy aspects of this newly developed summer resort, is interesting because the hotel there was built by Thomas Handasyd Perkins, uncle of Channing's wife.

38. "Cases of Delirium Tremens," *NEJMS* 8 (1819): 15–28. See Thomas Sutton, *Tracts on Delirium Tremens* (London: T. Underwood, 1813). John Ware later wrote a more important paper on delirium tremens: *Remarks on the History and Treatment of Delirium Tremens* (Boston: Hale, 1831).

39. "Medical Lectures," *NEJMS* 1 (1812): 406; "Lectures on Midwifery," *NEJMS* 2 (1813): 309. See also Admission Card to Midwifery Lectures by Walter Channing, M.D., Boston, November 9, 1813, issued to Mr. John Proctor, H MS c15, Countway Library.

40. Private lectures were not uncommon, as was shown in the case of Gorham and J. C. Warren. Nor was Channing the only person offering a private course of lectures on midwifery, though he was the best qualified to do so. Numerous advertisements in Boston newspapers give further evidence. See, for example, the *Columbian Centinal* (Boston) throughout the decade.

41. Harrington, *Harvard Medical School*, 1:406.

42. Harvard University, Harvard College Papers, vol. 8, August 21, 1815, Harvard University Archives.

43. James C. Mohr, *Doctors and the Law: Medical Jurisprudence in Nineteenth-Century America* (New York: Oxford University Press, 1993); Thomas Rogers Forbes, *The Midwife and the Witch* (New Haven: Yale University Press, 1966); Charlotte A. Borst, "Midwives in Early New England, 1620–1820: From Healer and Community Authority to Quack and Outsider" (M.A. thesis, Tufts University, 1977); Marland, *Art of Midwifery*.

44. WC to Edward Everett, December 31, 1818, Ms. Am. 2006 (28), BPL. Everett (A.B. Harvard 1811), "the most brilliant young graduate of recent years," was appointed Professor of Greek Literature in 1814 and spent the following four years studying in Europe before returning to Cambridge for a brief teaching career. He eventually became president of Harvard and is remembered today as the orator whose long-winded speech preceded Abraham Lincoln's Gettysburg Address. Morison, *Three Centuries of Harvard*, pp. 226–67.

45. Harvard College, Corporation Records, vol. 5, 1810–1819, October 14 and 16, 1816, Harvard University Archives.

46. WC, Miscellaneous notes, WC Papers II.

47. "Circular of the Medical School in Boston," *NEJMS* 12 (1823): 334. Channing's ten dollar fee in 1823 would be the approximate equivalent of $125 in year 2000 values.

48. Williams College is in the western part of Massachusetts, and Bowdoin College is in Maine, then still part of Massachusetts.

49. Warren, *Life of John Collins Warren*, 1:96–97; Harrington, *Harvard Medical School*, 1:339–407.

50. See, for example, WC to John Collins Warren, August 16, 1827, JCW Papers, vol. 13.

51. Harvard University School of Medicine, Minutes and Records of the Faculty of Medicine, vol. 1, November 1816 to April 1847, October 27, 1819, Countway Library.

52. Warren, *Life of John Collins Warren*, 1:116.

53. Massachusetts Medical Society, *Catalogue of the Honorary and Past and Present Fellows*; Burrage, *History of the Massachusetts Medical Society*, pp. 280–81.

54. *Columbian Centinal* (Boston), September 13, 1820.

55. See, for example, WC to Benjamin Vaughan, March 19, 1816, Benjamin Vaughan Papers, American Philosophical Society; WC to Benjamin Smith Barton, March 20, [1810], September 11, 1811, Benjamin Smith Barton Papers, American Philosophical Society. For the general interest in mineralogy, see John C. Greene, "The Boston Medical Community and Emerging Science, 1780–1820," in Cash et al., *Medicine in Colonial Massachusetts*, p. 193.

56. Greene, "The Boston Medical Community and Emerging Science," p. 196; "Museum of Natural History," *NEJMS* 5 (1816): 188–91; "Linnaean Society of New England," *NEJMS* 9 (1820): 311–13.

57. This was followed in 1820 by his *American Medical Botany*. For a while it looked as if Bigelow would be wooed back to Philadelphia, where he was being offered a chair. However, at the insistence of James Jackson, who was fearful of losing such a promising physician and scientist, Harvard offered Bigelow the newly endowed Rumford Professorship on the Application of Science to the Useful Arts, which provided an annual stipend, in addition to his professorship at the medical school. George E. Ellis, "Memoir of Jacob Bigelow, M.D., LL.D.," pp. 117–18; James Jackson to President John Thornton Kirkland,

October 10, 1816, Harvard College Papers, vol. 8, Harvard University Archives; Nathaniel Chapman to WC, December 21, 1816, B MS c25.3, Countway Library. See also Struik, *Origins of American Science*, pp. 169–70.

58. "Linnaean Society of New England," *NEJMS* 7 (1818): 94–95; "Linnaean Society of New England," *North American Review* 6 (1817–18): 141–42.

59. Theodore Lyman, Jr., and Amos Lawrence to Jacob Bigelow, WC, and F. C. Gray, October 15, 1822, B MS c25.3, Countway Library; Jacob Bigelow, F. C. Gray, and WC to President John Thornton Kirkland, December 12, 1822, Harvard College Papers, vol. 10, Harvard University Archives. John Collins Warren arranged for some of the Linnaean collection to go to the New England Museum and Gallery of Fine Arts, with the proviso that they be made available to medical students as well as to officers and faculty of Harvard College. Report to the Trustees of the Humane Society, August 6, 1824, JCW Papers, vol. 12.

60. Channing was admitted May 26, 1818. Conversation with Alexandra Olson, American Academy of Arts and Sciences.

61. John Adams is credited with inspiring the creation of the American Academy of Arts and Sciences, in part to prove that Boston could compete with Philadelphia, where the American Philosophical Society had been meeting since 1743. Struik, *Origins of American Science*, pp. 43–47; Brooke Hindle, *The Pursuit of Science in Revolutionary America, 1735–1789* (Chapel Hill: University of North Carolina Press, 1956), pp. 263–67.

62. See, for example, David B. Tyack, *George Ticknor and the Boston Brahmins* (Cambridge, Mass.: Harvard University Press, 1967); Lilian Handlin, *George Bancroft: The Intellectual as Democrat* (New York: Harper & Row, 1984); Herbert Baxter Adams, *The Life and Writings of Jared Sparks*, 2 vols. (1893; Freeport, N.Y.: Books for Libraries Press, 1970).

63. WC to Edward Everett, December 31, 1818, Everett Papers, BPL.

64. The *North American Review*, first issued in 1815, reflected the national pride that followed the War of 1812. Edward T. Channing succeeded Jared Sparks, who had followed William Tudor and Willard Phillips as editors. Edward Everett became editor after Channing's resignation. Adams, *Life and Writings of Jared Sparks*, 1:218–34. See also Handlin, *George Bancroft*, pp. 101–2; Doreen M. Hunter, *Richard Henry Dana, Sr.* (Boston: Twayne Publishers, 1987), pp. 20–41.

65. Edward Tyrrel Channing resigned the editorship when he became Boylston Professor of Rhetoric and Oratory at Harvard in 1819, having received an M.A. degree just before the appointment. He is credited with influencing many notable speakers and literary men, including Ralph Waldo Emerson, Oliver Wendell Holmes, Henry Wadsworth Longfellow, Charles Sumner, Edward Everett Hale, Henry David Thoreau, and Thomas Wentworth Higginson. Morison, *Three Centuries of Harvard*, pp. 216–17; "Edward Tyrrel Channing's 'American Scholar' of 1818," introduction by Richard Beale Davis, *Key Reporter* 26 (Spring 1961): 1–3; Richard Henry Dana, Jr., "Biographical Notice," in *Lectures Read to the Seniors in Harvard College*, by Edward T. Channing (Boston: Ticknor and Fields, 1856).

66. [WC], "Judge Tilghman's and Dr. Caldwell's Eulogies on Dr. Caspar Wistar, Late President of the American Philosophical Society and Professor of Anatomy in the University of Pennsylvania," *North American Review* 7 (1818): 136–41.

67. [WC], "Art. IX,—Histoire de la Médecine," *North American Review* 8 (1818–19): 221–53.

68. [WC], "On the Health of Literary Men," *North American Review* 8 (1818–19): 176–80. Nine additional articles found in the *North American Review* are also attributed to Walter Channing, either in the Index of Writers, p. 123, or by the names penned into the various

volumes at Widener Library, Harvard University. This would make him one of the more prolific writers in the early years of the journal. They are "Essay on American Language and Literature," 1 (1815): 307; "Reflections on the Literary Delinquency of America," 2 (1815): 33–43; "On the Fine Arts," 3 (1816): 194–201; a review of *An Elementary Treatise on Mineralogy and Geology,* 5 (1817): 409–29; a review of *Vegetable Materia Medica of the United States* and *American Medical Botany,* 6 (1818): 344–68; "On the Health of Literary Men," 8 (1818–19): 176–80; a review of *American Medical Botany,* 9 (1819): 23–26; a review of *Hints to my Countrymen,* 23 (1826): 467–70; and a review of *The Classical Reader* and *The Class Book of American Literature,* 24 (1827): 234–36. See William Cushing, *Index to the North American Review, Volumes 1–125, 1815–1877* (Cambridge: John Wilson and Son, 1878).

69. Nathaniel I. Bowditch, *A History of the Massachusetts General Hospital (to August 5, 1871)* (Boston: Printed by the Trustees, 1872); Leonard Eaton, *New England Hospitals, 1790–1833* (Ann Arbor: University of Michigan Press, 1957); Charles E. Rosenberg, *The Care of Strangers: The Rise of America's Hospital System* (New York: Basic Books, 1987). See also Margaret Gerteis, "The Massachusetts General Hospital, 1810–1865: An Essay on the Political Construction of Social Responsibility during New England's Early Industrialization" (Ph.D. diss., Tufts University, 1985).

70. Jackson and Warren were not acting de novo. There had been at least two bequests to the town of Boston designated for hospitals. Additionally, the Reverend John Bartlett, chaplain at the Almshouse, had already convened a meeting to lay before the public the overcrowded conditions that prevented adequate medical care for men and women whose indigent state was not caused by moral failure. Jackson and Warren had attended that meeting. Bowditch, *History of the Massachusetts General Hospital,* pp. 2–3; Guenter B. Risse, *Mending Bodies, Saving Souls* (New York: Oxford University Press, 1999), p. 345.

71. The original fifty-six incorporators represented the wealthiest and most influential leaders in the Commonwealth, and included John Adams, John Quincy Adams, and several Revolutionary War heroes, plus John Warren and Marshall Spring, both physicians. See Bowditch, *History of the Massachusetts General Hospital,* pp. 399–400, Gerteis, "Massachusetts General Hospital, 1810–1865," pp. 22–23.

72. Eaton, *New England Hospitals,* pp. 30–33.

73. In 1818, three years prior to the opening of the general hospital, and thanks to a large endowment from John McLean, the McLean Asylum for the Insane opened in Somerville, Mass., as a department of the Massachusetts General Hospital.

74. Whitehill, *Boston: A Topographical History,* pp. 71–72; Harold Kirker and James Kirker, *Bulfinch's Boston, 1787–1817* (New York: Oxford University Press, 1967).

75. Bowditch, *History of the Massachusetts General Hospital,* pp. 423–33.

76. James Jackson to the Trustees of the Massachusetts General Hospital, October 2, 1821, Massachusetts General Hospital, Archives and Special Collections. John Collins Warren did not have an assistant until 1823. According to Leonard Eaton, "The selection of Walter Channing as assistant physician in 1821 was probably the most important addition to the medical staff in those years." *New England Hospitals,* p. 117.

77. WC, Miscellaneous notes, WC Papers II.

78. Students paid additional fees to observe operations at the hospital. There were, however, relatively few operations in the early years. Beecher and Altschule, *Medicine at Harvard,* p. 38.

79. *Our First Men: A Calendar of Wealth, Fashion and Gentility* (Boston: published by all the booksellers, 1846), p. 47.

80. John Ware, "Account of Physicians in this Town—1817 & etc.," A. MS, Countway Library. The income attributed to Bigelow seems low and may be an error on Ware's part. In year 2000 dollars, Channing would have been earning between $10,000 and $15,000. "The Inflation Calculator," www.westegg.com. I am grateful to Peter Drummey for his guidance.

81. WC, April 20, 1811, Shattuck Papers, vol. 3, 1811–1819, MHS.

82. Shattuck and John Collins Warren were two physicians who married wealthy women.

83. Barbara H. Perkins to Margaret Searle, December 9, [1811], WC Papers II.

84. Susan Higginson Channing to Louise Higginson, July 13, 1812, HCC Papers; Margaret Searle Curson, Journal, vol. 5, January 13, 1813, b MS Am 1175.1, Houghton Library, Harvard University; Eliza Susan Quincy, Journal, September 16, 1814–September 30, 1821, winter 1814–1815, Quincy Family Papers, MHS.

85. Perkins and Jackson had traveled to England on board the same ship in 1799. Putnam, *Memoir of Dr. James Jackson*, pp. 206–13.

86. Quotation from Margaret Searle Curson, Journal, vol. 5, May 12, 1813, b MS Am 1175, Houghton Library, Harvard University. See also Edith Perkins Cunningham, *Owls Nest: A Tribute to Sarah Elliott Perkins* (Boston: Riverside Press, 1907), pp. 15–21; Tamara Plakins Thornton, *Cultivating Gentlemen* (New Haven: Yale University Press, 1989), pp. 89, 148, 157.

87. Eliza Susan Quincy, Journal, December 1814, Quincy Family Papers, MHS.

88. Others who were less complimentary found her self-willed, arrogant, and difficult to get along with. Eliza Perkins Cabot, "Reminiscences," Hugh Cabot Family Papers, Schlesinger Library, Radcliffe Institute for Advanced Study, Harvard University.

89. Cunningham, *Owls Nest*, pp. 21–22.

90. For Stephen Higginson, see *Dictionary of American Biography*, 9:15–16; Thomas Wentworth Higginson, *Life and Times of Stephen Higginson* (Boston: Houghton, Mifflin, 1907).

91. Margaret Searle Curson, Journal, vol. 2, July 21, 1812, b MS Am 1175.1, Houghton Library, Harvard University; Eliza Susan Quincy, Journal, December 1814, July 5, 1815, Quincy Family Papers, MHS; Elizabeth Perkins Cabot, "Reminiscences," Hugh Cabot Family Papers, Schlesinger Library, Radcliffe Institute for Advanced Study, Harvard University. Eliza Cabot attributed Barbara's personality to her mother's "high theories about her children. She gave them only dry bread for their supper and made them eat it standing."

92. Barbara Perkins to Margaret Searle, December 9, [1811], CF Papers. Lord Henry Home Kames (1696–1782), a Scottish lawyer, philosopher, and agriculturist, published *Elements of Criticism* (2 vols.) in 1762; Etienne Bonnot de Condillac (1715–1780), a French philosopher, published *La Logique* in 1780.

93. Margaret Searle Curson, Journal, vol. 4, September 1812; vol. 5, May 12, 1813, b MS Am 1175.1, Houghton Library, Harvard University.

94. Boston Register of Marriages, 1807–1828, Archives, Boston City Hall. It was the custom in Boston for brides to marry in the parlor of their parents' home and to follow the ceremony with a reception for relatives and close friends.

95. Many Federalists in Boston had bitterly opposed the War of 1812, from which they could see no advantage to New England, and deeply resented the interruption of trade that the war produced.

96. WC to Edward Everett, July 1, 1815, Everett Papers, BPL.

97. Barbara H. P. Channing to Margaret Searle Curson, n.d. [1815], CF Papers; William Ellery to Richard Henry Dana, August 19, 1815, Dana Family Papers, MHS.

98. Susan Higginson Channing to Mrs. William Russel, November 11, 1815; Susan Higginson Channing to Louisa Higginson, [November 15, 1815], HCC Papers.

99. WC to Lucy Russel, December 10, 1815, WC Papers II.

100. WC, List of Midwifery Cases, WC Papers III. Though physicians today would not deliver their own children, it was not uncommon in Channing's time. See, for example, Tyler Briggs, Diary, June 30, 1821, August [12?], 1835, B MS b258.1, Countway Library; William Thornton Parker, "Cases," December 24, 1849, H MS b48.1, Countway Library; Samuel Butler, "Journal of Cases Treated, beginning June 29, 1849," MSS, College of Physicians of Philadelphia, Pennsylvania, April 4, 1855.

101. Susan Higginson Channing to Lucy Russel, April 17, [1816], HCC Papers.

102. Edward T. Channing to Richard Henry Dana, February 7, 1812, Dana Family Papers, MHS; Susan Higginson Channing to Louisa Higginson, August 3, [1812], HCC Papers.

103. Susan Higginson Channing to Louisa Higginson, [August or September 1816], HCC Papers; WC to Lucy Russel, September 4, 1816, WC Papers II.

104. WC to Lucy Russel, September 4, 1816, WC Papers II.

105. See, for example, Susan Hale, ed., *Life and Times of Thomas Gold Appleton* (New York: D. Appleton, 1885), pp. 14–15. Appropriately, his house was on Pond Street.

106. Barbara Higginson Channing to Margaret Curson, January 21, [1818], CF Papers; Susan Higginson Channing to Louisa Higginson, November 25, 1817, HCC Papers. See also Susan to Louisa, September 1817.

107. William Ellery Channing to WC, December 25, 1822, WEC Papers.

108. Mendelsohn, *Channing the Reluctant Radical*, pp. 158–64; Adams, *Life and Writings of Jared Sparks*, 1:143.

109. Barbara Perkins Channing to Lucy Russel, n.d., CF Papers; Susan Higginson Channing to Louisa Higginson, April 26, 1819, HCC Papers.

110. "The Late Fever in Boston," *NEJMS* 7 (1819): 380–86; WC to Lucy Russel, September 1, [1819], WC Papers II.

111. My special thanks to Dr. Tim Brewer, who provided much useful information on this point.

112. Barbara H. Perkins, Journal, [no date], WC Papers III. I have been unable to find the source for this poem, despite the efforts of several librarians and literary friends. It does not seem likely that the poem was original with Barbara, since there is no evidence of other poetry written by her.

113. Susan Higginson Channing to Lucy Russel, January 7, 1821, HCC Papers.

114. Barbara H. Perkins, Journal, March, August, October 4, 1821, WC Papers III. Many pages were cut out from the journal by an unknown censor.

115. Susan Higginson Channing to Lucy Russel, July 31, 1822, HCC Papers. See also WC to Lucy Russel, August 5, [1822], WC Papers III.

116. See, for example, Catherine Maria Sedgwick to J. [Jane] Sedgwick, February 12, 1819, Catherine Maria Sedgwick Papers III, MHS.

117. Susan Higginson Channing to Lucy Russel, December 31, 1822, HCC Papers.

118. Samuel Gardner Perkins's mother was Elizabeth Peck Perkins. [Ogden Codman], *Gravestone Inscriptions and Records of Tomb Burial in the Granary Burying Ground, Boston, Massachusetts* (Salem, Mass.: Essex Institute, 1918).

119. Susan Higginson Channing to Lucy Russel, January 11, 1823, HCC Papers. Walter had been living in a house owned by his father-in-law. For details on the house, see Lewis Bunker Rohrbach, ed., *Boston Taxpayers in 1821* (Camden, Me.: Picton Press, 1988).

120. Charles T. Brooks, *William Ellery Channing, a Centennial Memory* (Boston: Roberts Brothers, 1880), p. 125.

121. Eliza Cabot to Catherine Maria Sedgwick, November 16, 1822, Catherine Maria Sedgwick Papers III, MHS.

122. Frederick T. McGill, Jr., *Channing of Concord: A Life of William Ellery Channing II* (New Brunswick: Rutgers University Press, 1967), pp. 1–5. McGill suggests that the Forbeses needed money and that Ellery's board was welcome income. Ellery later created a semi-autobiographical character named Leviticus, whose childhood experiences closely paralleled his own. The manuscript of "Leviticus" can be found in the William Ellery Channing Papers 1843–1901, Special Collections, Concord, Massachusetts, Free Public Library.

123. Susan Higginson Channing to William Ellery Channing, December 24, 1822, b MS Am 1755, Houghton Library, Harvard University.

124. William Ellery Channing to WC, December 25, 1822, WEC Papers, MHS.

125. Susan Higginson Channing to William Ellery Channing, December 24, 1822, b MS Am 1755, Houghton Library, Harvard University.

126. WC to Lucy Russel, July 17, 1823, WC Papers II.

Notes to Chapter 4

1. WC, "Labour, Lecture 35," Miscellaneous Lecture Notes, WC Papers II.

2. Strictly speaking, to be a midwife was to be "with the woman" at the time of childbirth (*mid* meaning with, *wife* in the sense of woman) and the word referred to females who had traditionally assisted during labor and delivery. In the eighteenth century, as British physicians began to attend parturient women, they were often called man-midwives. *Obstetrician* (derived from the Latin *ob*, before, and *stare,* to stand) likewise referred to someone stationed before the mother to receive the child, though increasingly with a professional connotation that excluded female midwives. *Accoucheur* or *accoucheuse* (from the French *coucher,* to put to bed) were simply the French terms. *Oxford English Dictionary.*

3. WC, Miscellaneous Lecture Notes, WC Papers II.

4. Channing recorded 195 cases from August 1811 to July 24, 1822. WC, List of midwifery cases, WC Papers III. For an analysis of Channing's casebook, see Kass, "Obstetrical Casebook of Walter Channing."

5. Channing was not unique in this respect. See Statement of Dr. Brown, 1819, vol. 9, Warren Papers, MHS: "Dr. Gorham and every other physician when they are called upon to attend in a case of midwifery take charge of the patient and retain the family if they can."

6. WC, Obstetrical Cases, April 29, 1829, WC Papers II. For Walter Channing Cabot, 1829–1920, see descendants of Samuel and Elizabeth Perkins Cabot, Cabot Family Genealogy, in Almy Family Papers, Schlesinger Library, Radcliffe Institute for Advanced Study, Harvard University.

7. See Chapter 13 for the Hildreth legacy.

8. Richard Henry Dana, Jr., *The Journal of Richard Henry Dana, Jr.*, ed. Robert F. Lucid (Cambridge, Mass.: Belknap Press of Harvard University Press, 1968), 1:355–56.

9. WC, *A Treatise on Etherization in Childbirth, illustrated by Five Hundred and Eighty-One Cases* (Boston: William D. Ticknor and Co., 1848), pp. 297–98.

10. For the first ten years of his practice Channing kept careful notes of each midwifery case in a small vellum-bound copybook. Thereafter, though he continued to keep records and made reference on several occasions to his casebooks, the only accounts extant are eighteen cases recorded in 1829 and eighty-seven cases detailed in his *Treatise on Etherization in Childbirth*. There are also references to his cases made by other physicians and observers, cases discussed in his lectures, at medical meetings, and in the journal articles and pamphlets that he wrote. Since most of these were meant for students or other physicians, they are preponderantly descriptions of difficult cases. Portions of this chapter appeared in Amalie M. Kass, " 'My brother preaches, I practice': Walter Channing, M.D., Antebellum Obstetrician," *Massachusetts Historical Review* 1 (1999): 78–94.

11. John George Metcalf, Lectures on Midwifery, at the Medical School of Harvard University, Boston, 1825 and 1826, Lecture 18, H MS b48.1, Countway Library.

12. Ibid.; Edward Jarvis, Dr. Walter Channing Jr.'s Lectures on Midwifery and Medical Jurisprudence, Lecture 24, B MS b271.1, Countway Library.

13. WC, "Polypus of the Womb," *BMSJ* 52 (1855): 89–95, 112–18, quotation p. 92.

14. Edward Channing, "Recollections of a Hitherto Truthful Man."

15. [WC], Fragment from the *New England Galaxy*, Miscellaneous, WC Papers II.

16. Jarvis, Dr. Walter Channing Jr.'s Lectures, Lecture 24, B MS b271.1, Countway Library. In retrospect this seems strange, for it would force the woman to push uphill in the final stage of labor. A possible explanation is that beds were often soft and the physician wanted to make certain that the woman's pelvis would be well supported.

17. WC, *Treatise on Etherization in Childbirth*, pp. 321, 190. Physicians preferred that their patients refrain from stimulating food and anything else that might excite the system. All physical organs were believed to affect one another and this was especially true of the stomach. See William P. Dewees, *A Compendious System of Midwifery* (Philadelphia: H. C. Carey and I. Lea, 1824), p. 192.

18. WC, "Sketches in Midwifery Practice," *BMSJ* 57 (1857): 229–36, quotation p. 232.

19. See Leavitt, *Brought to Bed*, pp. 13–35; Judith Walzer Leavitt, "Under the Shadow of Maternity," in *Women and Health in America*, ed. Judith Walzer Leavitt, 2d ed. (Madison: University of Wisconsin Press, 1999), pp. 328–46; Carl N. Degler, *At Odds: Women and the Family in America from the Revolution to the Present* (Oxford: Oxford University Press, 1981), pp. 59–65.

20. Susan Higginson to Fanny Searle, January 29, 1806, HCC Papers; Anna Cabot Lowell, Journal no. 10, April 1825–May 1827, Anna Cabot Lowell Papers II, MHS.

21. Elizabeth Sedgwick, Journal, 1824–1829, pp. 1–2, MS Am 1170, Houghton Library, Harvard University.

22. Sarah Watson Dana to Elizabeth Watson Daggett, July [1848?], Dana Family Papers, Schlesinger Library, Radcliffe Institute for Advanced Study, Harvard University.

23. William Ellery to Richard Henry Dana, March 10, 1814, Dana Family Papers, MHS; *Journal of Richard Henry Dana, Jr.*, 1:68.

24. Total fertility rates for white women in the United States have been estimated at 6.92 in 1810 (when Channing began his practice) and 5.21 in 1860, when he was ending his practice. See Linda Gordon, *Woman's Body, Woman's Right* (New York: Grossman Publishers, 1976), pp. 48–49. Contraception has been practiced in various forms for centuries, but societal expectations, lack of reliable biological knowledge, and the difficulties of birth con-

trol methods made it nearly impossible for most women. For a recent discussion of women's agency in controlling their own fertility, see Susan E. Klepp, "Revolutionary Bodies: Women and the Fertility Transition in the Mid-Atlantic Region, 1760–1820," *Journal of American History* 85 (1998): 910–45.

25. For childbirth and midwifery, see Jane B. Donegan, *Women and Men Midwives*; Nancy Schrom Dye, "History of Childbirth in America," *Signs* 6 (1980–81): 97–108; Claire E. Fox, "Pregnancy, Childbirth and Early Infancy in Anglo-American Culture, 1675–1830" (Ph.D. diss., University of Pennsylvania, 1966); Sylvia D. Hoffert, *Private Matters: American Attitudes toward Childbearing and Infant Nurture in the Urban North, 1800–1860* (Urbana: University of Illinois Press, 1989); Leavitt, *Brought to Bed*; Sally G. McMillen, *Motherhood in the Old South: Pregnancy, Childbirth, and Infant Rearing* (Baton Rouge: Louisiana State University, 1990); Catherine M. Scholten, " 'On the Importance of the Obstetrick Art': Changing Customs of Childbirth in America, 1760 to 1825," *William and Mary Quarterly*, 3d ser., 34 (1977): 426–45; Wertz and Wertz, *Lying-In*; Laurel Thatcher Ulrich, *A Midwife's Tale: The Life of Martha Ballard, Based on Her Diary, 1785–1812* (New York: Alfred A. Knopf, 1990).

26. See Shawn Johansen, "Before the Waiting Room: Northern Middle-Class Pregnancy and Birth in Antebellum America," *Gender and History* 7 (July 1995): 183–200.

27. WC, Obstetrical Cases, April 17, 1829, WC Papers II.

28. WC, "Sketches in Midwifery Practice," *BMSJ* 57 (1857): 233.

29. Susan Channing to Louisa Higginson, n.d. [April 1816], HCC Papers.

30. This notion of "moral influences" also applied to male patients and to non-obstetrical female patients. For example, medical students were taught that anxiety might affect pulse rates and that the pulse should not be taken until "the patient had been put at his or her ease." Rosenberg, *Care of Strangers*, p. 91.

31. [Anon.], Notes from Dr. Channing's Lectures on Midwifery, Boston, 1819, p. 14, B MS c79.4, Countway Library.

32. WC, Miscellaneous lecture notes, WC Papers II.

33. WC, Miscellaneous notes on obstetrics, WC Papers II.

34. [Anon.], Notes from Dr. Channing's Lectures, p. 14, B MS c79.4, Countway Library.

35. See Donegan, *Women and Men Midwives*, pp. 141–236.

36. Anna Cabot Lowell, Personal Journals, no. 20, July 26, 1832, Anna Cabot Lowell Papers II, MHS; Samuel A. Green to WC, February 14, 1831, WC Papers II; WC, Miscellaneous notes, WC Papers II.

37. John George Metcalf, Lectures on Midwifery, Lecture 18, H MS b29.2, Countway Library.

38. Ibid.

39. Dewees, *Compendious System of Midwifery*, p. 192; [anon.], Notes from Dr. Channing's Lectures, p. 12, B MS c79.4, Countway Library.

40. This makes sense empirically, because lying on the left side relieves the uterine aorta and sends more blood to the heart.

41. Edward Jarvis, Dr. Walter Channing Jr.'s Lectures, Lecture 23, B MS b271.1, Countway Library.

42. WC, "Notes of Difficult Labors, in the Second of which Etherization by Sulphuric Ether Was Successfully Employed Nineteen Years Ago," *BMSJ* 46 (1852): 113–16.

43. WC, Miscellaneous notes on obstetrics, WC Papers II.

44. WC, Obstetrical Cases, July 1, 1829, WC Papers II.

45. WC, Miscellaneous notes on obstetrics, WC Papers II.

46. WC, Miscellaneous lecture notes, WC Papers II.

47. [Anon.], Notes from Dr. Channing's Lectures, p. 92, B MS c79.4, Countway Library.

48. For this reason, Channing recommended that his students read the midwifery texts of Madame Boivin and Madame LaChapelle, explaining that these French midwives could best discuss pain in childbirth.

49. WC, "Retention of a Portion of the Placenta," *BMSJ* 67 (1862): 149–55.

50. WC, List of Midwifery Cases, October 22, 1816; WC, Cases, April 2, 1829, WC Papers II.

51. David Humphreys Storer, Lectures on Midwifery by Walter Channing, taken at the Medical College, Boston, 1824–1825, p. 140, B MS b8.1, Countway Library.

52. WC, Miscellaneous lecture notes, WC Papers II. The notion that civilization had weakened humans or caused diseases unknown in more primitive times has a long history. For a recent appraisal, see Charles E. Rosenberg, "Pathologies of Progress: The Idea of Civilization as Risk," *Bulletin of the History of Medicine* 72 (1998): 714–30.

53. WC, Miscellaneous notes on obstetrics, WC Papers II; Susan Higginson Channing to Julia Allen Channing, June 20, 1837, Allen Family Papers, Houghton Library, Harvard University. For comparative statistics regarding maternal mortality in Dublin and London hospitals vs. that in rural American practices, see Ulrich, *Midwife's Tale*, pp. 172–73. One problem with such comparisons is that the women who entered European hospitals for childbirth were usually very poor, whereas the American farm women were probably better nourished. Nonetheless, it was comparisons such as these between European and American mortality rates that led to conclusions such as Channing reached. See also Speert, *Obstetrics and Gynecology in America*, pp. 38–39.

54. WC, Miscellaneous lecture notes, WC Papers II.

55. Edward Jarvis, Dr. Walter Channing Jr.'s Lectures, Lecture 22, B MS b271.1, Countway Library.

56. WC, Miscellaneous notes, WC Papers II.

57. WC, List of Midwifery Cases, October 22, 1816, June 22, 1822.

58. Edward Jarvis, Dr. Walter Channing Jr.'s Lectures, Lecture 27, B MS b271.1, Countway Library.

59. As has been pointed out to me by Dr. J. Worth Estes and Philip Cash, bleeding appeared to produce relaxation though it was not true physiological relaxation.

60. The introduction of ergot in cases of childbirth has been discussed in note 8, Chapter 2. Experience had shown that the unpredictability of its effect and potential for harm to mother or fetus made its use questionable. In no case could it be used until the cervix was completely dilated and the head of the child presented. Channing gave ergot four times in 195 cases between 1811 and 1822. In each case the baby was stillborn, but we do not know whether the fetal death occurred prior to labor or during the birth process. Channing indicated that one mother thought her baby had been dead for some days.

61. It is difficult to understand why such crude instruments were used, although insertion of a sharp knife or pick may have been too threatening to consider. John George Metcalf, Lectures on Midwifery, Lecture 18, H MS b29.2, Countway Library; WC, Miscellaneous notes on obstetrics, WC Papers II. See also Harold Speert and Alan F. Guttmacher, *Obstetric Practice* (New York: Landsberger Medical Books, 1956), p. 263: "if all the requisite conditions for induction are confirmed, a sterile hook, tenaculum, or steel knitting needle is

carefully guided through the internal os and scraped against the presenting membranes until they are torn."

62. See, for example, WC, "A Case of Arm Presentation with Remarks," *NEJMS* 11 (1822): 30–37.

63. At the period of Channing's practice, saving the mother was generally considered more important than saving the child, should it be necessary to choose. For the change in physicians' views of craniotomy and cesarean section at the end of the nineteenth century, see Judith Walzer Leavitt, "The Growth of Medical Authority: Technology and Morals in Turn-of-the-Century Obstetrics," *Medical Anthropology Quarterly*, n.s., 1 (1987): 230–55.

64. WC, "Cases and Notes," *BMSJ* 56 (1857): 171.

65. Two hours after application of the lever the child was delivered. He was stillborn, but "was after much exertion made to breathe," though only for a few hours. WC, List of Midwifery Cases, October 22, 1816.

66. WC, "Cases and Notes," *BMSJ* 56 (1857): 172. In this case the uterus ruptured, so there was little chance of saving the woman, but the physicians did not know this until an autopsy was performed. Perhaps if forceps had been used the baby would have survived, since the head remained in the pelvis even after the rupture.

67. Edward Jarvis, Dr. Walter Channing Jr.'s Lectures, Lecture 29, B MS b271.1; John Barnard Swett Jackson, "Medical Cases and Autopsies, 1830–69," Case no. 410, December 24, 1832, H MS b72.4, Countway Library.

68. Edward Jarvis, Dr. Walter Channing Jr.'s Lectures, Lecture 29, B MS b271.1, Countway Library.

69. Rand may have been correct, since the baby was still high in the pelvis and forceps delivery at that stage could be dangerous to the mother. I thank Dr. Theodore Barton for helping me understand this and several other Channing cases.

70. WC, "Sketches in Midwifery Practice," *BMSJ* 57 (1857): 229–36. Channing did not identify the friend who made the comment quoted here, p. 235.

71. Ibid., quotation p. 235. It can be argued that use of instruments increased the possibility of puerperal fever, but physicians did not fully understand the connection between intervention and sepsis.

72. "Inflammation" was a commonly used descriptive term for infection. Puerperal fever, childbed fever, and peritonitis were the usual diagnostic terms for diseases that caused morbidity and mortality among childbearing women.

73. WC, Cases, July 28, 1829, WC Papers II.

74. See Speert, *Obstetrics and Gynecology in America*, pp. 150–57, for several cases of cesarean section in the United States, including a successful operation in Ohio reported in the *Western Journal of Medicine and Physical Science* 3 (1830): 485–89. There is no reference to this in Channing's lecture notes, which contain examples of cases from England, Ireland, and France. He did, however, instruct the students how the operation should be performed. David Humphreys Storer, Lecture Notes, January 14, 1824, B MS b8.1, Countway Library; John George Metcalf, Lectures on Midwifery, Lecture 24, H MS b29.2, Countway Library. See also J. J. Locker, "A Case of Caesarean Operation," *NEJMS* 8 (1819): 167–73. Channing was editing the *Journal* at the time of this publication.

75. WC, "Sketches in Midwifery," *BMSJ* 57 (1857): 233–34.

76. WC, Case dated November 10, 1863, Miscellaneous notes, WC Papers II. Channing used ether in this case, which made the forceps procedure less painful for the mother.

77. WC, "On the Transfusion of Blood," *BMSJ* 1 (April 1, 1828): 97–102. See also James

Blundell, "Experiment on the Transfusion of Blood by Syringe," reprinted from *Medico-Chirurgical Transactions* in *NEJMS* 8 (1819): 161–66. For Blundell, see Wilks and Bettany, *Biographical History of Guy's Hospital* (London: Ward, Lock, Bowden & Co., 1892), pp. 365–71.

78. WC, Cases, February 20, 1829, WC Papers II. The case notes do not begin with labor and delivery, which suggests that Channing was not involved until infection had become apparent.

79. WC, Miscellaneous lecture notes, WC Papers II. For therapeutics in obstetrics, see A. Clair Siddall, "Bloodletting in American Obstetric Practice, 1800–1945," *Bulletin of the History of Medicine* 54 (1980): 101–10; Wertz and Wertz, *Lying-In*, pp. 67–73; John S. Haller, Jr., *American Medicine in Transition, 1840–1910* (Urbana: University of Illinois Press, 1981), pp. 51–52, 161–63. For a general discussion of nineteenth-century therapeutics, see Haller, pp. 3–99; Charles E. Rosenberg, "The Therapeutic Revolution: Medicine, Meaning and Social Change in Nineteenth-Century America," in *The Therapeutic Revolution: Essays in the Social History of American Medicine*, ed. Morris J. Vogel and Charles E. Rosenberg (Philadelphia: University of Pennsylvania Press, 1979), pp. 3–25; William G. Rothstein, *American Physicians in the Nineteenth Century: From Sects to Science* (Baltimore: Johns Hopkins University Press, 1972), pp. 41–62.

80. Boston mortality statistics for Channing's time are unreliable, and in the absence of birth rates it is not possible to compare his data with other cities or other decades. James H. Cassedy, *American Medicine and Statistical Thinking, 1800–1860* (Cambridge, Mass.: Harvard University Press, 1984), pp. 1–24; Maris A. Vinovskis, "Mortality Rates and Trends in Massachusetts before 1860," *Journal of Economic History* 32 (1972): 184–213; Lemuel Shattuck, "On the Vital Statistics of Boston," *American Journal of the Medical Sciences*, n.s., 1 (1841): 369–401. For this and the preceding paragraph, see Kass, "Obstetrical Case Book of Walter Channing," pp. 509–12.

81. Edward Jarvis, Dr. Walter Channing Jr.'s Lectures, Lecture 25, B MS b271.1, Countway Library.

82. WC, "Miscellaneous Cases, Spina Bifida, Preternatural Labors, Erysipelatous Inflammation," *NEJMS* 15 (1826): 357–62.

83. Oliver Wendell Holmes is credited with coining the word *gynecology*, which derives from the Greek for women. Frederick N. Dyer, "Autobiographical Letter from Horatio Robinson Storer, M.D., to His Son, Malcolm Storer, M.D., Discussing the History of Gynæcological Teaching," *Journal of the History of Medicine and Allied Sciences* 54 (1999): 439–58.

84. WC, "Cases of Organic Diseases of the Womb and Its Appendages," *BMSJ* 36 (1847): 469–77.

85. WC, "Notes of Cases of Recent and Chronic Inversio Uteri," *BMSJ* 60 (1859): 229–34.

86. Ibid.

87. Hayward's experiments with repair of fistulae were only moderately successful and it was not until Marion Sims solved the problem of appropriate sutures that women who suffered the embarrassment and discomfort of fistulae could be helped. George Hayward, "Case of Vesico-vaginal Fistula, Successfully Treated by an Operation," *American Journal of the Medical Sciences* 24 (1839): 283–88; reprinted in *BMSJ* 21 (1839): 21–29. Channing was present at Hayward's first operation.

88. WC, "Never Too Late to Mend," *BMSJ* 61 (1859): 139–41. The remedy was essentially a very strong purgative.

89. *Boston Medical Police* (Boston: Snelling and Simons, 1808); *Rules and Regulations of the Boston Medical Association* (Boston: J. Belcher, 1811). For the Boston Medical Association and its efforts to fix prices for medical services, see Mark S. Blumberg, "Medical Society Regulation of Fees in Boston, 1780–1820," *Journal of the History of Medicine and Allied Sciences* 39 (1984): 303–38. Nighttime was specified as beginning at 11:00 P.M. and ending at 5:00 A.M. or sunrise, if later.

90. *Boston Medical Police* (Boston: Sewell Phelps, 1820). By contrast, in New York the fee for "common case of midwifery" ran from twenty-five to thirty-five dollars, "tedious or difficult labours" thirty-six to sixty dollars.

91. "Boston Medical Association," *BMSJ* 52 (1855): 326, 384–86.

92. WC, "Polypus of the Womb," *BMSJ* 52 (1855): 89–95, 112–18, quotation p. 91; WC, "Notes of Cases of Recent and Chronic Inversio Uteri," *BMSJ* 60 (1859): 229–34, quotation p. 232; WC, Miscellaneous notes on obstetrics, WC Papers II.

93. WC, "Cases and Notes," *BMSJ* 56 (1857): 197–98.

94. John Barnard Swett Jackson, "Medical Cases and Autopsies," no. 676, January 14, 1836; no. 527, May 21, 1834, H MS, b72.4, Countway Library.

95. WC, Miscellaneous notes, WC Papers II.

96. WC, "Case of Ruptured Womb, with Remarks," manuscript, WC Papers II.

97. WC, Miscellaneous lecture notes, Introductory lecture, 1822 and 1834, WC Papers II.

98. WC, "Cases," *BMSJ* 54 (1856): 432.

Notes to Chapter 5

1. Henry Codman to John Collins Warren, August 22, 1821, JCW Papers, MHS; the patient was diagnosed with syphilis. He was treated with cathartics, opium, and mercurials, but he died in the hospital on May 7, 1822. Massachusetts General Hospital, Medical Records, vol. 1, Massachusetts General Hospital, Archives and Special Collections.

2. Channing's continuous service, seventeen and a quarter years, was greater than any but Jackson, Warren, and George Hayward. Jackson's service from his initial appointment on April 6, 1817, until his resignation on October 13, 1837, adds up to twenty and a half years, but for four and a half years of that time there were no patients at the hospital. Warren, appointed on the same day as Jackson, remained attending surgeon until 1852. George Hayward, first chosen as assistant surgeon on March 19, 1826, advanced to chief in January 1838 and remained until April 1851, for a total of twenty-five years. Bowditch, *History of the Massachusetts General Hospital*, p. 410. The Asylum for the Insane, renamed McLean Hospital, was administered separately from the General Hospital, although the same trustees served both institutions.

3. WC to N. I. Bowditch, October 7, 1851, Archives and Special Collections, Massachusetts General Hospital.

4. James Jackson to N. I. Bowditch, July 15, 1828, Archives and Special Collections, Massachusetts General Hospital. The trustees had expressed a desire that occasional changes be made in the positions of assistant physician and assistant surgeon. Jackson's letter of nomination for Channing included a response to that concern. "I trust that the Trustees will not suppose that I do not pay sufficient attention to the suggestion in their vote." Warren replaced his assistants more frequently. The trustees had authorized three assistants for each

department and in 1829 John Ware became the second assistant physician. Bowditch, *History of Massachusetts General Hospital*, pp. 84, 410.

5. Eaton, *New England Hospitals*, p. 117. See also Rosenberg, *Care of Strangers*, pp. 58, 63.

6. Case no. 126, Massachusetts General Hospital, Medical Records, vol. 3, February 22–August 1, 1823, Countway Library.

7. Massachusetts General Hospital, Medical Records, vol. 85, December 28, 1837–February 2, 1838, Countway Library.

8. "Jackson came into Boston once a week, on Tuesdays, and always went through the wards with me, and aided me whenever the circumstances of the cases required." WC, Reminiscences, WC Papers II.

9. Initially, the apothecary served as house physician, but in 1828 the separate office of House Physician was created, and shortly thereafter House Surgeon was added. See Bowditch, *History of Massachusetts General Hospital*, p. 84.

10. For a variation on the family metaphor, see Rosenberg, *Care of Strangers*, pp. 42–43.

11. Massachusetts General Hospital, *Annual Report of Board of Trustees, A.D. 1828* [Boston, 1828], p. 2 (emphasis in original).

12. Massachusetts General Hospital, Visiting Committee Records, 1826–1830, October 16, 1827, Massachusetts General Hospital, Archives and Special Collections.

13. See Eaton, *New England Hospitals*, and Rosenberg, *Care of Strangers*. The physicians, as well as the trustees, did not want the hospital to replicate the Almshouse, where derelicts and alcoholics were housed together with the sick and mentally ill poor who stood little chance of recovery.

14. The average time that free patients remained in the hospital in 1838 was just under six weeks. Massachusetts General Hospital, *Annual Report of Board of Trustees, A.D. 1838* [Boston, 1838], p. 5.

15. Putnam, *Memoir of Dr. James Jackson*, p. 161.

16. See Rosenberg, *Care of Strangers*, introduction and Part I.

17. Bowditch, *History of Massachusetts General Hospital*, pp. 65, 70, 91, 124.

18. Massachusetts General Hospital, Trustee Minutes, vol. 2, 1818–1827, May 23, 1824, Massachusetts General Hospital, Archives and Special Collections.

19. See, for example, Rosenberg, *Care of Strangers*, p. 21.

20. WC to John Collins Warren, August 4, 1829, JCW Papers, vol. 14; Bowditch, *History of Massachusetts General Hospital*, pp. 91, 96; Eaton, *New England Hospitals*, pp. 185–86.

21. Massachusetts General Hospital, Medical Records, vol. 1, 1821–22, Massachusetts General Hospital, Archives and Special Collections.

22. Massachusetts General Hospital, Medical Records, book 10, December 20, 1824–April 16, 1825, January 1825, Countway Library.

23. Massachusetts General Hospital, *Annual Report, 1838*, p. 11. This number does not reflect the total number of patients cared for during the year, as there were patients already in the hospital at the beginning of the year.

24. Bowditch, *History of Massachusetts General Hospital*, pp. 91–92.

25. Massachusetts General Hospital, *Annual Report, 1838*.

26. Massachusetts General Hospital, Medical Records, book 10, December 20, 1824–April 16, 1825, January 1825, Countway Library.

27. In the first six months following the opening of the hospital, Jackson informed the

trustees, "there have been more cases of difficult and rare disease than in the private practice of a Physician in an extensive business in a year." *Address of the Trustees of the Massachusetts General Hospital, to the Subscribers and to the Public* [Boston, 1822], pp. 7–8.

28. Massachusetts General Hospital, Medical Records, vol. 82, August 14–October 3, 1837, Countway Library.

29. Eaton, *New England Hospitals*, p. 166.

30. WC, "Re-vaccination," *BMSJ* 1 (1828): 279–80. See also Bowditch, *History of Massachusetts General Hospital*, p. 81.

31. Bowditch, *History of Massachusetts General Hospital*, p. 102. See also *BMSJ* 6 (February–August 1832) and 7 (August 1832–February 1833) for many articles about the cholera epidemic; and Charles E. Rosenberg, *The Cholera Years* (Chicago and London: University of Chicago Press, 1987), Part 1.

32. James Jackson, John C. Warren, Walter Channing, and George Hayward to the Board of Trustees, January 7, 1827, cited in Eaton, *New England Hospitals*, p. 266 n. 32; Bowditch, *History of Massachusetts General Hospital*, pp. 73–74. See also George Hayward, "A History of the Erysipelatous Inflammation that Recently Appeared in the Massachusetts General Hospital," *NEJMS* 16 (1827): 292.

33. Eaton, *New England Hospitals*, p. 177. Although the transmission of infectious diseases was not understood, many physicians believed that bad air, whether as miasmas rising from bad soil or malaria from swamps, should be avoided—hence the need for good ventilation in hospitals.

34. WC, Medicine, WC Papers II. See Chapter 2.

35. For a discussion of these therapeutic changes, see John Harley Warner, *The Therapeutic Perspective* (Cambridge, Mass.: Harvard University Press, 1986); Rosenberg, *Care of Strangers*; Rosenberg, "The Therapeutic Revolution," pp. 3–25.

36. Eaton, *New England Hospitals*, pp. 169–74; Warner, *Therapeutic Perspective*, pp. 83–161.

37. For the Paris school, see Erwin H. Ackerknecht, *Medicine at the Paris School, 1794–1848* (Baltimore: Johns Hopkins University Press, 1967); and John Harley Warner, "Remembering Paris," *Bulletin of the History of Medicine* 65 (1991): 301–35.

38. Jacob Bigelow, *Self-limited Diseases* [Boston, 1835]; Warner, *Therapeutic Perspective*, pp. 26–31. In an annual address to the Massachusetts Medical Society, May 30, 1860, Oliver Wendell Holmes showed the extent to which he at least adhered to Bigelow's ideas. "I firmly believed that if the whole materia medica, *as now used*, could be sent to the bottom of the sea, it would be all better for mankind,—and all the worse for the fishes." "Currents and Counter-Currents in Medical Science," *Medical Essays, 1842–1882* (Boston: Houghton Mifflin, 1891), p. 203.

39. Massachusetts General Hospital, Medical Records, January 8, 1838, vol. 85, December 28, 1837–February 2, 1838, Countway Library.

40. Ibid., November 15, 1823, vol. 4, August 8–December 5, 1823, Countway Library.

41. Speert, *Obstetrics and Gynecology in America*, pp. 90–99. The Pennsylvania Hospital authorized a lying-in ward in 1793, but it did not become operational for another ten years. There is no indication from Channing's papers that he observed obstetrical cases there, but it is possible that he did. Thomas Chalkley James, Channing's professor of obstetrics during his student days in Philadelphia, was not named Physician to the Lying-In Department until after Channing had left Philadelphia.

42. Massachusetts General Hospital, Report on a Lying-in Department, October 1845, Massachusetts General Hospital, Archives and Special Collections.

43. M. A. DeWolfe Howe, *The Humane Society of the Commonwealth of Massachusetts: An Historical Review, 1785–1916* (Boston: printed for the Humane Society, 1918).

44. Ibid., p. 211.

45. Charles A. Lowell to Nathaniel I. Bowditch, December 29, 1830; [Board of Trustees] to Rev. Dr. Lowell, February 4, 1831, Massachusetts General Hospital, Archives and Special Collections. See also Frederic A. Washburn, *The Massachusetts General Hospital* (Boston: Houghton Mifflin, 1939), pp. 357–58.

46. To the Trustees of the Massachusetts General Hospital, November 25, 1845, Massachusetts General Hospital, Archives and Special Collections. Channing was no longer on the hospital staff so he was not an appropriate person to make the case, though he strongly supported it.

47. Massachusetts General Hospital, Report on a Lying-in Department, October 1845, Massachusetts General Hospital, Archives and Special Collections.

48. *By-Laws of the Massachusetts Charitable Fire Society, with the Act of Incorporation and Additional Act* (Boston: J. B. Chisholm, 1861); Henry H. Sprague, *A Brief History of the Massachusetts Charitable Fire Society* (Boston: Little, Brown, 1893).

49. *Report of the Boston Lying-In Hospital* (Boston: J. E. Hinckley & Co., 1833); Massachusetts Charitable Fire Society, Records, vol. 1, Minutes, April 8, 1831; vol. 3, Minutes of the Government of the Society, March 19, 1831, July 5, 1831; Rev. Charles Lowell to Thomas Jones, March 17, 1831, Papers of the Massachusetts Charitable Fire Society, MHS. See also Petition to the General Court, Boston, January 16, 1832, The Importance of an Establishment of a Lying-in Hospital in the City of Boston for indigent married women, Massachusetts State Archives, Boston. Also An Act to incorporate the Boston Lying-in Hospital, approved February 4, 1832, Massachusetts State Archives.

50. Speert, *Obstetrics and Gynecology in America*, pp. 91–93, 99–100.

51. WC to James Jackson, Jr., November 22, 1832, H MS c8.3, Countway Library.

52. The Boston Lying-in Hospital merged in 1966 with the Free Hospital for Women (primarily gynecology) to become the Boston Hospital for Women. In 1975 the Boston Hospital for Women merged with the Peter Bent Brigham (a large general hospital) and the Robert Breck Brigham (primarily rheumatology) and adopted the name Brigham and Women's Hospital in 1980. In 1994 Brigham and Women's Hospital and the Massachusetts General Hospital merged to form Partners Healthcare, so the Boston Lying-in is finally, if tangentially, now associated with the Massachusetts General Hospital.

53. Frederick C. Irving, "Highlights in the History of the Boston Lying-in Hospital," typescript, Massachusetts General Hospital, Archives and Special Collections. See also Frederick C. Irving, *Safe Deliverance* (Boston: Houghton Mifflin, 1942), pp. 61–103.

54. Massachusetts Charitable Fire Society, Records, vol. 3, Meeting of the Government of the Society, July 5, 1831, March 12, 1832, MHS.

55. Quotation from "Boston Lying-In Hospital," *The Medical Magazine* 1 (1833): 19–20.

56. The significant role of the directresses also demonstrates the degree to which many upper- and middle-class Boston women were engaged in important work in a home very different from their own. Many were wives of physicians.

57. *Rules and Regulations of the Trustees of the Boston Lying-in Hospital* (1838). See also *By-Laws of the Boston Lying-In Hospital*, "Article IV: A suitable Hospital shall be provided for the reception of married women, who may need the benefit of the Institution, which shall be afforded at as low a rate as may consist with its interest and existence."

58. Benjamin Rich, Thomas K. Jones, Charles Lowell, et al., Petition to the General Court, Boston, January 16, 1832, Massachusetts State Archives.

59. WC, "To the Trustees of the Massachusetts General Hospital," November 25, 1845, Massachusetts General Hospital, Archives and Special Collections; WC, "An Address to a Society for Obstetric Improvement," WC Papers II.

60. "Medical Intelligence," *BMSJ* 7 (1832): 130. See also Grenville Temple Winthrop to WC, June 4, 1833, WC Papers II. When Hale died in 1848, Channing wrote an obituary that appeared in the *BMSJ* 39 (1848): 334–41.

61. Irving, "Highlights in the History of the Boston Lying-in Hospital," p. 4. Extant hospital records cover only cases 1–253, 1832 to 1844. Of these, 173 occurred while Channing was on the staff. Boston Lying-in Hospital, Admissions 1832–1844, Countway Library. Subsequent record books seem to have been lost. David Storer published an analysis of 451 deliveries from 1832 to 1850: "Statistics of the Boston Lying-in Hospital," *American Journal of the Medical Sciences*, n.s., 20 (1850): 347–68.

62. Boston Lying-in Hospital, Admissions, 1832–1844, Case no. 42, Roach, August 11, 1834, Countway Library.

63. Eaton, *New England Hospitals*, p. 225. Minutes of trustee and committee meetings for this period also seem to have been lost.

64. Boston Lying-in Hospital, Admissions, 1832–1844, Case no. 140, Susan Brown, August 31, 1837, Countway Library.

65. Ibid., Case no. 31, Holmes, April 7, 1834.

66. Ibid., Case no. 17, Carner, August 3, 1833; Case no. 3, Yorke, January 1833; Case no. 9, Boga, March 21, 1833; Case no. 26, Goodenow, December 26, 1833.

67. Ibid., Case no. 19, Brazier, August 12, 1833; Case no. 75, Green, December 13, 1835.

68. Ibid., Case no. 24, Cors, October 30, 1833.

69. Ibid., Case no. 34, Currier, May 10, 1834. No postpartum difficulties or previous complaints were noted in the hospital record, though it must be remembered that the records were kept by the house physician.

70. Ibid., Case no. 66, Healy, July 20, 1835.

71. Ibid., Case no. 89, Locke, February 20, 1836; Case no. 108, Howes, November 11, 1836; Case no. 134, Franklin, July 15, 1837.

72. Ibid., Case no. 10, Oakes, May 4, 1833; Case no. 28, Sturtevant, March 18, 1834.

73. Ibid., Case no. 166, Frost, August 14, 1838.

74. Ibid., Case no. 149, Lombard, February 3, 1838; Case no. 147, Osborn, December 26, 1837.

75. In contrast with the conventional treatment administered at the Lying-in Hospital during its first period, when Horatio Storer became attending physician he frequently experimented with new treatments. See, for example, "Boston Lying-In Hospital," *BMSJ* 54 (1856): 38–39.

76. Boston Lying-in Hospital, Admissions, 1832–1844, Case nos. 42 and 131 (forceps); Case nos. 147 and 161 (perforator); Case no. 45 (lever), Countway Library. David Humphreys Storer reported 8 cases delivered by forceps and 2 craniotomies in 451 cases. Storer, "Statistics of the Boston Lying-in Hospital," p. 358.

77. These cases belie the accusation sometimes made by critics of medicalized midwifery that physicians deliberately used forceps to hasten delivery and reduce the time they needed to spend at the bedside.

78. WC, List of Midwifery Cases, 1811–1822, WC Papers III.

79. Boston Lying-in Hospital, Admissions, 1832–1844, Case no. 134 ("bad health for many years," including dysentery); Case no. 76 ("puerperal peritonitis"); Case nos. 82 and 161 (cause of death not given in case notes, but symptoms of puerperal fever are clearly described), Countway Library. Storer's paper does not give a total number of deaths, but mentions six cases of peritonitis, three of convulsions, two of diarrhea, two of utero-hemorrhage, one of phlegmasia dolens (thrombophlebitis leading to leg swelling), one of ascites, one of neuralgia, and one of typhus fever. He also mentioned that there had been "but four cases of lacerated perineum." "Statistics of the Boston Lying-in Hospital," pp. 360–67.

80. Boston Lying-in Hospital, Admissions, 1832–1844, Case no. 156, McCarthy, April 17, 1838.

81. Ibid., Case no. 76, Williams, December 21, 1835, to Case no. 82, Hammond, January 21, 1836.

82. Boston Society for Medical Improvement, Records, vol. 2, February 8, 1836, Countway Library. "Dr. Channing spoke on four cases of puerperal fever at the 'Lying In Hospital' one fatal."

83. WC, List of Midwifery Cases, 1811–1822, WC Papers III.

84. Boston Lying-in Hospital, Admissions, 1832–1844, Case no. 166, Frost, August 14, 1838, delivered September 29, baby died October 1; Case no. 168, Welch, entered August 24, 1838, delivered October 14, baby died October 16; Case no. 170, Ford, entered October 17, 1838, baby born November 9, Countway Library.

85. Starting in 1829, there were two assistant physicians, John Ware joining Channing at that level. In 1836 there was a further reorganization and James Jackson, Jacob Bigelow, and Channing were named attending physicians, J. B. S. Jackson assistant physician. The following year James Jackson retired and his place was filled by Enoch Hale. When Channing relinquished his post, John Ware became the third attending physician, along with Hale and Bigelow. See Bowditch, *History of Massachusetts General Hospital*, pp. 128, 135–39, 410.

86. WC to William Gray, January 22, 1839, Massachusetts General Hospital, Archives and Special Collections.

87. WC, Miscellaneous notes, WC Papers II; Bowditch, *History of Massachusetts General Hospital*, p. 148.

88. WC, Reminiscences, WC Papers II.

Notes to Chapter 6

1. "Medical Lectures in the Medical Institution of Harvard University," *NEJMS* 4 (1815): 392. According to this source, the lectures for 1815 began on the first Wednesday in November. In 1816 lectures began on the third Wednesday of November. *NEJMS* 5 (1816): 320. In 1827 the schedule was altered and the session, still thirteen weeks long, began on the third Wednesday in October. In 1831 it was decided to revert back to the November opening and to extend the session for an additional month. Harrington, *Harvard Medical School*, 2:474–76; "Medical School in Boston," *BMSJ* 10 (1834): 337–38. Harrington quotes from the statutes indicating a continuation of the October opening, but this is contradicted by announcements in the *Boston Medical and Surgical Journal* and by Channing's notes. The day and time for Channing's lectures varied during the first years he taught, but from 1821 on his class convened on Friday at 3:00 P.M., Tuesday and Saturday at 9:00 A.M.

Channing's comment in the epigraph referred to James Jackson's decision to share his lectures with John Ware. For an overview of medical education in this period, and especially of obstetrical instruction, see Martin Kaufman, *American Medical Education: The Formative Years, 1765–1910* (Westport, Conn.: Greenwood Press, 1976); William G. Rothstein, *American Medical Schools and the Practice of Medicine: A History* (New York: Oxford University Press, 1987); Lawrence D. Longo, "Obstetrics and Gynecology," in *The Education of American Physicians*, ed. Ronald L. Numbers (Berkeley: University of California Press, 1980), pp. 205–25.

2. Kirker and Kirker, *Bulfinch's Boston*, pp. 175–79.

3. Ibid., pp. 224–25; Harrington, *Harvard Medical School*, 1:405–6; William Workman, Ephemera, November 20, 1822, B MS c19.1, Countway Library; George Weed to Luther Ticknor, December 16, 1823, H MS misc., Countway Library.

4. "Some Account of Harvard University in Cambridge, Massachusetts," *NEJMS* 5 (1816): 125; Harrington, *Harvard Medical School*, 1:417–21. The professors' donation of books was supplemented by a gift from Benjamin Vaughan as well as the collections of the Boston Medical Library and the Boylston Medical Library, both of which predated construction of the new medical school. In 1816 the medical faculty provided that its meetings would rotate from house to house of the members and that a fine of three dollars should be imposed for failure either to give sufficient notice of a meeting at one's house or to secure a substitute if unable to host the meeting, and a fine of two dollars for absence from a meeting. These fines were added to the library fund.

5. Anna C. Holt, "A Medical Student in Boston, 1825–26," *Harvard Library Bulletin* 6 (1952): 176–92, 358–75, quotation p. 187.

6. William Wellington, "Biographical Sketches of the Obstetrical Society of Boston," in *Historical Sketch of the Obstetrical Society of Boston*, by Benjamin E. Cotting (Boston: David Clapp, 1881), pp. 60–61. Horatio Robinson Storer preserved a different aspect of Channing's lectures: "He was interesting but very discursive, & at times a little broad in his suggestions. I remember him telling the class that whether married or not, they should always be provided with a pot of rose ointment, to prevent in their own persons any local epithelial lesion, & to facilitate ingress." Dyer, "Autobiographical Letter from Horatio Robinson Storer, M.D.," pp. 439–58.

7. One of the students in Channing's final year of teaching accused him of being "desultory and amusing, reminding one of the style of his brother Edward." James Clarke White, *Sketches from My Life, 1833–1913* (Cambridge, Mass.: Riverside Press, 1914), p. 60.

8. Irving, *Safe Deliverance*, p. 102; Kelly and Burrage, *American Medical Biographies*, p. 205.

9. James Freeman Clarke, *Memorial and Biographical Sketches* (Boston: Houghton, Osgood, 1878), p. 172.

10. Dyer, "Autobiographical Letter from Horatio Robinson Storer, M.D.," p. 441.

11. Irving, *Safe Deliverance*, p. 83.

12. William Workman, Ephemera, February 8, 1823, B MS c19.1, Countway Library.

13. Samuel Wiswell Butler to L. M. Yale, November 14, 1839, H MS, Misc., Countway Library.

14. William Workman, Ephemera, February 1, 1823, February 11, 1825, B MS c19.1, Countway Library. The custom of annual parties continued for many years. See, for example, "Dr. Bigelow has given his party to the medical students" and reference to the "splendid parties" given by Dr. Warren and Dr. Hayward. Augustus Hannibal Burbank to Esther Burbank, November 30, 1846, February 14, 1847, B MS misc., Countway Library.

15. Henry Little to Charles Jarvis, [June] 29, 1823, B MS c11.3, Countway Library. For calculation, see "The Inflation Calculator," www.westegg.com.

16. William Workman, who kept a careful account of every penny expended, calculated that he spent $132.21 the first year and $126.30 the second year for professors' tickets, board, washing, firewood, and lights, as well as for expenses to and from Northampton. He also invested $47.21 in books and instruments. At the end of the second year there were the extra expenses for his diploma, graduation, and the travel to Boston and Cambridge and home again. In addition, he had to pay fees to the local physician who guided his practical medical education. To earn part of this money, Workman and others like him spent part of each year teaching school in their own or a nearby town. Workman, "Expenses of my Medical Education," Account Book, B MS c19.1, Countway Library. See also Henry Little to Charles Jarvis, [June] 29, 1823, B MS c11.3, Countway Library.

17. William Workman, Ephemera, January 20, 1825, B MS c19.1, Countway Library.

18. Holt, "Medical Student in Boston," p. 373.

19. Boston Society for Medical Improvement, Records, vol. 4, December 28, 1840, Countway Library.

20. WC, "Life and Living," manuscript, WC Papers II.

21. Holt, "Medical Student in Boston," p. 358; John George Metcalf, Lectures on Midwifery, at the Medical School of Harvard University, Boston, 1825 and 1826, November 16, 1825, H MS b29.2, Countway Library.

22. Lectures in anatomy and surgery (Warren), theory and practice (Jackson, followed by Ware), and chemistry (Gorham, followed by Webster) met six times a week. The smaller time allotted to midwifery and to materia medica is some indication of their relative unimportance in the curriculum.

23. Baudeloque's theories were taught by Dewees and other disciples of the French school.

24. WC, "Nourishment of the Fœtus in Utero," manuscript, WC Papers II. In his textbook on obstetrics, William P. Dewees discussed at great length the hypotheses by which impregnation is said to take place and concluded, "However philosophers may differ in the mode of application of the male semen to the female ovary, they all agree that it is either directly or indirectly essential to impregnation." *Compendious System of Midwifery*, pp. 61–63. Carl Ernst von Baer (1792–1876) is credited with being the first to discover the mammalian ovum and is considered the father of modern embryology. Garrison, *History of Medicine*, pp. 453–54.

25. WC, Miscellaneous lecture notes, WC Papers II.

26. This description of Channing's lectures is based on notes taken by John George Metcalf, David Humphreys Storer, and Edward Jarvis, all at the Countway Library; Dr. Walter Channing's Note Book of Lectures, Minot Papers, MHS; WC, Miscellaneous lecture notes, WC Papers II. It does not differ significantly from that of other instructors' lectures at the time. See, for example, Dewees, *Compendious System of Midwifery* (1824), or later, Fleetwood Churchill, *On the Theory and Practice of Midwifery* (Philadelphia: Blanchard and Lea, 1851).

27. Rothstein, *American Medical Schools and the Practice of Medicine*, pp. 53–55.

28. George L. Weed to Luther Ticknor, December 16, 1823, H MS misc., Countway Library. The art of wax modeling for medical teaching reached a peak in Florence at the end of the eighteenth and beginning of the nineteenth centuries. Thomas Schnalke, *Diseases*

in Wax: The History of Medical Moulage, trans. Kathy Spatschek ([Chicago]: Quintessence Publishing Co., 1995), esp. Chapter 7. According to the *NEJMS* 5 (1816): 412, "The department of Midwifery in the Medical College of Harvard University is enriched by the arrival from Europe of a superb female wax figure, designed to illustrate the physiology of pregnancy. This figure was executed at Florence, under the direction of learned and exact professors, and probably surpasses everything of the kind, which has appeared on this side the Atlantic." No trace of the figure can be found today. For models from Paris, see Report of the Midwifery Professors, Department of Harvard University, April 29, 1822, Reports to the Overseers, vol. 1, 1761–1825, Harvard University Archives.

29. WC to John Collins Warren, December 1835, JCW Papers, vol. 17.

30. Wellington, "Historical Sketch of the Obstetrical Society of Boston," p. 61.

31. WC, Miscellaneous medical lecture notes on midwifery and obstetrics, WC Papers II. See also Harrington, *Harvard Medical School,* 2:484.

32. "Dr. Robbins was in this afternoon . . . where were Briggs, Leverett and myself—and offered a midwifery case to Either of you gentlemen—whereupon Mr. Leverett said he should like it very much—& I suppose is now engaged in it." Henry Little to Charles Jarvis, June 1, 1823, B MS c11.3, Countway Library. The Almshouse was renamed the House of Industry in 1821, when it relocated from Leverett Street to South Boston.

33. New Medical School, undated, proposal in handwriting of WC, WC Papers II.

34. See, for example, Irving, *Safe Deliverance,* p. 84; Malcolm Storer, "The Teaching of Obstetrics and Gynecology at Harvard," *Quarterly of the Harvard Medical Alumni Association* 8 (1903): 427–45; Wertz and Wertz, *Lying-In,* p. 85.

35. John Collins Warren to President Kirkland, January 29, 1816, Harvard College Papers, vol. 8, Harvard University Archives. Warren was writing here about models that would be used for the instruction of students on the Cambridge side of the river.

36. Rothstein, *American Medical Schools and the Practice of Medicine,* p. 57.

37. J. Whitridge Williams, "The Introduction of Clinical Teaching of Obstetrics in the United States," *American Journal of Obstetrics* 50 (1904): 302–20; Carl T. Javert, "James Platt White: A Pioneer in American Obstetrics and Gynecology," *Journal of the History of Medicine and Allied Sciences* 3 (1948): 489–506; Wertz and Wertz, *Lying-In,* pp. 85–87; Virginia G. Drachman, "The Loomis Trial: Social Mores and Obstetrics in the Mid-Nineteenth Century," in Leavitt, *Women and Health in America,* pp. 166–74. White paid the woman ten dollars for her service. The implications of this episode regarding issues of class and attitudes toward immigrants are more than apparent.

38. Quoted by Lawrence Longo, "Obstetrics and Gynecology," p. 212.

39. "Demonstrative Midwifery," *BMSJ* 42 (1850): 257–58; "Demonstrative Midwifery—Trial for Libel," *BMSJ* 43 (1850–51): 55–57. The *BMSJ* reported that Dr. Bedford (presumably Dr. Gunning S. Bedford) had had an obstetrical clinic for teaching purposes at the University School of Medicine for three years.

40. WC, Miscellaneous medical lecture notes on midwifery and obstetrics, WC Papers II.

41. WC, "An Address to a Society for Obstetric Improvement," WC Papers II.

42. WC, "Bibliographical Notices," *BMSJ* 66 (1862): 295–99. The Lying-in Hospital moved in 1854 to Springfield Street, in Boston's South End, but closed two years later because of financial difficulties.

43. Medical jurisprudence was taught in conjunction with many medical subjects, including institutes of medicine (or medical theory) and chemistry. Some medical schools

provided lectures for practicing physicians, others for practicing lawyers. For a broad perspective on medical jurisprudence and the relationship of physicians and the legal system, see James C. Mohr, *Doctors and the Law: Medical Jurisprudence in Nineteenth-Century America* (New York: Oxford University Press, 1993). Also Chester R. Burns, "Medical Ethics and Jurisprudence," in Numbers, *Education of American Physicians*, pp. 271–89; Beecher and Altschule, *Medicine at Harvard*, pp. 53–54, 121–23.

44. I have found only one partial set of lecture notes from Channing's course, taken by David H. Storer from January 21 to February 24, 1824. Lectures on Midwifery and Medical Jurisprudence, January 21–February 24, 1824, Countway Library.

45. David Humphreys Storer, *An Address on Medical Jurisprudence delivered before the Fellows of the Massachusetts Medical Society at the annual meeting, May 28, 1851* (Boston: John Wilson and Son, 1851). In 1868 the annual discourse of the Massachusetts Medical Society revealed unchanging attitudes toward obstetrics. "It has always seemed to me remarkable that the subject of Legal Medicine . . . should in most of the schools be made so subordinate and be rated of such small importance as compared with the other courses usually taught; being attached, apparently as a pendant, usually to the chair of Obstetrics, and sometimes to that of Chemistry. Now this appears to be reversing the convenient and proper order of things, and there does not seem to be the slightest propriety in thus making the greater subsidiary to the less." Henry Grafton Clark, *Medical Jurisprudence* (Boston: David Clapp, 1868), p. 17.

46. WC, "A Medico-Legal Treatise on Malpractice and Medical Evidence—A Review," *BMSJ* 62 (1860): 233–41, 259–65, 300–307, quotation p. 300. Channing's essay is a review of a book by John J. Elwell. Channing used this review to discourse on criminal abortion, the physician's role in abortion, development of the English jury system, court procedures, malpractice, and his own experiences giving testimony in legal matters, both in and out of court. He gave little space to Elwell's ideas, though he enthusiastically recommended the book.

47. Ibid., quotation pp. 259–60.

48. Mohr, *Doctors and the Law*, p. 41.

49. Probably James D. Glassford, *An Essay on the Principles of Evidence and Their Application to Subjects of Judicial Inquiry* (Edinburgh: A. Constable & Co., 1820). The identity of Reid remains unknown.

50. WC, Introductory Lecture, undated; WC, Legal Medicine Notes, WC Papers II; David Humphreys Storer, Lectures on Midwifery and Medical Jurisprudence, Countway Library. Several authors (see, for example, Beecher and Altschule, *Medicine at Harvard*, pp. 53–54) have connected medical jurisprudence with midwifery because of the nineteenth-century medical belief that women were especially liable to insanity and other mental disorders because of their reproductive function. There is a hint of this theory in Channing's lectures on insanity, which taught that the most curable forms of insanity "are those which are connected with uterine functions." Most of his lecture focused on the manifestations of insanity in men. It was not until the latter part of the nineteenth century that physicians developed the more elaborate theory connecting women's diseases, mental and physical, with the uterus. See Chapter 13.

51. According to Harold Kirker and James Kirker, *Bulfinch's Boston*, pp. 180–83, the Austin-Selfridge case grew out of the intensity of Federalist-Republican political rivalries in the first decade of the nineteenth century. Charles Austin, a Harvard student, attempted to beat Selfridge on the head with a cane in revenge for a verbal attack Selfridge had inflicted

on his father, Benjamin Austin. Selfridge drew his pistol in defense and fired point-blank at Charles, who died on the spot. Selfridge was acquitted of charges of manslaughter.

52. See Kenneth Allen De Ville, *Medical Malpractice in Nineteenth-Century America: Origins and Legacy* (New York: New York University Press, 1990).

53. WC, "Medico-Legal Treatise on Malpractice and Medical Evidence," p. 303. These ideas about the limits of physician responsibility had been expressed by Judge Minot of Pennsylvania and were reprinted by Channing to represent his own view.

54. WC, Notes for a valedictory lecture, delivered to the students attending the midwifery course, 1837–38 (delivered January 30, 1838, and March 1, 1847), WC Papers II.

55. Walter Channing, Instructer [*sic*], Report of the Department of Obstetrics and Medical Jurisprudence, Academic Year 1826–27, Corporation Papers, 2d Series, 1826–1827, Harvard University Archives.

56. For example, William Workman's subject was "Digestion," John Flint's was "Fever," David H. Storer's was "Hearing in Fishes." "Medical Graduates in Harvard University in 1825, with the Subjects of Their Theses," *NEJMS* 15 (1825): 334. See also Harrington, *Harvard Medical School*, 1:476–77.

57. Rothstein, *American Medical Schools*, pp. 50–51; Ronald L. Numbers, "The Fall and Rise of the Medical Profession," in *Sickness and Health in America*, by Judith Walzer Leavitt and Ronald L. Numbers (Madison: University of Wisconsin Press, 1985), pp. 185–96. For the medical sects, see Norman Gevitz, ed., *Other Healers: Unorthodox Medicine in America* (Baltimore: Johns Hopkins University Press, 1988).

58. WC, Notes for a valedictory lecture, WC Papers II.

59. WC, Legal Medicine Notes, WC Papers II.

60. WC, Notes for a valedictory lecture, WC Papers II.

61. WC, "Of the Medical Profession and of its Preparation," *BMSJ* 33 (1845): 309–17, 329–37, 349–57.

62. WC, General Introductory Lecture to Medical Course, November 4, 1840, mss, WC Papers II. The title to this paper comes from the archivist, not from Channing. The date may not be accurate.

63. WC, "Of the Medical Profession and its Preparation," *BMSJ* 33 (1845): 331.

64. WC, General Introductory Lecture to the Medical Course, November 4, 1840, mss, WC Papers II.

65. WC, General Introductory Lecture, manuscript, WC Papers II. This is the manuscript for a different lecture from the General Introductory Lecture dated November 4, 1840. Channing is known to have delivered the introductory lecture in 1840, 1845, and 1853. In my opinion, the one cited here was written in 1840 and the manuscript cited in notes 62 and 64 was rewritten, delivered in 1845, and published in the *BMSJ* 33 (1845): 309–17, 329–37, 349–57.

66. "Summer Course of Lectures in Midwifery," *NEJMS* 15 (1826): 224; 16 (1827): 224; *BMSJ* 1 (1828): 159. See also Harrington, *Harvard Medical School*, 2:495.

67. Dale Cary Smith, "The Emergence of Organized Clinical Instruction in the Nineteenth-Century American Cities of Boston, New York and Philadelphia" (Ph.D. diss., University of Minnesota, 1979); William Frederick Norwood, *Medical Education in the United States before the Civil War* (Philadelphia: University of Pennsylvania Press, 1944), pp. 183–85; Rothstein, *American Medical Schools*, pp. 55–61.

68. WC, Reminiscences, WC Papers II; WC to President Kirkland, July 18, 1825, Corporation Papers, 1st series, supplements, 1825, Harvard University Archives. By this time,

Channing was living at the corner of Common and School Streets. According to the *American Medical Almanac* (1839), 1:21, Jackson and Channing's private school was known as the Boston Private Medical School, but this name was not used by Channing nor was it so designated in their advertisements.

69. Matriculating Book, Massachusetts Medical College, 1826–1850, Countway Library. This book lists each year's entering students, along with the name of their preceptors. The flyleaf, dated November 26, 1826, contains an excerpt from the Statutes and Laws of the University in Cambridge, Mass., written in Channing's hand. There is no way to verify the accuracy of the matriculating book, especially during the final years it supposedly covered.

70. "Medical Instruction," *BMSJ* 2 (1829–30): 544, 448. See also Warren, *Life of John Collins Warren*, 2:273. Warren and his associates never had many private pupils and gave up the arrangement around 1840.

71. John Ware, Articles of Agreement for Medical Instruction and Prospectus, April 26, 1830, H MS c7.4, Countway Library; "Private Med. School," *BMSJ* 3 (1830): 360. Ware was one of the editors of the *New England Journal of Medicine and Surgery* and its successor, the *Boston Medical and Surgical Journal*. In time he would be named Adjunct Professor of Theory and Practice and eventually replace Jackson as the Hersey Professor. Otis and Lewis were also Harvard medical graduates. Both had studied with John Collins Warren. After passage of the Anatomy Act in 1831, Winslow Lewis was named Demonstrator in Anatomy at the medical college.

72. John Ware to John Collins Warren, October 27, 1830, JCW Papers, vol. 15. Both schools charged seventy-five dollars for six months' and fifty dollars for three months' instruction.

73. Record of Pupils Reading, List of Pupils with Drs. Jackson & Channing & time of entrance, mss., Countway Library.

74. "Private Medical Instruction," *BMSJ* 12 (1835): 194–95.

75. The Marine Hospital, established during the administration of President John Adams, was financed by a small tax on seamen's wages. The Eye and Ear Infirmary was started in 1824 to address diseases not cared for at the Massachusetts General. Eaton, *Hospitals in New England*, pp. 23–25, 166–67.

76. Medical students were still being asked to rob graves, as Channing had done for John Warren the elder. John Collins Warren regularly imported bodies from a supplier in New York. John D. Godman to John Collins Warren, January 1, 1829, JCW Papers, vol. 14. Importing bodies from New York could present serious problems during the warm months and was occasionally a great embarrassment.

77. Warren, *Life of John Collins Warren*, 1:404–20; Harrington, *Harvard Medical School*, 2:651–67.

78. See Waite, "Development of Anatomical Laws in the States of New England"; Norwood, *Medical Education in the United States before the Civil War*, p. 400. The 1831 act was formally entitled "An Act more effectually to protect the Sepulchres of the Dead, and to legalize the Study of Anatomy in certain Cases," and was reproduced in *BMSJ* 4 (1831): 85–87. According to Philip Cash, cadavers became more plentiful in later years as the number of poor immigrants increased in Boston.

79. "Medical Instruction," *BMSJ* 10 (1834): 132. Jackson's son, James Jackson, Jr., in whom he had placed all his dreams and affection, died in April 1834. The younger Jackson had studied at Jackson and Channing's school, received his medical degree from Harvard,

and spent three years in Paris, where he was a protégé of Louis. He was thought to be a physician of unusual talents and much was expected of him, not only by his father, but by the rest of the medical establishment and the general public. He had been back from Europe only a few months when he became fatally ill with typhoid fever. The retirement of James Jackson, Sr., from the private medical school is only one sign of the devastating effect of his loss. See Chapter 7.

80. "Private Medical Instruction," *BMSJ* 19 (1838–39): 211.

81. Harrington, *Harvard Medical School*, 1:496–500.

82. "Dr. Lewis's Medical School," *BMSJ* 22 (1840): 80; "Private Medical Instruction," *BMSJ* 23 (1840–41): 71.

83. Harrington, *Harvard Medical School*, 1:501–5; Norwood, *Medical Education in the United States before the Civil War*, p. 184. See also *BMSJ* 36 (1847): 146–47, 266; 43 (1850): 128; 50 (1854): 259–62.

84. The trustees of the Massachusetts General Hospital were not enthusiastic about the move. Responding to a communication from John Collins Warren, they stated that they "cannot see any advantage to the hospital from building a medical school close by but could see some disadvantages." However, they did not object to the plan. Marcus Merton, Jr., to John Collins Warren, February 22, 1846, JCW Papers, vol. 22; Bowditch, *Massachusetts General Hospital*, p. 194.

85. "Hospital for Children," *BMSJ* 35 (1846): 348; Jacob Bigelow to John Collins Warren, July 24, 1846, Samuel A. Eliot to John Collins Warren, September 18, 1846, JCW Papers, vol. 22; "The Boston Society of Natural History," *BMSJ* 69 (1863–64): 23; Warren, *Life of John Collins Warren*, 2:4.

86. See Chapter 12.

87. See Chapter 13. WC to the President & Fellows of Harvard College, September 4, 1854, Harvard College Papers, vol. 21, 2d series; President James Walker to Walter Channing, September 18, 1854, Presidents' Papers, Harvard University Archives.

88. WC to John Collins Warren, January 24, 1838, JCW Papers, vol. 18. See also Warren, *Life of John Collins Warren*, 1:328.

89. The course offerings and faculty for 1853–54 were: Obstetrics and Medical Jurisprudence, Walter Channing, M.D.; Clinical Medicine and Materia Medica, Jacob Bigelow, M.D.; Theory and Practice of Medicine, John Ware, M.D., and Morrill Wyman, M.D.; Pathological Anatomy, J. B. S. Jackson, M.D.; Anatomy and Physiology, Oliver Wendell Holmes, M.D.; Principles and Operations of Surgery, Henry J. Bigelow, M.D.; and Chemistry, Professor J. P. Cooke. Fees for the entire course were $80; matriculation, $3; dissecting ticket, $5; and graduation, $20. Hospital and library, free. Channing opened the session with the General Introductory Lecture in November 1853. "Massachusetts Medical College," *BMSJ* 49 (1853): 192.

90. "Massachusetts Medical College," *BMSJ* 43 (1850–51): 128.

91. "Resignation of Professor Channing," *BMSJ* 51 (1854–55): 166.

92. David Humphreys Storer, *An Address Delivered at the First Medical Commencement of the Massachusetts Medical College, March 7, 1855* (Boston: John Wilson & Son, 1855).

Notes to Chapter 7

1. The Board of Selectmen, assisted by the School Committee and other specialty boards, provided day-to-day administration. Not everyone could vote. Not only were all

women excluded from the franchise, but property and religious restrictions also limited the number of voters. In 1820 the number of qualified voters was fewer than eight thousand. James M. Bugbee, "Boston under the Mayors," in *The Memorial History of Boston*, ed. Justin Winsor, 4 vols. (Boston: James R. Osgood, 1882), 3:217–92.

2. WC to Lucy Russel, n.d. [1825 or 1826], WC Papers III.

3. "It may be painful to talk of one who is lost to us here, but I think the sacrifice should be made for the children who could not know her. Nothing would induce me to speak of it to Father, I should so dread the effect." Barbara Channing to Lucy Russel, August 15, 1840, CF Papers.

4. WC to Barbara Channing, October 17, 1825; WC to "dear children," n.d., CF Papers.

5. For Round Hill, see Handlin, *George Bancroft*; Thomas Gold Appleton, *Life and Letters of Thomas Gold Appleton* (New York: D. Appleton, 1885).

6. McGill, *Channing of Concord*, pp. 4–7; Mary W. Poor, *Recollections of Brookline* (Brookline, Mass.: Brookline Historical Society, 1903), p. 23.

7. Susan Channing to Lucy Russel, January 30, 1831, HCC Papers.

8. WEC to WC, August 15, 1827, WEC Papers.

9. Channing purchased the house in 1833 for $12,500. Suffolk County Registry of Deeds, Book 368, pp. 170, 172, Suffolk County Court House, Boston.

10. William Henry Channing (1810–1884) was the son of Francis and Susan Higginson Channing. William Henry Channing to Barbara Channing, August 18, 1876, CF Papers.

11. WC to Lucy Russel, n.d. [1827], WC Papers III.

12. The youngest Dana child died shortly after her mother. Hunter, *Richard Henry Dana, Sr.*, p. 56.

13. WC to Richard Henry Dana, [1827], Dana Family Papers, MHS.

14. [WC], "The Book of Nature, by John Mason Good," *United States Review and Literary Gazette* 1 (1827): 407–17.

15. Hunter, *Richard Henry Dana, Sr.*, p. 78.

16. WC to Richard Henry Dana, February 11, 1828, Dana Family Papers, MHS.

17. Sparks spent six years as owner and editor of the *North American Review*, while beginning to turn his attention to historical research and writing. He visited Mount Vernon in 1827, where he collected many of the papers of George Washington, and spent 1828–1829 in France and England copying documents for his twelve-volume opus, *Diplomatic Correspondence of the American Revolution*, published in 1829 and 1830.

18. [WC], "Hints to My Countrymen," *North American Review* 23 (1826): 467–70; [WC], "The Classical Reader," *North American Review* 24 (1827): 234–36. The reviews were not signed, but they are attributed to Channing. William Cushing, *Index to the North American Review, Volumes 1–125* (Cambridge: John Wilson and Son, 1878).

19. WC to Jared Sparks, February 26, 1827, January 21, 1828, May 13, 1829, MS Sparks Papers 153, Houghton Library, Harvard University; Jared Sparks to WC, March 2, 1827, WC Papers II. See also Adams, *Life and Writings of Jared Sparks*, 1:353. For Howe, see Julia Ward Howe, *Reminiscences, 1819–1899* (Boston: Houghton Mifflin, 1899), pp. 85–86.

20. David Sears to WC, July 26, 1823, WC Papers II; Theophilus Parsons, Jr., to Theophilus Parsons, Esq., n.d. [September 1824], BPL.

21. See, for example, WC to Walter Channing, Esq. [Uncle Walter], n.d., WC Papers II; William Ellery Channing to WC, n.d., WEC Papers (microfilm reel 1, letters no. 9, no. 73); WEC to WC, July 20, 1824, Bostonian Society; WEC to WC, August 16, 1825, b MS Am 1610, Houghton Library; Susan Higginson Channing to William Russel, March 31,

1825; Susan Higginson, Jr., to Francis Higginson, [September 1828], HCC Papers. William's health was a genuine cause for concern; he had severely damaged it while a young man and was never robust thereafter.

22. Susan Channing to Lucy Russel, January 30, 1831, HCC Papers.

23. For "my dear Doctor Walter Channing," see Sophia Peabody to Maria Chase, March 30, 1829, Peabody Papers, Sophia Smith Collection, Smith College.

24. Cuba was a favorite destination for New Englanders seeking to regain their health. The sea voyage to the island and its warm climate were among the major attractions. WC to Sophia Amelia Peabody, August 12, 1828, November 17, 1828, September 20, 1828, October 11, [1829?], Berg Collection, New York Public Library. I am grateful to Megan Marshall for her help with the archives of the Peabody sisters. See also Mary Peabody to Miss R. Pickman, [1833], no. 653, Robert Straker Collection, Antioch College Library, Yellow Springs, Ohio. Channing was also physician to George Peabody, a brother of Sophia and Elizabeth Peabody. In a letter to his mother, George stated that a subsequent physician did "not make me feel that confidence in him that I felt in Doctor Channing." George F. Peabody to Mrs. Elizabeth P. Peabody, March 5, 1832, no. 589, Robert Straker Collection, Antioch College Library.

25. See, for example, Mary T. Peabody to Maria Chase, November 10, 1826; Sophia Peabody to Maria Chase, January 9, 1828, Peabody Papers, Sophia Smith Collection, Smith College.

26. WC, *A Case of Pericarditis* [Boston, 1834]. Channing had previously published "A Case of Rheumatism, with Disease of the Heart," *NEJMS* 14 (1825): 147–51, which described a similar disease. In this case the patient was a twenty-five-year-old woman.

27. Benedict F. Massell, *Rheumatic Fever and Streptococcal Infection* (Boston: Francis A. Countway Library of Medicine, 1997); Thomas G. Benedek, "Rheumatic Fever and Rheumatic Heart Disease," in *The Cambridge World History of Human Disease*, ed. Kenneth F. Kiple (New York: Cambridge University Press, 1994), pp. 970–77. Puerperal fever is associated with a different strain of the streptococcus.

28. Arthur Wayne Brown, *William Ellery Channing* (New York: Twayne Publishers, 1961), p. 123; Ruth M. Baylor, Miscellaneous notes, Ruth M. Baylor Papers, MHS. The society had originated with William Ellery Channing, who wanted to improve religious education for the children in his congregation.

29. February 9, 1830. Channing was one of the initial curators charged with supervision of the collections and served as a vice president in 1836–1837. Several other physicians, including John Ware, George Hayward, and David Humphreys Storer, were also prominent in the initial years of the society. John Collins Warren became president in 1847. Boston Society of Natural History, Records of the Recording Secretary, 1830–1836, Library, Boston Museum of Science. See also Augustus A. Gould, "Notice of the Origin, Progress, and Present Condition of the Boston Society of Natural History," *Proceedings of the Boston Society of Natural History* 1 (1841–44): 1–8.

30. Warren, *Address to the Boston Society of Natural History*; Boston Society of Natural History, *The Boston Society of Natural History, 1830–1930* ([Boston]: printed for the Society, 1930); Holt, "Medical Student in Boston," p. 187.

31. Report of Committee to provide lecturers, etc., October 22, 1829, Papers of the Boston Society for the Diffusion of Useful Knowledge, MHS. For Channing's lecture notes, see "Public Health," WC Papers II. For audience reaction, see Marc Friedlander and L. H. Butterfield, eds., *Diary of Charles Francis Adams* (Cambridge, Mass.: Belknap Press of Harvard University Press, 1968), 3:81, 88, 95–96. Channing's third lecture topic was the rela-

tionship of the natural environment to disease, a topic that interested many scientists and physicians who attributed fevers to bad air, wet soils, and abrupt changes of climate.

32. Notice signed by John Ware and Walter Channing, *NEJMS* 13 (1824): 336.

33. WC, "Case of Inversio Uteri with Comments," *NEJMS* 11 (1822): 264–69; "Case of Syphilitic Ulceration of the Larynx," *NEJMS* 12 (1823): 350–56; "Case of Rheumatism, with Disease of the Heart," *NEJMS* 14 (1825): 147–51; "On a Species of Premature Labour," *NEJMS* 14 (1825): 151–56; "On Blisters," *NEJMS* 15 (1826): 235–43; "Miscellaneous Cases, Spina Bifida, Preternatural Labors, Erysipelatous Inflammation," *NEJMS* 15 (1826): 357–70. Channing also published an article on "Bills of Mortality," calling for consistent nomenclature of disease so that bills of mortality (official lists of deaths giving diseases, ages, and sexes of the deceased) would be more useful for physicians and public officials. *NEJMS* 15 (1826): 225–34. The reviews were unsigned but give every indication of his authorship. See *NEJMS* 13 (1824): 139–53; *NEJMS* 14 (1825): 284–304; *New-England Medical Review and Journal* 1 (1827): 113–41. Also William P. Dewees to WC, July 10, 1825, WC Papers II.

34. By 1827 the *New England Journal* had become so unprofitable that the publisher was no longer willing to continue. Six hundred copies were printed per issue, but sales were closer to four hundred. Wells & Lilly to WC, October 6, 1827, JCW Papers, vol. 13.

35. With volume 16 (1827), the *New England Journal of Medicine and Surgery* was temporarily renamed *New-England Medical Review and Journal*, Ware and Channing continuing as editors. It was renamed again when Warren, Ware, and Channing assumed editorship of the merged journals, this time as the *Boston Medical and Surgical Journal*. Warren, *Life of John Collins Warren*, 1:236–43; *Boston Medical Intelligencer* 5 (1827–28): 582–83; Joseph Garland, "The New England Journal of Medicine, 1812–1968," *Journal of the History of Medicine and Allied Sciences* 24 (1969): 25–38.

36. WC, "On the Transfusion of Blood," *BMSJ* 1 (April 1, 1828): 97–102; "Inflammation of the Tongue," *BMSJ* 1:84–86; "Case of Tumor within the Abdomen," *BMSJ* 1 (1828): 784–89.

37. Warren, *Life of John Collins Warren*, 1:236–44; John Ware to JCW, February 1829; WC to JCW, February 28, 1829; John Cotton to JCW, March 12, [1829]; Ware to JCW, April 22, [1829]; JCW to Cotton, April 23, [1829]; Ware to JCW, April 23, 1829; Cotton to Ware, 1829, all vol. 14; Ware to JCW, Feb. 1830, vol. 15, JCW Papers.

38. See, despite some inconsistencies, Joseph Garland, "Medical Journalism in New England, 1788–1924," *BMSJ* 190 (1924): 870–79; Garland, "New England Journal of Medicine, 1812–1968"; Henry Burnell Shafer, "Early Medical Magazines in America," *Annals of Medical History* 7 (1935): 480–91.

39. See, for example, WC to H. W. Fuller, September 1, 1828; James Jackson to WC, January 30, 1829; WC to John Collins Warren, February 2, 1829; James Jackson to WC, May 8, 1829; WC to Henry Childs, December 11, 1829, B MS c75.2, Countway Library; Burrage, *History of the Massachusetts Medical Society*, pp. 281, 313, 377.

40. Burrage, *History of the Massachusetts Medical Society*, p. 466.

41. WC to Lucy Russel, n.d., WC Papers III; Elizabeth Palmer Peabody to Horace Mann, [fall 1834], typescript, Antioch College Library; WC to Richard Henry Dana, February 11, 1828, December 1828, Dana Family Papers, MHS; George Ticknor, *Life, Letters and Journals of George Ticknor*, 7th ed., 2 vols. (Boston: James R. Osgood, 1877), 1:390–91.

42. WC to Jared Sparks, January 21, 1828, MS Sparks Papers 153, Houghton Library, Harvard College; WC to Richard Henry Dana, [1828?], Dana Family Papers, MHS.

43. Susan Higginson Channing to Lucy Russel, March 20, 1831; Susan Channing, Jr.,

to Mary W. White, March 30, 1831, HCC Papers; Mary Elizabeth Channing, Journal, CF Papers.

44. Delano A. Goddard, "The Pulpit, Press and Literature of the Revolution," and Andrew P. Peabody, "The Unitarians in Boston," cited in Winsor, *Memorial History of Boston*, 3:119–22, 467.

45. Cash et al., *Medicine in Colonial Massachusetts*, pp. 49, 91–92, 95. John Clarke VI apprenticed to James Lloyd, studied midwifery in London, and expected to teach midwifery in Boston. Unfortunately, he died after giving just one set of lectures. Had the sixth John Clarke lived a longer life, he might well have become the first professor of midwifery at Harvard and Channing's career might have been very different.

46. Eliza Susan Quincy, Journal, November 28, 1814, July 4, July 5, 1815, and addendum, Quincy Family Papers, MHS. See also Anna Cabot Lowell, Personal Journal, March 26, 1831, March 31, 1832, Anna Cabot Lowell Papers II, MHS. Eliza Quincy was the daughter of Josiah Quincy, mayor of Boston and president of Harvard.

47. [Eliza Follen], "Obituary Notice of Mrs. Eliza Wainwright Channing," *Christian Register*, April 5, 1834; Elizabeth Peabody to Mary T. Peabody, April 6, 1834, Berg Collection, New York Public Library. Eliza Cabot had married Charles Follen, a German émigré who taught at Harvard.

48. Jonathan Mayhew Wainwright served at Christ Church in Hartford, Connecticut, and Trinity Church, New York, before coming to Boston in 1834. In 1838 he returned to New York as assistant minister and assistant rector at Trinity. In 1852 he was named provisional bishop of New York. Arthur H. Chester, *Trinity Church in the City of Boston* (Cambridge: John Wilson and Son, 1888). See also *Dictionary of American Biography*, 10:316–17; William B. Sprague, *Annals of the American Pulpit* (New York: Robert Carter and Brothers, 1859), 5:610–17. The number of Episcopalians in Boston was relatively small but, like the Unitarians, they represented the social and financial elite. Phillips Brooks, "The Episcopal Church," in Winsor, *Memorial History of Boston*, 3:447–66; Jane H. Pease and William H. Pease, "Whose Right Hand of Fellowship? Pew and Pulpit in Shaping Church Practice," in *American Unitarianism*, ed. Conrad Edick Wright (Boston: Massachusetts Historical Society and Northeastern University Press, 1989), pp. 181–206.

49. *Columbian Cential* (Boston), September 10, 1831.

50. Mary T. Peabody to Sally Gardner, May 1, 1834, H. Mann Papers, MHS; Eliza Channing to Lucy Russel, October 16, 1832, CF Papers. Mary's "rough edges" probably refers to the outspoken manner of which she was sometimes accused.

51. In May 1834 one of Susan's daughters, Susan Channing Higginson, named her newborn daughter Elizabeth Wainwright Higginson in memory of the woman who had so briefly been her aunt. Susan married her cousin Francis Higginson, M.D., for whom Walter had been preceptor as well as professor.

52. WC to James Jackson, Jr., November 22, 1832, H MS c8.3, Countway Library.

53. George Hayward to WC, March 20, 1833, WC Papers III.

54. "Massachusetts Medical Society," *BMSJ* 8 (1833): 241, 290. Channing's address was published in 1833 and 1836: *On Irritable Uterus* [Boston: n.p., 1833 and 1836]. As the annual orator, Channing was also required to eulogize recently deceased members of the society. Joshua Fisher had been president from 1815 to 1823 as well as a state senator. Channing gave an effusive memoir, praising his patriotism during the Revolutionary War, his enterprise in cotton manufacture, and his devotion to his medical patients. Channing admired Fisher's reliance on personal observations of disease and his determination to pre-

scribe accordingly. He also spoke of Fisher's interest in natural history and the professorship in that subject that he had endowed at Harvard. Asa Gray, an outstanding botanist, was Fisher Professor for nearly half a century. Burrage, *History of the Massachusetts Medical Society,* p. 104.

55. In 1813 Oliver Prescott of Groton, Massachusetts, gave the annual address, "On the Natural History and Medicinal Effects of Secale Cornutum, or Ergot," a topic more obstetrical than gynecological. Prescott's paper was published that same year and did much to stimulate interest in the use of ergot. Burrage, *History of the Massachusetts Medical Society,* p. 467; Speert, *Obstetrics and Gynecology in America,* pp. 181–82.

56. See Chapter 13.

57. Stevenson lived next door to Channing and was a particularly good friend. Channing mourned his premature death in 1835 and wrote a poem in Stevenson's memory, later published in a collection of his poetry, *New and Old,* p. 129.

58. Stevenson, Channing, and others who tried saline injections were onto something—but for the wrong reasons. According to Charles Rosenberg, their therapy was based on the finding that the blood of cholera victims contained more solids than liquids and the assumption that a proper balance would be restored by the injections. Rosenberg, *Cholera Years,* p. 67 n. 6. Subsequent cholera research has led to treatment by rehydration, either orally or intravenously, to replace lost water and salts. Reinhard S. Speck, "Cholera," in *Cambridge World History of Human Disease,* pp. 642–69. See also Norman Howard-Jones, "Cholera Therapy in the Nineteenth Century," *Journal of the History of Medicine and Allied Sciences* 27 (1972): 373–94.

59. J. Greely Stevenson, "Case of Cholera Treated by Saline Injections," *BMSJ* 7 (1832): 181–85; WC, "A Fragment of a Medical Autobiography," *BMSJ* 71 (1865): 351–58, esp. 355–56. Stevenson wrote that the initial improvement was due to the injection and that the subsequent deterioration could be ascribed to the feeble constitution of the patient, a twenty-two-year-old shoemaker. He raised questions about the possible effects of mercurials and stimulants he had received as well as the damage caused to the capillaries by offensive foreign matters, that is, the salts.

60. See, for example, WC, "Fragment of a Medical Biography," p. 356.

61. *Daily Evening Transcript* (Boston), June 1, 1833. The issues of gender and class, the change in values as the nation moved from an agricultural to an industrial society, and the tensions between the newer evangelical sects and traditional churches represented by the Avery case continue to intrigue historians and novelists. For many observers then and now the verdict was a travesty of justice. See, for example, Raymond Paul, *The Tragedy at Tiverton: An Historical Novel of Murder* (New York: Viking Press, 1984); Mary Cable, *Avery's Knot* (G. P. Putnam's Sons, 1981); and David Richard Kasserman, *Fall River Outrage: Life, Murder, and Justice in Early Industrial New England* (Philadelphia: University of Pennsylvania Press, 1986). Catherine Williams, *Fall River: An Authentic Narrative,* ed. Patricia Caldwell (New York: Oxford University Press, 1993), was written shortly after the trial to attack Avery and the Methodists and to defend the factory girls.

62. Sixty years later the Lizzie Borden ax murders again brought national attention to Fall River.

63. The Avery case is vividly described in George Howe, "The Minister and the Mill Girl," *American Heritage,* October 1961. The trial was reported in Benjamin F. Hallett, *A Full Report of the Trial of Ephraim K. Avery, charged with the murder of Sarah M. Cornell, before the Supreme Court of Rhode Island, at a special term in Newport, held in May 1833; with the Arguments of Counsel* (Boston: Daily Commercial Gazette and Boston Daily Advocate, 1833).

64. Howe, "The Minister and the Mill Girl," pp. 82–83; Kasserman, *Fall River Outrage*, pp. 129–30. See also *Memoirs of Jeremiah Mason*, ed. G. J. Clark (1873; Boston: Boston Law Book Co., 1917). Mason had been attorney general of New Hampshire and a United States senator from that state before moving to Boston in 1832.

65. WC, Miscellaneous notes on the Avery Trial, WC Papers II. The impeachment trial of Warren Hastings, first British governor-general in India, lasted from 1788 to 1795.

66. Ibid.

67. Frank Sanborn, "Ellery Channing on the Mystery of Shakespeare, with a Sketch of the Essayist," typescript, Concord Free Public Library, Concord, Massachusetts.

68. One of the physicians for the defense, Dr. Usher Parsons, had delivered lectures on anatomy in Rhode Island and Philadelphia but seems not to have been permanently associated with a medical faculty.

69. Hallett, *Full Report of the Trial of Ephraim K. Avery*, p. 198.

70. WC, Miscellaneous notes on the Avery Trial.

71. "Medical Evidence in Trial of Reverend E. K. Avery for the Murder of Sarah M. Cornell," *BMSJ* 8 (1833): 333–40; Kasserman, *Fall River Outrage*, p. 184. In the next issue of the *BMSJ*, a special communication criticized medical witnesses who leave an impression that medical testimony is at best very uncertain, and but little to be depended on, in making up a verdict. The two physicians who had examined Sarah's body were singled out for neglecting to gather sufficient evidence to ascertain from the outset if the case was suicide or murder. "Medical Jurisprudence," *BMSJ* 8: 350–51.

72. WC, Miscellaneous notes on the Avery Trial. According to Channing's notes, the encounter occurred "the afternoon of the day I returned." This has to be an error because the jury did not deliver its verdict until the following Sunday, June 2.

73. *Memoirs of Jeremiah Mason*, p. 361.

74. WC, Miscellaneous notes on the Avery Trial.

75. *Daily Evening Transcript* (Boston), June 7, 1833.

76. *Daily Evening Transcript* (Boston), June 14, 1833.

77. The foundation for the Bunker Hill Monument had been laid with great ceremony by General LaFayette in 1825. John Collins Warren, whose uncle Joseph Warren had died during the battle, was one of the prime movers in the Bunker Hill Monument Association. It took another seventeen years from the laying of the foundation to secure the money needed for completion of the structure. Nathaniel Dearborn, *Boston Notions* (Boston: Printed for Nathaniel Dearborn, 1848), pp. 282–85; Warren, *Life of John Collins Warren*, 1:209–11.

78. Eliza Wainwright Channing to Lucy Russel, October 16, 1832, CF Papers.

79. Eliza Follen to Catherine M. Sedgwick, April 2, 1834, Catherine Maria Sedgwick Papers III, MHS; William Ellery Channing to Jonathan Phillips, March 28, 1834, Phillips Papers, MHS.

80. The following description of Eliza's labor and death is based largely on letters written by Elizabeth Peabody to her sister Mary, March 22–24, March 28–31, 1834, Berg Collection, New York Public Library. Again I thank Megan Marshall for alerting me to these letters.

81. Elizabeth Peabody described the delivery as an operation, a term commonly used for any instrumented delivery.

82. Eliza Cabot Follen to Catherine Maria Sedgwick, April 2, 1834, Catherine Maria Sedgwick Papers III, MHS.

83. Many years later Ellery referred to the loss of his mother as the most difficult time

of his life, but it is not clear to which mother he was referring. He was not quite five years old when Barbara died. Francis B. Dedmond, "The Selected Letters of William Ellery Channing the Younger (Part One)," in *Studies in the American Renaissance*, ed. Joel Myerson (Charlottesville: University Press of Virginia, 1989), pp. 116–17.

84. Barbara Channing to Lucy Bradstreet Channing, December 2, [1839?], CF Papers.

85. Elizabeth Peabody to Mary Peabody, March 22–24, 1834, Berg Collection, New York Public Library.

86. James Jackson, *A Memoir of James Jackson, Jr., M.D.: with extracts from his letters to his father; and medical cases, collected by him* (Boston: I. R. Butts, 1835).

87. WC to James Jackson, Jr., November 22, 1832, B MS c8.3, Countway Library.

88. Eliza Cabot Follen to Catherine Maria Sedgwick, April 2, 1834, Catherine Maria Sedgwick Papers III, MHS; Elizabeth Peabody to Mary Peabody, April 3, 1834, Berg Collection, New York Public Library.

89. Mary Channing (daughter of William Ellery Channing) to Mary Peabody, October 4, 1834, Horace Mann Papers, MHS.

90. Susan Higginson Channing to Lucy Russel, May 28, 1834, HCC Papers.

91. WC to Lucy Russel, May 28, 1834, CF Papers.

92. Elizabeth Peabody used this expression describing the deaths of Eliza Channing and James Jackson, Jr. Elizabeth P. Peabody to Mary Peabody, March 30, 1834, Berg Collection, New York Public Library.

93. WC, "The Objects and Progress of the Society," address before the Boston Society of Natural History, May 20, 1835, WC Papers II. Channing urged the society to reach out to the public. He hoped its collections would be available for study by everyone, not just the members. He was especially eager to welcome children from the public schools and charities. See also Boston Society of Natural History, Records of the Recording Secretary, 1830–1844, May 20, 1835, Boston Museum of Science.

94. WC, *The Moral Uses of the Study of Natural History, in Introductory Discourse and Lectures Delivered before the American Institute of Instruction in Boston, August, 1835* (Boston: Charles Hendee, 1836), pp. 255–69. The American Institute of Instruction was organized in 1831 for the promotion and improvement of instruction in morality, science, and literature. Though the institute was based in Boston, its membership stretched from South Carolina to Vermont. Lecture topics at the 1835 weeklong meeting ranged from a discussion of the best way to inspire correct literary taste (Ralph Waldo Emerson) to the importance of physical education (John Collins Warren).

95. The case of the child who died from pericarditis, for example, occupied him from June to August 1834.

96. Lucy was unwell most of her life. Although retrospective diagnosis is difficult, the symptoms described by various members of the family suggest that she too had had rheumatic fever. See Susan Channing to Lucy Bradstreet Channing, October 13, [?], CF Papers.

97. Josephine E. Roberts, "Miss Peabody and Temple School," *New England Quarterly* 15 (1942): 497–508. Susan Wainwright, probably a niece of Eliza Channing; Mary Rogers, daughter of Walter's sister Mary; and Mary Ruth Channing, a daughter of William Ellery Channing, were also among the ten girls in the class. See also Frederick C. Dahlstrand, *Amos Bronson Alcott* (London and Toronto: Associated University Presses, 1982), pp. 109–29; and Bruce A. Ronda, *Elizabeth Palmer Peabody* (Cambridge, Mass.: Harvard University Press, 1999), pp. 112–42.

98. Charles Sedgwick, descendant of a notable family that had lived for several genera-

tions in western Massachusetts, was clerk of Berkshire County Court. His wife, Elizabeth Buckminster Dwight Sedgwick, had an equally impressive lineage. She conducted a small school for girls in her home, where Lucy spent several years. Mary Channing was also a student there, but for a shorter period. The novelist Catherine Maria Sedgwick, a sister of Charles, was a good friend of many Channings.

99. WC to Lucy Bradstreet Channing, September 16, 1836, CF Papers.

100. Uncle Edward was Boylston Professor of Rhetoric and Oratory, Uncle William was an Overseer, and of course his father was a professor and dean of the medical school. The burden of his family pedigree is suggested by McGill, *Channing of Concord*, pp. 9–15.

101. Ibid.; Robert N. Hudspeth, *Ellery Channing* (New York: Twayne, 1973), pp. 17–20. Ellery parodied Harvard in "The Youth of the Poet and the Painter," published in the *Dial* 4 (1843–44). For more about Harvard during this period, see Robert A. McCaughey, *Josiah Quincy, 1772–1864: The Last Federalist* (Cambridge, Mass.: Harvard University Press, 1974), pp. 163–78; and Morison, *Three Centuries of Harvard*, pp. 246–72.

102. WC to Lucy Bradstreet Channing, July 11, 1837, CF Papers.

103. WC to Mary Channing and Lucy Bradstreet Channing, January 15, 1837, CF Papers.

Notes to Chapter 8

1. WC, *Treatise on Etherization in Childbirth*, p. 136.

2. William Henry Channing to James Jackson, Jr., March 10, 1832, B MS c8.3, Countway Library.

3. Mary Wilder Tileston, ed., *Caleb and Mary Wilder Foote, Reminiscences and Letters* (Boston: Houghton Mifflin, 1918), p. 52. Several religious denominations continue to provide special prayers of thanksgiving for a new mother following safe delivery of her child. I thank Dr. Theodore Barton for reminding me of this.

4. "Puerperal Fever is probably the most fatal disease to which women in childbed are liable, and is by no means of rare occurrence." Churchill, *On the Theory and Practice of Midwifery*, p. 477. Nathaniel Hulme, with whose teaching Channing was familiar, had written that puerperal fever was "the most dangerous of all fevers . . . more fatal even than the plague or the smallpox." Channing taught that puerperal fever and the plague were equally dangerous. For Hulme, see Irvine Loudon, *Childbed Fever: A Documentary History* (New York: Garland Publishing, 1995), pp. xxxvii, 3–7.

5. See, for example, WC, "Observations on Puerperal Fever with Diarrhaea," *NEJMS* 2 (1813): 232–45; WC, "Practical Remarks on Some of the Predisposing Causes, and Prevention, of Puerperal Fever, with Cases," *NEJMS* 6 (1817): 157–69.

6. Hence the disease acquired a variety of names, including milk fever (because of the onset simultaneous with lactation), puerperal peritonitis, and puerperal septicemia.

7. Loudon, *Childbed Fever*, p. xxxvi.

8. See Charles A. Rosenberg, *Explaining Epidemics and Other Studies in the History of Medicine* (Cambridge: Cambridge University Press, 1992), pp. 293–304. Rosenberg aggregates theories regarding the causes of epidemics under three headings: configuration, contamination, and predisposition. See Loudon, *Childbed Fever*, pp. xxxviii–xliv.

9. Alexander Gordon, *A Treatise on the Epidemic Puerperal Fever of Aberdeen* (London: printed for G. G. and J. Robinson, 1795). See also George W. Lowis, "Epidemiology of Puerperal Fever: The Contributions of Alexander Gordon," *Medical History* 37 (1993): 399–410.

10. Gordon, *Treatise on the Epidemic Puerperal Fever of Aberdeen*, p. 3.

11. Ibid., pp. 98–99.

12. Weed was distinguished from puerperal fever by the brevity of the attack and the absence of abdominal tenderness. It was thought to be caused by cold air and that women with sensitive constitutions were especially prone to the disorder.

13. WC, "Practical Remarks on Some of the Predisposing Causes, and Prevention, of Puerperal Fever, with Cases," *NEJMS* 6 (1817): 157–69.

14. WC, *Cases of Inflammation of the Veins with Remarks on the Supposed Identity of Phlebitis and Phlegmasia Dolens* [Boston: 1830].

15. WC, "Practical Remarks on Some of the Predisposing Causes, and Prevention, of Puerperal Fever, with Cases," p. 169.

16. WC, Miscellaneous lecture notes, WC Papers II.

17. Edward Jarvis, "Dr. Walter Channing Jr.'s Lectures on Midwifery and Medical Jurisprudence," 1827–1829, January 12, 1828, pp. 135–37, B MS b271.1, Countway Library.

18. WC, Miscellaneous lecture notes (no. 53 Labour), WC Papers II.

19. Ibid. (no. 35 Labour), WC Papers II.

20. Boston Society for Medical Improvement, Records, vol. 1, Constitution and By-Laws of the Boston Society for Medical Improvement, Countway Library. After 1837 the society rented a meeting room. Channing was a stickler for well-run meetings and frequently reprimanded the members when they did not adhere to protocol.

21. Ibid., vol. 3, February 7, 1838, Countway Library.

22. Ibid., Anniversary Dinner, February 1837, Countway Library.

23. Ibid., Constitution and By-Laws, Countway Library. This is a separate volume containing a register of the members, not to be confused with Records, vol. 1, which is also called Constitutions and By-Laws. Vol. 1 contains the organizational records and minutes from February 19, 1828, to December 24, 1832. Channing signed his name on September 15, 1828, and was the nineteenth man to do so. The first group of signatures, headed by Zabdiel B. Adams, was dated February 19, 1828.

24. Ibid., Records, vol. 1, January 12, March 23, 1829, Countway Library. Eventually the museum came under the direction of John B. S. Jackson, whose passion for pathological anatomy helped make it an outstanding collection. Eventually it was transferred to the Harvard Medical School. See J. B. S. Jackson, *A Descriptive Catalogue of the Anatomical Museum of the Boston Society for Medical Improvement* (Boston: William D. Ticknor and Co., 1847).

25. Boston Society for Medical Improvement, Records, vol. 1, March 29, 1830, Countway Library. Erysipelas is an acute, widespread inflammation of the skin and subcutaneous tissues. It could cause septicemia and was often fatal. The infection is caused by the streptococcus, the same organism that causes puerperal fever and wound infections. A different strain of the streptococcus causes scarlet fever, throat infections, acute nephritis, and rheumatic fever. Most but not all cases of puerperal fever were due to the first strain, the beta hemolytic group A streptococci. See Ann G. Carmichael, "Erysipelas," in *Cambridge World History of Human Disease*, pp. 720–21.

26. The Minutes of the Society for Medical Improvement do not make clear whether these were Channing's patients or whether he had seen them in consultation.

27. Boston Society for Medical Improvement, Records, vol. 4, October 10, 1842, Countway Library.

28. Fisher also mentioned that the physician had a hangnail, which may have been the entrance point for infection. The physician eventually recovered. There is no record of the

eventual outcome for the second student, who went home when he became ill. Oliver Wendell Holmes presided at this meeting.

29. Boston Society for Medical Improvement, Records, vol. 4, November 28, 1842, Countway Library.

30. Holmes's preparation for his paper, as well as its reception by the medical community, is well described in Tilton, *Amiable Autocrat*, pp. 169–76. See also Loudon, *Childbed Fever*, pp. 43–63; and Cutter and Viets, *Short History of Midwifery*.

31. Boston Society for Medical Improvement, Records, vol. 4, January 9, 1843, Countway Library.

32. Ibid., January 23, 1843.

33. The full text of Holmes's paper can be found in C. N. B. Camac, ed., *Classics of Medicine and Surgery* (New York: Dover Publications, 1909, 1936), pp. 401–32.

34. Ibid., pp. 429–30.

35. For an analysis of issues of contagion and infection in puerperal fever, see Gail Pat Parsons, "Puerperal Fever, Anticontagionists, and Miasmatic Infection, 1840–1860: Toward a New History of Puerperal Fever in Antebellum America," *Journal of the History of Medicine and Allied Sciences* 52 (1998): 424–52.

36. Cutter and Viets, *Short History of Midwifery*, p. 139; Loudon, *Childbed Fever*, pp. xliv–xlix. See also K. Codell Carter and Barbara R. Carter, *Childbed Fever: A Scientific Biography of Ignaz Semmelweis* (Westport, Conn.: Greenwood Press, 1994).

37. Dorothy I. Lansing, W. Robert Penman, and Dorland J. Davis, "Puerperal Fever and the Group B Beta Hemolytic Streptococcus," *Bulletin of the History of Medicine and Allied Sciences* 57 (1983): 70–80; David Charles and Bryan Larsen, "Streptococcal Puerperal Sepsis and Obstetric Infections: A Historical Perspective," *Review of Infectious Diseases* 8 (1986): 411–21; Irvine Loudon, "Puerperal Fever, the streptococcus, and the sulphonamides, 1911–1945," *British Medical Journal* 295 (1987): 485–90.

38. Oliver Wendell Holmes, "The Contagiousness of Puerperal Fever," in the *New England Quarterly Journal of Medicine and Surgery* 1 (1842–43): 503–50. *The New England Quarterly Journal of Medicine and Surgery* was created in 1843 by several members of the Society for Medical Improvement who wanted to produce a more scholarly journal than the weekly *Boston Medical and Surgical Journal*. The two journals were intended not to compete but to supplement each other. David Clapp, Jr., was publisher of both. The *Quarterly Journal* lasted only one year.

39. Susan Higginson Channing and Lucy Ellery Channing to Lucy Bradstreet Channing, January 8, 1843; Susan Higginson Channing to Mary and Barbara Channing, January 29, 1843, CF Papers.

40. Boston Society for Medical Improvement, Records, vol. 4, February 27, 1843, Countway Library.

41. Ibid., March 11, 1844.

42. However, Channing was still describing "constitutional causes" for puerperal fever, in one instance citing active cathartic medicine, which produced violent diarrhea and vomiting and excited fever in a woman with "an epidemic constitution." WC, *Treatise on Etherization in Childbirth*, p. 374.

43. Boston Society for Medical Improvement, Records, vol. 6, March 14, 1849, Countway Library.

44. WC, "Puerperal Peritonitis," *BMSJ* 40 (1849): 274–76.

45. Boston Society for Medical Improvement, Records, vol. 6, May 14, 1849, Countway Library.

46. Ibid., vol. 6, May 12, 1851.

47. "Boston Medical Association," *BMSJ* 40 (1849): 183–84.

48. Holmes never had a large medical practice and so his experience in obstetrics would have been limited.

49. Hugh L. Hodge, *On the Non-contagious Character of Puerperal Fever: An Introductory Lecture, 11 October, 1852* (Philadelphia: T. K. and P. G. Collins, 1852).

50. Charles D. Meigs, *On the Nature, Signs, and Treatment of Childbed Fevers* (Philadelphia: Blanchard and Lea, 1854), p. 113; Meigs, *Obstetrics: The Science and the Art*, 2d ed. (Philadelphia: Blanchard and Lea, 1852), p. 631.

51. See J. Wister Meigs, "Puerperal Fever and Nineteenth-Century Contagionism: The Obstetrician's Dilemma," *Transactions and Studies of the College of Physicians of Philadelphia*, 4th ser., 41 (1973–74): 273–80. The author is a great-great grandson of Charles D. Meigs.

52. Oliver Wendell Holmes, *Puerperal Fever as a Private Pestilence* (Boston: Ticknor and Fields, 1855).

53. WC, "On the Contagiousness of Puerperal Fever," *BMSJ* 52 (1855): 293–99.

54. Channing strongly recommended Robert Gooch's essay "Peritoneal Fevers," published in 1829. "I know how intolerant 'young America' is of everything older than yesterday; but had I such relations with my profession as to believe that my recommendation of any writings as deserving the careful study of students and practisers of midwifery and its associated sciences, would avail anything, I know of few I could name which have better claims than Gooch's to their attention." *BMSJ* 52 (1855): 295n.

55. Quinine was no more likely to cure than any other drug. Its advantage would have been that it did not weaken the patient and thereby might help her recovery.

56. Oliver Wendell Holmes, "The New Century and the New Building of the Medical School of Harvard University," *BMSJ* 109 (1883): 361–68, quotation p. 362.

Notes to Chapter 9

1. The ether operation has been described many times. For an overview of the discovery and its implications for medicine, see Duffy, *Healers*, pp. 146–54; Martin S. Pernick, *A Calculus of Suffering: Pain, Professionalism, and Anesthesia in Nineteenth-Century America* (New York: Columbia University Press, 1985). Warren, *Life of John Collins Warren*, 1:381–92, presents Warren's account of the events surrounding the first operation and his view of the controversy that followed. Norman A. Bergman, *The Genesis of Surgical Anesthesia* (Park Ridge, Ill.: Wood Library—Museum of Anesthesiology, 1998), discusses attempts at anesthesia and relief of pain prior to the events at the Massachusetts General Hospital. For a biography of Abbott, see Leroy D. Vandam and John Adams Abbott, "Edward Gilbert Abbott: Enigmatic Figure of the Ether Demonstration," *New England Journal of Medicine* 311 (1984): 991–94.

2. Richard Wolfe points out that Morton is the sole source for Warren's remark, which has nonetheless become part of the ether story.

3. Emmet F. Horine, "Episodes in the History of Anesthesia," *Journal of the History of Medicine and Allied Sciences* 1 (1946): 521–26.

4. The controversy over the discovery of anesthesia involved Morton, Charles T. Jack-

son, a chemist who claimed he had suggested the use of sulphuric ether to Morton, and Horace Wells, a Hartford dentist who was once a partner of Morton's. There was much at stake for the three men, including a congressional medal and a monetary prize, as well as recognition from the French Academy of Science and the French Academy of Medicine. In 1851 Nathaniel Bowditch wrote that "the patience of the public has long since been wearied out by the ether controversy," and he listed twenty-six relevant pamphlets published in the first two years of ether's use. *History of the Massachusetts General Hospital*, pp. 212–14. For the most recent discussion, see Richard J. Wolfe and Leonard F. Menczer, eds., *I Awaken to Glory* (Boston: Boston Medical Library, 1994); and Richard J. Wolfe, *Fallen Idol: W. T. G. Morton and the Introduction of Surgical Anesthesia: A Chronicle of the Ether Controversy* (San Francisco: Norman Publishing, 2000).

5. See Henry R. Viets, "The Earliest Printed References in Newspapers and Journals to the First Public Demonstration of Ether Anesthesia in 1846," *Journal of the History of Medicine and Allied Sciences* 4 (1949): 149–69.

6. Boston Society for Medical Improvement, Records, vol. 5, November 9, 1846, Countway Library. The minutes do not record any remarks made by Channing.

7. "Insensibility During Surgical Operations Produced by Inhalation," *BMSJ* 35 (1846–47): 309–17.

8. Bigelow's letter to Francis Boott was published, along with the text of Henry J. Bigelow's paper, in the *Lancet* 1 (1847): 5–8.

9. A. Y. Youngson, *The Scientific Revolution in Victorian Medicine* (London: Croom Helm, 1979), p. 54.

10. For the French reaction to anesthesia, see Roselyne Rey, *The History of Pain*, trans. Louise Elliott Wallace, J. A. Cadden, and S. W. Cadden (Cambridge, Mass.: Harvard University Press, 1993), pp. 152–78.

11. Simpson (1811–1870) followed Hamilton in the chair of Medicine, Midwifery and the Diseases of Women and Children. In addition to his work with chloroform, he made many important contributions to obstetrics and gynecology, including papers promoting wider use of the uterine sound and the speculum in gynecological examinations, and development of the air-tractor as a replacement for forceps. See John A. Shepherd, *Simpson and Syme of Edinburgh* (Edinburgh: E. & S. Livingstone, 1969); Eve Blantyre Simpson, *Sir James Y. Simpson* (Edinburgh: Oliphant Anderson and Ferrier, 1896); and W. O. Priestly and H. R. Storer, *The Obstetric Memoirs and Contributions of James Y. Simpson, M.D., F.R.S.E.* (Philadelphia: J. B. Lippincott, 1855).

12. The first obstetric use occurred on January 19, 1847. Simpson communicated it to the Obstetric Society the following day. Simpson published an account in the *Monthly Journal of Medical Science* (1846–47): 639–40.

13. Several years later, Channing reported an earlier event in which sulphuric ether was given to a woman suffering severe pain in childbirth. Her husband, a professor of chemistry at Oberlin College, had experimented with sulphuric ether in preparation for his lectures. In the absence of a physician he tried to relieve his wife's agony by giving her ether. WC, Notes of Difficult Labors, in the Second of which Etherization by Sulphuric Ether Was Successfully Employed Nineteen Years Ago," *BMSJ* 46 (1852): 113–15; Boston Society for Medical Improvement, Records, vol. 7, February 23, 1852, Countway Library. The use of ether was not recorded at the time or repeated in subsequent labors of this woman. Thus, according to Channing's account, it was never acknowledged as the first use of anesthetic ether. There may have been other similar episodes.

14. F. Willis Fisher, "The Ether Inhalation in Paris" and "Letter from Paris—Ethereal Inhalation in Insanity and Obstetrics," *BMSJ* 36 (1847): 109–12, 172–74. Fisher, an American studying medicine in Paris, had received news of the discovery from Charles T. Jackson. The pioneer in obstetrical use in Paris was Baron Dubois, Clinical Professor of Midwifery. Dubois remained a skeptic even though none of his patients developed any serious problems from the use of anesthesia.

15. For the Longfellows and the first use of ether in childbirth in America, see Edward Wagenknecht, *Mrs. Longfellow: Selected Letters and Journals of Fanny Appleton Longfellow (1817–1861)* (New York: Longmans, Green, 1956); Edward Wagenknecht, *Longfellow: A Full-Length Portrait* (New York: Longmans, Green, 1955); Andrew Hilen, ed., *The Letters of Henry Wadsworth Longfellow* (Cambridge, Mass.: Belknap Press of Harvard University Press, 1972); Charles B. Pittinger, "The Anesthetization of Fanny Longfellow for Childbirth on April 7, 1847," *Anesthesia and Analgesia* 66 (1987): 368–69; and Douglas Campbell, "A Christmas Carol . . . and the Story behind It," *Harvard Magazine*, January–February 1991. I am grateful to Barbara Swartz for sending me the last item.

16. N. C. Keep, "Inhalation of Ethereal Vapor for Mitigating Human Suffering in Surgical Operations and Acute Diseases," *BMSJ* 36 (1847): 199–200.

17. WC to Prof. J. Y. Simpson, November 7, 1848, Royal College of Surgeons of Edinburgh. Simpson and others had credited Channing with being the first American to use ether in childbirth. In correcting that error for Simpson, Channing also specified that a midwife delivered the child.

18. N. C. Keep, "The Letheon Administered to a Case of Labor," *BMSJ* 36 (1847): 226.

19. Henry Wadsworth Longfellow to Charles Sumner, April 7, 1847, in Hilen, *Letters of Henry Wadsworth Longfellow*, 3:134.

20. Henry Wadsworth Longfellow to Zilpah Longfellow, April 8, 1847, in Hilen, *Letters of Henry Wadsworth Longfellow*, 3:134–35.

21. See letters from George S. Hillard and Francis Lieber quoted in Wagenknecht, *Longfellow: A Full-Length Portrait*, p. 243; and Hilen, *Letters of Henry Wadsworth Longfellow*, 3:134.

22. Fanny Appleton Longfellow to Anne Longfellow Pierce, n.d., in Wagenknecht, *Mrs. Longfellow*, pp. 129–30.

23. Genesis 3:16.

24. Boston Society for Medical Improvement, Records, vol. 5, April 26, 1847, Countway Library. Homans's use of anesthesia has been neglected, probably because he did not publish the case. I assume it was a normal delivery, as was Fanny Longfellow's.

25. WC, "A Case of Inhalation of Ether in Instrumental Labor," *BMSJ* 36 (1847): 313–18, quotation p. 314.

26. Ibid., p. 315.

27. See, for example, WC to James Y. Simpson, November 7, 1848, Royal College of Surgeons of Edinburgh; and WC, *Treatise on Etherization in Childbirth*, p. 26. Channing claimed that his operative midwifery case was the "second in which it had been at all used in this country in childbirth." This does not square with the announcement by Homans. See note 24 above. Moreover, an unidentified physician who responded to Channing's questionnaire for his *Treatise on Etherization in Childbirth* listed his cases seriatim, beginning April 17, 1847 (p. 345). The certainty of "firsts" in most things is very difficult.

28. WC, "Inhalation of Ether in a Case of Laborious Labor," *BMSJ* 36 (1847): 335–37.

29. WC, *Two Cases of Inhalation of Ether in Instrumental Labor* (Boston: n.p., 1847).

30. WC, "Cases of Inhalation of Ether in Labor," *BMSJ* 36 (1847): 415–19; WC, *Six Cases of Inhalation of Ether in Labor* (Boston: White and Potter, 1847).

31. Boston Society for Medical Improvement, Records, vol. 5, June 28, 1848, Countway Library. In the first table of cases, reported in WC, *Treatise on Etherization in Childbirth*, Homans has fifty-six cases, Channing forty-five, Storer forty, and Fisher thirty-three. However, Channing also described more than thirty additional cases of his in Tables 2 and 3 and the appendix.

32. [Anon.], "Ether in Childbirth," *BMSJ* 37 (1847–48): 264.

33. The word *etherization* was used by Channing for the effects of sulphuric ether, chloric ether, and chloroform. Although Channing used "Five hundred and eighty-one" in the title of his treatise, he actually described and analyzed a slightly larger number of cases.

34. For a study of the use of statistics in antebellum medicine, see Cassedy, *American Medicine and Statistical Thinking*.

35. The quotation is ascribed to "an old play." In September 1848, the same month as the appearance of Channing's treatise, Simpson published a summary account of 150 cases in his own practice, as well as accounts of the result of anesthesia in 95 cases at the Edinburgh Maternity Hospital and testimonies from physicians and hospitals in other parts of the British Isles. He did not tabulate his results. James Y. Simpson, *Anesthetic Midwifery: Report on its Early History and Progress* (Edinburgh: Sutherland and Knox, 1848).

36. There were also physicians who had experience with anesthesia but did not reply to the inquiry. Channing offered no explanation for their recalcitrance, but apologized for having possibly offended them.

37. Channing's use of statistics was rudimentary at best. The comparison group was eighteen cases. Fifteen maternal deaths and seventeen fetal deaths were reported, thus providing overwhelming evidence in favor of anesthesia. There was no way to determine the equivalence of the anesthesia and nonanesthesia cases. Nor do the small numbers in each subcategory permit meaningful conclusions.

38. Erasmus D. Miller, letter printed in WC, *Treatise on Etherization in Childbirth*, p. 355.

39. Nathaniel B. Shurtleff, letter printed ibid., p. 349.

40. William Thornton Parker, letter printed ibid., p. 352.

41. Abel L. Pierson, letter printed ibid., p. 339.

42. Daniel V. Folts, letter printed ibid., p. 351.

43. Woodbridge Strong, letter printed ibid., p. 346.

44. J. Bigelow, letter printed ibid., pp. 337–38.

45. Channing supported Charles T. Jackson's claims regarding the discovery of anesthesia. Jackson had been his student and was a friend and associate of his nephew William Francis Channing. Channing's letters in favor of Jackson were printed in the Congressional Report, No. 114, House of Representatives, 30th Cong., 2d sess., pp. 5–7.

46. WC, *Treatise on Etherization in Childbirth*, p. 24. See Martin Pernick, *A Calculus of Suffering*, for a discussion of benevolence as one of the factors that influenced many enthusiasts for anesthesia.

47. For an overview of physicians' reactions to anesthesia in childbirth, see John Duffy, "Anglo-American Reaction to Obstetrical Anesthesia," *Bulletin of the History of Medicine* 38 (1964): 32–44; and Leavitt, *Brought to Bed*, pp. 116–27.

48. WC, *Treatise on Etherization in Childbirth*, p. 40.

49. James Y. Simpson, *Answer to the Religious Objections Advanced against the Employment of Anesthetic Agents in Midwifery and Surgery* (Edinburgh: Sutherland and Knox, 1847).

50. For Noyes, see Samuel A. Eliot, ed., *Heralds of a Liberal Faith*, 4 vols. (Boston: American Unitarian Association, 1910), 3:269–74.

51. Many theologians and scholars have wrestled with the meaning of Genesis 3:16. For a modern interpretation, see Carol L. Meyers, *Discovering Eve: Ancient Israelite Women in Context* (New York: Oxford University Press, 1991).

52. James Y. Simpson to Charles D. Meigs, January 23, 1848, and Charles D. Meigs to James Y. Simpson, in *Medical Examiner and Record of Medical Science*, March 1848; both reprinted in WC, *Treatise on Etherization in Childbirth*, pp. 10–12.

53. Meigs relied on animal experiments conducted by the French physiologist Pierre Flourens. It was Flourens who suggested that anesthesia might cause death when it reached the vital node, or respiratory center. Rey, *History of Pain*, pp. 161–62.

54. Irving, *Safe Delivery*, p. 96; Leavitt, *Brought to Bed*, p. 117. See also Lewis C. Scheffey, "The Earlier History and the Transition Period of Obstetrics and Gynecology in Philadelphia," *Annals of Medical History*, 3d ser., 2 (1940): 215–24.

55. Channing reprinted Meigs's letter to Simpson in the *Treatise on Etherization in Childbirth*. It had already been published several times, including in the *Lancet* 1 (1848): 613–14 and the *Philadelphia Medical Examiner*, March 1848. Simpson's reply to Meigs, "Answer to the Objections to Anaesthesia in Midwifery, Adduced by Professor Meigs of Philadelphia," August 1, 1848, was published in James Y. Simpson, *Anaesthesia, or the Employment of Chloroform and Ether in Surgery, Midwifery* (Philadelphia: Lindsay & Blakiston, 1849), pp. 230–48.

56. WC, *Treatise on Etherization in Childbirth*, pp. 13–15.

57. [?] to WC, [1848], B MS c53.3, Countway Library.

58. J. F. B. Flagg, *Ether and Chloroform, Their Employment in Surgery, Dentistry, Midwifery, Therapeutics* (Philadelphia: Lindsay and Blakiston, 1851), p. 123.

59. Announcement for *A Treatise on Etherization in Child-birth*, by Walter Channing, M.D, *BMSJ* 39 (1848–49): 277–78; "Etherization in Child-birth," 302–3; "Opposition to New Doctrines—Etherization," 325; WC to James Y. Simpson, November 7, 1848, Royal College of Surgeons of Edinburgh.

60. [Edward Warren], "Art. II—A Treatise on Etherization in Childbirth, illustrated by Five Hundred and eighty-one cases," *North American Review* 68 (1849): 300–314.

61. Daniel F. Condie, "Reviews, Art. XVII," *American Journal of Medical Science*, n.s., 17 (1849): 99–115. For a modern-day appraisal of Channing's treatise, see Donald Caton, *What a Blessing She Had Chloroform: The Medical and Social Response to the Pain of Childbirth from 1800 to the Present* (New Haven: Yale University Press, 1999), pp. 32–37. Caton faults Channing for presenting contradictory evidence and for ignoring some that he should have observed, but he does recognize that Channing's support for anesthesia contributed to its acceptance by the profession. Some of Caton's other criticisms assume a scientific attitude and familiarity with controlled clinical trials that were not part of antebellum medicine.

62. Frederick C. Waite, *History of the New England Female Medical College, 1848–1874* (Boston: Boston University School of Medicine, 1950).

63. Samuel Gregory, *Man-Midwifery Exposed and Corrected* (Boston: George Gregory, 1848).

64. Ibid., p. 44.

65. Report of the Committee on Obstetrics, *Transactions of the American Medical Association* 2 (1849): 233–52, quotations p. 243.

66. Boston Society for Medical Improvement, Records, vol. 6, January 22, 1849, April

23, 1849, Countway Library. These papers were published in the society's *Transactions in American Journal of Medical Sciences*, n.s., 17 (1849): 343–49; 18 (1849): 41–46.

67. Boston Society for Medical Improvement, Records, vol. 6, March 24, 1851, Countway Library.

68. Ibid., November 14 and November 24, 1851.

69. WC, Miscellaneous lecture notes, WC Papers II.

70. WC, *Treatise on Etherization in Childbirth*, p. 319.

71. WC to James Y. Simpson, November 7, 1848, Royal College of Surgeons of Edinburgh.

Notes to Chapter 10

1. Wright, *The Transformation of Charity in Postrevolutionary New England.*

2. WC to Lucy Bradstreet Channing, July 7, 1846, CF Papers. Most of these titles are self-explanatory. The *Washingtonian* was a temperance journal; the *Voice of Industry* was published by the New England Association of Workingmen; the *Harbinger* was published by the Fourierist members of Brook Farm; the *Christian World*, a Unitarian weekly, was edited by Channing's brother George.

3. See Charles E. Rosenberg and Carroll S. Rosenberg, "Pietism and the Origins of the American Public Health Movement: A Note on John H. Griscom and Robert M. Hartley," *Journal of the History of Medicine and Allied Sciences* 23 (1968): 16–35, for the relationship of evangelical religion and sanitary reform, and Michael L. Dorn, "(In)temperate Zones: Daniel Drake's Medico-moral Geographies of Urban Life in the Trans-Appalachian West," *Journal of the History of Medicine and Allied Sciences* 55 (2000): 256–91, for an example of the relationship of the medical profession to social reform.

4. Daniel Drake, *Discourses Delivered by Appointment, Before the Cincinnati Medical Library Association, January 9th and 10th, 1852*, quoted in Dorn, "(In)temperate Zones," p. 256. At a lengthy meeting held in Boston to discuss the general principles of reform and the best means of promoting it, Channing was the only medical man in a group that included Ralph Waldo Emerson, Bronson Alcott, William Lloyd Garrison, Wendell Phillips, Theodore Parker, Samuel G. Howe, Maria Chapman, Eliza Follen, James and Lucretia Mott, and Charles Sumner. The Reverend Samuel May, Jr., to Mary Carpenter, May 29, 1847, in *William Lloyd Garrison, 1805–1879: The Story of His Life Told by His Children*, 4 vols., by W. P. Garrison and F. J. Garrison (New York: Century Co., 1889), 3:187–88.

5. "Dr. Channing's Discourse," *BMSJ* 33 (1845–46): 344.

6. WC to WEC, June 1803, WC Papers II. See Chapter 1.

7. For an overview of temperance, see Alice Felt Tyler, *Freedom's Crusade* (New York: Harper Torchbooks, 1944), pp. 308–50; Ronald G. Walters, *American Reformers*, rev. ed. (New York: Hill and Wang, 1998), pp. 125–46; William J. Rorabaugh, *The Alcoholic Republic: An American Tradition* (New York: Oxford University Press, 1979); and Ian R. Tyrrell, *Sobering Up: From Temperance to Prohibition in Antebellum America, 1800–1860* (Westport, Conn.: Greenwood Press, 1979). The fact that much of the Channing patrimony derived from the manufacture and sale of rum during the era of the slave trade cannot have been lost on Channing as he engaged in temperance work.

8. John Collins Warren recalled the custom at the end of the eighteenth century when grave gentlemen, and even clergymen, made a diurnal visit to particular friends or particular

taverns, where hot punch, porter, brandy and water, bread, and cheese were employed to facilitate consultation on topics of the day. Warren, *Life of John Collins Warren*, 1:15.

9. Tyler, *Freedom's Crusade*, p. 321. Per capita consumption on a national level during the thirty years following the Revolution was three times the amount used by average adults in the years after 1940. Robert L. Hampel, *Temperance and Prohibition in Massachusetts, 1813–1852* (Ann Arbor: UMI Research, 1982), p. 1. Not only were spiritous drinks inexpensive and readily available, but we must remember that water was often not safe and there were few other drinks such as the prepared fruit juices, sodas, and colas so popular today.

10. Constitution of the Massachusetts Society for the Suppression of Intemperance, quoted in WC, *Annual Address Delivered before the Massachusetts Temperance Society, May 29, 1836* (Boston: John Ford, 1836).

11. Lyman Beecher, *Autobiography*, II, quoted in Tyler, *Freedom's Crusade*, p. 323.

12. Published 1784. Rush did not criticize the use of beer, cider, and wine, but he objected strongly to distilled drinks as injurious to mental and physical health as well as to morality. Walters, *American Reformers*, p. 127.

13. Other Boston physicians prominent in the temperance movement at this time were John Ware, Joshua B. Flint, and George C. Shattuck. For a general discussion of the role of physicians in the temperance movement, see Cassedy, *American Medicine and Statistical Thinking*, pp. 40–45; and James H. Cassedy, "An Early American Hangover: The Medical Profession and Intemperance 1800–1860," *Bulletin of the History of Medicine* 50 (1976): 405–13.

14. Warren, *Life of John Collins Warren*, 1:232–33.

15. Adopted by the Massachusetts Medical Society, June 6, 1827. "Origin of the Massachusetts Society for the Suppression of Intemperance," in *The Physiological Effects of Alcoholic Drinks with Documents and Records of the Massachusetts Temperance Society* (Boston: Massachusetts Temperance Society, 1848), pp. 14–15, 22. See also "Massachusetts Medical Society," *NEJMS* 16 (1827): 332–33. In 1828 the medical society offered a prize for dissertations on intemperance. "Prize Dissertation," *BMSJ* 1 (1828): 784, 800. In 1832 a manifesto signed by seventy-five physicians of Boston reiterated the medical opposition to the use of ardent spirits. For examples of the attitudes of the profession, see John Forbes, "The Physiological Effects of Alcoholic Drinks" (1846), in Massachusetts Temperance Society, *Documents and Records of the Massachusetts Temperance Society*, pp. 113–91; *BMSJ* 4 (1831): 345–50; 15 (1836): 261–67; 23 (1840–41): 16; and 26 (1842): 390–95. The medical society continued to serve wine at its annual dinners until 1842, when the practice was abandoned. See *BMSJ* 26 (1842): 237; and 28 (1843): 364–65.

16. WC to Jared Sparks, May 13, 1829; WC to Sparks, December 5, [1831], MS Sparks Papers 153, Houghton Library, Harvard University.

17. WC, Notes for medical lectures, WC Papers II.

18. Daniel T. McColgan, *Joseph Tuckerman: Pioneer in American Social Work* (Washington, D.C.: Catholic University of America Press, 1940), p. 180. Joseph Tuckerman was a Unitarian minister who resigned his pastorate in Chelsea, Massachusetts, to become minister-at-large to the poor people of Boston. As such, he was active in many social reforms. Tuckerman was particularly influenced by William Ellery Channing, who had been a Harvard classmate and with whom he shared many beliefs, theological, philosophical, and social. See also John White Chadwick, *William Ellery Channing* (Boston: Houghton, Mifflin, 1903), pp. 323–27.

19. I am grateful to the late Dr. J. Worth Estes, Professor Emeritus of Pharmacology at

Boston University Medical School, for his help on this point. Tuckerman referred to Chamber's medicine and Reed's medicine, each obtained at a pharmacy bearing that name. He relied on Drs. Spooner and Lewis to care for the men and women who took the medicine, which evidently caused great distress to the patient. See Joseph Tuckerman, Diary, May 23–August 16, 1827, Tuckerman Papers, MHS; and Tuckerman's *Fourth Quarterly, or First Annual Report Addressed to the American Unitarian Association* (Boston: Bowles and Dearborn, 1827).

20. WC to John Collins Warren, August 16, 1827, JCW Papers, vol. 13; Massachusetts Temperance Society, *Documents and Records*, p. 18.

21. "Constitution of the Massachusetts Temperance Society," in Massachusetts Temperance Society, *Documents and Records*, pp. 42–47.

22. WC, *Thoughts on the Origin, Nature, Principles and Prospects of the Temperance Reform* (Boston: Council of the Massachusetts Temperance Society, 1834).

23. Channing held this post until 1848. George Faber Clark, *History of the Temperance Reform in Massachusetts, 1813–1883* (Boston: Clark & Carruth, 1888), pp. 17–18. Channing became secretary following the deaths of his friend Dr. J. Greely Stevenson, who had been recording secretary, and the Reverend Hosea Hildreth, who, as agent of the society, had also been corresponding secretary. See also *Twenty-Fourth Annual Report of the Massachusetts Temperance Society for the year ending May 27, 1836* (Boston: John Ford, 1836).

24. WC, *Annual Address delivered before the Massachusetts Temperance Society, May 29, 1836.*

25. Clark, *History of the Temperance Reform*, pp. 35–36.

26. See WC to John Collins Warren, January 24, 1838, JCW Papers, vol. 18.

27. WC to unidentified correspondent, June 4, 1839, WC Papers II.

28. Anti-temperance attitudes were also strong among some Unitarians who had vested interests in the manufacture or sale of liquor. The most notable example of this occurred at the Hollis Street Church, where the minister, John Pierpont, was an outspoken opponent of alcohol and most of the congregation were just as adamantly opposed to temperance. Pierpont almost lost his job because of the controversy. See Samuel A. Eliot, ed., *Heralds of a Liberal Faith*, 3 vols. (Boston: American Unitarian Association, 1910), 2:185–93. The financier J. P. Morgan was a grandson and namesake of Pierpont.

29. Hampel, *Temperance and Prohibition*, pp. 68–90.

30. Clark, *History of the Temperance Reform*, pp. 37–41; WC, Notes on Temperance Reform, WC Papers II. See also WC to Josiah Quincy, Jr., April 10, 1838, Mss Acc 2643, BPL; Samuel A. Eliot to WC, April 18, 1839, Autograph File, Houghton Library, Harvard University.

31. WC, Address to Temperance Society of Harvard University, and delivered before it, written February 1838, manuscript, WC Papers II.

32. William Ellery Channing to WC, August 6, 1838, WEC Papers. In his public utterances on temperance, William Ellery Channing proposed intellectual opportunities, alternative entertainments, and leisure occupations for the poor as a way to improve their lives and wean them from brawling, drunkenness, and other, less attractive activities. He also advocated physical education for youth and asylums for the treatment of inebriates. William Henry Channing, *Life of William Ellery Channing*, pp. 474–76; Mendelsohn, *Channing the Reluctant Radical*, pp. 206–7.

33. *Address of the Government of the Massachusetts Washington Total Abstinence Society to the Society and to the Public* (Boston: R. Newcomb–T. C. Fairfield, 1842); "Massachusetts

Washington Total Abstinence Society," *Christian World* (Boston), June 10, 1843. For the Washingtonian movement, see Hampel, *Temperance and Prohibition*, pp. 104–19; Walters, *American Reformers*, pp. 133–36; Clark, *History of the Temperance Reform*, pp. 49–54.

34. The American Statistical Society had been founded in Boston in 1839 to collect, preserve, and diffuse statistical information in many areas. See Cassedy, *American Medicine and Statistical Thinking*, p. 193.

35. WC to Lucy Bradstreet Channing, July 11, [1844], CF Papers.

36. Henry Jacob Bigelow to Jeffries Wyman, December 6, 1844, H MS c12.2, Countway Library.

37. John Shaw, *A Ramble through the United States, Canada, and the West Indies* (London: J. F. Hope, 1856), pp. 238–41. A typescript of this excerpt is in the Channing Family II Papers, MHS. This cholera was dysentery or summer complaint, a common summertime disorder, and not Asiatic cholera.

38. WC, Notes on Temperance Reform, manuscript, WC Papers II. For a discussion of Unitarian beliefs regarding the moral nature of man, see Daniel Walker Howe, *The Unitarian Conscience: Harvard Moral Philosophy, 1805–1861* (Cambridge, Mass.: Harvard University Press, 1970), pp. 45–68.

39. *BMSJ* 7 (1833): 386–87; *BMSJ* 12 (1835): 15–16, 224–25; *BMSJ* 18 (1838): 96; *BMSJ* 20 (1839): 113. In 1825 Mayor Quincy had commissioned a study of potential sites for the acquisition of an increased supply of water, but nothing had come of the report that was submitted to him. Winsor, *Memorial History of Boston*, 3:238. For a brief summary of the water history of Boston, see Fern L. Nesson, *Great Waters: A History of Boston's Water Supply* (Hanover, N.H.: University Press of New England, 1983).

40. Massachusetts Temperance Society, *Documents and Records*, January 21, 1837, pp. 71–72. Ten years previously, when the society first condemned intemperance, it advised that the most salutary drink for man is water. Massachusetts Temperance Society, *Documents and Records*, June 6, 1827, pp. 15–16.

41. Struik, *Origins of American Science*, pp. 255–58.

42. WC, *A Plea for Pure Water* (Boston: S. N. Dickinson, 1844); WC, *Parliamentary Sketches and Water Statistics* (Boston: Benjamin H. Greene, 1846).

43. WC, *Plea for Pure Water*, p. 24. One of the most outspoken critics of the plan to bring water from Long Pond and of a municipal water system supported by general taxation was Lemuel Shattuck, who later acquired fame as a pioneer in public health. Shattuck disagreed with the estimates of future demand for water and objected to the increased municipal debt and the political power that would result from a public water system. Lemuel Shattuck, *Mr. Shattuck's Letter to Jonathan Preston on the Water Question* (Boston: Samuel N. Dickson, 1845); John B. Blake, "Lemuel Shattuck and the Boston Water Supply," *Bulletin of the History of Medicine* 29 (1955): 554–62. Blake describes Shattuck as a hero who could err.

44. Nesson, *Great Waters*. See also Dearborn, *Boston Notions*, pp. 374–75.

45. WC, *Plea for Pure Water*, p. 27. Nonetheless, many described the new water as resembling weak tea.

46. For Boston's treatment of the poor, see Thomas H. O'Connor, "To Be Poor and Homeless in Old Boston," in *Massachusetts and the New Nation*, ed. Conrad Edick Wright (Boston: Massachusetts Historical Society, 1992), pp. 202–25. A few physicians shared Channing's concern for the poor, including John Ware and Henry I. Bowditch. Ware, the son and brother of Unitarian ministers, also shared Channing's religious beliefs. Bowditch,

also a Unitarian, was better known as a passionate abolitionist, but he was involved with some of the efforts on behalf of the poor.

47. For social conditions in Boston, see William H. Pease and Jane H. Pease, *The Web of Progress* (Athens: University of Georgia Press, 1991); Anne C. Rose, *Transcendentalism as a Social Movement, 1830–1850* (New Haven: Yale University Press, 1981); Walters, *American Reformers*, pp. 175–196; Eric Schneider, *In the Web of Class* (New York: New York University Press, 1992); McColgan, *Joseph Tuckerman*; Francis Tiffany, *Charles Francis Barnard, a Sketch of His Life and Work* (Boston: Houghton, Mifflin, 1895); and Edward Pessen, *Riches, Class, and Power: America before the Civil War* (New Brunswick: Transaction Publishers, 1990).

48. For the Unitarian response to poverty, see Howe, *Unitarian Conscience*, pp. 236–55.

49. Tuckerman and his associates in their ministry to the poor were largely inspired by William Ellery Channing's vision of social responsibility. "In those days, Dr. Channing stood forth clad in the robes of inspirer and prophet. Through the luminous beauty of his eyes shone the light and through the tones of his voice thrilled the emotions that revealed a diviner realm of life to others. But frail in health, and with a body so etherealized as to 'serve but as a pretext for keeping his soul a little longer on earth,' he was incapable of the physical strain involved in flinging himself against the hard realities and into the rough and tumble mêlée of practical philanthropic work. . . . Channing's part was to supply the vision and the sacred passion." Tiffany, *Charles Francis Barnard*, pp. 42–43.

50. For a discussion of other analyses, see Daniel J. Rothman, *The Discovery of the Asylum: Social Order and Disorder in the New Republic* (Boston: Little, Brown, 1971), Chapter 7.

51. Channing did not display much interest in Brook Farm, but his daughters Mary and Barbara were greatly attracted to it. Barbara visited several times. Her cousin and childhood schoolmistress, Sophia Dana Ripley, was one of the leaders of the community. Barbara Channing to Lucy Russel, February 20, 1841, April 8, 1842, August 29, [1842], CF Papers. See also Lindsay Swift, *Brook Farm, its Members, Scholars, and Visitors* (New York: Macmillan, 1900), esp. pp. 263–70; and John Thomas Codman, *Brook Farm, Historic and Personal Memoirs* (Boston: Arena Publishing, 1894).

52. WC, *An Address on the Prevention of Pauperism* (Boston: William D. Ticknor, 1843). Channing dedicated the address "To the memory of My Brother, William Ellery Channing." The selection of Walter Channing to deliver this address was unusual because the society was largely Congregational and Channing was by then identified with the liberal wing of the Unitarians.

53. Channing also discussed the New Amendment Poor Law, recently proposed in England, and its provision for medical care for the sick poor. According to his understanding of the legislation, medical men in each district would bid for the job and those whose bid was lowest would receive the post: "the question of skill may but slightly, if at all, enter; and the whole character of the profession must be most injuriously affected." Channing compared this to public education in the United States, "where a large fund has been owned by a state, the income of which has been devoted to the public instruction. It is notorious, that where this has been the case, incompetent persons have often been selected, because they have offered to work for the least compensation—the office of teacher has been degraded, and the best means of useful knowledge have been denied to the people." *Address on Pauperism*, p. 55.

54. Channing returned to the problems of working women when he described his European journey in *A Physician's Vacation*. See Chapter 12.

55. Channing's letters make frequent reference to household economies. Both his older daughters suffered from his unwillingness to spend money, especially Mary, who was described as well prepared to be the wife of a poor minister. Susan Higginson Channing to Julia Allen Channing, March 8, 1844, Allen Family Papers, Houghton Library, Harvard University.

56. Beginning in 1821, Boston had built new facilities for the poor along the South Boston shore. Over time additional buildings were added to the complex, which finally included the House of Correction, House of Industry, House of Juvenile Offenders, and House for the Insane. They were reputed to be well constructed and well managed. Dearborn, *Boston Notions*, pp. 213–14. Charles Dickens visited the House of Correction and other institutions situated in South Boston while in Boston in 1842 and was favorably impressed. *American Notes,* in *Complete Works of Charles Dickens* (New York: Harper and Brothers, n.d.), pp. 249–55.

57. The pamphlet received two friendly reviews, one in the *Christian World*, a weekly newspaper published by his brother George, and the other in the *Present*, a journal edited by his nephew William Henry Channing. Notices of New Publications, *Christian World*, October 28, 1844; Signs of the Times, *Present* 1 (1843): 141–44. Three years later, Channing reviewed the 1846 annual address of the Society for the Prevention of Pauperism for the *Harbinger*, a Fourierist journal published by George Ripley and other leaders of the Brook Farm experiment. *Harbinger* 2 (1846): 357–58.

58. WC to Barbara Channing, November 5, 1866, WC Papers II.

59. The Society for the Prevention of Pauperism (already referred to) and the Howard Benevolent Society were among the more prominent. They all had a strongly moralistic tone. There were also numerous female organizations intended to assist women in poverty.

60. Boston Employment Society, *Report of the Boston Employment Society* (Boston: Coolidge & Wiley, 1848). The Board of Directors included several ministers and men associated with other philanthropic organizations. None is identified with an M.D. except Channing.

61. See, for example, Thomas H. O'Connor, *Bibles, Brahmins, and Bosses: A Short History of Boston*, 3d ed. (Boston: Trustees of the Public Library, 1991), pp. 138–52; Handlin, *Boston's Immigrants*, esp. pp. 54–87.

62. See Boston Society for the Prevention of Pauperism, *Annual Report* (Boston: John Wilson and Son, 1855, 1856–57, 1857–58, 1859–60, 1860–61); Society for the Prevention of Pauperism, *Journal* (1851): 21; *Report of a Committee appointed at a Joint Meeting of the Howard Benevolent Society, Young Men's Benevolent Society, Society for the Prevention of Pauperism and Boston Employment Society* (Boston: Dutton & Westworth, 1851). Eventually the Society for the Prevention of Pauperism became the Industrial Aid Society.

63. Boston Society for Aiding Discharged Convicts, *Constitution and By-Laws* (Boston: White and Potter, 1847); *First Annual Report* (Boston: White and Potter, 1847); *Second Annual Report* (Boston: White and Potter, 1848). Channing was president from 1847 to 1854. There were several other organizations in Boston dedicated to improving the lot of prisoners, including the Prison Discipline Society.

64. Samuel G. Howe is best remembered as teacher to the deaf and dumb, but he was involved with many other liberal causes, including the Greek War for Independence, which Channing supported during the 1820s. Andrew was an abolitionist and mayor of Boston during the Civil War.

65. *The Prisoner's Friend*, April 1854.

66. Committee on the Expediency of Providing Better Tenements for the Poor, *Report*

(Boston: Eastburn's Press, 1846). See also Tilden G. Edelstein, *Strange Enthusiasm: A Life of Thomas Wentworth Higginson* (New Haven: Yale University Press, 1968), p. 39.

67. The committee based its assertions of childhood mortality on "Mr. Shattuck's calculation in 1845," a reference to Lemuel Shattuck, who was instrumental in establishing the annual registration of vital statistics in Massachusetts. Cassedy, *American Medicine and Statistical Thinking*, pp. 194–98; Barbara Gutmann Rosenkrantz, *Public Health and the State: Changing Views in Massachusetts, 1842–1936* (Cambridge, Mass.: Harvard University Press, 1972).

68. Committee on the Expediency of Providing Better Tenements for the Poor, *Report*, p. 11.

69. Pease and Pease, *Web of Progress*, pp. 28–29, 273 n. 19.

70. In 1831 Channing served on the Executive Committee of the Franklin Lectures, initiated by the Twelfth Congregational Society to provide lectures "for a class whose circumstances do not allow them to partake in the popular instruction so liberally provided in our city." WC to Jared Sparks, August 5, 1839, MS Sparks Papers 153, Houghton Library, Harvard University. See also Lewis G. Pray, *Historical Sketch of the Twelfth Congregational Society in Boston* (Boston: John Wilson and Son, 1863), pp. 27–28.

71. Rose, *Transcendentalism as a Social Movement*, p. 110; Dearborn, *Boston Notions*, pp. 199–200; *Mercantile Library Reporter*, March 1855, p. 76.

72. WC, "My Own Times," pp. 14–24, 38–47, 65–72. A copy of this talk at Widener Library, Harvard University, contains several notations made by Edward Tyrrel Channing correcting historical inaccuracies that he had found in the text. The second lecture was *The Law of Compensations: A Lecture delivered before the Mechanic Apprentices' Library Association*, February 20, 1855 (Boston: n.p., 1855).

73. In his instructions for disposal of his possessions after death, Channing directed that some of his books be sent to the Mechanic Apprentices' Library. "I can not forget the pleasure its members took in my Lectures to them, and how very pleasant have been that Society's anniversaries to me." WC to Barbara Channing, November 5, 1866, WC Papers II.

74. See Paul F. Boller, Jr., *American Transcendentalism, 1830–1860* (New York: G. P. Putnam's Sons, 1974), pp. 145–57.

75. In 1850 Channing gave a Lyceum Lecture in Haverhill, Massachusetts, that was even more confusing than *The Law of Compensations*. Titled "Man considered in his physical, intellectual and moral capacity," the talk included unusual examples of human ability to withstand extremes of heat and cold, "which made some of the 'green 'uns' stare," and proposed to an unsympathetic audience that there is no difference in the intellectual capacities of individuals. *Haverhill Gazette*, January 26 and February 9, 1850. See also Rufus Longley to WC, January 24, 1850, B MS c53.3, Countway Library.

76. WC, November 2, 1844, in S. E. Coues, Peace Album, MS Am 635, Houghton Library, Harvard University.

77. Secondary sources devoted to the peace movement include Merle Eugene Curti, *The American Peace Crusade, 1815–1860* (1929, reprint; New York: Octagon Books, 1965); Charles DeBenedetti, *The Peace Reform in American History* (Bloomington: Indiana University Press, 1980); Valarie H. Ziegler, *The Advocates of Peace in Antebellum America* (Bloomington: Indiana University Press, 1992); Tyler, *Freedom's Ferment*, pp. 396–413; and Walters, *American Reformers*, pp. 115–24. See also Eugene Perry Link, *The Social Ideas of American Physicians* (Selinsgrove, Pa.: Susquehanna University Press, 1992), pp. 143–44.

78. The peace movement inspired a poem titled "The Spirit of War," which Channing published in *New and Old*, p. 56:

You praise her prowess, and her conquests laud,
The shameful earnings of successful fraud:
She from the weak, in puny battle slain,
Hath borne the laurel of unmanly gain.
War is a coward in its plan and end,
And makes a slave of him it makes a friend.
Nay, worse, it kills for quarrel not its own,
And reaps a harvest by another sown. . . .

So have I seen some hungry hawk on high,
O'er the still vale delight his robber eye,
Till some bold bird, more daring than the rest,
Hops on the branch where hangs its silly nest;
Sudden the tuneless coward marks his prey,
And tears him bleeding from his native quay.

79. WC, *Thoughts on Peace and War, an Address delivered before the American Peace Society, at its annual meeting, May 27, 1844* (Boston: American Peace Society, 1844). Channing referred to the criticisms in his introduction to the published address. I have been unable to locate them in contemporary newspapers.

80. Many prominent members of the Federal Street Church opposed abolitionism, thereby compounding William Ellery Channing's ambivalence on the issue. However, when every Unitarian and Congregational church in Boston, including his own, refused their premises for a memorial service for Charles Follen, an ardent antislavery spokesman and one of William's dearest friends, he recognized the hypocrisy of his position and began to write and speak forcefully against slavery. See Edmund Spevack, *Charles Follen's Search for Nationality and Freedom, Germany and America, 1796–1840* (Cambridge, Mass.: Harvard University Press, 1997), pp. 246–49. For a review of WEC and slavery, see Mendelsohn, *Channing the Reluctant Radical*, pp. 223–70. Walter was also moved by Follen's death, which occurred when the ship *Lexington* caught fire and sank at sea en route from New York to Boston. He commemorated his friend in a poem, "Raising the Wreck of the Lexington," *New and Old*, pp. 30–33.

81. Frank Carpenter, Unitarian minister and Channing scholar, has written that William Ellery was an outspoken critic of "the inhuman, iniquitous and illegal slave-trade." Frank Carpenter, "Channing and Slavery," Newport, R.I., August 1994, personal communication to the author.

82. WC to Lucy Bradstreet Channing, July 31, 1840, CF Papers. With her father's encouragement, Barbara solicited their Beacon Hill neighbors for signatures on a petition condemning the annexation of Texas, but she discovered that Boston women were ignorant and unfeeling about slavery. Barbara Channing to Lucy Russel, December 15, 1845, CF Papers.

83. WC to Lucy Bradstreet Channing, July 7, 1846, CF Papers. Many leaders in the peace movement were also abolitionists. As war against slavery gathered force they found themselves increasingly conflicted. See Ziegler, *Advocates of Peace in Antebellum America*, for a good discussion of this point.

84. WC to Mrs. Maria Child Chapman, November 29, 1842, BPL; *Liberator*, November 18, November 25, December 2, 1842. Latimer was present at the meeting, having been

released from prison because of the public clamor. Though the legal issue was moot, the organizers went forward with the meeting, which gave them an opportunity for speech making and declarations against the "encroachment of the Slaveholding Power." *Liberator*, November 18, 1842. See also Bowditch, *Life and Correspondence of Henry Ingersoll Bowditch*, 1:133–35.

85. WC to Lucy Bradstreet Channing, August 1, [1844], CF Papers. See also *Liberator*, July 5, July 12, July 19, July 26, August 16, August 28, 1844; *Freeman* (Concord, Mass.), July 26, 1844; and Carlos Baker, *Emerson among the Eccentrics* (New York: Penguin Books, 1996), pp. 239–40.

86. James Russell Lowell, "On the Death of Charles Turner Torrey." Channing was invited to participate by Henry I. Bowditch, a medical colleague and friend who was among the most active antislavery men in Boston. Bowditch, *Life and Correspondence of Henry Ingersoll Bowditch*, 1:172–78. For the text of Lowell's poem, see *The Complete Poetical Works of James Russell Lowell*, Cambridge Edition (Boston: Houghton Mifflin, 1911), p. 104. For an account of the funeral, see *Liberator*, May 22, 1846.

87. The advent of black students coincided with an application from the first woman to seek admission to Harvard Medical School. This and the recent Parkman-Webster scandal may have added to the dilemma facing the faculty. See Chapter 12.

88. Harvard University, Faculty of Medicine, Minutes of Meetings, December 13, 1850, Countway Library. There were 116 students enrolled in the 1850–51 session, of whom 4 came from slave states. One hundred were New Englanders. Both the chairman and secretary of the protesting group were Bostonians. The most thorough discussion of the episode is Philip Cash, "Pride, Prejudice and Politics," *Harvard Medical Alumni Bulletin* 54 (December 1980): 20–25. Cash attributes the faculty timidity to the Parkman-Webster scandal. See Chapter 12.

89. Harvard University, Faculty of Medicine, Minutes, vol. 2, December 26, 1850, Countway Library.

90. Both men sponsored by the Colonization Society, Daniel Laing and Isaac Snowden, completed their medical education with Dr. Clarke, a surgeon at the Massachusetts General Hospital. Laing also studied in Paris before going on to Liberia. Delany, frustrated in his ambition and disillusioned about the treatment of blacks in the United States, became an important spokesman for black nationalism and traveled to Africa seeking a homeland for American blacks that would not be tainted by association with the American Colonization Society. During the Civil War he was the first black major commissioned in the Union army. See Amalie M. Kass, "Dr. Thomas Hodgkin, Dr. Martin Delany, and the Return to Africa," *Medical History* 27 (1983): 373–93.

91. WC to Edward Wade, [1854], BPL. The Constitution of the United States (Art. 1, Sect. 2) specified that five slaves would equal three free men when population was counted for purposes of taxation and representation. This rule, one of the compromises adopted at the Constitutional Convention of 1787, was revoked by the Fourteenth Amendment.

92. Edelstein, *Strange Enthusiasm*, pp. 39–43.

93. Ibid., p. 164.

94. Higginson was not guilty of the murder, but there is little doubt that he was one of the chief instigators of the attack. Channing's distress over the outcome of the Burns affair is described in a letter from Ann Weston to "Dear Folks," June 5, 1854, BPL.

95. The case of Anthony Burns was one of the most notorious events that preceded the Civil War. Burns was defended by Richard Henry Dana, Jr., son of Channing's cousin and

close friend. For Dana's account of the affair, see *Journal of Richard Henry Dana, Jr.* and Charles Francis Adams, *Richard Henry Dana: A Biography* (Boston: Houghton Mifflin, 1890). Albert J. Von Frank, *The Trials of Anthony Burns* (Cambridge, Mass.: Harvard University Press, 1998), is a more recent study of the Burns case.

96. WC to Edward Wade, [1854], BPL.

97. WC to Mary Higginson, January 1, 1865, CF Papers II.

98. Ibid.

99. Among those killed in the war was the son of Channing's friend and colleague John Ware. *BMSJ* 68 (1863): 245. Oliver Wendell Holmes's son and namesake, the future Supreme Court justice, was badly wounded in two battles.

100. Higginson was also a strong supporter of women's rights.

101. First Chronicles 22:8; WC to Mary Higginson, September 3, 1864, CF Papers II.

102. Draft in handwriting of WC, undated, CF Papers.

Notes to Chapter 11

1. WC, Retrospectus, WC Papers II. Channing was referring to daily newspapers.

2. Ibid. Barbara complained that her father was "the only Dr. who does not go away." She tried to persuade him to take a vacation, "but it would be as easy to move the Pyramids." Barbara Channing to Lucy Russel, November 21, 1849, CF Papers.

3. WC to Richard Henry Dana, October 4, 1841, Dana Family Papers, MHS; WC to Lucy Bradstreet Channing, July 9, [1844], CF Papers.

4. WC to Jared Sparks, May 3, 1849, April 29, 1851, September 3, 1855, MS Sparks Papers 153, Houghton Library, Harvard University.

5. Barbara Channing to Lucy Russel, August 4, [?], CF Papers.

6. Obituary in *BMSJ* 95 (1876): 237–38; Edward Channing, "Recollections of a Hitherto Truthful Man," p. 49.

7. WC to Louisa Higginson, March 9, 1844, CF Papers II.

8. WC to no person identified, n.d., [after 1852], WC Papers II.

9. Kate Sedgwick to Charles Sedgwick, April 5, 1841, quoted in McGill, *Channing of Concord*, p. 57.

10. Ralph Waldo Emerson to Samuel Ward, October 1839, in Baker, *Emerson among the Eccentrics*, p. 153. Using a nom de plume, Hal Menge, Ellery had previously published some poems in the *Boston Mercantile Journal* and the *New England Magazine*. McGill, *Channing of Concord*, pp. 21–25.

11. Ralph Waldo Emerson to Ellery Channing, January 30, 1840, in McGill, *Channing of Concord*, p. 43.

12. Barbara Channing to Lucy Russel, February 20, 1841, CF Papers; McGill, *Channing of Concord*, pp. 55–57. James Perkins had boarded with Walter before his marriage to Eliza and would have known Ellery well from those days. He tried to counsel Ellery prior to his departure for Illinois but without success. Perkins subsequently described his nephew as having a "misty and unreorganized mind" and a "thoroughly morbid mind" that would not listen to advice or obey commands. McGill, *Channing of Concord*, pp. 29–30. Barbara Channing excused her brother's failings. "He has not had from his infancy such a home and constant care and love as Charlie [Sedgwick] but has been left to prove his own character and struggle with peculiarities of temper. . . . what ever seems changeable or feeble is on the

surface not in the heart." Barbara Channing to Lucy Bradstreet Channing, July 1, 1838, CF Papers.

13. Eleanor Flexner, *Century of Struggle: The Woman's Rights Movement in the United States*, rev. ed. (Cambridge, Mass.: Belknap Press of Harvard University Press, 1975), pp. 66–68; Edward T. James, Janet Wilson James, and Paul S. Boyer, eds., *Notable American Women: A Biographical Dictionary*, 3 vols. (Cambridge, Mass.: Radcliffe College, 1971), 1:678–82. There is an extensive literature on Margaret Fuller, most recently a biography by Charles Capper, *Margaret Fuller: An American Romantic Life* (New York: Oxford University Press, 1992).

14. Ellery to Margaret Crane Fuller, September 5, 1841, Fuller Family Correspondence, vol. 15, Houghton Library, Harvard University.

15. Mary E. Channing and Barbara Channing to Kate Sedgwick, September 21, 1841, CF Papers.

16. Ellen Kilshaw Fuller to Margaret Crane Fuller, September 17, 1841, Fuller Family Correspondence, vol. 15, Houghton Library, Harvard University.

17. See Susan C. Higginson to Francis J. Higginson, September 20, 1841, HCC Papers; Ellen Kilshaw Fuller to Margaret Crane Fuller, September 17, 1841, Fuller Family Correspondence, vol. 15, Houghton Library, Harvard University.

18. Margaret Fuller to Ralph Waldo Emerson, September 8, 1841, September 16, 1841, in *The Letters of Margaret Fuller*, ed. Robert N. Hudspeth, 5 vols. (Ithaca: Cornell University Press, 1938), 2:230–32.

19. Ellery and Ellen were married September 24, 1841, by the rector of St. Paul's Protestant Episcopal Church. James Perkins was not authorized to perform marriages in Ohio, but he did attempt a semblance of approval by permitting the ceremony to be performed in his home. McGill, *Channing of Concord*, pp. 61–63.

20. James H. Perkins to William H. Channing, October 2, 1841, CF Papers.

21. The first three children (eventually of five) were Margaret, born May 23, 1844; Caroline Sturgis, born April 13, 1846; and Walter, born April 14, 1849. *Concord, Massachusetts, Births, Marriages, and Deaths, 1635–1850* (printed by the town, n.d.), pp. 398, 400, 402. They were all delivered by Dr. Josiah Bartlett. See Josiah Bartlett, Account Books, Concord Museum Collection on deposit at Concord Free Public Library.

22. The most egregious of these escapes was a journey to Italy in 1846, during Ellen's second confinement. Ellery raised $300 from friends, some of his father's included, justifying the trip as necessary for poetic inspiration. He spent sixteen days in Rome and was back in his own country in four months. McGill, *Channing of Concord*, pp. 87–89. His father was not well informed about the entire escapade. WC to Lucy Bradstreet Channing, July 7, 1846, CF Papers.

23. Thomas Wentworth Higginson to Sam Johnson, February 24, 1852, typescript, CF Papers II.

24. Ellen Kilshaw Fuller Channing to WC, August 3, 1847, B MS c53.3, Countway Library; Ellen Kilshaw Fuller Channing to Barbara Channing, n.d., CF Papers. Shortly after the birth of Margaret Fuller Channing, Walter visited Concord, and admired the baby, the house, and Ellen's skill as a housekeeper. Before leaving he gave Ellen a hundred dollars, "25 being for the baby." WC to Lucy Bradstreet Channing, July 9, [1844], CF Papers.

25. Emerson referred to William Ellery Channing as "Boston's bishop." Chadwick, *William Ellery Channing*, p. 353.

26. Ibid., pp. 415–21; William Henry Channing, *Life of William Ellery Channing*, pp. 689–98.

27. WC to George G. Channing, September 26, 1842, WC Papers II.

28. WC to William Ellery Channing, August 7, 1842, WC Papers II.

29. Susan Higginson Channing to Catherine Maria Sedgwick, October 3, [1842], Catherine Maria Sedgwick to Susan Higginson Channing, October 13, 1842, Catherine Maria Sedgwick Papers I, MHS. Other members of the family were also present at his sickbed, including Ruth Gibbs Channing, Susan Higginson Channing, William's daughter, and her husband. A local physician, Dr. Swift, had charge of the case.

30. The birth of the elder child, Mary, was recorded in WC, List of Midwifery Cases, July 16, 1822, WC Papers III.

31. WC to Lucy Russel, May 6, 1831, CF Papers. Channing feared that Mary and her children might someday become entirely dependent on the family and added, "God grant I may feel as I now do." For the death of Robert Rogers, see John Barnard Swett Jackson, Medical Cases and Autopsies, February 3, 1839, H MS b72.4, Countway Library. Rogers had been Channing's patient. See also Barbara Channing to Lucy Bradstreet Channing, March 15, 1839, CF Papers.

32. William Ellery Channing to Susan Higginson Channing, February 12, 1819, Pierpont Morgan Library, New York.

33. Massachusetts State Archives, Deaths, vol. 9, p. 103. No occupation, place of birth, or parentage was given. The will of Lucy Ellery Channing lists Henry as "gentleman," signifying no occupation. Trust Agreement for Estate of Lucy Channing, July 24, 1834, CF Papers II. See also Barbara Channing to Lucy Russel, April 17, 1841, October 15, 1843, CF Papers. North Bridgewater was later incorporated into the city of Brockton, Massachusetts.

34. For an account of the death and funeral of Washington Allston, see *Journal of Richard Henry Dana, Jr.*, 1:172–75, 182. Early in his career Allston painted portraits of several members of the family, including Francis Dana Channing, William Ellery Channing, and Lucy Ellery Channing. His wife Ann Channing was the model for one oil, perhaps two, as well as many sketches. William H. Gerdts and Theodore E. Stebbins, Jr., *A Man of Genius: The Art of Washington Allston (1779–1843)* (Boston: Museum of Fine Arts, 1979).

35. For Ann and Washington Allston in England and her death, see Jared B. Flagg, *The Life and Letters of Washington Allston, with Reproductions from Allston's Pictures* (New York: C. Scribner's Sons, 1892); and William Henry Channing, *Life of William Ellery Channing*, pp. 317–19. The cause of her death is unclear, though there are descriptions of sudden illness and a rapid decline.

36. Gerdts and Stebbins, *Man of Genius*, p. 60; [WC], "Washington Allston," *Christian World*, July 22, 1843.

37. [WC], "Washington Allston." The obituary was reprinted in the *Daily Advertiser* and in the *Christian Register*. Channing provided additional recollections for Richard Henry Dana, Sr., who assembled information about Allston from many friends and associates, intending to write a full biography. Dana continued to work on the book until he was too old to conclude it, but his notes became the basis for the first definitive biography, Jared B. Flagg, *The Life and Letters of Washington Allston*. See WC to Richard Henry Dana, July 19, 1844, Dana Family Papers, MHS.

38. Kate Sedgwick to Catherine Maria Sedgwick, April 21, 1842, Catherine Maria Sedgwick Papers II, MHS. This was William Francis Channing, the son of William Ellery Channing. He received a medical degree from the University of Pennsylvania in 1844 but abandoned medicine for scientific experimentation and made some important electrical inventions, including a fire alarm telegraph. *Dictionary of American Biography*, 4:8–9. Mesmer-

ism, introduced by the Austrian Franz Mesmer, taught that disease, particularly nervous disorders, was caused by the imbalance of an invisible magnetic fluid in the body. Cures depended on restoration of the fluid to its proper balance. Gevitz, *Other Healers*, p. 126.

39. WC to Lucy Russel, June 4, 1847, CF Papers.

40. It was common among Boston's wealthy families to leave the city every summer for surrounding towns such as Milton, Nahant, Beverly, and Brookline. The Channing daughters usually did a round of visits to various relatives who had taken up summer residence in these places. On this occasion, they were near Ruth Channing and her daughter Mary Eustis. George Channing and his family were also living in Milton.

41. Barbara Channing to Lucy Russel, August 7, 1847, CF Papers; Massachusetts State Archives, Deaths Reported in the Town of Milton, vol. 33, p. 120.

42. WC to Lucy Russel, [August 1847], CF Papers.

43. Baker, *Emerson among the Eccentrics*, p. 40. Lidian Emerson, Waldo's wife, spoke of Unitarianism as "cold and hard, with scarcely a firmament above it." See Howe, *Unitarian Conscience*, pp. 151–73, for attempts to remedy the "emotional lacks" of their religious practices.

44. For a brief period in the early 1850s Walter's daughter Barbara flirted with Catholicism. Previously, William Henry Channing had shown some interest in the Church of Rome but was dissuaded by his uncle William Ellery Channing. James Freeman Clarke to Barbara Channing, [1853], CF Papers; Van Wyck Brooks, *The Flowering of New England* (New York: E. P. Dutton, 1940), p. 251.

45. Clarke (1810–1888) was the step-grandson of James Freeman, one of the earliest Unitarian ministers in Boston. He attended Harvard College and Divinity School, where his classmates included William Henry Channing and Samuel May. He was a friend of Margaret Fuller and had studied the German and English philosophers who powerfully influenced transcendentalism in New England. While a minister in Louisville, Clarke edited the *Western Messenger*, the publication that spoke for Unitarianism in the trans-Appalachian states. Arthur S. Bolster, Jr., *James Freeman Clarke: Disciple to Advancing Truth* (Boston: Beacon Press, 1954); James Freeman Clarke, *Autobiography, Diary and Correspondence*, ed. Edward Everett Hale (Boston: Houghton, Mifflin, 1891). Bolster's biography is based on his Ph.D. dissertation (Harvard University, 1953) on file at Andover-Harvard Theological Library, Harvard University.

46. Chadwick, *William Ellery Channing*, pp. 354–55.

47. Bolster, *James Freeman Clarke*, p. 68.

48. Barbara Channing to Lucy Russel, February 20, 1841, CF Papers.

49. Church of the Disciples, Annals of the Church, January 30, 1841–June 20, 1852, Andover-Harvard Theological Library.

50. Church of the Disciples, Boston, Massachusetts, Declaration of Faith and Purpose, Signed April 27, 1841, Andover-Harvard Theological Library. The signing took place at the Peabody home above Elizabeth Peabody's bookstore on West Street.

51. Helen Cheever, "Highlights from Seventy Years of our History of One Hundred Years," read at the Women's Alliance, 1941. Church of the Disciples, Misc. Papers, Box 1, Andover-Harvard Theological Library.

52. Three charitable institutions emerged from concerns of the social meetings—the Temporary Home for Destitute Children, Children's Aid Society, and the Home for Aged Colored Women. Barbara Channing, the most idealistic of Channing's children, was one of the most active participants in these endeavors.

53. WC to James Freeman Clarke, July 8, 1842, Perry-Clarke Papers, MHS.

54. Theodore Parker, "The Transient and Permanent in Christianity," sermon delivered May 19, 1841. Quoted in Bolster, *James Freeman Clarke*, p. 149.

55. The secessionists formed another church, the Church of the Savior, with Robert C. Waterston as their minister. Waterston, minister at the Pitts Street Chapel, had publicly attacked Parker as an infidel. The Church of the Savior held its first meeting for worship March 2, 1845, and continued until 1854, when debt incurred by the cost of a new building forced its absorption by the Second Church. Records of the Second Church, Boston, vol. 39, Subscriptions; vol. 41, Records of the Society of the Church of the Savior, February 10, 1845, to 1854; vol. 43, Account Book, MHS. The Church of the Savior had good relations with the Church of the Disciples. George Channing maintained his friendship with Clarke. He continued to edit the *Christian World* for several years. In 1850, at the age of sixty, George was ordained an evangelist in the Unitarian church and was a successful preacher for the next two decades. *Christian Register*, October 9, 1852; Elizabeth Parsons Channing, *Autobiography and Diary*, pp. 1, 5.

56. Next to Walter Channing's signature on the pledge of membership in the Church of the Disciples is written, in a different hand, "withdrawn see church journal." I have not found anything in the church records, including Clarke's journals, to explain this mysterious notation. All the evidence points to Channing's continued participation in the church and his friendship with James Freeman Clarke. It is possible that he withdrew from membership when he moved to Dorchester, or later when he moved to Brookline.

57. Clarke, *Memorial and Biographical Sketches*, pp. 169–85.

58. Barbara Channing's interest in the Church of the Disciples fluctuated over time. At one point she found it more ritualistic and conventional than she had hoped; later she joined the Religious Union of the Associationists, led by her cousin William Henry Channing. The Associationists were greatly influenced by Fourierism and other radical proposals for social reform. Their intention was "to spread among mankind the Reign of Love—one—harmonious—universal." Among the members were the Ripleys and several others from Brook Farm. The Religious Union lasted from 1847 to 1850. Barbara was involved simultaneously with the Associationists and the Church of the Disciples. Record Book of the Religious Union of Associationists and James T. Fisher Papers, MHS. William Henry Channing has been described as the "most extreme embodiment, among the Church reformers, of the misty, ill-defined Transcendentalism which the public came to associate with the entire 'New School.'" William R. Hutchison, *The Transcendentalist Ministers: Church Reform in the New England Renaissance* (1959; Hamden, Conn.: Shoe String Press, 1972), p. 169. See also Rose, *Transcendentalism as a Social Movement*, pp. 144–45.

59. On a more mundane level, the Church of the Disciples may also have appealed to Channing because its members did not represent the fashionable part of Boston society. Julia Ward Howe, for example, preferred Clarke's church to any other in Boston for the same reason. Howe, *Reminiscences*, pp. 244–47.

60. WC to Lucy Russel, [August 1847], CF Papers.

61. Ibid.; WC to Lucy Russel, August 26, 1847; WC to Lucy Russel, [1851], CF Papers.

62. Bolster, *James Freeman Clarke*, p. 158; John A. Andrew to WC, October 26, 1849, B MS c53.3, Countway Library.

63. Clarke, *Memorial and Biographical Sketches*, pp. 174–75.

64. Barbara Channing to Lucy Russel, March 5, 1849, CF Papers.

65. Olney Cole to WC, October 23, 1847, November 4, 1847; Mehetable E. Cole to

WC, November 25, 1847, January 1, 1850; Rufus Longley to WC, January 24, 1850, B MS c53.3, Countway Library. The Coles, who begged Channing to come to Providence on behalf of their daughter, worried about his fees, but promised to "do the best we can by you" and prepared a turkey dinner in anticipation of his visit. For whatever reason, Channing did not remain for the meal.

66. For a good exposition of this position, see John Ware, "Success in the Medical Profession," *BMSJ* 43 (1851): 496–522.

67. In addition to the papers and *Treatise on Etherization in Childbirth*, already cited in Chapter 9, Channing's contributions to the *Boston Medical and Surgical Journal* during these years (1840–1854) include: "Of the Medical Profession and its Preparation" (introductory lecture delivered to the medical class of Harvard University, November 5, 1845), 33 (1845–46): 309–17, 329–37, 349–57; "Dr. Murphy's Lectures on Midwifery" (review), 35 (1846–47): 298–99; "The Late John Revere, M.D.," 36 (1847): 292–95; "Cases of Organic Diseases of the Womb and Its Appendages," 36 (1847): 469–77; "Females and their Diseases" (a review of Charles D. Meigs), 37 (1847–48): 438–41; "Memoir of Enoch Hale," 39 (1848–49): 334–41; "Puerperal Peritonitis" (letter to the editor), 40 (1849): 274–76; "Sketch of Dr. John D. Fisher," 42 (1850): 117–21; "Notes of Difficult Labors, in the Second of which Etherization by Sulphuric Ether Was Successfully Employed Nineteen Years Ago," 46 (1852): 113–15; "Professional Reminiscences of Foreign Travel," 47 (1852–53): 303–9, 326–34, 363–69, 393–400; "Hydrophobia" (letter to the editor), 50 (1854): 10–12.

68. WC, "Notes on Anhæmia, principally in its connections with the Puerperal state, and with Functional Disease of the Uterus; with Cases," *New England Quarterly Journal of Medicine and Surgery* 1 (1842): 157–88. For comments on the paper, see Irving, *Safe Deliverance*, pp. 84–85; Herbert Thoms, *Chapters in American Obstetrics*, 2d ed. (Springfield, Ill.: Charles C. Thomas, 1961), pp. 137–38; Walter Radcliffe, *Milestones in Midwifery* (Bristol, Eng.: John Wright and Sons, 1967), p. 82; Jeremy M. Norman, ed., *Morton's Medical Bibliography*, 4th ed. (Aldershot, Eng.: Scholar Press, 1991), no. 3116. Irving refers to Channing's paper as the first description of "the pernicious-like type of anemia which on rare occasions complicates pregnancy." Thoms calls the paper "the first recorded description of so-called hemolytic anemia of pregnancy." *Morton's Medical Bibliography* calls it the first description of "pernicious anemia of pregnancy." In the light of contemporary hematology, none of those descriptions fits Channing's paper. I am grateful to Dr. Mortimer Greenberg for helping me place Channing's paper in the context of modern hematological knowledge.

69. It is possible that the anemic women observed by Channing had developed their disease before delivery, especially since bloodletting was frequently practiced during pregnancy to relieve the plethora associated with the puerperal state. Inadequate diet can also produce an anemic condition in pregnant women. Thus, what Channing saw could have been severe iron deficiency anemia or folic acid deficiency anemia, either of which is preventable or can be easily remedied in modern obstetrical practice. It is unlikely that the cases described by Channing were pernicious anemia as that term is used by hematologists today. The disease now called pernicious anemia is due to vitamin B12 deficiency caused by the patient's lack of a factor (known as intrinsic factor) necessary for absorption of vitamin B12 from food and usually present in gastric juice.

70. Channing objected to the imprecision of the word "anæmia," which strictly used means "without blood." Did anæmia mean an external symptom (colorless state of the skin), the lack of blood (quantity), or altered condition of the blood (quality)? His conclusion was that it was the altered condition of the blood caused by a process gone awry.

71. Maxwell M. Wintrobe, *Hematology: The Blossoming of a Science* (Philadelphia: Lea & Febiger, 1985), pp. 9–19. The same year that Channing's paper appeared, Gabriel Andral published a monograph on hematology that included a discussion of anemia in pregnancy but not as a disease consequent to delivery.

72. See William Osler, "Puerperal Anæmia, and Its Treatment with Arsenic," *BMSJ* 119 (1888): 454–55, for a case of puerperal anemia that came under the care of an outstanding American clinician. Though the patient's blood could be analyzed more extensively than that in Channing's cases, and arsenic seemed an effective cure, Osler pointed out how much remained unknown about the disease. He credited Channing with the "first article on pernicious or essential anæmia."

73. WC, "Physical Education," *Journal of Health and Monthly Miscellany* 1 (1846): 170–72, 193–97, 225–30, 295–99.

74. Harvard University, Faculty of Medicine, Minutes of Meetings, September 4, October 2, 1854.

75. For the Parkman murder and trial, see Harrington, *Harvard Medical School*, 2:639–47; Morison, *Three Centuries of Harvard*, pp. 282–86; George Bemis, *Report of the Case of John W. Webster* (Boston: C. C. Little and J. Brown, 1850); Robert Sullivan, *The Disappearance of Dr. Parkman* (Boston: Little, Brown, 1971); Helen Thomson, *Murder at Harvard* (Boston: Houghton, Mifflin, 1971). For a fanciful version of the events, see Simon Schama, *Dead Certainties (Unwarranted Speculations)* (New York: Knopf, 1991).

76. For a description of the Parkman Professorship of Anatomy, see William Bentinck-Smith and Elizabeth Stouffer, *Harvard University History of Named Chairs, Professorships of the Faculties of Medicine and Public Health, 1721–1991* (Cambridge, Mass.: Secretary to the University, 1991–1995), pp. 219–20. Parkman had studied medicine in Europe and became an expert in treatment of the insane. He wanted to be appointed superintendent of McLean Hospital but was passed over.

77. Nathan Cooley Keep, the dentist who provided anesthesia to Fanny Longfellow, had been Parkman's dentist and had made the dental plates by which Parkman was identified. His testimony at the trial was crucial to conviction. William Thomas Green Morton, already fighting for recognition as the sole discoverer of anesthesia, disputed Keep's testimony when he was called to the stand. "Medical Evidence in the Trial of Prof. Webster," *BMSJ* 42 (1850): 173–83.

78. Harrington, *Harvard Medical School*, p. 640.

79. *BMSJ* 41 (1849–50): 366, 386; 42 (1850): 124–25, 162–67, 173–82, 186, 197–200, 202–3, 222–26, 228, 400, 478, 480, 498–99, 518; 43 (1850–51): 105–6.

80. Sullivan, *Disappearance of Dr. Parkman*, p. 186.

81. Cash, "Pride, Prejudice and Politics," 20–25.

82. John White Webster to WC, June 1, 1850, B MS misc., Countway Library.

83. WC, Miscellaneous notes, WC Papers II. "[L]ines with rhyming ends" from WC, "Newport Reunion Address."

84. [WC], *New and Old*.

85. In 1942, Frederick Irving noted, "at present a copy reposes in the rare-book department of the Boston Public Library, which seems to be the best place for it. . . . [I]t is evident that Dr. Channing could bestride a Pegasus no better than he could drive a horse." *Safe Deliverance*, p. 102. There are also copies of the book at the Houghton Library and Countway Library.

86. "To Loneliness," *New and Old*, p. 119.

87. "To Authority," ibid., p. 120.

88. "To Duty," ibid., p. 122.

89. WC to Lucy Russel, November 28, 1851, CF Papers.

90. Ibid.

91. WC to Jared Sparks, May 3, 1852, MS Sparks Papers 153, Houghton Library, Harvard University; Jared Sparks to WC, May 5, 1852, H MS Misc., Countway Library. See also Abbott Lawrence, Envoy Extraordinary and Minister Plenipotentiary of the United States of America, Legation of the United States, London, June 1, 1852, H MS Misc., Countway Library. Channing was also recommended to the American ministers in Berlin, Paris, St. Petersburg, and Madrid, who facilitated his journey. Several other Americans working abroad were also helpful.

92. WC to Lucy Russel, May 9, 1852, CF Papers.

93. For details of the journey, see WC, Physician's Vacation, and WC, "Professional Reminiscences of Foreign Travel," BMSJ 47 (1852–53): 303–9, 326–34, 363–69, 393–400.

94. On the other hand, he did not go to Switzerland or Italy, which were often destinations of Americans traveling in Europe.

95. WC, Physician's Vacation, pp. 200–201.

96. Ibid., pp. 514–17.

97. Undoubtedly the physician was Karl Edouard Marius Levy. In the BMSJ, Channing referred to Dr. Braun as Dr. Brown. There are many misspellings and misidentifications in the BMSJ articles and in A Physician's Vacation.

98. Carter and Carter, Childbed Fever; Ignaz Semmelweis, The Etiology, Concept, and Prophylaxis of Childbed Fever, ed. and trans. K. Codell Carter (Madison: University of Wisconsin Press, 1983).

99. Channing also praised the St. Petersburg maternity ward for successfully preventing puerperal fever. WC, "Professional Reminiscences of Foreign Travel," BMSJ 47 (1852): 330.

100. Ibid.

101. Ibid., p. 333.

102. James Syme (1799–1870), a highly successful surgeon and Professor of Clinical Surgery at Edinburgh, was one of the first European surgeons to adopt ether anesthesia. William Sharpey (1802–1880), a native Scot, spent most of his professional life as Professor of Anatomy and Physiology at University College, London. Robert Christison had been Professor of Medical Jurisprudence and was Professor of Materia Medica and Therapeutics at the University of Edinburgh at the time of Channing's visit.

103. In Manchester, Channing met Dr. Charles Clay, another pioneer in gynecology. Channing admired Clay's operations for removal of diseased ovaries, though he was not prepared himself to perform such daring surgery.

104. Ether too can cause fatalities, but Channing remained wedded to its use, perhaps because of the habitual loyalty of Boston's medical establishment to their colleagues at the Massachusetts General Hospital.

105. Journal of Richard Henry Dana, Jr., 2:509–10; WC to Lucy Russel, May 15, 1860, CF Papers.

106. Boston Society for Medical Improvement, Records, vol. 7, October 25, 1852, Countway Library.

107. Barbara Channing to Lucy Russel, July 17, [1853], CF Papers. Barbara published a fictional account of her travels in Italy. The volume was dedicated "To the memory of

Ellen Fuller Channing" and published anonymously. *The Sisters Abroad; or an Italian Journey* (Boston, Whittemore, Niles & Hall, 1857).

Notes to Chapter 12

1. Hydropathy, or the water cure, was first popularized in Europe during the 1820s by Vincent Preissnitz and introduced to the United States during the 1840s. It relied on large quantities of water, used externally and internally, to cure disease and maintain health. Susan E. Cayleff, *Wash and Be Healed: The Water-Cure Movement and Women's Health* (Philadelphia: Temple University Press, 1987); Katherine Kish Sklar, " 'All Hail to Pure Cold Water!' " and Ann Douglas Wood, " 'The Fashionable Diseases': Women's Complaints and Their Treatment in Nineteenth-Century America," both in Leavitt, *Women and Health in America*.

2. Homeopathy, based on the teaching of Samuel Hahnemann, a German practitioner, had two fundamental principles: the law of similia, which said that diseases can be cured by drugs that produce in a healthy person the same symptoms as those of a sick person; and the law of infinitesimals: the smaller the dose the more effective the cure. Thus, homeopathic medicine was administered in increasingly small dilutions, always after they were "excited and enabled to act spiritually upon the vital forces." Martin Kaufman, "Homeopathy in America: The Rise and Fall and Persistence of a Medical Heresy," in Gevitz, *Other Healers*, pp. 99–112; Haller, *American Medicine in Transition*, pp. 104–19.

3. "Massachusetts Homeopathic Fraternity," *BMSJ* 29 (1843–44): 226, 258–59.

4. Notes on homeopathy, hydropathy, "bed cases," insanity, and the nervous system, Miscellaneous manuscript, n.d., WC Papers II.

5. Susan E. Cayleff, "Gender, Ideology, and the Water-Cure Movement," in Gevitz, *Other Healers*, p. 88.

6. Incomplete mss. on homeopathy, n.d., WC Papers II.

7. Constipation was a common complaint in nineteenth-century cities where diet was limited, especially during the winter months, when fresh fruits and vegetables were scarce, and people were not in the habit of drinking water, often for good reason (as shown in Chapter 10).

8. Later in the century, the Massachusetts Medical Society was forced to expel members who practiced homeopathy or consulted with homeopaths.

9. Miscellaneous notes on obstetrics, WC Papers II.

10. Notes on 10 miscellaneous cases, mss., n.d., WC Papers II. Channing's grandson Edward told the story differently. In his version, Barbara had become enamored of homeopathy and her father swallowed her pills to prove their ineffectiveness. Edward Channing, "Recollections of a Hitherto Truthful Man," p. 6. Perhaps both incidents occurred.

11. Haller, *American Medicine in Transition*, pp. 209–17; John Duffy, *From Humors to Medical Science*, 2d ed. (Urbana: University of Illinois Press, 1993), pp. 85–87. See also *BMSJ* 17 (1837–38): 368–69; 22 (1840): 143–44, 242; 31 (1844–45): 323–24; 34 (1846): 263, 302, 426; 36 (1847): 305–7.

12. See Warren, *Life of John Collins Warren*, 2:14–16, 28–29; "American Medical Association," *BMSJ* 40 (1849): 279–83. John Collins Warren was elected the next president of the AMA.

13. WC, "American Medical Association," *BMSJ* 40 (1849): 299–304, 362–64.

14. Charles D. Meigs to WC, March 13, 1852, WC Papers II. See also "Special Commit-

tees of the American Medical Association," *BMSJ* 44 (1851): 428. One reason for Channing's unwillingness to cooperate may have been his intention to leave for Europe in mid-May.

15. Some changes were instituted in 1858 with the creation of a summer school, which meant that a student would receive instruction for most of the year. Written examinations were also planned, but according to some scholars, the Civil War disrupted implementation. See Harrington, *Harvard Medical School*, 2:534–38.

16. The issue that confronted physicians was "criminal abortion," or the deliberate destruction of the fetus to end a pregnancy. Spontaneous expulsion of the fetus during the first six months of pregnancy was also called an abortion; after that period it was a "premature delivery." Both were considered to be "untoward events." See Churchill, *On the Theory and Practice of Midwifery*, pp. 179–80.

17. David H. Storer, Notebook, Walter Channing [lecture on jurisprudence], February 11, 1824, B MS b8.1, Countway Library (emphasis added). See also WC, Miscellaneous notes for a lecture on the causes of abortion, WC Papers II.

18. See, for example, WC, "Infanticide," Miscellaneous lecture notes, WC Papers II; Dewees, *Compendious System of Midwifery*, pp. 111–15; Thomas Percival, *Percival's Medical Ethics*, ed. Chauncey D. Leake (Baltimore: Williams & Wilkins, [c. 1927]), pp. 133–42; and Theodric Romeyn Beck, *Elements of Medical Jurisprudence* (Albany, N.Y.: Webster and Skinner, 1823), Chapter 8.

19. David H. Storer, Notebook, Walter Channing [lecture on jurisprudence], February 11, 1824, B MS b8.1, Countway Library.

20. Charles W. Chauncy, Boston Medical Records, 1821–23, 2 vols., Lecture, December 21, 1821, vol. 1, CB 1823.13, Countway Library. The full text of one of Channing's lectures on the causes of miscarriage can be found among the miscellaneous manuscripts in the WC Papers II.

21. It is unlikely that, in treating cases of delayed or suppressed menses, Channing was facilitating an abortion, since his diagnosis would include attention to other signs of pregnancy. There is no evidence that he ordered violent purgatives or emetics that might induce an abortion.

22. For birth control during this period, see Gordon, *Woman's Body, Woman's Right*; Degler, *At Odds*; and Janet Farrell Brodie, *Contraception and Abortion in Nineteenth-Century America* (Ithaca: Cornell University Press, 1994).

23. At this time, graduating medical school students did not make formal pledges to obey the Hippocratic oath or other statements of ethics. Nonetheless, they were aware both of the Hippocratic teaching, which forbade a physician administering an abortifacient, and of Percival's ethics. Percival, *Percival's Medical Ethics*, pp. 132–33; Dale C. Smith, "The Hippocratic Oath and Modern Medicine," *Journal of the History of Medicine and Allied Sciences* 51 (1996): 484–500.

24. James C. Mohr, *Abortion in America* (New York: Oxford University Press, 1978), esp. pp. 46–118.

25. "Criminal Abortions," *BMSJ* 30 (1844): 302–3. The editor of the journal identified "the vast amount of wickedness" perpetrated by abortionists with infanticide in "heathen" China. See also *BMSJ* 31 (1844–45): 124; 32 (1845): 45.

26. Boston Society for Medical Improvement, Reports, vol. 5, June 24, 1844, January 11, 1847, Countway Library. At another meeting, Channing described a patient who had consumed a quarter-pound of ergot and developed severe peritonitis. Most likely, both examples were the same woman. Or perhaps the minutes taken at the first meeting contained

an error. Vol. 6, August 11, 1851. Attempts at self-abortion were also reported at meetings of the Boston Society for Medical Observation. See Boston Society for Medical Observation, Records, vol. 4, June 2, 1851, Countway Library. The Boston Society for Medical Observation was founded in 1846 by some of the younger physicians associated with the Boylston Medical School.

27. Boston Society for Medical Improvement, Reports, vol. 6, June 23, 1851, February 28, 1853, Countway Library. See also Mohr, *Abortion in America*, pp. 48–53; and Carroll Smith-Rosenberg, "The Abortion Movement and the AMA, 1850–1880," in her *Disorderly Conduct* (New York: Alfred A. Knopf, 1985), pp. 225–28.

28. Boston Society for Medical Improvement, Reports, vol. 6, May 12, 1851, Countway Library.

29. Hugh Lenox Hodge, Professor of Obstetrics at the University of Pennsylvania, criticized abortion in his 1839 lectures, using the argument that fetal life existed before quickening. Hugh Lenox Hodge, *An Introductory Lecture to a Course on Obstetrics*, cited in Brodie, *Contraception and Abortion in Nineteenth-Century America*, p. 266.

30. "Punishment of Criminal Attempts at Abortion," *BMSJ* 32 (1845): 45; Mohr, *Abortion in America*, pp. 120–24.

31. David Humphreys Storer, *An Introductory Lecture before the Medical Class of Harvard University* (Boston: David Clapp, 1855). The portion omitted in this published version was later printed at the instigation of Horatio Storer in *Journal of the Gynecological Society of Boston* 6 (1872): 194–203.

32. Storer did qualify his remarks on contraception by saying that he was giving a hypothesis without "sufficient data to warrant me in stating positively the fact." On the consequences of abortion he had no doubts.

33. "Bibliographical Notices," *BMSJ* 53 (1855): 409–11. The editor referred to "*the crime of procuring abortion* and the scarcely less heinous offence of *preventing impregnation*." See Frederick N. Dyer, *Champion of Women and the Unborn, Horatio Robinson Storer, M.D.* (Canton, Mass.: Science History Publications, 1999), pp. 80–87, for one explanation for the suppression of Storer's lecture.

34. For the "physicians' crusade," see Mohr, *Abortion in America*, Chapter 6; Smith-Rosenberg, "The Abortion Movement and the AMA"; and Leslie J. Reagan, *When Abortion Was a Crime: Women, Medicine, and Law in the United States* (Berkeley: University of California Press, 1997), esp. pp. 1–18.

35. Horatio R. Storer to Malcolm Storer, October 30, 1901, quoted in Dyer, *Champion of Women and the Unborn*, p. 68.

36. Suffolk District Medical Society, Records, Special Meeting, May 9, 1857, Report of Committee on Criminal Abortions, Countway Library; "Extracts from Records of the Suffolk District Medical Society," *BMSJ* 56 (1857): 281–84; "The Report Upon Criminal Abortions," *BMSJ* 56 (1857): 346–47; "Annual Meeting of the Massachusetts Medical Society," *BMSJ* 56 (1857): 383–86; Dyer, *Champion of Women and the Unborn*, pp. 101–32; Mohr, *Abortion in America*, pp. 148–59.

37. "Annual Meeting of the Massachusetts Medical Society," *BMSJ* 56 (1857): 383–86.

38. Suffolk District Medical Society, Records, Special Meeting, May 9, 1857, Report of Committee on Criminal Abortions, Countway Library.

39. WC, "Effects of Criminal Abortion," *BMSJ* 60 (1859): 134–42; WC, "A Medico-Legal Treatise on Malpractice and Medical Evidence—A Review," *BMSJ* 62 (1860): 233–41, 259–65, 300–307. The second citation here refers to a review written by Channing of a

treatise on jurisprudence written by John J. Elwell. It gave Channing an opportunity to give his views on criminal abortion.

40. WC, "Effects of Criminal Abortion," *BMSJ* 60 (1859): 135.

41. WC, "A Medico-Legal Treatise," *BMSJ* 62 (1860): 237.

42. Ibid., p. 236.

43. WC, "Death of Charlotte Bronte," *BMSJ* 57 (1857): 94–97.

44. WC, "Infanticide," Miscellaneous lecture notes, WC Papers II.

45. Theodric Romeyn Beck, *Elements of Medical Jurisprudence*, pp. 185–97; WC, Miscellaneous notes, WC Papers II.

46. WC, Miscellaneous papers, WC Papers II.

47. American Medical Association, *Transactions* 12 (1859): 27–28, 75–77.

48. WC, Will, February 3, 1866, WC Papers II.

49. "A Physician," *Remarks on the Employment of Females as Practitioners in Midwifery* (Boston: Cummings and Hilliard, 1820). This pamphlet is frequently criticized by feminist scholars as an example of medical misogyny. See Edna Manzer, "Woman's Doctors: The Development of Obstetrics and Gynecology in Boston, 1860–1930" (Ph.D. diss., Indiana University, 1979), pp. 15–20, 345 n. 38; Donegan, *Women and Men Midwives*, p. 131; Wertz and Wertz, *Lying-In*, p. 56; and Regina Markell Morantz-Sanchez, *Sympathy and Science: Women Physicians in American Medicine* (New York: Oxford University Press, 1985), pp. 25–26.

50. For a similar contemporary view, see the preface written by John W. Francis in Thomas Denman, *Introduction to the Practice of Midwifery* (New York: Bliss & White, 1821).

51. Notice to the public, signed by James Hamilton, M.D., Professor of Midwifery, University of Edingburgh [sic], April 28, 1817. *Columbian Centinal* (Boston), December 24, 1819, January 1, 1820. Hamilton stated that Mrs. Alexander had also attended "the Edingburgh [sic] General Lying In Hospital, where she had every opportunity of improvement in the line of her profession."

52. James Jackson, letter printed and circulated to the public, Boston, September 17, 1818, Countway Library; Warren, *Life of John Collins Warren*, 1:220, 2:275–76. Jackson did not give up his obstetrical practice, except for consultations, until 1825. Warren continued to practice obstetrics somewhat longer, although he ceased doing forceps deliveries in 1818.

53. Thomas T. Hewson to John Collins Warren, April 12, 1818, JCW Papers, vol. 9. According to a note signed "Justus," "the leading physicians of Boston sent out a circular, recommending the establishment of an institution for the education of females in the Art and Science of Midwifery." *BMSJ* 40 (1849): 87.

54. "Notice to the Public," *Columbian Centinal* (Boston), December 24, 1819, January 1, September 16, 23, 30, 1820, January 24, 27, February 17, 1821.

55. "Boston Medical Association," *BMSJ* 62 (1860): 309.

56. "A Physician," *Remarks on the Employment of Females as Practitioners in Midwifery*, pp. 5–11.

57. Ibid., pp. 4–5.

58. Ibid., p. 7.

59. Ednah D. Cheyney, in Winsor, *The Memorial History of Boston*, 4:347. Mrs. Alexander died September 15, 1845. Her obituary was printed in the *Boston Liberator*. Cited by Samuel Gregory, *Man-Midwifery Exposed and Corrected* (Boston: George Gregory, 1848), p. 21.

60. Samuel A. Green to WC, February 14, 1831, WC Papers II. This case is discussed in Chapter 4. See note 36 and accompanying text, case of Mrs. L.

61. The earliest attribution of the pamphlet to Channing is in William Cushing, *Initials and Pseudonyms: A Dictionary of Literary Disguises*, 2d ser. (New York: T. Y. Crowell, 1888), and is the basis for a similar reference in Samuel Halkett and John Laing, *Dictionary of Anonymous and Pseudonymous English Literature*, new and enlarged ed., ed. James Kennedy, W. A. Smith, and A. F. Johnson (Edinburgh: Oliver and Boyd, 1926), and in Robert B. Austin, *Early American Imprints: A Guide to Works Printed in the United States, 1668–1820* (Washington: U.S. Dept. of Health, Education, and Welfare, Public Health Service, 1961). The pamphlet is attributed to Channing by the National Union Catalogue, the National Library of Medicine, and the College of Physicians of Philadelphia. The copy at the Boston Public Library has a pencil notation, "gift of John Ware to library, 1852, 9 May," and is listed under his name. The Countway Library of Medicine also attributes it to Ware. The William R. Perkins Library at Duke University has a copy acquired from the Boston Public Library that has a penciled notation on the cover attributing it to Dr. Ware. Nonetheless, Duke lists the author as Walter Channing. The American Antiquarian Society's copy identifies the author as "Dr. Ware of Boston." Charles Shoemaker, comp., *A Checklist of American Imprints* (New York: Scarecrow Press, 1964), lists both Channing and Ware. Finally, the Library of Congress, New York Academy of Medicine, and Research Libraries Group computer network (RLIN) simply attribute the pamphlet to "Physician."

62. Most extant copies of the pamphlet have no marking to indicate the authorship, but there are three exceptions. One mentioned in the above note is at the Boston Public Library. The second, at the College of Physicians of Philadelphia, is inscribed, "to Isaac Hays, M.D. from the author," and the third, at the Countway Library of Medicine, Boston, is inscribed, "S. Webber from the author." A handwriting expert who studied these inscriptions along with writing samples from Channing and Ware concluded that the inscriptions were written by Ware. Barbara Harding Associates to author, April 28, 1997.

63. George H. Lyman, "The Interests of the Public and the Medical Profession," *Medical Communications of the Massachusetts Medical Society* 12, no. 1 (1875): 17–37 (also 2d ser., vol. 8, part 1 [Boston: David Clapp and Son, 1875]). I was fortunate to find this reference in Edna Manzer, "Woman's Doctors," pp. 15–20, 345 n. 38.

64. John Ware, *Success in the Medical Profession. An Introductory Lecture Delivered at the Massachusetts Medical College, November 6th, 1850* (Boston: David Clapp, 1851).

65. See Chapter 9. Gregory, *Man-Midwifery Exposed and Corrected*.

66. Ibid., preface.

67. Enoch Carter Rolfe, a graduate of Bowdoin Medical College, lectured on obstetrics and diseases of women. The other professor, William Mason Cornell, had been a minister before receiving a degree in medicine from Berkshire Medical College. He edited the *Journal of Health*, the publication in which Channing's paper "Physical Education" appeared in 1847. See Chapter 11. Cornell was a temperance advocate, which may explain Channing's affinity. Waite, *History of the New England Female Medical College*, pp. 18–19.

68. Ibid., pp. 26–37.

69. See Mohr, *Abortion in America*, pp. 102–14, for a discussion of the complex relationship between abortion and nineteenth-century feminists.

70. Suggestions have been offered that Elizabeth Blackwell had applied to schools in Boston during her extensive search for admission to medical school. If so, as dean, Channing would have known it. His nephew William F. Channing was a friend of Blackwell's, so perhaps he instigated the inquiry. Unfortunately, there are no records of applications received by Harvard at this period. Blackwell's autobiography refers to "twelve country

schools" to which she applied after being rejected in Philadelphia and New York but does not specify to which colleges she wrote. Elizabeth Blackwell, *Pioneer Work in Opening the Medical Profession to Women* (London and New York: Longmans, Green, 1895), p. 52; "Female Physicians," *BMSJ* 37 (1848): 506–7; Ruth J. Abram, ed., *"Send Us a Lady Physician": Women Doctors in America, 1835–1920* (New York: W. W. Norton, 1985), p. 72; Nancy Ann Sahli, *Elizabeth Blackwell, M.D. (1821–1910)* (New York: Arno Press, 1982), p. 103 n. 98.

71. Harvard University, Faculty of Medicine, Minutes, July 19, 1847, Countway Library; Harvard College, Papers, vol. 15, 2d series, July 19, 1947, p. 63, Harvard University Archives; Harvard College, President and Fellows, August 14, 1847, Harvard Medical School, Dean's Office Files, 1839–1900, Box 3, Countway Library.

72. Harriot Kezia Hunt, *Glances and Glimpses; or, Fifty Years Social, Including Twenty Years Professional Life* (Boston: John P. Jewett, 1856).

73. Harvard University, Meetings of the President and Fellows of Harvard College, Minutes, December 27, 1847, Harvard University Archives; Harvard College, President and Fellows, December 27, 1847, Harvard Medical School, Dean's Office Files, 1839–1900, Box 3, Countway Library; *BMSJ* 37 (1847–48): 405, 506–7.

74. Hunt, *Glances and Glimpses*, p. 266.

75. Harvard University, Faculty of Medicine, Minutes, November 23, 1850, Countway Library. Ware's affirmative vote seems curious in view of his lecture three weeks previously opposing the entrance of women to the medical profession. On the other hand, Ware was one of the two professors (Channing the other) who voted against rescinding admission of the three black students.

76. Harvard College, President and Fellows, November 30, 1850, Harvard Medical School, Dean's Office Files, 1839–1900, Box 3, Countway Library; Oliver Wendell Holmes to Harriot Kezia Hunt, December 5, 1850, in Hunt, *Glances and Glimpses*, p. 268.

77. Blackwell, *Pioneering Work*, p. 95.

78. "Females Attending Medical Lectures," *BMSJ* 37 (1847): 405.

79. A newspaper report quoting the student resolutions was reprinted in Hunt's autobiography, *Glances and Glimpses*, p. 270. This seems to be the only record of the resolutions.

80. Harvard University, Faculty of Medicine, Minutes, December 12, December 13, 1850, Countway Library.

81. Beecher and Altschule, *Medicine at Harvard*, pp. 461–74; Nora N. Nercessian, *Worthy of the Honor: A Brief History of Women at Harvard Medical School* (n.p.: President and Fellows of Harvard College, 1995).

82. Agnes C. Vietor, *A Woman's Quest: The Life of Marie E. Zakrzewska, M.D.* (New York: D. Appleton, 1924), is based on autobiographical notes and correspondence. For Zakrzewska and for the New England Hospital for Women and Children, see also *Notable American Women*, 3:702–4; Virginia G. Drachman, *Hospital with a Heart* (Ithaca: Cornell University Press, 1984); Mary Roth Walsh, *"Doctors Wanted: No Women Need Apply": Sexual Barriers in the Medical Profession, 1835–1975* (New Haven: Yale University Press, 1977); Morantz-Sanchez, *Sympathy and Science*.

83. An exception was Horatio Storer, who was the resident surgeon in the early years of the hospital because there were no women in Boston adequately trained in surgery. Storer resigned in 1866 after refusing to accept supervision by the trustees. His successor was a woman.

84. Many of the men who favored women's rights, including women's right to medical education and professional status, were also prominent in the antislavery movement, most

notably William Lloyd Garrison, Theodore Parker, Frederick W. G. May, and Samuel Sewell. Two of Channing's nephews, Dr. William F. Channing and the Reverend William H. Channing, were abolitionists as well as advocates of women's rights. They also supported Zakrzewska in the early years of her career. The three Channings have been confused in some of the literature describing Zakrzewska's career, including the autobiography edited by Agnes Vietor. See *Woman's Quest*, pp. 185, 244.

85. Vietor, *Woman's Quest*, p. 277; New England Hospital for Women and Children, *Annual Reports* (Boston: Prentiss & Deland, 1866, 1870).

86. According to Zakrzewska, John Ware did not support the general concept of women doctors but he viewed her and her colleagues as exceptions. He laughed heartily when she "told him that the exceptions would multiply by the hundreds." Vietor, *Woman's Quest*, p. 254.

87. A Committee of the Board of Directors, *History and Description of the New England Hospital for Women and Children, Codman Avenue, Boston Highlands* (Boston: n.p., 1899), p. 10.

88. Vietor, *Woman's Quest*, p. 332.

89. For an overview of health reform, see Martha H. Verbrugge, *Able-Bodied Womanhood: Personal Health and Social Change in Nineteenth-Century Boston* (New York: Oxford University Press, 1988), Chapter 3; Regina Markell Morantz, "Making Women Modern: Middle-Class Women and Health Reform in Nineteenth-Century America," in Leavitt, *Women and Health in America*, pp. 346–58.

90. Ladies Physiological Institute, Secretary's Reports, 1850–1859, Schlesinger Library, Radcliffe Institute for Advanced Study, Harvard University.

Notes to Chapter 13

1. Joseph Channing [either an error in transcription or mistranslation of Giovanni], June 10, 1853, Concord Vital Records, transcript card, Concord Free Public Library, Special Collections. He was named Giovanni in remembrance of Margaret Fuller's husband, the Marchese d'Ossoli, who drowned off Fire Island along with Margaret and their son while returning from Italy in 1850. The child was always called Eugene, the name of one of Ellen's brothers. At the request of Ralph Waldo Emerson, Ellery and Henry David Thoreau went to Long Island to search for any of Margaret's possessions that had washed ashore. McGill, *Channing of Concord*, p. 105; Baker, *Emerson among the Eccentrics*, pp. 313–14.

2. Ellery Channing II, Journal, July 24, 1853, b MS Am800.6, Houghton Library, Harvard University.

3. WC to Mary Higginson, October 3, 4, 5, 1853; Ellen Kilshaw Fuller Channing to T. W. Higginson, October 4, 1853, CF Papers.

4. Ellen Kilshaw Fuller Channing to Thomas Wentworth Higginson, [November 1853], CF Papers.

5. Ellen Kilshaw Fuller Channing to Thomas Wentworth Higginson, [November 1853]; T. W. Higginson, Memorandum, November 14, 1853; WC to Mary Higginson, November 14, 1853; T. W. Higginson to Mary Higginson, [November 15, 1853]; WC to Mary Higginson, November 16, 1853; T. W. Higginson to WC, November 18, [1853], CF Papers.

6. WC to Mary Higginson, October 3, 1853, CF Papers.

7. Ellery was not neglected by his friends in Concord. He dined frequently at the Thoreau home and with the Emersons and was received by other neighbors when he chose to

accept their invitations. At the end of his life he lived with Franklin Sanborn, another Concord neighbor, and Sanborn's wife.

8. WC to Mary Higginson, October 3 and 4, 1853; WC to Lucy Russel, November 14/15, 1853; T. W. Higginson to Louisa Higginson, November 18, 1853, CF Papers II; Susan Higginson to Mary White Foote, December 25, 1853, in *Mary Louisa Higginson, Life & Letters, 1832–1856*, ed. Amy W. Cabot and Elizabeth Hamlen, 2:114 (typescript in CF Papers). This Susan Higginson is a daughter of Susan and Francis Channing and the wife of Francis Higginson.

9. Ellen reported that Ellery was "driven by the Furies" and seemed "to hate & loathe me so that he can hardly bear to be in the room with me." She feared that if they separated he would have no one to talk to, no one to unburden himself to, and would be unable to release his morbid thoughts. Ellen to T. W. Higginson, [November 1853], CF Papers.

10. WC to Mary Higginson, October 4, 1853, CF Papers.

11. WC to Mary Higginson, December 10, 1853; WC to Ellery Channing (written by T. W. Higginson), December 13, 1853, CF Papers.

12. "To the Editor," *BMSJ* 49 (1853–54): 330.

13. Ellen Kilshaw Fuller Channing to Mary Higginson, June 25, 1854, CF Papers.

14. WC to the President & Fellows of Harvard College, September 4, 1854, Harvard College Papers, vol. 21, 2d series; President Walker to Walter Channing, M.D., September 18, 1854, Presidents' Papers, Harvard University Archives; WC to Dr. C. E. Ware, corresponding secretary of the Massachusetts Medical Society, September 4, 1854, Countway Library; WC resignation, September 4, 1854, from records of the American Academy as transmitted by Alexandra Olson to author.

15. WC, To the Editors, October 6, 1854, *BMSJ* 51 (1854–55): 226.

16. The trustees of the Boston Lying-in Hospital on Washington Street decided to relocate because the original building was badly in need of repair. The new hospital on Springfield Street was larger, more elaborate, and more costly than its predecessor. It did not attract the increased number of patients that had been anticipated, indicating—among other things—that women continued to prefer home deliveries. After two years of serious deficits, the hospital was closed. It reopened again in 1873 on McLean Street, close to the Massachusetts General Hospital and the medical school. See Irving, *Safe Deliverance*, pp. 120–28. See WC, Book Review, *The Principles and Practice of Obstetrics. By Gunning S. Bedford*, in *BMSJ* 66 (1862): 295–97, for WC's criticisms of the hospital.

17. WC, *Physician's Vacation*.

18. WC to T. W. Higginson, n.d., CF Papers II; WC to Lucy Russel, July 21, 1856, CF Papers; WC to Richard Henry Dana, August 5, 1856, Dana Family Papers, MHS; WC to Lucy Russel, November 29, 1856, CF Papers.

19. [Anon.], "A Physician's Vacation; or, a Summer in Europe," *North American Review* 84 (1857): 265–66.

20. See note in WC, "The Bed Case," *BMSJ* 63 (1860): 162; [WC], "Fragment of a Medical Autobiography," *BMSJ* 71 (1865): 351–58. There are also manuscript portions of an autobiography in the Channing Papers but no indication of how a book might have been structured.

21. [WC], "Fragment of a Medical Autobiography," *BMSJ* 71 (1865): 350–58. The article was unsigned but the author is unmistakable.

22. WC, "Smallpox," *BMSJ* 62 (1860): 89–95. Although Benjamin Waterhouse had been the first to successfully vaccinate in the United States, Channing remained faithful to

Jackson, who had hoped to claim that honor (see Chapter 3). From 1811 to 1837, when vaccination was compulsory in Boston, the death rate per 100,000 was 2.7. From 1837 to 1855 vaccination was entirely voluntary. After 1855 vaccination was required but enforcement was largely neglected. The death rate was 52.1 per 100,000 from 1855 to 1872, which shows the effect of no requirement after 1837 and unenforced vaccination after 1855. Jonathan E. Henry, "Experience in Massachusetts and a Few Other Places with Smallpox Vaccination," *BMSJ* 185 (1921): 221–28.

23. WC, "Spiritualism," *BMSJ* 56 (1857): 333–38; WC, "Death after Taking Laudanum—Poisoning by Aconite, by Alleged Spiritual Communication," *BMSJ* 56 (1857): 449–56.

24. WC, "Cases and Notes," *BMSJ* 56 (1857): 169–74, 193–98, quotations pp. 195, 171.

25. WC, "The Bed Case," *BMSJ* 63 (1860): 72–80, 92–99, 112–19, 134–42, 152–63. Also published as *Bed Case: Its History and Treatment* (Boston: Ticknor and Fields, 1860).

26. WC, "The Bed Case," *BMSJ* 63 (1860): 138.

27. WC, "Cases from My Notebook," *BMSJ* 62 (1860): 517–24.

28. See Carroll Smith-Rosenberg and Charles E. Rosenberg, "The Female Animal: Medical and Biological Views on Woman and Her Role in Nineteenth-Century America," in Leavitt, *Women and Health in America*, pp. 111–30; originally published in the *Journal of American History* 60 (September 1973): 332–56.

29. See Smith-Rosenberg, "The Hysterical Woman: Sex Roles and Role Conflict in Nineteenth-Century America," in her *Disorderly Conduct*, pp. 197–216; and Ann Douglas Wood, " 'The Fashionable Diseases': Women's Complaints and Their Treatment in Nineteenth-Century America," in Leavitt, *Women and Health in America*, pp. 222–38; originally published in the *Journal of Interdisciplinary History* 4 (1973): 25–52.

30. WC to Mary [Molly] Higginson, October 5, 1858, CF Papers II. Charles Trueworth Hildreth died in 1845 at the age of forty-five. He had been admitted to the Massachusetts Medical Society in 1823. Massachusetts Medical Society, *Catalogue of the Honorary and Past and Present Fellows, 1781–1931* (Boston: Massachusetts Medical Society, 1931), p. 118.

31. William Wellington, *Biographical Sketches of the Obstetrical Society of Boston* (Boston: David Clapp & Son, 1881), p. 62.

32. Docket no. 41930, Elizabeth F. Hildreth, Will, 1858, Suffolk County Probate Records.

33. WC to Mary [Molly] Higginson, October 18, 1858, CF Papers II.

34. "Massachusetts Benevolent Medical Association," *BMSJ* 59 (1858): 304–5.

35. Schedule of personal and real property belonging to Dr. Walter Channing, January 1, 1869, WC Papers III.

36. WC, Retrospectus, WC Papers II; Irving, *Safe Deliverance*, p. 103.

37. Schedule of personal and real property. His total wealth was estimated on January 1, 1869, as $102,430. Channing thought some of the figures were low.

38. "Annual Meeting of the Massachusetts Medical Society," *BMSJ* 60 (1859): 365–67, quotation p. 367. *Gualtheria procumbens* is creeping wintergreen (partridge berry) and is the basis for medicinal wintergreen. One of its properties is methyl salicylate. My thanks to Kristina Jones for her help.

39. "Annual Meeting of the Massachusetts Medical Society," *BMSJ* 62 (1860): 387–90, quotation p. 390.

40. WC to Mary Higginson, April 1860, WC Papers III; "Election of Dr. Channing to

the Obstetrical Society of London," *BMSJ* 62 (1860): 47. The Obstetrical Society of London held its first meeting in 1858. Radcliffe, *Milestones in Midwifery*, p. 95.

41. Dr. William Read has been credited with stimulating interest in such an organization. The first meeting was convened by him with help from Charles G. Putnam and Charles E. Buckingham. See Cotting, *Historical Sketch of the Obstetrical Society of Boston*. Putnam, a son-in-law of James Jackson, was one of Channing's most trusted colleagues and had been a consultant at the Boston Lying-in Hospital. Buckingham succeeded David Humphreys Storer as Professor of Obstetrics at Harvard.

42. "[A]lthough we have not the prodigious advantages afforded by an enormous population as in London, nor the opportunities to be obtained from special hospitals like most foreign societies," it was the founders' hope that "the efforts of a comparatively small but united body of intelligent members may furnish satisfactory results." Obstetrical Society of Boston, Records, December 7, 1860, Countway Library.

43. WC to William Cranch Bond Fifield, December 2, 1859, B MS c3.2, Countway Library.

44. Obstetrical Society of Boston, Records, January 5, 1861, Countway Library.

45. Ibid., January 12, 1861.

46. Ibid., March 2, 1861.

47. Cotting, *Historical Sketch of the Obstetrical Society of Boston*, p. 13.

48. In 1694 Frederick Dekkers of Leiden first detected albumen in urine by boiling it with acetic acid. John C. Lever, of Guy's Hospital, London, is credited with publishing in 1843 the first findings of albuminous urine in connection with puerperal convulsions. Garrison, *Introduction to the History of Medicine*, pp. 271, 605.

49. Cotting, *Historical Sketch of the Obstetrical Society of Boston*, pp. 13–20, 26.

50. The Obstetrical Society of Boston is still in existence. It meets monthly from October to April and has a membership of about 160, plus associate members. I am grateful to Dr. Jerome Federschneider for information about present-day activities of the society.

51. Cotting, *Historical Sketch of the Obstetrical Society of Boston*, pp. 30–34.

52. Rosemary Stevens, *American Medicine and the Public Interest*, 2d ed. (Berkeley: University of California Press, 1998), pp. 202–4.

53. Ibid., pp. 34–54.

54. "List of Fellows, since the Institution of the Society," *Transactions of the Edinburgh Obstetrical Society* 1 (1868–69): vii–viii. Charles D. Meigs and Dr. Storer were named Fellows at the same time. That was most likely Horatio Storer and not his father. See Dyer, *Champion of Women and the Unborn*, p. 267.

55. For Storer's view, see Frederick N. Dyer, "Autobiographical Letter from Horatio Robinson Storer, M.D., to His Son, Malcolm Storer, M.D., Discussing the 'History of Gynecological Teaching.' "

56. Channing did report one severe negative reaction to sulphuric ether. "Its effects were unlike any I have observed during or after inhaling ether." Fortunately, he was able to restore breathing. WC, "On Some Diseases of the Female Urethra," *BMSJ* 54 (1856): 89–96; published also as a separate pamphlet, *On Some Diseases of the Female Urethra* (Boston: Press of the Boston Medical and Surgical Journal, 1856).

57. WC, Miscellaneous notes, WC Papers II.

58. M. V. Hecker to WC, April 3, 1856, WC Papers II.

59. WC, "A Case from my Note-Book," *BMSJ* 67 (1862): 29–31.

60. WC, *On Some Diseases of the Female Urethra*, pp. 11–12; WC, "Notes of Cases of

Recent and Chronic Inversio Uteri," *BMSJ* 60 (1859): 229–34; WC, "Sketches in Midwifery Practice," *BMSJ* 57 (1857): 229–36; WC, "Cases," *BMSJ* 54 (1856): 389–95, 431–36.

61. WC, *On Some Diseases of the Female Urethra*.

62. *Transactions of the American Medical Association* 2 (1849): 234; Deborah Kuhn Mc-Gregor, *From Midwives to Medicine* (New Brunswick: Rutgers University Press, 1998), esp. p. 152; Donegan, *Women and Men Midwives*, pp. 156–57.

63. WC, "Inversion of the Womb," *BMSJ* 60 (1859): 547–49.

64. WC, "Retention of a Portion of the Placenta," *BMSJ* 67 (1862): 149–55.

65. WC, "Painless Delivery, Hæmorrhage, Turning, Recovery," *BMSJ* 71 (1864): 229–32.

66. Massachusetts Medical Society, Records of the Society, typescript, May 29, 1866, Countway Library; WC, "Asiatic Cholera," manuscript, WC Papers II.

67. See, for example, Jacob Bigelow, "Whether Cholera Is Contagious," *BMSJ* 74 (1866): 89–92; H. W. King, "Is Asiatic Cholera Contagious?" *BMSJ* 74 (1866): 248–252; Rosenberg, *Cholera Years*, pp. 175–225.

68. Ellen Kilshaw Fuller Channing to Thomas Wentworth Higginson, [August or September 1855], CF Papers.

69. Ibid. In her letter to Higginson, Ellen incorporated some of the language from her correspondence with Ellery in an attempt to explain how and why she had decided to renew their relationship.

70. Barbara Channing to Lucy Russel, July 20, 1856, CF Papers.

71. Barbara Channing to Lucy Russel, March 28, 185[6], CF Papers.

72. Barbara Channing to Mary Higginson, [September 22, 1856], MS Am 1611, Channing Family Letters, Houghton Library, Harvard University.

73. Barbara Channing to Mary Higginson, [September 25, 1856], typescript, CF Papers. Personal conversation with staff at Mt. Auburn Cemetery, April 26, 2000. Among those who most suffered from Ellen's death was her mother, Margaret Crane Fuller, who outlived both of her daughters.

74. T. W. Higginson to Richard F. Fuller, November 18, 1856; Fuller to Higginson, November 28, 1856; Higginson to Fuller, November 29, 1856, CF Papers.

75. Edward Channing, "Recollections of a Hitherto Truthful Man," pp. 7–8. The child's birth was registered in Abington. At that time, he was named Henry F. Channing. Massachusetts Births, 1856, vol. 106, p. 359, Massachusetts State Archives, Boston.

76. WC to Mary Higginson, [1856?] and April 1860, WC Papers III.

77. WC to Mary [Molly] Higginson, n.d. and April 1860, WC Papers III.

78. WC to Mary Higginson, n.d., WC Papers III.

79. WC to Mary [Molly] Higginson, April 1860, WC Papers III.

80. McGill, *Channing of Concord*, p. 156.

81. According to McGill, *Channing of Concord*, pp. 153–61, in 1865 Ellery sold the house on Main Street where he had lived so unhappily with Ellen and moved to a smaller house on Middle Street, purchased for him by his father. This may not be accurate. Ellery received $2500 for the house on Main Street. The new house was purchased by him for $2200. Thus, there seems to be no reason for his father to have provided the money. McGill's information was based on an interview in 1932 with a granddaughter-in-law of Ellery's. For both deeds, see Middlesex County Registry of Deeds, vol. 959, pp. 101–2; vol. 962, pp. 126–27.

82. Mason, *Re-Union of the Sons and Daughters of Newport, R.I.*, p. 92.

83. WC to Barbara [Babby] Channing, August 25, 1859, b MS Am 1610, Houghton Library, Harvard University.

84. Edward Channing, "Recollections of a Hitherto Truthful Man," p. 9.

85. WC to Mary Higginson, January 1, 1865, CF Papers.

86. Suffolk County Registry of Deeds, vol. 888, p. 85.

87. James W. Spring, *Boston and the Parker House* (Boston: J. R. Whipple, 1927); George Gibbs Channing to WC, October 24, 1872, CF Papers. I am grateful to Mr. Jerry Dunfey and Mr. Mike Knapp for guiding me to information about the Parker House, known today as the Omni Parker House.

88. Norfolk County Registry of Deeds, book 335, p. 304. Channing paid $15,000 for land and buildings on Dorchester Avenue (formerly Turnpike). Channing resold the property to its original owner, John J. May, when he moved to Brookline. Suffolk County Registry of Deeds, April 29, 1871, book 1046, p. 103.

89. Edward Channing, "Recollections of a Hitherto Truthful Man," p. 10; WC to Walter Jr., May 5, 1866, WC Papers III.

90. WC to Martha Stearns, June 3, 1866, WC Papers III.

91. "Reports of Medical Societies, Norfolk District Medical Society," *BMSJ* 76 (1867): 308, 513–14, 530.

92. For the death of Edward, see Barbara Channing to Lucy Russel, February 12, [1856], CF Papers; Richard H. Dana, Jr., *The Journal of Richard Henry Dana, Jr.*, 2:684–85. Walter visited Edward on the day of his death but did not remain for the end.

93. WC, Notes for a paper on dysmenorrhea, WC Papers II. This was probably the paper given to the Norfolk District Medical Society; see note 91.

94. WC to Walter Channing, Jr., October 31, [18]68, WC Papers III.

95. WC to George G. Channing, October 5, 1868, WC Papers II.

96. After his return from Europe, Walter Jr. decided to specialize in mental illness, eventually becoming one of the major alienists (as psychiatrists were called) in New England. One wonders if his interest in mental illness was due at least in part to his father's strange behavior.

97. Walter Channing to Mrs. Mary C. E. Barnard, April 15, 1868, WC Papers II.

98. The annexation of Dorchester by Boston became official on January 4, 1870. Samuel J. Barrows, "Dorchester in the Last Hundred Years," in Winsor, *Memorial History of Boston*, 3:599–600.

99. "Married at Indiana Place Chapel, Follen Cabot of Brookline, 25 years, son of Frederic Cabot to Caroline Sturgis Channing, aged 19; Married Sept. 6, 1870 at the house of Dr. Walter Channing, Dorchester (Boston) Thatcher Loring, aged 26 to Margaret Fuller Channing, daughter of W. Ellery Channing of Concord and Ellen Fuller, aged 26." Church of the Disciples, Records, Andover-Harvard Theological Library, Harvard University. For purchase of the Brookline house, Norfolk County Registry of Deeds, Abbot & ux. to Channing, July 8, 1870, book 395, p. 66; Williams to Loring, June 26, 1876, book 481, p. 1. Channing erased the debt by deducting the amount from her share of his estate. Norfolk County, Probate Court no. 3446, first codicil.

100. In the early part of the twentieth century, the High Street Hill area where Channing had lived became known as Pill Hill because so many doctors had their homes there. It is presently a National Register District and a Local Historic District. Greer Hardwicke and Roger Reed, *Images of America, Brookline* (Charleston, S.C.: Arcadia Publishing, 1998), p. 51.

101. WC to Walter Channing, Jr., May 13, 1866, WC Papers III. The full sentence read "for my children are my chief joy" but, since he was telling Walter that it gave pleasure to be able to serve him, it is safe to infer that Channing was referring to his grandchildren.

102. *Brookline, Jamaica Plain and West Roxbury Directory for 1871* (Boston: Dean, Dudley, 1871); Directory of Brookline, 1873–74; Brookline Atlas, 1872; telephone conversation with Brookline Public Library; Edward Channing, "Recollections of a Hitherto Truthful Man," pp. 9–10. The house Channing rented belonged to Miss Sarah Searle, whose family were close friends of Channing's for more than fifty years.

103. WC to George G. Channing, September 10, 1872, WC Papers II.

104. Norfolk County Probate Court, no. 3445, October 29, 1874. In the court order Channing was declared to be "insane and incapable of taking care of himself," but the term "insane" had a different connotation from today's popular meaning. In the nineteenth century, it was not uncommon for a family to use the probate courts to protect assets when there were indications that an elderly person might do something unwise with the estate. Conversation with Elizabeth Bouvier, Court Archivist, Massachusetts State Archives.

105. Walter Channing, second codicil, October 14, 1870, filed August 4, 1876, Norfolk County Probate Court. At the time of his death, Channing's estate was valued at $92,618. Executor's Inventory, Norfolk County Probate Court, December 13, 1876. Channing's wealth in year 2000 dollars would have been around a million and a half dollars.

106. Elizabeth Parsons Channing, *Autobiography and Diary*, pp. 30, 33.

107. Deaths Reported in the Town of Brookline for the year 1876, vol. 284, p. 215, Massachusetts State Archives.

108. Clarke, *Memorial and Biographical Sketches*, pp. 169–85.

109. WC, "Life and Living," manuscript, WC Papers II.

Selected Bibliography

Adams, Herbert Baxter. *The Life and Writings of Jared Sparks*. 2 vols. 1893; Freeport, N.Y.: Books for Libraries Press, 1970.

Arney, William Ray. *Power and the Profession of Obstetrics*. Chicago: University of Chicago Press, 1982.

Baker, Carlos. *Emerson among the Eccentrics*. New York: Penguin Books, 1996.

Baltzell, E. Digby. *Puritan Boston and Quaker Philadelphia: Two Protestant Ethics and the Spirit of Class Authority and Leadership*. New York: Free Press, 1979.

Bartlett, Josiah. "A Dissertation on the Progress of Medical Science." *Medical Communications and Dissertations of the Massachusetts Medical Society* 2 (1813): 235–70.

Bemis, George. *Report of the Case of John W. Webster*. Boston: C. C. Little and J. Brown, 1850.

Beecher, Henry K., and Mark D. Altschule. *Medicine at Harvard: The First 300 Years*. Hanover, N.H.: University Press of New England, 1977.

Bell, Whitfield J. "Medicine in Boston and Philadelphia: Comparisons and Contrasts, 1750–1820." In Cash et al., *Medicine in Colonial Massachusetts, 1620–1820*.

Bigelow, Jacob. *Self-limited Diseases*. [Boston, 1835].

Blackwell, Elizabeth. *Pioneer Work in Opening the Medical Profession to Women*. London and New York: Longmans, Green, 1895.

Blake, John B. *Public Health in the Town of Boston, 1630–1822*. Cambridge, Mass.: Harvard University Press, 1959.

Blumberg, Mark S. "Medical Society Regulation of Fees in Boston, 1780–1820." *Journal of the History of Medicine and Allied Sciences* 39 (1984): 303–38.

Boller, Paul F., Jr. *American Transcendentalism, 1830–1860*. New York: G. P. Putnam's Sons, 1974.

Bolster, Arthur S., Jr. *James Freeman Clarke: Disciple to Advancing Truth*. Boston: Beacon Press, 1954.

Bowditch, Nathaniel I. *A History of the Massachusetts General Hospital (to August 5, 1871)*. Boston: Printed by the Trustees, 1872.

Bowditch, Vincent. *Life and Correspondence of Henry Ingersoll Bowditch*. 2 vols. Boston: Houghton, Mifflin, 1902.

Bowen, George Lovering. *James Lloyd II, M.D. (1728–1810) and His Family on Lloyd's Neck*. [n.p.]: privately printed, 1988.

Brodie, Janet Farrell. *Contraception and Abortion in Nineteenth-Century America*. Ithaca: Cornell University Press, 1994.

Brown, Arthur Wayne. *William Ellery Channing*. New York: Twayne Publishers, 1961.

Browne, Howard S. "Newport's Revolutionary Physicians." *Newport History* 54 (Winter 1981): 19–24.

Burrage, Walter. *A History of the Massachusetts Medical Society, 1781–1922*. Norwood, Mass.: privately printed, 1923.

Carter, K. Codell, and Barbara R. Carter. *Childbed Fever: A Scientific Biography of Ignaz Semmelweis*. Westport, Conn.: Greenwood Press, 1994.

Cash, Philip. "Setting the Stage: Dr. Benjamin Waterhouse's Reception in Boston, 1782–1788." *Journal of the History of Medicine and Allied Sciences* 47 (1992): 5–28.

Cash, Philip, and Yoshio Higomoto. "Further Information Concerning Dr. Benjamin Waterhouse's Appointment as Harvard's First Professor of Medicine." *Journal of the History of Medicine and Allied Sciences* 49 (1994): 419–28.

Cash, Philip, Eric H. Christianson, and J. Worth Estes, eds. *Medicine in Colonial Massachusetts, 1620–1820*. Boston: Colonial Society of Massachusetts, 1980.

Cassedy, James H. *American Medicine and Statistical Thinking, 1800–1860*. Cambridge, Mass.: Harvard University Press, 1984.

Caton, Donald. *What a Blessing She Had Chloroform: The Medical and Social Response to the Pain of Childbirth from 1800 to the Present*. New Haven: Yale University Press, 1999.

Cayleff, Susan E. *Wash and Be Healed: The Water-Cure Movement and Women's Health*. Philadelphia: Temple University Press, 1987.

Chadwick, John White. *William Ellery Channing, Minister of Religion*. Boston: Houghton, Mifflin, 1903.

Channing, Edward. "Recollections of a Hitherto Truthful Man," typescript. Courtesy of Willard P. Fuller, Jr.

Channing, Elizabeth Parsons. *Autobiography and Diary*. Boston: American Unitarian Association, 1907.

Channing, George G. *Early Recollections of Newport, R.I., from the Years 1793 to 1811*. Newport, R.I.: A. J. Ward; Charles E. Hammett, Jr., 1868.

Channing, William Henry. *Life of William Ellery Channing, D.D.* Boston: American Unitarian Association, 1880.

Churchill, Fleetwood. *On the Theory and Practice of Midwifery*. Philadelphia: Blanchard and Lea, 1851.

Clark, George Faber. *History of the Temperance Reform in Massachusetts, 1813–1883*. Boston: Clark & Carruth, 1888.

Clarke, James Freeman. *Autobiography, Diary and Correspondence*. Ed. Edward Everett Hale. Boston: Houghton, Mifflin, 1891.

———. *Memorial and Biographical Sketches*. Boston: Houghton, Osgood, 1878.

Comrie, John D. *History of Scottish Medicine*, 2d ed. 2 vols. London: Wellcome Historical Medical Museum, 1932.

Corner, George W. *Two Centuries of Medicine: A History of the School of Medicine, University of Pennsylvania*. Philadelphia: J. B. Lippincott, 1965.

Cott, Nancy F. *The Bonds of Womanhood*. New Haven: Yale University Press, 1977.

Cotting, Benjamin E. *Historical Sketch of the Obstetrical Society of Boston*. Boston: David Clapp, 1881.

Crane, Elaine Forman. *A Dependent People: Newport, Rhode Island in the Revolutionary Era*. New York: Fordham University Press, 1985.

Curti, Merle Eugene. *The American Peace Crusade, 1815–1860*. 1929. Reprint, New York: Octagon Books, 1965.

Cutter, Irving S., and Henry R. Viets. *A Short History of Midwifery*. Philadelphia: W. B. Saunders, 1964.

Dana, Richard Henry, Jr. *The Journal of Richard Henry Dana, Jr.* 3 vols. Ed. Robert F. Lucid. Cambridge, Mass.: Belknap Press of Harvard University Press, 1968.

Dearborn, Nathaniel. *Boston Notions*. Boston: Printed for Nathaniel Dearborn, 1848.

DeBenedetti, Charles. *The Peace Reform in American History*. Bloomington: Indiana University Press, 1980.

Dedmond, Francis B. "The Selected Letters of William Ellery Channing the Younger (Part One)." In *Studies in the American Renaissance*. Ed. Joel Myerson. Charlottesville: University Press of Virginia, 1989, pp. 115–218.

Degler, Carl N. *At Odds: Women and the Family in America from the Revolution to the Present*. Oxford: Oxford University Press, 1981.

De Ville, Kenneth Allen. *Medical Malpractice in Nineteenth-Century America: Origins and Legacy*. New York: New York University Press, 1990.

Dewees, William P. *A Compendious System of Midwifery*. Philadelphia: H. C. Carey and I. Lea, 1824.

Donegan, Jane B. *Women and Men Midwives: Medicine, Morality and Misogyny in Early America*. Westport, Conn.: Greenwood Press, 1978.

Drachman, Virginia G. *Hospital with a Heart*. Ithaca: Cornell University Press, 1984.

———. "The Loomis Trial: Social Mores and Obstetrics in the Mid-Nineteenth Century." In Leavitt, *Women and Health in America*, pp. 166–74.

Duffy, John. *From Humors to Medical Science*, 2d ed. Urbana: University of Illinois Press, 1993.

———. *The Healers: A History of American Medicine*. Urbana: University of Illinois Press, 1979.

———. *The Sanitarians*. Urbana: University of Illinois Press, 1990.

Dye, Nancy Schrom. "History of Childbirth in America." *Signs* 6 (1980–81): 97–108.

Dyer, Frederick N. *Champion of Women and the Unborn, Horatio Robinson Storer, M.D.* Canton, Mass.: Science History Publications, 1999.

———. "Autobiographical Letter from Horatio Robinson Storer, M.D., to His Son, Malcolm Storer, M.D., Discussing the 'History of Gynecological Teaching.' " *Journal of the History of Medicine and Allied Sciences* 54 (1999): 439–58.

Eaton, Leonard. *New England Hospitals, 1790–1833*. Ann Arbor: University of Michigan Press, 1957.

Edelstein, Tilden G. *Strange Enthusiasm: A Life of Thomas Wentworth Higginson*. New Haven: Yale University Press, 1968.

Ellis, George E. "Memoir of Jacob Bigelow, M.D., LL.D." Massachusetts Historical Society, *Proceedings* 17 (1879–80): 383–467.

Flagg, Jared B. *The Life and Letters of Washington Allston, with Reproductions from Allston's Pictures*. New York: C. Scribner's Sons, 1892.

Forbes, Thomas Rogers. *The Midwife and the Witch*. New Haven: Yale University Press, 1966.

Fowler, William M., Jr. *William Ellery: A Rhode Island Politico and Lord of Admiralty*. Metuchen, N.J.: Scarecrow Press, 1973.

Garland, Joseph. "The New England Journal of Medicine, 1812–1968." *Journal of the History of Medicine and Allied Sciences* 24 (1969): 25–38.

Garrison, Fielding H. *An Introduction to the History of Medicine*, 4th ed. Philadelphia: W. B. Saunders Co., 1929.

Gevitz, Norman, ed. *Other Healers: Unorthodox Medicine in America.* Baltimore: Johns Hopkins University Press, 1988.

Gordon, Alexander. *A Treatise on the Epidemic Puerperal Fever of Aberdeen.* London: printed for G. G. and J. Robinson, 1795.

Gordon, Linda. *Woman's Body, Woman's Right.* New York: Grossman Publishers, 1976.

Grant, Alexander. *The Story of the University of Edinburgh during its First Three Hundred Years.* 2 vols. London: Longmans, Green, 1884.

Green, Samuel A. *History of Medicine in Massachusetts: A Centennial Address delivered before the Massachusetts Medical Society at Cambridge, June 7, 1881.* Boston: A. Williams, 1881.

Greenleaf, Robert W. *An Historical Report of the Boston Dispensary for One Hundred and One Years, 1796–1897.* Brookline, Mass.: Riverdale Press, 1898.

Gregory, Samuel. *Man-Midwifery Exposed and Corrected.* Boston: George Gregory, 1848.

Haller, John S., Jr. *American Medicine in Transition, 1840–1910.* Urbana: University of Illinois Press, 1981.

Hallett, Benjamin F. *A Full Report of the Trial of Ephraim K. Avery, charged with the murder of Sarah M. Cornell, before the Supreme Court of Rhode Island, at a special term in Newport, held in May 1833; with the Arguments of Counsel.* Boston: Daily Commercial Gazette and Boston Daily Advocate, 1833.

Hampel, Robert L. *Temperance and Prohibition in Massachusetts, 1813–1852.* Ann Arbor: UMI Research, 1982.

Handlin, Lilian. *George Bancroft: The Intellectual as Democrat.* New York: Harper & Row, 1984.

Handlin, Oscar. *Boston's Immigrants.* Cambridge, Mass.: Belknap Press of Harvard University Press, 1959.

Harrington, Thomas F. *The Harvard Medical School: A History, Narrative and Documentary, 1782–1905.* 3 vols. New York: Lewis Publishers, 1905.

Hodge, Hugh L. *On the Non-contagious Character of Puerperal Fever: An Introductory Lecture, 11 October, 1852.* Philadelphia: T. K. and P. G. Collins, 1852.

Hoffert, Sylvia D. *Private Matters: American Attitudes toward Childbearing and Infant Nurture in the Urban North, 1800–1860.* Urbana: University of Illinois Press, 1989.

Holmes, Oliver Wendell. *Puerperal Fever as a Private Pestilence.* Boston: Ticknor and Fields, 1855.

Holt, Anna C. "A Medical Student in Boston, 1825–26." *Harvard Library Bulletin* 6 (1952): 176–92, 358–75.

Howe, Daniel Walker. *The Unitarian Conscience: Harvard Moral Philosophy, 1805–1861.* Cambridge, Mass.: Harvard University Press, 1970.

Howe, Julia Ward. *Reminiscences, 1819–1899.* Boston: Houghton Mifflin, 1899.

Howe, M. A. DeWolfe. *The Humane Society of the Commonwealth of Massachusetts: An Historical Review, 1785–1916.* Boston: printed for the Humane Society, 1918.

Hunt, Harriot Kezia. *Glances and Glimpses; or, Fifty Years Social, Including Twenty Years Professional Life.* Boston: John P. Jewett, 1856.

Hunter, Doreen M. *Richard Henry Dana, Sr.* Boston: Twayne Publishers, 1987.

Hutchison, William R. *The Transcendentalist Ministers: Church Reform in the New England Renaissance.* 1959; Hamden, Conn.: Shoe String Press, 1972.

Irving, Frederick C. *Safe Deliverance.* Boston: Houghton Mifflin, 1942.

Johansen, Shawn. "Before the Waiting Room: Northern Middle-Class Pregnancy and Birth in Antebellum America." *Gender and History* 7 (July 1995): 183–200.

Kass, Amalie M. "'Called to her at three o'clock AM': Obstetrical Practice in Physician Case Notes." *Journal of the History of Medicine and Allied Sciences* 50 (1995): 194–229.

———. "'My brother preaches, I practice': Walter Channing, M.D., Antebellum Obstetrician." *Massachusetts Historical Review* 1 (1999): 78–94.

———. "The Obstetrical Casebook of Walter Channing, 1811–1822." *Bulletin of the History of Medicine* 67 (1993): 494–523.

Kasserman, David Richard. *Fall River Outrage: Life, Murder, and Justice in Early Industrial New England.* Philadelphia: University of Pennsylvania Press, 1986.

Kaufman, Martin. *American Medical Education: The Formative Years, 1765–1910.* Westport, Conn.: Greenwood Press, 1976.

Kelly, Howard A. *Cyclopedia of Medical Biography.* 2 vols. Philadelphia: W. B. Saunders, 1912.

Kelly, Howard A., and Walter L. Burrage. *American Medical Biography.* Baltimore: Norman Remington Co., 1920.

King, Lester S. *Transformations in American Medicine, from Benjamin Rush to William Osler.* Baltimore: Johns Hopkins University Press, 1991.

Kirker, Harold, and James Kirker. *Bulfinch's Boston, 1787–1817.* New York: Oxford University Press, 1967.

Klepp, Susan E. "Revolutionary Bodies: Women and the Fertility Transition in the Mid-Atlantic Region, 1760–1820." *Journal of American History* 85 (1998): 910–45.

Leavitt, Judith Walzer. *Brought to Bed: Childbearing in America, 1750–1950.* New York: Oxford University Press, 1986.

———, ed. *Women and Health in America.* Madison: University of Wisconsin Press, 1984.

———, ed. *Women and Health in America,* 2d ed. Madison: University of Wisconsin Press, 1999.

Leavitt, Judith Walzer, and Ronald L. Numbers. *Sickness and Health in America.* Madison: University of Wisconsin Press, 1985.

Litoff, Judith Barrett. *American Midwives, 1860 to the Present.* Westport, Conn.: Greenwood Press, 1978.

Loudon, Irvine. *Childbed Fever: A Documentary History.* New York: Garland Publishing, 1995.

———. "The Making of Man-Midwifery, Essay Review." *Bulletin of the History of Medicine* 70 (1996): 507–15.

Manzer, Edna. "Woman's Doctors: The Development of Obstetrics and Gynecology in Boston, 1860–1930." Ph.D. diss., Indiana University, 1979.

Marland, Hilary, ed. *The Art of Midwifery: Early Modern Midwives in Europe.* London and New York: Routledge, 1993.

Mason, George Champlin. *Newport Illustrated.* New York: D. Appleton, 1854.

———. *Re-Union of the Sons and Daughters of Newport, R.I., August 23, 1859.* Newport, R.I.: Fred. A. Pratt, 1859.

Massachusetts Temperance Society. *The Physiological Effects of Alcoholic Drinks, with Documents and Records of the Massachusetts Temperance Society.* Boston: Massachusetts Temperance Society, 1848.

McColgan, Daniel T. *Joseph Tuckerman: Pioneer in American Social Work.* Washington, D.C.: Catholic University of America Press, 1940.

McGill, Frederick T., Jr. *Channing of Concord: A Life of William Ellery Channing II.* New Brunswick: Rutgers University Press, 1967.

McGregor, Deborah Kuhn. *From Midwives to Medicine.* New Brunswick: Rutgers University Press, 1998.

McMillen, Sally G. *Motherhood in the Old South: Pregnancy, Childbirth, and Infant Rearing.* Baton Rouge: Louisiana State University, 1990.

Meigs, Charles D. *Obstetrics: The Science and the Art,* 2d ed. Philadelphia: Blanchard and Lea, 1852.

———. *On the Nature, Signs, and Treatment of Childbed Fevers.* Philadelphia: Blanchard and Lea, 1854.

Mendelsohn, Jack. *Channing the Reluctant Radical.* Boston: Little, Brown, 1971.

Mohr, James C. *Abortion in America.* New York: Oxford University Press, 1978.

———. *Doctors and the Law: Medical Jurisprudence in Nineteenth-Century America.* New York: Oxford University Press, 1993.

Morantz-Sanchez, Regina Markell. *Sympathy and Science: Women Physicians in American Medicine.* New York: Oxford University Press, 1985.

Morison, Samuel Eliot. *Three Centuries of Harvard.* Cambridge, Mass.: Belknap Press of Harvard University Press, 1963.

Nercessian, Nora N. *Worthy of the Honor: A Brief History of Women at Harvard Medical School.* N.p.: President and Fellows of Harvard College, 1995.

Nesson, Fern L. *Great Waters: A History of Boston's Water Supply.* Hanover, N.H.: University Press of New England, 1983.

Norwood, William Frederick. *Medical Education in the United States before the Civil War.* Philadelphia: University of Pennsylvania Press, 1944.

Numbers, Ronald L., ed. *The Education of American Physicians.* Berkeley: University of California Press, 1980.

O'Connor, Thomas H. *Bibles, Brahmins, and Bosses: A Short History of Boston,* 3d ed. Boston: Trustees of the Public Library, 1991.

Pease, William H., and Jane H. Pease. *The Web of Progress.* Athens: University of Georgia Press, 1991.

Percival, Thomas. *Percival's Medical Ethics.* Ed. Chauncey D. Leake. Baltimore: Williams and Wilkins [c. 1927].

Pernick, Martin S. *A Calculus of Suffering: Pain, Professionalism, and Anesthesia in Nineteenth-Century America.* New York: Columbia University Press, 1985.

Pessen, Edward. *Riches, Class, and Power: America before the Civil War.* New Brunswick: Transaction Publishers, 1990.

Putnam, James Jackson. *A Memoir of Dr. James Jackson.* Boston: Houghton, Mifflin, 1905.

Radcliffe, Walter. *Milestones in Midwifery.* Bristol, Eng.: John Wright and Sons, 1967.

Reagan, Leslie J. *When Abortion Was a Crime: Women, Medicine, and Law in the United States.* Berkeley: University of California Press, 1997.

Rey, Roselyne. *The History of Pain.* Trans. Louise Elliott Wallace, J. A. Cadden, and S. W. Cadden. Cambridge, Mass.: Harvard University Press, 1993.

Risse, Guenter B. *Mending Bodies, Saving Souls.* New York: Oxford University Press, 1999.

Rorabaugh, William J. *The Alcoholic Republic: An American Tradition.* New York: Oxford University Press, 1979.

Rose, Anne C. *Transcendentalism as a Social Movement, 1830–1850.* New Haven: Yale University Press, 1981.

Rosenberg, Charles E. *Explaining Epidemics and Other Studies in the History of Medicine.* Cambridge: Cambridge University Press, 1992.

———. *The Care of Strangers: The Rise of America's Hospital System.* New York: Basic Books, 1987.

———. *The Cholera Years.* Chicago and London: University of Chicago Press, 1987.

Rosenkrantz, Barbara Gutmann. *Public Health and the State: Changing Views in Massachusetts, 1842–1936.* Cambridge, Mass.: Harvard University Press, 1972.

Rosner, Lisa. "Thistle on the Delaware: Edinburgh Medical Education and Philadelphia Practice, 1800–1825." *Social Medicine* 5 (1992): 9–42.

Rothman, Daniel J. *The Discovery of the Asylum: Social Order and Disorder in the New Republic.* Boston: Little, Brown, 1971.

Rothstein, William G. *American Medical Schools and the Practice of Medicine: A History.* New York: Oxford University Press, 1987.

———. *American Physicians in the Nineteenth Century: From Sects to Science.* Baltimore: Johns Hopkins University Press, 1972.

Sahli, Nancy Ann. *Elizabeth Blackwell, M.D. (1821–1910).* New York: Arno Press, 1982.

Scholten, Catherine M. " 'On the Importance of the Obstetrick Art': Changing Customs of Childbirth in America, 1760 to 1825." *William and Mary Quarterly,* 3d ser., 34 (1977): 426–45.

Schneider, Eric. *In the Web of Class.* New York: New York University Press, 1992.

Semmelweis, Ignaz. *The Etiology, Concept, and Prophylaxis of Childbed Fever.* Trans. and ed. K. Codell Carter. Madison: University of Wisconsin Press, 1983.

Shattuck, Lemuel. "On the Vital Statistics of Boston." *American Journal of the Medical Sciences,* n.s., 1 (1841): 369–401.

Shryock, Richard H. *Medicine in America: Historical Essays.* Baltimore: Johns Hopkins University Press, 1966.

Simpson, James Y. *Anesthetic Midwifery: Report on its Early History and Progress.* Edinburgh: Sutherland and Knox, 1848.

———. *Answer to the Religious Objections Advanced against the Employment of Anesthetic Agents in Midwifery and Surgery.* Edinburgh: Sutherland and Knox, 1847.

Smith, Dale Cary. "The Emergence of Organized Clinical Instruction in the Nineteenth-Century American Cities of Boston, New York and Philadelphia." Ph.D. diss., University of Minnesota, 1979.

Smith-Rosenberg, Carroll. *Disorderly Conduct.* New York: Alfred A. Knopf, 1985.

Speert, Harold. *Obstetrics and Gynecology in America: A History.* Chicago: American College of Obstetricians and Gynecologists, 1980.

Sprague, Henry H. *A Brief History of the Massachusetts Charitable Fire Society.* Boston: Little, Brown, 1893.

Storer, David Humphreys. *An Address on Medical Jurisprudence delivered before the Fellows of the Massachusetts Medical Society at the annual meeting, May 28, 1851.* Boston: John Wilson and Son, 1851.

———. "Statistics of the Boston Lying-in Hospital." *American Journal of the Medical Sciences,* n.s., 20 (1850): 347–68.

Story, Ronald. *The Forging of an Aristocracy: Harvard and the Boston Upper Class, 1800–1870.* Middletown, Conn.: Wesleyan University Press, 1980.

Sullivan, Robert. *The Disappearance of Dr. Parkman.* Boston: Little, Brown, 1971.

Thacher, James. *American Medical Biography.* Boston: Richardson & Lord and Cotton & Bernard, 1828.

Thoms, Herbert. *Chapters in American Obstetrics,* 2d ed. Springfield, Ill.: Charles C. Thomas, 1961.

Tilton, Eleanor M. *Amiable Autocrat: A Biography of Dr. Oliver Wendell Holmes*. New York: Henry Schuman, 1947.

Tyack, David B. *George Ticknor and the Boston Brahmins*. Cambridge, Mass.: Harvard University Press, 1967.

Tyler, Alice Felt. *Freedom's Crusade*. New York: Harper Torchbooks, 1944.

Tyrrell, Ian R. *Sobering Up: From Temperance to Prohibition in Antebellum America, 1800–1860*. Westport, Conn.: Greenwood Press, 1979.

Ulrich, Laurel Thatcher. *A Midwife's Tale: The Life of Martha Ballard, Based on Her Diary, 1785–1812*. New York: Alfred A. Knopf, 1990.

Verbrugge, Martha H. *Able-Bodied Womanhood: Personal Health and Social Change in Nineteenth-Century Boston*. New York: Oxford University Press, 1988.

Vietor, Agnes C. *A Woman's Quest: The Life of Marie E. Zakrzewska, M.D.* New York: D. Appleton, 1924.

Vogel, Morris J., and Charles E. Rosenberg, eds. *The Therapeutic Revolution: Essays in the Social History of American Medicine*. Philadelphia: University of Pennsylvania Press, 1979.

Wagenknecht, Edward. *Longfellow: A Full-Length Portrait*. New York: Longmans, Green, 1955.

———. *Mrs. Longfellow: Selected Letters and Journals of Fanny Appleton Longfellow (1817–1861)*. New York: Longmans, Green, 1956.

Waite, Frederick C. "The Development of Anatomical Laws in the States of New England." *New England Journal of Medicine* 233 (1945): 716–26.

———. *History of the New England Female Medical College, 1848–1874*. Boston: Boston University School of Medicine, 1950.

Walsh, Mary Roth. *"Doctors Wanted: No Women Need Apply": Sexual Barriers in the Medical Profession, 1835–1975*. New Haven: Yale University Press, 1977.

Walters, Ronald G. *American Reformers*, rev. ed. New York: Hill and Wang, 1998.

Warner, John Harley. *The Therapeutic Perspective*. Cambridge, Mass.: Harvard University Press, 1986.

Warren, Edward. *Life of John Collins Warren with the Autobiography and Journals*. 2 vols. Boston: Ticknor and Fields, 1860.

Wertz , Richard W., and Dorothy C. Wertz. *Lying-In: A History of Childbirth in America*. New York: Free Press, 1977.

Whitehill, Walter Muir. *Boston: A Topographical History*. Cambridge, Mass.: Belknap Press of Harvard University Press, 1963.

Willard, Sidney. *Memories of Youth and Manhood*. 2 vols. Cambridge, Mass.: John Bartlett, 1855.

Williams, Catherine. *Fall River: An Authentic Narrative*. Ed. Patricia Caldwell. New York: Oxford University Press, 1993.

Wilson, Adrian. *The Making of Man-midwifery: Childbirth in England, 1660–1770*. Cambridge, Mass.: Harvard University Press, 1995.

Winsor, Justin, ed. *The Memorial History of Boston*. 4 vols. Boston: James R. Osgood, 1882.

Wolfe, Richard J. *Fallen Idol: W. T. G. Morton and the Introduction of Surgical Anesthesia: A Chronicle of the Ether Controversy*. San Francisco: Norman Publishing, 2000.

Wright, Conrad. *The Liberal Christians: Essays on American Unitarian History*. Boston: Beacon Press, 1970.

Wright, Conrad Edick. *The Transformation of Charity in Postrevolutionary New England*. Boston: Northeastern University Press, 1992.

———, ed. *American Unitarianism*. Boston: Massachusetts Historical Society and Northeastern University Press, 1989.

———, ed. *Massachusetts and the New Nation*. Boston: Massachusetts Historical Society, 1992.

Youngson, A. Y. *The Scientific Revolution in Victorian Medicine*. London: Croom Helm, 1979.

Ziegler, Valarie H. *The Advocates of Peace in Antebellum America*. Bloomington: Indiana University Press, 1992.

Walter Channing Bibliography

Published Books and Pamphlets

An Address on the Prevention of Pauperism. Boston: William D. Ticknor, 1843.

Annual Address Delivered before the Massachusetts Temperance Society, May 29, 1836. Boston: John Ford, 1836.

Bed Case: Its History and Treatment. Boston: Ticknor and Fields, 1860.

A Case of Pericarditis. [Boston: n.p., 1834].

Cases of Inflammation of the Veins with Remarks on the Supposed Identity of Phlebitis and Phlegmasia Dolens. [Boston: n.p., 1830].

The Law of Compensations: A Lecture delivered before the Mechanic Apprentices' Library Association (February 20, 1855). Boston: n.p., 1855.

The Moral Uses of the Study of Natural History, in Introductory Discourse and Lectures Delivered before the American Institute of Instruction in Boston, August, 1835. Boston: Charles Hendee, 1836.

New and Old. Boston: n.p., 1851.

Of the Medical Profession, and of Its Preparation, An Introductory Lecture, Read before the Medical Class of Harvard University, November 5, 1845. Boston: D. Clapp, Jr., 1845.

On Irritable Uterus. [Boston: n.p., 1833 and 1836].

On Some Diseases of the Female Urethra. Boston: Press of the Boston Medical and Surgical Journal, 1856.

Parliamentary Sketches and Water Statistics. Boston: Benjamin H. Greene, 1846.

A Physician's Vacation. Boston: Ticknor and Fields, 1856.

A Plea for Pure Water. Boston: S. N. Dickinson, 1844.

Six Cases of Inhalation of Ether in Labor. Boston: White and Potter, 1847.

Thoughts on the Origin, Nature, Principles and Prospects of the Temperance Reform. Boston: Council of the Massachusetts Temperance Society, 1834.

Thoughts on Peace and War, an Address delivered before the American Peace Society, at its annual meeting, May 27, 1844. Boston: American Peace Society, 1844.

A Treatise on Etherization in Childbirth, illustrated by Five Hundred and Eighty-One Cases. Boston: William D. Ticknor, 1848.

Two Cases of Inhalation of Ether in Instrumental Labor. Boston: n.p., 1847.

Selected Journal Articles and Excerpts

"Address of Dr. Walter Channing, at the Re-Union at Newport, in Behalf of its Returned Sons and Daughters." In George C. Mason, *Re-Union of the Sons and Daughters of Newport, R.I., August 23, 1859*. Pp. 76–77.

"American Medical Association." *BMSJ* 40 (1849): 299–304, 362–64.

"Art. IX,—Histoire de la Médecine." *North American Review* 8 (1818–19): 221–53.

"The Bed Case." *BMSJ* 63 (1860): 72–80, 92–99, 112–19, 134–42, 152–63.

"A Case." *BMSJ* 69 (1863): 329.

"A Case from an Old Common-Place Book." *BMSJ* 67 (1862–63): 212–14.

"A Case from my Note-Book." *BMSJ* 67 (1862): 29–31.

"A Case of Arm Presentation with Remarks." *NEJMS* 11 (1822): 30–37.

"A Case of Inhalation of Ether in Instrumental Labor." *BMSJ* 36 (1847): 313–18.

"Case of Inversio Uteri with Comments." *NEJMS* 11 (1822): 264–69.

"A Case of Rheumatism, with Disease of the Heart." *NEJMS* 14 (1825): 147–51.

"Case of Tumor within the Abdomen." *BMSJ* 1 (1828): 784–89.

"Cases." *BMSJ* 54 (1856): 389–95, 431–36.

"Cases and Notes." *BMSJ* 56 (1857): 169–74, 193–98.

"Cases from My Notebook." *BMSJ* 62 (1860): 517–24.

"Cases of Delirium Tremens." *NEJMS* 8 (1819): 15–28.

"Cases of Inhalation of Ether in Labor." *BMSJ* 36 (1847): 415–19.

"Cases of Organic Diseases of the Womb and Its Appendages." *BMSJ* 36 (1847): 469–77.

"Death after Taking Laudanum—Poisoning by Aconite, by Alleged Spiritual Communication." *BMSJ* 56 (1857): 449–56.

"Death of Charlotte Bronte." *BMSJ* 57 (1857): 94–97.

"Effects of Criminal Abortion." *BMSJ* 60 (1859): 134–42.

"The Fine Arts." *North American Review* 3 (1816): 194–201.

"A Fragment of a Medical Autobiography, or a Case Reported by the Patient." *BMSJ* 71 (1865): 351–58.

"Hints to My Countrymen." *North American Review* 23 (1826): 467–70.

"Inversion of the Womb." *BMSJ* 60 (1859): 547–49.

"Judge Tilghman's and Dr. Caldwell's Eulogies on Dr. Caspar Wistar, Late President of the American Philosophical Society and Professor of Anatomy in the University of Pennsylvania." *North American Review* 7 (1818): 136–41.

"The Late John Revere." *BMSJ* 36 (1847): 292–95.

"Of the Medical Profession and of its Preparation." *BMSJ* 33 (1845): 309–17, 329–37, 349–57.

"A Medico-Legal Treatise on Malpractice and Medical Evidence—A Review." *BMSJ* 62 (1860): 233–41, 259–65, 300–307.

"Miscellaneous Cases, Spina Bifida, Preternatural Labors, Erysipelatous Inflammation." *NEJMS* 15 (1826): 357–70.

"My Own Times, or 'Tis Fifty Years Since." *Monthly Miscellany and Journal of Health* 1 (1846): 14–24, 38–47, 65–72.

"Never Too Late to Mend." *BMSJ* 61 (1859): 109–13, 135–43.

"Notes of Cases of Recent and Chronic Inversio Uteri." *BMSJ* 60 (1859): 229–34.

"Notes of Difficult Labors, in the Second of which Etherization by Sulphuric Ether Was Successfully Employed Nineteen Years Ago." *BMSJ* 46 (1852): 113–15.

"Notes on Anhæmia, principally in its connections with the Puerperal State, and with Functional Disease of the Uterus; with Cases." *New England Quarterly Journal of Medicine and Surgery* 1 (1842): 157–88.

"Observations on Puerperal Fever with Diarrhaea." *NEJMS* 2 (1813): 232–45.

"On Reflections on the Literary Delinquency of America." *North American Review* 2 (1815): 33–43.

"On the Contagiousness of Puerperal Fever." *BMSJ* 52 (1855): 293–99.

"On the Health of Literary Men." *North American Review* 8 (1818–19): 176–80.

"On the Transfusion of Blood." *BMSJ* 1 (April 1, 1828): 97–102.

"Painless Delivery, Hæmorrhage, Turning, Recovery." *BMSJ* 71 (1864): 229–32.

"Physical Education." *Journal of Health and Monthly Miscellany* 1 (1846): 170–72, 193–97, 225–30, 295–99.

"Polypus of the Womb." *BMSJ* 52 (1855): 89–95, 112–18.

"Practical Remarks on Some of the Predisposing Causes, and Prevention, of Puerperal Fever, with Cases." *NEJMS* 6 (1817): 157–69.

"Professional Reminiscences of Foreign Travel." *BMSJ* 47 (1852–53): 303–9, 326–34, 363–69, 393–400.

"Puerperal Fever with Diarrhaea." *NEJMS* 2 (1813): 232–44.

"Puerperal Peritonitis." *BMSJ* 40 (1849): 274–76.

"Remarks on Diseases Resembling Syphilis, with Observations on the Action of Those Causes Which Produce Them." *NEJMS* 1 (1812): 65–68, 139–50, 245–50, 377–82.

"Retention of a Portion of the Placenta." *BMSJ* 67 (1862): 149–55.

"Re-vaccination." *BMSJ* 1 (1828): 279–80.

Review of *American Medical Botany*, 1819 edition. *North American Review* 9 (1819): 23–26.

Review of "Dr. Murphy's Lectures on Midwifery." *BMSJ* 35 (1846–47): 298–99.

Review of *An Elementary Treatise on Mineralogy and Geology. North American Review* 5 (1817): 409–29.

Review of "Females and their Diseases." *BMSJ* 37 (1847–48): 438–41.

Review of *Vegetable Materia Medica of the United States* and *American Medical Botany. North American Review* 6 (1818): 344–68.

"Sketches in Midwifery Practice." *BMSJ* 57 (1857): 229–36.

"Smallpox." *BMSJ* 62 (1860): 89–95.

"Spiritualism." *BMSJ* 56 (1857): 333–38.

"Washington Allston." *Christian World*, July 22, 1843.

Index

Page numbers in italic indicate illustrations.